THE NEW FACE OF ASIAN PACIFIC AMERICA

Numbers, Diversity & Change in the 21st Century

Edited by

Eric Lai &
Dennis Arguelles

THE NEW FACE OF ASIAN PACIFIC AMERICA

Numbers, Diversity & Change in the 21st CENTURY

Edited by

Eric Lai &
Dennis Arguelles

AsianWeek, San Francisco
with
UCLA's Asian American Studies Center Press
in cooperation with the
Organization of Chinese Americans
and the
National Coalition for
Asian Pacific American Community Development

**The New Face of Asian Pacific America:
Numbers, Diversity and Change in the 21st Century**

Co-Editors *Eric Lai, M.A. and Dennis Arguelles, M.A.*
Associate Editor (including photos and maps) *Cindy Chew, M.A.*
Copy Editor *Caroline R. Knapp*

Library of Congress Cataloging-in-Publication Data

Lai, Eric Yo Ping, 1969–
The new face of Asian Pacific America : numbers, diversity, and change in the 21st century / edited by Eric Lai and Dennis Arguelles.
p. cm.
Includes bibliographical references and index.
ISBN 0-9665020-3-5 (softcover)
1. Asian Americans—Social conditions. 2. Pacific Islander Americans—Social conditions. 3. Asian Americans—Ethnic identity. 4. Pacific Islander Americans—Ethnic identity. 5. Asian Americans—Statistics. 6. Pacific Islander Americans—Statistics. 7. United States—Population. 8. United States—Ethnic relations. I. Title.

E184.O6L35 2003
305.895'073'090511—dc21

2002156209

ISBN 0-9665020-3-5

Printed in the United States of America.
Consolidated Printers, Inc. (Berkeley, California)

10 9 8 7 6 5 4 3 2 1

Book Team
Book & Cover Design *David Quintero, David Quintero Design, Inc.*
Layout *Enzo Lombard-Quintero, David Quintero Design, Inc.*
Graphics and Charts *Olivia Nguyen* and *Melany dela Cruz, M.A.*
Advisors *Christine Chen, Lisa Hasegawa,* and *Don Nakanishi, Ph.D.*

Table of Contents

Section IV. Culture and Society

Foreword

The genesis of *The New Face of Asian Pacific America* and *AsianWeek* newspaper was the vision of my late father, Mr. John T. C. Fang.

My father emigrated from China in the early 1950s, and lived in America for the last 40 years of his life. During that time, he adopted America as his home, and like many before, and many since, he became a product of two cultures: not just Asian and not just American, but both—Asian American.

Throughout his life in America, my father was deeply concerned with the betterment and welfare of his fellow Asian immigrants—and of those Asian Pacific Americans who, like his three sons, were born in America and not fluent in their native language. He saw a need for a national publication—and for books—which would unite the community through the common thread of English.

He started *AsianWeek* in 1979, the first English-language weekly newspaper for Asian Pacific Americans, nationwide. Since then, it has become the link for American-born Asians to better understand their community; it has become a bridge for Asian immigrants to better understand mainstream American culture. It is also the primary vehicle for mainstream America to learn of the concerns and aspirations of the country's fastest-growing community.

The New Face of Asian Pacific America is a continuation of what we have achieved at *AsianWeek*.

With its expert analysis of the issues facing the Asian Pacific American community, its deft editing, and its outstanding graphs and photographs, there is little doubt in my mind that this book will not only serve as a source of tremendous pride for the APA community, but will also become an indispensable resource in defining a changing-America in the years to come.

I would like to thank the *AsianWeek* staff, and the staff at the University of California, Los Angeles, for their professional, painstaking, and tireless efforts to produce this landmark publication. Special thanks to Eric Lai, Tony Wong, Cindy Chew, Neela Banerjee, and Jennie Sue for their work on this project. I would also like to acknowledge the efforts of my mother, Florence, and wife, Daphne, whose inspiration gave me the determination to begin and finish this project.

Sincerely,
James Fang
President
AsianWeek
January, 2003

This book is dedicated to

John T. C. Fang

Founder and Publisher of *AsianWeek*

1927 – 1992

List of Tables, Maps and Charts

SECTION III: GEOGRAPHY

Chapter 1: California

Chapter 2: Northeast

Chapter 3: Hawai'i

Chapter 4: West

Chapter 5: Canada

Chapter 6: Midwest

Chapter 7: South

SECTION IV: CULTURE AND SOCIETY

Chapter 2: Popular Culture

Chapter 3: Education

Chapter 4: Politics

Chapter 5: Work

Chapter 6: Health

Chapter 7: Business and Hi-Tech

Chapter 8: Gays and Lesbians

NOTE: Population maps are not the most precise source for exact population figures, especially at the county or census tract level. Please refer to the text, tables, or the U.S. Census website (*www.census.gov*) for definitive statistics.

Introduction

There are three kinds of lies: lies, damned lies, and statistics.

—Mark Twain, quoting 19th century British statesman, Benjamin Disraeli.

Far too often and for far too long, statistics have been used to paint an inaccurate portrait of the Asian Pacific American community, often to its detriment. In the late 19th century, immigration statistics were used to foment fears of a "yellow peril," justify restrictive immigration quotas and discourage Asian workers from settling in the United States. In the late 20th century, statistics were used to portray Asian Pacific Americans as a monolithic Model Minority, a community in which everyone was well-educated and well-off, a concept that is often used to drive a wedge between minority communities.

With *The New Face of Asian Pacific America,* we hope to correct some of those misperceptions by arming the reader, whether he or she is a scholar, activist, service provider, policymaker, corporate analyst or just an interested individual, with the most comprehensive set of statistics and figures on Asian Pacific Americans at the dawn of the new millennium.

This book strives to provide an accurate depiction of Asian Pacific America, relying on the latest 2000 Census data as well as the expertise of renowned scholars, researchers and activists. It profiles over ten distinct ethnic groups (Chinese, Filipino, etc.) and "groupings" (i.e. South Asians), provides geographic and regional analyses and includes essays on a wide range of issue-specific areas such as labor, education, business and religion, just to name a few.

Numbers, diversity and change

The 2000 Census underscores two characteristics of the Asian Pacific American community that have distinguished it for several decades: growth and diversity. In April 2000, the Asian Pacific American population numbered approximately 12.5 million, or 4.5 percent of the total U.S. population. This was up from approximately 7.3 million and 3 percent of the U.S. population in 1990.

Groups like Japanese and Korean Americans saw population growth slow, unlike Asian Indian and Filipino Americans, who saw their populations explode during the economic boom of the 1990s and the resultant need for skilled foreign workers.

On the surface, it appears Asian Pacific Americans have achieved much, and 2000 Census and other data support this impression. Asians had the highest median family and household incomes, owned the most expensive homes, and were the best-educated among all groups, topping even non-Hispanic whites during the past decade.

At the same time, Asians' individual (per capita) income lagged more than ten percent behind that of non-Hispanic whites (Native Hawaiians and Pacific Islanders were 40 percent lower). And higher home values? That can be explained in large part by the propensity of Asians to live in expensive urban areas in high cost-of-living states like Hawai'i, California and New York. Educational attainment? Far from being a race of math/computer whizzes, the Asians allowed to immigrate to America under U.S. policies have been those with technical backgrounds and better educations. Moreover, 2000 Census data showed that many Asians remained impoverished, unemployed, and less-educated than the average American.

In addition to growth, there has been change: APAs moved out of traditional strongholds like Hawai'i, California and New York, to greener fields like Georgia, Nevada, and North Carolina—driven out by high costs of living or lured there by jobs

Asian Pacific America by the numbers

– Total APA population in 2000, incl. hapas: **12,504,636***

– Total Asian Americans and Pacific Islanders in 2000 of a single race only: **10,641,833****

– Total Asian Americans in 2000, incl. hapas: **11,898,828**

– Asian Americans who are more than one race, 2000: **13.9 percent**

– Total NHPIs in 2000, incl. hapas: **874,414**

– NHPIs who are more than one race, 2000: **54.4 percent**

– Total Asian Pacific Islanders in 1990: **7,273,662*****

– APA population growth from 1990 to 2000, incl. hapas: **71.9 percent**

– APA population growth from 1990 to 2000, single-race only: **46.3 percent**

– People who are of mixed Asian American AND Pacific Islander ancestry, 2000: **268,606**

– Largest APA ethnicity in 2000, incl. hapas: **Chinese, 2,734,841**

– Smallest listed APA ethnicity in 2000, incl. hapas: **Ni-Vanuatu, 18******

– Largest APA state population: **California, 4,321,585**

– Smallest APA state population: **Wyoming, 4,588**

– Fastest-growing APA population by state, 1990-2000: **Nevada, 225.5 percent**

– Slowest-growing APA population by state, 1990-2000: **Hawai'i, 25.2 percent**

– Highest percentage of APAs in overall population: **Hawai'i, 70.8 percent**

– Lowest percentage of APAs in overall population: **West Virginia, 0.7 percent**

– National median single-race Asian household income, 1999: **$51,908**

– National median single-race NHPI household income, 1999: **$42,717**

– National median household income, 1999: **$41,994**

– Percentage of single-race Asian households in poverty, 1999: **12.6 percent**

– Percentage of single-race NHPI households in poverty, 1999: **17.7 percent**

– Percentage of all households in poverty, 1999: **12.4 percent**

*Unless stated otherwise, we define APAs as anyone of part-Asian or part-NHPI descent, therefore including all mixed-race people of part-Asian or part-NHPI ancestry.

**Includes Asian Americans or Pacific Islanders who are of more than one ethnicity, i.e. Chinese-Indians, Vietnamese-Thai-Koreans, Samoan-Native Hawaiian, etc.

***1990 Census was last one in which Asian Pacific Islanders were considered a single race. Also, the 1990 Census did not ask respondents if their ancestry consisted of more than one race. It is unclear what proportion of mixed-race Asian Pacific Islanders marked themselves as API or their other race.

****From Tables 4, Census 2000 Briefs on Asian and NHPI Populations.

Many thanks to Elizabeth Grieco of the Migration Policy Institute, Melany dela Cruz of UCLA's Census Information Center, Andy Yan of the Asian American Federation of New York, and Paul M. Ong at UCLA for cross-checking and verifying our numbers.

and other opportunities. Today, more than one-third of the Vietnamese American population lives in the South, as do more than one-fifth of the Indian and Korean American populations.

The New Face is the first public policy book of its kind to analyze these changes, using the latest data available from the 2000 Census.

Why the "P" in APA?
For the first time the Census identified Native Hawaiians and Pacific Islanders separately from Asian Americans and revealed that, on the whole, they had a much different socioeconomic experience than Asian Americans. This justified years of lobbying and educating by NHPI activists to be identified as a separate race category.

We applaud the decision by the Census Bureau to separate Asian Americans and Pacific Islanders. In our view, it not only enables NHPI communities to receive greater visibility and services they might have been previously denied due to the prevailing Model Minority myth, but it also highlights the cultural diversity within the APA community, which is one of its most distinguishable characteristics.

In the naming of this book, the term Asian Pacific America was chosen in an attempt to be as inclusive as possible while being linguistically economical. We understand the term is not universally embraced. However, we hope whatever the book arguably lacks in accurate semantics it makes up for in its content and sincerity to shedding light on the diverse characteristics, experiences and issues of all Asian American and Pacific Islander communities.

The 2000 Census was also the first time that individuals could identify themselves as being of more than one race or ethnicity. It was a good decision: the total multiracial American population in 2000 stands at around 6.8 million, with about 1.8 million of them being part-Asian or part–NHPI. The demographic difficulty that arises, however, is the possibility of double- or triple-counting multiracial individuals; the psychological difficulty is in deciding whether or not mixed-race or mixed-ethnic individuals are "one of us."

We believe that the ideal of an APA community—one that recognizes the differences among its various subgroups, yet can act together as a unified social and political force—remains important. With unity comes greater numbers; with greater numbers comes increased representation; with increased representation comes the potential to create social change.

For these reasons and more, we have chosen to publish the combined APA population total in preference of separate Asian American or NHPI totals whenever possible. Furthermore, we have also consciously chosen to include hapas, i.e. those APAs of more than one race or ethnic background in our population counts, rather than exclude them, as many previous 2000 Census-based studies have tended to do. For, as Wei-Ming Dariotis and Theresa Williams-Leon write in their chapters on mixed-race individuals and culture, hapas are increasingly identifying with their APA side, even as they create a community of their own.

The result? The numbers were not only groundbreaking—this is the first time they have been published anywhere outside of *AsianWeek*—they are also startling: 12.5 million APAs total, and nearly 2.1 million hapas, making them the second-largest APA sub-group in 2000, behind only the (single-race) Chinese. By 2010, hapas could very well be the largest, depending on birthrates and immigration policies in the post-Sept. 11 era.

The Problem of Comparing 1990 and 2000 Populations

The introduction of multiracial and multiethnic categories in the 2000 Census, besides allowing the counting of mixed-race or "hapa" people for the first time, also created a problem for demographers: How to compare 2000 population figures with previous years? Because earlier ten-year Censuses did not ask respondents if they were more than one race, most demographers have opted to use the smaller "alone" population counts in 2000, which typically exclude mixed-race and even mixed-ethnic respondents, depending on the context.

The assumption seems to be that in 1990 and previous years, mixed-race or mixed-ethnic people of part-Asian or part-NHPI ancestry would have—given only one choice by the Census—tended to NOT choose Asian or NHPI. In fact, there has been little hard evidence showing that is true or that the opposite case—that mixed-race APIs in 1990 and earlier tended to identify themselves as API instead of white or black— etc. was true.

Given that ambiguous situation, and given this book's preference to include hapas and mixed-ancestry people wherever possible, we've opted to use the largest, most "inclusive" population counts in 2000. As a result, our figures for percentage increases in 2000 versus previous ten-year Censuses may appear higher than those appearing in other publications.

Graphics
Most of the data contained in this book is freely available at the U.S. Census' website, *www..census.gov*, in particular, the American Factfinder (*http://factfinder.census.gov*) section. However, this book takes that data and presents it in an easier to understand format. We hope the more than 50

informative maps, along with the over 100 charts and infographics, make this book both a valuable and accessible resource. Cindy Chew, our multi-tasking associate editor, generated most of the raw maps and charts with the help of Melany dela Cruz at UCLA. Olivia Nguyen is the graphic artist who created the wonderful final versions of the maps and graphics you see in this book.

Thanks must also be extended to Katia Segre-Cohen and Craig Cornelius at Geolytics, Inc. (www.geolytics.com), which generously donated its Census CD software for use in generating the maps. Geolytics' software is used by more than 2,800 libraries, universities and government agencies to provide accurate, easy-to-use census-based demographic and/or geographic information system (GIS) data. Thanks to Larry Shinagawa of Ithaca College for helping to create this relationship.

Acknowledgments
There are many people we'd like to thank who helped make *The New Face* come to fruition.

Many thanks to individuals in our partnering organizations, including Christine Chen, Executive Director of the Organization of Chinese Americans, the leading group representing Chinese Americans nationwide, and Lisa Hasegawa, Executive Director of the National Coalition for Asian Pacific American Community Development (CAPACD), the first organization dedicated to the housing and community development needs of Asian Americans and Pacific Islanders.

Our colleagues at *AsianWeek* were pillars of support and advice. At *AsianWeek*, we'd especially like to thank Neela Banerjee, Tony Wong, and Jennie Sue, as well as Russell Hoch and Cindy Blair at our sister company, Grant Printing.

We'd also like to thank Florence Fang and James Fang, the president of *AsianWeek*. It was James who had the inspiration to authorize the production of an Asian American Guide to the 1990 Census, and a successive volume in 2000, which grew into the book you are now holding in your hands.

At the UCLA Asian American Studies Center, we'd like to recognize Don Nakanishi, Mary Kao, Russell Leong, Charles Ku and Brandy Worrall for their advice and assistance. Thanks to Paul Ong of the UCLA Lewis Center for Regional Policy Studies for his thoughtful guidance. Melany dela Cruz, the Center's Census Project Coordinator, deserves special recognition for her technical and research support. Finally, we thank Wayne Kei and Barbara Harris of the U.S. Census Bureau's Customer Liaison Office for helping us establish the Asian Pacific American Community Development Data Center, which we operate in conjunction with CAPACD.

Others who offered invaluable advice: Gary Okihiro, at Columbia University; *AsianWeek* columnist, Phil Tajitsu Nash; 'Yellow Journalist,' Bill Wong; Frank Wu, of Howard University; Grace Ebron, at AltaMira Press; Elizabeth Grieco, at the Migration Policy Institute; Nicholas Jones, of the Race Statistics Branch of the U.S. Census Burea; K.V. Rao, of Bowling Green University, Jin Sook Lee, of the Asian Pacific American Labor Alliance, AFL-CIO; and too many others to list here.

Our hardworking associates on the book include: Cindy Chew, who wore a dizzying number of hats, including associate editor, and editor of photos and maps; Caroline R. Knapp, our eagle-eyed copyeditor; and Enzo Lombard–Quintero and David Quintero, who joined us late but still managed to do fantastic work on the layout and design of the book, CD-Rom, and website.

And many thanks go to the generous contributions of our contributing photographers: Corky Lee, perhaps the premier documentarian of the APA experience today, for his fantastic photos, Cory Lum of the *Honolulu Advertiser* for contributing his photographs of his hometown of Hawai'i, Kieran Ridge and Hiromi Oda for their photographs documenting the Bay Area's APA gay and lesbian community, and Santi Suthininithet and Dylan Maddux for their music photos.

A special thanks to Kim Wong at State Farm, the corporate sponsor of *The New Face of Asian Pacific America*, without whose generous support this book would not have been possible.

Last but not least, we'd like to thank our respective families and loved ones. Eric: his parents Juey-Hong and Li-Huey and his brother Bruce, and, of course, his wife Tina. Dennis: his family and friends for always serving as a reminder to him of what is most important in life.

—Eric Lai and Dennis Arguelles
Co-Editors
January, 2003

SECTION I
OVERVIEW

Diversified Growth

Over the last 150 years, Asian Pacific Americans have emerged as a distinct, noteworthy population. The fate of Asian America has always been intertwined with U.S. immigration policy, which has determined its population size, shaped its ethnic composition, and defined its socioeconomic character. The first part of this chapter explores this phenomenon by covering the demographic history and changes in Asian America, focusing on the last half-century.

The second part of this chapter discusses the experiences of Native Hawaiians in Hawai'i, which, despite an exodus to the mainland during the later half of the twentieth century, remains home to the majority of Native Hawaiians in the United States. The history of this indigenous population is one of tragedy and near genocide in the face of colonialism as well as resilience and recovery in recent decades.

Part I: Asian Pacific Americans: growth and diversity

Although Asian Pacific Americans comprised less than one percent of the total U. S. population in 1960, they increased their share to just under four percent by 2000, including hapas, those of mixed ancestry. In absolute numbers, the Asian Pacific American population grew from just under 1 million in 1960 to 10 million in 2000—a tenfold increase. The Census predicted that this rapid growth will continue through the next two decades, with Asian Pacific Americans projected to number about 19.6 million and comprise an estimated 6 percent of the nation's population by 2020.

This population increase poses a policy challenge to the Asian Pacific American community and to the nation as a whole. A proactive approach requires us to do more than just react to today's pressing problems. We must create a vision ensuring a just and equitable place for Asian Pacific Americans in American society and the economy—a position that enables APAs to contribute to the building of a truly multicultural society. One way to move in that direction is to understand current and future demographic patterns and trends. Such an understanding provides insights to the struggles and conflicts in the educational, economic, and

Photo: Corky Lee

In the 21st century, it is projected that U.S.-born Asians will begin to make up a larger proportion of the population, while Asian immigration will slow down.

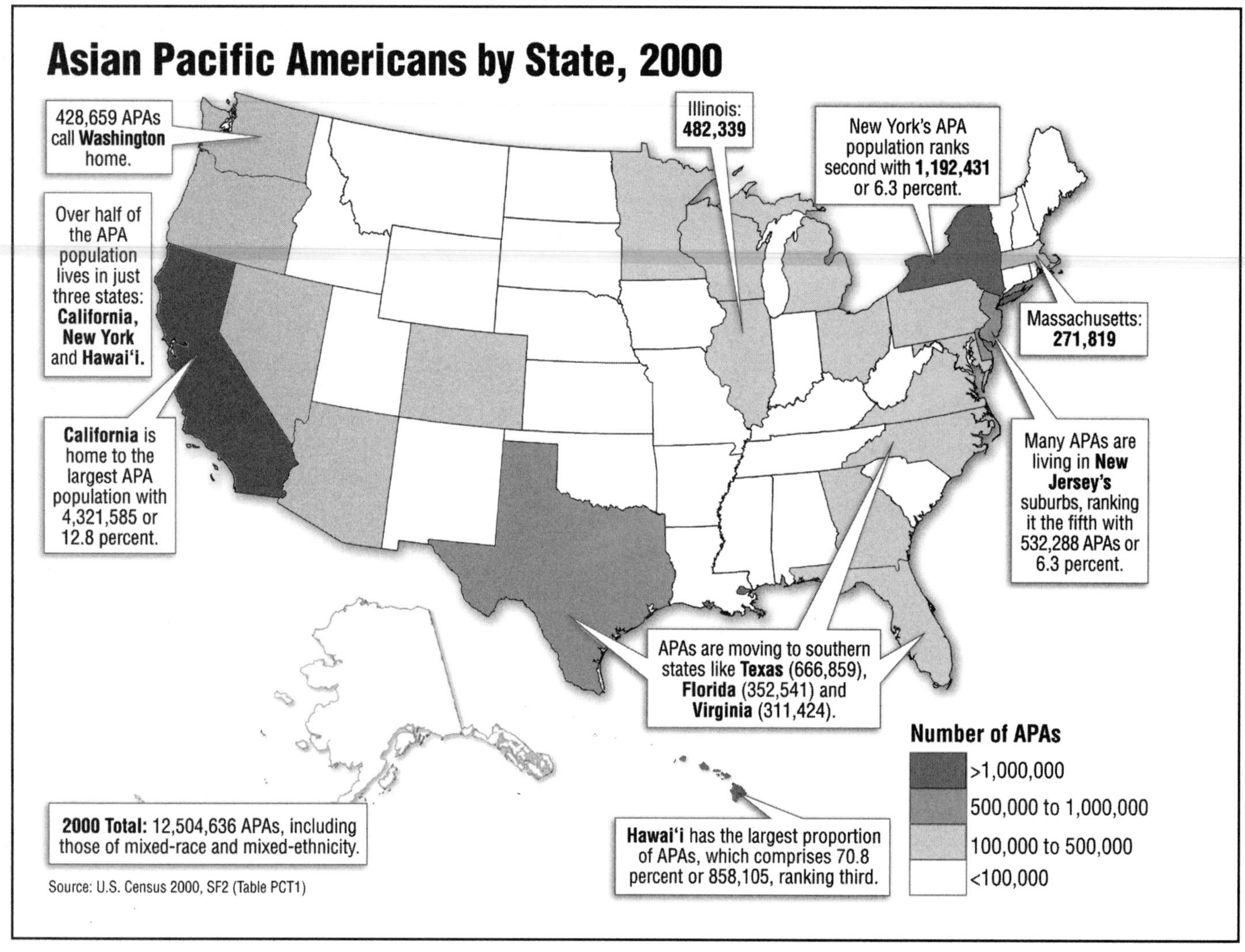

social service arenas, along with interracial and interethnic relationships.

Asian immigrants and U.S. immigration policy, 1830–1965

The history of immigration legislation is central to understanding how Asians were targeted and excluded on the basis of race. Throughout the second half of the nineteenth century and the first part of the twentieth, Asians immigrated primarily to pursue economic opportunity. The Chinese were the first group of Asians to arrive in the United States. By the 1830s, several Chinese sugar companies were already operating in Hawai'i; the first group of 195 Chinese contract laborers arrived in 1852 to produce sugar. Larger numbers of Chinese began arriving in the American West after gold was discovered in California in 1848. Between 1851 and 1860, over 41,000 Chinese immigrants arrived in the United States from China. In 1865, the Central Pacific Railroad Company began recruiting Chinese laborers. Chinese immigration jumped to nearly 65,000 in 1861–70 and then to over 124,000 in 1871–80.

By the 1870s, the Chinese had become the largest racial minority in the Golden State, and whites, including many immigrants, viewed these Asians as unwelcome economic competitors and heathens incapable of being assimilated. Nativism and racism converged into a regional-based movement with national implications. The Chinese Exclusion Act of 1882 restricted entry to individuals based on nationality and

All Asian American population projections up to year 2025 were made before the Census Bureau had confirmed it would split Asian Pacific Islanders into separate racial categories and also count mixed-race people. To maintain consistency within the chapter, all population figures and projections exclude hapas, or those of mixed-race or mixed-ethnicity. The rest of the book *does* include hapas in its population counts.

prevented Chinese immigrants from becoming naturalized citizens. This resulted in the Asian Pacific American population growing by less than 2,000 persons between 1880 and 1890. Over the next half-century, this pattern repeated itself as other Asians immigrated to the United States and became targets of anti-immigrant hostilities and legislation.

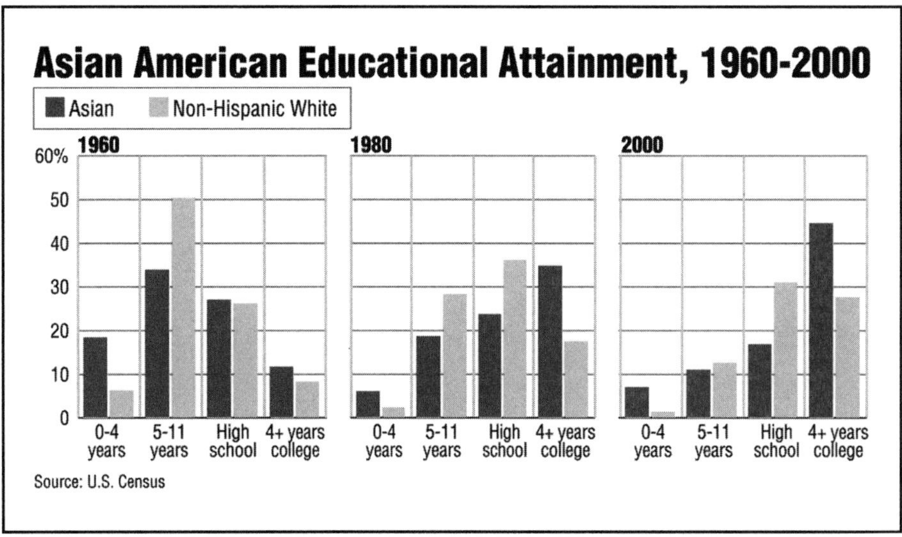

Japanese, Filipinos, and Koreans were recruited as contract laborers to work on Hawaiian sugar plantations in the late 1800s. Japanese laborers arrived on the mainland in significant numbers after the 1900 Organic Law voided labor contracts in Hawai'i. Immigration from Japan jumped from just over 2,200 persons between 1881 and 1890 to nearly 130,000 between 1901 and 1910. In the late 1920s, Filipinos became the largest group of Asian farm laborers along the Pacific Coast, though Japanese, Asian Indian, and Korean tenant farmers were also prevalent in scattered locations. Asian Indian immigration in this early period reached its zenith of over 4,700 immigrants in between 1901 and 1910 and hovered around 2,000 persons per decade until the 1950s. These new sources of immigration were the primary reason the Asian Pacific American population grew in the years after Chinese immigration was barred.

However, anti-Asian sentiment continued to grow alongside Asian immigration. The 1917 Immigration Act delineated a "barred zone" from whence no immigrants could come. This act was promulgated specifically to prevent future Asian Indian immigration. The 1924 Immigration Act tightened existing exclusions to deny entry to virtually all Asians, establishing a quota on the Asia-Pacific triangle. Finally, the passage of the 1934 Tydings-McDuffie Act eliminated Filipinos' status as U.S. nationals and established immigration quotas of only 50 persons a year. This act significantly curbed the wave of immigration coming from the former U.S. commonwealth. By the late 1930s, these curbs in immigration would result in the Asian Pacific American population being dominated by the American-born citizens. Census data reveals that the Asian Pacific American population grew by a scant 55 persons between 1930 and 1940.

Ironically, the trend toward ending racial restrictions on immigration came soon after one of this nation's darkest moments in race relations. In 1942, under the guise of protecting national security, the United States incarcerated 110,000 Americans of Japanese ancestry, two-thirds of whom were American citizens by birth. The United States repealed the Chinese Exclusion Act in 1943, but at the same time gave China an annual immigration quota of only 105. International pressure on the United States to eliminate racial restrictions on immigration increased as the country emerged as a major global power after World War II. The Luce-Cellar bill of 1946 established small immigration quotas for Asian Indians and Filipinos, and a 1947 amendment to the War Brides Act allowed Chinese American veterans to bring brides into the United States. These acts contributed a small spike in the growth in the number of foreign-born Asians during the 1940s. Despite this, by 1960 the share of foreign-born Asians in the population had reached an all-time low of 32 percent.

Post-1965 growth

During the latter third of the 20th century, renewed large-scale immigration led to a recomposition of the Asian Pacific American population by nativity and ethnicity. The 1965 passage of the Hart-Cellar Act, which lifted discriminatory and restrictive quotas and ordinances, led to tremendous growth of the Asian Pacific American population. From 1960 to 1970, the share of foreign-born Asians rose 18 percent to 38 percent, helped by immigration flows that nearly tripled during the decade. From 1970 to 1980, the share of foreign-born Asians jumped to 63 percent of the Asian population as

Married Households with Children by Race, 2000

Race of Householder	% Married
Total	**66.3%**
Asian alone	80.2%
Non-Hispanic white alone	75.5%
Hispanic alone	60.7%
NHPI alone	57.7%
American Indian alone*	50.4%
Black alone	33.7%

*Includes Alaska natives

Source: U.S. Census 2000, SF1, Table P28A-I

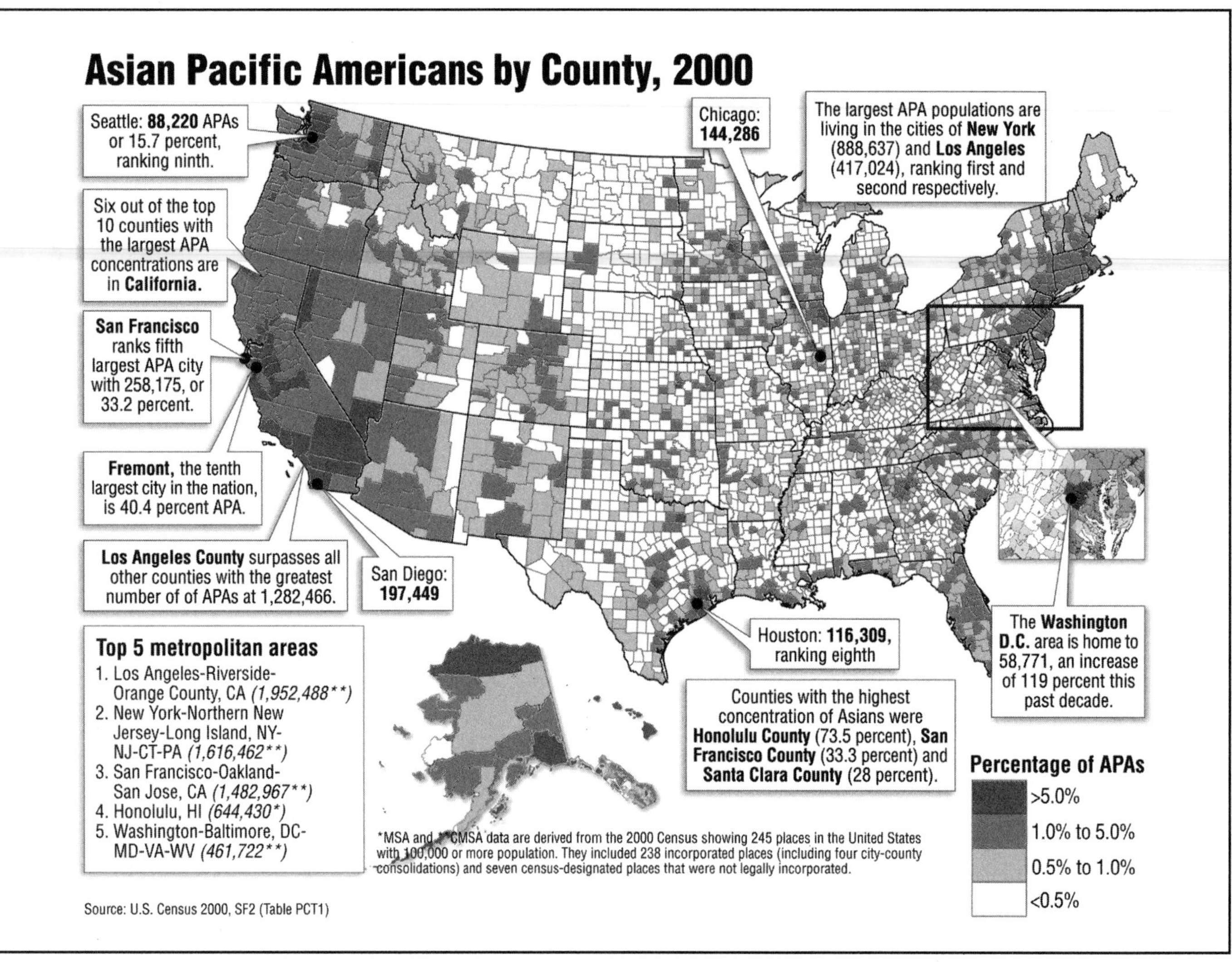

immigration increased nearly four-fold. The share of foreign-born Asians has slowly increased through 2000 to approximately 68 percent. Immigration has clearly been a major source of Asian population growth in the United States since 1960.

Projections show, however, that immigration will slow in the 21st century, and that U.S.-born Asians will begin to make up a larger proportion of the population over the next twenty years. By 2020, the Census estimates that foreign-born Asians will comprise about 55 percent of the population. Within the Asian population, however, the percentage of foreign-born varies drastically by ethnicity. Japanese Americans have the lowest foreign-born share, reflecting their long presence in this country and low rate of recent immigration. Vietnamese Americans and other Southeast Asian populations have the highest foreign-born shares, reflecting the influx of refugees from these countries since the 1980s.

Changes in geographic distribution of the Asian population

Since Asians first began arriving in the United States, they have been concentrated on the West Coast, primarily in California and Hawai'i, drawn by economic opportunity and existing networks. The West was home to 100 percent of Asian Pacific Americans according to the 1860 Census. External pressures, such as persecution in California, forced some of these early immigrants to seek new opportunities elsewhere in America. However, the West's share of Asians did not drop below 90 percent until after 1940. Even in 1960, the vast majority of Asians were still concentrated in the West; fully 71 percent of the U.S. Asian population lived in two states, California and Hawai'i. No other region had even 10 percent of the total Asian Pacific American population.

By 1980, the West's share of Asians had fallen to 57 percent, due to declines in Hawai'i's Asian population and internal migration of the Asian population. The increased dispersion of the Asian Pacific American population was partially the result of refugee resettlement programs. U.S. government policies initially placed

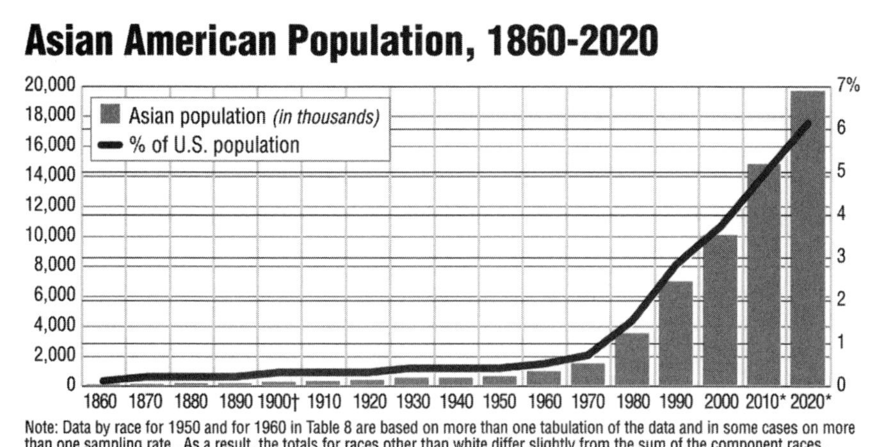

Note: Data by race for 1950 and for 1960 in Table 8 are based on more than one tabulation of the data and in some cases on more than one sampling rate. As a result, the totals for races other than white differ slightly from the sum of the component races.
*Projections
†1900 data includes Asian Americans in Alaska and Hawai'i; previous years did not, hence the jump in population.
Source: Barringer; U.S. Census

Southeast Asian refugees around the country, trying to minimize their impact on local service providers and particular communities and, it was believed, to speed up their assimilation into the host society. Consequently, refugees were much less concentrated in the West and Northeast than other immigrants. Still, no region other than the West had even 20 percent of the nation's Asian Pacific American population. In comparison, only 19 percent of the general U.S. population lived in the West; 22 percent lived in the Northeast; 26 percent lived in the Midwest; and 33 percent lived in the South.

In 2000, 48 percent of Asians still lived in the West, with the South experiencing the greatest percentage growth of this population. California's total population is 13 percent Asian and continues to have the largest number of each of the six largest Asian groups—Asian Indian, Chinese, Filipino, Japanese, Korean, and Vietnamese. Despite greater geographical distribution, however, Asians are still disproportionately concentrated in the West as compared with both the non-Hispanic white population and the general population. Non-Hispanic whites are concentrated in the South (34 percent) and Midwest (27 percent). Only 8 percent of non-Hispanic whites lived in California in 2000, compared with 35 percent of the Asian population. The general U.S. population distribution closely mirrors the non-Hispanic white distribution, with well over 50 percent of the population living the South and Midwest regions of the country.

Projections based on Census data show that Asian Pacific Americans will experience moderate dispersion throughout the nation by 2020. However, two-fifths of the net growth in population will be in California. By 2020, there will be more Asian Pacific Americans in California than the total for 46 other states (excluding New York, Hawai'i, and Illinois); Asian Pacific Americans will make up nearly 18 percent of the state's population. The New York/New Jersey area will also become an Asian Pacific American center, with nearly 2.5 million people.

Changes in ethnic composition of the U.S. Asian population

The U.S. Asian population has grown more ethnically diverse since 1960, though some similarities to the past remain. In 1960, the Japanese were the largest national-origin group in the U.S., with 50 percent of the total Asian population. By 2000, Japanese made up only 8 percent of the Asian total at about 800,000 people. The Chinese population has remained relatively stable at roughly a quarter of the total Asian population from 1960 through 2000. In 2000, they comprised about 2.4 million people. Filipinos have been another historically significant group. Their share of the Asian population, after rising in 1980, has settled to about 18 percent.

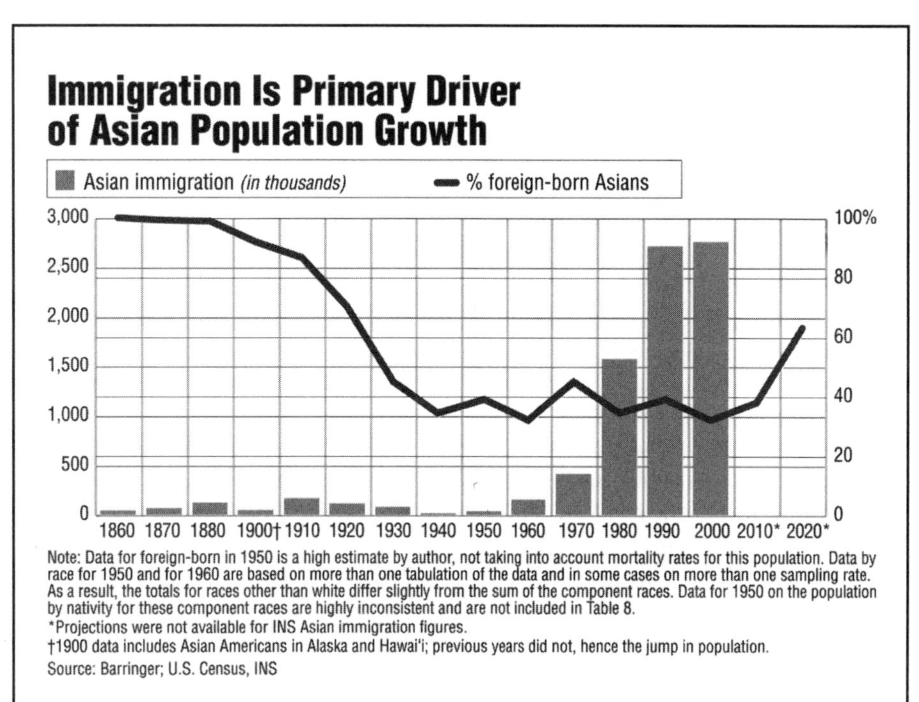

Note: Data for foreign-born in 1950 is a high estimate by author, not taking into account mortality rates for this population. Data by race for 1950 and for 1960 are based on more than one tabulation of the data and in some cases on more than one sampling rate. As a result, the totals for races other than white differ slightly from the sum of the component races. Data for 1950 on the population by nativity for these component races are highly inconsistent and are not included in Table 8.
*Projections were not available for INS Asian immigration figures.
†1900 data includes Asian Americans in Alaska and Hawai'i; previous years did not, hence the jump in population.
Source: Barringer; U.S. Census, INS

Chino Latinos?

APAs of the Hispanic variety

Some are Japanese or Chinese whose ancestors immigrated generations ago to Latin America before coming to the United States. Others are Filipinos who lived in Mexican-American barrios and used their Spanish surnames and language ability to blend into the community. And still others are the products of mixed-race marriages between Asian Pacific Americans and Latinos.

In 2000, there were more than 400,000 APAs who marked themselves as also being Hispanic. That's an increase of around 100,000 from 1990, when 305,000 Asian Pacific Islanders identified as being also Hispanic.

This may perplex some: how is it possible to be of a single race and also Hispanic? For an answer, there is the Census Bureau's methodology, which has treated Hispanics (or Latinos) as an ethnicity, not a race, since it first began quizzing respondents in 1980. In the 2000 Census, respondents were first asked if they considered themselves Hispanic; then immediately afterwards they were asked to which races they belonged.

The reason for this clumsy methodology is the difficulty in pinning down exactly what makes one Hispanic. Its lowest common denominator seems to be the ability to speak Spanish (though this is not always true). But people who reported to the Bureau that they were Hispanic run the gamut from dark-skinned descendents of Aztec Indians to blond-haired, blue-eyed Cubans of mostly Spanish extraction. And as we see from the above figures, there is also a substantial population of Asians, Native Hawaiians and Pacific Islanders who also see themselves as Hispanic.

About one in 40 Asians reported themselves as Hispanic. According to Leo Estrada, a demographer at UCLA, a large percentage of these are older Filipino Americans. Many immigrated to America straight into Latino or Mexican neighborhoods, or were employed as migrant farmworkers, cannery workers and other jobs alongside Hispanics. Many Hispanic Asians are descendents of Chinese, Japanese and Korean workers and business people from countries like Peru, Ecuador, Brazil, who immigrated to the United States. Others are descendents of Chinese workers who were forced out of California in the late 1800s to nearby Mexican border towns, from where they eventually re-emigrated into the United States.

The percentage of NHPIs reporting themselves as Hispanic is markedly higher: almost 15 percent, or nearly one in seven. This Hispanic-NHPI contingent has its origins in Hawai'i. Puerto Ricans were imported to the islands to work on the pineapple plantations in the late 19th century, says Estrada. Around the same time, Mexicans were brought to Hawai'i to work as cowboys. These Latinos stayed and intermarried with local Native Hawaiians. Their descendents today live in Hawai'i or on the mainland in cities with large Hawaiian expatriate populations, such as Seattle, Los Angeles, San Francisco, and Las Vegas.

New York City, especially Brooklyn, has a large population of Asian Indians who arrived by way of the Caribbean. But Estrada says that those Asian Indians tend not to identify themselves as Hispanic. He also says that people from former Portuguese colonies such as Brazil tend not to identify themselves as Hispanic or Latino.

In 1960, just 6 percent of all Asians (56,000 people) were included in an "Other" category that covered Asian Indians, Koreans, Vietnamese, and other groups. Since the 1980s, the most significant growth has occurred in the Southeast Asian and Asian Indian populations. The Asian Indian share of the population has more than tripled over the last two decades, now totaling nearly 1.7 million. Increasing numbers of Southeast Asians refugees and families have been resettled in the United States. The Vietnamese population has grown to over 1 million people and 11 percent of the Asian population, which is roughly comparable to the size of the Korean population. While their absolute numbers are small, and no one ethnic group included over 200,000 members in 2000, the growth of this segment of the Asian population as a whole has been staggering. Fully 11 percent of Asians, or over 1 million people, reported their ethnicity as Cambodian, Hmong, Laotian, Bangladeshi, Pakistani, Thai, Indonesian, or one of about ten other categories. Projections show that Asian Indians and Southeast Asians will continue to experience a higher growth rate than the total Asian Pacific American population through 2020. The Chinese population will remain the largest group, due in part to continued immigration from many sources, including ethnic Chinese from Southeast Asian countries.

Changes in educational attainment

Increased immigration since 1960 has led not only to increasing ethnic diversity of the Asian population but also to changes in socioeconomic status. Asians were never a monolithic group. Even early immigrant workers who came to seek economic opportunities in the American West varied in the ways they were recruited, the work they sought, their ethnicity, and their education. Recent waves of immigration have made the diversity of Asian Pacific Americans even more striking. One of the primary areas in which we see this increased diversity is in levels of educational attainment, which is a primary determinant of socioeconomic status.

Cities with Largest Hispanic APA Populations, 2000

Metro area	Number of APAs also Hispanic	% of APAs also Hispanic
Los Angeles-Riverside-Orange County, CA **	68,403	3.5%
Honolulu, HI*	45,599	6.3%
New York-Northern New Jersey-Long Island, NY-NJ-CT-PA**	38,272	2.4%
San Francisco-Oakland-San Jose, CA**	37,364	2.5%
San Diego, CA*	15,262	4.8%

Note: Due to overcounting of mixed-race people, figures slightly exceed actual number of individuals that are Hispanic and APA.
*MSA: Stands for Metropolitan Statistical Area.
**CMSA: Stands for Consolidated Metropolitan Statistical Area.
Source: U.S. Census 2000, SF1, Table P10

Hispanics by Race, Nationwide, 2000

Race	Number of Hispanics	% of national Hispanic pop.	Total national pop.	% that is Hispanic
Total	**37,659,799**	**100.0%**	**288,764,438**	**13.0%**
White	18,753,075	49.8%	216,930,975	8.6%
Some other race	16,750,841	44.5%	18,521,486	90.4%
American Indian	674,601	1.8%	4,119,301	16.4%
NHPI	126,265	0.3%	874,414	14.4%
Black	1,035,683	2.8%	36,419,434	2.8%
Asian	319,334	0.8%	11,898,828	2.7%

Note: Due to double-counting of mixed-race people, the total exceeds actual U.S. population of 281.4 million. Race categories are either race alone or in combination with one or more other races.
*Includes Alaska natives.
Source: U.S. Census 2000, SF1, Table P10

Most Hispanics of APA origin reside in areas with large APA populations: California, Hawai'i, urban centers such as Chicago and New York City, etc. But the areas with the highest percentage of Hispanics among their APA population are in southern border states like Texas and New Mexico.

Of course, most Hispanics did not count themselves as APA. About half of the 35.3 million Hispanic Americans said they were white, with another 42 percent marking "Some Other Race." Estrada says that factors such as the proximity of other self-identifying Hispanics, social class, skin color, number of years in the United States, are all used by Hispanics to decide whether to mark themselves as white or Some Other Race.

It's a compromise that leaves many dissatisfied, including some Hispanic or Latino activists, who are pushing for Hispanic/Latino to be recognized as its own race for the next Census. If that happens, it could drastically reduce the number of APAs in 2010 who identify themselves as Hispanic.

—Eric Lai

During the late 1960s and 1970s, the United States experienced a severe shortage of high-skill workers, and the Hart-Cellar Act of 1965 enabled the country to recruit foreign workers to fill the gap. Since the 1980s, one-third of the engineers and medical personnel in the U.S. labor market have come from abroad—mostly from India, China, Taiwan, and the Philippines. In fact, over 60 percent of immigrants from India and Taiwan reported having attained college degrees.

On the other hand, U.S. policy and involvement in Southeast Asia contributed to increased poverty and instability in the region for thousands of Cambodians, Vietnamese, and Laotians. As of 1996, more than one million refugees from these three countries alone have been admitted to the United States. Many of these refugees come from agrarian societies and have grown up in war-torn countries. They have few transferable skills and little formal education. Less than 5 percent of immigrants from Cambodia and Laos reported earning college degrees according to pre-Census 2000 figures.

The combination of these factors results in the overrepresentation of Asians at both ends of the educational spectrum. A higher percentage of Asians than non-Hispanic whites have completed 4 or more years of college, according to the 2000 Census. This has held true since 1960. At the same time, five times as many Asians as non-Hispanic whites have 0 to 4 years of education (7.0 percent versus 1.3 percent in 2000). Although the percentage of people with such low levels of education has decreased for both non-Hispanic whites and for Asians since 1960, the disparity between the two racial groups has actually increased. Asians were three times as likely as non-Hispanic whites to have 0 to 4 years of education in 1960 and in 1980.

Part II: Native Hawaiians in Hawai'i: challenged paradise

The size, racial composition, and socioeconomic character of the Native

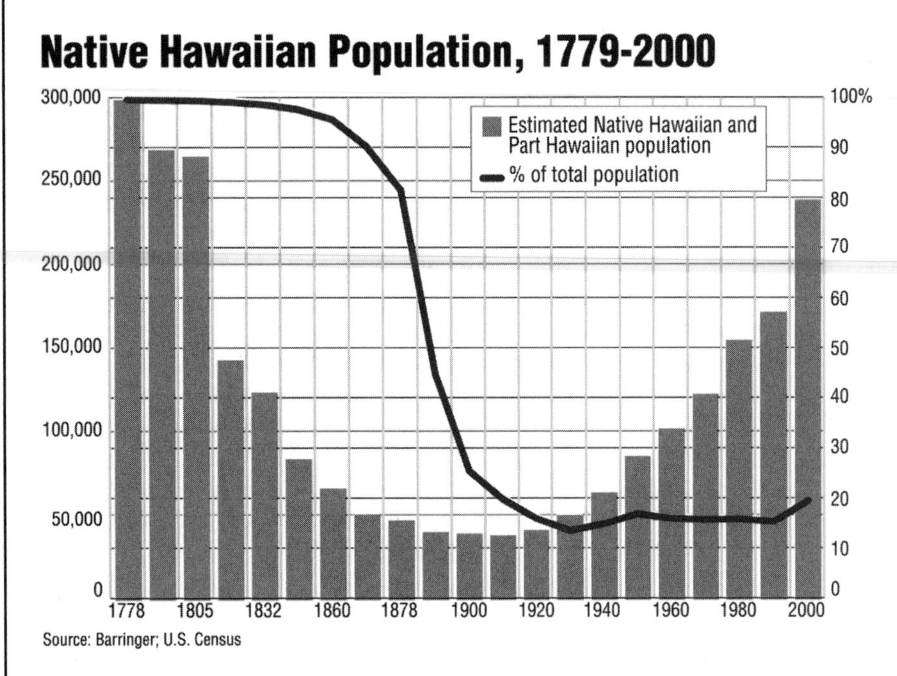

Hawaiian population have been forever altered by contact with the West. Despite a high rate of interracial marriage, Native Hawaiians are not fully or equally incorporated into the dominant society. Socioeconomic statistics show that they are below parity with the dominant groups in Hawai'i. Native Hawaiians have been marginalized by a territorial and state educational system that has failed to provide an adequate education. There are signs of positive changes that can redress some of the historical wrongs, but the future remains uncertain.

Long-term population trends

Native Hawaiians have undergone a long history of decline both in number and in socioeconomic status with a recovery only evident in recent decades. The landing of Captain James Cook in 1778 marked the beginning of their first sustained contact with the West as well as the start of this decline. The population of the islands at this time consisted of indigenous Polynesian peoples. The Office of Hawaiian Affairs (OHA) estimates the Native Hawaiian population in 1778 at about 300,000, but other estimates are considerably higher. Foreign contact introduced epidemics such as small pox, measles, whooping cough, and influenza to Hawai'i as well as venereal diseases that resulted in sterility, miscarriages, and death. The tragic consequence was a drastic decline of the local population. A century after Cook's landing, the Native Hawaiian population had dropped to less than one-sixth of its original size.

The next half-century (from 1878 to 1930) was marked by an overall shift in the racial composition of the island's total population. Although the first century of sustained contact with the West nearly decimated the Native Hawaiian population, they still constituted a large majority of the total population (82 percent in 1879). The Native Hawaiian population continued to decrease in absolute number until 1910, followed by a slow increase in the 1920s and 1930s. During this same period, the number of non-Native Hawaiians grew by thirty times, from about 10,000 to 314,000. The growth was driven by immigration from Asia and settlers from the mainland, as Hawai'i made the transition to a plantation economy. Immigrants provided the labor required for the back-breaking plantation work. In the three decades following Hawai'i's annexation by the United States in 1898, more than 250,000 foreign laborers arrived, mostly from Japan and the Philippines, with small numbers from Korea, Puerto Rico, Portugal, and Spain. By 1930, Native Hawaiians constituted less than one-sixth (14 percent) of the island's population.

According to Census data, 1910 and 1930 proved to be a turning points for Native Hawaiians. The absolute count reached a nadir in 1910 and has steadily increased in each subsequent decade. Since 1930, the long-term growth rate of the Native Hawaiian population (including full- and part-Native Hawaiians) has been equal to or greater than the growth rate of the non-Native Hawaiian population. By the end of the century, there were nearly a quarter million persons who identified themselves as being either full- or part-Native Hawaiian, comprising nearly one-fifth of the state's population.

Racial transformation of the Native Hawaiian population

The Native Hawaiian population has not only grown since 1910, but it has also been transformed by interracial marriages with whites and Asians. This

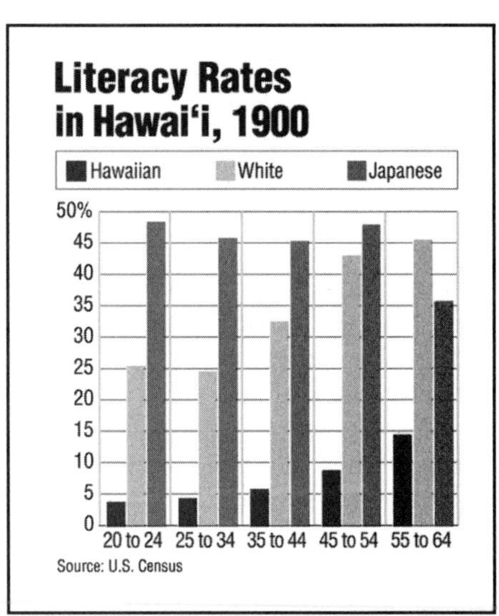

has led to a remarkable growth of the part-Native Hawaiian population. However, this phenomenon makes enumerating the Native Hawaiian population problematic because racial and ethnic identity are fluid in racially mixed populations and are influenced by both personal experience and larger social and economic forces.

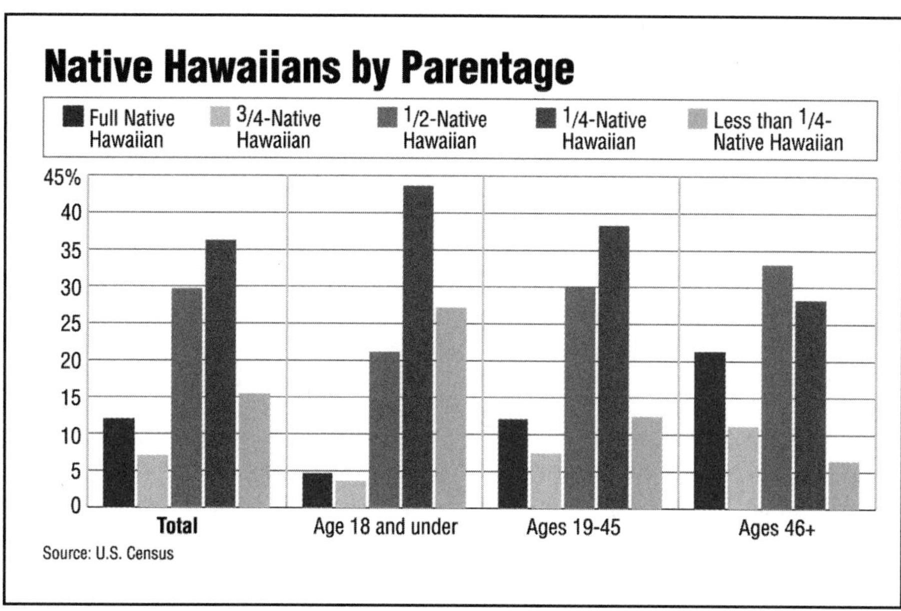

At the beginning of the nineteenth century, there were relatively few part-Native Hawaiians. A half-century later, there were still less than one thousand part-Native Hawaiians out of a total 73,000 Native Hawaiians. While the part-Native Hawaiian population grew for the rest of the nineteenth century, they remained a minority (21 percent) at the turn of the twentieth century. Nonetheless, the transition in the composition was progressing generation after generation. By 1930, part-Native Hawaiians became a majority of the combined full- and part-Native Hawaiian population. By 1959, when the U.S. claimed Hawai'i as a state, full-Native Hawaiians comprised only a tenth of the Native Hawaiian population (11,000 were Native Hawaiian, and 91,000 were part-Native Hawaiian).

If the results of the 2000 Census are taken literally, then there has been a remarkable recovery of the population that can be considered full-Native Hawaiian. One-third of the inclusive count of nearly 240,000 Native Hawaiians (those who checked the "Native Hawaiian" category alone or in combination with another race category) self-identified as being only Native Hawaiian. Given the small base of full-Native Hawaiians in earlier decades, it is likely that many of those identifying only with the Native Hawaiian category have some non-Native Hawaiian ancestry.

The 2000 health interview survey conducted by the state of Hawai'i provides an alternative and more detailed profile of the racial composition of the Native Hawaiian population. In the survey, Native Hawaiian is defined in two ways. Overall, 4 out of 5 who had some Native Hawaiian ancestry were less than one-half Hawaiian, and less than one out of 8 reported only Native-Hawaiian heritage. As might be expected, the proportion of respondents who identified themselves as full Hawaiian was strongly related to age. The elderly population had the highest proportion of "full Native Hawaiians," but the youth population was dominated by part-Hawaiians. Of Hawaiians age 46 and above, 21 percent were full Native Hawaiian, and 11 percent were three-quarters Native Hawaiians. Only 5 percent of Hawaiians age 18 and under were full Native Hawaiians, while 71 percent were one-quarter or less Native Hawaiian.

This survey also provides information on how Native Hawaiian adults classified themselves racially. An overwhelming majority of those who are least three-quarters Native Hawaiian by parentage classify themselves racially as Native Hawaiian alone. Surprisingly, over 25 percent of those who are no more than one-quarter Native Hawaiian by parentage also classify themselves the same way, choosing to define themselves racially as only Native Hawaiian. On the other hand, 24 percent of those who are one-quarter Hawaiian and 47 percent of those who are less than one-quarter Hawaiian do not define themselves as either Native Hawaiians or part-Native Hawaiian. These data reveal that the individual-level concept of being Native Hawaiian is based not only ancestry but also on whether the person self-identifies with the population and its culture. The surprisingly large number of those selecting only Native Hawaiian as their racial identity in the 2000 Census signals a growing desire to reclaim Native Hawaiian roots. This suggests that for

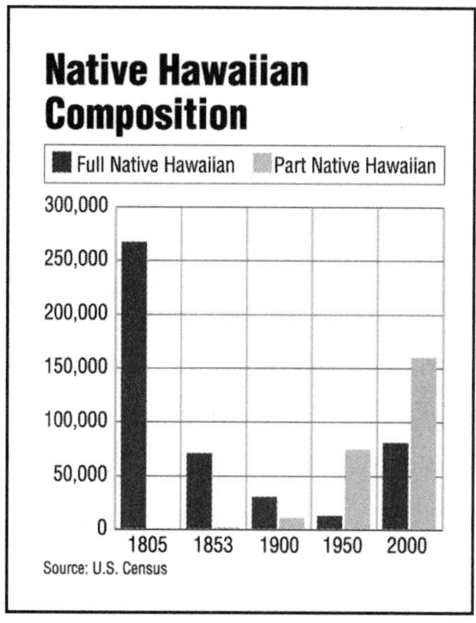

many, interracial marriage is associated with acculturation into the Native Hawaiian community rather than into the dominant society.

Educational attainment

According to mainstream sociology, a high rate of interracial marriage is a component and strong indicator of assimilation, but this is not the case for Native Hawaiians. As the statistics in the previous section reveal, many part-Native Hawaiians see themselves as members of the Native Hawaiian population. Just as important, socioeconomic indicators show that Native Hawiians have not been fully incorporated as equals. This is evident in Native Hawaiian educational attainment, a key determinant of social and economic status. Relative to other groups, Native Hawaiians have lower levels of educational attainment, and those who identify as Native Hawaiian alone are even more disadvantaged. The story is more complex when viewed historically.

Just after annexation, the 1900 Census data show that Native Hawaiians had a substantially lower illiteracy rate than did whites or Japanese. This was partially a result of the efforts by missionaries to "educate" the indigenous population in the pre-U.S. period. Despite the high literacy rate, four-in-ten Native Hawaiians did not speak English. This suggests literacy in the Native Hawaiian language. The Japanese at the time had a higher illiteracy rate and a higher proportion of non-English speakers because this population was primarily composed of immigrants with little education. At the end of "independence" (in reality a period of shared power with whites), Native Hawaiians were the most educated group on the island.

The 1950 Census, taken about a decade prior to Hawaiian statehood, shows the adverse impact of U.S. territorial control on Native Hawaiian socioeconomic status. White adults emerged on top in terms of educational attainment. Compared to both Native Hawaiians and Japanese, whites were much more likely to have at least a high school degree or some college and were much less likely to have less than a high school education. This reversal of educational patterns was partly due to the migration of better-educated whites to the territory rather than simply the result of the state's educational system. The Japanese caught up with the Native Hawaiians, due in part to the growing dominance of the second generation. Given the history of the Japanese in Hawai'i, this improvement in educational attainment was produced by the state's education system. Looking at only younger adults (those under 35), Japanese had higher median educational attainment than Native Hawaiians, indicating that gap would only grow over time. The Native Hawaiians had fallen behind, documenting the territory's failure to adequately educate this population.

Educational attainment during the latter half of the twentieth century is linked to the performance of the state of Hawai'i. By 2000, when a college education is the most important indicator of educational attainment (and socioeconomic success), the Japanese are closing the gap on whites but are still in second place. The Native Hawaiians (full and part), however, are now clearly behind. Where nearly 50 percent of Japanese and over 40 percent of whites ages 25-39 had attained a college education in 2000, just 16 percent of Native Hawaiians (both full and part) had attained this level of education. This disparity is due in part to the fact that Native Hawaiian students perform worse than average in public schools, so they are less able to gain entry into four-year colleges and universities. One consequence is that Native Hawaiians are underrepresented at the University of Hawai'i. For many, getting a college education outside of Hawai'i is not a viable option. Because of lower educational attainment, Native Hawaiians tend to earn less and are less able to accumulate wealth in terms of homeownership.

—Paul M. Ong and Loh-Sze Leung

The authors would like to acknowledge the contributions of Theresa Cenidoza and Melany dela Cruz.

Census, Consensus? APAs and Multiracial Identity

In the last decade, community leaders and scholars have been calling for expanding the definition of who is Asian Pacific American. We are examining more and more the multiplicity and hybridity within and across Asian American and Pacific Islander communities, while simultaneously emphasizing the complex and ever-shifting interrelationships with non-APAs that transgress the black-white framework. It is precisely within this debate that bi-racial and multiracials within APA communities are contesting their marginalized positions and vying for centrality.

All areas of policy-making and policy implementation designed to impact APAs explicitly and implicitly affect bi-racial and multiracial APAs, whether one is talking about K-12 public schools, university admissions, public health matters, poverty, immigration and language rights, affirmative action, race and ethnic relations or cultural preservation. This chapter raises several issues and urges APA social service agencies, multiracial organizations, and educational institutions to begin thinking about actively incorporating multiracial APAs into our various community agendas.

The 1990s: grappling with the interracial marriage and the multiracial phenomena

Interracial marriages have increased by more than 800 percent since the 1960s, signaling major shifts as to how race informs interpersonal relations, attraction, and mate selection. In May 1996, a *New York Times* article reported that of the 1.5 million interracial marriages counted by the Census, 31 percent had an Asian spouse. In 1990, according to sociologist Larry H. Shinagawa, 31.2 percent of all APA husbands and 40.4 percent of APA wives were intermarried, whereas 18.9 percent of APA husbands were inter-ethnically married and 12.3 percent were inter-racially married. Nearly 52 percent of Japanese American women and 40.2 percent of Filipino American women were intermarried.

Photo: AP Wide World

Though the multiracial APA community has become more visible in recent years, the community faces sensitive issues of acceptance and recognition from the APA community as a whole.

Multiracial people of part-APA descent make up about a quarter (27.3 percent) of the total 6.8 million

Single-race vs. Multi-race APAs

	Alone	Multi-race	% larger†
APAs	10,641,833	1,862,803	17.5
Asian	10,242,998	1,655,830	16.2
Native Hawaiian*	398,835	475,579	119.2
Indian	1,718,778	180,821	10.5
Other South Asian	219,963	51,420	23.4
Chinese (all)	2,577,675	302,160	11.7
Filipino	1,908,125	456,690	23.9
Japanese	852,237	296,695	34.8
Korean	1,099,422	129,005	11.7
Vietnamese	1,169,672	54,064	4.6
Indonesian	44,186	18,887	42.7
Hmong	174,712	11,598	6.6
Thai	120,918	29,365	24.3
Samoan	96,756	36,525	37.7
Native Hawaiian only	145,809	255,353	175.1
Guamanian or Chamorro	59,487	33,124	55.7
Tongan	29,940	6900	23

*Includes Pacific Islanders.
†Includes multi-race.
Source: U.S. Census 2000, "Asian Population: 2000" Briefs, Table 4 and "Native Hawaiian and Other Pacific Islander Population: 2000"

multiracial population (this does not include multiethnic hapas, such as Japanese-Bangladeshis, or Hawaiian-Guamanians). Of the 1,037,420 children from interracial households identified by the 1990 Census, nearly one half (466,580) were in families where one parent was marked "Asian" (at the time, this category included both Asians and Pacific Islanders) and the other parent was white. Thus, it was no surprise when nearly a quarter million people indicated a multiracial designator through a "write in" campaign for their race/ethnicity. Among the "write-ins," mixed Asian ancestry designations were quite notable.

As a result of the 1990 Census data and active lobbying by multiracial organizations like Project R.A.C.E. (Re-classify All Children Equally), the Association of MultiEthnic Americans, and the Hapa Issues Forum, the 2000 Census let individuals check off multiple races—rather than choose only a single one as before—to delineate multiple racial heritages. This raised serious questions as to how monoracial minority communities, particularly APAs who represent such a significant percentage of the multiracial population, would be impacted by the multiple check-off option in terms of their numbers and resource allocation. While the issue of official multiracial recognition continues to draw out differences among opponents and proponents, one emergent trend is imminent, "that a multiracial identity is a viable identity for some Asian Americans."

Bi-raciality and multiraciality since 2000

The 2000 Census signified a critical challenge to old methods of gathering and analyzing racial statistics. It has also made way for more accurate racial statistics in the politically engineered racial enumeration game.

Overall, multiracial individuals make up 14.9 percent of the total 12.5 million APA population (multiethnic APAs make up another 1.5 percent). APAs of non-multiracial heritage totaled more than 10.6 million, making up about 3.8 percent of the total population (including multiracial APAs brings the total up to 12.5 million, or about 4.4 percent of the population). Multiracial APAs make up an even bigger percentage of the overall multiracial population. Bi-racial people that are part-APA make up about one-quarter of the total 6.4 million "two-race" population. Of the overall multiracial population (from two to six races, according to the Census form), there are nearly 1.86 million APAs of two or more races, or 27.3 percent.

So what does this tell us about APAs? While racial blending via intermarriage and interracial sexual unions between Asians and non-Asians have always existed, interracial unions and marriages between Asians and non-Asians did not take major hold until after World War II, due to racial mores, institutional barriers, and the racial position of Asians in America.

In addition to the 2000 Census findings, the hyper-visibility of multiracial APA celebrities in American popular culture, such as Tiger Woods, Ann Curry, Lou Diamond Phillips, Apolo Ohno, Sean Lennon, Dean Cain, Kristin Kreuk, Keanu Reeves, Sophia Choi, Dwayne Johnson (The Rock), and others, also send a powerful message that bi-racial and multiracial Asian Americans and Pacific Islanders are now an integral part of everyday American public life. Though many APA communities have come to recognize how common interracial families are today—as regularly highlighted in popular Asian American print media like *Yolk, Pacific Citizen*, and *AsianWeek*—it still appears that interracial couples, families, and multiracial individuals occupy a tenuous membership within APA communities as a whole.

And even as the Census Bureau was beginning its reporting of the results,

political conservatives with persistent advocates such as Ward Connerly, had already launched their "color blind" racial campaign (i.e. the racial privacy initiative), an extension of California's Proposition 209, to deny existing structural racial inequalities and to eliminate race-based social policies designed to address these inequities. Rather than problematizing "racial inequality," these advocates have naively or sinisterly put forth that if we erase "race" from public policy concerns, then, it will disappear (and presumably, so too will "racism" be washed away with the stroke of this initiative).

What is most disturbing about the "colorblind" racial movement is that the growing presence of multiple-race or bi-racial and multiracial populations has been offered as a reason for why race and race-based policies have outlived their purpose. Incidentally, representatives of groups like the Association of MultiEthnic Americans and the Hapa Issues Forum—many of whom are themselves multiple-race identified individuals and interracially married with multiracial children—have opposed the "colorblind" racial philosophy. Perhaps, the rallying cry should be: "Not in Our Name!"

Ironically, throughout the 1990s, racial minority communities and civil rights organizations voiced concern and even opposition to any recognition of multiple racial identifications during the struggle for a "check all that apply" option for the 2000 Census. APAs, whose various communities experienced high outmarriage rates, were no exception. They too were suspicious as to how this information would be utilized and how this might affect the allocation of resources for their communities. For instance, some socioeconomically-challenged groups feared a loss in government funding if their numbers appeared to suddenly drop. With Proposition 209 and now the racial privacy initiative, many concerns of APA communities and organizations in California were not unfounded. In fact, multiple racial identification can also be employed to increase a community's numbers.

Some groups, like the Hmong and Vietnamese, see their populations increase by less than ten percent. But others, like the Filipinos, Japanese, Native Hawaiians, and most of the Pacific Islander groups, grow substantially. The Native Hawaiian community, when including multiracial members, grows 175 percent. Perhaps the consideration of multiple ethnic and racial combinations in counting Asian Americans and Pacific Islanders could be of great use in understanding community needs and demographic trends, without necessarily falling into the zero-sum trap of outmarriage equaling loss of numbers.

Policy areas to consider

From the moment one is born, one is identified racially on record. Through interpersonal experiences, self-identification, and socially imposed identification in schools, in employment, and on government forms, individuals are racially designated. Thus, each individual, through his or her unique and shared experiences with others, comes to identify him or herself as parts of racial groups and ethnic communities throughout his or her life course. And these identifications can shift, depending on who is making the official designation and because of changes in one's life experiences.

I do not advocate any one way that individual multiracial APAs ought to identify themselves. But by designation and definition, policies that affect APA "parent groups" affect multiracial individuals. Because of this, to single out specific policies regarding bi-racial and multiracial Asian Americans and Pacific Islanders may not be so urgent. Nevertheless, many multiracial APAs are choosing to identify with and claim themselves as members of APA communities. For this reason, I look at six general policy areas that may specifically affect multiracial APAs.

1) Public schools

Accurate ethnic and racial counts are key for school administration and policymaking, and can help APA communities. Most of the speculation thus far has been on how accurately tracking multiracial APAs would cause APA groups to lose numbers. Indeed, the exact opposite can occur: keeping better track of multiracial APAs whose physical appearances and names do not reflect their APA ancestry could actually increase APA numbers and representation.

Recommendation: In addition to increasing the numbers of examples and texts about minority groups in general (as the current dearth of histories and texts about Asian Americans and other racial minorities in the U.S. public school curricula is beyond abominable), let's add more examples of interracial families and multiracial individuals. Making what students learn in the classroom pertinent to both the content of their educational materials and their everyday lives is critical. This would be beneficial to multiracial and monoracial students, alike.

2) Public health

Perhaps the most important area relating to multiracial APAs. It is important to identify biological characteristics (not to be mistaken for the pseudo-scientific/socio-political concept of race), including genetic histories and frequencies for blood, organ, and bone marrow donorship, as well as the genetic disposition toward certain kinds of illnesses and diseases, ranging from drug and alcohol addiction, diabetes, hypertension, cancers, osteoporosis, and strokes to getting HIV.

Recommendation: APA community health and social service agencies must begin strategic outreach programs to interracial families and multiracial individuals. A massive campaign to collect and to bank health data on interracial families and multiracial APAs for blood, organ, and bone marrow donorship purpose needs to be undertaken. Pacific Islanders, of whom many are multiracial, have many health risks and complications due to their dispossessed status. It is more critical than ever to have accurate health statistics in order to meet their health needs.

3) Amerasians

The philanthropic work of those like Pearl S. Buck has been most notable in addressing the "dilemma" of Amerasians in Asia. However, after 100 years of American colonial and military legacy in Asia, it is long overdue for the U.S. government and the military to redress Amerasian children and their families throughout Asia and the Pacific. Right after World War II, the Japanese American Citizen's League played a pivotal role in getting the War Brides Acts of the late 1940s passed into legislation, mostly to help Japanese American servicemen and their native Japanese fiancées (though it helped Asian women and Amerasian children of many other ancestries).

Recommendation: The option to choose life in Asia and/or life in America should be granted to all Amerasians from all parts of Asia. Similar legislation to the Homecoming Act of 1987 needs to be introduced for the benefit of all Amerasians, but especially for those from Okinawa, Cambodia, South Korea, Thailand, and the Philippines, who have been long forgotten. In the way American fathers are required to meet paternal obligations through child support in the United States, the U.S. military and the U.S. government need to establish a mandate for American civilian and military personnel who have children overseas to meet their parental obligation and to provide financial support for their Amerasian children until legal adulthood. To address the historical, social and economic concerns of Amerasians will require pan-ethnic collaboration by many APA agencies and multiracial organizations to lobby the U.S. government and U.S. military.

4) Disadvantaged status

From 1977 until the recent 2000 Census, the Office of Management and Budget, which oversees the U.S. Census, had designated five racial categories. In 2000, Native Hawaiians and Pacific Islanders, who represent less than 1 percent of the total U.S. population, were separated into their own category. Also, for the first time, multiple racial designations were made possible.

Presumably, multiracial people who check more than one racial category would be able to continue qualifying as historically disadvantaged minorities for federally mandated special considerations in university admissions and employment. However, this has been a point of major contention for racial minority communities, who have found the "chameleon qualities" of bi-racial and multiracial people (understandably so) to be based on individual opportunism at the expense of traditional racial minorities who fought vigorously for these gains and who still desperately need specific kinds of resources and special recognition to counter the structural barriers that limit community progress.

Some, such as Henry Der from the National Coalition for an Accurate Count of Asians and Pacific Islanders, have even asked whether or not biracial and multiracial people warrant their own racial category—a racial category, which of course, assumes a shared history and collective sense of identity—for the purposes of specific provisions and the intended benefits of Federal laws and programs. Der put forth, ". . . biracial or multiracial persons have the burden to document what distinct experiences or disadvantagement, in contrast to persons of protected single race backgrounds. . ."

Recommendation: In the way that some Asian Americans, like Japanese Americans and Chinese Americans, are no longer treated as disadvantaged minorities in certain instances, some combinations of bi-racial and multiracial Asian Americans should not have access to programs designed to offset structural inequalities for underrepresented APA populations. However, so long as structural inequalities persist and the Office of Management and Budget attempts to monitor the progress of various racial and ethnic communities through racial record-keeping and data tabulations—as it should—APA-descent multiracial individuals must remain part of these federal guidelines. With proponents of the racial privacy initiative attempting to drive U.S. racial policy, this issue seems to be of critical importance to single-race and multiple-race identified individuals who will be affected detrimentally if structural inequalities are not honestly addressed in school admissions, the workplace, etc.

5) Indigenous status of Pacific Islanders

Native Hawaiians, Chamorro people, and Samoans from American Samoa have a significantly different U.S. incorporation history than most Asian American groups. As indigenous peoples to geographic locations that are now integral parts of the United States, there are urgent legal, social, political and medical matters that certain Pacific Islander groups face. Many of their issues and concerns mirror the experiences of American Indians and Native Alaskans.

The Native Hawaiian Sovereignty Movement has been an example of how sharply different many Native Hawaiians experience "Hawai'i as the 50th State" than do Asian Americans. Although including Pacific Islanders into the APA count often benefits Asian Americans, there may be times when it is necessary to support the separate social and political identity of Pacific Islanders.

Recommendations: There are serious health concerns, land and tenant struggles, water usage rights, right to self-determination, etc. that face Native Hawaiians in Hawai'i, the Chamorro people in Guam, and Samoans in American Samoa. Asian Americans must educate themselves on their social, political, cultural, and legal relationship to the continual decline in Pacific Islander ways of life and Asian American organizations and institutions must determine ways in which they can serve as allies to the various groups and factions within Pacific Islander communities.

Interestingly, in Hawai'i, for example, a minimum 50 percent Native Hawaiian descent is necessary for access to Hawaiian Homelands. Considering that most of those who are part Hawaiian are less than 50 percent by ancestry, this designation may be a clever way of preventing the United States from meeting its legal obligations to Native Hawaiians. Though, in the case of attending the private Bishop Estate-run Kamehameha Schools, one only needs to prove any amount of Native Hawaiian ancestry. In order for the United States and the state of Hawai'i to fulfill their promises to Native Hawaiians, perhaps, it may be time to challenge the 50 percent policy and for Asian Americans to support Native Hawaiians in their efforts to access Hawaiian Homelands through other measures besides being 50 percent Native Hawaiian.

6) Outreach and awareness

Acceptance and inclusion of interracial couples and multiracial Asian Americans into Asian America's community-based schools, churches, voluntary ethnic associations, and civil rights organizations will require extensive community awareness and education efforts. The San Francisco-based Hapa Issues Forum has been at the forefront, forging connections with various APA communities.

Recommendation: Educational outreach programs on multiracial Asian Americans should be part of every Asian American organization. Multiracial identity workshops should be part of every Asian American conference. Multiracial Asian Americans should be represented at all levels of decision-making for APA communities. In particular, APA communities need much education on the realities and complex identity experiences of Asian-descent and Pacific Islander-descent multiracials of African American, Latino, Native American, and other racial/ethnic minority backgrounds. Though Asian European Americans report their share of marginalized experiences in APA communities, particular emphasis must be made on the acceptance and inclusion of multiracial APAs who are not of part-European ancestry.

Conclusion

The 2000 Census seems only to confirm that APA communities have always been, are becoming more so, and will most likely remain one of the most "important socio-political site[s] of racial reconfiguration and ethnic re-articulation." For at least two decades, the shared sentiment of scholars and community leaders has been that APA communities are undergoing significant shifts in their demographic composition. Along with population movements such as immigration and migration, interracial and interethnic unions often in the form of legal marriages, have been cited as leading causes for these changes. APA communities continue to become increasingly complex, pan-organizational, transnational, and ever-changing, so much so that these adjectives which connote "diversity" have become stereotypically passe and cliched. Yet, fundamental shifts in APA communities are real, occurring at a more rapid pace.

The faces, the names, and the social realities of bi-racial and multiracial Asian Americans and Pacific Islanders reflect one of the many transformative processes taking place within and across APA communities in which race, ethnicity, gender, class and transnational statuses are converging on both interpersonal and institutional levels. APA community and identity boundaries are, therefore, all the more subject to dissent from within and contestation from without. Multiracial APAs who embody this simultaneity of dissent from within and contestations from without are one of many dynamic forces and untapped resources within and across APA communities. The discussions of centering and amalgamating bi-racial and multiracial Asian Americans and Pacific Islanders into APA communities afford our communities an opportunity to confront and eradicate hierarchically racialized and gendered APA identities, as well as reassess and re-organize the increasingly transcultural and transnational arrangements of APA communities in America.

—Teresa Williams-Leon

The Write-In Race

It happened again. My wife was coming back from enrolling my daughter in a new school. And she was livid. She was waving one of those forms they give you. And she was going amok. All it took was that one question, the one that asks about your child's race. All you have to do is check the box.

Easier said than done. A simple question in a monochromatic era of the past, but we're practically to the next century. Genes know no borders. With all the mixing and criss-crossing, which box do you check, especially if you're half-Asian and half-something else? And what if the "something else" has it's own derivations? There isn't a box big enough for just my side of the family, let alone my wife's. There aren't enough boxes for the entire world.

U.S. Census officials like to put everyone in a little box: white, black, American Indian and Alaskan native, Asian and Pacific Islander, Hispanic or Spanish. This, of course, is a threat to any interracial family harmony. Huge family arguments have erupted over whose side gets to designate the box on the form.

My daughter, for example, is half-Filipino. She's also a quarter-Irish. A little bit of Scotch (not on the rocks). But trying to make the answer Census-ready is enough to put a marriage on the rocks.

"She's Filipino," I say to my wife proudly. "Mark the box."

"No she's not," she says, a sudden stickler for accuracy and a new devotee of identity politics. "What about me?"

She was unconvinced that, with whites still a majority in the nation, we should give my daughter to the Filipinos to "help them out." So we compromised. She got to mark down whatever she wanted – just as long as she gave all three of our dogs a much needed bath.

But this is not the best way to settle this matter. Still, the dogs were, as they say, "so clean you could eat off them." And the school district got its form.

And my daughter? My wife marked the box "other."

The Census Bureau has finally become sensitive to these family squabbles. Starting with the 2000 Census, for the first time, officials have created an unprecedented new category. Welcome all those of "some other race." The Census folks have exploded the box, and given us some room to see if our descriptive power matches our procreative ingenuity. The new Census form, unveiled in Los Angeles, will now allow people to write in their own ethnicity.

That's right. Now you can write in your ethnicity. But this poses its own problems. First, we'll need an acronym for "some other race." "SOR" raises a homonym that plays too much into the right-wing folks who denounce "grievance politics." We shouldn't be sore about anything, though we've waited a long time to be recognized.

I like the term "SOMOR," as in "I really hated the choices the Census Bureau gave me, so here are SOMOR to consider." It's estimated that there are 5 million people potentially affected by the multi-race change. Maybe more. That's just it. We don't know.

Some don't want to know. There are those who are threatened with knowing how many mixed race people are out there. Oddly enough, some civil rights folks claim that this new category will take away from Asian, black, and Latino numbers. In other words, we lose our fair share of the political pie if we take a stand on pride and heritage—and truth. If we create smaller minorities, we lose. It's a new version of divide and conquer.

Emil Guillermo goes amok figuring out how to identify his hapa daughter to the Census.

Photo: Emil Guillermo

I don't see it that way. I'd rather we see a more accurate picture of the new America. But to help out the folks at the Census, and to make sure we're not overly creative, here are some new write-in categories for people to use.

For example, I've long believed that Filipinos are really Asian Hispanics. We're in the vicinity of China, but we genuflect to the pope, thanks to those damn Spanish explorers. The country is named after King Philip of Spain, after all. I say Filipinos should write down "Aspanic."

Some others in Emil shorthand:
Asian-white: Assites.
Black-white: Blites.
Hispanic-white: Hispites.
Japanese-white: Nippites.
Chinese-black: Chigroes.
Hispanic-black: Blaspanics.

What about my daughter? We borrowed a term coined by our friend at the University of Connecticut, Angela Rolla, herself the mother of two beautiful mixed-race Filipino-Caucasian kids. What does Rolla call them? Cauca-pinos.

From Gold Mountain to Globalization

Over the last two decades, close to 13 million individuals have immigrated to the United States. This impressive scale of human migration is aggrandized by the diversity of cultures among these new Americans. Despite the continuing anti-immigration sentiments and the xenophobic behavior of some in the United States, the flow of immigration continues to reinvent the American identity and its reflection in American cities.

Nowhere is this more obvious than in California, where over 26 percent of all immigrants to the United States have arrived since 1980. While a significant amount of attention has focused on Latino immigration to California during the last two decades, Asian immigration has also loomed large. Over 2 million Asian immigrants arrived in the United States during the 1990s; 34 percent chose California as their destination.

In 1990, California's Asian community was 2.8 million, and during the ensuing decade it increased to 3.8 million in 2000. This growth is primarily due to immigration, and secondarily to births. From 1990 to 1998, Asian immigration brought 2.2 million new individuals to the U.S., 766,000 of whom settled in California. This meant that of the 969,000 people who moved to California during that time, 79 percent were recent immigrants. This level of immigration has led to a constant re-invention of Asian Pacific American identity, as old and new "Asians" meet to articulate a uniquely hyphenated identity that is as much rooted in the American sociopolitical structure as it is in the global Asian diaspora.

Photo: AP Wide World

Angel Island, once California's point of entry for new immigrants on the West, processed close to one million immigrants, mostly from China and Japan, from 1910 to 1940.

What is in a name?

In the United States, the word Asian can be a source of confusion for many readers who are not familiar with this arbitrary demographic taxonomy. For example, western Asia, which includes the Arab world, Israel, Turkey, Iran, and Afghanistan, is summarily excluded. "Asian" in the United States appears to be a racialized identity that is politically created and geographically inaccurate. In that light, we may have arrived at a point in the political identity of the United States when deconstruction of demographic meta-categories, as well as other ethno-national identities, may

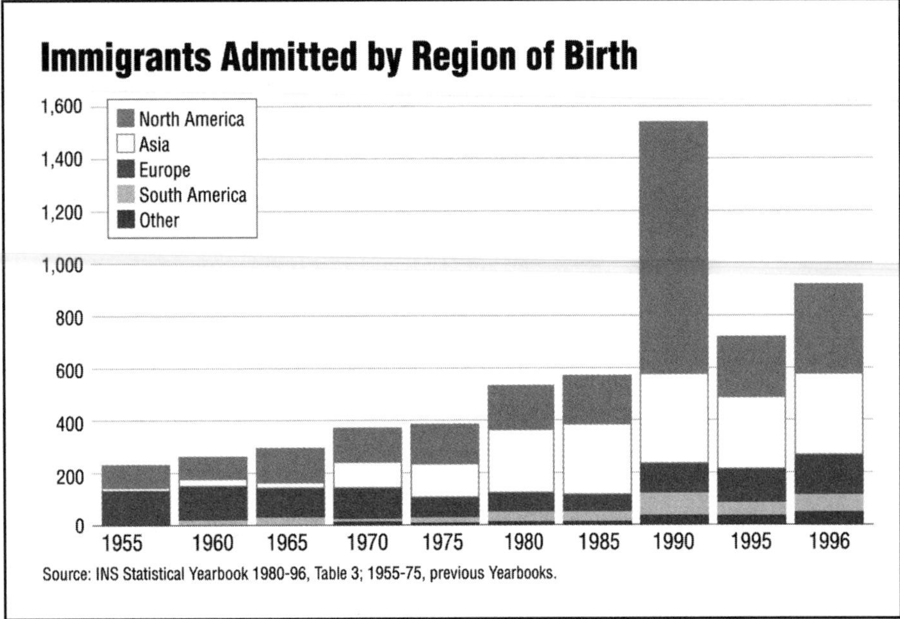

Source: INS Statistical Yearbook 1980-96, Table 3; 1955-75, previous Yearbooks.

be necessary, in order to stem the seeming profusion of banal terminologies in the everyday discourse on multiculturalism. We need to examine the need for continental identities in the face of emergent emphasis on the local.

While the adequacy of terms such as "Asian," "Latino," "African American," and "White" in describing a group of people is doubtful, the apparent political necessity for maintaining and nurturing such ambiguous terms is interesting. What does the word Asian, then, really imply? How does one hyphenate two continents to create the Asian-American identity? If Asian and American implicitly exclude certain peoples and countries, how inclusive is the hyphenation of the two of them? Like others, I use "Asian" for the purpose of compatibility with other narratives and analyses. However, I remain unconvinced of its adequacy and appropriateness.

Pattern and magnitude of immigration

From 1820 to 1998, 63 million individuals immigrated to the United States. Among these, close to eight million have been Asian. But close to one-fifth of all immigrants—and more than four-fifths of Asian immigrants—arrived to the United States during the 80s and 90s. These 12.8 million individuals represent a new "peopling" phase in the dynamics of American demography.

Unlike their early 20th century predecessors, the new immigrants are mainly from Latin America and Asia, and the latter group alone provided close to seven million immigrants. Fueled by a growing post-WW II economy and a shift in immigration policy, the new immigrants have arrived in the United States to fill a range of niches from professional to industrial and service sector jobs. Despite declining annual immigration rates, Asian immigrants continue to fuel the growing Asian population of the United States.

Immigrants increasingly chose California as their state of residence. From 1980 to 1998, California's share of annual U.S. immigration averaged slightly over 26 percent. The popularity of the greater Los Angeles area—about one in ten immigrants between 1983-1998 chose it as home—has turned it into a new Ellis Island. Today in Los Angeles County, over one-third of all residents are foreign-born.

Asian immigration

With 2.2 million immigrants, Asian countries were the source of about 31 percent of total U.S. immigration from 1990 to 1998. While the annual number of Asian immigrants declined from a high of 302,542 in 1994 to 172,174 in 1998, California remains the leading destination. As of 1998, California was still receiving more than 32 percent of its documented immigrants from the listed Asian

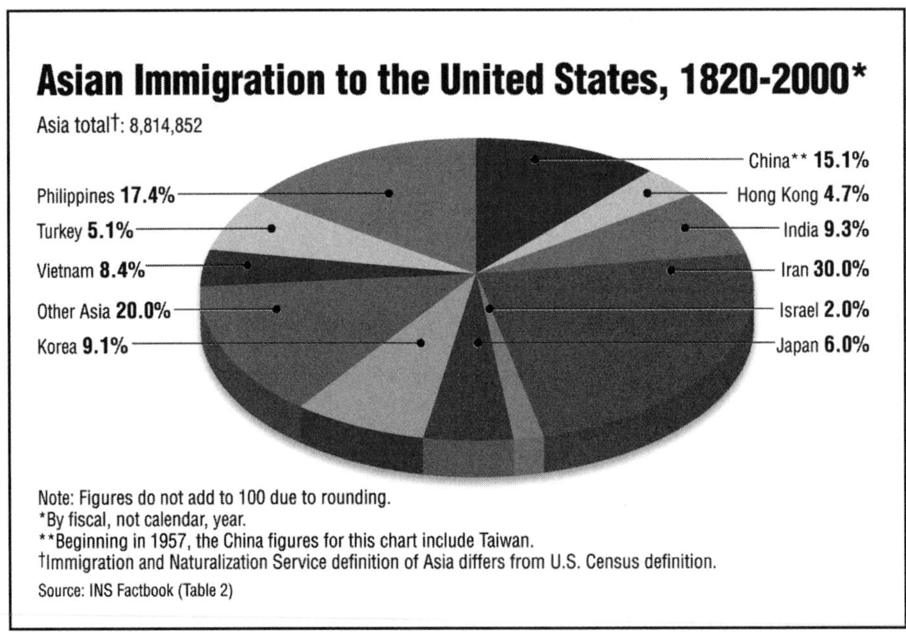

Note: Figures do not add to 100 due to rounding.
*By fiscal, not calendar, year.
**Beginning in 1957, the China figures for this chart include Taiwan.
†Immigration and Naturalization Service definition of Asia differs from U.S. Census definition.
Source: INS Factbook (Table 2)

countries. For the country as a whole, Asians still provide over 26 percent of the annual immigration.

Among the top 10 nations sending Asian immigrants to the United States from 1990 to 1998, the Philippines, China, Vietnam, India, Korea, Pakistan, and Taiwan appear every year. The Philippines was the single largest source of Asian immigration. Meanwhile, seven leading countries supplied 1.9 million, or 85 percent, of all Asian immigrants in the 1990s. For California, this pattern remains consistent with the national picture, with the only difference that Hong Kong replaces Pakistan on the top ten list during the 1990s.

While it appears that California attracts a significant number of Asian immigrants to the United States, the level of attraction varies from one nationality to the next. For example, 46.2 percent of Taiwanese chose California as their state of intended residence in the 1990s, but only 29.7 percent of Korean immigrants came to this state. Only 19.6 percent of Asian Indian immigrants chose California. As such, the sociopolitical identity of the Asian Pacific American community varies from one region to the next. Assuming current immigration patterns continue to hold, California's Asian community will be largely defined by Filipinos, Vietnamese, Chinese, including Taiwanese and people from Hong Kong, Asian Indians, Koreans—plus the long-established Japanese American population, for whom immigration has been in decline since World War II.

In addition to their changing national origins, new immigrants are demographically different, as well. For example, whereas older immigrants were mostly young men, by the 1980s and 1990s, women became the majority and the average age of immigrants was on the rise, as well. Therefore, a typical immigrant is no longer a young male, but an older married female. This is also true for Asians, and even more pronounced among Asian immigrants to California. This suggests that we can expect a stronger set of Asian cultural communities, where extended family structures will contribute to a longer maintenance of cultural identities, and hence a political machine for asserting a group's particularistic rights.

Where Asian immigrants go

Asian immigrants in the 1990s went mainly to four states: California, New York, Texas, and New Jersey (in that order). These states collectively received about 1.3 million, or 58 percent, of all Asian immigrants, with California taking about one-third by itself. With the exception of Illinois, the Midwestern and Rocky Mountain states receive few Asian immigrants. However, Asians have chosen both "frost-belt" and "sun-belt" states as their places of intended residence. The logic of this geography rests on previously established Asian communities, as well as on economic opportunities available in major American cities. The 2000 Census results indicate that in addition to the four states listed, Washington and Hawai'i continue to house a significant portion of the APA population.

New Asian immigrants primarily moved to areas where pockets of Asian communities already existed. Looking at ZIP codes, 15 attracted more than 5,000 immigrants during the 1990s. With a total Asian immigration share of over 95,000 (i.e. over 12 percent of all the Asian immigrants in California during this period) these ZIP codes identify the core of Asian communities in California. Unsurprisingly, these ZIP codes are mainly in the larger urban areas of Los Angeles, Orange County, San Diego and the Bay Area, but the fact that Orange County is the leading destination may be of interest to some. ZIP code 92683, located in the city of Westminster, nicknamed "Little Saigon" for its thriving Vietnamese community, attracted over 10,000 Asians during the 1990s, followed by numbers ranging from 6,800 to 8,000 in three other ZIP codes in the Bay Area.

While Los Angeles County's share of Asian immigrants is over 210,000 during this period, only three of the 15 largest ZIP codes of Asian concentrations (i.e., over 5,000) appear in this county. In order of magnitude, these ZIP codes are 91754, 91801 and 90701. As expected, they are to be found in Alhambra, Monterey Park and Artesia, where a large APA population had already existed in 1990. As such, Asian immigration has not only provided a numerical boost to the APA population in the state, but the geographic specificity with which the 1990s immigration has occurred points to a political strengthening of specific regions within the state. These are typically contested places, where the numerical growth

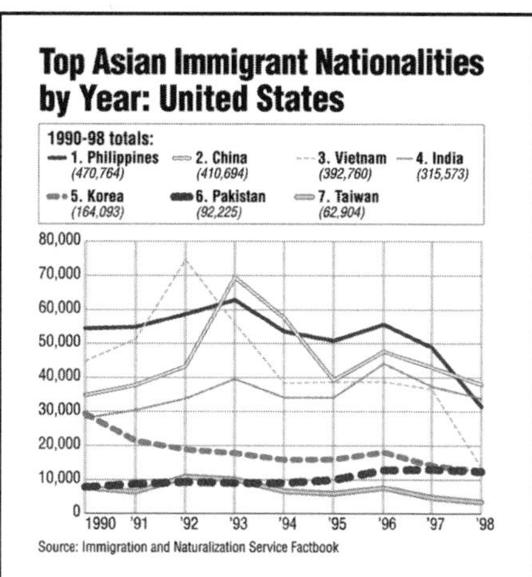

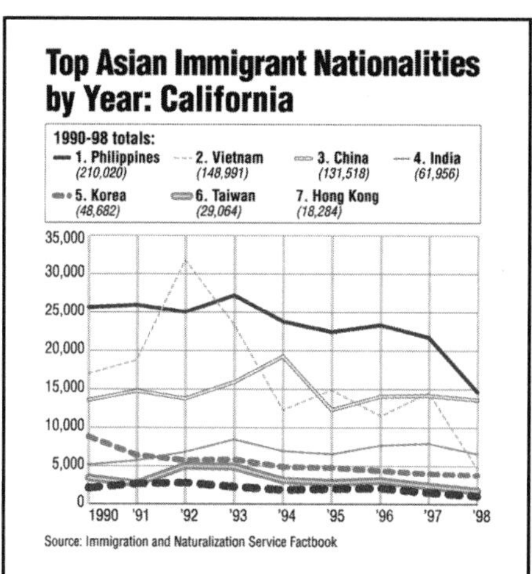

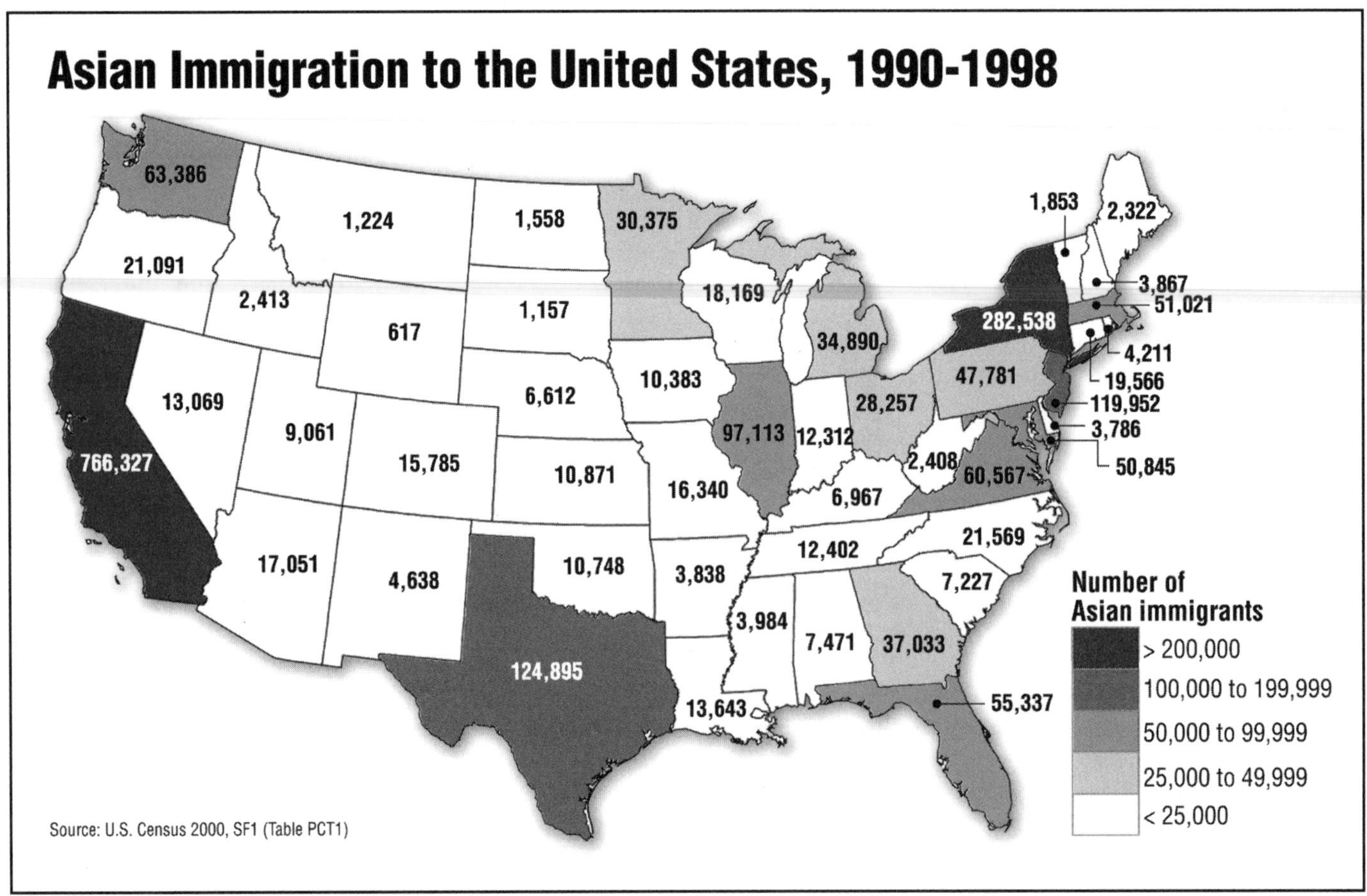

of Asians may have become equated with their need for the appropriate political representation and socioeconomic infrastructure.

Challenging perceptions of homogeneity

Despite the political adoption of a single nomenclature, the APA community and its immigrant subset are far from being a homogenous population. More so than Latinos, the APA community is divided by linguistic, religious, national identity and political affiliations. As such, it would be a mistake to interpret the immigration pattern of Asians as a singular demographic event. In fact, the internal diversity of the APA community necessitates a micro-level analysis of this population. While this volume will make significant strides in that arena, I wish to explore this diversity by showing how Korean immigration deviates significantly from other Asian groups.

As Dr. Eui-Young Yu illustrates elsewhere in this volume, Koreans have been in America since the earlier part of the 20th century; however, on the eve of the 1965 Immigration Act, the Korean American population was less than 70,000. In fact, the documented Korean immigrants from 1903 to 1964 were numbered at only about 22,300, but political events in Korea and the impact of the 1965 Immigration Act led to an increased flow of Koreans to the United States after 1970. By 1975, when the annual immigration rate of Koreans stabilized at around 30,000 per annum, Korea had become the third largest source of immigrants to the U.S. During the 70s, the Korean community grew by 417 percent, which was three times larger than the growth rate of the entire Asian population. With 357,000 Koreans in the U.S. at the beginning of the 1980s, Korean communities began to thrive in the decade to come and Koreatown became a popular word in Southern California and elsewhere, in any discussion of Korean American communities.

The emergence of Los Angeles as the geographic center of the Korean American community was no accident. In Los Angeles County, the Korean population grew nearly six-fold from 1970 to 1980—bigger even than the four-fold increase in the whole country. Korean immigration and its geographic orientation provided a rich example of an emerging middle class immigrant community with aspirations of social, political and economic ascendance.

During the 1980s, Korean immigrants continued to arrive in the United States in large numbers and the annual immigration rates never fell below 30,000. By 1990, the Korean community had grown to 799,000 in the United States and 144,000 in Los Angeles County. This was a doubling of the population

Over two million Asian immigrants arrived in the United States during the 1990s; almost exactly one-third chose California as their destination.

at both geographic scales in one decade. However, despite this impressive growth, the 1990s were to pose a challenge to the continued growth and concentration of this population.

Immigration from Korea dropped below 30,000 after 1990 and reached its lowest level in 1998. While some may attempt to explain the decreasing Korean immigration as a result of the 1992 civil unrest in Los Angeles, the reality was that numbers were declining before that. It is more plausible that the lower Korean immigration rate is due to the long-term rise in Korean economy and living standards, problems with the American economy, and the rise of anti-immigration sentiments in the United States.

At the same time that their immigration rates were declining, Korean immigrants were decreasingly choosing to live in California. By 1998, less than 4,000 Koreans were declaring California as their intended state of residence. Within California, new Korean immigrants were also dispersing into new neighborhoods. For example, while the top ten ZIP codes of Korean destination in 1990 received about 2,600 Korean immigrants, in 1998, the same ZIP codes attracted only 750 Korean immigrants. This declined even more quickly than overall Korean immigration. Korean immigrants not only began to find newer areas to settle, but also were decreasingly congregating in large numbers. By 1998, the highest ZIP code of destination (i.e. 11354) attracted only 147 immigrants. However, that ZIP code did not even appear on the list in 1990. Therefore, not only did New York, rather than Los Angeles, provide the ZIP code with the largest recipient of Korean immigration, but the level of concentration is also less than it was during the earlier part of the decade.

Korean immigration patterns displayed signs of further deviation from the Asian norm. For example, while Asian female immigrants continued to outnumber males in the 1990s, this gender gap gradually declined among Koreans. One explanation is that there are now many Korean families in the United States, meaning that marriages between those in Korea and the United States, and the resulting family reunification, has gradually declined among Koreans. This suggests that Koreans have acquired their hyphenated Americanness through longer residences (over three decades by now), and that their community benefits from a larger presence of extended families.

There is no doubt that Koreans remain an important part of the APA community, despite their declining immigration rate. Furthermore, more than any other APA groups, Korean Americans are establishing communities in diverse locations around the United States. Alabama, Alaska, New Hampshire, Missouri, North Dakota, and South Dakota, are among the states where more than 15 percent of the APA population are Korean. This suggests Koreans are taking root in the United States and moving beyond the need for high levels of proximity to large ethnic enclaves. While estimating the impact of the 1992 civil unrest in Los Angeles on Korean geographic patterns is not an easy task, it is difficult to deny that this event may have created a significant demographic process through which the Korean community has begun to diffuse geographically.

Whatever the cause, Korean Americans appear to be different in important ways from the rest of the APA community. First, with a declining immigration rate, second and third generation Korean Americans are becoming sizable. Second, while Korean enclaves such as L.A.'s Koreatown will remain an icon of ethnic identity, they will lose their importance gradually as an economic center for new immigrants.

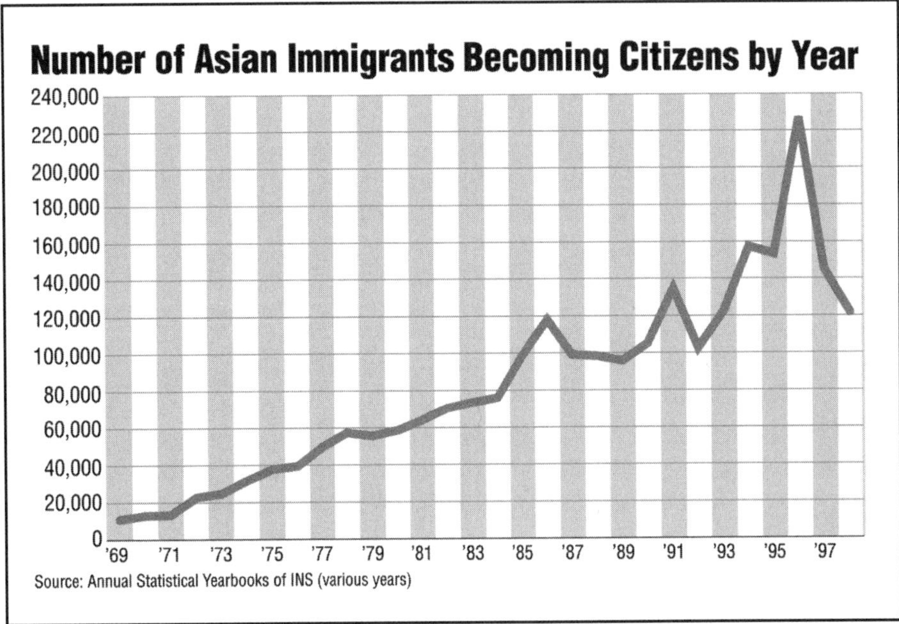

Shift in Asian orphan adoption

Asian children adopted by Americans, often referred to as trans-racial adoptees, used to be mostly Korean Americans. In Minnesota, for example, the influence of the Lutheran Church led many Korean Americans there to be adopted by local families—and grow up with distinctly un-Korean names like Kristen Jensvold and Robert Kerry. The aftermath of the Vietnam War and the plight of orphans and Amerasian children led to a rise in the adoption of Southeast Asian orphans and children.

By the 1990s, however, adoption of Chinese babies by Americans, virtually all of them girls, was becoming dominant. The Chinese Government's one-child policy for families was intended to limit population growth. But some parents, wishing for a son, would abandon their girls or give them up for adoption. In 2000, nearly 5,000 Chinese babies were brought over for adoption, according to the INS, 97 percent of those girls.

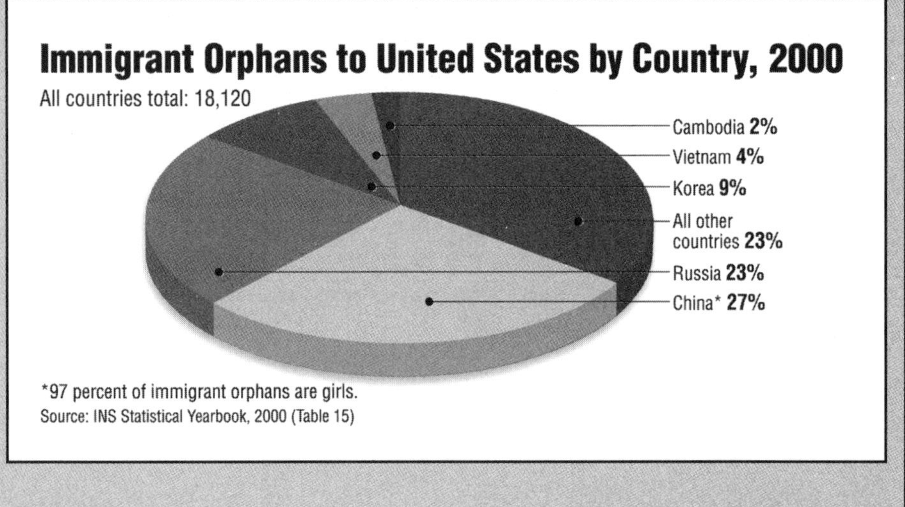

Korean immigration to the United States may yet become strong again, given possible changes in global and local economies (as well as politics). However, a large time gap between one group of immigrants and the next may produce differentiated identities that will fracture the community along the lines of new and old—an experience familiar to Chinese Americans. Given the complexity of Asian identity, the internal nuances of subgroups and their evolving patterns point to an interesting future of heterogeneity among APAs.

Conclusion

By 2020, the overall APA population will reach close to 19.6 million—a sizable community whose role in the political decision-making process cannot be ignored. The challenge for the APA community will lie in its willingness to participate in the political process. This will include increased citizenship and voting rates, as well as creating an APA political machine that ensures a full hearing for this community's particularistic demands on the American political system. Given the growing naturalization rates among APAs, especially during the first half of the 1990, it is possible to create such a political force in the United States.

This does not suggest a deviation from the American system of government, but a convergence on it, while emphasizing the second half of the hyphenated identity. Without a doubt, while APAs may seek their cultural values from the Asian or Pacific Islander component of their compound identity, succeeding in the United States will depend on their willingness to extract from their American-ness a commitment to political participation. What we may see by 2020 and beyond is a lesser pronouncement of geographic enclaves and higher virtual cohesion along political, economic, and intellectual dimensions.

Still, much will depend on the sociopolitical environment of the United States and its attitude toward immigrant and minority communities. However, given the American participatory political system, it is possible to create better socioeconomic and political experiences for specific communities. The degree to which this must be accomplished at specific geographic locations is indicative of deficiencies in the sociopolitical conditions of the host country. If a pan-APA identity can be a tool to assure equity in a system that only responds to "pressure groups," the maintenance of APA identity will be necessary regardless of its cultural ramifications. Sociopolitical negotiations of the next few decades will determine the degree to which APA identity will become a cultural category or a political organizing tool in the United States.

—Ali Modarres

The Model Minority?

If you have ever walked the streets of San Francisco's Chinatown and seen the tiny "single resident occupancy" units that more often than not house entire families, if you know Asian immigrant women who work in sewing factories making below minimum wage, if you have ever talked to immigrant youth who are struggling to graduate from this country's urban high schools—you know that not all Asian Pacific Americans have achieved the American dream.

Nevertheless, APAs continue to be labeled model minorities, with statistics giving credence to this notion. According to the 2000 Census, compared to the national average, Asian Americans were more likely to grow up in two-parent homes. They earned the highest median family income and graduated from college at disproportionately high rates.

At the same time, however, the Census also revealed a highly divided population, split between the haves and have-nots. In short, the Census results served as a reminder of gross inequities that remain stubbornly intact in 21st century.

Many APA community groups were aware of these inequities long before the release of the 2000 Census. In fact, in an effort to confront discrimination, Native Hawaiian/Pacific Islander (NHPI) activists lobbied successfully to create a separate category for their population. By doing so, they believed statistics would reveal NHPIs as an underclass, a community that still faces barriers to participating fully in American society.

Indeed, the 2000 Census indicated that and more. For the first time, the Census classified NHPIs into a distinct group, comprised of Native Hawaiians, Samoans, Tongans, "other Polynesians," Guamanians, "other Micronesians," Melanesians and Pacific Islanders "non-specified." The Asian American population consisted of Chinese, Filipino, Japanese, Asian Indian, Korean, Vietnamese, Cambodian, Hmong, Laotian, Thai and "other Asians."

In almost all socioeconomic categories, African Americans and Latinos fared the worst, while non-Hispanic whites maintained their position as the privileged class. For example, the national poverty rate was 12.4 percent,

Photo: Corky Lee

One in seven Asian children live in poverty, according to Census statistics. More than one in five NHPI children grows up poor.

Household Size by Type, 1999

ALL HOUSEHOLDS	
TOTAL	**105,539,122**
1-person household	**27,203,724**
Male householder	11,569,038
Female householder	15,634,686
2-or-more-person household	**78,335,398**
Family households	**72,261,780**
Married-couple family	**55,458,451**
With own children under 18 years	25,674,582
No own children under 18 years	29,783,869
Other family	**16,803,329**
Male householder, no wife present	**4,302,568**
With own children under 18 years	2,190,654
No own children under 18 years	2,111,914
Female householder, no husband present	**12,500,761**
With own children under 18 years	7,369,167
No own children under 18 years	5,131,594
Nonfamily households	**6,073,618**
Male householder	3,570,290
Female householder	2,503,328

Note: 77 percent of family households involve married couples.
6 percent of all single-parent family households are headed by men with no wife present.
17 percent of all family households are headed by women with no husband present.

Source: U.S. Census 2000, SF3, Tables H85 and HCT42, P10 and P146A-I

but broken down, the proportion was 8.1 percent for non-Hispanic whites, 22.6 percent for Latinos and 24.9 percent for African Americans.

Among these segregated classes were Asian and NHPI Americans. In most categories, the socioeconomic statistics for Asian Americans mirrored the statistics for non-Hispanic whites, and the numbers for NHPIs more closely matched those for Latinos and African Americans.

Other data indicates even further division within the Asian American population. Thus, while it may appear Asian Americans have achieved the American dream, a closer look at the statistics shows a highly diverse population, one in which a sizeable number continue to struggle.

The following is a summary of the socioeconomic status of Asian Pacific Americans in the year 2000. The socioeconomic data used here provides information for only the "alone" categories for Asians and NHPIs. Because data regarding hapas was available only as part of the "Two Race or more" category, this group was excluded from the APA totals.

Population and immigration

The single-race Asian Pacific American population grew substantially in the past 10 years to 10,550,602 (3.7 percent of the population) from 6,876,394 (2.8 percent of the population). The APA population was also relatively young, with median ages of 32.7 and 27.5, respectively, for Asian Americans and NHPIs, compared to the national median of 35.3.

Asian Americans were, by and large, an immigrant population. In 1990, 65.6 percent of Asian Americans were born in foreign countries. In 2000, the proportion increased to 68.9 percent, while just 11.1 percent of the total U.S. population was foreign-born. Unlike the stereotype of being foreigners clinging to their old country, Asian Americans became naturalized citizens at high rates: 49.9 percent versus 40.3 percent of the total foreign-born population.

Given these statistics, it is no surprise that language remained one of the biggest barriers for Asian Americans. In 2000, 2.6 percent of the 105,539,122 U.S. households spoke an Asian language, the most common being Chinese, Korean, Vietnamese and Tagalog. Of those Asian-language households, 29.2 percent—or 801,253 households—were linguistically isolated, meaning all the adults in the household (high school age and older) had some limitation in communicating in English. Moreover, of 9,520,205 Asian Americans 5 years old and over, 39.5 percent (3,760,480) did not speak English "very well," and 3.4 percent (326,064) did not speak English at all.

By contrast, the NHPI population—a large proportion of which was Native Hawaiian—was less likely to be foreign-born and less likely to face language barriers. Still, Census numbers indicated an increased presence of foreign-born NHPIs, 13 percent in 1990 versus 19.9 percent in 2000. Of the 347,400 Pacific Islanders 5 years old and over, 15.0 percent (52,110) did not speak English "very well"; and 1.2 percent (4,270) did not speak English at all.

Family values

Asian Americans tended to come from larger families and were more likely to grow up in two-parent households than any other group. On the other hand, though NHPIs, like Asian Americans, had larger than average families, they were less likely than average to come from two-parent homes.

Nationwide, family size decreased over the past decade. In 2000, the average was 3.14 persons for all U.S. families (compared to 3.2 in 1990), 3.61 persons for Asian American families (compared to 3.8 in 1990), and 4.05 for NHPI American families (compared to 4.2 in 1990).

The proportion of Asian American families maintained by a husband and wife in 2000 remained stable over the past decade at 82.2 percent, higher than the national average of 76.7. The proportion of married-couple families among NHPI family households, however, was significantly lower, at 71.2 percent.

Meanwhile, Asian American family households were less likely than average to be headed by women (with no husbands present), while NPHI family households were more likely to be headed by women. In 2000, 17.3 percent of all U.S. families fell into this category; the ratios for NHPI family households and Asian American family households were 18.8 percent and 11.4 percent respectively.

Place of Birth by Citizenship Status and Race, 1999

	General population	Non-Hispanic white alone	Hispanic alone	Black alone	Asian alone	NHPI alone
TOTAL	**281,421,906**	**194,514,140**	**35,238,481**	**34,361,740**	**10,171,820**	**378,782**
% foreign-born that are citizens	40.3%	54.5%	27.8%	44.5%	49.9%	40.1%
Native	**250,314,017**	**187,673,608**	**21,080,664**	**32,261,875**	**3,159,618**	**303,305**
Born in state of residence	168,729,388	123,193,684	15,806,739	23,215,912	2,310,188	176,480
Born in other state in the United States	78,057,078	63,150,088	3,607,235	8,769,562	726,278	77,202
Northeast	*18,563,204*	*16,119,105*	*763,315*	*1,281,057*	*173,525*	*4,622*
Midwest	*21,969,267*	*19,739,212*	*455,338*	*1,251,906*	*129,708*	*5,769*
South	*25,301,191*	*17,759,452*	*1,067,588*	*5,744,410*	*146,884*	*9,530*
West	*12,223,416*	*9,532,319*	*1,320,994*	*492,189*	*276,161*	*57,281*
Born outside the United States	3,527,551	1,329,836	1,666,690	276,401	123,152	49,623
Puerto Rico	*1,439,674*	*47,522*	*1,371,646*	*68,534*	*3,572*	*1,496*
U.S. Island areas	*166,960*	*38,569*	*14,984*	*48,391*	*10,919*	*42,792*
Born abroad of American parent(s)	*1,920,917*	*1,243,745*	*280,060*	*159,476*	*108,661*	*5,335*
Foreign-born	**31,107,889**	**6,840,532**	**14,157,817**	**2,099,865**	**7,012,202**	**75,477**
Naturalized citizen	12,542,626	3,729,229	3,939,732	934,367	3,502,021	30,284
Not a citizen	18,565,263	3,111,303	10,218,085	1,165,498	3,510,181	45,193

Source: U.S. Census 2000, SF3 (Tables P21, PCT63A-I)

The relatively small fraction of single-mother households among Asian Americans may be a reflection of the low rate of out-of-wedlock births among Asian American women. According to the U.S. Census Survey, 31 percent of the women sampled who gave birth between June 1999 and June 2000 did so while unmarried, much higher than the 15 percent ratio for Asian Pacific American women. (NHPIs were not considered in a separate category.)

That said, it is apparent that among APA families which are not traditional two-parent homes, men played a larger role than average. For example, men headed 6.0 percent of all U.S. family households where wives were absent, a lower proportion compared to that for NHPI family households, 9.3 percent. Moreover, of single-parent homes, nationally, 25.6 were headed by men; for Asian Americans and NHPIs, the ratios were, respectively, 33.9 percent and 33.1 percent.

Homeownership and housing

For many APAs, particularly Chinese American immigrants, owning a home is an ultimate goal, one that symbolizes both permanence and status. However, APAs are less likely than average to be homeowners. While nationally, 66.2 percent of households lived in owner-occupied housing, the proportion was much lower for people of color: 53.2 percent for Asian Americans, 46.3 percent for African Americans, and 45.5 percent for NHPIs.

It is apparent, though, that both NHPI and Asian American homeowners tended to occupy property that was more expensive than average. Considering California, Hawaii and New York were the three states with the largest APA populations—and were also states with the most expensive real estate prices—this makes sense.

The median value for all owner-occupied housing units was $118,800. For Asian American and NHPI owner-occupied units the median values were $199,300 and $160,500, respectively, higher than the median values of homes owned by other groups, including $123,400 for non-Hispanic whites, $105,600 for Latinos, and $80,600 for African Americans. Among all owner-occupied housing units, 20.2 percent were worth $200,000 or more. Between Asian American and NHPI homeowners, however, 49.8 percent and 34.8 percent, respectively, owned property worth $200,000 and up. By contrast, the ratios were 22.4 percent of non-Hispanic white homeowners, 14.6 percent of Latino homeowners, and 7.5 percent of African American homeowners.

Among those with mortgages, non-Hispanic whites dedicated the lowest percent of their household income to owner costs, 21.1 percent. The rate for African Americans was just above that at 21.7 percent, and for Asian Americans, NHPIs and Latinos, the proportions rose to 24.3 percent, 24.7 percent and 24.9 percent respectively.

When it comes to living conditions, Asian Americans appeared to have a greater propensity for residing in crowded areas, presumably because of their tendency to live in urban cities. Indeed, 18.5 percent of Asian American households lived in structures containing 20 or more units, versus 12.8 per-

Percentage of Children Born Out-of-Wedlock, by Race, 2000

Group	Percentage
Non-Hispanic white alone	26%
Black alone	62%
Asian Pacific American alone	15%
Hispanic alone	30%

Source: U.S. Census Bureau, Current Population Survey, June 2000

cent of black households, 12.1 percent of NHPI households, 12.4 percent of Latino households, and 6.7 percent of non-Hispanic white households.

Interestingly, the fraction of blacks and non-Hispanic whites sharing rooms was much smaller compared to those other groups, 8.5 percent and 1.9 percent respectively. Of the rooms occupied by Asian Americans, 20.5 percent were shared by 1.01 or more occupants. For NHPIs, the ratio was 25.7 percent, and for Latinos, 29.3 percent.

Education

Americans became an increasingly educated population in the past decade. In 1990, 78 percent of all Asian Americans and 76 percent of all NHPIs 25 years or over were at least high school graduates; the national rate was 75 percent. In 2000, the rate increased to 80.4 percent nationally, and 80.4 percent and 78.3 percent respectively for Asian Americans and NHPIs.

Notably, Asian Americans received higher education at astounding rates: 44.1 percent of Asian Americans 25 years and over attained bachelor's degrees or higher (master's degrees, Ph.D.s or professional degrees), compared with 27 percent of non-Hispanic whites, 14 percent of African Americans, 13.8 percent of Pacific Islanders and 10.4 percent of Latinos.

At the other end of the spectrum, 19.6 percent of all Americans 25 years old and over had no high school diploma. Non-Hispanic whites had the smallest ratio of people in this category, 14.5 percent. Asian Americans were next with 19.6 percent, followed by NHPIs with 21.7 percent, African Americans with 27.7 percent, and Latinos with 47.6 percent.

Despite the impressive educational achievements of Asian Americans, it must also be pointed out that a smaller proportion of Asian Pacific American women attained at least a high school diploma than average. While nationwide the proportion was 80.7 percent, slightly lower percentages of NHPI women (78.4 percent) and Asian American women (77.8 percent) fell into this category.

Labor

The unemployment rate further substantiated a pattern of bifurcation among the races. For people 16 years and older in the civilian labor population, the national unemployment rate was 5.8 percent; for non-Hispanic whites, 4.3 percent; and Asians, 5.1 percent. However, for Latinos, the proportion was 9.3 percent; NHPIs, 10.9 percent; and African Americans, 11.6 percent.

Overall, however, NHPIs were working at record rates. For the population of people 16 years and older, 66.2 percent of NHPIs participated in the labor market, compared to 63.9 percent nationwide. Meanwhile, non-Hispanic whites, Asian Americans, African Americans and Latinos participated at rates of 64.9 percent, 63.3 percent, 61.4 percent and 60.2 percent respectively.

Of mothers 16 years old and older, Latinos and Asian Americans were the most likely to be full-time parents. Nationwide, 60 percent of mothers were in the labor force, versus 49.5 percent of Latinos and 56.5 percent of Asians. Non-Hispanic white mothers participated in the labor market at a rate of 61.0 percent, NHPI mothers at 61.2 percent and African American mothers at 71.3 percent.

Business

Increasingly, APAs became business owners in the 1990s. According to the 1997 Economic Census, 4.3 percent of all U.S. firms were APA-owned (785,480 out of 18,431,456). The number of such firms increased 30.2 percent from 1992 from 603,426, and showed a 68.4 percent change in sales and receipts during that same period.

Income

In 2000, Asian American earned the highest median family income, $59,324, compared to the national average of $50,046. Non-Hispanic white families trailed with $54,698. NHPI families had a median income of $45,915, followed by Latinos with $34,397, and African Americans with $33,255.

Still, because APA families were larger than average, in terms of per capita income, they earned significantly less than non-Hispanic whites ($24,819). The per capita incomes for Asian Americans, NHPIs, blacks and Latinos were $21,823, $15,054, $14,437 and $12,111 correspondingly.

Similar to the statistics for overall median family income, those for women showed that Asian American women were paid higher average incomes than any other racial group. While the national median earning for women was $27,194, Asian Americans in this category made $31,049. Non-Hispanic whites followed with $28,265; NHPI women with $25,694; African American women with $25,589; and Latino women with $21,634.

Housing Units Worth More than $200,000, by Race of Owner, 1999

	Percentage
General population	20.2%
Black alone	7.5%
Asian alone	49.8%
NHPI alone	34.8%
Hispanic alone	14.6%
Non-Hispanic white alone	22.4%

Source: U.S. Census 2000, Tables H84 and HCT41

For many Asian Pacific Americans, particularly Chinese American immigrants, owning a home is an ultimate goal, one that symbolizes both permanence and status. However, Asian Pacific Americans are less likely than average to be homeowners.

While Asian Americans appeared to be doing relatively well in terms of income, statistics that break down the numbers in terms of ethnicity—due in 2003 when the Census Bureau releases the next round of data from the 2000 Census—are sure to tell a different story. Just as creating a new category for NHPIs indicated large disparities between the average Asian American and the average NPHI, data broken down by ethnicity should show other gaps, as it did in 1990.

For example, in 1990, APAs earned the second highest per capita income. However, that statistic did not expose the divide between ethnic groups. In this case, Japanese Americans earned the highest per capita income of all racial and ethnic groups, $19,373, compared to the national average of $14,143. Meanwhile Hmong Americans, also grouped in the Asian category, had among the lowest per capita income averages, $2,692.

The division in the Asian population is further evidenced in other household income data. While 23.1 percent of Asian American households earned over $100,000, a greater proportion than any other group including the 17.5 percent of non-Hispanic whites, the proportion of Asian American households earning below $20,000 was 13.8, higher than the 10.9 percent of non-Hispanic white households.

Again, NHPIs, Africans and Latinos trailed the rest of Americans; 11.2 percent of NHPI families earned over $100,000, as did just 7.1 percent of African Americans and 6.7 percent of Latinos. Inversely proportional to that, the ratio of NHPIs earning below $20,000 was 18.3 percent; for Latinos and African Americans, the rate was 26.5 percent and 30.4 percent, respectively.

Poverty

Once more, the notion of a segregated society was reinforced by data on poverty rates. In 2000, the national poverty rate was 12.4 percent. Asian Americans were just at that level, 12.6 percent, but significantly above the rate for non-Hispanic whites, 8.1 percent. The statistics for other groups were more sobering: 17.7 percent of NHPIs lived in poverty, as did 22.6 percent of Latinos and 24.9 percent of African Americans.

At the same time, the ratio for women living in poverty was 9.1 percent for non-Hispanic whites, 12.7 percent for Asian Americans, 18.7 percent for NHPIs, 24.2 percent for Latinos, and 26.7 percent for African Americans.

Among Asian Americans, seniors and children were more likely than average to be poor. While only 0.6 percent of non-Hispanic white seniors lived below the poverty line, 12.3 percent of Asian American seniors were in this category. NHPI seniors were better off, with 11.5 percent reporting they lived below the poverty line. For black and Latino seniors, the proportions were 19.6 percent and 23.5 percent respectively.

In addition, Asian Pacific American children faced poverty at heightened rates, though black and Latino children were more at risk. Non-Hispanic white children had the lowest rate of poverty at 9.3 percent, followed by Asian Americans at 14.3 percent, Pacific Islanders at 22.7 percent, Latinos at 27.8 percent and African Americans at 33.1 percent.

Conclusion

The APA community is a highly diverse population, arguably more so than any other racial group. While some families have been in the United States for five generations or longer, many more are recent immigrants. From the Indian hi-

Poverty Status by Age and Race, 1999

TOTAL POPULATION	General population	Non-Hispanic white alone	Hispanic alone	Black alone	Asian alone	NHPI alone
Total	**273,882,232**	**189,785,997**	**34,450,868**	**32,714,224**	**9,979,963**	**364,909**
Income below poverty level	33,899,812	15,414,119	7,797,874	8,146,146	1,257,237	64,558
Total percent under poverty level	12.4%	8.1%	22.6%	24.9%	12.6%	17.7%
Child poverty rate (under 18 years old)	16.6%	9.3%	27.8%	33.1%	14.3%	22.7%
Elderly poverty rate (over 65 years old)	9.9%	7.8%	19.6%	23.5%	12.3%	11.5%

Source: U.S. Census 2000, SF3 (Tables P87 and P159A-I)

Photo: Corky Lee

APAs have larger family sizes compared to other groups, one big reason their median household income is higher. But counting all members of extended family units tells a different story.

tech worker to the village farmer from Laos, they come to this country with varying degrees of education, skills and financial resources.

That said, it is no wonder that race-based census data, while giving an overview of the community, fails to express the diversity within the population. Regardless of statistics that support the idea of the model minority, there remain a sizable proportion of APAs whose quality of life remains dismally poor. This is revealed in data expressing linguistic isolation, in statistics that delineate lower-level incomes, and in numbers that reveal poverty rates.

The social capital variables of each group are key indicators of socioeconomic success. For example, Professor Curtiss Takada Rooks of San Jose State University, points out that demographic analysis of Chinese immigrants since 1950 has shown a clear distinction between upper-class and working-class immigrants. Those who arrive in this country with strong educational and professional backgrounds are much likelier to achieve success compared with those with weaker social capital.

Still, the question must be asked why, overall, APAs—and particularly those in the "Asian" category—have surpassed other minority groups according to almost all socioeconomic indicators?

It is a question that cannot be answered simply. Many different theories offer possible explanations. One proposes that Confucian ideology, which dominates the thinking of most East Asian countries, teaches Asian immigrants the tools for success in capitalist America. Confucianism articulates the importance of education and family, as well as the value of competition, order and hard work. Generally, people hailing from Confucian-bound societies—Korea, Japan, China—have excelled in the United States, while those from Buddhist-influenced counties—Laos and Cambodia for instance—have succeeded to a lesser extent.

Geographical factors may also contribute to the success of Asian immigrants. Like Latinos, Asian Americans are a majority foreign-born population. However, unlike Latinos, most Asians travel vast distances to a new continent in order to immigrate, knowing that it will be difficult if not impossible to return to their homelands. Many sacrifice everything, setting new roots in the United States, so that their children will have a better future. Their high rate of becoming naturalized citizens—49.9 percent of foreign-born Asian Americans and 40.1 percent of foreign-born NHPIs versus 27.8 percent of foreign-born Latinos—is one indicator of their strong desire to assimilate.

Housing Units by Mortgage Status and Owner's Race, 1999

	All households	Non-Hispanic white alone	Hispanic alone	Black alone	Asian alone	NHPI alone
Housing units with a mortgage	1,088	1,095	1,061	937	1,540	1,261
Housing units without a mortgage	295	299	263	262	344	291

Source: U.S. Census 2000, SF3, Tables HCT45A-I

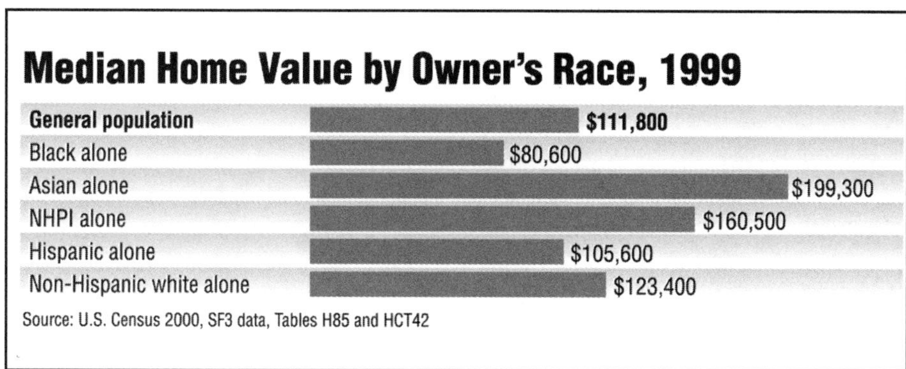

Why African Americans still lag behind the rest of this country in terms of socioeconomic standards is the topic of another discussion. However, looking at U.S. history, and the residual effects left by that history, it is apparent that more work needs to be done to right past wrongs. In contrast to African Americans, few if any Asian Americans came to this country by force. They have faced institutionalized discrimination, but undoubtedly to a lesser extent than African Americans.

Rather, Asian Americans come to the United States, generation after generation, full of optimism and the belief that America is indeed the land of opportunity. Whether in sweaty sewing factories, overcrowded urban schools, or the city ghettos that are the first homes of many immigrants, APAs still believe in the American dream.

Surely, that spirit is a factor in their success.

—*Joyce Nishioka*

SECTION II
ETHNICITY

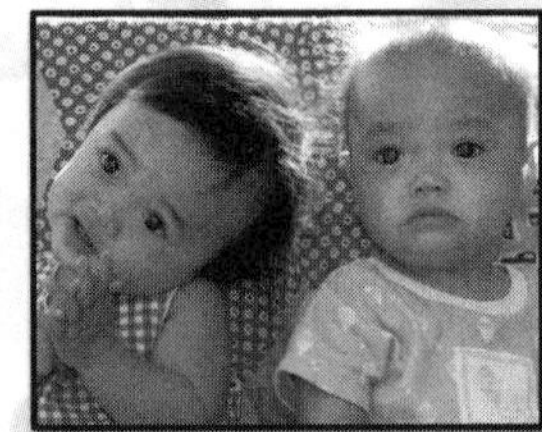

Once Excluded, Now Ascendant

Chinese Americans are the oldest and largest ethnic group of Asian ancestry in the United States. They have endured a long history of migration and settlement that dates back to the late 1840s, including some 60 years of legal exclusion. With the lifting of legal barriers to Chinese immigration after World War II and the enactment of a series of liberal immigration reforms since the passage of the Hart-Celler Act of 1965, the Chinese American community has increased more than ten-fold. The community grew from 237,292 in 1960 to 1,645,472 in 1990 and to 2,879,636 (which includes the Taiwanese population and some 447,051 mixed-race persons) in 2000.

Much of this tremendous growth is due to immigration. According to the U.S. Immigration and Naturalization Service (INS), 1,465,117 immigrants were admitted to the United States from China, Hong Kong, and Taiwan as permanent residents between 1961 and 1998—nearly half of them between 1991–1998 alone. China has been on the INS list of top ten immigrant-origin countries in the United States since 1980.

The U.S. Census also attests to the big part played by immigration. As of 1990, foreign-born Chinese accounted for more than two-thirds of the ethnic Chinese population in the United States. Despite high rates of immigration, however, the foreign born share of the ethnic population dropped substantially to 47 percent in 2000, indicating that the Chinese American population in the 21st century will steadily grow more from child-bearing by those already in the country than by those arriving from the other shore of the Pacific Ocean. This chapter offers a demographic profile of Chinese Americans and discusses some of the important implications of drastic demographic changes for community development.

Photo: Corky Lee

Today, the Chinese American community must face unique issues that involve their growing incorporation into American society.

Historical demographic trends

The Chinese American community has remained an immigrant-dominant community, even though members of this ethnic group arrived in the United States at a much earlier time than many Southern and Eastern European-origin groups, such as Italians and Jews, and than any other Asian-origin groups. While the majority of Italian, Jewish, and Japanese Americans are maturing into third and fourth generation since their respective groups' arrivals in the

United States, Chinese Americans at the dawn of the 21st century are primarily made up of first and second generation—47 percent foreign-born and another 20 percent U.S.-born with foreign-born parentage. The third generation (U.S.-born with U.S.-born parentage) accounts for 33 percent.

Chinese American Population, 1890-2000

Year	Number of Chinese Americans	Sex ratio*	% born in United States	% born in California
1890	107,475	2,679	0.7%	67.4%
1900	118,746	1,385	9.3%	38.5%
1910	94,414	926	20.7%	38.4%
1920	85,202	466	30.1%	33.8%
1930	102,159	296	41.2%	36.6%
1940	106,334	224	51.9%	37.2%
1950	150,005	168	53.0%	38.9%
1960	237,292	133	60.5%	40.3%
1970	435,062	110	53.1%	39.1%
1980	812,178	102	36.7%	40.1%
1990	1,645,472	99	30.7%	42.9%
2000	2,879,636	99	52.9%**	40.0%

*Males per 100 females.
**Estimated from the 2000 Current Population Survey.
Source: U.S. Census of the Population, 1970-2000

Legal exclusion that lasted more than 60 years between 1882 and 1943 explains the twisted demographic development prior to World War II. In the mid-19th century, most Chinese immigrants arrived in Hawai'i and the U.S. mainland as contract labor, working at first in the plantation economy in Hawai'i and in the mining industry on the West Coast and later on the transcontinental railroads west of the Rocky Mountains. These earlier immigrants were almost entirely from the Canton region of South China and intended to stay only as long as it took to "dig" enough gold to take home.

But few realized their gold dreams; many found themselves instead easy targets of discrimination and exclusion. In the 1870s, white workers' frustration with economic distress, labor market uncertainty, and capitalist exploitation turned into anti-Chinese sentiment and racist attacks against the Chinese. Whites accused the Chinese of building "a filthy nest of iniquity and rottenness" in the midst of the American society and driving away white labor by "stealthy" competition and called the Chinese the "yellow peril," the "Chinese menace," and the "indispensable enemy."

Photo: Judi Parks

More than half of Chinese Americans in 2000 were born in the United States. Four out of five of those U.S.-born Chinese were born in California.

In 1882, the U.S. Congress passed the Chinese Exclusion Act, which was renewed in 1892 and later extended to exclude all Asian immigrants until World War II. The number of new immigrants arriving in the United States from China dwindled from 123,000 in the 1870s to 14,800 in the 1890s, and then to a historically low number of 5,000 in the 1930s. This trend did not change significantly until Congress repealed the Chinese Exclusion Act in 1943.

Moving eastwards

Legal exclusion, augmented by extra-legal persecution and anti-Chinese violence, effectively drove the Chinese out of the mines, farms, woolen mills, and factories on the West Coast. As a result, many Chinese laborers already in the United States lost hope of ever fulfilling their dreams and returned permanently to China. Others, who could not afford the return journey (either because they had no money for the trip or because they felt ashamed to return home penniless),

Photo: Corky Lee

The Chinese American community has remained an immigrant-dominated community, with the first and second generations comprising 67 percent of the population.

gravitated toward San Francisco's Chinatown for self-protection.

Still others traveled eastward to look for alternative means of livelihood. Chinatowns in the Northeast, particularly New York, and the mid-West grew to absorb those fleeing the extreme persecution in California. Consequen-tly, the proportion of Chinese living in California decreased in the first half of the 20th century, and the ethnic Chinese population grew slowly with a gradual relaxation of the severely skewed gender imbalance.

The ethnic Chinese population growth rate went up and down decade by decade, but basically remained stagnant in the span of half a century from 1890 to 1940. The gender imbalance for Chinese was nearly 27 males per single female in 1890. That dropped steadily over time, but males still outnumbered females by more than 2:1 by the 1940s.

The shortage of women combined with the "paper son" phenomenon and the illegal entry of male laborers during the exclusion era stifled the normal development of the Chinese American family. In 1900, less than 9 percent of the Chinese American population was U.S.-born. Since then, the share of the U.S.-born increased significantly in each of the succeeding decade until 1960. Accordingly, the proportion of children under 14 years of age increased substantially from a low of 3.4 percent in 1900 to a high of 33 percent in 1960. During and after World War II, more women than men were admitted to the United States as war brides, but the annual quota of immigrant visas for the Chinese was only 105 after the lifting of the Chinese Exclusion Act. In the 1950s, hundreds of refugees and their families fled Communist China and arrived in the United States.

These demographic trends led to the birth of a visible second and third generation between the 1940s and 1960s, during which the U.S.-born outnumbered the foreign born population. In 1960, over 60 percent of the Chinese American population was U.S.-born. However, the absolute number of the U.S.-born population was relatively small and much younger (a third was under age 14) than the average U.S. population. Even today, members of both second and third generations are still very young and have not yet come of age in significant numbers compared to the first generation, according to estimates culled from U.S. Census Current Population Survey data in 1998-2000. The 2000 Current Population Survey indicates that in the second generation, 44 percent of Chinese Americans are under 17 years old and 10 percent are between 18 and 24 (compared to 8

Cities* with Highest Proportions of Chinese Americans, 2000

	Number of Chinese Americans	% of total population
Monterey Park	26,810	44.6%
Arcadia	19,676	37.1%
San Gabriel	14,581	36.6%
Alhambra	31,099	36.2%
Rosemead	17,441	32.6%
Rowland Heights	15,740	32.4%
Temple City	10,269	30.8%
Hacienda Heights	13,551	25.5%
Cupertino	12,777	25.3%
San Francisco	160,947	20.7%
Diamond Bar	11,396	20.2%

*Population of at least 30,000

Source: U.S. Census 2000

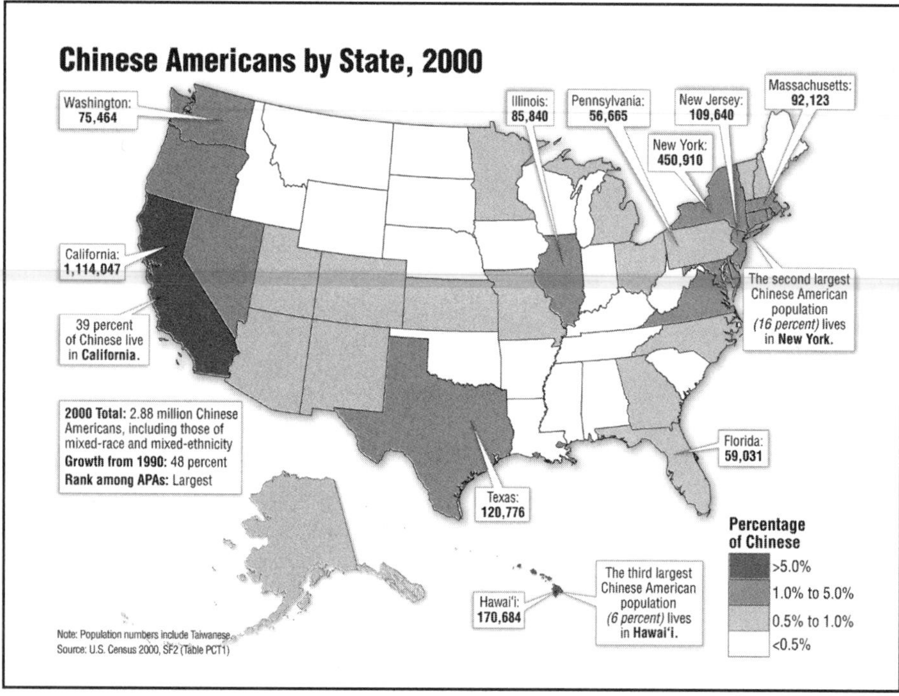

percent under 17 and 8 percent between 18 and 24 in the first generation).

Contemporary Chinese Americans: intra-group diversity

In much of the pre-World War II era, the Chinese American community was essentially an isolated bachelors' society consisting of a small merchant class and a vast working class of sojourners whose homeland was mainland China and whose lives were oriented toward an eventual return to that homeland. Since World War II, and particularly since the enactment of the 1965 Hart-Cellar Act, the ethnic community has experienced unprecedented demographic and social transformation from a bachelors' society to a family community. The ten-fold growth of the Chinese American population from 1960 to 2000 is not merely a matter of numbers but marks a turning point in the social development of the ethnic community and its group members. What characterizes the social transformation is the tremendous within-group diversity in terms of places of origin, socioeconomic backgrounds, patterns of geographic settlement, and modes of social mobility.

Contemporary Chinese immigrants have arrived not only from mainland China but also from the greater Chinese Diaspora—Hong Kong, Taiwan, Vietnam, Cambodia, Malaysia, and the Americas. In Los Angeles, for example, 23 percent of the Chinese American population was born in America, 27 percent in mainland China, 20 percent in Taiwan, 8 percent in Hong Kong, and 22 percent from other countries around the world, as of 1990. Linguistically, Chinese immigrants come from a much wider variety of dialect groups than in the past. For example, all ethnic Chinese share a single ancestral written language (varied only in traditional and simplified versions of characters), but speak numerous regional dialects—Cantonese, Mandarin, the Min dialect, Hakka, Fujianese, Chaozhounese, and Shanghainese—that are not easily understood outside the group.

Contemporary Chinese immigrants have also come from diverse socioeconomic backgrounds. Some arrived in

Photo: Cindy Chew

The contemporary Chinese American population includes people immigrating from mainland China, Hong Kong, Taiwan, Southeast Asia—and even Latin and South America, and elsewhere.

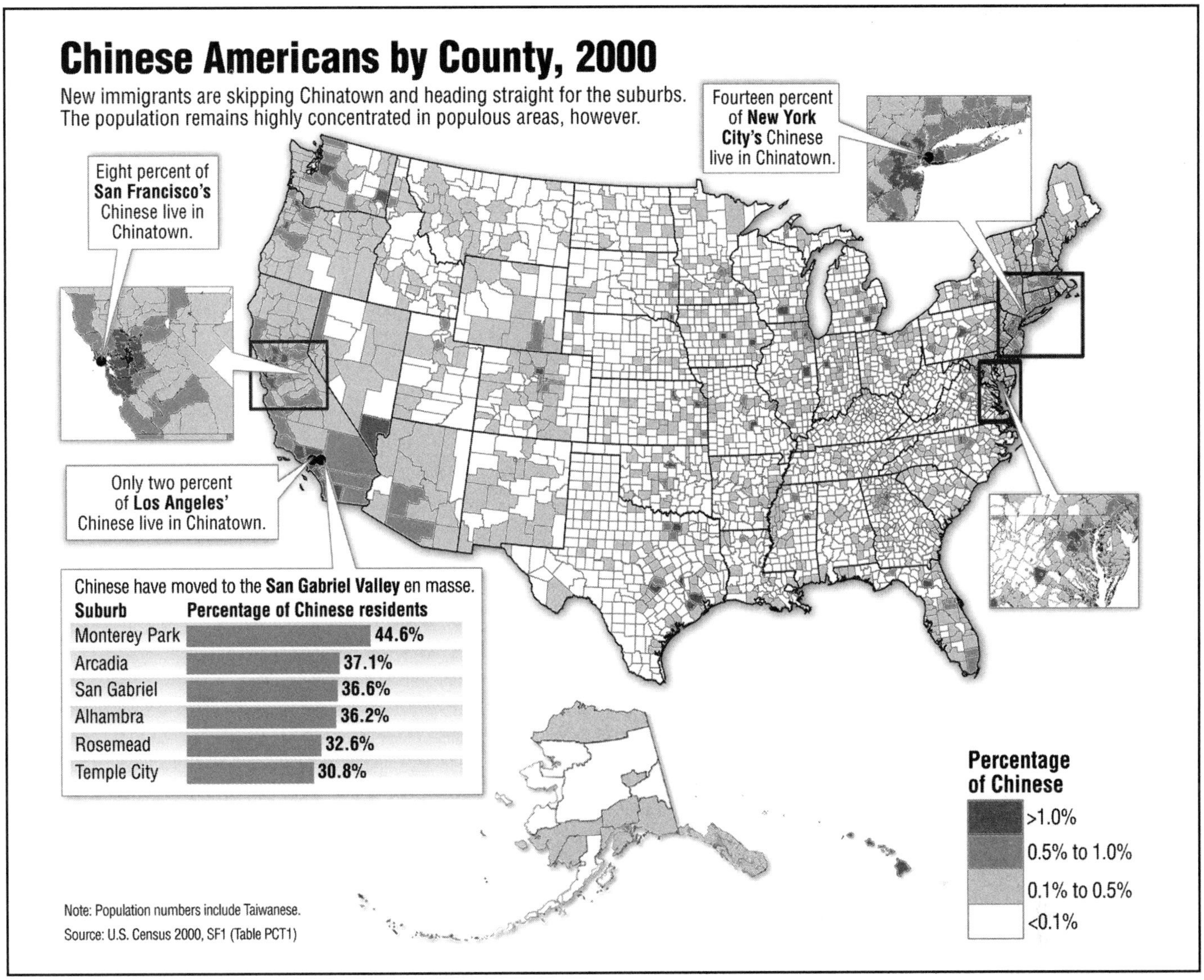

Chinese Americans by County, 2000

New immigrants are skipping Chinatown and heading straight for the suburbs. The population remains highly concentrated in populous areas, however.

Eight percent of **San Francisco's** Chinese live in Chinatown.

Fourteen percent of **New York City's** Chinese live in Chinatown.

Only two percent of **Los Angeles'** Chinese live in Chinatown.

Chinese have moved to the **San Gabriel Valley** en masse.

Suburb	Percentage of Chinese residents
Monterey Park	44.6%
Arcadia	37.1%
San Gabriel	36.6%
Alhambra	36.2%
Rosemead	32.6%
Temple City	30.8%

Percentage of Chinese

>1.0%
0.5% to 1.0%
0.1% to 0.5%
<0.1%

Note: Population numbers include Taiwanese.
Source: U.S. Census 2000, SF1 (Table PCT1)

the United States with little money, minimum education, and few job skills, which forced them to take low-wage jobs and settle in deteriorating urban neighborhoods. Others came with family savings, education and skills far above the levels of average Americans.

Nationwide, levels of educational attainment among Chinese Americans were significantly higher than those of the general U.S. population in both 1980 and 1990, and skill level increased over time. The 1990 Census showed that 41 percent of Chinese Americans at productive ages (aged 25 to 64) have attained four or more years of college education, compared to 21 percent of non-Hispanic whites. Immigrants from Taiwan displayed the highest levels of educational attainment with 62 percent having completed at least four years of college, followed by those from Hong Kong (46 percent) and from the mainland (31 percent). Professional occupations were also more common among Chinese Americans than among non-Hispanic whites (36 percent vs. 27 percent). The annual median family income for Chinese Americans was $34,000 in 1989, compared to $30,000 for the national median family.

While major socioeconomic indicators are above the national average, the trend of bifurcation is equally striking, especially among immigrants from the mainland. For example, as of 1990, almost 40 percent of immigrants from China do not have high school diplomas, compared to 8 percent of those from Taiwan, 18 percent of those from Hong Kong, and 22 percent of all Americans.

Where they live

The settlement patterns of Chinese Americans today are characterized by concentration as well as dispersion. Geographical concentration, to some extent, follows a historical pattern: Chinese Americans continue to concentrate in the West and in urban areas. One state, California, accounts

A people of their own: Taiwanese Americans

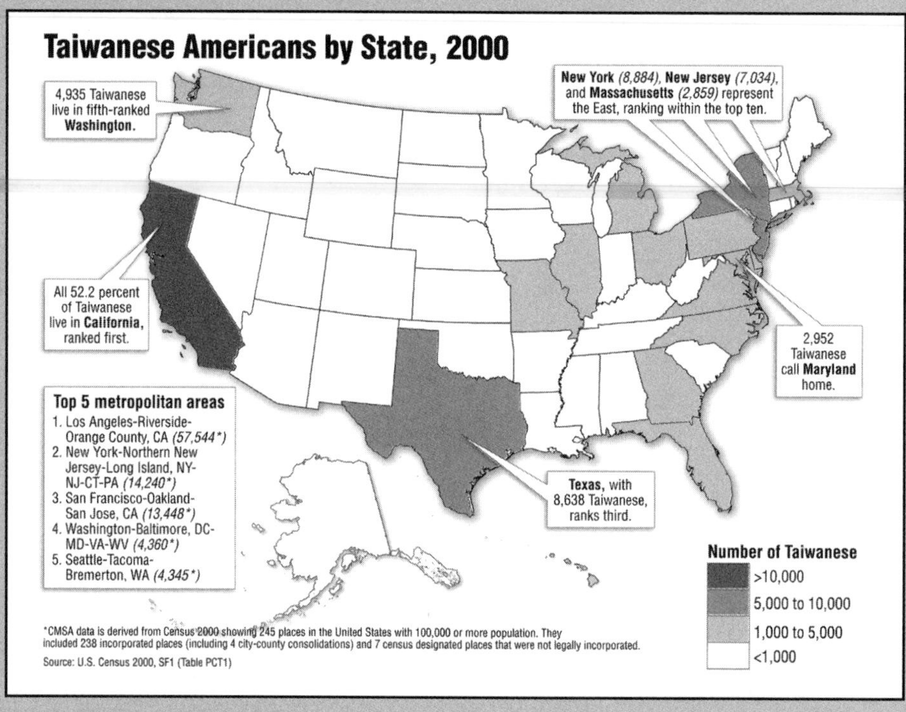

Compared to the roughly 2.7 million Chinese living in America, the Taiwanese American population is a tiny drop in the bucket. The 2000 Census counted just 144,795 Taiwanese Americans in the United States, with more than 75,000—or about half—living in California (there are also Taiwanese clustered around Washington D.C., Houston, and the suburbs of New York City).

Like the Cantonese or Shanghainese, the Taiwanese are ethnically Chinese, though, like the above groups, they speak their own dialect in addition to Mandarin. Still, there are important reasons why Taiwanese Americans maintain a distinct identity. After being defeated by the Communists, the Nationalist government—along with a million and a half Chinese—fled the mainland for the island of Taiwan in the late 1940s, where they established a U.S.-backed government. But repression during the early days of the regime—many Taiwanese opponents to the nationalists were killed or imprisoned—as well as the quashing of local traditions bred resentment.

Most native Taiwanese, unlike the newer arrivals, fiercely oppose reunification with the mainland. Today, Taiwan is no longer ruled by a military government, but by the Democratic Progressive Party (DPP), which represents the majority native Taiwanese population. The DPP firmly opposes reunification with China.

Like most other Asian groups, the Taiwanese first started coming to the United States in large numbers during the mid-1960s under provisions in the new immigration laws that allowed in the skilled and highly-educated. As a result, the Taiwanese American population is mostly well-educated and well-off: among Taiwanese 25 years or older, 60 percent had a bachelor's degree or better in 1990, compared to a rate of 40 percent among Chinese, and 20 percent among all APAs.

for 40 percent of all Chinese Americans (1.1 million). New York accounts for 16 percent, second only to California, and Hawai'i for 6 percent.

However, other states that have historically received fewer Chinese immigrants have witnessed phenomenal growth, such as Texas, New Jersey, Massachusetts, Illinois, Washington, Florida, Maryland, and Pennsylvania. Among cities with populations over 100,000, New York City (365,000), San Francisco (161,000), Los Angeles (74,000), Honolulu (69,000), and San Jose (58,000) have the largest numbers of Chinese Americans. Small suburban cities in Los Angeles and the Bay Area also have extraordinarily high proportions of Chinese Americans in the general population. As shown in Table 2, there are 11 cities of over 30,000 people in the United States in which Chinese Americans share over 20 percent of the city's population.

Traditional urban enclaves, such as Chinatowns in San Francisco, New York, Los Angeles, Chicago, and Boston, continue to exist and to receive new immigrants, but they no longer serve as primary centers of initial settlement, as many new immigrants, especially the affluent and highly skilled, are bypassing inner cities to settle into suburbs immediately after arrival. For example, as of 2000, only 2 percent of Chinese immigrants in Los Angeles, 8 percent in San Francisco, and 14 percent in New York live in old inner-city Chinatowns.

The majority of the Chinese American population is spreading to outer areas or suburbs in traditional gateway cities as well as in centers of new Asian settlement across the country. Most of the cities with the

Among those employed 16 years or older, 82 percent of Taiwanese Americans were either in "managerial and professional specialty occupations" or "technical, sales and administrative occupations," compared to 67 percent for all Chinese and 58 percent in the general population, in 1990. The average family income in 1990 was more than $62,000, versus $51,931 for all Chinese, and $43,803 for the general population. At the same time, 11.2 percent of Taiwanese families in 1990 were below the poverty level—higher than the overall population's figure of 10 percent.

Though Taiwanese communities can be found all over the United States, the unofficial capital of Taiwanese America is the Los Angeles suburb of Monterey Park. More than 61 percent of the population in the year 2000 was Asian, with the largest slice being Taiwanese immigrants.

Monterey Park's transformation into "Little Taipei" is due almost single-handedly to the late Chinese American real estate developer, Frederic Hsieh. In 1970, two years before Hsieh bought his first property in Monterey Park, the city was about 50 percent white, 34 percent Hispanic, and 15 percent Asian, with the majority of the Asians being Japanese. Hsieh promoted Monterey Park to the new, increasingly-moneyed immigrants just then arriving from Taiwan and Hong Kong, who were seeking an alternative to settling in Chinatowns in San Francisco and New York. Cleverly, Hsieh translated Monterey Park in Chinese into Mengtelu Gongyuan, meaning "Lush, Very Green Park." He promoted the city's telephone area code 818—as the number 8 is considered lucky by the Chinese and many other Asians—and the suburb's good schools, always a factor for immigrant families.

In 1977, Hsieh told Monterey Park's incredulous Chamber of Commerce, "You may not know it, but [Monterey Park] will serve as the mecca for Chinese business."

By the 1980s, Hsieh's vision had come true. In 1996, at least two-thirds of Monterey Park's 5,000 businesses were owned by Chinese. Monterey Park had a Chinese mayor, and a predominantly Asian city council.

The influx brought a backlash. "Will the last American to leave Monterey Park please bring the flag?" read a sign at a local gas station. The city council debated whether to make English the official language and force businesses to put up English language signs. The conflict eventually subsided, and Monterey Park and the neighboring suburbs are now a relatively shining example of a multicultural community.

By the late 1990s, immigration from Taiwan slowed. The country's standard of living had risen; there was less economic incentive to leave. In 1989, 13,974 Taiwanese immigrated to the United States; ten years later, the number was barely half of that.

Also, many of the wealthier, more-established Chinese and Taiwanese had moved east to suburbs like San Marino or South Pasadena, or south to Orange County suburbs like Tustin and Anaheim Hills. But Monterey Park remains the cultural and business capital of Taiwanese in Los Angeles and, by extension, in the rest of the country.

—Eric Lai

highest proportions of Chinese are new immigrant suburbs that have become middle class immigrant cities only after the mid-1980s. As of 2000, half of all Chinese Americans live in suburbs. However, recent residential movements of Chinese Americans into ethnically concentrated suburban communities have tipped the balance of power, raising nativist anxiety of ethnic "invasion" and anti-immigrant sentiment.

Making it in America: different routes

Modes of social mobility among Chinese Americans also vary because of tremendous socioeconomic diversity. Three predominant modes are noteworthy. The first mode is the familiar time-honored path of starting at the bottom and moving up through hard work. This route is particularly relevant to those with limited education, few marketable job skills, and little familiarity with the larger labor market. In the post-industrial era, the globalized and restructured economy has fewer and fewer middle rungs in the mobility ladder. As a result, low-skilled workers starting at the bottom may well be trapped there with little chance of upward mobility even when they work hard.

The second mode is the incorporation into professional occupations in the mainstream economy through educational achievement. It has become evident in recent years that Chinese American youths enroll in colleges and graduate with bachelor and master degrees in disproportionate numbers. While many college graduates may have an easier time gaining labor market entry, however, they often encounter a greater probability of being blocked by a glass ceiling as they move up into managerial and executive positions.

Photo: Cindy Chew

Though no longer the primary centers of initial immigrant settlement, Chinatowns like those in New York and San Francisco still thrive commercially and continue to serve a contemporary immigrant population.

The third mode is ethnic entrepreneurship. Since the 1970s, unprecedented Chinese immigration, accompanied by the tremendous influx of human and financial capital, has set off a new stage of ethnic economic development. From 1977 to 1987, the U.S. Census reported that the number of Chinese-owned firms grew by 286 percent, compared to 238 percent for Asian-owned firms, 93 percent for black-owned firms, and 93 percent for Hispanic-owned firms. From 1987 to 1997, the number of Chinese-owned businesses continued to grow at a rate of 180 percent (from less than 90,000 to 252,577). As of 1997, there was approximately one ethnic firm for every 9 Chinese and for every 11 Asians, but only one ethnic firm for every 42 blacks and one for every 29 Hispanics. Chinese-American owned business enterprises made up 9 percent of the total minority-owned business enterprises nation-wide, but 19 percent of the total gross receipts, according to the 1997 Economic Census.

While ethnic entrepreneurship creates numerous employment opportunities for both entrepreneurs and co-ethnic workers, it also leads to problems that leave some workers behind in their pursuit of upward mobility. These problems include labor rights abuses, over-concentration of jobs with low wages, few chances for promotion or advancement, poor working conditions and few, if any, fringe benefits.

Conclusion

The current demographic trends mirror the linguistic, cultural, and socioeconomic diversity of the Chinese American community and its multi-faceted life in the United States. These trends suggest that the community is being transformed from a predominantly immigrant community to a native ethnic community at the dawn of the 21st century. While issues and challenges directly relevant to immigration and immigrant settlement continue to occupy a central place in community affairs, new issues and challenges concerning citizenship, civil rights, interethnic/interracial coalitions, and political incorporation have acquired a high degree of urgency.

The future of Chinese Americans, foreign-born and U.S.-born alike, is intrinsically linked to the diversity of immigration and to the current social stratification system into which today's immigrants and their children are supposedly assimilating. Learning how to negotiate the culture of diversity and to redefine oneself in the new racial and ethnic stratification system is not only imperative but also inevitable.

—*Min Zhou*

Swimming with and against the Tide

Filipino American Demographic Changes

Introduction

As the United States continues to endure various social and political conditions under the global restructuring of the economy, the nation-state boundaries that once existed are becoming blurred. Immigration from Asia, Latin America, and the Caribbean to the United States has been on the rise and created a minority-majority in some states. The Filipino American population has benefited from this trend. The second-largest APA group overall—with 2.36 million Filipinos in 2000, including those of mixed-race or mixed-ethnic heritage—Filipinos follow only the Chinese Americans (2.88 million). The Filipino American population grew by 66 percent from 1.42 million in 1990, both from immigration and domestic-born children. It's part of what makes Filipino Americans so diverse—in geographical origin and dialect, culture-wise and socioeconomically, and in levels of acculturation and length of residence in the United States.

We begin with a brief historical overview of Filipino Americans and the immigration legislation that has both invited and excluded them. From this, we can view the growth of the Filipino American community and how it was perceived over time. We will also compare and contrast where Filipinos live in America, on a national, state and metropolitan level. And we close with a discussion of how these changes have impacted Filipino Americans in terms of social, economic, and political upward mobility, particularly in the aftermath of Sept. 11.

The racial and ethnic diversity of the Filipino American community is based on its unique history with the United States.

The growth of Filipino America, 1930-2000

The decennial census first began categorizing ethnic groups with origins from Asia or Pacific Islands in the late 1800s. From 1850 to 1890, Chinese and Japanese were enumerated in selected states initially and then included on the printed schedules thereafter. In comparison, Filipino Americans have been counted by the decennial Census for over a century, but were first recognized as a separate category—rather than lumped in the "other" category—in 1930. The Filipino American population first started booming after the Philippines became a territory of the United States in 1898. They arrived as

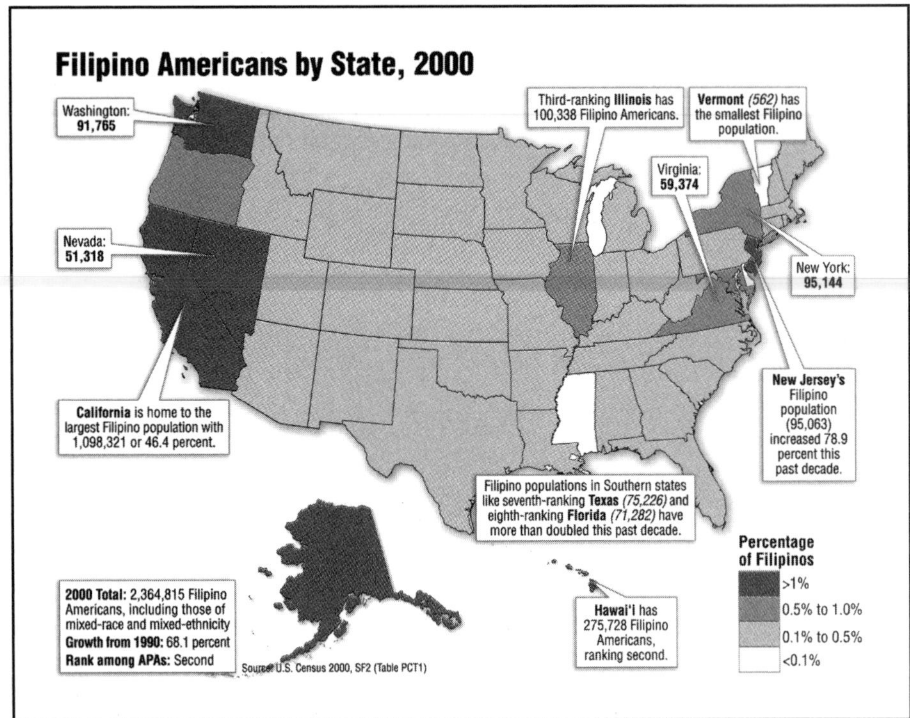

laborers, mostly in agriculture and domestic service, and as students. By 1930, the Filipino American population numbered 45,026, according to the Census Bureau.

Since 1970, the Filipino population has grown nearly seven times, from 336,731 to 2,364,815, making up almost one percent of the national population. This includes hapas of part-Filipino ancestry, who make up 22 percent of the Filipino American population—the third-highest rate among major APA groups (behind Native Hawaiians and Japanese).

The end of World War II and the globalization of the production process created the political, social and economic conditions to bring about another influx of immigration from Asia. The passage of the 1965 Immigration Act, which removed "national origins" quotas, changed the pattern of immigration to the United States significantly, as more professional and middle-class immigrants joined working-class immigrants to find better economic opportunities in America.

History of immigration laws

It is difficult to generalize about the Filipino American community, as it is comprised of several distinct groups, differentiated across and within by origins of immigration, socioeconomic characteristics, dialect, geographical origin, and levels of acculturation. What unifies them is that American self-interest, translated into government political and economic policies is what brought them here.

Filipino university students to the United States, called *pensionados*, were the first formal immigrants. Congress passed the Pensionado Act in 1903 for foreign policy reasons: to educate and bind current and future Filipino leaders to the American colonial administration. In exchange for each year of education in the United States, *pensionados* were required to work for the civil service government in the Philippines for the same length of time. Although the *pensionado* program lasted from 1903 to 1938, the total number of immigrants was only about 14,000, and the majority of them returned to the Philippines to fulfill their contract.

The first wave of Filipinos to enter and remain in significant numbers immigrated to Hawai'i from 1906 to 1935. They were first recruited to work in the Hawaiian sugar and pineapple plantations, and later the farms of California as migrant laborers. A series of political events, including American international and economic politics both in the United States and the Philippines, were key. Prior to 1906, Hawaiian sugar plantations had relied first on Chinese and then Japanese laborers. These workers were viewed as problematic, however, causing the government to end first Chinese immigration (Chinese Exclusion Act of 1882) and then severely restrict Japanese (the 1907 to 1908 Gentlemen's Agreement).

A new source of cheap agricultural labor was needed. Coincidentally, the integration of the Philippines by the United States into the capitalist world market as an export agricultural economy resulted in the loss of small family-owned farms. Amid promises of monetary success, young displaced male Filipinos with minimal educations and bleak economic futures readily chose to immigrate to the United States—especially since their status as American nationals after the Spanish-American War made it easy to do so. By 1934, 119,470 Filipinos had immigrated to Hawai'i. Only 8,952 were women—it was believed that restricting Filipino women from entering the United States would deter the establishment of Filipino American communities and encourage an eventual return to the Philippines. After demand for cheap farm workers in California emerged during the 1920s, about 45,000 Filipinos from Hawai'i and the Philippines immigrated there and other parts of the West Coast.

Beginning in the 1920s and exploding by the 1930s, sentiment against Filipinos took a decidedly hostile turn, culminating in aggressive physical attacks. Filipinos were viewed as a social menace and an economic threat to

whites. Legislative testimony in California documented negative stereotypes that focused on the sexual prowess of Filipino males. Initially, Filipinos had not been barred from marrying white women. However, concerns of racial purity and mixed-race offspring prompted lawmakers to amend anti-miscegenation laws to include Filipinos. The Tydings-McDuffy Act of 1935 limited immigration from the Philippines by granting it independence, which reclassified Filipinos as aliens, and then limiting their immigration to 50 individuals per year.

The National Origins Act favored European immigration by establishing quotas for each nation based on two percent of the total foreign-born population in the United States in 1898. As a result, 98 percent of all immigrants continued to arrive from Europe. Occasionally, restrictions to both the Tydings-McDuffy Act and the National Origins Act were rescinded, if American agricultural corporations in Hawaii indicated a need for additional Filipino laborers.

Despite restrictive exclusionist policies, anti-Filipino sentiments were so intense that it was not enough to just limit immigration. A social and legal movement ensued to send Filipino immigrants back to the Philippines. Federal legislation in the form of the Repatriation Act of 1936 provided free transportation back to the Philippines on the condition that Filipinos forfeit their right of ever returning to the United States. Very few took advantage of the offer.

In spite of anti-miscegenation laws, there remain today American-born children and grandchildren of this first wave of Filipinos. Most are multi-racial or multi-ethnic, and grew up in farm laborer camps and followed the agricultural work. They tend to have lower educations and incomes than their foreign-born counterparts.

Exclusionism did not abate until the advent of WWII, which forced the United States to lessen its restrictions on immigration, but only by a bare minimum. The United States' need to establish good war-time relations with the Philippines, China, and India prompted Congress in 1946 to raise the quota on Filipino immigrants to 100 per year. As in the past, exceptions to quotas were made. Thousands of Philippine-born Filipinos were recruited to serve in the military, especially the Navy, where they took jobs mostly as stewards and cooks. This population comprises the second wave of immigration and an important segment of the Filipino population in the United States today.

From 1935 to 1964 immigration from the Philippines was minimal. After the 1965 Immigration Act, Filipinos began arriving in the United States, for education, for work, and to escape the repressive political regime of President Ferdinand Marcos. This resulted in a significant brain drain of highly-educated Filipinos. Unlike earlier immigrants who were largely farm workers and military personnel, the new Filipino immigrants were professionals, many in the medical fields. Within a few years, less than a tenth of the Filipino immigrants were laborers; two-thirds were professional and technical workers.

As the need for professionals began to be filled, policies restricting Filipino immigration were once again implemented. During 1976, Congress passed legislation requiring that professionals could only enter the country at the request of an employer under the Eilberg Act. Further restrictions under the Health Professionals Education Assistance Act required that all foreign medical professionals take and pass an examination before being allowed into the United States. Once in the United States, professional degrees and licenses earned in the Philippines often went unrecognized, leaving many immigrants underemployed and paid low wages. For example, a registered nurse might be hired as a nursing assistant. Due largely to preferences for certain occupations like nursing, the post-1965 immigrants tended to be female. All in all, this third wave of Filipino immigration wrought major demographic changes in gender and class in the Filipino American community.

Since the 1980s, U.S. immigration policy, such as the Immigration Reform and Control Act, has aimed to restrict immigration from Asia, Latin America and the Caribbean—making Filipinos and other immigrants targets of selective deportations, interrogation, and racial profiling.

Settlements

The earliest Filipino American settlement dates back to Louisiana in the late 1800s. Today, Filipinos are dispersed throughout the nation, but most still live in California and Hawai'i, a legacy of the laborers who worked the fields and canneries of the West Coast in the early 1900s and created communities and social networks there.

In 2000, seven of the ten cities with the largest Filipino populations were in California. Most grew out of social networks formed by military relationships between the Philippines and the United States, starting with the building of U.S. bases in the Philippines during the Spanish-American War.

The bases heavily recruited Filipinos for enlisted positions and civilian jobs. By 1987, "the United States bases were the second largest employer after the Philippine government, providing jobs and an annual salary totaling more than $96 million to over 68 thousand Filipinos," according to scholar Yen Le Espiritu.

Many enlisted Filipinos were sent to bases in the United States, and then stayed. San Diego's Filipino community is a direct outgrowth of the Naval base there. So are the communities in Long Beach, Calif., Norfolk, Va., Bangor, Maine and Bremerton, Wash., and Honolulu, where post-retirement employment in shipyards and defense factories proved profitable.

More recently, economic opportunities have lured Filipinos to states like Nevada. In cities like Reno and Las Vegas, Filipinos occupy jobs within the tourism industry as employees in hotels, shops and restaurants, and in the health care industry, primarily as nurses. Of the top five states, the Filipino population of Nevada grew the most, at 427 percent, with Washington (201 percent), Alaska (200 percent) and New Jersey (181 percent) following far behind. These figures were calculated by taking the 2000 Census' Filipino "in combination" population and dividing it by the 1990 Census' Filipino population.

The majority of foreign-born Filipinos who were naturalized in 2000 reside in areas where Filipino Americans are most concentrated. The big exception is Hawai'i, where the skyrocketing costs of housing and living have forced many Filipinos to leave. California is a popular choice. Earlier waves of Filipino immigrants went to urban areas, but today's Filipinos are moving out to the suburbs. From 1990 to 2000, the percentage of Filipino Americans living in the suburbs grew from 51.7 percent to 57.5 percent.

Age and gender

Most Filipino Americans are between the ages of twenty-five and fifty-four. 55 percent are women, which is not surprising, as more than six in ten Filipino immigrants in 2000 were women, according to the INS. Three major factors explain why female immigration is on the rise: preference and non-preference quotas; globalization of the economy has created a feminization of labor; and export-led growth strategy has weakened the Philippine's domestic market economy.

According to researcher Saskia Sassen, new Asian immigration—increasingly thought of as middle-class and professional immigration—is now paving the way for poorer immigrants and undocumented ones, too. In the 1970s women became the majority of legal immigrants. Most came without their husbands or children. From 1972 to 1979, women represented 45.6 percent of all immigrants admitted legally under the preference category of skilled and unskilled workers in short supply. In addition, women made up more than half of the 290,000 admitted under the non-preference immigrant category, which consist of the spaces that become available when the preference quotas are not fully used. This immigration trend has continued into the 1980s and 1990s.

At the same time, the Philippine economy shifted towards exporting goods. This change shrunk economic opportunities in rural areas and brought about the feminization of labor: women were recruited from the country to the cities for industrial jobs because, generally, they are more patient, docile, and dexterous than men. Having moved once for work, these women are now potential overseas immigrants.

Foreign investment and production for export contributes to the development of economic, cultural, and ideological linkages with more industrialized countries. These linkages tend to promote emigration both directly and indirectly. Sassen explains, "For men and women alike, the disruption of traditional ways of earning a living and the escalation of export-led development make entry into wage labor increasingly a one-way proposition." With traditional economic opportunities in the rural areas shrinking, it becomes difficult, if not impossible, for workers to return home if they are laid off or unsuccessful in their job search. Sassen further asserts,

All these trends have contributed to the formation of a pool of potential migrants in developing countries such as the Philippines, South Korea, Taiwan, and the countries of the Caribbean basin. People uprooted from their traditional ways of life, then left unemployed and unemployable as export firms hire newer workers or move production to other countries, may see few options but emigration, especially if an export-led growth strategy has weakened the country's domestic market economy.

Moreover, Americanization programs have made Filipinos into potential immigrants through education, language and ideology. Thus, immigration abroad becomes a serious option because of economic trends and the preference of industrialized countries for English-speaking immigrants.

Contemporary Asian immigration trends

In 1980, the Philippines replaced China and Japan as the Asian country sending the largest number of immigrants to the United States. By the 1990s, the Philippines sent more immigrants than any country except Mexico. For undocumented immigrants in 1996, the Philippines was one of three countries in the top fifteen outside of North or South America. An estimated 95,000 of the estimated five million undocumented or illegal immigrants came from the Philippines, ranking sixth (Mexico was first with 2.7 million undocumented immigrants living in the United States).

The portion of the Filipino American population that is foreign-born is declining: from 69 percent in 1990 to 50 percent between 1998 and 2000 (29 percent were second generation and 21 percent were third generation or later).

In the latter half of the twentieth century, immigration from the Philippines and China has been roughly equal in size. South Asian immigration has pulled ahead, however, and may cause their populations to exceed those of Filipinos or Chinese

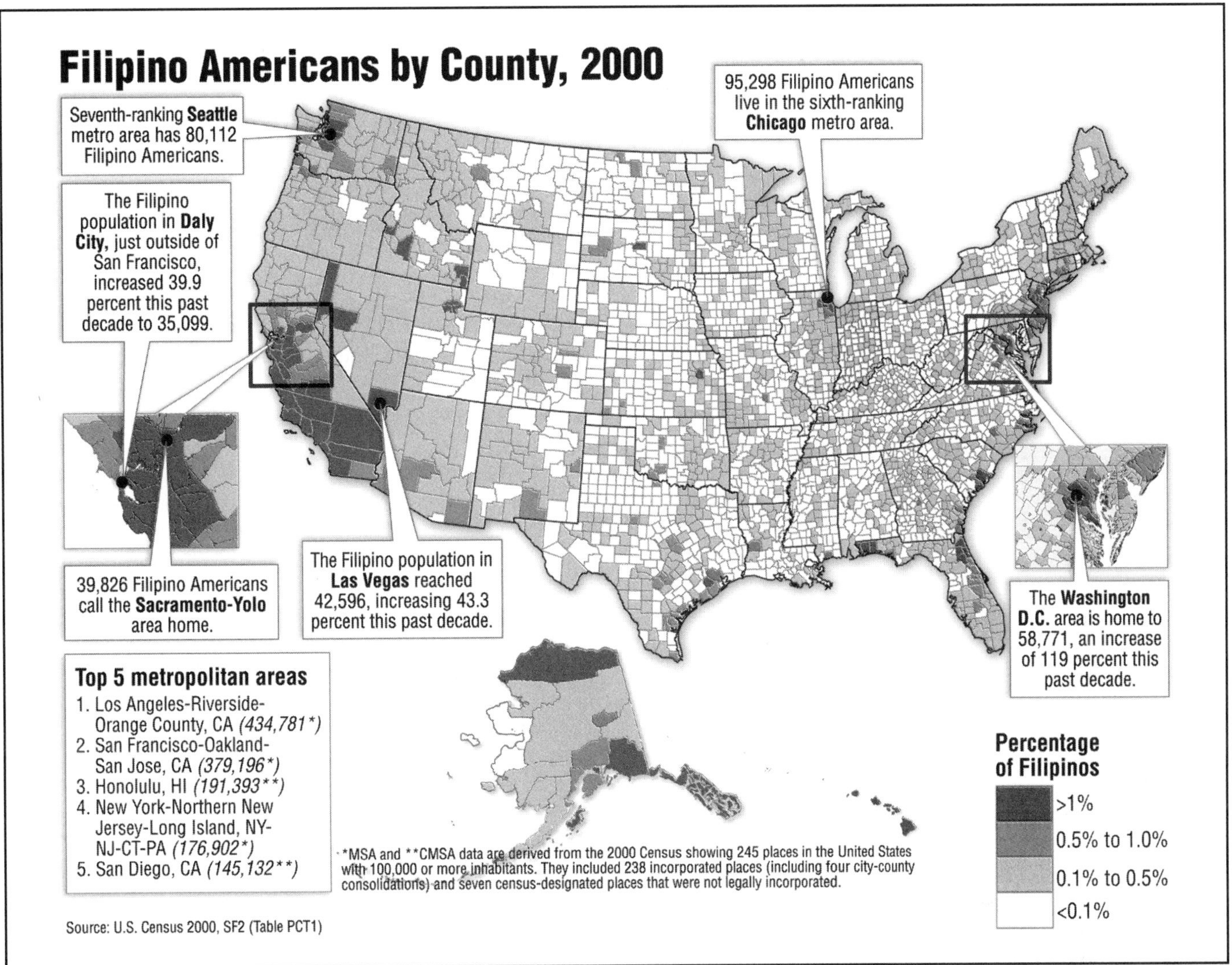

soon. As a result of increasing immigration to the United States and the number of undocumented immigrants present illegally in the country during the last decade, the debate on immigration reform spurred anti-immigrant sentiments and raised questions about who is worthy of benefiting from economic, social, and political opportunities.

Opportunities and challenges in the 21st century

The demographic changes of the last decade have had a significant impact on the Filipino American community in terms of social, economic, and political upward mobility, particularly in the aftermath of Sept. 11.

Present day immigration legislation

U.S. immigration legislation has allowed many Filipinos to seek better opportunities here in America, but in recent years the opposite has occurred. In 1986, Congress enacted the Immigration Reform and Control Act to provide solutions to escalating illegal immigration through increased enforcement, employer sanctions, and legalization. That same year, the passage of the Immigration Marriage Fraud Amendments enacted stiff penalties for marriage fraud. The 1990 Immigration Act limited the number of family-sponsored preference visas, which continue to decline each year. Instead, employment-based preferences—mostly temporary—are on the rise and have become the foremost means of entry for Filipinos to the United States. The Illegal Immigration and Reform and Immigrant Responsibility Act of 1996 passed strict new measures to discourage those tempted to enter without inspection or to overstay temporary visas for lengthy periods. If apprehended, undocumented persons face immediate deportation and the possibility of being barred from re-entry to the United States for life.

More recently, the Absconder Apprehension Initiative was developed as part of the U.S. Department of Justice's anti-terrorist campaign and as a consequence of Sept. 11. As a result, record high numbers of Filipinos are being deported. As one Philippine consulate official in San Francisco revealed, "INS agents now bring over an average of four Filipinos per working day." The initiative directs the FBI, the INS, the U.S. Marshals' Service and all U.S. attorneys to form special "apprehension teams," which aim to locate and deport an estimated 314,000 alien fugitives known as "absconders," with priority on males who come from "al Qaeda active nations." The Philippines was identified by the Department of Justice as such because of the doings of the Abu Sayyaf terrorists in Basilan Island, despite the fact that it is only one of 7,100 islands in the Philippines.

Although Philippine President Arroyo was among the very first heads of state to declare support for the anti-terrorist war declared by President George W. Bush and to offer facilities and resources to the United States, no protections have been offered to prevent innocent legal or illegal Filipinos from being victims of racial profiling, interrogation, and selective deportation. The upsurge in deportations may partly explain the decrease in foreign-born Filipinos from 1998 to the present. Together, these immigration policies have reversed the tides of opportunity and have made it more difficult for illegal and legal immigrants to move-up the ladder of social mobility, let alone eke out a modest living in the United States.

Recruitment of Nurses and Teachers

The economic mobility of Filipino Americans continues to be hampered by the global restructuring of the economy. In times of crisis, the United States has relied on the surplus of Filipino workers, particularly women, to fill jobs considered "unwanted" by natives. In the last thirty years, many large American cities have recruited Filipino nurses to meet shortages in their hospitals. Recently, Filipino school teachers are also in demand, due to the colonial, English-speaking schools set up when the Philippines was a U.S. territory. Potential Filipino teachers still must pay their own way to America and fork over application and processing fees; teacher-strapped school districts are enjoying a free lunch in this regard.

As a result, many Filipinos occupy low-wage and middle-wage sector jobs that offer very little opportunity to advance up a higher-paying career ladder. As more second and third generation Filipinos earn better educations, hopefully the move towards greater economic mobility can be accomplished.

Contradictions: Filipino veterans and airport screeners

Political mobility of Filipino Americans remains in flux. After WWII ended, Filipino veterans who fought side-by-side American troops were told they were not entitled to full veterans' benefits, ranging from hospital and nursing home care, to pensions, life insurance, etc. Despite mass organizing efforts, Filipino veterans have been unable to secure full veterans benefits.

Filipino airport screeners once dominated the ranks at Bay Area airports such as Oakland, San Jose, and San Francisco. But after the terrorism of Sept. 11, hundreds of Filipino screeners have been laid off, despite decades of experience. The newly-created Transportation Security Administration which now oversees airport security refused to hire non-U.S. citizens. These jobs—once mostly held by minorities—are increasingly going to whites. And the new federal jobs are much better-paid, as the old private security screeners were often paid minimum wage.

"About 50,000 non-citizens are serving in the military. To say they can fight to protect national security but they can't work in airports as screeners seems unjust," said Ben Wizner, an attorney for the ACLU of Southern California. Filipino screeners are fighting back, though. In mid-November 2002, a U.S. District Court Judge ruled that barring non-U.S. citizens was unconstitutional, and granted a temporary injunction allowing non-U.S. citizens to re-apply for their old screener jobs. Groups like People's Association of Working Immigrants (PAWIS) were planning further action to help laid-off workers. These episodes show how Filipinos still have a long way to go in terms of becoming a major political force. Filipinos will remain second-class citizens until they unite effectively with other APA groups to have their voice heard.

Conclusion

Filipinos continue to be one of the largest APA groups due to immigration and increased childbearing. Filipino immigration has decreased during the past decade, and there is no telling whether it will once again be on the rise. But the continuing nurse and teacher shortage will mean significant streams of low-/semi-skilled and skilled workers from the Philippines will continue to emigrate.

Segments of the Filipino American population are succeeding. An increasing majority of Filipinos is moving to the suburbs, which is one marker of economic success. The relatively young and middle-aged population and increasing educational attainment levels also indicates that second and third generation Filipino Americans will possess greater employment and earnings opportunities than their parents. SF4 data available in late 2003 will provide greater insight and help ensure that resources are distributed equitably. What is known is that Filipino Americans remain a population that is diverse on many levels that must be seen in relation to, not in isolation of, each other.

—Melany Dela Cruz & Pauline Agbayani-Siewert

Thanks to Victor Viesca, Dennis Arguelles, Joe Montano, and Terry Valen for offering their knowledge and encouragement.

Instant Identity: The Emergence of Asian Indian America

Asian Indians are one of the fastest growing immigrant communities in the last two decades in the United States, passing one million in population for the first time in the year 2000. Not only is the community young and fast-growing, it has only been counted with any degree of accuracy in the last twenty years. Statistical data on Asian Indian Americans at a national level before 1980 is spotty and inaccurate.

Before 1980, the U.S. Census did not have a separate category for Asian Indians. Prior to that change, there was only a single "Indian" category, which conflated those of Asian Indian origin and Native Americans. The confusion at the policy level was perhaps understandable. The general populace didn't know what to think of Asian Indians. A 1978 opinion survey found eleven percent of respondents saw Asian Indians as white, fifteen percent considered them black, 23 percent said brown, while 51 percent were befuddled enough to choose "other" or not answer at all!

In 1975, a leading Asian Indian American group, the Association of Indians in America (AIA), wrote to the U.S. Government's then-Civil Rights Commission, expressing that "Indians are different in appearance; they are equally dark-skinned as other non-white individuals and are, therefore, subject to the same prejudices." The AIA efforts resulted in a separate racial category of "Asian Indian." But confusion still reigned, as the Government was ineffective at communicating the new separate Indian category. Recent studies question the accuracy of that count.

What we do know for sure is that Asian Indian Americans were the fastest-growing APA group in the last decade, and are the third largest, behind only Chinese and Filipinos. The 2000 Census counted 1,678,765 people who were of only Asian Indian decent. An additional 40,013 people were mixed Asian Indian in combination with one or more Asian ethnic groups, i.e. Asian Chinese. There were also another 180,821 people who reported being Asian Indian in combination with one or more other race, i.e. white, black, or American Indian. The phenomenal growth was partly caused by a shortage of software engineers and computer scientists during the high-tech boom of the 1990s, a shortage that was filled by importing engineers from India.

Photo: Corky Lee

Asian Indians are the fastest-growing APA group in the last decade, as young working-age people and their children are contributing to the community's largely young population.

Although Indians had been coming to the United States since the early 1800s, no significant immigration took place

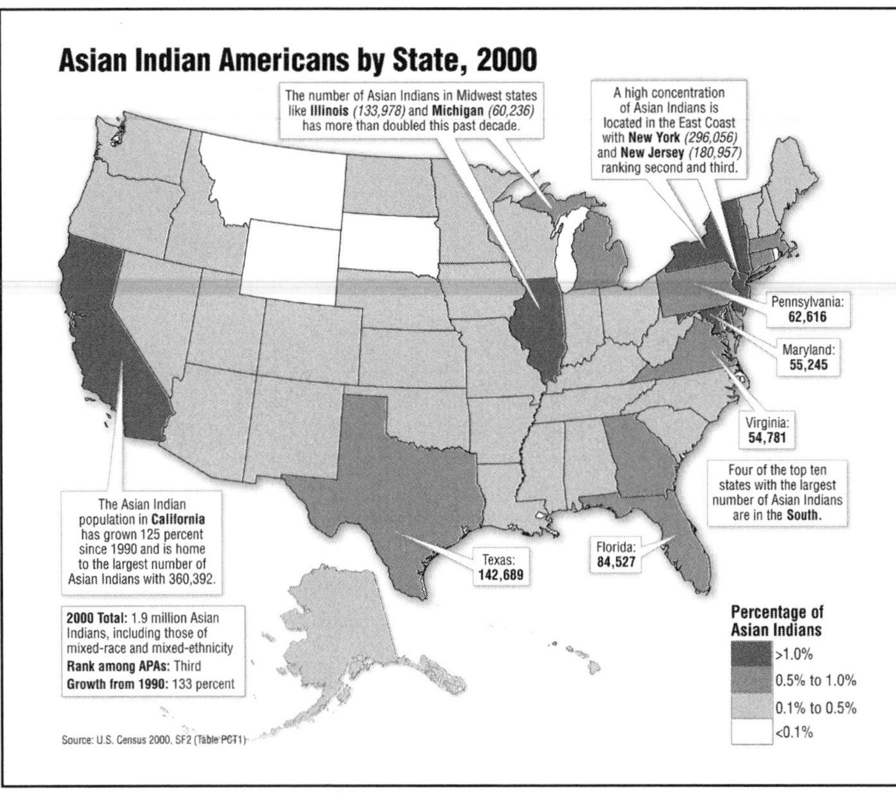

until after World War II, after restrictions on Asians were lifted towards the war's end by President Franklin D. Roosevelt. Immigration of Asian Indians did not pick up until 1965. Only 7,629 immigrants from South Asia are said to have arrived in the United States by 1965. Because of this, and because of the known confusion of Asian Indian with American Indian, all of our calculations for Asian Indian Americans in 1980 and prior excluded those born in the United States and 50 years or older.

Demographic profile

The 1980 Census recorded 387,223 Asian Indians in the United States based on the race question. However, one 1996 study by Rao showed that the number of Asian Indians in 1980 may have been as high as 414,780—or 7 percent higher—if one factors in place of birth (India) or ancestry (Asian Indian) as well. This number was arrived after making misclassification adjustments on all those aged 50 and over who marked Asian Indian and born in the United States. They are assumed to be Native Americans who marked the wrong box.

The misclassification error had a huge impact: there was a flurry of conflicting research in the 1980s that showed that U.S.-born Asian Indians had an unemployment rate five times that of other APA groups. This particular error seems to have been reduced by 1990. Using strict criteria of satisfying all three questions in 1980—race, ancestry, and place of birth—there were 363,760 Asian Indians.

In 1990, the Census counted a total of 815,447 Asian Indians, an increase of 125.6 percent over 1980. Asian Indians were the fourth-largest Asian group after the Chinese, Filipinos, and Japanese. Most of the population growth is due to new immigrants rather than births. That has been a fact since 1965, with the loosening of American immigration quotas. In 1990, the U.S. Government further spurred immigration by creating, for the first time, separate categories for family-sponsored, employment-based, and diversity of immigrants. The 2000 Census counted nearly 1.7 million non-mixed Asian Indians, a 100 percent increase over 1990, and an increase of almost five times over the 1980 population.

An East-West Center study of Asian Indians in the United States based on 1980 Census data concluded that Asian Indians are extremely well-assimilated economically, but very diversified in other areas such as cultural, religious, and other dimensions. According to the 1990 Census, Indians had the highest median household income, family income, per capita income, and annual median income ($40,625) of any foreign-born group. They also ranked first in holding stocks and individual retirement accounts (IRAs), in rates of educational achievement, and in the attainment of managerial or professional positions in a 1991 survey of five Asian Pacific American groups, according to Bruce LaBrack, in the article on South Asians in the 1997 book, *Our Cultural Heritage: A Guide to America's Principal Ethnic Groups.*

However, a review of the most popular Asian Indian newspaper in the United States suggests that marital, economic, childcare, and child custody issues are becoming common. As the diversity of the immigrant population increases, it is expected that social problems and tensions are likely to increase as well. The adaptation of American customs among second generation Asian Indians that differ from those of their parents are contributing to this end.

The Asian Indian American population is dominated by young working-age people. Nearly four in ten are between the ages of 20 and 40. The true figure may have been even higher; some temporary immigrant workers (such as H1 visa holders) and their families might not have completed the 2000 Census forms due to confusion

Early Indian arrivals

Indians had come to the United States as early as 1820. But the distance and restrictive immigration quotas meant that by the end of the 19th century, less than 800 Indians are recorded to have emigrated here.

No wonder that when four Sikhs were allowed to land in San Francisco on April 6, 1899, it was a newsworthy event. "The quartet formed the most picturesque that has been seen on the Pacific Mall dock for many a day," reported the *San Francisco Chronicle*. "They hope to make their fortunes here and return to their homes in the Lahore district, which they left some twenty years ago."

It was unclear what happened to those Sikhs, but soon many other Sikhs followed, also seeking their fortunes. Small Sikh male worker communities soon sprang up all along the West Coast. From the early 1900s until 1922, there were up to 100 Hindus working at a timber mill near Portland, Oregon. The Sikhs lived in a "Hindu Alley," recalled old-timers to the the *Daily Astorian* newspaper in 1973, and made Indian food like chapatti. The Indians kept to themselves, but were known by the locals for their prowess at wrestling.

In San Francisco, a Hindu temple was dedicated in 1908. In the Central Valley city of Stockton, California, the first organized society of Sikhs was formed in 1911, with a temple built the following year. And in 1912, six Indians enrolled as students at UC Berkeley.

Relations were not always so harmonious, as Indians were seen as a threat for jobs by local workers. In 1907, in the city of Bellingham, Washington, a mob of about 500 men attacked boarding houses and mills, forcing about 300 Indians to flee. And restrictive laws, such as the 1913 Alien Land Law in California aimed at preventing Chinese and Japanese from owning and farming land, also affected Indian immigrants.

—*Eric Lai*

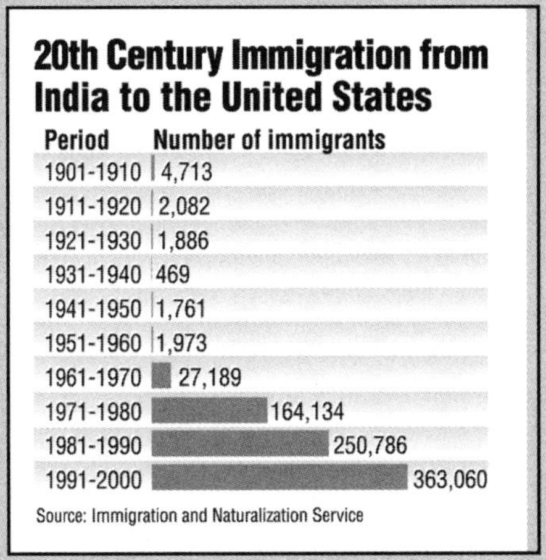

20th Century Immigration from India to the United States

Period	Number of immigrants
1901-1910	4,713
1911-1920	2,082
1921-1930	1,886
1931-1940	469
1941-1950	1,761
1951-1960	1,973
1961-1970	27,189
1971-1980	164,134
1981-1990	250,786
1991-2000	363,060

Source: Immigration and Naturalization Service

over whether they should complete the Census forms (they were supposed to). About 8.5 percent of the Asian Indian American population is below 15 years old; only 5.6 percent is age 50 or over. The proportion of those 55 years and over—virtually all of them foreign-born and first generation immigrants—is growing slowly.

Preliminary analysis of the 2000 Census data shows that the excessive number of Asian Indian elderly (particularly women) reported in the 1980 and 1990 Censuses has almost disappeared, presumably due to fewer Native Americans marking Asian Indian by mistake. The Asian Indian community is not only very young compared to the white population, it is aging slowly. The median age changed from 28.9 years in 1990 to 30 years old in 2000. The number of children underage, young adults 25 to 34 years old and those 50 years old and more, grew more than 100 percent during the 1990s. The increase in young adults is due to the temporary worker program and the high-tech job boom, while the young children are mostly due to those same young adults.

Where were they born?

Slightly more than one-quarter of the Asian Indians in the United States were born in the United States. 51.3 percent were born in India; another ten-plus percent were born in other countries such as Pakistan, Bangladesh, and Guyana, where a sizable Indian population lives. That leaves about 15 percent born in other parts of the world, such as the Caribbean, evidence of the wide scope of the Indian diaspora (see the "Indo-Caribbeans" sidebar).

With so many young Asian Indian Americans, the percentage of Asian Indian Americans born in the United States will no doubt increase. The 2000 Census data shows that only 20 percent of Indian immigrants had come to the United States before 1980, and fifty percent had arrived by 1990. The implication is that about half of Asian Indian immigrants came just during the 1990s.

What is happening to marriage?

Arranged marriage has been an Indian cultural tradition. Asian Indian American newspaper articles continue to extol the virtues of arranged marriages and bringing one's spouse from a far-off country despite little knowledge of the future soul mate. Though the data does not permit an exhaustive analysis, the data from the last three Censuses confirm that divorce and separation is still rare among Asian Indian Americans. 51 percent of Asian Indians are married and about 42 percent are never married or less than 16 years old. There are more never-married men (about 58 percent) than never-married women (42 percent). This conforms with the traditional Indian male sojourner pattern, in which single men are more likely to

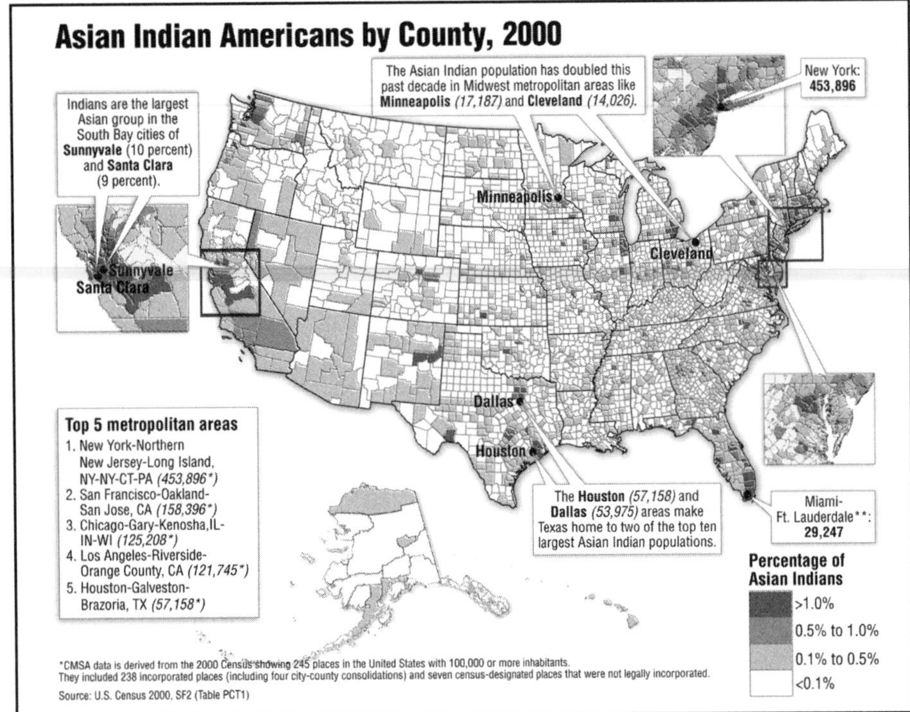

migrate first for work, whereas single women are less likely to travel.

Only 2.8 percent in 2000 were either divorced or separated. While not exactly comparable, a 1996 U.S. Census survey found that 10.3 percent of women and 8.2 percent of men in the general population were currently divorced. Of the 2.8 percent divorced Asian Indian population, about 57 percent are women. The widowed population was 2.8 percent in 2000. About 83 percent of the widowed are women, most likely living with their children.

Living arrangements
Traditional family arrangements abound among Asian Indians. About 83 percent of Asian Indian households are nuclear households and about six percent of households have extended family members, including siblings, parents, etc. An insignificant number of households have a cohabiting partner (0.3 percent). The highest median age by state for Asian Indian was 35.8 years old for men and 35 for women, both in Hawaii. South Dakota has the lowest median age among males and females. The average family size nationwide was 3, with New York's average the highest at 3.78 per family.

There are few unmarried Asian Indian households. The highest percentage in 2000 was found in Montana, at 5.6 percent. That's puzzling, and suggests the same old misclassification problem whereby Native Americans and Asian Indians were conflated.

The total number of children Asian Indian women had was not yet available for 2000 at press time. However, it was falling. In 1980, the completed fertility rate for women aged 45-49 was 3.2 children. In 1990, it fell significantly to just 2.48 children per woman aged 45-49.

Languages spoken
73 percent of Asian Indian Americans speak a language besides English; only 20 percent cannot. These 20 percent are probably second generation Asian Indian Americans.

Mobility status
About 79 percent of Asian Indians stayed in the same house and apartment for the last year. Only five percent moved from their last location within the United States in the last twelve months, while about fifteen percent moved from a foreign location to the United States. These fifteen percent are new arrivals setting up families in the United States for the first time. Nevada and the District of Columbia have the highest percent of households having a relative living with them (15.27 percent). There are many states where ten percent or more households had a relative living with them at the time of the 2000 Census. The reason? Many young adult immigrants bring their parents to help them with new children and in setting up a new household.

Educational attainment
The educational attainment of Asian Indians far exceeds those of local populations for any given marital status or age group. It is important to note that most Asian Indians allowed to emigrate to the United States have completed their bachelor's or master's degree. This selectivity is an important factor that contributes to higher levels of education among Asian Indian Americans. It is one reason that Asian Indians are so well-off economically. According to the Census, Americans with doctoral degrees will earn about $3.4 million over their lifetimes, while those with professional degrees will earn $4.4 million. That compares to people with high school educations, who will earn an average of just $1.2 million.

The 2000 Census data shows that about 54 percent of Asian Indians held a professional or college education. Among Asian Indians 20 years or older, only 25 percent have high school diplomas or lower, with the remaining 75 percent population having some college or professional degree. One in five Asian Indians over age 20 has a master's degree (23.3 percent among males and 15.3 percent among females). The percentage of those over age 20 with doctoral degrees is four percent. Here, the

Indo-Caribbeans—a large but invisible community

Ethnic Indians first began arriving in the United States from the Caribbean beginning in the 1970s. Indo-Caribbeans, as they are known, are a substantial community—estimates place between 150,000 and 250,000 in New York City alone—but no one is sure exactly how large nationwide. The Census does not track Indo-Caribbeans separately; they may identify themselves as Asian Indian or Pakistani, or choose the Caribbean country of origin.

Indians were brought by the British to the Caribbean beginning in the first half of the 19th century as indentured workers. The majority went to three countries—Guyana, Trinidad and Tobago, and Suriname—but others went to Jamaica, St. Lucia, and other countries up until the early 20th century. Even today, Indians comprise about half of the population of Guyana, while in Trinidad and Tobago, Indians comprise about forty percent of the population.

In New York City, Indo-Caribbeans are most visible for their small businesses and restaurants. The latter blend Indian and Caribbean cuisines—rotis and dal alongside jerk chicken, all served with Red Stripe beer.

Indo-Caribbeans share the experience of being multiple migrants who grew up under a colonial system. And all of them share a sense of being a blend of two if not three cultures, dominated by a sense of nostalgia for the old country—India, in most cases—coupled with a slight alienation from their brethren straight from India.

"What the Asian Indians have been saying—and this is what Caribbean Indians have said to me—is that they feel their culture is of a higher standard than Caribbean Indians," one Indo-Caribbean told journalist Matthew Strozier in a 1997 article that appeared on the website IndiaInNewYork.com.

The Indo-Caribbean community in the United States is more diverse than it first appears to outsiders. Many Indo-Caribbeans have retained regional and ethnic identities from India, while simultaneously assimilating values and identities from their Caribbean host country, and their present home, the United States. Thus, an Indo-Caribbean may identify him or herself, depending on the context, with his or her ancestors' home region, i.e. Madras, modern-day Pakistan, etc., his or her adopted homeland, i.e. Guyana or Suriname, and what city or county he or she comes from there, and where he or she now lives in the United States.

The American identity has become more salient with younger people. Dr. Moses Seenarine, a professor at Hunter College where he teaches Caribbean history and politics, writes that in New York City, there have been conflicts at social clubs and events between Indo-Caribbean youths from Queens, Brooklyn, and the Bronx.

Religion is also a major differentiator among Indo-Caribbeans, one which is conflated with caste and socioeconomic class. Seenarine writes that Indo-Caribbean society in the United States is "divided into predominantly underclass and working class families, and a small number of middle class families who control almost all of the community organizations, media and businesses."

Seenarine is skeptical of the prospects for improving relations between Indo-Caribbeans of vastly different socioeconomic means. He writes: "The class biases and exploitation of this small middle class results in the silencing and pauperization of the vast majority of the community. Attempts at mobilizing the community are often motivated by business or religious interests, and to date there are no community based centers for Indo-Caribbean children, women, or seniors. Not surprisingly, the vast majority of poor Indo-Caribbeans in the United States remain untouched by the various community organizations and media, and there is a growing division between them and the dominant middle class."

—*Eric Lai*

gender differences are more significant: five percent among men and two percent of women. In terms of professional degrees, 5.6 percent of men and 5 percent of women had professional degrees in 2000.

Where do they work and how much do they make?

The average salary earned by an individual Asian Indian worker in 2000 was $29,745. The difference is wide between the sexes: males' average annual salary was $40,551, compared to $16,078 for females. These gender differences closely follow the educational differences noted earlier and the type of employment sought by Asian Indian males and females. When the Census Bureau releases the PUMS data in 2004, researchers will be able to determine exactly what gender and race differentials exist in salaries after controlling for education.

There are ongoing debates on whether Asian Indians should be included in affirmative action policies, and whether businesses owned by Asian Indians should qualify for minority status. For instance, some Chinese Americans in San Francisco protested against including Asian

Indians among beneficiaries of a city-wide affirmative action program aimed at under-represented Asian Pacific Americans. There were similar protests and proclamations in Ohio and other states against including Asian Indian-owned businesses in the list of minority-owned businesses that benefit from preferential hiring and bidding policies.

Where do the Asian Indians live?
Asian Indians are highly concentrated in the Northeastern part of the United States. About 35 percent live there, with more than 400,000 Asian Indians calling the New York City metropolitan area home. Southern and Western regions of the United States serve as homes to more than half of Asian Indians. The San Francisco Bay Area has the highest percentage of Asian Indians.

Summary and Conclusions:
The demographics of Asian Indians in 2000 were very favorable for them to advance socioeconomically as a group. The percentage of young, working people is very high relative to the number of elderly and children. Provided with equal opportunity, this youthful community looks set to achieve high levels of education, climb the occupational ranks, and increase their incomes and wealth. While Asian Indians do boast the highest median household income for any ethnic group in the country, the mainstream media often ignores the possibility that their incomes may lower than whites with similar educations and degrees. Furthermore, the 2000 Census showed that many Asian Indian households had relatives living with them—meaning that the larger average household size is a big reason for the larger household incomes. Finally, the concentration of Asian Indians predominantly in East and West Coast cities, means that the higher cost of living there also offsets any gains in household incomes. The bottom line is that it is very likely that when one controls for educational achievement and experience, Asian Indians may still be earning significantly lower wages than majority population with similar characteristics (though such a definite conclusion is beyond the means of this chapter).

—*K.V. Rao*

Methodology

The Census asks four questions that can be used to count Asian Indians, though all have their individual difficulties. First, a direct question on race included "Asian Indian" as one of the 14 categories of race that also has Indian (American). In the 1970 U.S. Census, Asian Indians were included in the white racial category while Chinese, Filipinos, Japanese, and Koreans were counted as "other." Similarly, Asian Indian babies were registered with race as "white" in official birth records, making it difficult to count the number of children born at that time. The short forms used by many elementary schools across the United States also counted Asian Indian youngsters as white. Thus, many traditional sources of demographic information are unhelpful when studying Asian Indians.

The second question asks where a person was born and when they arrived to the United States, if foreign-born. These two sub-questions provide information on citizenship status and immigration status besides their country of origin. One of the problems with this question is that persons who immigrated before the independence of India in 1947 might have been born in what is now called Pakistan.

The third question is about the languages spoken at home. It is difficult to identify Asian population on the basis of one of the several Indian languages spoken at home. For example, the native language of many native Indians is English, and they speak it regularly at home. The issue of identification is also complicated by the fact that many Pakistanis, Sri Lankans, Bangladeshis, Burmese, Nepalese and several other nationals speak one or other Indian languages.

The fourth and the last question is on ancestry, used for the first time in 1980. This helps draw out ethnic backgrounds of non-immigrants, or those of a certain ethnicity who may have resided in another country before emigrating to the United States, i.e. Indians who emigrated from the Caribbean.

Unfortunately, using any of these questions alone to track the Asian Indian American population would be inaccurate and possibly undercount it. One problem is that most Asian Indians are not familiar with the term "race" in their native country. The divisions discussed in Indian society are usually by religion or caste but not by race. Ancestry is another confusing term and it gets even more complicated when interracial and inter-caste marriages are involved. For instance, only 62 percent of Asian Indians in 1990 marked themselves as being of Asian Indian ancestry. Place of birth information is also faulty: only about half indicated their place of birth as India in 1980 and 1990. For instance, some estimates place the number of Indians who immigrated to the United States from the Caribbean Islands at as many as 250,000, most of them living in the New York City metropolitan area.

The data from this chapter was drawn from: the five percent sample of the U.S. Public Use Micro-data Sample (PUMS) data of 1980; one percent PUMS from the 1990 Census; summary file tabulations from the 2000 Census; and results from recently-released Census Supplementary Survey (CSS) PUMS files. Statistics are for all states nationwide. Appropriate weights have been applied to get nationally representative numbers from the various samples.

Entrepreneurs par Excellence

As the new millennium dawned, Korean Americans reached a number of important milestones. For the first time, the Korean American population topped the one million mark. Korean American businesses also topped $45 billion in sales. The oft-noted Korean American propensity for entrepreneurship was also confirmed by 2000 Census results that showed that a Korean American was more likely than a member of any other APA ethnic group to run his or her own business. This chapter examines the state of Korean Americans today, their past and their upcoming prospects.

Immigration: a 20th century phenomenon

The history of Koreans in America has been steered by political and economic conditions in the United States as well as in Korea, racial dynamics in the United States, and the very characteristics of the immigrants themselves. Some 7,000 Koreans were recruited and brought to Hawai'i as plantation laborers, from January 1903 to July 1905. Most of these immigrants were young bachelors. They were brought in to meet the labor demand on the Hawaiian plantations after a series of laws barring Chinese labor immigration were enacted. The frequent strikes by Japanese laborers in Hawai'i and rising anti-Asian sentiments in California also discouraged Japanese immigration. Plantation owners were looking for alternate sources of immigrant labor.

Before the door was completely closed in 1924, about 1,100 Korean "picture brides" were brought in. These brides were better educated than their male partners, and brought life and hope to the predominantly bachelor community. They led their husbands from Hawaiian farms to Honolulu and California, and actively took part in church activities and independence movements that helped free their homeland from Japanese colonial rule.

Students and political exiles constituted the third group of early Korean immigrants who landed on the American shores. Between 1899 and 1909, 64 students arrived. Between 1910 and 1924, about 540 political exiles came by way of China or Europe, without passports. Approximately 289 Korean students arrived with passports issued by the Japanese government between 1921 and 1940. These political exiles and students provided significant leadership in the pre-World War II Korean American community. Syngman Rhee, who later became the first president of the Republic of Korea, and Ahn Chang Ho, another political activist, are well known examples.

Photo: Christopher Andrew

The Korean population in the United States has grown more than fifteen-fold in the past three decades, pushing the group over the one million mark in 2000.

Between 1924 and 1945, no Korean immigrants were admitted to the United States. The federal immigration laws enacted in 1924 barred immigration

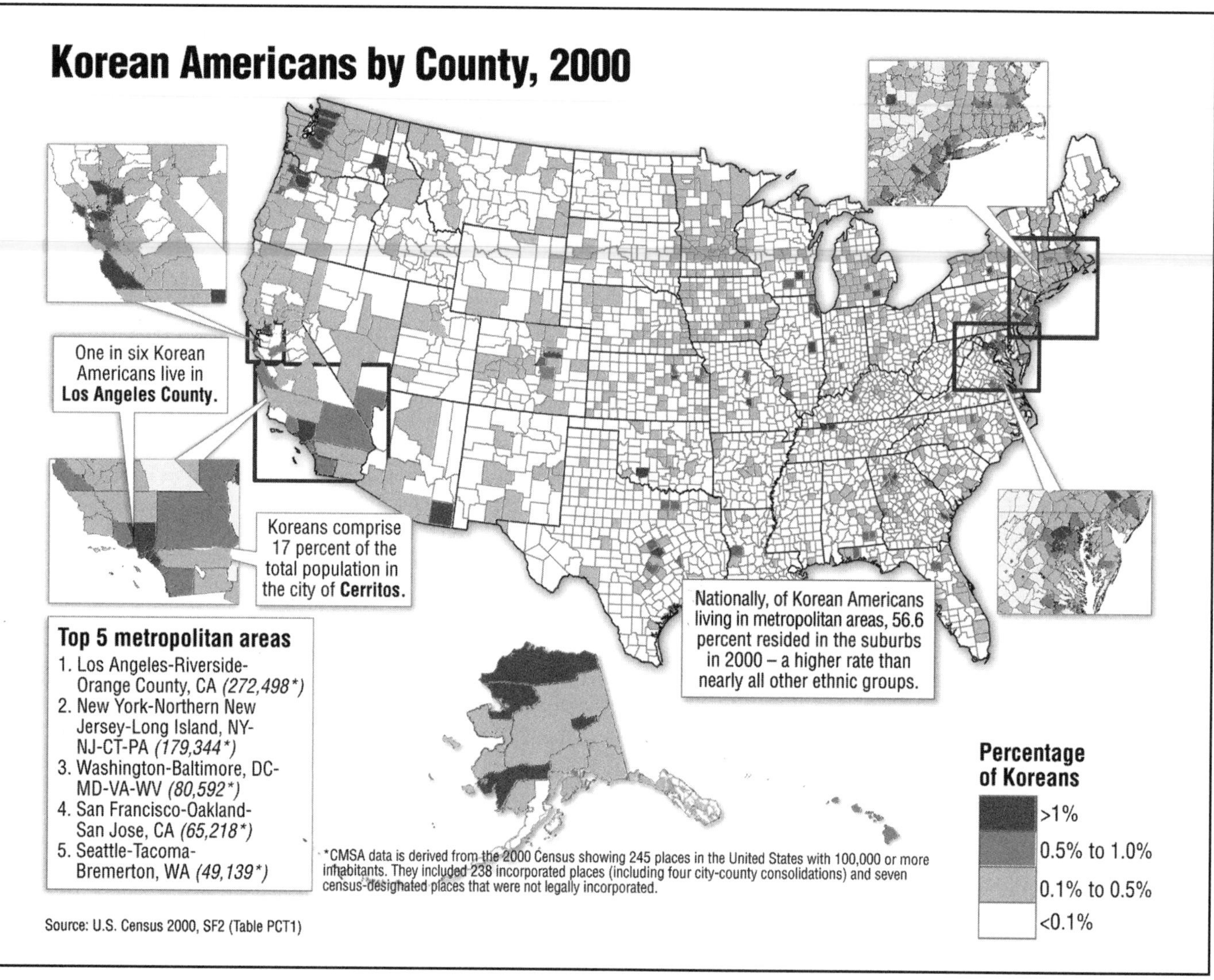

from Asian countries. The U.S. Immigration and Naturalization Service did not start to compile Korean immigration statistics until 1948. Nevertheless, the small group belonging to the first-wave of Korean immigrants organized a strong community and actively participated in the independence movement for Korea. Due to a great imbalance in the numbers of Korean American men versus Korean American women, and anti-miscegenation (interracial marriage) laws of the time, many of the first wave of immigrants stayed single throughout their lives. As a result, the Korean population, concentrated in Hawai'i and California, remained static at around 10,000 until 1950.

American intervention in the Korean War (1950-53) triggered the second wave of Korean immigration. American soldiers stationed in Korea brought home Korean brides, arranged adoption of war orphans to American homes, and sponsored students to come to the United States. Between 1951 and 1964, approximately 6,500 brides, 6,300 adopted children, and 6,000 students came to this country. These three groups have been a significant component of the Korean immigration to the United States ever since. The number of Koreans who have immigrated to this country as adopted children, or brides of Americans, since the Korean War is more than 100,000 for each respective group.

As a by-product of the civil rights movements of the 1950s and 1960s and due to changing dynamics of international relations, major changes were instituted in the U.S. immigration laws in 1965. The national origin quota system based on race was abolished. As a result, for the first time Koreans were able to immigrate to the United States as families. Until this time, Korean immigrants were mostly individuals in special categories—laborers, students, picture brides, war brides, and orphans.

After 1965, students-turned professionals were able to apply for permanent residence visas in the United States under provisions of the Hart-Cellar Act. Between 1965 and 1970, they were a

major component of Korean immigration. Sub-sequently, these professionals, along with wives of U.S. servicemen, petitioned for their spouses, siblings, and parents to immigrate as well. Since 1970, close relatives of permanent residents or citizens have comprised an overwhelming majority of the Korean immigrants coming to America.

Until the most recent decade, the number of Korean immigrants to the United States had grown exponentially every decade since the Korean War. Only 107 Koreans were admitted as immigrants during the 1940s. By the 1970s, that had grown to 267,638 Korean immigrants, constituting 6 percent of the total immigrants admitted to the United States in the 1970s, and ranked third in number behind only the Mexicans and Filipinos.

A total of 778,899 Korean immigrants were admitted to the United States between 1941 and 1998. Unlike Japanese immigration, which has remained basically steady since the 1950s, and Chinese immigration, which exploded at the same time and continues to grow, Korean immigration peaked during the 1980s. Annual admittance has steadily declined since 1987. The number of Korean immigrants admitted in 1998 was only 13,691, one of the lowest levels recorded since 1972. Between 1991 and 1998, Korea's ranking among countries sending immigrants to the United States dropped sharply to fourteenth.

Population size
Still, the historically steady and substantial inflow of immigration from Korea has accelerated the growth of the Korean population in the United States. Since 1970, when it was about 70,000, the Korean population has increased more than fifteen-fold to 1.07 million in the year 2000 (1.23 million when including Koreans who are part-Asian, and mixed race).

The Korean population grew 35 percent between 1990 and 2000, while the U.S. total population increased only 13 percent. During the decade, the Asian population as a whole grew 48 percent, second to the Hispanic population growth rate of 58 percent. On the other hand, the white population grew only six percent, showing the lowest growth rate among the major racial groups. Among APAs, Indians, Vietnamese and Chinese outpaced the Koreans.

Three basic types
Ethnically, and/or racially, mixed Koreans account for 12.34 percent of all Koreans. The percentage of multi-ethnic Koreans, mixed with other Asians, accounts for 1.84 percent, while multi-racial Koreans account for 10.50 percent. The Koreans' rate of mixing with other ethnic or racial groups is among the lowest of the largest 15 Asian American groups (among larger Asian American populations, the Japanese show the highest rates, while Vietnamese show the lowest).

The percent of multi-ethnic and/or racial Koreans varies greatly from state to state. The rate is highest for Koreans in Hawai'i. Many of the U.S.-born descendants of the first-wave Koreans who immigrated at the turn of the twentieth century still live in Hawai'i and their out-marriage rate is very high. Thus, 43 percent of all persons of Korean heritage in Hawai'i are persons of mixed ethnic and/or racial heritage—14.5 percent mixed with other Asians, and 28.6 percent with other races. The proportion of mixed heritage persons among Koreans in Hawai'i is even higher than that of the Japanese (32 percent).

In the continental United States, states with a relatively small number of Koreans, such as North Dakota, Idaho, New Mexico, Arkansas and Oklahoma, tend to show a high percentage of mixed-heritage Koreans. More than a quarter of all Koreans in these states are ethnically or racially mixed. Korean women married to American soldiers and Korean children adopted to American homes have been a significant component of Korean immigration since the Korean War and they tend to settle all over the United States. Children born to these Koreans apparently raised the rate of mixed heritage persons in these states.

On the other hand, states with a relatively large number of Koreans, such as California, New York, New Jersey and Maryland, show a relatively low rate of mixed-heritage Koreans. These are also the states where a large number of more recent immigrant families have settled. In these states, persons of mixed-heritage constitute less than 8 percent of all Koreans. Propinquity is apparently a factor here. If people of a common ethnic heritage live close to each other, the chances are higher that they will meet and marry one another.

Where Koreans live
Koreans, like most other Asian Americans, have traditionally been concentrated in the Western part of the United States. 44 percent of Koreans live in the West, compared to 22 percent of the general population. Nevertheless, the geographic distribution has changed significantly since the 1960s, as Koreans have been quicker than other APAs to disperse themselves across the wider regions of the United States (see map). Travelers are likely to find at least one or more Korean churches with a sign written in Hangul characters in most metropolitan cities in America.

Perhaps what's most remarkable is the increase in the numbers of Korean Americans in the South. There, the population of Korean Americans grew 46 percent between 1990 and 2000. During that decade, the Korean population in Georgia increased fastest, at 88 percent. High growth rates were also noticeable among other states on the Atlantic coastal region, such as North Carolina, Tennessee, Delaware, Florida and Virginia. This relatively high presence of Koreans compared to

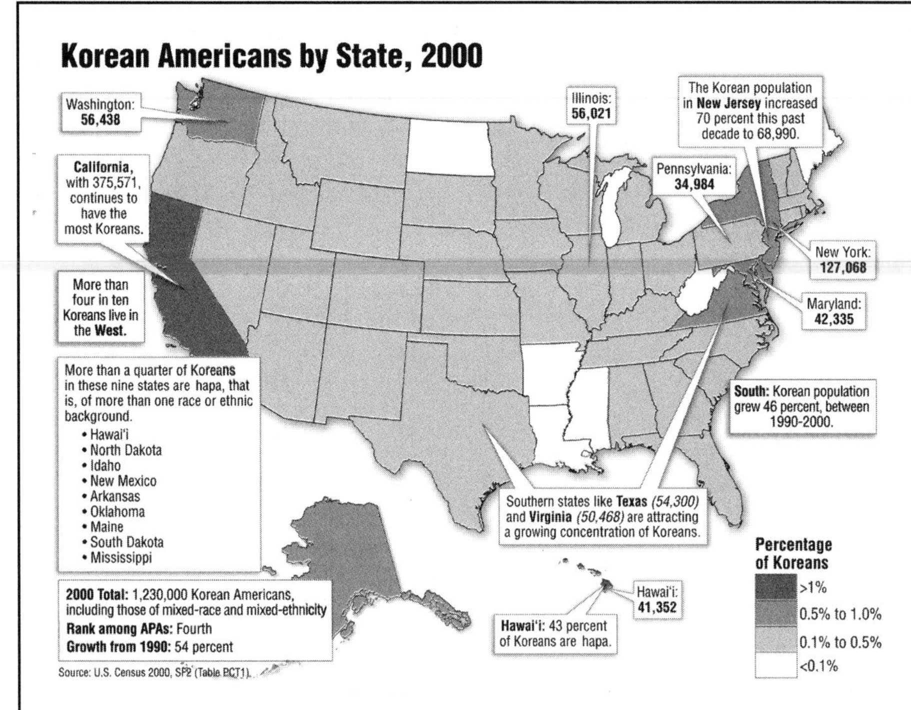

other APAs may be due to the preponderance of Koreans who run retail businesses in cities scattered around the South.

While many Korean businesses are in the urban city centers, most Koreans make their homes in the suburbs of these big metropolises. Korean immigration to the United States since 1965 has been typically an urban-to-urban migration, from large urban centers of South Korea to large metropolitan areas of the United States. About 57 percent live in the suburbs, though—one of the highest rates among major racial/ethnic groups, topped only by Indians (59 percent). For the general population, about 50 percent live in the suburbs, while 30 percent live in central cities. Finding a good school for their children is one of the most important factors that Korean parents consider in looking for a neighborhood in which to settle down, which is why they choose the suburbs when they can.

Despite their above-noted diaspora throughout the South, Koreans as a whole are still concentrated in just a few large metropolises. Southern California leads the way. More than a quarter million Korean Americans live in the area defined by the Census as the Los Angeles-Riverside-Orange-San Bernardino-Ventura, Calif. Consolidated Metropolitan Statistical Area (CMSA). Next is the conglomerate encompassing New York City and the surrounding metropolitan areas of New York, Northern New Jersey, Connecticut, and Pennsylvania. Forty percent of all Koreans in the United States are found in these two regions. Nearly three-quarters of Koreans in the U.S. live in one of thirteen large metropolitan areas.

The dynamic nature of population redistribution becomes clearer when we look at changes among states and cities. California continues to be the state with the largest number of Koreans, with growth rates that kept pace with the overall Korean American growth rate. New York's growth rate, 25 percent, was significantly lower than the national average, though it still maintains the rank of second in size in 2000. Movement of Koreans to Illinois slowed during the 1990s, while in New Jersey, it barreled up to 70 percent. This was in part due to a heavy influx of Koreans to the New Jersey suburbs around New York City.

What we can draw from this is this: while Koreans have relatively high concentrations in certain parts of the country, these rates are still lower than those of most other APAs. The Chinese and Japanese, for example, are much more concentrated in western states like California and Hawai'i, respectively. Also, we see that when Korean Americans live in the same metropolitan area, they collect together into multiple scattered neighborhoods, rather than inhabiting a single one.

For example, in Los Angeles County, where one in six Korean Americans lives, there are six distinct areas where Koreans are concentrated: 1) Koreatown, 2) the Diamond Bar–Rowland Heights-Walnut area, 3) the Downey-Cerritos-La Mirada area, 4) the Gardena-Torrance-Palos Verdes area, 5) the Glendale-La Crescenta-La Canada area, and 6) the Northridge suburb in the San Fernando Valley. Korean churches, Korean supermarkets, and many other types of Korean firms serving mainly their own ethnic clienteles are found in these areas. Koreans constitute a significant minority of the resident population in all of these areas. In Koreatown, Koreans constitute about 20 percent of its total population. In the city of Cerritos, Koreans comprise 17 percent of the total population. In La Crescenta and La Canada, the Korean share is 14 percent and 11 percent, respectively. In Diamond Bar, it is 10 percent.

Koreatown is the central business district of the wider Korean community in Southern California; the other five clusters serve as mere satellite communities. Most of the high-level service firms and organizations such as

law firms, accounting firms, political and community associations serving Koreans are located in Koreatown. Between 1990 and 2000, Koreatown greatly expanded its boundary to upscale residential communities westward. The Korean population in Koreatown increased from 35,000 to 47,000 during this decade. The dispersed clustering pattern of Koreans exhibits a clear contrast to the Chinese pattern. Chinese appear to be mostly concentrated in a single West-East stretch extending from Monterey Park to Chino Hills.

Work

Koreans are entrepreneurs par excellence. Surveys conducted in Los Angeles, Chicago, New York, and Atlanta confirm that about one-third of Korean immigrant households engage in a self-owned business, about one-fifth in professional work, and the rest in other salaried occupations. In the 1970s, a typical newly-arrived family would start a small business after a few years of work on assembly lines or with maintenance companies. Nowadays, many start business shortly after arrival thanks to the strong economy and liberalization of foreign exchange laws in Korea.

The 1997 U.S. Economic Census confirmed many of the anecdotal pictures of Korean business patterns that have been reported in Korean newspapers. With more than 135,000 businesses, Koreans rank third among APAs, after the Chinese and Indians. But their tendency to enter into business is one of the highest among all minority ethnic/racial groups. For instance, the rate of Korean business ownership is 71 percent higher than their share of the population. This bests other business-minded populations such as the Japanese (47 percent higher), Chinese (41 percent higher), Indians (34 percent higher), Vietnamese (17 percent higher), and less-business-oriented groups such as the Filipinos (32 percent lower than the general population), Hispanics (54 percent lower), and African Americans (68 percent lower).

Korean business ownership varies greatly by type of industry. The Korean population constitutes only one out of 260 Americans, but one in 67 retail trade firms are owned by Koreans. Koreans are also highly concentrated in apparel and accessory stores, food stores, and general merchandise stores. In each industry, one in 33 stores is Korean-owned. Koreans also own a high percentage of clothing factories, eating and drinking places, personal services stores, and local and interurban passenger transit services, i.e. taxis.

The high concentration of Koreans in these types of industries partly explains the high dispersion for Koreans over wide regions. These firms are mostly labor intensive and family, or individually, operated businesses and the heavy concentration of Koreans in these areas reflect their relatively short immigration history in this country. The high concentration in these types of retail and personal services is also observed among Vietnamese, whose immigration history is even more recent than that of Koreans.

Why do Koreans concentrate in small business? Potential profitability is one obvious reason. But the more important reason may be the feeling of mastery of the work environment. One critical issue that Korean immigrants face is that of status inconsistency and the ensuing erosion of self-esteem. A majority of Korean immigrants earned college degrees and held professional jobs before moving to America. Language difficulties and unfamiliarity with American culture prevent many from finding a satisfactory job commensurate with their education and work experience. Their options are: 1) work in a safe but lower-status and less rewarding job, or 2) operate their own business in a risky and difficult environment. Running one's own business is difficult and risky, but gives psychological satisfaction of being one's own boss and a status of *sajangnim*, or "president" in Korean. Many immigrants therefore opt for entrepreneurship.

Despite their relatively short tenure in the United States, Korean business firms appear to be doing well. The average annual sales and receipts per Korean-owned firm is $339,000. This is less than those of the Japanese ($511,000), Chinese ($420,000), and Asian Indian ($405,000), and is far less than the national average ($891,000) for all firms. But it is far higher than those of Hispanic- ($155,000), Filipino- ($131,000), Vietnamese- ($95,000), and African American- ($86,000) owned firms. In terms of the number of employees, Korean firms also stand in the middle of the economic hierarchy.

The data clearly show that within the American business structure and its clear racially-based hierarchy, Korean-owned firms occupy a "middleman" minority status—sandwiched between the dominant group (non-Hispanic whites) and less powerful classes (African Americans and Hispanics).

To compete successfully, Korean small business owners work long hours, mobilize family labor, and ethnic resources. Husband and wife team up to operate the family business without vacations or weekends. Grown-up children also help during the after-school hours. Despite the stereotypes, not all Korean businesses are located in impoverished inner-city neighborhoods. Similar to their choice of residence, Koreans locate their businesses over wide areas, in suburban as well as in inner-city areas. The author's 1989 survey of Korean businesses in Southern California revealed that about one-half of Korean-owned businesses were located in the suburbs. Only 27 percent of the Korean-owned businesses had Hispanics and/or African Americans as their major clientele.

Leading Businesses Operated by Koreans and Chinese, 1997

		KOREAN			CHINESE		
Rank	Overall	Number	% of overall	Ratio*	Number	% of overall	Ratio*
All industries	**20,821,934**	**135,571**	**0.65%**	**1.71**	**252,577**	**1.21%**	**1.41**
1. Apparel and accessory stores	127,848	6,317	4.94%	13.00	1,922	1.50%	1.75
2. Food stores	216,067	10,336	4.78%	12.59	6,323	2.93%	3.40
3. General merchandise stores	35,027	1,269	3.62%	9.53	391	1.12%	1.30
4. Apparel and other textile products	54,889	1,884	3.43%	9.03	2,854	5.20%	6.05
5. Textile mill products	8,213	226	2.75%	7.24	101	1.23%	1.43
6. Eating and drinking places	493,313	10,182	2.06%	5.43	37,614	7.62%	8.87
7. Personal services	1,348,554	22,619	1.68%	4.41	16,932	1.26%	1.46
8. Local and interurban passenger transit	116,993	1,590	1.36%	3.58	3,022	2.58%	3.00
9. Wholesale trade – non-durable goods	309,731	3,727	1.20%	3.17	10,352	3.34%	3.89
10. Leather and leather products	5,251	54	1.03%	2.71	109	2.08%	2.41

*Concentration ratio is the proportion in each industry group divided by proportion of population of each race/ethnic group.
Source: U.S. Economic Census, 1997

Epilogue

Koreans enthusiastically responded to the liberalization of U.S. immigration laws in the 1960s by moving, in large droves, to the United States. Immigration rates accelerated during the 1970s and 1980s. The total population now numbers more than 1.2 million, including those of mixed Korean heritage. Koreans have become a visible and significant minority in this multi-ethnic and multi-cultural nation. This hard-working, highly educated, and actively organized ethnic community is increasing its stake in the American society. The impact will be tremendous very soon when the second-generation of Korean Americans reach adulthood.

As the Korean community reaches a stage where it can finally become a viable participant in American political and economic affairs, the community also appears to be slowing down its growth, population-wise. The population size has a significant bearing not only to the political empowerment of Korean Americans, but also on the country they left behind. In this closely-tied global village, the communities of Koreans, Japanese and Chinese living in the United States are having a significant effect on the bilateral and multilateral relationships among Korea, China, and Japan—effects which will only increase in the future.

During a relatively short period in America, Korean immigrants have concentrated in building an economic base for themselves and for their children. That translates into moving to places where they can find both profitable business opportunities and good schools for their children. For some, that means locating in poor urban minority-dominated ghettos; for others, it means moving into middle-class suburbs. Their lives involve mingling with both the poor and wealthy, the majority and the minority.

The latest Census results already show a significant relationship between the strong upward mobility of Koreans and their population redistribution pattern. The effect of living in a multi-racial and multi-cultural society is also impacting their Korean ethnic identity: already, there are significant numbers of multiethnic and multi-racial Koreans. This mixed Korean population will no doubt increase with the second and succeeding generations, as the Japanese American before them so clearly demonstrated.

—*Eui-Young Yu*

Race Relations: Los Angeles Riots and the Korean-African American Conflict

Introduction

Ten years later, the 1992 Los Angeles riots remain the worst civil disturbance in recent American history, exposing the deepening racial and class divisions in the United States. The divisions between the haves and have-nots, minority and majority, immigrants and natives, and even between the many "minority" groups, exacerbated distrust, fear and hopelessness. With groups perceiving that they are vying against each other to grab a shrinking piece of the pie, racial and ethnic conflicts in Los Angeles have proliferated in the aftermath of the riots. On the other hand, the riots increased racial and ethnic awareness and opened up dialogue between people who previously had nothing but superficial interaction with one another. Additionally, Asian American, African American, white and Latino riot victims shared frustration and anger with the government for not providing adequate compensation for their losses.

For Korean Americans, the riots had a profound economic, psychological and ideological impact. When the smoke cleared, Korean Americans were among those suffering the heaviest losses: 2,280 Korean-owned stores had been looted, burned or damaged, amounting to about $400 million in losses. A survey conducted eleven months after the riots showed that almost 40 percent of Korean Americans in Los Angeles were thinking of leaving. Another study found that more than half of Korean businessmen were facing a "very difficult" financial situation. Psychological damage suffered by victims of the riots still lingers and is very much part of their daily life. A survey conducted by

the Korean American Inter-Agency Council (KAIAC) found that 15 percent of college-age youth had dropped out of school because of the riots. Many Korean Americans lost faith in the "American Dream" and began to wonder about their place and the purpose of life in America. Despite the painful, tragic and traumatic experience of the riots, Korean Americans have gained much; in particular, they learned many valuable lessons about what it means to be a minority in America.

Economic factors: underlying ethnic tensions

The "middleman minority" theory proposed by a number of scholars suggests that their economic niche causes immigrant groups like Koreans to experience friction with all three of the key segments of the local population: customers, competitors and labor unions. In other words, Korean merchants cannot avoid friction with the African American community because of the built-in conflictual relationship with their African American customers. At the same time, Korean merchants face hostility from African American merchants who charge that they are driving them out of business by undercutting prices. It is easy to see how the problem can be exacerbated when the sellers are "immigrants" and the buyers are poor.

Indeed, the root cause of the inter-ethnic conflict appears to be economic survival. African American complaints against Korean merchants often focus on the following economic issues:

- Korean merchants do not hire African American workers.
- They overcharge African American customers for inferior products.
- They do not contribute their profits back to the African American community.

In other words, African Americans perceive Korean merchants as a threat to their own economic survival. Some African Americans perceive Korean merchants as a part of long line of "outsiders" coming to exploit their community. However, a majority of African American customers indicated, "It does not matter who serves them as long as they receive good service." Mindful of these complaints, many Korean businesses have begun to contribute to African American civic and voluntary organizations.

Social and cultural factors: underlying conflicts

Cultural misunderstandings fuel and escalate confrontations. African American customers complain that Korean merchants treat them with disrespect and say the merchants can't communicate with them (though I must emphasize that this is not the root cause of the Los Angeles riots, as the mainstream media was wont to theorize).

Korea is one of the most homogeneous societies in the world, claiming to have one language, one culture, and one ethnicity. "Monocultural people (i.e., Koreans) doing business in a multi-cultural society are potentially problematic. Particularly, the South Central Los Angeles is probably the worst place Koreans can come into," declared Larry Aubry of Los Angeles County Human Relations Commission. "Koreans don't know how to interact with customers." And again, "it is clear [Korean immigrants] are hard-working and industrious. But there's a high degree of resentment being bred against them in the African American community," Melanie Lomax, vice president of the National Association for the Advancement of Colored People (NAACP), told the *Los Angeles Times*. "Both groups are not particularly educated about the other's cultural heritage."

Koreans and African Americans differ on what is proper etiquette in the business setting. According to a 1989 study by Ella Stewart, Korean merchants most frequently mentioned loudness, bad language, and shoplifting as inappropriate behaviors by black patrons, stating that African American patrons should have shown respect and courtesy, and should have apologized more frequently. African American patrons most frequently mentioned Korean merchant/employees' negative attitude—being ignored and being watched constantly, as well as having money thrown back to them on the counter—as inappropriate behaviors.

Faced with what they consider an inappropriate act, Korean merchants usually react in one of two ways: by ignoring the customer, or by getting angry and confronting him or her. Being totally ignored by a merchant is an especially sensitive issue for many African American patrons, who regard it as a direct insult to their humanity, according to Stewart, regardless of the ethnicity of the merchant.

"I patronize the gas station because a Korean lady always greets me with 'hello' and never forgets to say 'have a nice day,'" one African American resident of South Central Los Angeles told me in an interview. "Across from that gas station, there is an African American-owned gas station. But he has never said hello or been friendly to me, so I patronize the Korean-owned gas station."

Korean merchants in general lack historical understanding or awareness of the American civil rights movement and U.S. race relations. Many, though, are willing to learn. A Korean language book I wrote, *Who African Americans Are*, went into a third printing within three months. Still, ignorance and cultural misunderstandings contribute to tensions, though they are not the root causes. A pre-existing volatile and conflictual relationship between the two groups must be examined more closely. How Korean merchants and African American residents interact plays a critical role in either minimizing or exacerbating tension.

Clash of ideologies

Unaware of the history of oppression and exploitation of minority groups by white America, Korean immigrants believe that America is a "land of opportunity" for all. Korean immigrants often show little respect toward African American customers who are frequently unemployed and dependent upon government programs. Many Korean immigrants believe that African Americans should not blame anyone except themselves for their misery and misfortune. Korean immigrants aren't aware that African American slums are a direct outcome of racial discrimination in employment, housing, education and politics.

Becoming an independent entrepreneur represents success to many African Americans, while it is nothing more than an avenue for making a living to many Korean immigrants. And although some businesses have become successful, the majority of Korean-owned mom-and-pop stores are struggling to make ends meet. "I know that I can't make much money in this business," said one Korean merchant.

Confrontations derive from the different historical, economic and ideological experiences of the two groups. African Americans, who have learned to stand up for their rights because of historical persecution and oppression, will not tolerate attacks on the most important thing they have left—their dignity.

Root causes of the Los Angeles riots

The Los Angeles riots of 1992 involved not only whites and blacks but also Asians, Koreans, Latinos and other groups. Some have characterized them as "bread riots" suggesting a lower-class uprising. One woman who participated in looting explained that "this was the first time she could get shoes for all six of her children at once." The looting and burning may have been an articulation of genuine grievances and protest against social and economic conditions that oppressed and discriminated against poor minorities. Several factors had contributed to frustration and the worsening of conditions for residents of South Central Los Angeles: closure of local factories and the loss of jobs, the rise of neo-conservative politics, dissatisfaction with the law enforcement and justice system, and the arrival of new Latino immigrants and Asian merchants.

The closure and relocation of manufacturing plants and factories in the United States for cheaper environs such as Asia and Mexico had caused displacement and unemployment among African American workers. This de-industrialization of the American economy during the 1970s and 1980s was the U.S. corporate response to the economic crisis created by increasing global competition. "Runaway shops" and overseas investment were an aggressive tactic by capitalists to regain competitiveness and increase profits. Commentators like Barry Bluestone and Bennett Harris noted that by the early 1980s, "every newscast seemed to contain a story about a plant shutting down, [or] another thousand jobs disappearing from a community." Unemployment was no longer the problem of the poor. The middle-class workers in traditional manufacturing industries such as steel, rubber, and automotive were the hardest hit, as they had no prospect of finding equivalent employment.

Republican administrations have succeeded in manipulating and dominating the language of the "politics of race." Over the past few decades, they have successfully pointed the finger at the victims of racism and repeatedly scapegoated immigrants or minorities for societal problems. It is important to note that anti-Asian sentiment and violence has increased in an atmosphere of neo-conservative public policies, which scapegoat and blame victims. Furthermore, some argue that the neo-conservative policies of the Republican administrations pitted minority groups against each other in the form of Korean-African American and Latino-African American tensions and increased the rise of anti-minority violence during the 1980s.

The problem of police brutality was also a major issue for African Americans living in the inner city. The Los Angeles Police Department (LAPD) long had a reputation for brutalizing African American suspects, or simply stopping and harassing young African American men just because they fit a "description" or were in the wrong neighborhood. "If I am walking down the street and see some gang-bangers on the one side and LAPD car on the other, I am not really sure which group I'm more afraid of. But actually, I feel more threatened by the police," one youth said. This distrust and enmity between the police and African American and Latino youths contributed to the explosion in 1992. As a result, various commissions after the riots recommended systematic changes in the LAPD to establish a positive relationship with Los Angeles's diverse communities.

Great awakening: the lessons of the Los Angeles riots

Korean Americans had been fairly invisible prior to the 1992 riots. In trying to rebuild after the riots, Korean American storeowners discovered just how politically isolated they were. No one from City Hall or Sacramento paid any attention to the needs of Korean American victims. "What they experienced on 29 and 30 April was a baptism into what it really means for a Korean to become American in the 1990s," wrote Elaine Kim, a professor of Comparative Ethnic Studies at UC Berkeley.

Many Korean Americans felt that they had been scapegoated as the cause of America's racial problems by media and politicians. K.W. Lee, a prominent journalist, wrote, "A minority's minority— voiceless and powerless—has

My Father, L.A. Riot Survivor

I was in my sophomore year of college, busy writing papers, when the court announced the Rodney King verdict — not guilty. Soon afterwards, the city of Los Angeles went ablaze, in a catastrophic event known to Korean Americans as *Sa-i-gu*.

Appa ("Dad" in Korean) had opened a small grocery store in South Central Los Angeles in 1991. He had chosen this location because there was little competition from bigger stores like Safeway or Ralph's. Like many Korean business owners, Appa found a niche by going to where other businesses would not.

Crime was common. Appa's register counter was raised a foot above the ground so he could watch his customers. Sometimes, he would catch thieves swiping small items like candy and soda. His merchandise was his livelihood; but many of his customers resented being spied upon.

When I used to visit him at the store, I could sense his anxiety. At first he tried to befriend his customers. When that didn't work, he would scream at them, angry at their disrespect for his attempts at kindness.

Appa was even robbed at gunpoint once during the first few months of opening the store. My father was not hurt, and the assailant was never caught. A rapport between Appa and his customers never really developed. And tensions increased after a Korean American store owner shot a 15-year-old black girl in Los Angeles for trying to steal a $1.79 bottle of orange juice in March 1991. The woman was arrested and charged with murder, but was later acquitted.

When the Los Angeles police officers that beat Rodney King were acquitted in court, racial tensions in the community erupted. Like the Jewish business owners during the Watts riot of 1965, Korean business owners in South Central Los Angeles became the victims of rage and discontent from African Americans.

Appa received a warning call from his friend who urged him to leave that day. Appa grabbed his money bag, jumped into his car and left the store. Shortly afterwards, rioters broke in. They rummaged through all of his belongings, and stole food and merchandise.

The next morning, Appa returned to his store and observed the damage from a nearby alley. The store was in shambles.

"I had nothing," Appa recounted. "I only had fire insurance, and it was not only a fire. The main thing was that I didn't want to lose my life. If I fought them, they would kill me."

Not all Koreans stood on top of the roofs of their businesses with guns. Most were like my father. They lost not only their source of income, but their dignity as human beings. But Appa is not disillusioned, nor does he seek sympathy. A year after the riots, Appa opened a new store in Central California, hundreds of miles away from Los Angeles. To our family's relief, it is a much safer place.

—Ji Hyun Lim

been singled out for destruction by a politically powerful but economically frustrated minority." In the aftermath of the riots, Korean Americans realized they were vulnerable, exploitable, and underrepresented. Political empowerment became a specific, concrete and immediate goal for Korean Americans, and they began to take appropriate measures.

The riots caused many second generation Korean Americans to see things from their parents' eyes for the first time. Born and raised in America, many had tried to separate themselves from their parents who spoke broken English and seemed to understand little about American ways of life. A second-generation Korean American student wrote, "I used to just consider myself an American, usually neglecting to express my ethnic background. I was embarrassed and ashamed, because many Koreans had established a negative image among the media and the African Americans."

Reclaiming "Korean-ness" brought a new sense of Korean American ethnic identity and activism. On May 2, 1992, about 30,000 people, mostly Korean Americans, attended a peace rally in the heart of Koreatown, protesting the lack of police protection during the riots and calling for racial harmony in the city. This rally marked a truly historic moment of unity among Korean Americans.

Political empowerment

When four Korean American candidates won elections held shortly after the Los Angeles riots of 1992, it appeared that Korean Americans had finally made gains in achieving a degree of political power. These elections were hailed as a milestone achievement for a Korean American community that had been searching for a "voice" to be actively involved in the political dialogue of mainstream America.

The National Korean American Service & Education Consortium (NAKASEC) was founded in 1994 in Los Angeles. Among other activities, NAKASEC launched a "Justice for Immigrants" campaign to educate the public about the vicious nature of anti-immigrant

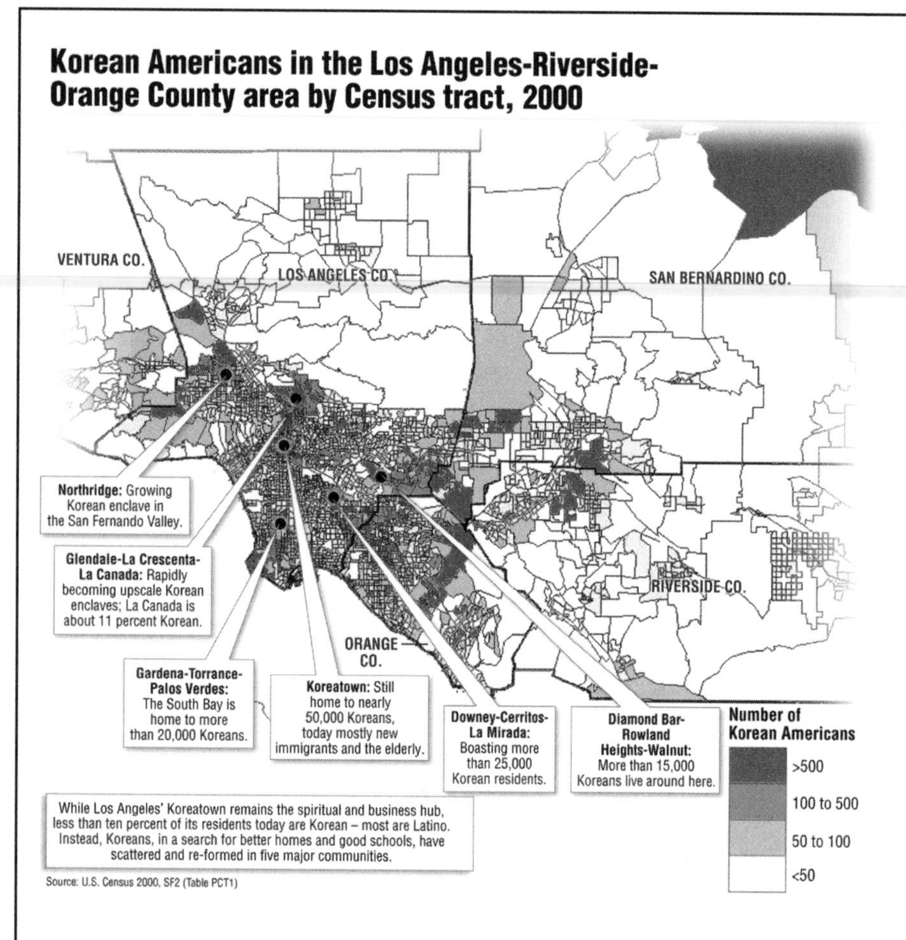

legislation, a campaign that garnered the support of 20 other organizations. NAKASEC may be the first step towards the formation of a national civil rights organization for Korean Americans, though it still needs to build a solid foundation and broader supports within the Korean American community to be more effective.

Multiethnic coalition building

The riots taught Korean Americans that they must adjust their thinking and behavior to live in a multiethnic society. They also realized that being reared in a homogeneous society was ill preparation for life in a multiethnic metropolis. During the riots, Korean-language media, especially radio stations, functioned as a life-line to desperate listeners. Korean Americans show great interest in learning about Latino and African American history and culture. Korean-language newspapers, television and radio stations continue to inform, educate and enlighten the community about African American and Latino experiences.

There was also an active attempt to promote mutual understanding between the aggrieved groups in Los Angeles. Thus arose groups such as the Black-Korean Christian Alliance, scholarships for African American students, etc. Unfortunately, apart from the Black-Korean Christian Alliance, most of the projects have been short-lived. There has been an effort to establish a Korean and African American Human Relations Council to solve inter-ethnic conflicts with dialogue exchange of ideas and culture, and mutual understanding. If it were successful, the natural next step would be to include Latinos as coalition partners.

Conclusion

Ten years after the riots, Los Angeles is still without a plan to address the fundamental urban needs underscored by the economic and demographic restructuring of the past two decades. The lack of vision, plans, resources and leadership poses major challenges for the city as it tries to rebuild its economic base and human relations between its many diverse communities.

Korean Americans have not been able to fully recover from the riots. The calamity did increase solidarity among Korean Americans, as well as raise multiethnic consciousness. And yet, a decade later, the lessons Korean Americans learned from the riots have not produced concrete plans of action. The Korean American community must establish local and national networks and institutions in order to economically and politically empower themselves.

—Edward Taehan Chang

Overcoming the Past and Building a Future

For Southeast Asian Americans, the new millennium marked several significant events. The year 2000 marked the twenty-fifth anniversary of the resettlement program that began in the mid-1970s and lasted for two decades. From refugees to full American citizens, the Vietnamese American and Chinese Vietnamese American communities have grown to a total of 1.22 million members, making them the fifth-largest group among APAs. However, the influx of refugees that powered this growth is winding down considerably, due to economic and political changes in Vietnam as well as U.S. immigration policies regarding Vietnam and Southeast Asia as a whole. There are indications that the second generation of Vietnamese Americans is quickly maturing and ready to take over the many tasks of community organizing and building. In this article, "Vietnamese" will be used to refer to both Vietnamese Americans and Chinese Vietnamese Americans, unless explicitly stated otherwise.

Regional settlement

Socio-political dimensions as well as urban changes are among the factors that determine regional make-up. California, for example, saw slow growth in its Vietnamese population during the 1990s, as births and new immigration were counterbalanced by Vietnamese residents leaving the state for places like the South that offered cheaper housing and job opportunities. Along with these changes, the number of Vietnamese in enclave cities such as San Jose, Westminster and Garden Grove remained steady.

Community leaders maintain that the Vietnamese continued to be undercounted in 2000, primarily for two reasons: underreporting by the Vietnamese themselves; and because many Chinese Vietnamese identified themselves simply as "Chinese" rather than "Vietnamese." The Vietnamese population, 282,000 according to the 1980 Census, has grown fourfold in two decades. It more than doubled from 1980 to 1990, jumping to 593,213. Ten years later, this population nearly doubled to 1.22 million, including multi-racial and multi-ethnic Vietnamese, who were counted for the first time in 2000.

Photo: David Kawashima

While immigration from Vietnam is expected to level off, the community is expected to continue to grow with the addition of American-born Vietnamese.

Background to migration

In the late sixties, there were half a million American military personnel in Vietnam. By contrast, there were less than 4,000 identified Vietnamese

A Longing for Return: The Emerging Field of Vietnamese American Literature

Vietnamese American literature is a new field, one that emerged only three decades ago as the Vietnamese American community rapidly developed after the Vietnam War. The literature cannot be understood outside the context of its emergence, namely the arrival of refugees after the war. Many left by plane in 1975; others left after the Communist takeover by boat, and were usually of lesser means.

Because initially most fled Vietnam fearing for their lives, the theme of return, more so than issues of assimilation and racism as was the case for early Asian American immigrant writers, is central to Vietnamese American writers.

The theme of return has changed over time, however. In memoirs, return is conducted through adult memory. Examples include Truong Nhu Tang's *A Vietcong Memoir* (1985), Nguyen Ngoc Ngan's *The Will of Heaven* (1982), and Nguyen Kien's *The Unwanted* (2001). Return is also expressed through the creative reporting of one's parents' story and memory, or through family history that spans a few generations, as in *Sacred Willow* (2000) by Duong Van May Elliot.

Return also occurs through the blurred and fragmented lenses of childhood memory, as in Cao Lan's *Monkey Bridge* (1997). After the U.S. Government lifted its trade embargo in 1994, stories of physical return to Vietnam emerged: Truong Tran and Hoang Chuong's *The Book of Perception* (1999), and Mong Lan's *Song of the Cicadas* (2001). In Linh Dinh's collection of short stories *Fake House* (2000), return takes place through the fictional incarnations of Vietnamese, Vietnamese American and white American characters.

Early efforts

Early texts were written in Vietnamese and published in literary magazines that focused mostly on homeland politics from a South Vietnamese perspective. They were mostly written by military officials and intellectuals denouncing the Communist regime. But with a new generation, stories are moving away from politics to focus on personal experience or fiction.

Early Vietnamese American writers had difficulties being published. For political reasons, their stories were unwanted by mainstream America. Many conservatives did not want to hear their stories, because of their guilt for having abandoned their allies. Others did not want to be reminded of the national defeat and international fiasco. Body counts needed to be forgotten; it was the end of a frightening game. The Domino Theory predicting the fall of neighboring countries to Communism proved to be as ephemeral as smoke.

Meanwhile, liberals were not interested in listening to the stories of those like the Vietnamese who had fought with American forces against Communism. In this context, and also because their writing did not conform to traditional American notions of literature, early Vietnamese American texts were published by small presses and did not receive wide distribution.

One exception was Le Ly Hayslip's *When Heaven and Earth Changed Places* (1989), which was made into an Oliver Stone film, *Heaven and Earth.* It is the story of a young woman who initially worked for the Viet Minh fighting against French colonialism and is subsequently trapped in the infernal machinery of war. It might still be the most popular and well-known Vietnamese American text. A moving story, it has also been criticized for appealing to a dominant understanding of the war, which tends to glorify the North Vietnamese and dehumanize the South Vietnamese and depicts Vietnamese women as embodying all the suffering of Vietnam.

In 1994, two books helped establish the genre of Vietnamese American memoir. They were Jade Ngoc Quang's *South Wind Changing* and Nguyen Qui Duc's *Where the Ashes Are.* These books did not focus on ideology or politics, but on personal experience. In *South Wind,* we follow the story of a student who is captured and sent to a re-education camp, simultane-

immigrants in the United States. Few could predict that by the year 2000, Vietnamese would be so visible in so many urban centers around the United States. Take California, where there are 447,000 Vietnamese, with notable clusters of new immigrants in Little Saigon in Orange County, the Tenderloin District of San Francisco and San Jose in Silicon Valley. Giving a new facelift to many dilapidated urban downtown areas, Vietnamese immigrants are revitalizing malls and business centers and creating safer streets through hard work. There were five major waves of Vietnamese immigration to the United States. The events of April 1975 triggered the first wave, when over 100,000 sought a way to escape as South Vietnam was taken over by the Communists from the North. The second movement came during the 1978 "boat people" phenomenon. Thousands of Vietnamese fled to neighboring countries, most of them in rickety, overcrowded boats. The result was one of the most massive relief efforts in United Nations history. Refugee camps were set up in many parts of Southeast Asia to cope with the outflux. Volunteer efforts and a sympathetic U.S. administration under President Jimmy Carter encouraged this outflow of Vietnamese. As more refugees languished in camps in countries which

ously describing the horrors of that experience and the tenuous relationship that develops between a guard and a prisoner. In *Where the Ashes Are*, we read the story of a father and son, focusing once again on the life of a prisoner, a theme systematically avoided in popular discourse. Some have argued that the book's relative lack of popularity comes from the fact that it narrates dual stories to an audience accustomed to the psychological development of one character alone. Writer Monique T.D. Truong has argued that these two stories have been constrained by the authors' self-imposed pressure to serve as witness and survivor of the larger group.

Next generation

To be Vietnamese American and write about Vietnam, or returning there after 1994, is a different story. Those who immigrated to the United States as children have grown up in the American educational system. They acquired what scholar Trinh T. Minh-Ha called the "master's language" and the culture embedded within it. When the United States lifted its nineteen-year economic embargo, Vietnam became the new frontier for business entrepreneurs and travelers, a place in which politicians such as Senator John McCain could once again evoke heroism in war. New kinds of narratives emerged. Like Cao Lan's *Monkey Bridge* (1997) and Andrew X. Pham's *Catfish and Mandala* (1999), they were written by younger Vietnamese Americans. More similar to other early Asian Pacific American writers from the earlier part of the 20th century, they try to articulate their hybrid identity, and what it means to live in between various cultures and plays of power.

Sacred Willow (2000) by May Elliot is unique in the sense that it is written by a woman who came to the United States as a student in the 1960s, way before the end of the Vietnam War. A family saga that spans four generations, the book attempts to talk about Vietnam apart from the war. In this book, we see the impossible choice given to South Vietnamese government leaders and the human cost inflicted by the continuous foreign intervention in Vietnam. Nguyen Kien's *The Unwanted* (2001) is also unique because it is one of the few stories written by an Amerasian. Nguyen came to the United States in the 1980s. His story tells of the tragic fate of an Amerasian child in Communist Vietnam.

A younger generation of writers is increasingly trying to redefine the Vietnamese American experience on its own terms. Linh Dinh's *Fake House* (2000) and Monique T.D. Truong's *The Book of Salt* mark a deviation from previous genres. These authors have publicly stated that they felt restricted by the expectation that they write from the perspective of former war refugees. Instead, they chose to write about topics in which neither the United States nor their personal experiences are the center of the book. *Fake House* is a collection of provocative short stories written from the perspective of characters that are not necessarily Vietnamese-born. *The Book of Salt* is a novel about a Vietnamese cook living in Paris in the 1920s.

These two stories serve as reminder that to define Vietnamese American literature only within the framework of the Vietnam War tends to stereotype Vietnamese American culture while obscuring the details and diversity in the population. It also perpetuates a dominant discourse that situates the United States at the center. The Vietnam War was indeed never about Vietnam nor was it about the Vietnamese people: it was merely the continuation of American efforts to situate itself as the world superpower through military and cultural domination.

—Isabelle Thuy Pelaud

were not always willing to provide asylum, the United States set up the Orderly Departure Program to alleviate the situation and allow these refugees entrance into U.S. borders.

In 1987, the Amerasian Homecoming Act brought over children of American military and civilian personnel stationed and assigned to Vietnam during the conflict. These children of war were supposed to be reunited with their fathers, but only a handful reconnected. A total of over 30,000 Amerasians and their immediate family members were resettled in America during the late eighties and early nineties. And through its Humanitarian Operations program, the United States also admitted thousands of Vietnamese—mostly former South Vietnamese soldiers, political prisoners and their families—who had suffered under Communist re-education programs.

Finally, in the mid-nineties, the Resettlement Opportunities for Vietnamese Returnees program was established to admit those who had languished in Southeast Asian camps, unable to prove their refugee status and go to the West. They returned to Vietnam to be given another chance of being re-interviewed for possible resettlement in the United States.

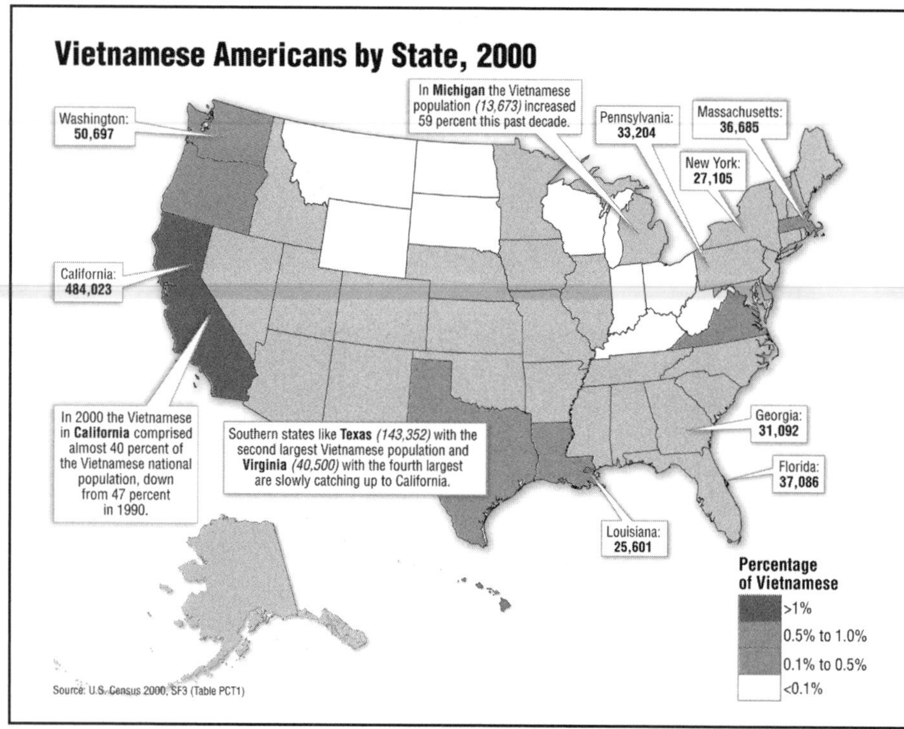

These five major movements lasted over twenty-five years, making it the longest refugee program since the exoduses of Hungarians and Cubans.

Unlike regular immigrants trying to adjust to a new environment, forced immigrants like the Vietnamese are usually less-prepared for the new society; many had little English language skills to begin their new life. They needed a number of services set up jointly by government agencies and non-profit groups. Programs ranging from English language training to employment development were established to assist these new immigrants during their initial resettlement.

A policy to scatter the Vietnamese refugees around the country with a number of sponsors was implemented in order to minimize the impact on host communities. But within a few years, many Vietnamese, especially those settled in isolated, rural locales. moved to urban areas with warmer weather and large Asian immigrant populations. This secondary internal movement of migration led to the concentration of Vietnamese in the West Coast and the South.

Ethnic Chinese Vietnamese

The Chinese had settled in Vietnam for centuries, with immigration picking up in the 20th century. They comprised less than an estimated two percent of the total population in 1975. While the cultures were similar, the Chinese in the South, in particular, were less integrated with their hosts. Most were in business occupations such as trade, services, finance, and manufacturing industries. Most spoke Chinese—usually Cantonese or Fujian dialects—more fluently than Vietnamese. Though the Chinese Vietnamese community boasted a dense network of kinship relations that made them economically powerful, they remained politically vulnerable. Only those of Vietnamese ethnicity, both before and after 1975, were able to freely participate in politics and civic life. That made the ethnic Chinese an easy scapegoat for the country's economic problems.

Chinese Vietnamese resettlement in the United States can be divided into three periods. The first migration occurred at the end of 1977, after the political dispute between China and Vietnam started. The Communist government of Vietnam ordered a sweeping campaign against all business merchants. Many lost their homes and were sent to farms. An estimated 30,000 Southern Chinese Vietnamese merchants and 150,000 dependent family members were affected. The Chinese Vietnamese remaining in the cities were denied government-controlled jobs; their children were denied admission to universities. At the same time, all young men were drafted to fight the war against the Khmer Rouge in Cambodia.

The chaotic and somewhat discriminatory policies against the Chinese Vietnamese from 1977 to 1980 led to a mass exodus of Chinese Vietnamese—estimated between 400,000 to 500,000—seeking freedom in neighboring countries such as China, Hong Kong, Indonesia, Malaysia and Thailand. The majority of these refugees found a way to resettle in the United States, taking advantage of the Refugee Act of 1975.

From 1980 to 1985, Vietnam's economic crisis brought about a second exodus. The entire country was seriously short of consumer goods and food due to a number of factors: the banning of private sector enterprises, government mismanagement, the U.S. economic embargo, and the loss of skilled labor and capital investment. In addition, the high rate of unemployment prevented any hope for economic recovery. In this environment, escaping by a leaky fishing boat seemed like a worthwhile risk. By the end of 1987, more than 55 percent of the Chinese Vietnamese remaining in South Vietnam had relatives living in one of twenty other countries worldwide, with the highest concentration in America.

Vietnam's political situation took a major turn in 1986. A new economic

reform program, Doi Moi, relaxed restrictions on private businesses so that they could revive. The government encouraged private businesses to invest and participate in collective partnership economic industries with the state. Fewer boat people were willing to risk their lives to leave an improving Vietnamese economy. At the same time, the ODP program started bringing in immigrants from Vietnam to the United States. Unlike the initial refugees, most of whom fled for their lives, today's immigrants are simply seeking better social and economic opportunities.

According to Khanh Tran's 1993 book, *The Ethnic Chinese and Economic Development in Vietnam*, a conservative estimate of the Chinese Vietnamese population in Vietnam in 1976 was 1.5 million, 85 percent of which lived in the South. In 1978, an estimated 220,000 left Vietnam for other Southeast Asian countries by boat, and 230,000 left for China by crossing the border in the north. By 2000, a total of 600,000 Chinese Vietnamese had left their adopted country to resettle in the United States, Australia and other countries of the West. The actual number of Chinese Vietnamese is unclear; the U.S. Census does not differentiate between the two. But many estimates place the percentage of Chinese Vietnamese at about one-third of the Vietnamese American population.

Pattern of settlement

Like other Asian immigrants, Vietnamese immigrants tend to gravitate toward urban areas. New enclaves have changed the face of entire blocks or inner city areas. The remarkable growth surprised not only geographers and census takers, but also politicians and government officials counting on support from the APA community. The Vietnamese American community is becoming a recognizable force in political and economic landscape. For example, in Orange County alone, nearly 45,000 firms were owned by APAs in 1997—with the majority owned by Vietnamese.

Vietnamese concentrations by region

Among the four major Census regions,

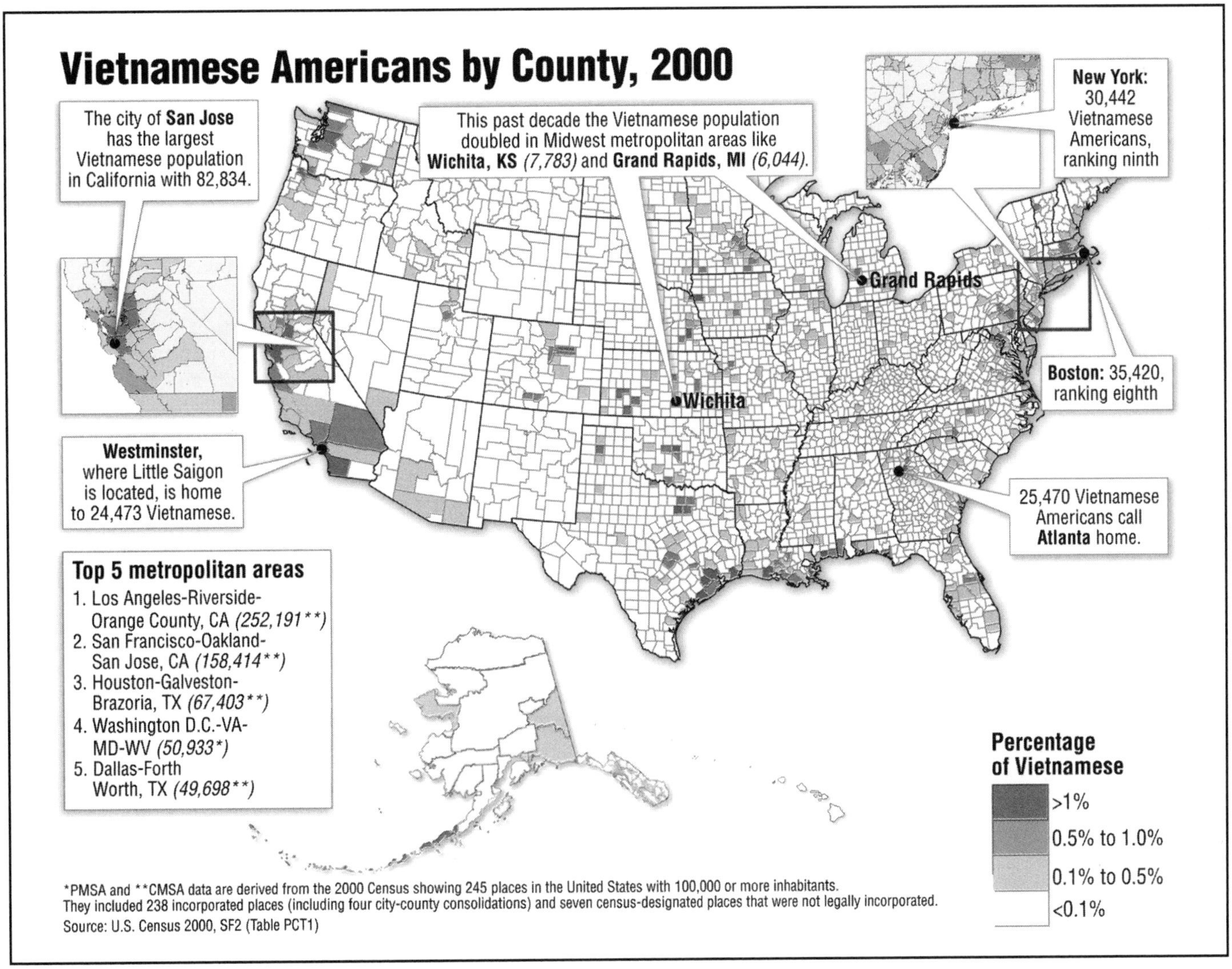

Vietnamese Americans by County, 2000

The city of **San Jose** has the largest Vietnamese population in California with 82,834.

This past decade the Vietnamese population doubled in Midwest metropolitan areas like **Wichita, KS** *(7,783)* and **Grand Rapids, MI** *(6,044)*.

New York: 30,442 Vietnamese Americans, ranking ninth

Grand Rapids

Wichita

Boston: 35,420, ranking eighth

Westminster, where Little Saigon is located, is home to 24,473 Vietnamese.

25,470 Vietnamese Americans call **Atlanta** home.

Top 5 metropolitan areas

1. Los Angeles-Riverside-Orange County, CA *(252,191**)*
2. San Francisco-Oakland-San Jose, CA *(158,414**)*
3. Houston-Galveston-Brazoria, TX *(67,403**)*
4. Washington D.C.-VA-MD-WV *(50,933*)*
5. Dallas-Forth Worth, TX *(49,698**)*

Percentage of Vietnamese

- >1%
- 0.5% to 1.0%
- 0.1% to 0.5%
- <0.1%

*PMSA and **CMSA data are derived from the 2000 Census showing 245 places in the United States with 100,000 or more inhabitants. They included 238 incorporated places (including four city-county consolidations) and seven census-designated places that were not legally incorporated.

Source: U.S. Census 2000, SF2 (Table PCT1)

the West Coast has the largest Vietnamese population, with a total of 564,424. The Southern states were next with a total of 335,679. The rest resided in the Northeast and the Midwest.

The West Coast has been a magnet for the Vietnamese ever since the mid-seventies. Refugees were first processed at many western cities, like San Francisco, Los Angeles, and Seattle—cities that already had large existing Asian populations. This drew many Southeast Asians during the 1980s, when they relocated from their initial resettlement locations. Businesses and social service agencies have flourished in these localities, facilitating the relocation of many Vietnamese immigrants to regions with warmer climate and far more employment opportunities.

While California remains the state with the largest Vietnamese population, 447,000, the percentage of Vietnamese living in California decreased during the 1990s. The downward trend of the electronics industry in which many Vietnamese were employed, coupled with unaffordable housing, prompted the departures. Economic growth in places like Texas, Florida and Louisiana attracted a great number of Vietnamese. New Orleans attracted numerous Vietnamese and has experienced population growth because of its fishing opportunities, strong Catholic community, and mild climate. California in 2000 comprises 40 percent of the total Vietnamese population, down from 47 percent in 1990.

New numbers warrant our attention: in the Northeast, there were 115,000 Vietnamese, while the Midwest was close behind at 107,000. The South registered 336,000 Vietnamese. The population increase in the Midwest is a major shift from the 1990s. In fact, over the past decade, the Vietnamese population doubled in cities like Wichita, to more than 7,000, and to nearly 6,000 in Grand Rapids.

Vietnamese concentration by state

California's Vietnamese population grew 60 percent during the 1990s. The Golden State still attracts a lot of Vietnamese from other parts of the country, along with new immigrants from Vietnam. But states like Florida (33,190), Massachusetts (33,962) and Texas (143,352) are catching up slowly. Virginia and Georgia also broke the 30,000 barrier. In Michigan, the Vietnamese population increased 59 percent to 13,673 and Nebraska had 6,364 Vietnamese, with the capital city of Lincoln accounting for 3,765. These figures reflect a trend of Vietnamese moving to cities with good economies and cheap housing.

Current issues and future trends

Many Vietnamese came to the United States with literally nothing but the shirts on their backs. They were not well prepared for their new society, for as refugees, it was not clear at all that they would eventually end up in America. In the 1990 Census, about one-quarter of Vietnamese were considered to be living in poverty. That compares to a 14 percent poverty rate among all APAs, and 13 percent for the population as a whole. Only 17 percent of Vietnamese Americans aged 25 or older had a college degree in 1990. Six out of ten Vietnamese Americans aged five or older told the Census that they did not speak English "very well." The per-capita annual income was $9,033 for Vietnamese in 1990, compared to $14,420 for the total population, and $13,368 for all APAs.

Given the fact that funds and resources were phased out during the 1990s, when the U.S. Government slowly phased out programs for Southeast Asians, the Vietnamese are faring well today. Socioeconomic statistics on Vietnamese Americans from Census 2000 were not available at the time of this writing, but there is plenty of evidence that Vietnamese Americans made many gains during the 1990s. Restaurants, and small businesses such as nail salons, food stores, and import-export shops, are niches where many Vietnamese are finding economic success. In 1997, Vietnamese owned 97,764 businesses employing 79,035 people with $9.3 billion in sales. About 16 percent of the businesses were retail shops, which reaped nearly $3 billion in sales.

Vietnamese politicians are emerging. Tony Lam is a member of the city council for Westminster, where "Little Saigon" is located, while Van Tran is the mayor pro tempore of the nearby suburb of Garden Grove. Dr. Van Hanh Nguyen is the National Director of the Office of Refugees Resettlement.

Granted, different waves of Vietnamese immigrants are adapting with different tactics and varying levels of success. Amerasians, for instance, tended to emigrate to the United States in their teen years, with poor educations from back home. Many have had a more challenging time.

The United States' lowering of its trade embargo with Vietnam, along with the liberalization of the political climate in Vietnam, have greatly affected immigration trends. While there are still a small number of Vietnamese immigrants awaiting admission and resettlement in the United States, they are the last of this Southeast Asian phenomenon of the last century. Now, issues of intergenerational differences, family changes, political involvement and empowerment, as well as the development of economic centers around the United States, are becoming more important for forward-looking Vietnamese Americans. A second-generation of Vietnamese Americans that see themselves as Americans rather than unwilling exiles is emerging. Compared to other established APA communities, the Vietnamese and Chinese Vietnamese Americans face a unique challenge. But the future looks positive based on past achievements.

—Chung Hoan Chuong and Minh Hoa Ta

The Rise of a Nikkei Generation

In the spring of 2001, rather startling Census information reported that the Japanese American population was shrinking. Census Bureau statistics revealed that the Japanese American population had fallen from about 848,000 in 1990 to 797,000 in 2000. The explanations given for the apparent decrease included low birth rates, high rates of outmarriage and assimilation, and low levels of immigration. But a year later, the Census Bureau issued a second set of more detailed figures, showing that there are 1.15 million Americans who claimed at least partial Japanese ancestry.

The apparent discrepancies in the two population figures were due to a change in the 2000 Census that allowed individuals to be classified as being of more than one race or ethnic group. Under this system almost 797,000 persons were reported as Japanese only. Another 350,000 were reported as Japanese in combination with one or more other racial/ethnic ancestries. The total Japanese American population, including mixed-race and mixed-ethnic people, is thus over 1.1 million.

Census methodology had significant effect

In the 1990 Census (and in earlier years), a person could choose only one racial category. As a result, only some of the mixed-ancestry people who are part-Japanese were included. An unknown number of part-Japanese people were counted in some other category. Therefore the 1990 "Japanese" count of 848,000 is larger than the number of people who were only of Japanese ancestry, but smaller than the number of persons with any Japanese ancestry.

The 1990 and 2000 Census figures, therefore, cannot be directly compared; it is not completely certain whether the Japanese American population has increased or decreased. However, a rough estimate of population change can be made, and it appears likely that the population grew. Assuming that the 1990 count of 848,000 included half of the mixed-ancestry Japanese American population, then calculating a 2000 population that includes half of the mixed ancestry Japanese Americans (972,500) yields an increase over the decade of about 18 percent, which is in line with Japanese American population trends over the last thirty years. It is also slightly greater than the growth rate for the United States population overall, which was less than 13 percent.

Photo: Gregory Urquiaga

More aging Japanese Americans are moving back into Japantown areas like Little Tokyo in Los Angeles, taking advantage of businesses there and reconnecting with their community.

The confusion caused by the two forms of Census data is understandable, but why was the notion of a decreasing

Thirty percent of the total Japanese American population is of mixed-ancestry, and perhaps half the population is made up of post-World War II immigrants and their offspring.

Japanese American population so plausible to many? Perhaps the social patterns and ethnic images of Japanese Americans based on the portion of the community founded by the immigrants of a century ago, and the extremely dramatic events they experienced, obscured important recent changes in the community. It would seem that the significance and size of the mixed-ancestry Japanese American population and of contemporary Japanese immigration are commonly underestimated.

Historical trends: Growing slowly, but steadily

Size: In spite of the perception of shrinking numbers, the historical statistics show the exact opposite. The Japanese American population has increased by well over 100,000 in every decade since the 1950s. Put another way, the population has nearly doubled since 1970, and is more than triple the 1950 count. Although the rate of increase is mild compared with other APA groups, the number of Japanese Americans has been slowly but steadily growing for decades.

Age: With a median age of 36.5 years of age in 1990, the Japanese American population was older than the overall U.S. population (33.0 years), and the overall Asian American population (30.4 years). Foreign-born Japanese, at a median age of 38.5 years, were older than U.S. native Japanese (median 35.3 years).

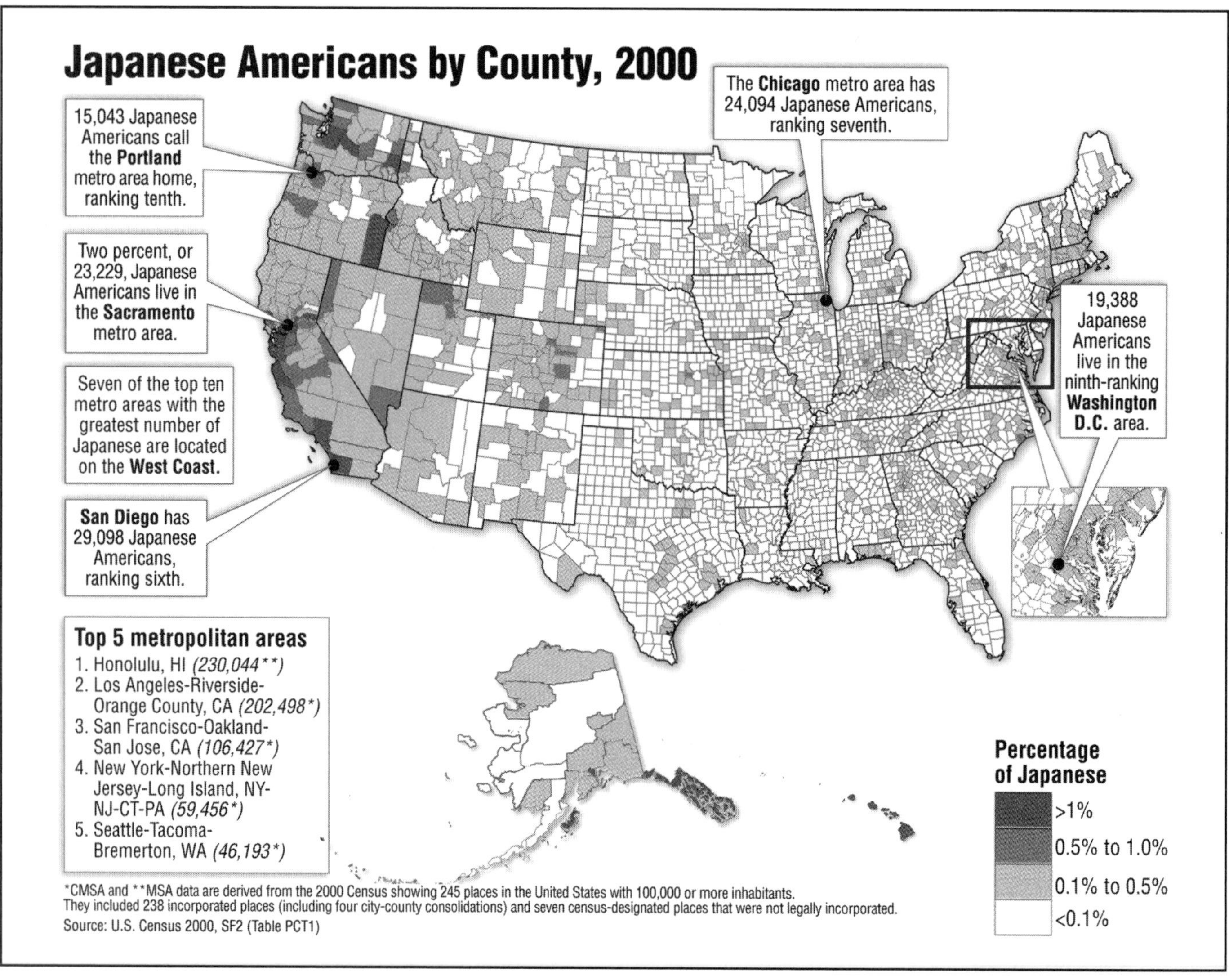

Sex ratio: The sex ratio was slightly skewed, with females making up 54 percent of the total Japanese American population. U.S. natives were evenly divided, at 50-50. But 63 percent of foreign-born Japanese immigrants were female.

Settlement patterns: Japanese Ameri-cans remain concentrated in the areas where Japanese immigrants first settled in the late 19th century. Over 60 percent live in two states, California (34 percent) and Hawai'i (26 percent). Almost 73 percent live in the West, with the rest distributed in three other regions, the Northeast (9 percent), North Central (8 percent), and the South (11 percent). There has been some dispersion in the pattern over the last 30 years, but it is a matter of greater growth outside the historic core areas, rather than a loss at the core. For example, from 1970 to 2000, California's share of the total has dropped two percent, even as its Japanese American population has grown from 213,000 to nearly 394,000. Hawai'i lost 11 percentage points while the number of Japanese Americans there grew from 217,000 to 297,000.

Estimating the number of children of contemporary Japanese immigrants

First, we looked at the fertility rates ("children ever born") of foreign-born Japanese women, which were derived from the "20%" sample of the 1990 Census. At that time, the total number of children ever born to Japanese women between 15 and 44 years of age was 80,879. The number of children born to women 45 and older was not published. However, there were 80,091 women in this age group. The fertility rate of the women between 35 and 44 years of age (the oldest category reported), 1.638 children, was used as the lifetime fertility rate of women 45 and older. On that basis, the total number of children for this group is estimated as at least 131,189 children (= 80,091 x 1.638). Combining the figures for the two age groups, the total number of children born to women over age 15 is 212,068 (=80,879+131,189).

There are several sources of inaccuracy of the estimate, beginning with the origin of the baseline data as an extrapolation from the 20% sample.

Three items decrease the estimated number of children:

(1) The fertility rate for the 45 and older group is probably higher than that of the 35-44 group, given the additional possible childbearing years as well as historical and sociological trends towards fewer children per woman.

(2) The number does not include children whose fathers are foreign-born Japanese immigrants and whose mothers are non-Japanese.

(3) The number of grandchildren of immigrants is not included. The oldest of the children are now over fifty years old, and some are grandparents themselves.

At the same time, the total 1990 count for Japanese did not include all hapas, a substantial portion of whom had foreign-born Japanese mothers. In calculating the proportion of children of immigrants in the Japanese American population, the first condition decreases the numerator (number of children), and the second decreases the denominator (total Japanese American population).

—Dean S. Toji

Immigration patterns

The Japanese American population was established by immigration in two major historical periods—before and after World War II. In the eight decades before World War II, roughly 450,000 Japanese migrated to the United States (including Hawai'i when it was an independent country, then a U.S. territory). The greatest concentration began in 1885, with the start of the mass labor migration, and ended in 1924, when the United States forbade immigration by "aliens ineligible to citizenship," pointedly targeting the Japanese who had not been completely blocked by earlier anti-Asian immigration laws.

Most of these migrants returned to Japan; but approximately one-fifth remained in the United States. This first major wave of Japanese immigration established the Japanese American community. The majority of Japanese immigrant (issei) women arrived from 1908–1924, entering as wives of men previously settled in the United States, and the resulting concentrated period of family formation produced the first American-born generation, the nisei. A post-WWII baby boom generation, the sansei, reached its peak in the early 1960s. There was a tight age cohort structure to the first three generations, whose members were relatively close in age and historical experience. Although the current generation of young people is sometimes referred to as yonsei (or the fourth generation), this age cohort is a much more complex mixture of ethnic, racial, and intergenerational backgrounds.

During the second ("contemporary") period of Japanese immigration, from the end of the World War II to the present, roughly one quarter million Japanese have immigrated to the United States. According to the Immigration and Naturalization Service, 239,070 Japanese immigrants came to the United States from 1945 to 2000. The pace of immigration has been fairly consistent for the last fifty years, averaging 5,000 per year since 1952, and has actually increased in the last decade. By the time this book is published, post-WWII immigration will probably have passed 250,000.

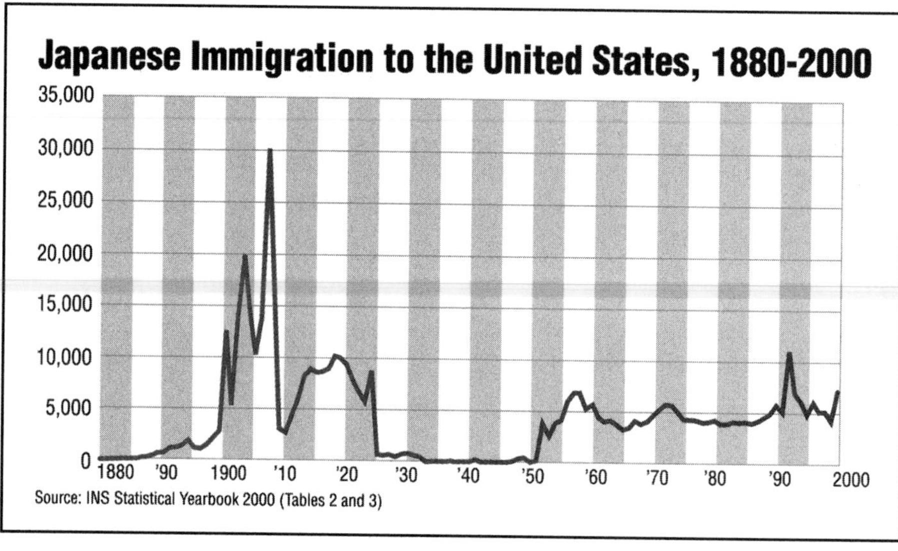

Source: INS Statistical Yearbook 2000 (Tables 2 and 3)

Japanese immigration is seen by many, including Japanese Americans themselves, as being small or of negligible size. But in absolute numbers, it has been as large as other sizeable Asian immigrant groups. During the period from 1965 (when racial restrictions on Asian immigration were finally removed) to 2000, there were 176,000 Japanese immigrants, a number similar to Pakistanis (204,000) Thais (150,000), Cambodians (206,000), Hmong (186,000), and Laotians (198,000). Or, here is another way to get a sense of the magnitude of contemporary Japanese immigration. During World War II, about 120,000 Japanese Americans were held at some time in the concentration camps. The number of post-World War II Japanese immigrants is more than double the number of Japanese Americans who were sent to camps.

Japanese-born wives of American citizens account for perhaps half of all Japanese immigrants to the United States. Japan was long one of the major sources of immigrants who came to the United States as spouses of American citizens. From 1945 to 1985, it was the sixth largest source of foreign spouses (mostly female) immigrating to the United States. During that period, the 84,000 foreign-born spouses made up well over half (55 percent) of the 154,000 immigrants from Japan. The husbands include Japanese Americans as well as Americans of other backgrounds.

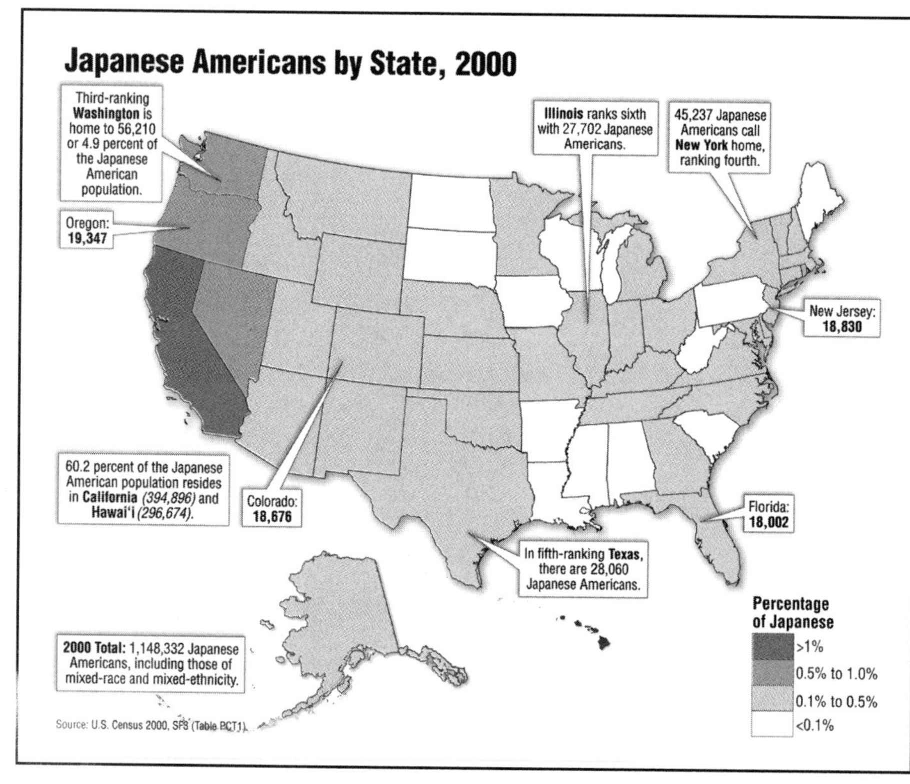

Source: U.S. Census 2000, SF3 (Table PCT1).

Native vs. foreign born

Over two-thirds of all Japanese Americans were born in the United States—the highest proportion among all APAs. 347,539 foreign-born respondents named Japan as their place of birth, or 30.2 percent of the total Japanese American population, according to 2000 Census 2000 data. In the 1990 Census, when the total Japanese American population was reported at 847,562, the number of the foreign-born were 280,686, or 33 percent of the total, according to the Census Bureau's profile of the foreign-born U.S. population.

The foreign-born population as enumerated by the Census includes, in addition to immigrants, other individuals who are here on temporary visas (such as college students, and business people and their families) and who may or may not intend to become settled immigrants. Nevertheless, this group has been a source of immigration by conversion to immigrant status from other entry visas.

Japanese Population in the United States, 1900-2000

Year	Population†	Change from Previous Decade: Number	Change from Previous Decade: Percent
1900	85,716		
1910	152,745	67,029	78.2%
1920	220,596	67,851	44.4%
1930	278,743	58,147	26.4%
1940	285,115	6,372	2.3%
1950	326,379	41,264	14.5%
1960	464,332	137,953	42.3%
1970	591,290	126,958	27.3%
1980	700,974	109,684	18.5%
1990	847,562	146,588	20.9%
2000*	1,148,032	300,470	35.5%
2000**	796,700	-50,862	-6.0%

†Includes territories of Hawai'i and Alaska, 1900-1950.
*Persons identified as entirely or partially Japanese.
**Persons identified as Japanese only.

Source: U.S. Census, 1900-2000

The children of the second wave of immigration

In addition to making up nearly a third of the Japanese American population, the significance of immigrants is even larger when we take into consideration their American-born children and grandchildren. There is no data available that directly measures this group, but a rough estimate can be made that there were well over 200,000 children of contemporary Japanese immigrants in 1990 (see factbox). Added together, post-World War II Japanese immigrants and their offspring may amount to over one-half of the total Japanese American population.

Intermarriage trends

Japanese American intermarriages to non-Japanese, which were once very few due to anti-miscegenation laws, segregation, and ethnic preferences, have risen very rapidly since the end of World War II. The proportion of intermarried Japanese American individuals rose from perhaps 10 percent in the 1950s, to about 30 percent in 1980, to over 40 percent in 1990. The trend is almost certain to continue; in 1990, about three-quarters of young U.S.-born Japanese American married adults were wed to non-Japanese, according to 1990 and 1996 research by demographers Larry Shinagawa and Gin Yong Pang.

Women make up nearly two-thirds of all intermarried Japanese Americans; the proportion is elevated by the large proportion (55 percent) of intermarried immigrant women. The race of intermarriage partners has also changed. The second period of immigration began with international marriages, most of which were also interracial marriages. In the early post war period, intermarriages were predominantly between Japanese immigrant women and white American men. In the 1960s and 1970s, marriages between American-born Japanese Americans and white Americans became the dominant intermarriage pattern. In the 1980s, there was a shift towards marriages to other Asian Americans. In 1990, marriages with other Asians rose to become the majority of Japanese American intermarriages.

[One caveat: the above figures are only rough estimates from the published research. There is no national scale study for the whole time period, and the various studies use different measures of intermarriage. The estimates for the 1950s to the 1980s are from a publication of Japanese American National Museum in 2001, citing Kitano & Kikumura (1973) and Kitano et al (1984), studies which count marriages recorded during selected years in Los Angeles County (in both articles) and also Hawai'i (in the latter). Shinagawa and Pang's research is based on 1980 and 1990 Census samples for California, and counts the number of existing marriages, regardless of when or where they occurred.]

Japanese American intermarriage was once assumed to represent assimilation to the white American majority. But this newer trend suggests the Asian Americanization of Japanese Americans. This was a trend common among Asian Americans. In fact, among the U.S.-born, Japanese Americans did not have the highest intermarriage rate—Chinese Americans did—although this was not as apparent because of a smaller percentage of U.S.-natives among Chinese Americans.

The emergence of mixed-ancestry Japanese

The rising number of intermarriages has inevitably led to the emergence of a large and growing mixed-ancestry Japanese American population. Almost 70 percent of the total Japanese American population is identified as entirely Japanese, and over 30 percent are partially Japanese in various combinations with other Asians and other (non-Asian) races. Combinations with other races (white, black, American Indian, Pacific Islander, or some other race) make up 25 percent of the total, while combinations with other Asians make up about 10 percent. An overlapping category, people who are part-Japanese and both mixed with other races and other Asians, makes up five percent of the total.

The Japanese had the highest proportion of mixed-ancestry members among the dozen largest Asian groups, at 31 percent. Asians reported an overall mixed-ancestry rate of 16 percent, far higher than whites and blacks (less

Japanese American Population, 2000

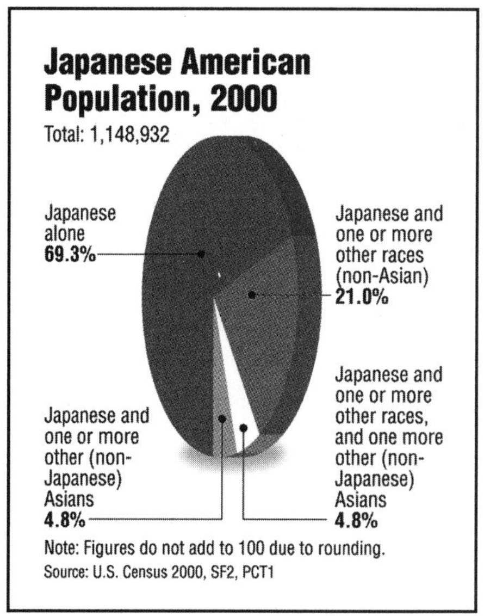

Note: Figures do not add to 100 due to rounding.
Source: U.S. Census 2000, SF2, PCT1

Returning to Little Tokyo

Once a mainstay for L.A.'s Japanese Americans, Little Tokyo's brick-inlaid shopping promenade, touristy boutiques and clichéd sushi restaurants now attract a mostly white, mid-thirties lunch crowd, along with a few Japanese tourists.

Yet back in the shade, watching the crowds go by, sit three old-timer nisei: Harold Okumoto, 72; Richard Hongo, 76; and Yashitaka "Bones" Kawahara, 72.

"Tell her how old you really are," joked one as the three greeted visitors. "He's 76. I'm only 72."

They acknowledge only obliquely that their neighborhood has changed. "Nothing's changed except most of my friends are all up there now," Okumoto said, pointing upward, towards the blue sky.

"Nothing's changed," he said, prompting Hongo to add, "One year from now, same thing."

The three men are increasingly representative of Little Tokyo. More aging Japanese Americans, some unable to drive, have been moving there to take advantage of the close proximity of businesses in the area.

Yet despite the area's commercial lure, Lisa Sugino of the Little Tokyo Service Center acknowledges that Little Tokyo, 10 minutes east of Koreatown, is overdue for a renaissance.

"Most of our growth came from the influx of Japanese corporations and international students," Sugino said, adding that businesses have for years been dependent on foreigners and Japanese American suburbanites.

"We got hit pretty hard from the L.A. riots. [We] lost 25 to 40 percent in business revenues in Little Tokyo. People were afraid to come down here," she said.

Before those memories had faded, the Asian crisis hit, exacerbating the economic decline in the small area bounded by Temple Street, Main Street, Fourth Street and Alameda Street. "There's this ebb and flow, but we'd like there to be more flowing."

Sugino's center has begun a new crime-prevention campaign to attract more visitors back to the 1,500-resident neighborhood. So far, she said, it seems to be working.

"There's more a sense of security. It's made a better experience for visitors for them to come back. The area is still hurting but there are a lot of plans to make it better."

And as more and more Japanese Americans are aging, Sugino sees more of "a general feeling of people wanting to return to their roots," she said. "There's a resurgence of taiko and sports leagues. It's a feeling of people wanting to go back to something they know."

—AsianWeek

than five percent), but substantially below American Indians (40 percent) and Native Hawaiians and Pacific Islanders (55 percent).

The age breakdown was not available at the time of writing, but it is certain that mixed-ancestry Japanese Americans are a much higher proportion of the younger age groups than of the overall Japanese American population. The mixed Japanese American population will continue to increase with the likely continuation of the rising trend of intermarriage rates.

Demographically, the future of the Japanese American community—if not the present—will increasingly depend on the inclusion of Japanese persons of mixed ancestry, and on these mixed-ancestry Japanese Americans identifying themselves as such.

"Nikkei": giving contemporary meaning to a diverse and complex ethnic group

This article treated the various aspects of Japanese American demographics discussed as representing separate patterns. But it is important to note that these aspects—early immigration and the several American-born generations that followed, contemporary immigration after WWII, intermarriage, and Japanese Americans of mixed ancestry—are in fact overlapping patterns. For example, some Japanese Americans born in the United States married Japanese immigrants—thus a portion of the children of contemporary immigrants may also be considered both sansei and yonsei (or more). Also, multiracial Japanese Americans include both immigrants and U.S. natives. A lag in grasping the growing complexity and diversity of today's Japanese American community has contributed to misperceptions of the 2000 Census reports, and the belief that the community is shrinking. By the 1970s, the word nikkei, meaning people of Japanese descent (usually those outside of Japan) started to be used by some, as a broad, inclusive term encompassing the growing diversity among Japanese Americans.

—Dean S. Toji

Seeking Recognition and the Return of Aloha

The Native Hawaiian people are determined to preserve, develop and transmit to future generations their ancestral territory, and their cultural identity in accordance with their own spiritual and traditional beliefs, customs, practices, language, and social institutions.

Public Law 103-150, Senate Joint Resolution of Apology to the Hawaiian people by the U.S. Congress and the President of the United States, November 23, 1993

The truth and significance of this statement by the U.S. Congress is at the heart of the most important human rights issue facing Hawai'i's people in the new millennium.

Na Hawai'i, the Native Hawaiian people, are descendants of the original inhabitants of the island archipelago, Hawai'i. Oral traditions passed on through chants, legends, myths and *mo'oku'auhau*, or family genealogies, trace the origins of the Native Hawaiian people to early Polynesian ancestors and beyond them to the life forces of nature itself.

According to these genealogies, Native Hawaiians are the living descendants of Papa, the earth mother and Wakea, the sky father. Ancestral deities include Kane of the living fresh water sources; Lono of the winter rains and the life force of agricultural crops; Kanaloa of the deep foundation of the earth, the ocean and its currents and winds; Ku of the thunder, war, fishing and planting; and Pele of the volcano. Thousands of deities of the forest, the ocean, the winds, the rains and other elements of nature are acknowledged as ancestors by Native Hawaiian families.

The Native Hawaiian population was estimated between 400,000 and 800,000 in 1778, the year that British explorer Captain James Cook arrived in Hawai'i. By 1810, King Kamehameha I had established a central monarchy, following a series of battles in which he defeated rival chiefs of the islands utilizing Western gunboats and weapons. This monarchy was overthrown in 1893 by U.S. naval forces, allied with American merchants, sugar planters and missionaries who had settled in the islands. In 1898, the U.S. Congress claimed control over the islands through an annexation agreement with the Republic of Hawai'i, a government established by the American merchant, planter and missionary settlers. Throughout the years of foreign settlement of the islands, the Native Hawaiian people succumbed to introduced continental diseases which, due to their lack of genetic immunity, grew to epidemic proportions.

Photo: Cory Lum

Native Hawaiians, whose traditional folklore states that they are living descendants of the earth and sky, seek rights to access private and public lands for religious and cultural reasons.

Such diseases included cholera, measles, whooping cough, influenza, leprosy, and tuberculosis. By 1900 the pure Native Hawaiian population declined to 29,800, with another 7,800 Hawaiians of mixed ancestry.

Hawaiian population in 2000

At the beginning of the 21st century, the total population of Hawai'i numbers 1.2 million. Whites and those of part-white ancestry are the largest group, numbering 476,100, or about 40 percent of the population. Japanese and part-Japanese number 296,674, or about one-quarter of the population, while Filipinos and part-Filipinos number 275,700, or 23 percent of the population. Native Hawaiians and part-Native Hawaiians in Hawai'i number 239,655, comprising 20 percent of the population.

Because the 2000 Census combines the mixed race categories with the pure race categories, the figures add up to more that 100 percent of the population due to double counting of those with mixed ancestry. And Hawaii's population contains many of mixed ethnicity or mixed-race. At best, the census provides a rough demographic sketch of Hawai'i. In the most recent estimate of pure Native Hawaiians in 1984, the Office of Hawaiian Affairs (OHA) calculated that there were 8,244 persons with 100 percent Native Hawaiian ancestry. At that time, the OHA also estimated that there were 72,709 people of 50 percent to 99 percent Native Hawaiian ancestry.

According to the 2000 Census, another 161,500 persons with Hawaiian ancestry live in the continental United States. Among these are students attending American colleges and universities and those who have secured high-paying jobs in their chosen profession upon graduation. Studies indicate that higher-paying, better quality jobs and the lower cost of housing and living expenses in the continental United States contribute to the emigration from Hawai'i.

In Hawai'i, Native Hawaiians earn lower incomes, hold lower-status jobs, and have the highest rate of unemployment of all the ethnic groups in the islands. By contrast, the descendants of Caucasian, Japanese and Chinese immigrants earn higher incomes and hold a greater portion of the managerial and professional jobs in Hawai'i. A significant percentage of Native Hawaiians earn incomes that are insufficient to provide for their families and thus receive public assistance to supplement their incomes. Among these, some depend entirely upon welfare support to meet their day-to-day needs.

As of 2001, Native Hawaiians make up 37 percent of the recipients of welfare assistance to needy families and 44 percent of the food stamp recipients, despite making up just 20 percent of the population. Native Hawaiians also comprise 39 percent of the adult inmate population in state correctional facilities. Native Hawaiians have high rates of risk factors for cardiovascular disease and cancer and, due to low incomes which hinder access to health care, suffer mortality rates that are higher than other ethnic groups in Hawai'i for heart disease, cancer, stroke and diabetes. The life expectancy for Native Hawaiians is shorter by eight years than the ethnic group with the highest life expectancy in Hawai'i.

Hawaiian rights under attack

At the turn of the 21st century, complicated issues related to the rights and entitlements of Native Hawaiians have arisen. Under the U.S. Constitution, indigenous minorities have rights that ethnic and racial minorities do not. For instance, Native American tribes are recognized as domestic dependent nations, with inherent powers of self-governance and self-determination, for whom the federal government sustains a trust responsibility. The 1977 American Indian Policy Review Commission defined the relationship that exists between the tribes and the government as premised on a "special trust that must govern the conduct of the stronger toward the weaker." This status has been extended to Eskimos, Aleuts, and Native Alaskans under the Alaskan Native Claims Settlement Act.

The recognition of Native Hawaiians as an indigenous people similar to Native American tribes is critical to sustaining their rights and entitlements under American law, to which other ethnic minorities in Hawai'i are not entitled. What are these rights and entitlements? One is the right of those

What a Difference an "n" Makes

Native Hawaiian: any individual who is a descendent of the aboriginal people who, prior to 1778, occupied and exercised sovereignty in the area that now constitutes the State of Hawai'i.

native Hawaiian (note small 'n'): refers to those who are of at least 50 percent Native Hawaiian ancestry. Under the law, only native Hawaiians are beneficiaries of the Hawaiian Home Lands. The Ceded Public Lands Trust has two beneficiaries—native Hawaiians and the general public. As part of the general public, Native Hawaiians are also beneficiaries of this trust.

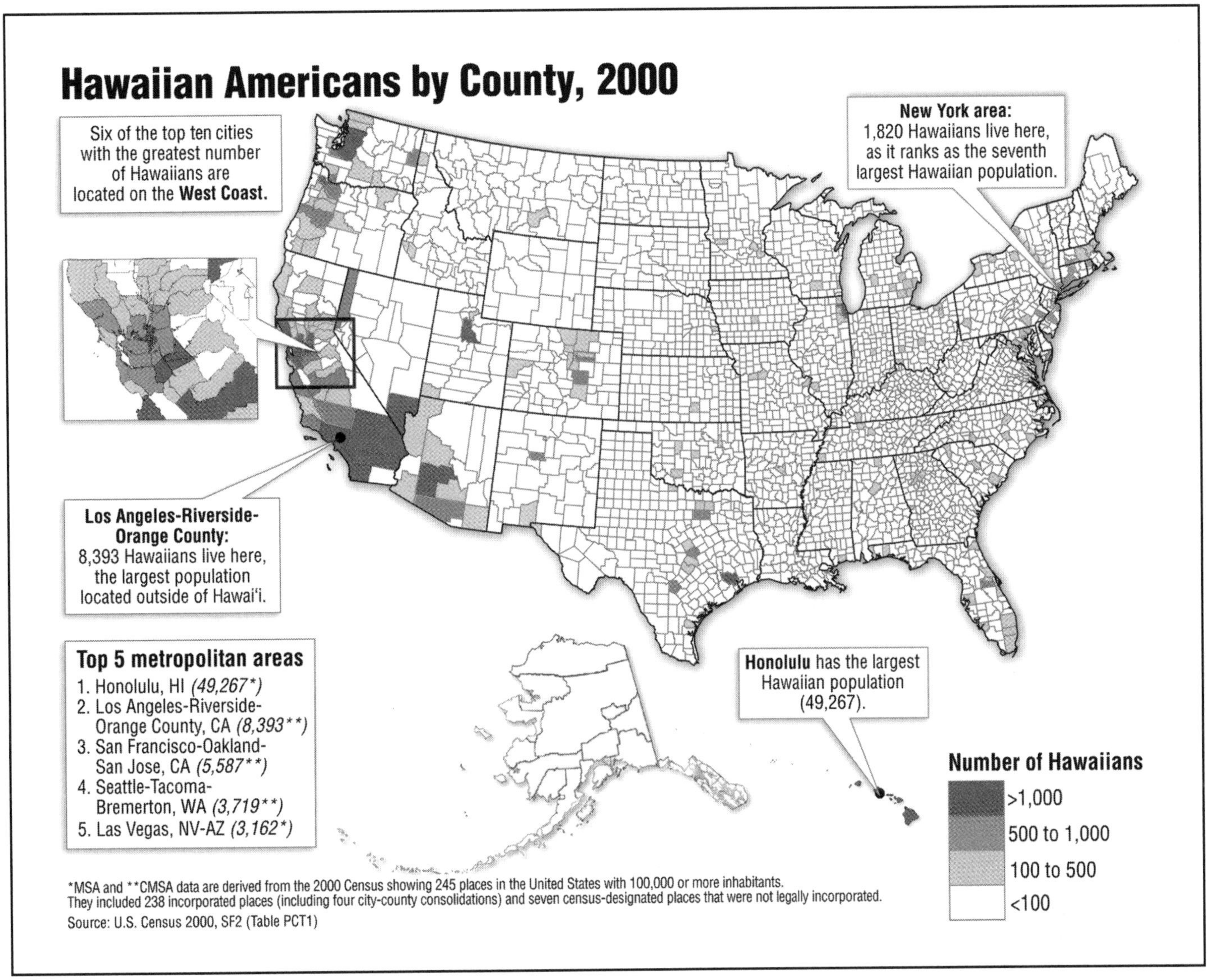

Hawaiian Americans by County, 2000

Six of the top ten cities with the greatest number of Hawaiians are located on the **West Coast.**

New York area: 1,820 Hawaiians live here, as it ranks as the seventh largest Hawaiian population.

Los Angeles-Riverside-Orange County: 8,393 Hawaiians live here, the largest population located outside of Hawai'i.

Honolulu has the largest Hawaiian population (49,267).

Top 5 metropolitan areas

1. Honolulu, HI *(49,267*)*
2. Los Angeles-Riverside-Orange County, CA *(8,393**)*
3. San Francisco-Oakland-San Jose, CA *(5,587**)*
4. Seattle-Tacoma-Bremerton, WA *(3,719**)*
5. Las Vegas, NV-AZ *(3,162*)*

Number of Hawaiians

- >1,000
- 500 to 1,000
- 100 to 500
- <100

*MSA and **CMSA data are derived from the 2000 Census showing 245 places in the United States with 100,000 or more inhabitants. They included 238 incorporated places (including four city-county consolidations) and seven census-designated places that were not legally incorporated.

Source: U.S. Census 2000, SF2 (Table PCT1)

with more than 50 percent Native Hawaiian blood to benefit from the 200,000 acre Hawaiian Homelands Trust and a portion of the revenues from the 1.2 million acre ceded public lands trust managed by the State of Hawai'i. The portion of revenues from the ceded public lands trust for those with more than 50 percent Native Hawaiian blood is managed by the OHA. Another right is the ability to access private and public lands for subsistence, cultural and religious purposes. Around 23,000 Native Hawaiians live on these Hawaiian homelands. Native Hawaiian rights are also recognized in the Water Code of the State of Hawai'i—meaning that stream waters where native aquatic life flourish and which flow into taro pond fields cannot be diverted. Finally, the Hawaiian language is an official language of the state.

In February 2000, the U.S. Supreme Court ruled that the elections of the trustees of the OHA, in which only Native Hawaiian beneficiaries were allowed to vote, were unconstitutional because they used race-based qualifications, violating the 15th Amendment. In the subsequent November 2000 election for OHA trustees, all registered voters in the state were allowed to cast votes and to run for these offices.

The U.S. Supreme Court, in its ruling, raised some fundamental questions regarding the status of Native Hawaiians:

May Congress treat the Native Hawaiians like Native American tribes? And has Congress in fact determined that their status is as such?

May Congress delegate to the State of Hawai'i the authority to preserve that status? And has Congress already delegated to the State Government of Hawai'i the authority to preserve that status?

A "No" answer could radically undermine the rights that Native Hawaiians currently enjoy. Indeed, the Court

Recognition of Native Hawaiians

Federal Recognition of Native Hawaiians

From 1906 to 1998, the U.S. Congress exercised its constitutional authority in furtherance of the trust relationship with the native people of Hawai'i through the enactment of 183 federal laws which explicitly include Native Hawaiians in the class of Native Americans.

1921 Hawaiian Homes Act—Sets aside 200,000 acres of ceded public lands for exclusive homesteading by native Hawaiians.

1938 Kalapana Extension Act—Rules that Kalapana native Hawaiians and those accompanied by them can fish and gather and apply for homesteads in the Volcanoes National Park.

1959 Admission Act—In a pact with the new state of Hawai'i, the Hawaiian Homelands Program was to continue under management of the State of Hawai'i. Betterment of the conditions of Native Hawaiians is one of the five purposes for the "ceded public lands trust." The other four purposes include education; farm and home ownership; public improvements; and public uses.

1974—Hawaiians are included in the definition of Native Americans for the purpose of benefiting from moneys appropriated under the Native American Programs Act for education, health, job training, etc.

1993 Public Law 103-150/Apology—Apologizes to the Native Hawaiian people for the U.S. role in the illegal overthrow of the Hawaiian government and acknowledges that the ceded public lands were acquired through that illegal act.

February 23, 2000—U.S. Supreme Court gives its decision in Rice v. Cayetano.

October 23, 2000—The Department of the Interior and the Department of Justice recommend federal recognition of Native Hawaiians similar to that of Native Americans.

State recognition of Native Hawaiians (from the Hawai'i State Constitution):

Article V. Section 4: English and Hawaiian are the official languages of Hawai'i.

Article X. Section 4: The State shall promote the study of Hawaiian culture, history and language.

Article XII. Adopts the Hawaiian Homes Commission Act and sets aside 30 percent of the revenue from sugar leases and water licenses for the native Hawaiian rehabilitation fund.

Article XII. Section 4: Native Hawaiians and the general public are the beneficiaries of the Ceded Public Lands Trust.

Article XII. Section 5: Establishes the Office of Hawaiian Affairs.

Article XII. Section 7: The State reaffirms and shall protect all rights, customarily and traditionally exercised for subsistence, cultural and religious purposes and possessed by ahupua'a tenants who are descendants of native Hawaiians who inhabited the Hawaiian Islands prior to 1778, subject to the right of the State to regulate such rights.

Water Code Section 174C-101: Native Hawaiian Water Rights

(c) Traditional and customary rights of ahupua`a tenants are protected. Such traditional and customary rights include, but are not limited to, the cultivation or propagation of taro on one's own kuleana and the gathering of hihiwai, opae, `o`opu, limu, thatch, ti leaf, aho cord, and medicinal plants for subsistence, cultural, and religious purposes.

Native Hawaiian Vote

In July 1996, 81,507 ballots were mailed out to registered Hawaiian voters asking, "Shall the Hawaiian people elect delegates to propose a Native Hawaiian government?" A total of 30,423 ballots were cast, representing 37 percent of the registered voters. Of these, 22,294 (73.28% of the ballots cast) voted YES and 8,129 (26.72% of the ballots cast) voted NO.

The return of Kaho'olawe

Under state law, the island of Kaho'olawe is being held as a trust for eventual transfer to a sovereign Hawaiian entity.

seemed to open the door to future legal challenges on the status of Native Hawaiians when it stated that

It is a matter of some dispute, for instance, whether Congress may treat the native Hawaiians as it does the Indian tribes. Compare Van Dyke, The Political Status of the Hawaiian People, 17 Yale L. & Pol'y Rev. 95 (1998), with Benjamin, Equal Protection and the Special Relationship: The Case of Native Hawaiians, 106 Yale L.J. 537 (1996).

Suddenly, the status, rights and entitlements which Native Hawaiians had enjoyed throughout the 20th century could be legally challenged out of existence. Moreover, the Supreme Court ruling seemed to contradict the policy of the U.S. Congress toward Native Hawaiians.

Beginning in 1906 and through 1998 the U.S. Congress, in effect, recognized a trust relationship similar to that of Native Americans, with the native people of

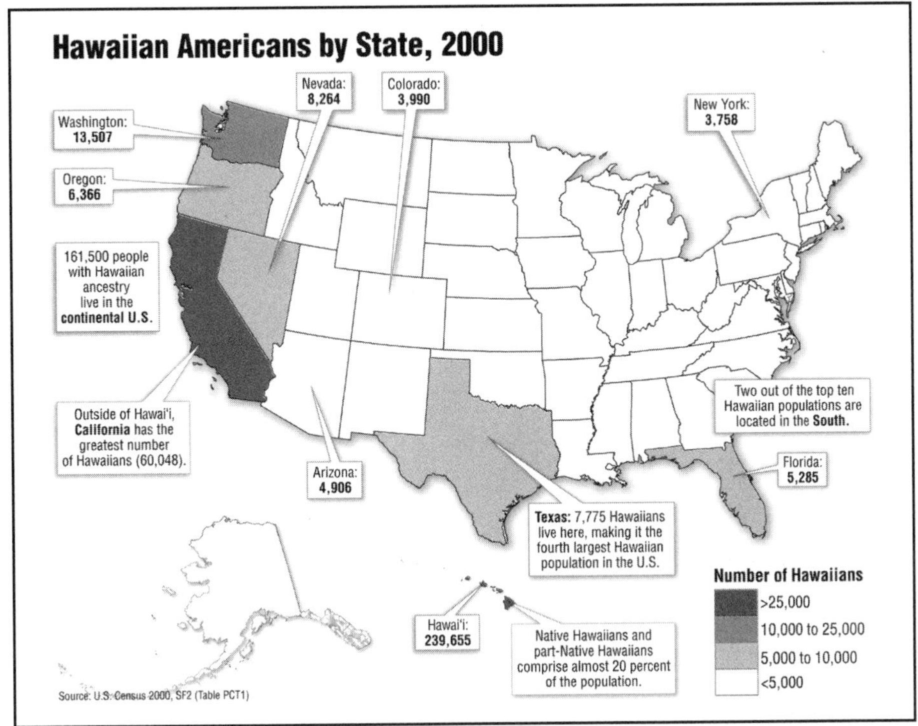

Hawai'i through the enactment of 183 federal laws, which explicitly included Native Hawaiians in the class of Native Americans. Some of the laws extended federal programs set up for Native Americans to Native Hawaiians, while other laws represented recognition by the U.S. Congress that the United States bore a special responsibility to protect Native Hawaiian interests. But none of the laws extended an explicit and formal recognition that Native Hawaiians are a sovereign people, with the right of self-governance and self-determination.

Legal maneuverings

In light of the ruling, Hawai'i's congressional delegation, led by Senators Daniel Akaka and Daniel Inouye, drafted and introduced the Akaka Bill to unambiguously clarify the trust relationship between Native Hawaiians and the United States. While the bill failed to pass in 2000 and 2001, the Hawai'i congressional delegation vows to continue to introduce the bill until it is passed. When passed, the bill would formally and directly extend the federal policy of self-determination and self-governance to Native Hawaiians, as Hawai'i's indigenous native people.

Opponents of Native Hawaiian recognition successfully lobbied Republican congressmen to oppose the bill in 2000 and 2001. Calling themselves Aloha For All, the group is supported by the National Coalition for a Color Blind America. Their web site, www.aloha4all.org, states their opposition to the Akaka Bill as follows:

This legislation is dangerous to the people of Hawai'i and to the sovereignty of the United States. It is an attempt to divide the thoroughly integrated people of Hawai'i along racial lines. It would partition the State of Hawai'i by setting up an apartheid regime to which only kanaka maoli *(the name Native Hawaiians prefer to call themselves) could belong . . . One of the most troubling aspects of the Akaka bill is its attempt to create an Indian tribe where none currently exists. It would be the first time in history when Congress recognizes a currently non-existent political entity and then puts in place a procedure to populate it.*

The Aloha For All group claims that all residents of Hawai'i are Hawaiian and that the limitation of any benefits to those who are "racially Hawaiian" is discriminatory and violates the 14th Amendment of the U.S. Constitution.

In 1990, only 56 percent of the residents of the islands were born in Hawai'i. The large percentage of residents living in Hawai'i who were born elsewhere contributes to the lack of appreciation of the historic rights and entitlements of Native Hawaiians as descendants of the original people who settled and developed a sophisticated social system in the islands. However, the future of human rights in Hawai'i lies in the recognition of the status, rights and entitlements of Native Hawaiians lies. Many non-Hawaiians claim they bear no obligation to reconcile with the descendants of Native Hawaiians for the injustices that occurred decades ago by persons to whom they bear no relation. However, non-Hawaiians in Hawai'i benefit from the results of those historical injustices, while Native Hawaiians bear the burden.

In addition, the U.S. Congress and the President, in Public Law 103-150—the Apology Resolution cited above—outlined a series of historical injustices for which they acknowledge responsibility and apologized "to Native Hawaiians on behalf of the people of the United

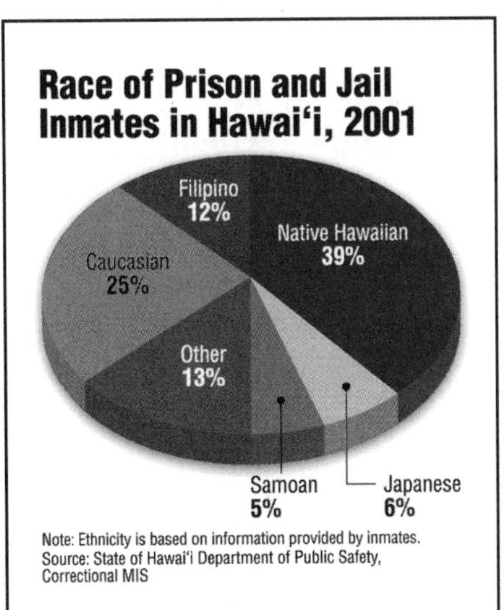

States." The Apology resolution also committed the Congress and all the people of the United States to a process of reconciliation with the Native Hawaiian people.

A 1999 Public Opinion Survey conducted by SMS Research and Marketing Services for the Office of Hawaiian Affairs among a random sample of Native Hawaiians and non-Hawaiians indicated that there was widespread awareness of the sovereignty issue among the general population of Hawai'i—but no majority opinion about how to resolve it. Among the Native Hawaiians who were surveyed, 47 percent favored some form of sovereignty for Native Hawaiians, 21 percent were undecided or did not know and 32 percent opposed sovereignty. Among non-Native Hawaiians, 42 percent favored some form of sovereignty, 25 percent were undecided or did not know and 34 percent opposed it. Among all those who supported sovereignty—both Native Hawaiian and non-Native Hawaiian—30 percent did so because they felt a need to correct past wrongs and because Native Hawaiians deserve sovereignty. Among the Native Hawaiians who opposed sovereignty, 36 percent believed that Native Hawaiians are not ready for sovereignty and 23 percent believed that sovereignty is impractical or impossible. Among the non-Native Hawaiian opponents, 21 percent believed that sovereignty would be unfair to non-Native Hawaiians. Indeed, one of the central arguments of the Aloha for All group is that Native Hawaiian sovereignty will cause resentment and undermine the spirit of aloha in contemporary Hawai'i.

Photo: Cory Lum

Native Hawaiians and part-Native Hawaiians comprise 20 percent of the population mix in Hawai'i's predominanty white, Japanese, and Filipino ancestry.

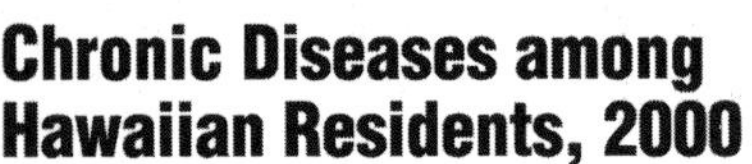

Chronic Diseases among Hawaiian Residents, 2000

(Rates per 1,000)

Health indices	Native Hawaiians	Other races	State of Hawaii
Arthritis	38.3	81.8	71.7
Asthma	139.5	71.5	86.5
Diabetes	49.0	45.1	45.9
High blood pressure	116.8	151.9	144.2
High cholesterol	85.6	146.6	133.1
Overweight	333.5	359.8	354.0

Note: The rates for asthma and diabetes in Native Hawaiians are among the highest of six chronic conditions monitored in Hawai'i. Arthritis and high cholesterol rates for Native Hawaiians are much lower than for the rest of the state.

Source: Office of Health Status Monitoring, Hawai'i State Department of Health

Hawaiians have a saying, *Aloha mai no, aloha aku*—When love is given, love should be returned. Native Hawaiian people have given aloha to newcomers and their descendants for generations. Sovereignty advocates believe that now is the time for aloha to be acknowledged and returned to the Native Hawaiian people and their descendants. The Akaka Bill introduced by Hawai'i's congressional delegation would provide an avenue for both the people of Hawai'i and the U.S. Congress to correct the historic injustices they have suffered collectively as a people, and enable them to exercise self-determination through self-governance, in order to heal as a people.

While federal recognition would represent a culmination of a century-old trust relationship between Native Hawaiians and the U.S. Congress, it would also constitute a small first step in the re-establishment of the first Native Hawaiian government since the overthrow of the Hawaiian monarchy in 1893.

—Davianna McGregor

Recognizing Identity Beyond the Categories

"No man is an island."

To quote this famous phrase accurately from the 16th century English poet John Donne: "No man is an Island, entire of itself; every man is a piece of the Continent, a part of the main."

And if the U.S. Census Bureau has any say in the matter, Pacific Islanders are now considered part of our continent as well.

Since 1960, the year after Hawai'i became the 50th state, Pacific Islanders have not had many choices about how to identify themselves on the Census questionnaire. Originally, two categories were included on the decennial Census questionnaire—and they were only for the state of Hawai'i. The two choices were: "Hawaiian" and "Part Hawaiian." But in 1970, the term "Hawaiian" appeared on the questionnaire for every state except Alaska. "Hawaiian" remained the only Pacific Islander group listed separately until 1980, when "Guamanian" and "Samoan" were added to the Census questionnaire. That year, the Census counted about 260,000 Native Hawaiian and Pacific Islanders.

In 1990, the category "Other Asian or Pacific Islander" was added to the questionnaire along with a write-in area for all unspecified groups of Polynesian, Micronesian or Melanesian cultural backgrounds. The 1990 Census counted 365,000 NHPIs, a 41 percent increase over 1980.

Photo: AP Wide World

Religion, along with sports and jobs, has had a significant effect on initial Pacific Islander immigration and eventual group settlement in states like Utah, Texas and Kansas.

In response to calls by Native Hawaiian and Pacific Islander activists, the Census Bureau split NHPIs off from Asians to become a sixth basic racial category, along with the existing white, black, American Indian, Asian, and Some Other Race (Hispanic or Latino is treated separately by the Census; members of any of those races may be Hispanic or Latino, though, in practice, most Hispanics or Latinos mark themselves as Some Other Race).

Respondents were also offered the option of picking one or more race categories to identify themselves. Thus, the Census 2000 data can be divided

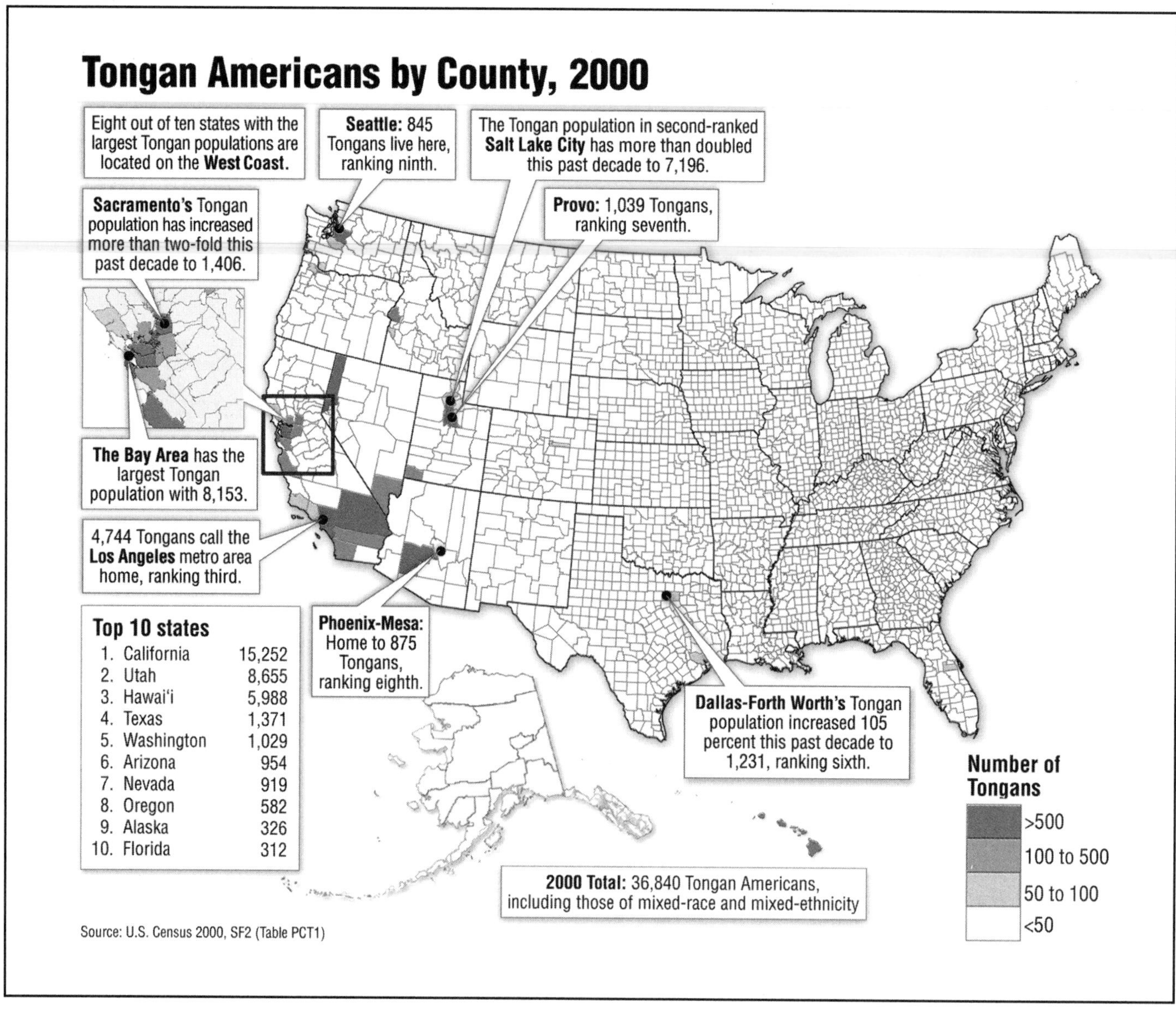

between monoracial (a.k.a. "race alone") and multiracial people ("race in combination"). As the Census questionnaires became more precise, divining what the exact NHPI population is became more difficult, especially since a huge proportion—more than half of all NHPIs—are of multiracial ancestry.

Examining the 2000 Census report on the NHPI population, we see an increase of about 34,000 or 9.3 percent, from roughly 365,000 people in 1990 to roughly 399,000 in 2000, using the NHPI-alone numbers. When including multiethnic and multiracial NHPIs, for the same dacade we see an increase of about 509,000, or 140 percent, to about 874,000 total in 2000. Compared with the overall population growth of 13 percent during the 1990s, the growth of NHPIs, especially when including multiracial NHPIs, was significant.

Also, Pacific Islanders residing in the U.S. Island Areas of Guam, American Samoa, the Commonwealth of the Northern Mariana Islands, and the U.S. Virgin Islands are completely excluded by the Census.

Dissecting the numbers further, three-fourths (73 percent) of NHPIs lived in

In this chapter, all population totals include both Native Hawaiians and Pacific Islanders, and include monoracial members as well as multiethnic and multiracial NHPIs. However, all socioeconomic data, such as median household income, educational attainment, poverty status, etc. are all calculated including only monoracial NHPIs.

Considerations for looking at Pacific Islander alone vs. alone and in combination population numbers

Pacific Islander alone:
Respondents reporting a single race as one or more of the detailed Pacific Islander groups (i.e. "Tongan and Samoan") but no other race.

Pacific Islander alone or in combination:
Respondents identifying themselves as entirely or partially Pacific Islander, reporting themselves as one of the detailed Pacific Islander groups and in combination with one or more other races (i.e. black, white, etc).

Compared to all other races, the Pacific Islander population had a much higher proportion of respondents reporting more than one race. It was also the only race where the number of respondents reporting two or more races was higher than the number reporting a single race. The total alone or in combination number indicates a significant overcount due to the fact that each detailed Pacific Islander group tallies of the number of the Pacific Islander responses rather than the number of respondents. Pacific Islanders identifying themselves as several detailed Pacific Islander groups are counted several times. For example, a respondent reporting "Samoan" and "Tongan" would be included in both the Samoan and Tongan numbers. Therefore, a completely accurate count of Pacific Islanders presents a challenge because each detailed group overcount is adding to the overcount of the overall total population.

Pacific Islander Population by Detailed Group "Alone" vs. "Alone or in Combination," 2000

POLYNESIAN	Pacific Islanders alone	Pacific Islanders alone or in combination with other races
Samoan	91,029	133,281
Tongan	27,713	36,840
Tahitian	800	3,313
Tokelauan	129	574
Polynesian, not specified	3497	8,796
MICRONESIAN		
Guamanian or Chamorro	58,240	92,611
Mariana Islander	60	141
Saipanese	195	475
Palauan	2,228	3,469
Carolinian	91	173
Kosraean	157	226
Pohnpeian	486	700
Chuukese	367	654
Yapese	236	368
Marshallese	5,479	6,650
I-Kribati	90	175
Micronesian, not specified	7,509	9,940
MELANESIAN		
Fijian	9,796	13,581
Papua New Guinean	135	224
Soloman Islander	12	25
Ni-Vanuatu	6	18
Melanesian, not specified	147	315
Other Pacific Islander	40,558	174,912
TOTAL	**248,960**	**487,461**

Source: U.S. Census Bureau, Census 2000

the thirteen-state Western region, fourteen percent lived in the South, seven percent lived in the Northeast, and six percent lived in the Midwest. More than half, or 58 percent, of the NHPI population lived in just two states: Hawai'i (282,667) and California (221,458). Other states with large NHPI populations include Washington, Texas, New York, Nevada, Florida, and Utah.

Among the U.S. cities with populations of 100,000 or more, Honolulu had the largest NHPI population with 58,130, followed by New York City with 19,203, and Los Angeles with 13,144. San Diego had the largest proportion of NHPIs, at 0.9 percent of the total population, followed by Los Angeles, at 0.4 percent, and Phoenix, at 0.3 percent.

Detailed Pacific Islander groups

Native Hawaiians, who make up nearly 45 percent of the entire NHPI population, are discussed in multiple chapters elsewhere in this book. With that in mind, I focus on the other Pacific Islander groups—from the familiar, such as the Samoans or Guamanians, to the lesser-known, such as the Chuukese (natives of the Truk Islands) to the Yapese.

Samoan migration and settlement

There are more than 130,000 Samoans living in the United States, with about two-thirds of monoracial ancestry and another third of multiracial ancestry. That's nearly a threefold growth from the 1990 population of 49,345. Like

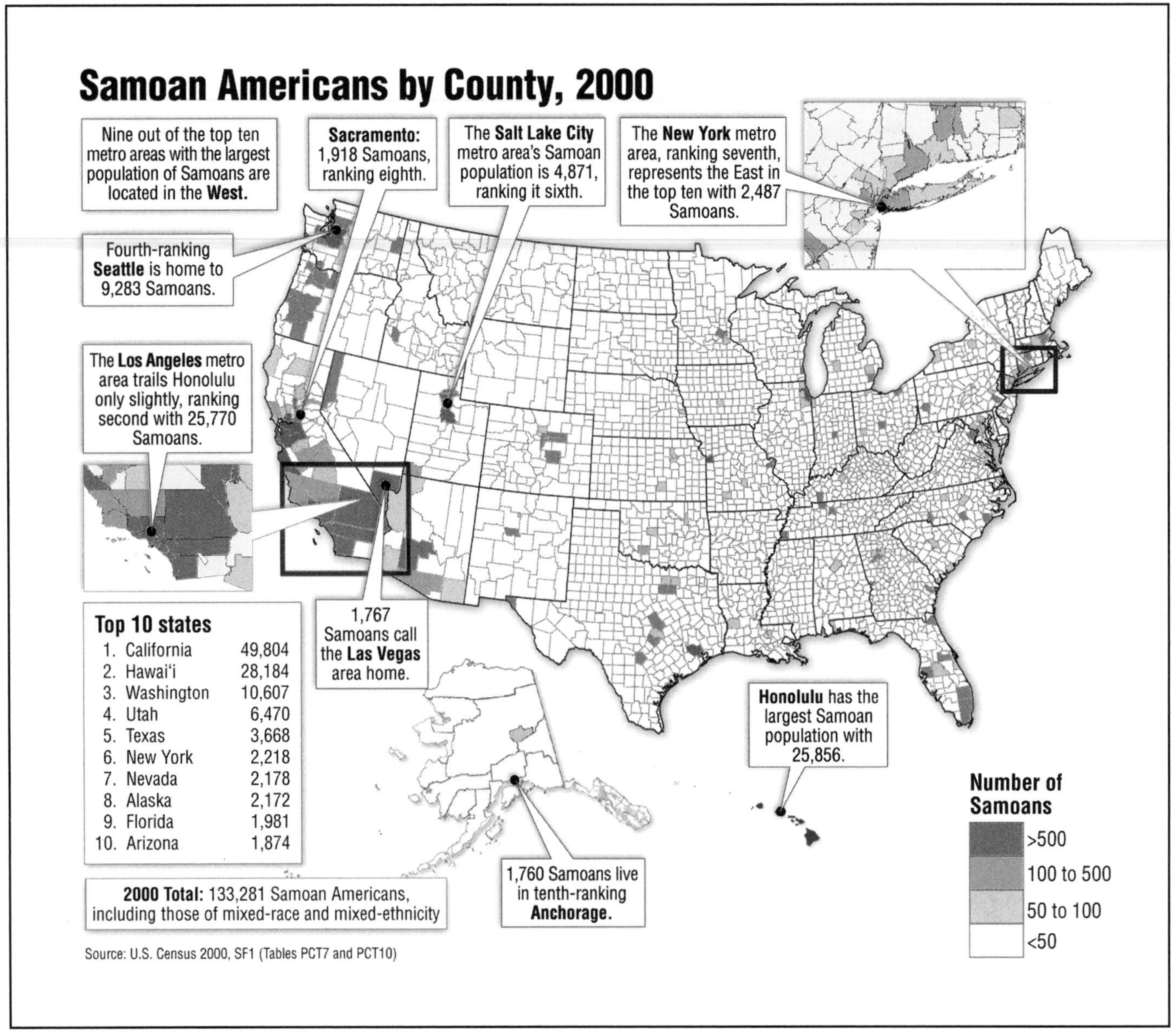

the Native Hawaiians, they are considered Polynesians, and are theorized to have migrated from the west (the East Indies, the Malay peninsula or the Philippines) as far back ago as 1,000 B.C.E. Europeans landed on the islands in 1722 in search for the "great unknown southern continent." The French explorer, Captain Louis-Antoine de Bougainville passed through the region in 1768 and named it the "Navigator Islands."

But the greatest influence on Samoan culture came from the Western missionaries who converted the population and brought religious life to its inhabitants (most Samoans are Christian with elements of Samoan tradition also honored).

Today, the islands are divided up into American Samoa and Samoa. The former is only 76 square miles, has a population of around 67,000, and sends a delegate to the U.S. Congress (as does Guam, discussed later). Samoa, known as Western Samoa until 1997, is an independent nation with islands totaling 1,090 square miles, and a population of 179,058. With nearly double the number of Samoans in the United States versus the population remaining in American Samoa, emigration of Samoans abroad is obviously high. The economy of American Samoa remains undeveloped; nearly one-third of workers are employed in the fishing or canning industry. Tourism has not taken off. Money sent back from Samoan expatriates remains a major part of the economy.

In recent years, one of American Samoa's main exports has been football

players. There are more than 200 playing Division I college football, and 28 in the NFL, reported ESPN in 2002. They include stars like San Diego Chargers linebacker Tiaina "Junior" Seau.

Guamanian or Chamorro: past and present

After Samoans, the next-largest NHPI group are the natives of the island of Guam, also known as Chamorro. There are only about 157,000 people living on today's multicultural Guam, of whom about half are Chamorro. So like American Samoa, a larger number of Chamorro actually live abroad—in the United States, there are nearly 93,000 people of pure or part-Chamorro descent. That compares to about 63,000 in 1990, and 40,000 in 1980.

The Chamorro are also theorized to have arrived from the Malay Peninsula around 1500 B.C.E. Part of the Micronesia chain of islands, Guam and its native Chamorro people have a violent history of conflict with outsiders, starting with Portuguese explorer Ferdinand Magellan's stop there in 1521.

In 1668, Jesuit priests arrived from Spain on a mission to convert the islanders to Catholicism with help from a small garrison of soldiers. But as the Catholics took over and traditional hierarchies eroded, a bloody Chamorro insurgence began. By the late 1600s, the rebellions, combined with influenza and smallpox epidemics, caused the Chamorro population to dwindle from an estimated 100,000 to about 5,000. The majority of survivors were women and children. Spanish soldiers and Filipino men were brought in to help repopulate the island, diluting the pure Chamorro bloodlines.

During World War II, the Japanese occupied Guam for 31 months before American forces recaptured the island in 1944. Today the U.S. military maintains a large, albeit declining, presence in Guam, with 23,000 military personnel and their families living on the island. Though the government has lobbied to free Guam from its "unincorporated" U.S. territory status, the island has yet to be granted the Commonwealth recognition given Puerto Rico. And although the people are given U.S. citizenship, they do not vote in U.S. presidential elections.

Economically, the growing tourist industry catering to Japanese visitors has helped offset the military downsizing. But the ongoing slump in the Japanese economy has hurt tourism to Guam in the last decade, and undoubtedly contributed to many Guamanians coming to the United States. The largest populations of Chamorro in the United States are in Hawai'i and West Coast cities like Los Angeles, San Francisco, San Diego, and Seattle. More than one third live in California alone; about six in ten live in California, Washington, Texas, Hawai'i and Florida.

Micronesia's archipelagos: symbol and struggle for Pacific Islander identity

Perhaps most interesting are the 200,000-odd Pacific Islanders who did not identify with being either Native Hawaiian, Samoan, Guamanian, or Tongan. This is not a surprising number when one considers the diversity within the Pacific Islands themselves and the various cultures. More than 2,100 islands make up the region known as Micronesia, covering an area of the Pacific Ocean as wide as the continental United States.

There are three major archipelagoes: the Marshalls, Carolines, and Marianas. History has witnessed these islands pass through the hands of Spanish, German and Japanese colonial rule before becoming a U.S.-administered United Nations strategic trusteeship following World War II. The arrangement became known as the Trust Territory of the Pacific Islands (TTPI).

Changes in How the Census Counts Pacific Islanders, by Decade*

1960	Number
"Hawaiian" or "Part Hawaiian"†	
1970	
Hawaiian††	
1980	**259,566**
Native Hawaiian	
Samoan	
Guamanian	
1990	**365,024**
Polynesian	283,885
Native Hawaiian	205,501
Samoan	*57,679*
Tongan	*16,707*
Micronesian	54,970
Guamanian	*47,754*
Melanesian	7,218
2000	
NHPI†††	**874,414****
Polynesian	
*Native Hawaiian**	*401,162*
*Samoan**	*133,281*
Tongan	*36,840*
Tahitian	*3,313*
Tokelauan	*574*
Polynesian, not specified	*8,796*
Micronesian	
*Guamanian or Chamorro**	*92,611*
Mariana Islander	*141*
Saipanese	*475*
Palauan	*3,469*
Carolinian	*173*
Kosraean	*226*
Pohnpeian	*700*
Chuukese	*654*
Yapese	*368*
Marshallese	*6,650*
I-Kiribati	*175*
Micronesian, not specified	*9,940*
Melanesian	
Fijian	*13,581*
Papua New Guinean	*224*
Solomon Islander	*25*
Ni-Vanuatu	*18*
Melanesian, not specified	*315*
Other Pacific Islander	174,912

†Only for state of Hawaii
††Every state except Alaska
†††Split off from Asian as separate racial category
*Indicates categories listed on 2000 Census questionnaire; all other categories must be checked as "Other Pacific Islander" and written by respondent.
**Census does not list all multiethnic combinations; totals for each detailed ethnicity will add up to more than NHPI total.
Source: U.S. Census

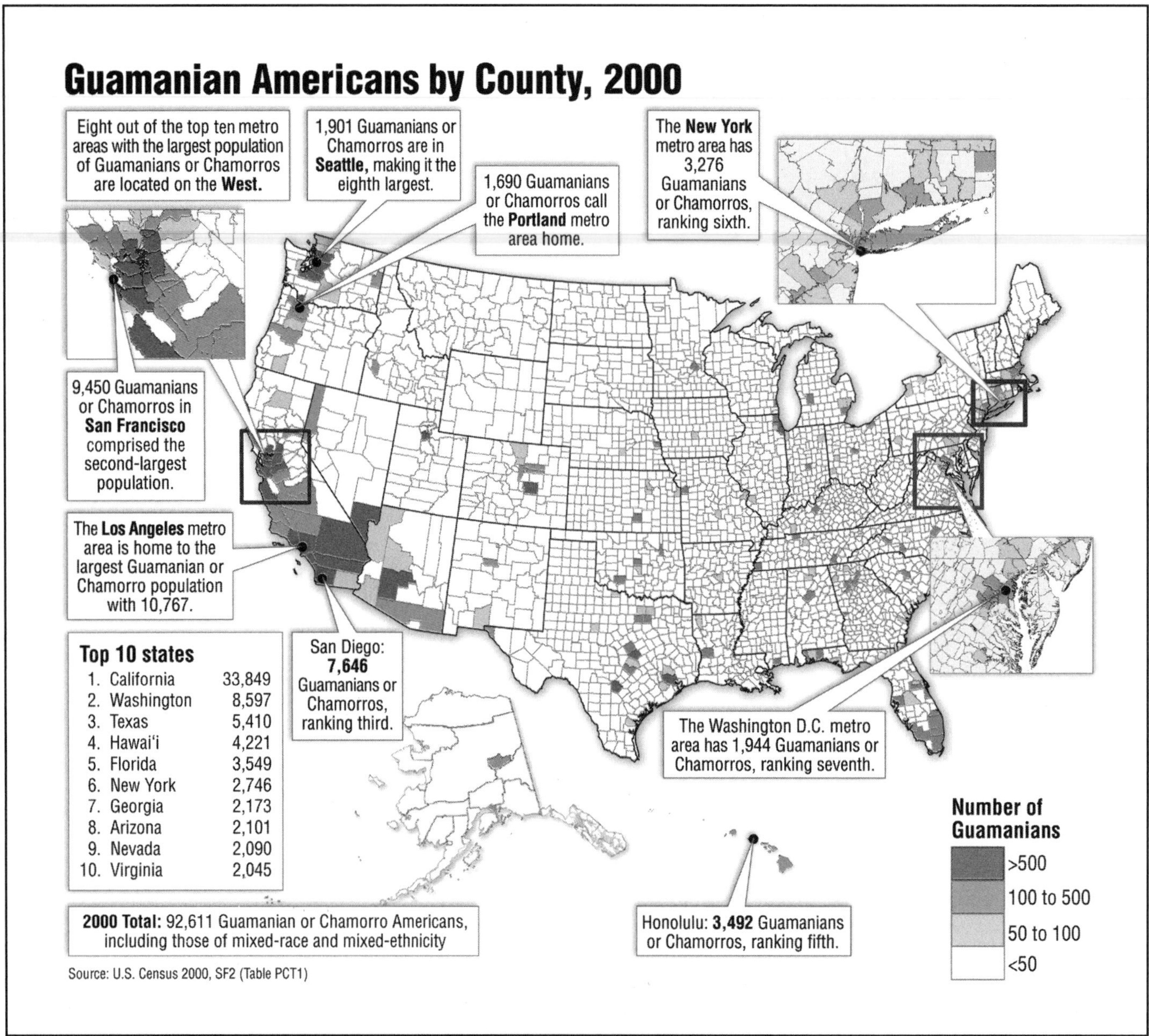

Under Navy control, the islands were handed over to the U.S. Dept. of the Interior in 1951 and divided into six administrative districts: the Marshalls, Ponape, Truk, Marianas, Yap and Palau, with Kosrae later added on. By the 1970s, the districts had begun voting to end the TTPI arrangement. After the U.S. fulfilled its obligations in 1986, the U.N. officially dissolved the TTPI in 1990. Palau was the last of the TTPI districts to end its trustee status in 1994.

Today, the original TTPI districts have been replaced with four separate, self-governing districts: the Commonwealth of the Northern Marianas; the Federated States of Micronesia, comprised of Kosrae, Pohnpei (Ponape), Chuuk (Truk) and Yap; the Republic of the Marshall Islands; and the Republic of Palau (Belau).

The islands remain undeveloped economically, though big business, in the form of fishing, tourism (catering to the Japanese, mostly), and garment factories (especially in the city of Saipan on the Northern Mariana islands), has arrived to varying degrees. While these islands are not necessarily less populated than American Samoa or Guam (Tonga, for instance, has a population of more than 100,000), the fact that they are not formally connected to the United States means that far fewer natives of these islands have emigrated to America.

Socioeconomic story

Besides the cultural and ethnic differ-

ences between Asians and Pacific Islanders, one of the main motivations for NHPI activists to fight for separate racial recognition by the Census Bureau was the very real socioeconomic differences between the groups. Indeed, while some NHPIs have very high incomes and educations, a disproportionate percentage are impoverished, have lower educations, and may require or need public assistance, which is often tied directly to demographic studies and population counts like the Census. The model minority myth surrounding Asian Americans, which obscures problems with disadvantaged members of the group, was hurting NHPIs, too. Note: due to limitations in the way data has been released by the Census Bureau, the following socioeconomic discussion includes both Native Hawaiians and Pacific Islanders, but only monoracial members.

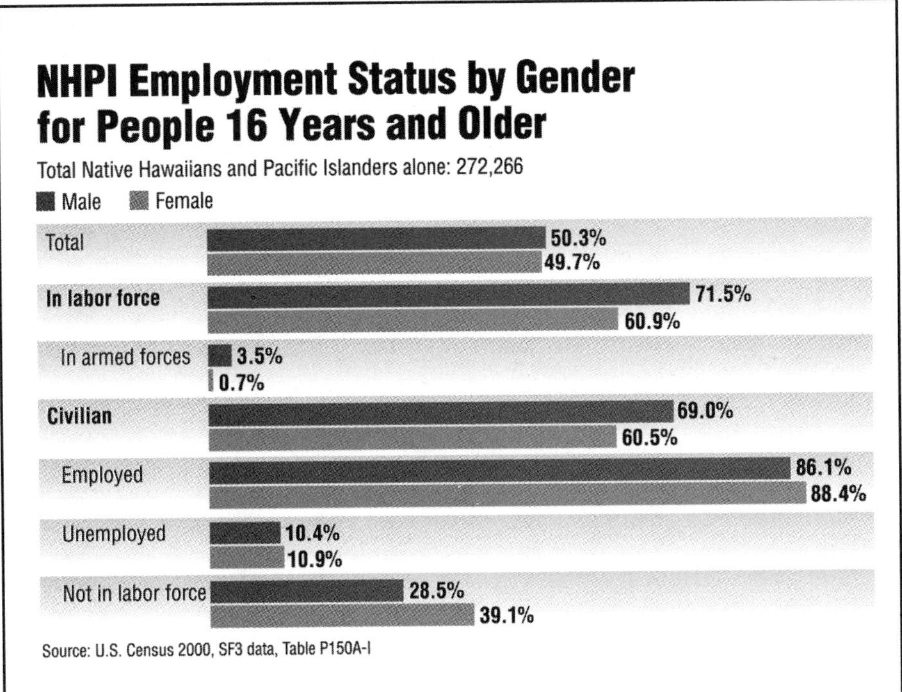

Income

In terms of aggregate figures, NHPIs tend to lag behind most other groups. The per-capita income in 1999 for NHPIs was $15,054. That is 37 percent lower than the $23,918 per capita income for whites, 31 percent lower than the $21,823 figure for Asians, and 30 percent lower than the overall population's per capita income of $21,587.

Among the 50 states, North Dakota ($45,993) ranked the highest in NHPI per capita income, followed by New Jersey ($23,745), South Carolina ($21,638), Iowa ($21,436) and Virginia ($20,761).

For NHPIs, the median earnings (dollars) in 1999 for full-time workers age 16 years or older were $28,457, with men earning $31,030 and women earning $25,694. In contrast, Asians earned about $36,051, with males earning $40,650 and females $31,049, while the overall U.S. population posted median earnings in 1999 of $32,098, with males earning $37,057 and females $27,194.

NHPIs posted their highest median earnings of $36,635 per full-time worker in Washington D.C., with females earning $44,318 and men $18,875. Connecticut ($31,610) was second in median earnings per full-time worker, followed by Minnesota ($31,216) and California at ($31,128).

Surprisingly, North Dakota, with an NHPI population of just 157, posted the highest earnings for non-full-time NHPI workers with an average of $57,857. Female full-time workers earned $58,393, while full-time male workers earned $31,250.

By household, NHPIs had a median income in 1999 of $42,717—higher than the overall U.S. median figure of $41,994, though lower than the Asian figure of $51,908. How is that possible, when we've seen earlier that median and per-capita figures for NHPI individuals are lower? Simply because NHPIs and Asians tend to have larger families and more workers per household. NHPIs (alone) have an average household size of 3.6, versus 3.11 for Asians alone and 2.59 for the general popula-

NHPI Poverty Rates Around the United States, 2000

Rank	Metro area	Poverty rate	State	Poverty rate
1	New York-Northern New Jersey-Long Island, NY-NJ-CT-PA**	23.0%	New York	25.9%
2	Honolulu, HI*	21.2%	Hawai'i	21.4%
3	Los Angeles-Riverside-Orange County, CA**	19.3%	Texas	16.8%
4	Seattle-Tacoma-Bremerton, WA**	14.5%	California	15.7%
5	San Francisco-Oakland-San Jose, CA **	10.8%	Washington	15.5%

*MSA: stands for Metropolitan Statistical Area.
**CMSA: stands for Consolidated Metropolitan Statistical Area.
Source: U.S. Census 2000, SF3 (Table P159)

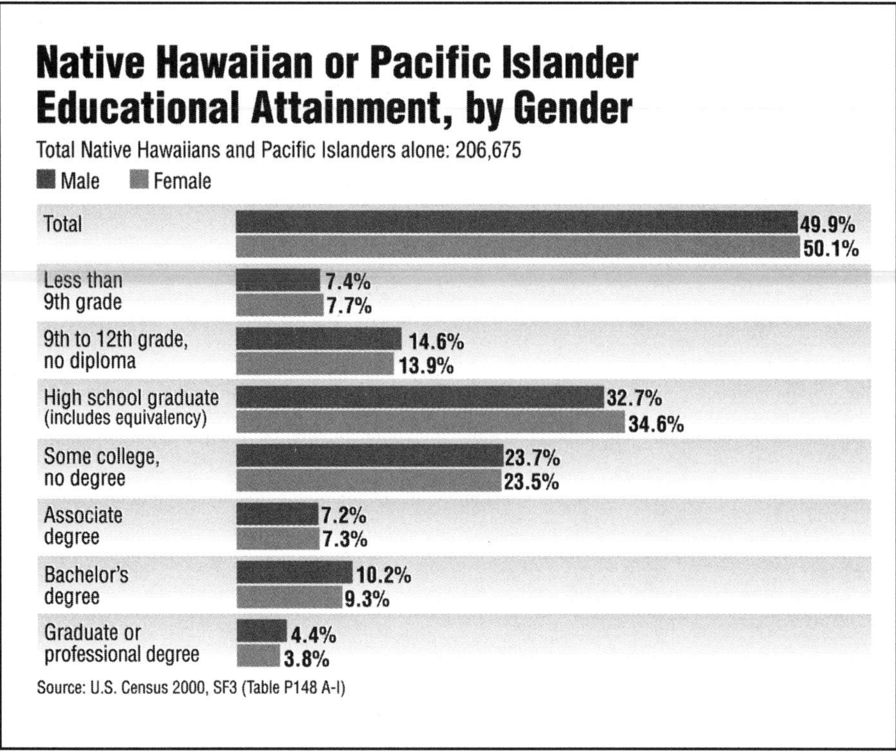

tion. By family size, NHPIs were also the largest, at 4.05, versus 3.61 for Asians (alone) and 3.02 for the overall population. At the time of writing, the Census had not released statistics on the median number of workers per family/household for the overall population or by race, so this theory could not be confirmed.

Employment

Pacific Islanders had a relatively high rate of unemployment. The unemployment rate for the general population is around 5.7 percent. For NHPI men, it is 10.4 percent, and for NHPI women, it is 10.9 percent. In general, that is lower than American Indians, about the same as blacks, and higher than Asians (4.9 percent for men and 5.3 percent for women), Hispanics, and non-Hispanic whites.

School and educational attainment

The percentage of NHPIs enrolled in school or college as of 2000 was 35.4 percent, which ranked higher than both the 26.1 percent of whites and 33.5 percent of Asians. That may be indicative of the relative youthfulness of the NHPI population living in America more than anything else. The median age for the general population is 35.3 years old; for Asians, it is 31.1 years old, while for NHPIs it is just 25.4 years old. Only those who marked Some other Race had a younger median age, of 24.8 years old (most of them are Hispanic or Latino).

The rate of choosing private schools—a more expensive, albeit prestigious proposition—was generally lower for NHPIs than for other groups, though the difference was not huge. Among nursery school through twelfth grade students, nine percent of NHPIs attended private schools, versus 14.9 percent for Asians and 16.8 for non-Hispanic whites. Meanwhile, 26.6 percent of NHPI college students attended a private college or university, lower than Asians (28.8 percent) but higher than non-Hispanic whites (25.9 percent).

However, in educational attainment for those 25 years or older, NHPIs do lag significantly. In the total population, about one quarter of the population has a bachelor's degree or more, with 18.5 percent holding a graduate, professional, or doctoral degree. Among Asians, 44.1 percent have a bachelor's degree or more, while 17.5 percent have a graduate, professional or doctoral degree. Among NHPIs, only 13.8 percent have a bachelor's degree and only 4.1 percent have a graduate degree or higher. However, around eight in ten of NHPIs are high school graduates.

Conclusion

If there's something to be learned from examining the historical experiences of Pacific Islanders, from Samoa to Guam to the Marshalls, Carolines and Marianas, perhaps it's that we as human beings still cherish our unique cultural identity and independence even more than making arrangements to be another "piece of the continent."

As for the next decade's Census report, instead of falling in line with that antiquated idiom, "No man is an island," perhaps the U.S. Census Bureau would be better served to contemplate employing George Orwell's *Animal Farm* slogan "all animals are equal but some are more equal than others."

—*Edmund Moy*

The Invisible Immigrants

Cambodian Americans

Cambodians, also known as the Khmer, started arriving in the United States two decades ago in the aftermath of the Vietnam War. Survivors of a terrible genocide, nearly all of the more than 200 thousand Cambodian Americans of single and mixed-descent counted by the 2000 Census were once refugees or are children of refugees.

The Refugee Act of 1980 codified and strengthened the U.S. policy of aiding individuals fleeing persecution. Of the approximately 1.64 million refugees who have arrived in the United States since 1983, 39 percent fled from either Cambodia, Laos or Vietnam. The Refugee Act also strengthened today's asylum adjudication process and created a federal Office of Refugee Resettlement (ORR). Cambodians Americans were among the earliest beneficiaries of the ORR's programs.

Photo: AP Wide World

Despite having to overcome difficult refugee experiences, Cambodians in America are working towards becoming active and prosperous members of their community.

While those pro-immigrant and humanitarian policies helped the Cambodian American population grow quickly during the 1980s and early 1990s, recent immigration trends have had an unfortunate and detrimental impact upon the Cambodian American community. A prime example is the June 2001 ruling by the U.S. Supreme Court, which found that it was illegal for the Immigration and Naturalization Service (INS) to hold a Cambodian man indefinitely if it cannot deport him in a reasonable time. At the time, Cambodia was one of the few countries that did not accept deportees.

Until this decision, despite civil and human rights concerns, individuals who had already served their criminal sentences were re-incarcerated and, in some instances, held for years in INS

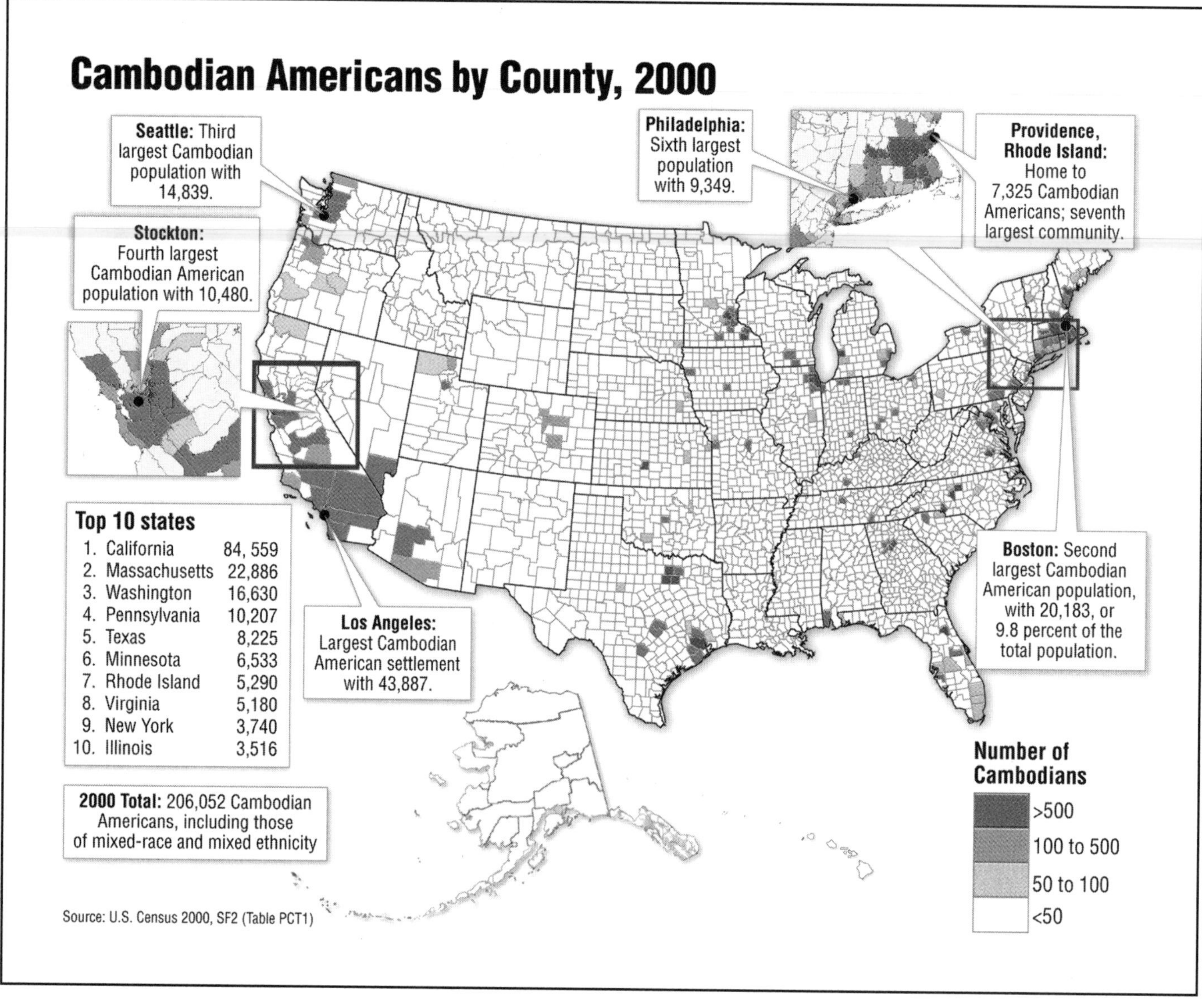

detention facilities and contracted jails across the country. Rather than release such people, the U.S. Government instead increased its efforts to make Cambodia accept deportees. Such a repatriation agreement was signed in the spring of 2002. In June of that year, six Cambodians were deported, with more slated for forced removal.

Looking back at a troubled past

Located in the heart of Southeast Asia, Cambodia is a small country about the physical size of the state of Oklahoma, bordered by Laos, Vietnam, and Thailand. The country, despite being officially neutral, inevitably found itself embroiled in the Vietnam War and its own Communist uprising in the form of the Khmer Rouge, led by Pol Pot. From 1969 to 1973, the U.S. secretly conducted air-bombing raids on North Vietnamese troops over the Cambodian border, despite Cambodia's neutrality.

The bombings caused Cambodian civilian casualties and damage to land and property that added to ever-increasing anti-American sentiment and a rise in the support for the communist Khmer Rouge. The carpet-bombing of Cambodia's countryside by American B-52s has been identified as one of the most important factors in the rise of Pol Pot and the Khmer Rouge. When U.S. forces withdrew from the region in 1975, the Khmer Rouge soon defeated the U.S.-dependant Cambodian government.

After taking power in April 1975, the Khmer Rouge began to implement a wholesale restructuring of Cambodian society with the intent of creating an agrarian socialist state. The mechanism for this change was forced labor camps and the systematic murder of all political opposition, those of minority ethnic groups, individuals from religious, professional and educated segments of society, and all others who questioned

the new order. The Khmer Rouge dissolved institutions such as banks, hospitals, schools, stores, religion, and attempted to unravel the fabric of the family. Children were separated from their parents to work in mobile groups or as soldiers.

In proportion, the genocide in Cambodia rivals that of the Jewish holocaust. During the Khmer Rouge's reign from 1975 to 1979, about one-third of the Cambodian population died by starvation, torture or execution—2 million in total. In 1979, the Vietnamese government wrested control of the country, putting an end to Khmer Rouge rule. With the fall of the Khmer Rouge and Vietnamese occupation, 600,000 refugees fled to refugee camps along the Thai border. Although refugees began arriving in the United States after the fall of Cambodia in 1975, the overthrow of the Khmer Rouge in 1979 marked the true beginning of the Cambodian mass exodus and arrival in America.

Immigration patterns

The 1980 Census was the first to count Cambodians in the United States. It found 16,044, of which nearly half that number (7,739) had been admitted as refugees. During the 1980s, liberal refugee admission policies helped the Cambodian American population increase nine times to 149,047 in the 1990 Census. According to INS statistics, 114,064 Cambodians were admitted as refugees during the 1980s.

Refugee admissions tapered off sharply in the 1990s. From 1991 to 1998, only 6,150 Cambodians were admitted as refugees, according to the INS. The Cambodian community continued to grow, according to the 2000 Census. There are 171,937 Cambodians of single descent, a 13 percent increase over 1990, and 206,052 Cambodians, including those of mixed-race and mixed-ethnicity.

It should be noted that measuring the demographics of the Cambodian American community has historically been challenging; it is widely suspected that the community is repeatedly undercounted by the Census Bureau. A 1992 report sponsored by the Center of Survey Methods Research of the Census Bureau identified language barriers, mistrust of strangers and the government, and unusual residence and household composition as significantly affecting Census counts. That report recommended that "Cambodian" should be added to the list of Asian ethnicities in the Census questionnaire form to make it easier for respondents to identify themselves. Although there is a growing recognition that overly-broad ethnic categories can obscure communities with special needs, the Census Bureau declined to add "Cambodian" to its 2000 Census questionnaire.

Policy and societal challenges

Despite their unique position as Asian holocaust survivors and refugees, Cambodian Americans are still largely overlooked by policy makers. Since the implementation of 1996 immigration and welfare reform laws, Cambodians have been caught up in a dragnet of immigration policies and social service policies that limit benefits to non-citizens and require the mandatory detention and deportation of those convicted of crimes.

Although a number of Cambodians have managed to find success in the United States, many continue to face challenges related to their refugee resettlement experience. The donut shop business in California has felt the hand of Cambodian American entrepreneurship. It is estimated that as much as 90 percent of California's 5,000 independent donut shops are Cambodian owned. However, the community as a whole, according to 1990 Census data available at the time of this writing, still deals with a high poverty rate (47 percent), poor English fluency (56 percent are rated as "linguistically isolated"), and low levels of educational achievement (only 6 percent of Cambodians over the age of 25 have a bachelor's degree from a university).

Learning English is a challenge for many Cambodians, who by and large arrived with a lack of formal education. The Khmer Rouge genocide decimated the educated and professional classes. As a result, Southeast Asian refugees (not including the Vietnamese), of whom Cambodians are a prominent percentage, have the lowest educational level, averaging just 3.1 years of schooling before arriving in the United States. Refugees from Latin America have 11.0 years of schooling; refugees from Africa have 7.5 years before coming to America, according to an ORR report.

This language barrier has made it difficult for many first-generation Southeast Asian Americans to become full-fledged citizens because they are unable to pass the English-language portion of the citizenship test. Due to the fact their parents have not become citizens, the 1.5 generation of Cambodian Americans (young people who arrived as infants or small children but have largely grown up in America) remain non-citizens. This has made them particularly vulnerable to changes in U.S. policies directed broadly at "aliens" or non-citizens.

The legacy of the Cambodian holocaust creates some of the most challenging barriers to Cambodian American political empowerment. Having survived near-starvation, violence, and torture, many Cambodians in this country still continue to struggle with day-to-day survival and consequently lack interest in civic participation. Because of their histories of being oppressed by the government, some Cambodians continue to harbor fear and distrust of the government and remain largely ignorant of their civic responsibilities.

Upcoming data from the 2000 Census is expected to show improved statistics in areas like education, poverty, and language fluency, due to more second and third generation Cambodian Americans. The implication of how current U.S. policies are negatively impacting the Cambodian American community exposes need for greater representation, advocacy and civic participation on their behalf. In looking at the past twenty years of Cambodian American history, it is clear that the community has come along way in a short period, but there is still much work to be done. Through greater civic and political participation, Cambodian Americans can guide their own course, empower themselves, and foster positive community development.

—*Porthira Chhim*

The Hmong in America

The Hmong people are an ethnic group whose origins go back about 3,000 years in China. Most Hmong—about eight million—still live in southwestern China. Another four million live in the Southeast Asian countries of Thailand, Burma, Laos and Vietnam, where they immigrated during the 19th century following centuries of persecution in China. There, they existed mostly as farmers living in rural areas.

Photo: Corky Lee

The Hmong population in Minnesota has grown substantially in the past decade, settling mostly in St. Paul, where the cost of living is much cheaper than California.

Before 1975, there were just a handful of Hmong in America, most of them university students from Thailand or Laos. The first Hmong migration of notable size to the United States began with the fall of Saigon and Laos to Communist forces in 1975. Many Hmong had worked with pro-American anti-Communist forces during the conflicts in Vietnam and Laos. As a result, they were subject to violence and retribution in Laos. Many Hmong escaped Laos to Thailand where they were incarcerated in refugee camps.

First wave settlement

From the late 1970s to the mid-1990s, large numbers of Hmong refugees were resettled in the United States. The peak was 1980, when 27,000 Hmong refugees were admitted. From 1981 to 1986, the number of Hmong refugees slowed to a few thousand each year, but admissions picked up again between 1987 and 1994, when about 56,000 Hmong refugees were accepted. After 1994, Hmong refugee admissions slowed to a trickle as most of the Thai camps were by now empty, with the remaining Hmong repatriated to Laos. Also, Hmong immigration based on family reunification remains low, especially compared to other Southeast Asian ethnic groups.

Where did the Hmong settle? With the first wave that arrived in the late 1970s and early 1980s, voluntary resettlement agencies consciously tried to disperse the Hmong around the country in a number of locales. At that time, sizeable Hmong populations could be found in East Coast cities like Providence, Rhode Island and Philadelphia, Pennsylvania; in Midwestern cities like Chicago, Des Moines, Iowa, and Kansas City, Kansas; and the western cities of Denver, Colorado, Missoula, Montana, Tulsa, Oklahoma, and Salt Lake City, Utah.

This strategy, however, proved unsuccessful in many instances. Several thousand Hmong, for instance, were settled in a poor, predominantly African American neighborhood in west Philadelphia, where they encountered much hostility and violence. Most of the Hmong moved out within several years. Also, many Hmong wished to be reunited with family and clan members. These reasons led to a massive shift of the Hmong population in the mid-to-late 1980s to central California cities like Fresno, Stockton and Merced, and,

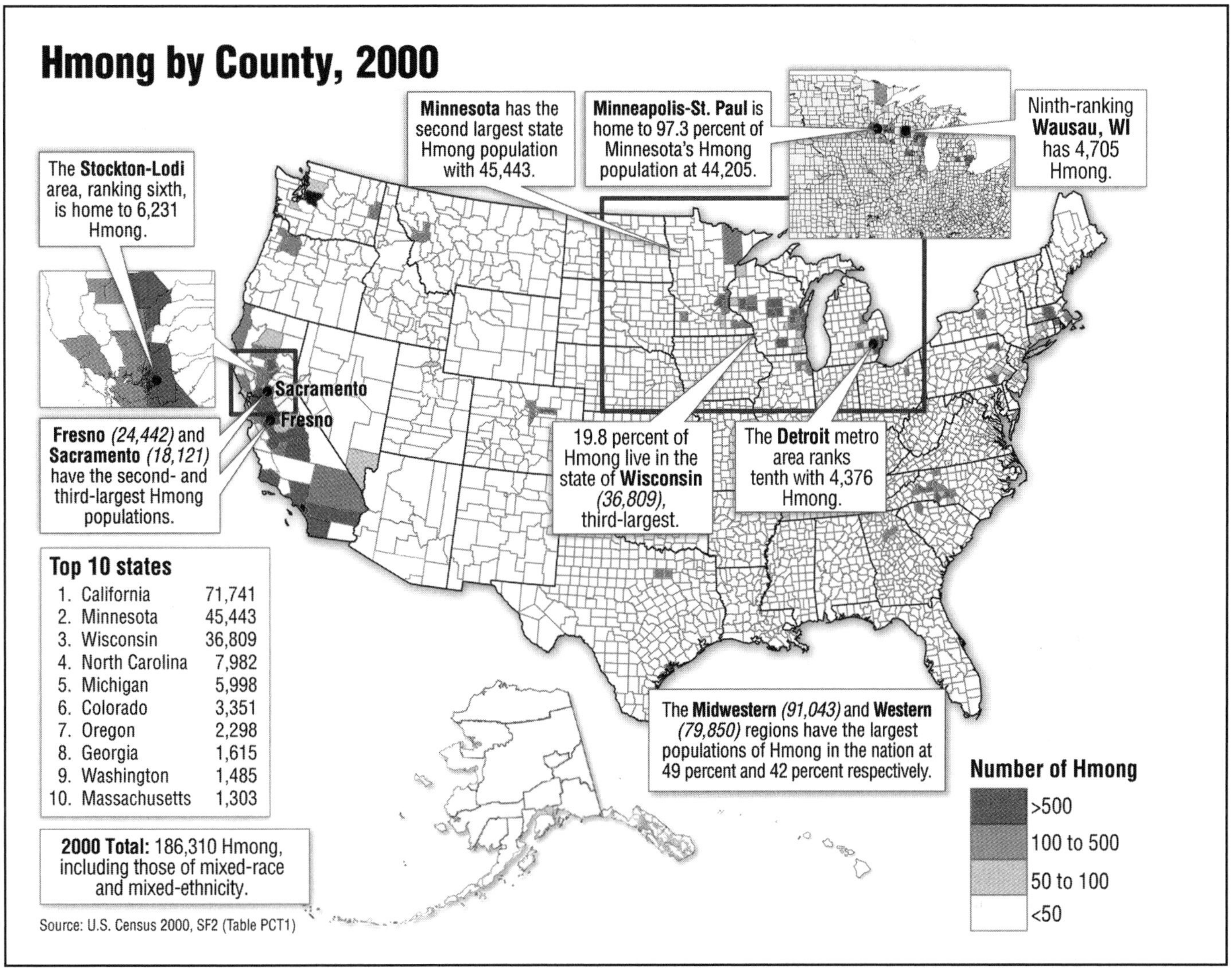

Hmong by County, 2000

The **Stockton-Lodi** area, ranking sixth, is home to 6,231 Hmong.

Minnesota has the second largest state Hmong population with 45,443.

Minneapolis-St. Paul is home to 97.3 percent of Minnesota's Hmong population at 44,205.

Ninth-ranking **Wausau, WI** has 4,705 Hmong.

Sacramento

Fresno

Fresno *(24,442)* and **Sacramento** *(18,121)* have the second- and third-largest Hmong populations.

19.8 percent of Hmong live in the state of **Wisconsin** *(36,809)*, third-largest.

The **Detroit** metro area ranks tenth with 4,376 Hmong.

Top 10 states

1.	California	71,741
2.	Minnesota	45,443
3.	Wisconsin	36,809
4.	North Carolina	7,982
5.	Michigan	5,998
6.	Colorado	3,351
7.	Oregon	2,298
8.	Georgia	1,615
9.	Washington	1,485
10.	Massachusetts	1,303

The **Midwestern** *(91,043)* and **Western** *(79,850)* regions have the largest populations of Hmong in the nation at 49 percent and 42 percent respectively.

2000 Total: 186,310 Hmong, including those of mixed-race and mixed-ethnicity.

Number of Hmong

- >500
- 100 to 500
- 50 to 100
- <50

Source: U.S. Census 2000, SF2 (Table PCT1)

to a lesser extent, to Minnesota and Wisconsin. By 1990, Fresno and Central Valley cities like Sacramento, Stockton and Merced were the center of Hmong American population and community life. Census figures show that by far the largest Hmong population at this time was found in California, followed by Minnesota, Wisconsin, Michigan and Colorado. The 1990 census counted 94,439 Hmong Americans across the United States.

Heading to the Midwest and South

During the 1990s, the Hmong moved again: away from the West and towards the Midwest and the South. This shift was epitomized by the emergence of Minneapolis and St. Paul as the unofficial capitals of Hmong America, taking over from Fresno. About half of Hmong today live in the Midwest, mostly in Minnesota, Wisconsin and Michigan, compared to 41 percent in 1990. Meanwhile, the proportion of Hmong in the Western states fell to 42 percent in 2000 from 55 percent in 1990. Nine out of ten in the West lived in California, with much smaller communities found in Colorado, Oregon, Washington and Alaska. Around 6 percent of the Hmong now live in the South, an impressive increase from just 1.3 percent in 1990. This movement was focused within a few states, such as North and South Carolina. In 2000, the Hmong population numbered in the Northeastern states remained very small, at just 2 percent.

By 2000, there were 169,428 Hmong numbered in America, representing a nearly 90 percent increase in the population from 1990. Many agree, however, that the figure is probably a significant undercount. The Twin Cities claimed 40,707 Hmong residents. Second was Fresno, California, with 22,456. After Fresno, the largest Hmong populations in the United States in 2000 were found in Sacramento-Yolo, Milwaukee-Racine, and Merced.

Why did Minneapolis-St. Paul emerge as the new Hmong American capital? The opportunity to make a better life seems to be at the heart of things.

"The cost of living is cheaper here than in California," Lee Pao Xiong, president of the Urban Coalition in St. Paul, told the Associated Press. "The quality of education is better here, and jobs are available here."

Xiong said he's recruited 10 families from his own extended family to come here from California in recent years. "They came here and they found jobs within a month or two and are making ten, eleven, twelve dollars an hour," he said.

A 2002 community directory provides listings of 13 Hmong community organizations and 39 Hmong religious congregations in the Minneapolis-St. Paul area. Whereas many Hmong in California's Central Valley have taken up their old occupations of farming, those in Minneapolis have found jobs working in factories. But there is a substantial emerging class of Hmong small business owners—many of them congregated near St. Paul's University Avenue, also known for its Vietnamese businesses—and college-educated Hmong professionals going into fields like law, medicine, and non-profit management. Hmong are opening restaurants serving Lao or Thai cuisine, though traditional Hmong dishes are available upon request. And the United States' first Hmong politician, a 32-year-old female lawyer named Mee Moua, was elected to the Minnesota State Senate in 2002.

In the Twin Cities metro area, most Hmong live in St. Paul, which also hosts an annual New Year celebration and a summer sports tournament that attracts thousands of Hmong to visit from around the United States.

Steady climb into the middle class

The Hmong came to America less-prepared for the modern capitalistic society of their new home than most other immigrant groups. Most had been farmers in their native country, and did not graduate from high school or the equivalent. As a result, many Hmong families when they first arrived were forced to go on public assistance. In 1990, the median Hmong household income was about $11,000, compared to $30,356 among all Americans. 67.1 percent of Hmong lived below the poverty line in 1990, compared to about 13 percent of all Americans.

In 1990, only 15 percent of Hmong owned their homes. While income data for Hmong had yet to be released at the time of this writing, housing data from the 2000 Census shows considerable upward socioeconomic movement, as many Hmong settled into stable or more lucrative jobs. 54 percent of Hmong owned their homes by 2000, reported the *Minneapolis Star-Tribune* newspaper. While homeownership was low in California at just 19.3 percent, it was around 55 to 60 percent in states like Minnesota, Wisconsin, Michigan, and North Carolina.

Culture

Traditionally, the Hmong favor large families with many children. Some of this can be explained by the Hmong's traditional farming roots. As a result, Hmong households average more than six persons per house or apartment in Minnesota and Wisconsin, compared to about 2.5 persons among the entire population. This helps explain the huge Hmong American population growth between 1990 and 2000, despite the decline in refugee admissions after 1994. These demographic trends suggest the Hmong population will continue to be among the fastest growing Asian group in the United States in the coming decades.

The large number of Hmong children also makes the population very youthful. Around half or more of the Hmong in California, Minnesota, Wisconsin, North Carolina, and Michigan were under 18 years old in 2000—compared to about a quarter within the general population.

The Hmong are a fairly tight-knit group; many community leaders are old clan leaders or politicians from Laos and are their descendents and relatives. For instance, the Hmong general Vang Pao, who commanded the Hmong forces fighting against the Communist North Vietnamese, remains a political leader for many Hmong in America. After escaping Laos, Vang Pao moved to Orange County, California, and helped found a leading Hmong organization, Lao Family Community. Lao Family Community has branches nationwide, many of them run by people close to Vang Pao or his actual relatives.

Still, there is a new generation of Hmong leaders emerging. They are young, well-educated, and not necessarily willing to be as beholden to old loyalties based on clan affiliation. Cleaved along this generational divide, the younger leaders support the reform of some aspects of Hmong culture that may clash with American customs. For instance, Hmong womens' groups have campaigned against polygamy, domestic violence, and teenage brides—not common but not unheard of among more traditional Hmong. Other leaders are trying to tackle the increasing number of Hmong youth being lured into gangs.

And others are trying to encourage Hmong entrepreneurship, a traditional route to the middle-class for immigrants but one less common with the Hmong. Vang Pao, for instance, has established a program with St. Thomas University in St. Paul to provide technical assistance to Hmong small businesspeople. While Hmong Americans certainly face a number of challenges, they are moving forward into a brighter future.

—Mark E. Pfeifer

Laotian Americans: You're From Where?

Laotian Americans are a very diverse group of people, like the geography of their home country, which is simultaneously tropical and mountainous. Laos is approximately the size of Great Britain, but unlike that island nation, Laos is sparsely populated and landlocked, wedged between Burma (Myanmar), Cambodia, China, Thailand, and Vietnam. While usage standards differ, one increasingly popular trend is to use the term "Laotian" to refer to all people from Laos, regardless of their ethnicity. Since another section of this chapter focuses exclusively on Hmong Americans, who are predominantly from Laos, this section focuses on all of the other Laotian American groups.

As this short piece makes clear, Laotian Americans continue to be diverse in practically every respect: they speak several different languages in the home, follow many different religions, are dispersed throughout the United States, and fill niches at every point along the socioeconomic scale.

History and Culture

According to the 2000 Census, 198,203 Laotian Americans (not including Hmong, but including mixed-race and mixed-ethnicity Laotians) live throughout the United States. Nearly all of them either arrived in this country as refugees or are the children of refugees. Laotian refugees began to arrive in 1975, when the Communist Pathet Lao defeated the U.S.-supported government of Laos. Resettlement in the U.S. increased dramatically in the late 1970s and 1980s, after hundreds of thousands of Laotians fled across the Mekong River to Thailand seeking safety in refugee camps.

Resettled refugees from Laos are extremely diverse in terms of culture and language. The dominant group are the Lao Loum, or Lowland Lao, who make up seven-tenths of the population back in Laos. But there are many ethnic minority groups, including the Hmong, most of whom come from upland areas, thus earning them the broad label, Highland Lao.

One such ethnic minority is the Khmu, from the highlands of northern Laos, who are one of the smallest refugee groups in the United States. An estimated half million Khmu live in the mountainous regions of northern Thailand, northern Laos, northwestern Vietnam, and southwestern China. The ancient homeland of the Khmu is thought to be the area around the city of Luang Prabang in northern Laos. Today, about 4,000 Khmu live in the United States. More than half live in California, in tight-knit communities around the San Francisco Bay area and in Stockton.

Forced to flee conflict many times, the Thaidam people are sometimes referred to as "professional refugees." Uprooted from northern Vietnam in 1954 when the French were defeated, the Thaidam fled to Laos where they lived for only twenty years before seeking asylum again in 1975. About 3,000 Thaidam live in the United States, primarily in Iowa. With a warm welcome from the people of Iowa, the first group of Thaidam came to Des Moines and others quickly followed. Des Moines soon became known as the "free capital of the Thaidam people." Ethnically and linguistically, the Thaidam are related to the Lao and other "Tai" groups.

Community challenges as refugees

Because of their refugee status, Laotian Americans face many issues and challenges. Having been exiled from their country to start their lives over again, many Laotians are still facing economic hardship, lack of higher learning opportunities, lack of resources, and lack of cultural traditions, values, and language from their homeland. These issues have led to many problems that the community still faces today, namely juvenile delinquency, unemployment, and intergenerational differences.

As for the Iu-Mein (or Yao) ethnic group, an estimated 20,000 arrived in the United States beginning in 1981. Originally from China, the subsistence-farming Iu-Mien lived in small, mountain communities in Laos. Like the Hmong, they became targets of the Pathet Lao because of their participation with Americans in the "secret war" in Laos. This group arrived without a written language, little exposure to wage labor, and very little experience with formal schooling.

Because of these pre-existing conditions, many Iu-Mien lack the type of skills that today's workforce requires. They have to settle for jobs that require minimal skills to no skills at all, and as a result, they must double their time, or work two jobs just trying to make ends meet. One major consequence is that the children are left at home with little or no supervision. These children consequently suffer academically, because help is unavailable to them in their home environments. Because formal schooling is still a new concept to many of these ex-refugees, the concept of education and educational resources is far out of reach and will remain so unless something is done to introduce the importance of formal education to them. Much more needs to be done in order for these parents, and the Laotian community as a whole, to realize that success in education is a family journey, not just one child or one student's path.

Another current problem in the community is the high rate of Laotian American youth going to prison, reportedly the highest rate among all Southeast Asian youth. Many reasons can be cited for this problem, but lack of parental involvement is a major factor.

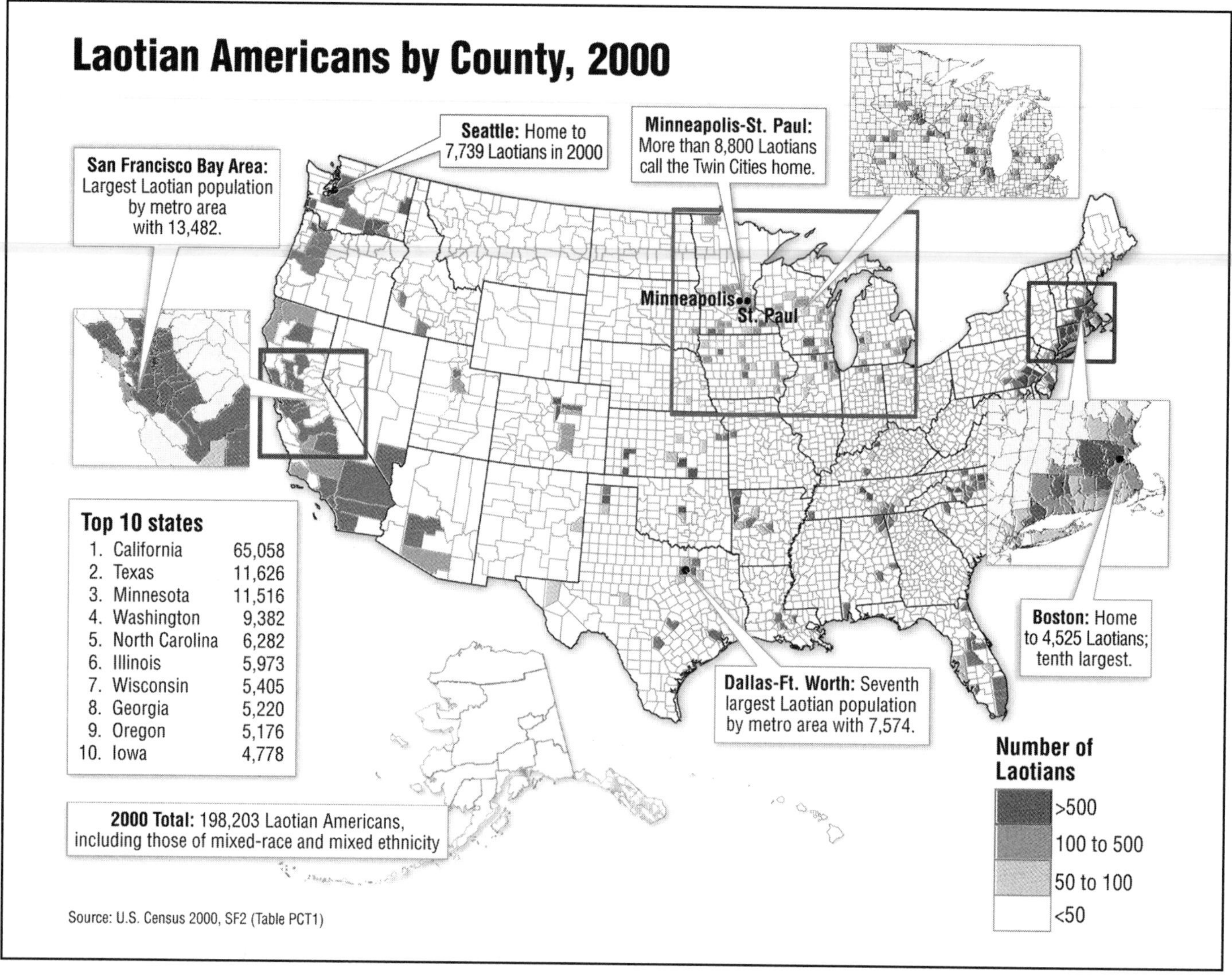

Grassroots network for educational success

A total of 105,477 refugees arrived in the United States from Laos between 1979 and 1981, so federally-funded mutual assistance centers throughout the country were formed for these "first wave" refugees; however, many of these centers eventually closed due to lack of funding. Then from 1986 to 1989, a total of 52,864 "second wave" Laotians arrived. Since many mutual assistance centers no longer exist, many older Laotian American immigrants have returned to the community to establish grassroots organizations to help more recent Laotian immigrants. Currently, many non-profit organizations, such as the Southeast Asian Resources Action Center (SEARAC), Laotian American National Alliance, and the Lao American Women Association are playing key roles in the continuous support and advocacy for Laotian Americans.

Regardless of the initial challenges of adapting to a new country, many Laotians are able to find a means of fulfilling their educational goals, managing to overcome obstacles to higher learning. The student network database from the *Lao Vision* magazine website documents and profiles many success stories. Take Soulinhakhath Steve Arounsack who has succeeded despite having very little parental involvement or financial contribution. Through scholarship and grants, Arounsack has earned his bachelor and master's degree and is currently a Ph.D. student at the University of California, Davis. While some students have the ability to succeed, unfortunately not all students have the resources available to them to achieve higher learning—lack of financial resources remain a major challenge. As a result, many are forced, like their parents, to join the workforce with little or no skills, where they must work overtime just to make ends meet. Higher education and gainful employment are still a rare commodity in the Laotian American community, bringing the "model minority" fallacy to light.

Most young refugees or children of refugees attribute their success to a growing network of Laotian Student

Associations at college campuses. These associations provide academic support as well as a strong network of students who share similar cultural experiences. Student and professional groups are also influential, servicing the Laotian community. Satjadham (SJD), a Lao literary group on the Internet, promotes culture, tradition, and language through classical and new literature of Laos to first-generation Laotian Americans. SJD boasts more than 100 members—many are refugees or children of refugees, holding advanced degrees. *Lao Vision* magazine, founded by Kag Khetsavanh (a refugee himself) acts as a forum for educational, intergenerational, cultural, and traditional discussion for younger or first-generation Laotian Americans in the United States.

Maintaining cultural identity

One concern that the community now faces is declining cultural practices—which include traditions, values, and language—among a newer generation of Laotian Americans dispersed throughout the country. The 2000 Census figures show just how scattered the Laotian American community is. Predictably, the largest states are California, with around 65,000 Laotians and Texas, with nearly 12,000. But there are many Laotians scattered in the Midwest (Minnesota, Illinois, Wisconsin, and Iowa), and southern states like Georgia and North Carolina. This dispersal challenges a traditionally concentrated and inclusive community. Such Laotian American enclaves now exist, though still rare, in those states with a greater number of Laotian Americans, such as New Iberia in Louisiana, San Diego and Fresno in California, and the Washington D.C. metropolitan area.

The traditional Laotian American family extends beyond a nuclear one, with grandparents and elders serving as respected household leaders. The term "immediate family" includes everyone whose bloodline can be traced within the family. The grandparents, and in some cases, great-grandparents, act as a channel of communication, teaching culture, tradition, and language to the next generation within the extended family structure. Elders continue to pass down many folktales and stories to first generation Laotian Americans through oral tradition, an important aspect of Laotian culture. The oral culture is a significant teaching tool for the elders because many can only speak, but not write, in their own language; so telling *nitaan* (folklores and fables) is their way of sharing their wisdom and learning with younger family members.

Because heritage, culture, and language serve as solid family foundations, the widening cultural gap between older and younger generations has had a significant effect on family structure. Parent-child communication is directly linked to success in society and how cultural traditions and values are passed down. But language barriers between Laotian-speaking parents and their English-speaking children are making them unable to share their unique Laotian and American experiences with each other.

Most Lowland Lao practiced Theravadha Buddhism in Laos. It's a practice they have carried on in the United States, one which has been very helpful for community-building purposes. The Laotian community in the Washington D.C. area for example, gathers at Watlao Buddhavong (Lao Buddhist Temple), in Catlett, Virginia, to celebrate Buddhist holidays and rites. Thousands of Laotians across the nation gather there annually to celebrate Pimai (Lao New Year) in April and the Laotian national independence holiday, which occurs on July 19th. These temples provide a place for interaction among different generations of Laotian Americans and offer weekend language school and other classes like classical dance and music. Because the Lowland Lao have a long-established written language and a history of formal education through Buddhist temples, these classes are merely a continuation of the tradition of learning via temple teaching.

While embracing a new life in the United States, many Laotian Americans continue strictly to practice Laotian traditions through their wedding ceremonies, New Year celebrations, and Buddhist festivals and rites in their daily lives.

Conclusion

From 1975 to 1999, a total of 241,892 Laotian refugees have arrived in the United States. Because Laotian American settlement remains relatively new, more resources and assistance are needed in order for the community to successfully adapt to mainstream society. More importantly, social scientists and other professionals must make the distinction between those who are refugees and those who are immigrants. Different data should be collected, and other factors must be considered before this group can be or should be put on the same page as other Asian Pacific Americans. Social issues, such as gainful employment, higher learning, and familial harmony begin with education, resources, and opportunities for Laotian American community. The "know-how" and "show-me-how" must be shared within the community and within the society.

Ethnic division among Laotian Americans signifies the rich culture and abundant diversity. While embracing the differences, Laotian Americans must realize that one unified voice is a key to social, educational, and political advancement in the United States. As a people of a shared native land in a new nation, they must question, challenge, and demand their rights and privileges through this unified voice. Let's start with the Census count of Laotian Americans, which many of us believe is an undercount. Then add a new ethnic category to the 2010 Census, where Laotian Americans will be allowed to check the same box and specify their ethnicity, i.e. "Laotian American, Lowland Lao ethnicity." This would lead to an accurate count and fair representation of the ethnic diversity of Laotian Americans.

Within the grassroots community, it's also important that all generations of Laotian Americans—past, present, and future—focus on the common issues that face the community. Laotian ethnic diversity aside, one voice will be stronger than the myriad of voices that exist in the community today.

—Toon Phapphayboun, with contribution from Max Niedzwiecki of the Southeast Asia Resource Action Center.

Unveiling the Face of Invisibility: Exploring the Thai American Experience

When you think of "Thailand," what comes to mind? The image of the "Land of Smiles?" The sex industry? Spicy food? It is important that dominant perceptions are challenged and redefined by exploring the ethnic-specific experiences and diversities within the Thai American community. The unique history of Thai immigrants and their struggle for legitimacy within the Asian Pacific American coalition and the mainstream culture will offer a deeper understanding of Thai Americans.

Unlike the more established Asian ethnic groups such as the Chinese and Japanese communities, who first began immigrating in the late nineteenth century, the majority of Thai Americans came to the United States after the passage of the 1965 Immigration Act eliminated the national origins quota system and enabled more Asians to enter the United States. About 27 percent of all Thai Americans came prior to 1975.

Early and contemporary immigration patterns

Between 1965 and 1975, students and professionals made up the first wave of Thai immigrants. The majority of the students sought a Western education because university degrees would mean social advancement in Thailand. The first wave of Thai immigrants settled predominantly east of the city of Hollywood near Los Angeles and other areas of Los Angeles County.

While many Thai immigrants did return to Thailand, the myth of the "American Dream" continued to lure many other Thai immigrants to America. During the second wave, between 1970 and 1980, public protests against the military dictatorship led many Thais to immigrate to other countries such as the United States. Along with the rising political tension, Thailand experienced increasing U.S. presence during the Vietnam War. Consequently, many Thai women married American servicemen who were stationed on military bases in Thailand, which were not removed until 1976. In addition, thousands of Thai nurses responded to the U.S. demand for nurses during this decade and brought their children with them.

The third wave of Thai immigration spans from 1980 to the present, as more students as well as professionals come to America. Because of the decreasing economic opportunities in Thailand, many Thais, especially from rural areas, entered the United States as "undocumented" immigrants and became the new "cheap labor" source in such labor-intensive industries as garment sweatshops.

The birth of Thai Town and other Thai communities

According to a study conducted by the Thai Community Development Center (CDC), there are about 50,000 Thais living and working in Southern California. The largest Thai American community is in Los Angeles, with about 22,000 Thais. In Southern California, Thai families can find a support network and seek social services from churches such as the Wat Thai Buddhist Temple in North Hollywood and community centers like the Thai CDC. To accommodate the growing numbers of Thai immigrants in Los Angeles, the Royal Thai Consulate was established in 1980 to help with immigration policies and legal services.

There are growing numbers of Thai people uncounted by the U.S. Census: undocumented Thais and those who are mixed races (Laotian-Thai, Chinese-Thai, Cambodian-Thai) who may be classified as "Other Asian." Thus, exact figures of Thais in the United States are unknown. According to the 2000 Census, there are 150,283 Thais, including those who reported being Thai mixed with another Asian ethnicity (i.e. Chinese-Thai) or another race such as white or black—or just about one percent of all APAs.

The Thai American community is growing more dispersed, with an emerging population of Thais on the East Coast, particularly in New Jersey. Many Thai immigrants are students and plan to get their education at Ivy League universities, whereas others have established Thai restaurants and markets. Like other Asian immigrants, many first-generation Thais start their own businesses, such as in the restaurant industry. As such, Thai immigrants choose an alternative path of socioeconomic mobility and develop a kind of

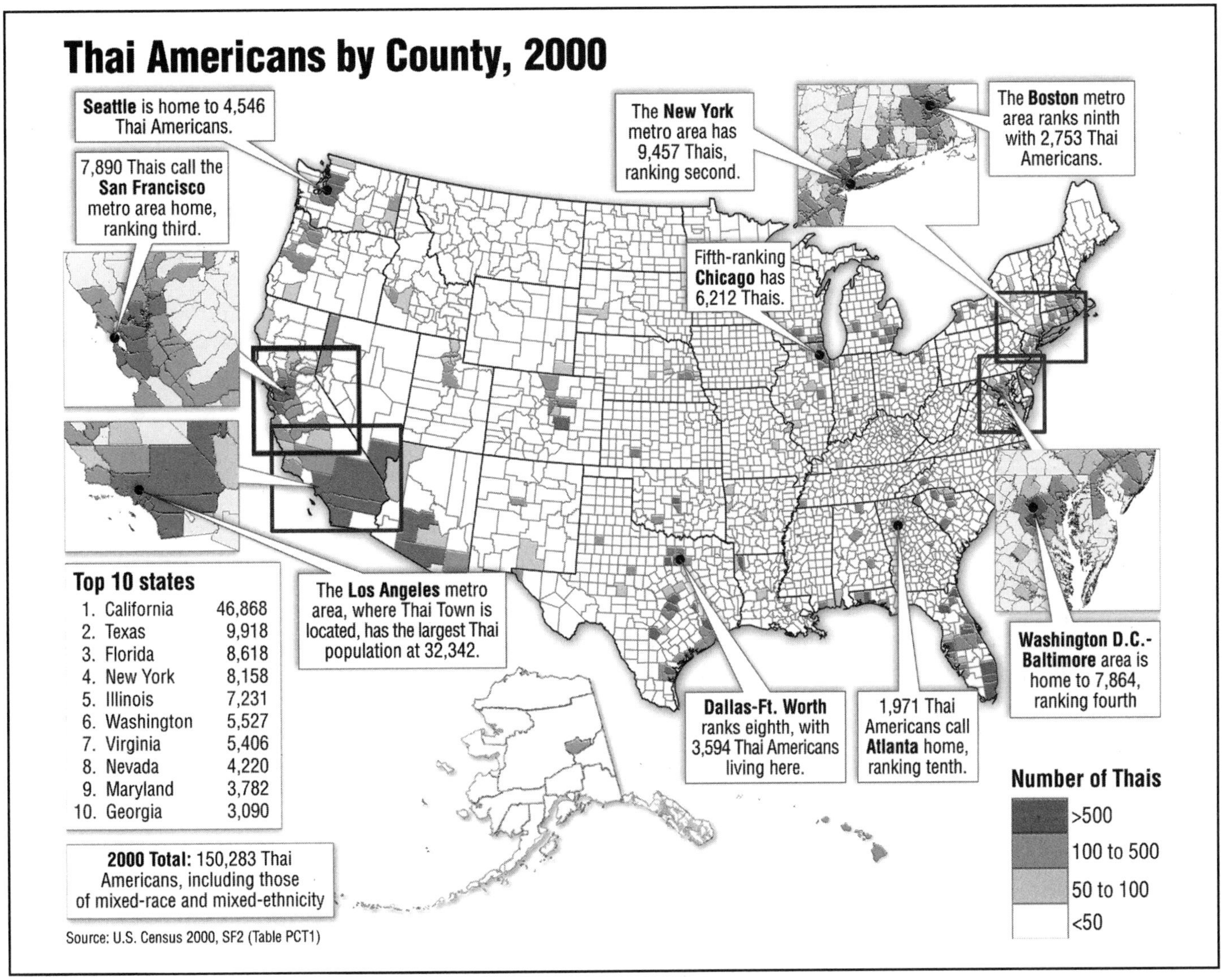

Thai Americans by County, 2000

Seattle is home to 4,546 Thai Americans.

7,890 Thais call the **San Francisco** metro area home, ranking third.

The **New York** metro area has 9,457 Thais, ranking second.

The **Boston** metro area ranks ninth with 2,753 Thai Americans.

Fifth-ranking **Chicago** has 6,212 Thais.

The **Los Angeles** metro area, where Thai Town is located, has the largest Thai population at 32,342.

Dallas-Ft. Worth ranks eighth, with 3,594 Thai Americans living here.

1,971 Thai Americans call **Atlanta** home, ranking tenth.

Washington D.C.-Baltimore area is home to 7,864, ranking fourth

Top 10 states

1.	California	46,868
2.	Texas	9,918
3.	Florida	8,618
4.	New York	8,158
5.	Illinois	7,231
6.	Washington	5,527
7.	Virginia	5,406
8.	Nevada	4,220
9.	Maryland	3,782
10.	Georgia	3,090

2000 Total: 150,283 Thai Americans, including those of mixed-race and mixed-ethnicity

Number of Thais
>500
100 to 500
50 to 100
<50

Source: U.S. Census 2000, SF2 (Table PCT1)

"ethnic enclave economy," a concept formulated by scholars Alejandro Portes and Min Zhou.

Given the fact that Thais in the United States are a relatively new community, how do Thai Americans figure in the larger APA coalition? Thai Americans are making strides to claim a sense of legitimacy and visibility through creation of Thai Town and community organizations. Located between Normandie and Western Avenues in Los Angeles, Thai Town was officially established in October 1999 and offers both the Thai community and visitors restaurants, entertainment, local businesses, and shopping.

Annually, the Thai community comes together to enjoy Thai Culture Day, which takes place in Thai Town on the last Sunday in September and celebrate with a parade of native costumes, art exhibits, and demonstrations of *muay Thai* (or Thai kick-boxing). One of the most important aspects of "Thai Town" is the economic possibilities it has provided for the Thai people. Chancee Martorell, director of Thai CDC, says the organization is assisting twenty-five Thais from the working-poor class to start their own businesses in Thai Town.

Preserving culture in America

Many older Thais have shared Thai culture with their children by involving them in such activities as Songkran (the water festival in April) and celebration of the King and Queen's birthdays (November and August, respectively) at the Wat Thai Buddhist Temple. In addition to being a place of worship for about 90 percent of Thais in Southern California, the Wat Thai Buddhist Temple serves as a space where the Thai second generation can explore their connection with their ancestral homeland. The temple provides workshops and classes on Thai language, dance, and the arts.

Other temples have emerged to serve the Thai families dispersed throughout

Southern California. The Buddhist Temple of America located in Ontario, California, was founded by my late father, Dr. Zhalermwudh Thongthiraj, who believed in fostering Thai unity and spreading Buddhist teachings to fellow Thais as well as non-Thais interested in learning about Buddhism.

Besides churches, there is an emerging leadership network among Thais that is making significant steps to bringing more visibility to the Thai American community. Established in 1994, the Thai CDC has worked passionately to empower and improve the working conditions of low-income Thais, such as in the 1995 El Monte Sweatshop case, in which 72 undocumented Thai immigrants were forced to sew clothes in slave-like conditions for up to 84 hours a week, as well as to advocate humane labor and immigration policies. The Thai CDC has become a key factor to increasing the legitimacy of Thai Americans, particularly in Southern California, by providing social and legal services to the Thai people, and developing leadership among Thai Americans through community service.

Photo: Corky Lee

A relatively new community in the United States, Thai Americans are making efforts to maintain a sense of cultural identity while finding a place for themselves in American society.

What has also helped bring more legitimacy and visibility to Thai Americans is the development of the "Thai American Experience" class at UCLA, the first of its kind in the nation. A few of the challenges of this course are 1) to enable Thai Americans to re-connect to their "native" or "ancestral" heritage and redefine what it means to be a "Thai American," "Thai Chinese," or "Thai Filipino" and 2) to acknowledge the historical experiences of Thai Americans not just as victims of institutional discrimination (e.g., the 1917 Immigration Law barred the immigration of those living in the "Asiatic Barred Zone" which included Thailand, then known as "Siam"), but also as potential agents of social change.

The future of the Thai community

As the Thai American community continues to grow in numbers and visibility, there are still prospects and challenges for Thai Americans to mainstream into American society. The Thai CDC is working in overdrive to ensure greater access to social services and economic opportunities, even taking calls from Thai people in Alaska. Director Martorell hopes the Thai CDC will work with Los Angeles city officials to "beautify" Thai Town—adding cultural symbols and a fountain in front of the Thai shopping plaza—as well as to continue their community economic development projects. The Thai CDC plans to work together with the Asian Pacific Islander Small Business Program to help the most in-need entrepreneurs through workshops and individualized business counseling. Thus, the future of the "Thai American" community lies in creating more leadership and educating others about ethnic-specific issues impacting the Thai people.

The Thai American community is part of the larger APA coalition and together, all Asian ethnic groups, in direct and subtle ways, challenge the stigma of being "perpetual foreigners," defined by mainstream representation of Asians as un-American and inassimilable.

—*Rahpee Thongthiraj*

New Communities and New Challenges

South Asian Americans have their origins in the present-day countries of Bangladesh, Bhutan, India, Nepal, Pakistan, and Sri Lanka. They have a long history of small and sporadic migration to the United States, but the immigration policy changes of the 1960s triggered an impressive movement of people from South Asia to the United States in the last three decades.

Collectively, people of South Asian origin constitute one of the largest Asian Pacific American populations, with Asian Indians alone ranking third in size among APAs. Individually, South Asian groups are dramatically smaller, yet each has experienced significant growth in the last decade. The number of Bangladeshi Americans, for example, increased nearly four times, from approximately 12,000 in 1990 to 57,412 (including multi-racial or multi-ethnic persons) in 2000. This chapter will delineate some of the historical and contemporary demographic features of South Asian Americans. It will focus on the less-studied groups, the Bangladeshi, Pakistani, Nepali, and Sri Lankan Americans.

Twentieth century immigration

The first measurable numbers of South Asians began arriving on the West Coast of the United States at the beginning of the 20th century. They formed one of the successive waves of Asians who made up workers in the developing West, building railroads, clearing and cultivating the rich agricultural lands of California, reclaiming the desert in the Southwest, and working in the lumber industry in Oregon and Washington. As with other Asian groups, South Asians were at first welcomed, but soon excluded by restrictions imposed at ports of entry and ultimately by legislation that limited Asian migration in 1917 and virtually ended it in 1924.

Photo: Corky Lee

The South Asian community in the United States has increased dramatically, with many immigrants reuniting with already-established relatives.

Between 1899 and 1924 immigration figures show that approximately 7,700 individuals whose "country of last permanent residence" was India entered the United States. Less than half of these immigrants remained in the United States. This group was comprised mainly of young or middle aged men. Only about a dozen women came from India during this period. A few hundred of the male immigrants did marry in the United States, mainly with Mexican immigrants or Mexican American women in California and

What comprises South Asia?

"South Asia" is a flexible term that refers to the geographic area that extends from Sri Lanka and the Indian subcontinent north to the borders of Burma, China, Afghanistan, and Iran. It commonly includes the countries of Bangladesh, Bhutan, India, Nepal, Pakistan, and Sri Lanka, which are linked together through language, culture, religion and a shared history. At the time of the earliest migrations of South Asians to America, India, Pakistan, and Bangladesh were part of British colonial India. When British rule ended in 1947, the region was divided into two independent countries: India, and East and West Pakistan. After a civil war in 1971, East Pakistan became the independent nation of Bangladesh. Bhutan, Nepal, and Sri Lanka (known as Ceylon until 1972) are counted among South Asian countries. Some studies also include the Maldives, a small island nation southwest of Sri Lanka, and Afghanistan, which shares a long border with Pakistan.

The term "South Asian American" is not widely used by individuals of South Asian origin. More often people identify themselves by country of origin such as Bangladeshi American or by linguistic-regional backgrounds such as Tamil, Bengali or Punjabi. Yet "South Asian" is frequently used by community activists and organizers addressing the common challenges that these groups face within their communities, as ethnic Americans, or as immigrants of color. The term also has currency among academics, policy analysts, and youth or student groups. Many of the latter use the term to forge solidarity and to acknowledge their shared cultural, historical, and linguistic roots.

The feasibility and efficacy of a collective South Asian identity or designation continues to be debated. In addition to historical, linguistic, and cultural connections, South Asian Americans often live in close proximity, occupy similar economic niches, belong to the same professional organizations and workers unions, and experience like challenges as they make a place for themselves in American society. Current scholarly studies frequently take an inclusive stance, making a serious effort to address wider South Asian American issues. Such collective works include a representation of South Asian American voices providing comparative perspectives on topics such as women's issues, politics, labor, and race. Many of these volumes include selections of art and literature (see list of sources at the back of this book for titles).

One major concern about using the "South Asian American" label is that it can easily become just another term for "Asian Indian American." Asian Indian numbers in the United States, and in South Asia for that matter, overwhelm and often obscure other groups from the region. In order to maintain some presence and visibility, many South Asian American groups prefer to maintain and rally around their own national identity. Still, South Asian American is likely to remain one of the layers of identity that individuals draw upon. It will continue to possess cultural meaning, as well as convey political positioning in much the same way that Asian Pacific American has come to be used.

—Jane Singh

the Southwest. Many South Asian immigrants remained single, in part, because of the anti-miscegenation laws that prohibited marriages across racial or color lines.

In spite of their small numbers, the first wave of immigrants built a resilient community that managed to organize itself both socially and politically. The majority of these immigrants came from a northern province of British India, the Punjab, an area that today straddles both India and Pakistan. Common language, culture, and reasonably close proximity on the West Coast enabled them to establish religious, social, and political institutions in places such as Stockton and San Francisco in California and Vancouver in the province of British Columbia in western Canada.

During this period, the first individuals from present-day Sri Lanka and Bangladesh arrived in very small numbers. Yamau Kira, a native of Ceylon, came to the United States in 1913. He opened one of first South Asian restaurants in New York City, the Ceylon-India Inn. By the 1940s, merchant seamen from what is now Bangladesh began settling in the states of New York and New Jersey. They established the first Pakistani American Association in New York in 1947.

After the Immigration Act of 1924, South Asian migration was a mere trickle. The first major change took place in 1946 when the United States Congress passed the Luce-Cellar Bill that made Indian immigrants eligible for naturalization, provided for family reunification, and established an annual quota of 100 new immigrants from India. The following year, the newly formulated countries of India and Pakistan won independence from Britain. The 1946 provisions were extended to other South Asian countries as well. By 1952, there were further changes in United States immigration law, but the number of new arrivals from South Asia remained insignificant until the racially-biased national origins quotas were abolished in 1965.

Post-1965 changes

The decades-long civil rights movement and shifting foreign policy led to the Hart-Cellar Act, which eliminated the racial criteria that had limited Asian migration. South Asian numbers began to increase. In 1965, immigration records show 769 South Asians entering the United States. By 1970 the numbers were 11,884 and by 1980 they reached 27,912. Among South Asians, Indians and Pakistanis showed the most dramatic changes with 187 Pakistanis admitted in 1965 and 4,265 in 1980. Indian immigrants numbered 582 in 1965 and 22,607 in 1980. In 1980, South Asians made up 12.8 percent of all Asian immigrants admitted.

The provisions of the 1965 law focused on both family reunification and manpower needs in the United States. In the immediate decade following immigration reforms, the majority of South Asians entered the United States as professionals and skilled workers. These immigrants were allowed to bring their spouses and underage children. Others, who had come during the 1950s and 1960s on a temporary basis as students or scholars, were able to convert their visas to permanent resident status.

By the late 1970s, domestic policy changes made it more difficult for foreign-trained physicians and other professionals such as engineers to qualify for admission to the United States. However, South Asian migration maintained a steady pace due to the increase of individuals immigrating under family preference categories. Those who had come earlier were now sponsoring their parents, siblings and their respective families.

Population

The South Asian population in the United States has grown substantially during the last three decades. Census figures show over 407,252 South Asian Americans in 1980, 919,626 in 1990, and approximately 2.2 million in 2000. During the 1990s alone, nearly every South Asian group more than doubled in size. When counted "alone or in combination with other races," Pakistani Americans numbers grew by 151.1 percent, Sri Lankans by 124.1 percent, and Bangladeshis by 385 percent. By comparison, the overall "alone or in combination" APA population increased 72.2 percent. With the exception of Asian Indians, South Asian population figures are still relatively small, but the sustained pattern of growth over the last two decades is striking.

Demographic variations

South Asian migration and settlement patterns show both parallels and divergences. It is important to recognize the distinctive patterns of each group to appreciate the particular factors impacting on South Asians in their movement to the United States, their distribution within the United States, and the demographic characteristics that shape each group.

Largest Sri Lankan Populations, 2000

Top 5 metropolitan areas	
L.A.	5,194
New York	4,558
Washington D.C.	2,135
S.F. Bay area	1,275
Boston	729

Top 5 states	
California	7,212
New York	3,480
Maryland	1,430
Texas	1,384
New Jersey	1,357
TOTAL	**24,587**

Note: There are 20 states with less than 100 Sri Lankans.

Source: U.S. Census Bureau, Census 2000 Summary File 2 (PCT1)

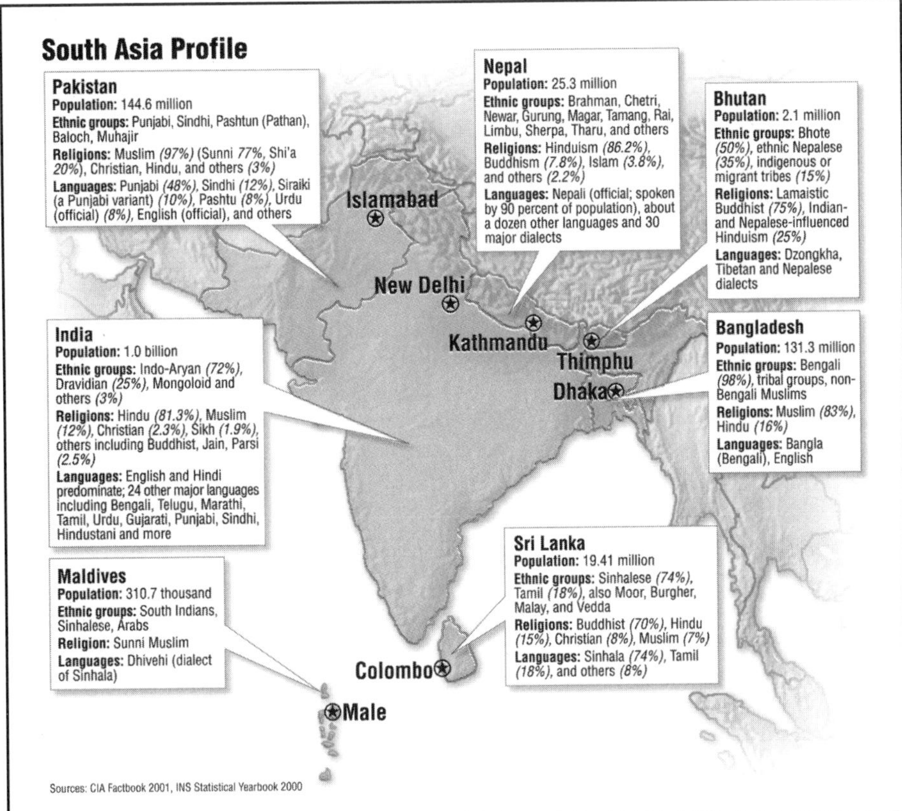

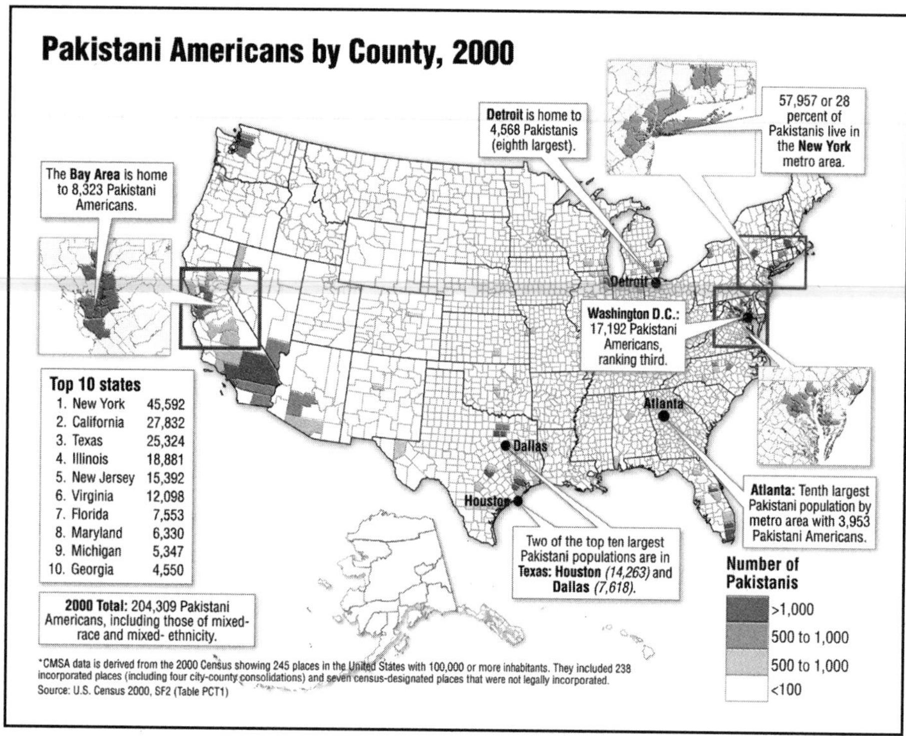

Bangladeshi Americans constituted the fastest-growing group among all Asians during the last decade. Still relatively small, the current growth rates herald the possibility of significant growth in the future. Of the 7,215 Bangladeshis who were admitted in 2000, 65 percent came as relatives of existing U.S. residents, 9.4 percent were allowed in for job reasons, and 23.8 percent came in the diversity program. The diversity category is the result of the 1990 Immigration Act's lottery program, instituted to enable and encourage immigration from countries that were not already sending large numbers.

Bangladeshis only began to appear in United States immigration figures after 1971, when Bangladesh became an independent nation. Prior to this time, from the 1950s and onward, they had been counted as Pakistanis and had entered mainly as students. In the 1970s and 1980s, they entered primarily as professionals and skilled workers but also as students. By 1990, there were increasing socioeconomic differences within this group as more family members, with different educational levels, began to arrive. The 1990 Immigration Lottery program also brought people from more diverse backgrounds

Bangladeshi Americans work a wide range of occupational niches. Beyond those who have professional or skilled jobs, many have gone into small businesses. In New York, where there is the highest concentration of Bangladeshi Americans, a majority work in the restaurant and transport industries. A 1991 survey showed that Bangladeshi Americans applied for over ten percent of the driving permits for taxis, just ahead of Asian Indians who made up 9.9 percent of the applicants, according to an article in the journal *Migration World*. In California, Bangladeshis can be found in the hi-tech industry working at all wage levels, from engineers and company owners to production line workers.

Nearly fifty two percent of Bangladeshi Americans reside in New York. Other concentrations are in California, Texas, New Jersey, Michigan, and Virginia. Growth and dispersion of the community is occurring—in Georgia, the Bangladeshi population grew from 135 in 1990 to 1,283 in 2000. In another possible population shift, Bangladeshi Americans have been moving from New York to Michigan in large numbers to take jobs in small factories in the Detroit area that produce automobile parts.

People from present-day Pakistan were among the first South Asians to immigrate to the United States. Many of these early arrivals married and settled on the West Coast, particularly in California, where there are families who trace their roots back to the early 1900s. After Pakistan became an independent nation in 1947, there were

South Asian Immigration to United States, 1990-2000

YEAR	BANGLADESH	BHUTAN	MALDIVES	INDIA	PAKISTAN	NEPAL	SRI LANKA	TOTAL
1990	4,252	1	0	30,667	9,729	184	976	**45,809**
1991	10,676	2	1	45,064	20,355	174	1,377	**77,649**
1992	3,740	1	0	36,755	10,214	212	1,081	**52,003**
1993	3,291	2	2	40,121	8,927	257	1,109	**53,709**
1994	3,434	2	0	34,921	8,698	257	989	**48,301**
1995	6,072	2	1	34,748	9,774	312	960	**51,869**
1996	8,221	8	1	44,859	12,519	431	1,277	**67,316**
1997	8,681	6	1	38,071	12,967	447	1,128	**61,301**
1998	8,621	6	1	36,482	13,094	476	1,085	**59,765**
1999	6,046	4	0	30,237	13,496	453	903	**51,139**
2000	7,215	3	1	42,046	14,535	617	1,123	**65,540**
TOTAL	**70,249**	**37**	**8**	**413,971**	**134,308**	**3,820**	**12,008**	**634,401**
% OF TOTAL	**11.1%**	**0%**	**0%**	**65.3%**	**21.2%**	**0.6%**	**1.9%**	**100%**

Source: Statistical Yearbook 2000, INS (Table 3)

a handful of individuals who came under the family reunification provisions of United States immigration law. More Pakistanis came as students from the 1950s to the early 1960s.

After 1965, Pakistanis entered as professional and skilled workers, as did other South Asians. Pakistanis continued to come on temporary student visas as well, a pattern which persisted into the last decade. Many student visa holders eventually apply to stay permanently in the United States due to the dim economic prospects back in their home country. In 1990, over 4,000 students came from Pakistan.

During the 1990s, Pakistani American numbers grew by 88.7 percent when counted alone or 151.1 percent when counted "in combination with other races." In 2000, 73 percent of new Pakistani immigrants entered the United States through family preference categories, 13.6 percent through employment-related preferences, and 12.1 percent under the diversity program. Among immigrants whose visas were adjusted to permanent residents in 2000, there were 257 students, 730 temporary workers, and 23 refugees.

The Pakistani American community is socio-economically diverse. Similar to other South Asians, this group shows a broad range of educational attainment. The 1990 Census recorded that 25.3 percent of Pakistani Americans had four years of college and 25.4 percent had post-graduate degrees. By comparison, the overall APA numbers with the same degrees were 22.7 percent and 13.9 percent, respectively. On the other end, the 1990 Census revealed that 15.1 percent of Pakistani Americans were high school graduates only and 16.6 percent did not have high school diplomas. In terms of language ability, 30.1 percent were categorized as not speaking English "very well" and 14 percent as linguistically isolated, or unable to speak English. Income levels for both U.S. and foreign-born Pakistanis showed that 12.2 percent were below the poverty line in 1990.

Photo: Corky Lee

The New York metropolitan area is home to the largest concentration of Pakistani Americans in the United States.

Pakistani Americans have varied occupations. According to the 1990 Census, 33.5 percent held managerial and professional positions, 35.2 percent worked in technical, sales, or administrative positions, 10.2 percent had service jobs, and 20.5 percent worked in areas such as production, fabrication and as laborers. Self-employment accounted for 7.9 percent. In 1990, 67.9 percent of working age Pakistani Americans were in the labor force, comparable to the overall APA rate of 67.4 percent and national rate of 65.3 percent.

As the tenth-largest APA community, Pakistani Americans are widely distributed across the country. Over 48 percent of Pakistani Americans live in New York, California, and Texas, with 22.3 percent in New York and 13.6 percent in California. The Texan population grew 232 percent in the last decade, from 7,627 to 25,324. Other states such as North Carolina and Georgia had even faster growth, at rates of 369 percent and 264 percent, respectively.

Sri Lankan Americans make up one of the smaller South Asian communities, with approximately 25,000 individuals recorded in the last census. Concentrated in California, their numbers went from 3,385 in 1990 to 7,212 in 2000. Other states where they reside in some numbers include New York, Maryland, Texas and New Jersey. The three metropolitan centers with the most Sri Lankan Americans are, in order, Los Angeles, New York, and Washington D.C.

As with other South Asian groups, Sri Lankan numbers increased steadily after 1965. In the 1980 Census, just 2,923 Sri Lankans were counted. This number grew to 10,970 in 1990. Civil war in Sri Lanka since the early 1980s prevented many individuals visiting the United States from returning home. Many students and others on temporary visas were allowed to stay as permanent residents. However, only nine Sri Lankans fleeing the war between 1980 and 1990

Will Sept. 11 unify or divide the South Asian community?

On the bleak streets of Jersey City, Indian residents of the once-blighted and still struggling city-center became familiar with a steady stream of racial hatred beginning in 1986 that lasted for almost a year. The assaults took the forms of slurs, violent threats, graffiti, and, in some cases, chasing and shoving people as they walked the streets.

"We'd be in the car, and some white person walking by would slap the hood and yell, 'Damn Hindus!' Or, little kids would run up ... and yell, 'Damn, Hindu!' and run away," remembers Raahi Reddy, who lived as a teenager in Jersey City with her family during what became known as the "Dotbuster attacks." A group inciting the violence called itself "The Dotbusters," in reference to the red *bindi*, traditionally worn by Indian women on their foreheads.

The racial hostilities came to a head when one Indian man was beaten to death and another one severely injured in two separate attacks. The "Dotbusters" episode later came to represent a critical moment in shaping the Indian American community's racial and political consciousness.

Almost two decades later, New Jersey is still a flashpoint in the South Asian American landscape. In 2002, Passaic County on the eastern edge of the state is one of the major holding sites for immigrant detainees caught in the post-Sept. 11 dragnet. At least 1,200 people have been arrested and held in INS detention or deported. Of these, about 40 percent are Pakistanis. Several hundred detainees of Middle Eastern and Muslim background are still being held in area jails.

"We saw extremely high and concentrated levels of state violence that our community has not seen before in this country. Immediately that state violence took local forms, manifested in racial violence and hate crimes against Arabs, Muslims, and South Asians," says Monami Maulik, a community organizer with Desis Rising Up and Moving (DRUM) in Jackson Heights. "For myself, living in this country for 20 years and doing immigrant organizing for the past six or seven years, it has been one of the most intense periods. I've never seen anything like it. I don't think my parents have either."

DRUM organizes poor and working class immigrants, many of them undocumented. In the past 15 years, this population of mostly low-income workers—taxi drivers, newsstand operators, domestic workers—has grown tremendously in New York City. They are the latest wave in what has been something of a sea change over the last two decades of South Asian immigration in America. From a predominantly professional, educated class of Indian emigrés post-1965, the flow of immigration has created a South Asian community of almost 800,000 in New York and 2.2 million nationwide—without counting undocumented residents who also make up an increasing number of the population. Also, many of the new immigrants are Pakistani and Bangladeshi as well as Indian.

"After the '80s you see South Asians in many walks of life, whereas before the stereotype was of doctors and engineers," says Tito Sinha, a New York lawyer and activist. "Demographic change allowed for new types of social and political activity. No longer was it just cultural associations or big fundraisers for political candidates, but people organizing around workplace issues and exploitation."

The earlier generation of immigrants, whose introduction to U.S. society was often smoothed by English fluency, high education, and professional jobs, tended to identify with their home country, caste, religious, and career affiliations. Most didn't see themselves as racial minorities in the sense of being placed in a hierarchy within American society, according to Madhulika Khandelwal, a professor of Asian American studies at Queens College.

were given asylum in the United States; the majority went to Canada, where many have settled in the Toronto area. With the 1991 changes in United States asylum laws, Sri Lankans seeking refugee status have been allowed to remain in the country while their cases are under review. Between 1991 and 1998, 321 Sri Lankan refugees became permanent U.S. residents.

In 2000, 44.4 percent of Sri Lankans entered the United States as relatives of existing residents or citizens, 32 percent in employment categories, and 21 percent in the diversity program. In the same year, 539 Sri Lankans entering on temporary visas were able to adjust their status to permanent resident. Among those were 70 students, 176 temporary workers, and 125 visitors for business or pleasure. There were no refugees admitted among those whose visas were adjusted to permanent residents, according to the INS tables for fiscal year 2000.

In the 2000 Census, Nepali Americans numbered 9,399 when counted "alone or in combination." Nepali annual immigration rose steadily from 184 in 1990 to 617 in 2000. In 2000, 40.6 percent of Nepalis came as relatives, 41.8 percent came through jobs, and 16.8 percent in the diversity category. 96 students and 70 temporary workers had their visas adjusted to "permanent resident" in 2000.

"In the last 10 years, a different kind of voice has emerged," Khandelwal says. "The U.S.-reared generation is much more aware of the American context, its racial and political demands about identity and social issues."

Khandelwal pegs the 1990s as a time when distinct strands began to take hold in the community fabric. Along with the younger generation stepping to maturity, women's leadership, queer identity, and other progressive voices became more prominent. Emerging emphasis on political struggle with social injustice, or on civic participation for more moderate groups, were part of the shift away from home-country divisions and toward a new South Asian identity.

This was the backdrop when the twin towers fell.

"For me it is very noticeable that 9/11 happens and suddenly South Asia is on the map," Khandelwal says. "This is the first time I saw the term in national media in such a big way."

Hundreds of hate crimes, including documented murders, and incidents of racial profiling or work discrimination were reported against South Asians in the months after Sept. 11. A disproportionate number of incidents were aimed at members of the 225,000 Sikh Indians in the United States, who were seemingly targeted due to the turbans and long beards the men traditionally wear. This despite the fact the Sikh religion is actually distinct from Islam (and Hinduism, for that matter). Meanwhile, Pakistanis were further impacted by INS detention.

"This is baptism by fire," says Nasir Gondal, president of the Council on American-Islamic Relations of New York. "The Pakistani community is not established or organized enough to deal with these kinds of demands."

An effective response to the current situation has had to confront such challenges as the still-deep class cleavages within the South Asian population, as well as the escalating tensions of the conflict between Pakistan and India over Kashmir. Reluctance to take a stand against post-Sept. 11 repression because of fear has also been a challenge in building a larger base of immigrant communities.

"I've heard people use as a rationale not to become involved the fact that these are immigration violators, so they don't deserve any rights," says Debasish Mishra, a member of South Asian Leaders of Tomorrow in New York City. "We have to stand up and take a principled stance. Regardless of whether these people are documented or undocumented, they are still part of our community."

On the flip side, the realization that no one is really protected against racial attack has also pushed more people to political awareness and activity. "There has been movement by more established groups, but it's difficult because it's new territory for some of them," says Sinha. "They're not used to the position of standing up for the community in this way, but more and more are realizing that they have to."

As the South Asian community grapples with new and urgent struggles against repression, the process itself of defining these issues will shape the next definitions of the community's identity, according to Khandelwal.

"It's a very important, crucial time for South Asians, Asian America, and the rest of America, because it's really about civil rights for everyone," she says. "By talking about South Asians in this context we are looking at the bigger picture."

—*Tram Nguyen*

The small group of Nepali Americans is linked across the United States by community organizations, newsletters, and bulletins. Besides a national group called the Nepalese American Council, the Nepal Embassy lists 21 regional organizations such as the Nepali Association of Oregon, which describes its goal as providing support and cultural context for the 150 Nepalis and their families who make their homes in Oregon and southern Washington.

Other South Asian groups

Some numbers are available for other groups counted among South Asians. In 2000, there were 212 Bhutanese and 51 Maldivians in the "alone or in combination" count. Few demographic details are available at this point about these particular populations. Among other groups of South Asian origin that come to the United States from the South Asian diaspora are immigrants from the Guyana, Surinam, the Caribbean and Fiji. Several of these communities, which include second generation-plus individuals along with new arrivals, constitute sizeable populations in different parts of the country. In New York, Indo-Caribbean American residential patterns and numbers are being taken into account in studies on reapportionment of New York State Assembly districts. These numbers are currently being extrapolated from the Census.

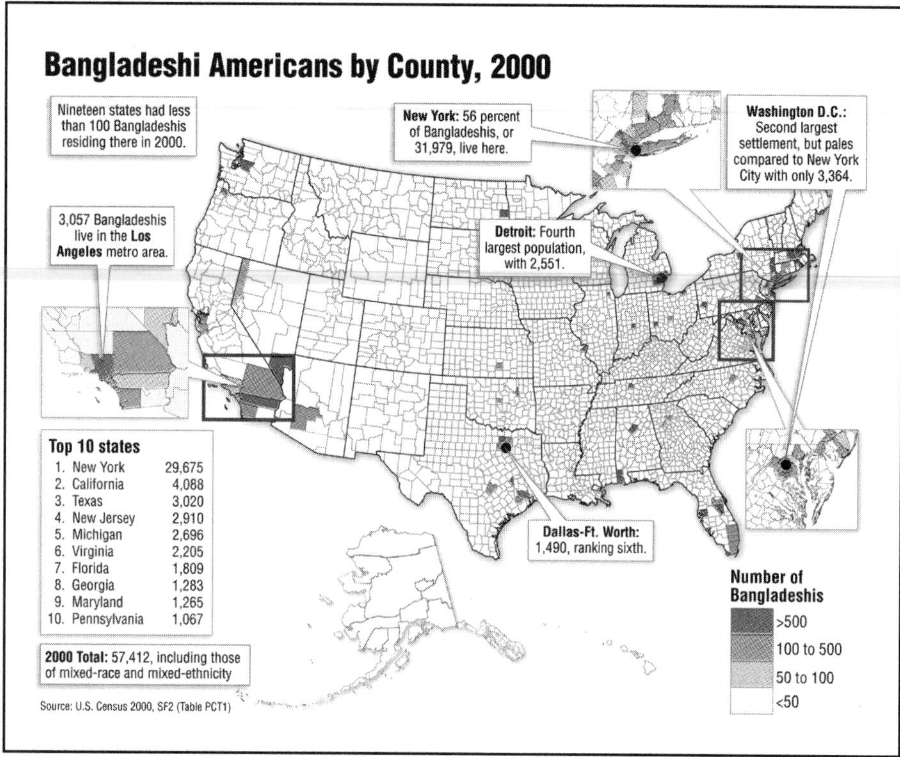

Trends and contemporary concerns

Preliminary figures from the 2000 Census show South Asian Americans demonstrating dynamic growth and settlement patterns during the last decade. Emerging data will provide a better profile on specific features of each group. Since most of the South Asian groups examined fall into the "Other Asians" category, their demographic characteristics often are left out of APA Census overviews and summaries. It is important that policymakers, community organizers, and scholars access and examine the data as they become available in order to develop a more comprehensive picture of each group.

At the beginning of the 21st century, South Asian communities are poised for vigorous development. While each will have its own distinctive trajectory, there are many ways that South Asians could come together to address common concerns. During the 1990s, more South Asian Americans have built coalitions with each other and with other Asian Americans, immigrant groups, and people of color. The post-Sept. 11th backlash is an unfortunate example of why concerned citizens are increasingly joining forces. Responding to hundreds of attacks on South Asian Americans, and, in some cases, people who look South Asian, Muslim, or Arab, several new organizations, such as South Asian American Leaders of Tomorrow, have been established to take action against these dangerous and sometime deadly incidents of hate violence. Additionally, Asian American advocacy groups have provided legal services and resource information to those facing job and housing discrimination, racial profiling, and INS searches and detentions because of their South Asian or Middle Eastern ethnicity.

On another front, South Asian American women have founded numerous organizations in the last decade and a half to address women's issues, from domestic abuse to the adverse impact of immigration policies. With regards to policy, these groups have contested regulations such as the 1986 Amendments Act and H-1B visa provisions that place restrictions on persons in the country on spousal visas. Most of these visa-holders are women who are deprived of autonomous immigrant rights by such measures, a critical factor for those who find themselves in troubled marriages.

Finally, as emerging populations, South Asian Americans are attentive to current and future immigration policy trends that may impact their communities. The desire to maintain favorable immigration laws, such as those ensuring family reunification, will likely prompt South Asian Americans to work in coalitions to preserve and foster such policies.

—Jane Singh

A Community Based on Shared Difference

In the year 2000, there were around 2.1 million Asian Pacific Americans of mixed heritage, or what today is increasingly being called "hapa." Originating in Hawai'i to describe those of mixed white and Hawaiian descent, the term hapa has caught on during the last decade to describe those of part-APA ancestry. It describes both those of mixed-ethnicity like Laotian-Chinese or Hawaiian-Samoan, or of mixed-race, such as Japanese-Fijian, or Chinese-Thai-European-African-Native American (like Tiger Woods).

The 2000 Census was the first time that the Census Bureau attempted to count the numbers of both mixed-race and mixed-ethnicity people. It was about time: not only is the hapa population fast-growing, it's already sizeable. With 2.1 million members, hapas constitute the second-largest APA subgroup, behind only the Chinese. By the next Census, depending on immigration and birthrate trends, hapas could very well top all other APA sub-groups in population size.

What are the implications for how we discuss race and ethnicity today? Indeed, the emerging hapa community makes the terms that are used today—by the U.S. Census, by the general populace—not just problematic, but potentially obsolete.

Let's start by trying to make sense of the U.S. Census. This is no easy task, first because of the confusing terms used by the Census Bureau, and second because of our own social confusion over terms like "race" and ethnicity. Words describe reality and determine the way we think about things. Terminology is always changing to reflect new social realities. One of the terms in a state of flux is "race."

Photo: AP Wide World

The hapa community includes trans-racial adoptees—Asian children raised by white parents.

True colors?

Race is a scientifically-useless category; biologically-speaking, there is only one human race. Socially and politically, however, race is a very meaningful category. There have been many different racial categorization systems in the past, dividing humanity into three, 30 or even 50 races. The dominant system in the United States today divides us into five groups: white, yellow, brown, red, and black. This system reflects a way of thinking about race that emphasizes a hierarchy placing white, defined as "pure," above everything else. The more geographically-based terms are European, Asian, Latino, Native, and African. Although these categories are obviously incomplete, leaving out many (for example, Pacific Islanders), they are preferred because they emphasize geographic origin rather than a fictitious biological division of humanity into separate races. Because of the racism inherent in the idea of separate races, I prefer not to use terms like "multiracial" or "biracial," but rather to talk about Asians and Pacific Islanders of mixed heritage.

Dividing people by the much more specific category of ethnicity is more useful in some contexts and less useful in others (when trying to aggregate numbers, for example). Ethnicity is also difficult to define—it is more than biology, more than heritage. To "be Chinese," for example, is not as simple as it might initially seem. Is a person Chinese if she was born in Australia of parents who were born in Indonesia, of parents who were born in China? What if one of those grandparents from China was Jewish with ancestors from Europe? Ethnicity is heritage plus culture—and culture, by definition, changes over time.

Origins of "hapa"

"Hapa" is a Native Hawaiian word, originally meaning simply "part" or "mixed," with no racial or ethnic meaning. It became associated with the phrase *hapa haole* during the influx of European immigrants, many of whom intermarried with the *ali'i*, or land-owning class, of Native Hawaiians. Thus, the first hapas were of the upper class. Later, as Japanese immigrants were imported as plantation labor, the Japanese Hawaiian population adopted the term hapa, mostly to refer to people of mixed Japanese and European heritage.

In the late 1980s and early 1990s, the term hapa gained increasing usage with the Japanese American community on the West Coast. In 1992, students at UC Berkeley founded the Hapa Issues Forum, addressing issues of ethnic diversity within the Japanese American community. The founding members included AfroAsians as well as EurAsians (a spelling I use to emphasize Asian-centricity), thus breaking the EurAsian meaning of hapa. Within a year or two, mixed-heritage APAs of other ethnicities joined the group and adopted the term, thus expanding it beyond a specifically Japanese or Native Hawaiian focus. Today, the term hapa includes AfroAsians, EurAsians, Latin Asians, Native Asians, and mixed APAs. The hapa community also includes trans-racial adoptees, such as Koreans or Chinese raised by white parents.

The racial terms used in the 2000 Census include the obvious as well as the obscure. The six basic racial categories are white, black or African American, Asian, American Indian or Alaskan Native, Native Hawaiian or Other Pacific Islander, and Some Other Race. The most obscure of these is Some Other Race, which corresponds, more or less, to Latino or Hispanic. Technically, Latino is not a racial category, as even the federal Office of Management and Budget recognizes that Latino is more of a general cultural designation, including people of every racial category.

Out of 11.9 million Asian Americans, 1.7 million, or 14 percent, are Asian as well as one or more other races—in other words, they are hapa. The numbers are actually more complicated. There are an additional 223,593, or 2 percent, who were only of the Asian "race" but were of more than one Asian ethnicity, i.e. Vietnamese-Korean, or Chinese-Japanese-Indian. Altogether, about 16 percent, or nearly one-in-six, of all APAs are hapa.

The same situation exists with the nearly 900,000 Pacific Islanders, but to an even greater degree. More than half (55.4 percent) of Pacific Islanders are mixed with some other race. Around one-third (30.7 percent) of Pacific Islanders, in fact, also claim part-Asian descent. Meanwhile, the percentage of Pacific Islanders of only mixed-ethnic background, i.e. Hawaiian-Samoan, is just around one percent.

I have a friend from college who revealed to me that, despite his blue eyes and Scandinavian surname, his great grandfather was Chinese—a fact his family still found shameful. Thus, when we talk about these numbers it is important to remember that they do not occur in a void. Race matters in our society, and because it does, people's understanding of their own racial and ethnic heritage is often shaped by family secrets and socialized meanings. The idea of racial or ethnic purity is simply that—an idea, a constructed notion of extreme weight and importance, but certainly not a biological fact or truth.

Mixed-race —defined as having one parent of Asian or Pacific Islander descent, and another of some other race, such as white, African American, or American Indian. As of the 2000 Census, which is the first to define Asians and Pacific Islanders of different "races," someone with one Asian parent and one Pacific Islander parent, is also technically mixed-race.

Mixed-ethnicity—defined as having parents of more than one Asian or Pacific Islander group, but not some other "race." Thus, a Pakistani-Chinese or Tongan-Hawaiian would be considered an individual of mixed ethnicity, but a Pakistani-Hawaiian would be considered someone of mixed-race, according to the way the Census divides Asians from Pacific Islanders.

How we calculated the hapa population

While data on race has been collected since the first U.S. Census in 1790, the 2000 Census was the first in which respondents were able to select more than a single racial category. Another change in 2000 was that Asians and Pacific Islanders, previously considered a single "race," were now split into two separate racial categories. That complicates things when trying to calculate the combined APA population or the hapa population. That's because, since the Census counts responses rather than respondents, there is an overlap in individuals who are both part-Asian and part-Native Hawaiian or Pacific Islander. Without accounting for that, we would have an overcount.

Still, calculating the hapa population is relatively straightforward. This is how we did it, a method which was verified and endorsed by Nicholas A. Jones, an analyst at the Census Bureau's Racial Statistics Branch.

Step 1: Find the number of multi-ethnic Asians (i.e. Pakistani-Chinese, Indian-Japanese, etc.): 223,593

Step 2: Find the number of multi-ethnic Native Hawaiians and Pacific Islanders (i.e. Hawaiian-Samoan): 9,223

Step 3: Find the number of multi-racial Asians (i.e. Korean-American Indian): 1,655,830

Step 4: Find the number of multi-racial Native Hawaiians and Pacific Islanders (i.e. Guamanian-White, Hawaiian-Chinese): 475,579

Step 5: Determine the overlap between the multi-racial Asian and multi-racial Native Hawaiian and Pacific Islander populations. That is, we want to count all of the individuals who are both part-Asian *and* part-NHPI. These people would be double-counted if we simply added populations 3 and 4.

The way we do this is to look at the 2000 Census population data and add up all the various salient race combinations, such as "Asian-NHPI" or "Black-Asian-NHPI-American Indian" or "White-Asian-NHPI" or even "White-Asian-NHPI-Black-American Indian-Some Other Race." The result—268,606—is subtracted from numbers one through four. Note: this overlap number is also key for determining the total APA population.

The resulting total hapa population for 2000 is 2,095,619. The total APA population – which is derived by adding up the Asian Alone, NHPI Alone, Asian In Combination and NHPI In Combination populations, and then subtracting the APA overlap figure, is 12,504,636.

Hapas, then, comprise 16.8 percent of the total APA population. Compared to other Asian/NHPI Alone ethnic groups, hapas would rank second-largest, behind only the Chinese population.

Other relevant figures:

Percent of all Native Hawaiians and Pacific Islanders that are part Asian: 30.7 percent

Percent of all Asians that are also part-Native Hawaiian Pacific Islander: 2.3 percent

Percent of hapas among all Native Hawaiians and Pacific Islanders: 55.4 percent

Percent of hapas among all Asians: 15.8 percent

Percent of mixed-race population that is either part-Asian or part-Native Hawaiian Pacific Islander: 27.3 percent

Because 2000 was the first year the Census counted people of mixed heritage, it is difficult to determine the growth rate of the hapa population. According to the Census Bureau, "The decision to use the instruction 'mark one or more races' was reached by the Office of Management and Budget in 1997 after noting evidence of increasing numbers of children from interracial unions and the need to measure the increased diversity in the United States." According to Bureau research, the number of children living in mixed-race families (which includes non-APAs of mixed-race) was around 460,000 in 1970. This more than doubled to 996,070 children in 1980, and doubled again to reach almost 2 million in 1990, when it accounted for 4 percent of all children in households.

This is by no means merely a recent phenomenon. Early Asian immigrants, particularly Chinese, Filipinos, and Sikh Indians, came to the United States under restrictive laws that prevented significant numbers of women of these populations from arriving, until the Immigration Act of 1965 significantly altered this situation. The Japanese were the only exception: Japanese women were able to come to the United States due to the Gentleman's Agreement of 1907, as well as because of a pre-existing Japanese cultural practice known as "Picture Brides" in which couples would court and marry via letters and pictures. Before the 1950s, most Asian immigrants were deemed "aliens ineligible for citizenship" meaning that they were

Does skin color matter? The politics of interracial APAs

Cindy, a Japanese American woman, was always considered a rebel of sorts within her family, but when she began dating an African American man, she committed her biggest act of defiance.

"You know if you have children and get divorced, it's not going to be easy to get re-married again," her mother warned, implying that no man would marry a woman with half-black children. From her father came more disapproval. "Our relatives aren't going to like that. There's going to be talk in the family."

Like many Asian American parents, Cindy's parents would have preferred that she find an Asian man, or even a white one. But Cindy's decision to date an African American has forced her, like many others in her situation, to confront startling and intense levels of racism within their own families.

According to a study by professors Larry Shinagawa and Gin Yong Pang, about a quarter of Asian Americans were in interracial or interethnic relationships according to Census data from 1990. However, in only a small fraction of those relationships is one partner African American or Latino, in part due to conflicts that can arise with family members.

Pang asserts that the acceptance of an individual's significant other is inherently tied to a hierarchy of color, consciously or unconsciously observed.

"If there is a color hierarchy among the races, it seems to get darker at the bottom," Pang said, pointing out that in traditional Asian cultures, dark skin signifies a lower class standing. "Some people I have interviewed said, 'My parents don't want me to marry out but if I do, that person better be white . . . rather than Hispanic or black.'"

This correlation between skin color and social status, Pang argues, often means that African American partners must possess exceptional credentials to merely be acknowledged by some Asian American families.

In Cindy's case, her boyfriend's economic standing—he is a highly-paid professional with a house near the beach and a master's degree—did little to sway her parents opinion.

"My parents were very skeptical of my boyfriend, as opposed to my [white] brother-in-law, who they accepted right off the bat," Cindy said.

"A white person will be much better tolerated and accepted into the circle,

considered inassimilable and unwanted in the American melting pot. However, these male laborers often found ways around these tactics designed to leave them in so-called "bachelor societies."

Chinese Americans: early unions with the Irish

Late 19th and early 20th century Chinese male immigrants in New York City often intermarried with the Irish immigrant women who lived near them. This experience is documented in the short fiction and journalism of Chinese American writer, Edith Eaton (pen name Sui Sin Far), who herself was the daughter of a British father and Chinese British mother. Eaton's writing also documents intermarriage in San Francisco's Chinatown. Most of these early intermarriages were of Asian men and European women. Current Chinese American outmarriages are more likely to be Chinese American women marrying European American men.

Of course, the category "Chinese American" is rather difficult to quantify. Many people listed as Singaporean, Malaysian, Thai, Burmese etc. may be ethnically Chinese while identifying nationally with these other countries. The 2000 Census breaks it down into three distinct categories: "Chinese, except Taiwanese;" "Indo Chinese;" and "Taiwanese." These categories added together yield a total population of 2.9 million (though this no doubt leaves out many people who might also be considered "Chinese"). Around 15.5 percent of Chinese are hapa.

Diaspora and diversity: South Asian Americans

Early Sikh immigrants to California often intermarried with Mexican American women; business partners often sought pairs of sisters to marry. This occurred in the early part of the 20th century, particularly in California's Central Valley, where there is a large, fairly-affluent land-owning farming community composed of their descendents. More recent information on Sikh intermarriage is hard to come by.

There were 1.9 million Asian Indians counted in the 2000 Census; of these, about 11.6 percent were Asian Indian hapa. Indeed, the population of South Asian Americans of mixed heritage (including Asian Indian, Pakistani, Sri Lankan, and Bangladeshi) is nearly 300,000. This reflects the increasing multiculturalism of the United States, as well as the scattered Indian diaspora, both abroad and in the United States. Of any APA ethnic group, Indian Americans are the least concentrated in particular communities or cities, preferring instead to disperse widely.

One out of three: Japanese Americans

Nearly one third (30.6 percent) of Japanese Americans are hapa. This number reflects the high outmarriage rate in

because a white spouse symbolizes American society," Pang said. "But when it comes to blacks or Hispanics forget it—they're not real Americans. They're not given that equal footing or standing unfortunately because of that racism we've internalized."

Much of the parental concern regarding interracial marriages to African Americans or Latinos, according to Pang, also stems from concern that their child and future grandchildren might experience racism as a result of the relationship. Despite this fear, some couples say they haven't encountered such blatant racism.

Linda Forrest is a Chinese American who has been married to her African American husband Thomas for more than two decades.

"There have been people in later years since we've been married where I could see the surprise in their face, but that doesn't happen too often," said Forrest. "I think whites see [us] as two minorities, so who cares. And blacks don't have much of a problem with me because I'm not white.

"My parents would have objected more if I married a Japanese American than an African American," Forrest said. "My mother lived through the war and suffered the atrocities of the Japanese."

The Forrests were not the only interracial couple to gain such a warm reception from family and friends. When Janice Mirikitani, a Bay Area author and poet, and the Rev. Cecil Williams were married, her parents initially opposed the match. Mirikitani's mother changed her opinion of the marriage once she came to know Williams.

"My mother is a loving and sweet woman and she came to see that Cecil is that kind of person also. Now she says to me 'you're so lucky to be married to such a good man,'" Mirikitani said.

About the worst Mirikitani and Williams have experienced together are instances where people refuse to acknowledge their union.

"It's very strange how people stereotype the marriage," Mirikitani said. "By white people I'll be asked if I'm the chauffeur, because it's inconceivable to them that I could be the wife. I've been asked if I'm the caterer, the maid, the florist."

—*AsianWeek*

the post-internment camp era among the Japanese nisei (second generation) and sansei (third generation), but it also includes the children of the so-called Japanese war brides from the 1950s and 1960s. Many Japanese American hapas grew up on U.S. army bases in Japan or the United States, isolated from the larger Japanese American community.

Japanese Americans of mixed heritage are not just a post-World War II phenomenon, however. This is evidenced by the fact that, despite anti-miscegenation laws specifically forbidding the Japanese from intermarrying with European Americans, the U.S. Government's War Relocation Authority in 1942 imprisoned at least 700 Japanese of mixed heritage, and approximately 1,400 Japanese married to non-Japanese, as well as a few of their spouses.

Hapa or mestizo?: Filipino Americans

After Japanese Americans, Filipino Americans report the next highest percentage of people of mixed heritage among APAs, at 21.8 percent. But due to their larger numbers, Filipino hapas—more than half a million—rank as the single largest contingent.

Because of the Philippines' status as a U.S. protectorate/colony—dating back to the U.S.-Philippines War of 1898—Filipinos were considered until 1946 to be U.S. nationals, though not citizens. This gave them somewhat flexible immigration rights. This, coupled with an imposed American-style educational system, encouraged Filipinos to emigrate to the United States.

The U.S.-Philippines War also gave rise to a small but significant population of African American-Filipinos, living mostly in the Philippines. Their ancestors were African American soldiers who were convinced to desert, because of their own or their parents' recent status as slaves. The nascent Filipino democratic government also argued that as people of color, African Americans should not fight the "white man's" war against their brothers. Given the use of the term "nigger" by U.S. soldiers and press to describe Filipinos, it is no surprise that many African American soldiers switched sides and became leaders in the Philippine Army. Their descendants are now beginning to investigate this interesting history.

Filipino American outmarriage was also encouraged by the limited number of Filipinas immigrating into the United States, relative to the number of Filipino men. Until the crucial Immigration Act of 1965, early Filipino male immigrants found themselves caught between low numbers of their countrywomen and anti-miscegenation laws that prevented intermarriage with European American women. Unions had to be extra-legal or kept quiet, until anti-miscegenation laws were finally overturned, culminating in the 1967 Supreme Court decision, Loving v. Virginia.

Filipinos have intermarried with African Americans and Native Americans at somewhat higher rates than other Asian ethnic groups. The continued U.S. military presence in the Philippines since World War II has also contributed to a mixed heritage population in the Philippines, some of whom eventually immigrate to the United States.

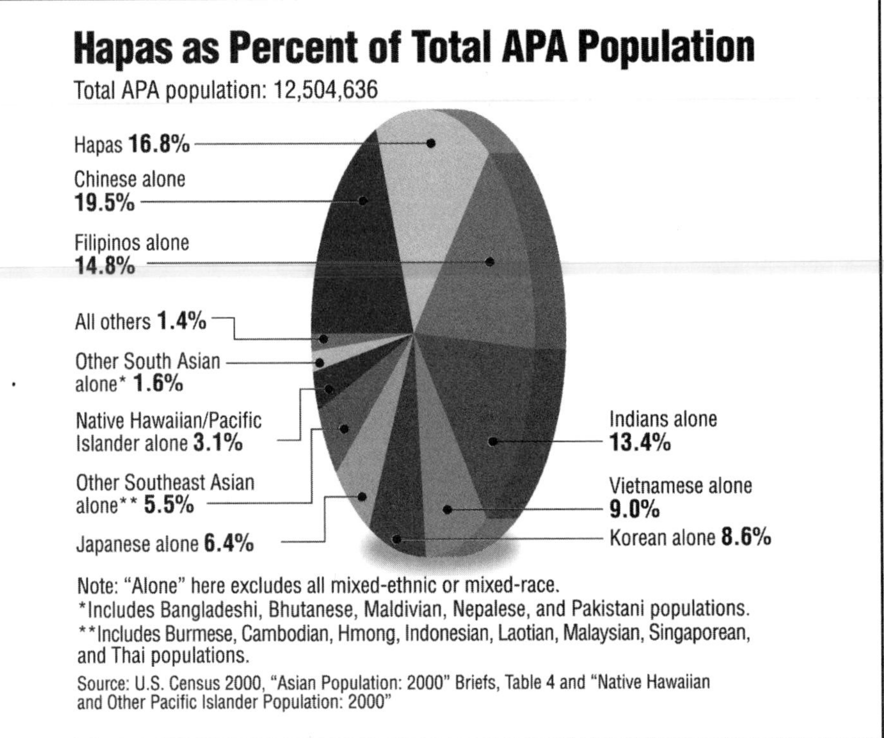

Note: "Alone" here excludes all mixed-ethnic or mixed-race.
*Includes Bangladeshi, Bhutanese, Maldivian, Nepalese, and Pakistani populations.
**Includes Burmese, Cambodian, Hmong, Indonesian, Laotian, Malaysian, Singaporean, and Thai populations.
Source: U.S. Census 2000, "Asian Population: 2000" Briefs, Table 4 and "Native Hawaiian and Other Pacific Islander Population: 2000"

TRAs and hapas: Korean Americans
12.3 percent of Korean Americans are hapa. Many are a legacy of the Korean War, or of the continued U.S. military presence in Korea. What is not clear from the Census data is what percentage of Korean Americans are transracial adoptees, adopted mostly by European Americans. Tens of thousands of Koreans, many of mixed heritage, but not all, have been adopted in the United States and other UN countries since the end of the Korean War.

Korean immigration to the United States developed later than other groups. Most of those immigrants came after 1965; many arrived already married with their families. The result? Fewer first-generation Koreans were likely to marry non-Koreans than were the first-generation Chinese and Filipinos arriving in the early 20th century.

Less than one in ten: Vietnamese Americans
Of the six largest Asian American groups, Vietnamese Americans are the least likely to report being of mixed heritage, with only 8.3 percent being hapa. While the majority of these may be of the Vietnamese Amerasian population, born during the U.S. involvement in Vietnam (of African American, Latino, Native American, other Asian American and European American fathers), some are also from current Vietnamese American outmarriage, and some also derive from earlier French colonial involvement in Vietnam. Somewhat undocumented is the large number of people of mixed Chinese and Vietnamese heritage, descended from large Chinese settlements over several generations in Vietnam.

Unique history: Hawai'i
The history of interethnic mixing in Hawai'i bears note not only because it boasts the largest percentage of APAs of mixed heritage, but also because it is the origin point for the word hapa, which is now being used (and some would say appropriated) by many APAs of mixed heritage as an inclusive term of identity and community.

Like the American Indians, the Native Hawaiian population was decimated by the European arrival. Reflecting the islands' diversity today, the Native Hawaiian population is heavily intermixed with other races and ethnic groups. Of the more than 282,000 Native Hawaiians and Pacific Islanders in Hawai'i, around 60 percent are of mixed heritage. All in all, 21.4 percent of Hawai'i's total 1.2 million population is multiracial, the majority of these being people of mixed Asian, Hawaiian, or Pacific Islander heritage.

Portrait of a hapa community: new directions
The communities of APAs of mixed heritage are diverse and complex. What is currently emerging as a hapa community challenges traditional definitions of community that are based on shared ethnicity, culture, tradition, language, food, etc. Many people still consider the term hapa to be limited to EurAsians of Japanese heritage, so do not feel the term embraces them. However, organizations like Hapa Issues Forum; classes on mixed heritage in Asian American Studies; and the publication of books like *The Sum of Our Parts, Intersecting Circles*: the voices of hapa women in poetry and prose, and Kip Fulbeck's autobiographical novel, *Paper Bullets*, in which he uses the term hapa to describe himself, are creating a sense of collective identity through this common terminology.

Hapa terms

Amerasian: a term refering to people of blended "American" and Asian ancestry—with the assumption often being that the American side is European American or African American, and from a father who was in the military and served in a war in Asia—usually in Korea, Japan, or Vietnam. The relatively high number of enlisted people of color, and the diversity of "American" ethnicities, is often ignored. This term has occasionally been used as a catch-all for Asians of mixed heritage, but is now often used with specificity to refer to the groups outlined above.

Anti-miscegenation: a term developed specifically to create a sense of fear and loathing of "racial mixing"—or "miscegenation" and its perpetrators, "miscegenators." A previous term, "amalgamation," did not convey enough negativity. Intermarriage, including that through mechanisms such as the War Brides Act, occurred anyway, despite the fact that the last anti-miscegenation laws were not actually eradicated until 1967, with the Supreme Court case, Loving v. Virginia.

Outmarriage: the more colloquial term for what sociologists call "exogamy" or marriage outside the group. This can refer to racial, ethnic, class or religious groups. One limitation of this term is that it accounts only for traditional heterosexual marriage, while failing to consider gay, lesbian, bisexual or transgender relationships, or non-marriage oriented heterosexual relationships. By all accounts, any kind of partnering outside one's ethnic or racial group engenders significant social issues.

Trans-racial adoptees: a term referring to children who are adopted outside of their "racial" group, it includes many Asians of mixed biological heritage. This raises the question: To which racial group do they belong? Frequently linked to orphaned war babies, trans-racial adoption is often sponsored by church communities connected to Christian adoption agencies in Asia—particularly in Korea and China. Domestically, trans-racial adoptions usually involve African American children and European American parents. But just as important is the forced adoption of American Indian children for the purposes of acculturation. Parallels are found in the forced adoption of aborigines in Australia in the 1950s and 1960s, a group sometimes referred to as the "Stolen Generation." In some states, like Minnesota, Asian trans-racial adoptees make up some of the largest number of Asian Americans. Whether or not trans-racial adoptees have high outmarriage rates (and "out" of which group?) has yet to be studied.

War bride: Originally conceived during World War II to allow for the immigration of European brides of U.S. servicemen, the War Brides Act of 1945 soon came to encompass Asian spouses of military personnel as well. This included the spouses of some Asian American soldiers. This is, for example, the way the Chinese American community was able to begin revitalizing itself after decades of discriminatory laws preventing the immigration of Chinese women. For several decades, Japanese women married to U.S. military personnel provided the largest influx of Japanese immigrants, but they were often not incorporated into traditional Japanese American communities because they would typically live in small towns or near military bases, with their husbands (a phenomenon is documented in Velina Hasu Houston's award-winning play, *Tea*). "War bride" is often inaccurately used to refer to any Asian woman married to an American serviceman, whether or not they actually met during war. The stigma of the term is that it implies a desperation and low-class status on the part of the Asian woman, and perhaps even that she was a prostitute or "bar girl."

—*Wei Ming Dariotis*

Yet we are still faced by the limits of this emerging community. Who belongs? Who is outside this community? Trans-racial adoptees certainly fit into the idea of "Asians of mixed heritage," which is used as a synonym for hapas. Can we legitimately claim Tiger Woods as hapa, even if he chooses a term like "Cablinasian" to describe himself? Like the Lesbian Gay Bisexual Transgender community, which often struggles with claiming celebrities whose behavior might indicate that they are or were LGBT, but who do not or did not lay claim to that identity, hapas often lay claim to celebrities who may not recognize themselves as part of this emerging community. And how do we avoid the pitfalls of ethnic identity—the ethnic nationalism, for example, that limits and restricts who can belong? Is being hapa more like being Lesbian Gay Bisexual and Transgender than like being Chinese? Or is the value of hapa-ness in that it challenges us to think about ethnic identities in a new way?

From looking at the statistics on hapas, those who are part-white outnumber all other hapas by a large margin. About 58 percent of hapas today, or 1.21 million, are part-white. Part-black hapas comprise 10 percent of the hapa population, while part-American Indian hapas comprise 6.3 percent of the hapa population. 17 percent of the hapa population is part-Some Other Race, which, as discussed earlier, is mostly made up of so-called "Hispanics" and Latinos.

While hapas of Native Hawaiian and Pacific Islander descent and Filipino ancestry rank first and second, overall, hapas of East Asian ancestry, especially Chinese and Japanese, predominate. What this means is that our community is primarily East Asian and white, not only in numbers, but also in positions of leadership and power. Most of the academics leading hapa studies are EurAsian—white and Chinese or Japanese.

The aforementioned Hapa Issues Forum is housed in the Japanese Community and Cultural Center of Northern California, and most of its seven chapters are located on prestigious college campuses, like UC Berkeley or Stanford, which contributes further to the economic and social elitism of the organization. These are simply facts, due to historical circumstances as well as contemporary social realities; what they mean, however, is that efforts to construct a hapa community must pay particular attention to the differences within our community. Like the APA community at large, hapas also have to contend with divisive hierarchies of race, class, gender, sexuality, and even ethnicity.

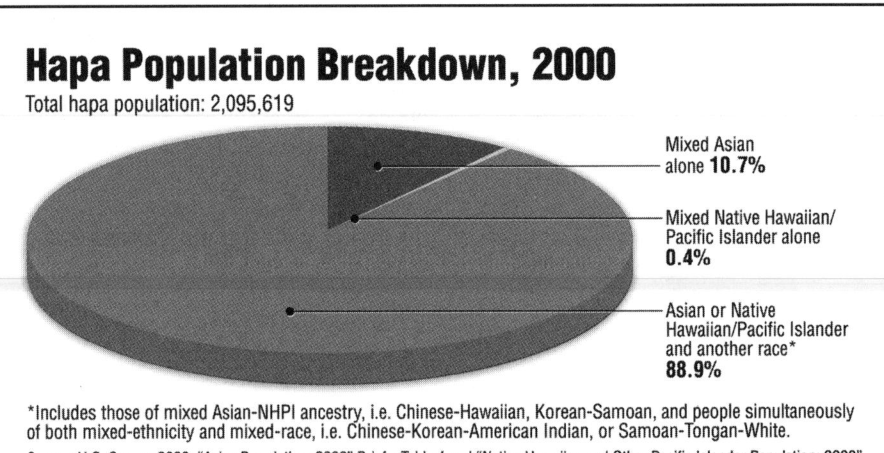

*Includes those of mixed Asian-NHPI ancestry, i.e. Chinese-Hawaiian, Korean-Samoan, and people simultaneously of both mixed-ethnicity and mixed-race, i.e. Chinese-Korean-American Indian, or Samoan-Tongan-White.

Source: U.S. Census 2000, "Asian Population: 2000" Briefs, Table 4 and "Native Hawaiian and Other Pacific Islander Population: 2000"

What does it mean to be Asian Pacific American?

Pan-ethnicity may have been born of the 1970s Asian American Movement, but it has yet to come of age. Within my Asian American Studies classes at San Francisco State University, my APA students overwhelmingly report an ethnic hierarchy within the APA community. This is demonstrated by their (often first generation) parents' desires that they date or marry first within their own ethnic group, then other Asians or Pacific Islanders, by a strict formula. While the formula may vary, the idea of a hierarchy remains rigidly the same. How are we to construct an APA "pan-ethnicity"—or an idea of ourselves as APA before our individual ethnic groups, if we maintain such a hierarchy —or if we ignore it? When asked, "What are you?" I used to list my parents' ethnicities: Chinese, Greek, Swedish, Scottish, English, German, and Pennsylvania Dutch—but that list was never my own identity. We are more than the sum of our parts.

Sure, within the hapa community we sometimes find ourselves bonding over shared ethnicities (whether it be Indian, Thai, or Pennsylvania Dutch), but ultimately it is the fact of our being hapa that draws us together, just as in the larger APA community, it is usually our shared identity that is more important than our individual ethnicities. To be APA is to be racialized, but to be APA also means to choose APA as a positive identity—not just based on ephemeral similarities ("we all eat rice") but because our differences are interesting to us. What it means to be hapa is to be recognized as a full APA and not "just half" or some other fraction of a whole identity. What began in the so-called "Biracial Baby Boom" of the late 1960s and early 1970s has proved to be more than an expression of free love, or an experience of war time: mixed heritage people are reaching critical mass in numbers and attaining the power to create identities and communities.

Hapas Among Various Asian and Pacific Islander Groups

	Non-hapa	Two or more ethnic groups only	Two or more races/ethnicities	Total hapas *(in millions)*	TOTAL† *(in millions)*
All APAs	83.2%	n/a	16.8%	2.10	12.50
Asian	84.2%	1.9%	13.9%	1.80	11.90
Native Hawaiian*	44.6%	1.1%	54.4%	0.48	0.87
Indian	88.4%	2.1%	9.5%	0.22	1.90
Chinese	84.5%	5.0%	10.5%	0.45	2.90
Filipino	78.2%	2.4%	19.3%	0.51	2.40
Japanese	69.3%	4.8%	25.8%	0.35	1.10
Korean	87.7%	1.8%	10.5%	0.15	1.20
Vietnamese	91.7%	3.9%	4.4%	0.10	1.20
Other South Asian**	74.8%	6.3%	18.9%	0.07	0.27
Other Southeast Asian***	81.8%	5.5%	12.7%	0.15	0.84
Other Asian	39.8%	5.3%	54.9%	0.22	0.37

*Includes Pacific Islanders.
**Includes Bangladeshi, Bhutanese, Maldivian, Nepalese, Pakistani and Sri Lankan populations.
***Includes Burmese, Cambodian, Hmong, Indonesian, Laotian, Malaysian, Singaporean and Thai populations.
†Detailed numbers and percentages add up to more than overall APA total due to double-counting of mixed-race people.

Source: U.S. Census 2000, "Asian Population: 2000" Briefs, Table 4 and "Native Hawaiian and Other Pacific Islander Population: 2000"

However, constructing a community that is based in difference requires that we acknowledge and honor the process of discovery. We are engaged in a collective effort to actively create a community that is often based on little more than the experience of being asked, "What are you?" As Emily Leach, the President of UC San Diego's chapter of Hapa Issues Forum, puts it:

"As a hapa, I look ... to validate my experiences and not remain the superficial, exotically beautiful, genealogical amalgam that seemingly everyone makes me out to be. I've never met a hapa who would deny the energy that exists among a group of hapas ... while we build on this sense of recognition, we must remember to actively consider always that the need for a hapa community has arisen from a sense that we did not have a place in the other ethnic communities we may have felt connected to. Thus, we must always be vigilant in maintaining open borders to our community; the difficulty is in knowing how, when, and why to have borders of any kind. How do you create a community based on inclusivity rather than exclusivity?"

Ultimately, what the 2000 Census numbers can tell us is something of the shape and position of people that we may categorize as Asians and Pacific Islanders of mixed heritage. Shaping these individuals, and their families, into a kind of community will be an ongoing struggle.

In California, "Over half a million hapas were recognized as a direct result of the Census Bureau's decision to collect data on people of mixed-race heritage," says Sheila Chung, executive director of Hapa Issues Forum. "These data not only provide more accurate information on race, but help to challenge our invisibility in the API community."

The numbers are just numbers, what we do with them is to create meaning. In the case of the hapa community, part of that is creating visibility and creating space in which to exist, through which to be recognized. We need not only to be seen by others, however; we must also begin to see ourselves and each other—in all our similarities and differences.

—Wei Ming Dariotis

SECTION III
GEOGRAPHY

A Community of Communities

Introduction

As one of the historical and contemporary centers for the Asian Pacific American population in the United States, California is both a bellwether of APA trends and an oracle of their future. As one travels through the geographic and statistical layers of the 1990 and 2000 U.S. Census in the state, one pattern is clear: Asian Pacific America in California is changing. The terrain is far from homogenous, composed of varied topographies of subethnicities, income disparities, and geographic distribution.

While immigration has continuously reshaped the state from 1990 to 2000, changes in how the U.S. Census counts APAs have meant that many communities which were once overlooked can now find voices in numbers. California's APAs are emerging as a diverse community of communities dispersed throughout the state. The state's shifting APA demographic landscape is presenting new challenges for policy makers, community activists, and scholars.

Apples to durians?: the changing Census of a changing state

For this chapter, we will be using a number of Asian and Pacific Islander categories from 1990 and 2000 Census Summary Files One, Two, and Three. In general, when simply counting populations, we tend to use inclusive numbers that include people of part- or mixed-ancestry, also known as hapas. In cases where the inclusive numbers are not available—as in the SF3 socioeconomic data—we examine Asian and NHPI groups "alone," that is, excluding hapas.

Another problem is caused by the splitting of 1990's combined Asian Pacific Islander category into separate Asian and Native Hawaiian/Pacific Islander categories in 2000, making comparisons of socioeconomic data between the two Censuses imperfect. Given all these caveats, our methods are not perfect, but the constant refinement of how the Census counts APAs, begins to paint a representative portrait of APA communities in the United States.

Photo: Cindy Chew

California's increasingly diverse APA population is reflected in a growing population of groups like the Vietnamese, Koreans and Asian Indians, adding to the already large Chinese and Filipino concentrations in the state.

Portrait of the APA population, 1990 to 2000

Overall APA numbers

California has consistently been home to the largest Asian Pacific American population, a pattern that continues in

Detailed APA Populations, 1990-2000: California

	1990		2000			
			ALONE*		ALONE AND IN COMBINATION**	
	Total	Percentage	Total	Percentage†	Total	Percentage
Filipino	733,941	25.8%	918,678	21.3%	1,098,321	25.4%
Chinese (excluding Taiwanese)	713,423	25.1%	980,642	22.7%	1,114,047	25.8%
Japanese	320,730	11.3%	288,854	6.7%	394,896	9.1%
Vietnamese	276,759	9.7%	447,032	10.3%	484,023	11.2%
Korean	259,908	9.1%	345,882	8.0%	375,571	8.7%
Asian Indian	154,122	5.4%	314,819	7.3%	360,392	8.3%
Native Hawaiian or Pacific Islander	103,126	3.6%	116,961	2.7%	221,458	5.1%
Laotian	60,627	2.1%	55,456	1.3%	65,058	1.5%
Cambodian	71,178	2.5%	70,232	1.6%	84,559	2.0%
Hmong	49,343	1.7%	65,095	1.5%	71,741	1.7%
Thai	30,461	1.1%	36,525	0.8%	46,868	1.1%
Other Asian††	74,217	2.6%	7,581	0.2%	11,986	0.3%
Taiwanese			*62,317*	1.4%	*75,412*	1.8%
Bangladeshi			*3,044*	0.1%	*4,088*	0.1%
Pakistani			*20,093*	0.5%	*27,832*	0.6%
Sri Lankan			*5,775*	0.1%	*7,212*	0.2%
Indonesian			*5,585*	0.1%	*29,710*	0.7%
Malaysian			*1,948*	0.0%	*4,282*	0.1%
TOTAL	**2,847,835**	**100.0%**	**3,746,519**	**86.7%**	**4,477,456**	**103.6%**

*i.e. excluding hapas
**i.e. including hapas
†Actual APA total in California is 4,321,585. Adding up detailed subethnicities using either method will lead to an undercount or an overcount.
††Includes Taiwanese, Bangladeshi, Pakistani, Sri Lankan, Indonesian, and Malaysian for 2000 and excludes them for 1990.
Source: U.S. Census 1990 and 2000, SF1 and STF1

2000. With an APA population of 4,321,585, California, by far, has the largest Asian population out of all 50 states. New York's 1,192,431 APAs follow California as a distant second, and Hawai'i ranks third (858,105 APAs). Asian Pacific Americans in California make up about 13 percent of the state's population which is not the highest percent in the United States. Hawai'i, at 71 percent, has the highest proportion of APAs in the general population. Interestingly, Washington and New Jersey, at seven and six percent, respectively, have the third and fourth highest percentage of APAs in the population.

Statewide APA subethnic populations

Within these overall population numbers, the diversity among APAs in California has grown and changed from 1990 to 2000. In 1990, apart from the Filipinos, who were the largest APA group, and the Vietnamese, who were fourth, the other large APA groups were all East Asian. The smallest identified APA groups, by contrast, were all Pacific Islander.

These trends continued in the 2000 Census. Including hapas, the Chinese pulled ahead of the Filipinos in California. The next three groups, the Vietnamese, Japanese and Koreans, in that order, had less than half of the population of either the Chinese or Filipinos. Using the single-race figures, the Chinese are still the largest, followed closely by the Filipinos, and then, at a distance, the Vietnamese, the Koreans, and the Asian Indians, whose growth during the 1990s was fueled by tech industry-related immigration. The Japanese, the fourth largest APA population when including hapas, falls to sixth when excluding them. This particular example illustrates the growing hapa population and its influence, particularly for the Japanese community, a trend that will likely continue in future Censuses.

Almost every Asian and Pacific Islander subethnicity grew over the last decade. For conservative estimates, we compared the 1990 data with the single-race 2000 figures. By percentage, the Asian Indian community in California has seen the largest growth, as its population doubled (104 percent) over the last 10 years, followed by the Vietnamese (61 percent), Chinese (37 percent), Korean (33 percent), and Hmong (32 percent). By raw numbers, the Chinese population grew the most (267,219), followed by the Filipinos (184,737),

Median Household Income by Race, 1999: California

TOTAL POPULATION	United States	Black alone	Asian alone	NHPI alone	Hispanic alone	Non-Hispanic white alone
United States	$41,994	$29,423	$51,908	$42,717	$33,676	$45,367
California	$47,493	$34,956	$55,366	$48,650	$36,532	$53,734

Source: U.S. Census 2000, SF3, Tables P37 and P148B, D, E, H, I)

Vietnamese (170,293), and Asian Indians (160,697).

Immigration is the engine

Much of the growth of APAs in California, as well as the rest of the country, has historically been and continues to be driven by immigration. According to the weighted tabulations from the Census Community Supplementary Survey, there were about one million "new" Asian immigrants residing in California in 2000. A little over one fifth were born in the combined areas of China, Hong Kong, and Taiwan. Nearly as many came from Southeast Asia (Cambodia, Lao, and Vietnam). Another fifth were born in the Philippines, and a tenth came from India. About one in fifteen were born in Korea. The rest were born throughout Asia, South Asia and other parts of the world (e.g. Canada).

The socioeconomic landscape of California APAs in 2000

Median Household Income

With a median household income of $55,366, Asian households are above the state-wide median household income of $47,493 and had the highest median household income out of all racial groups in California for the 2000 Census. Examining the two extremes of the household income spectrum (the less than $25,000 and the over $100,000 categories), 23 percent of Asian households earned less than $25,000 a year while 22 percent of Asian households earned more than $100,000 a year. Native Hawaiians and Pacific Islanders, on the other hand, are only slightly higher than the state median household income at $48,650. 22 percent of NHPIs earned less than $25,000 while 13 percent earned more than $100,000.

In 1990, the state-wide median household income was $35,798. APA households had a median income of $47,973, with 31 percent of APA households earning less than $25,000 and 7.5 percent earning more than $100,000.

Per capita Income

The picture is not so rosy when looking at per capita income. Asians in California actually lagged the state-wide average for all races combined. Meanwhile, non-Hispanic whites in California had a per capita income of $31,700—44 percent higher than Asians. NHPIs, meanwhile, had a California per capita income of $15,610—lower than blacks and comparable to Native Americans.

Educational Attainment

Asians are the best-educated group in California. Sixty six percent of Asian adults age 25 and older have at least some college education in 2000, higher than the state average of 57 percent. At the same time, nineteen percent of Asians lacked a high school diploma, also lower than the state average of 23 percent. Interestingly, those Asians with less than a ninth grade education are on par with the state average of eleven percent.

For NHPIs, the educational attainment statistics are very different from the Asian numbers and are significantly lower than the state average. For the same age group, 45 percent of NHPIs have at least some college education, 23 percent do not have their high school diplomas, and 8 percent of NHPIs have less than a ninth grade education.

These numbers are a slight decrease from their 1990 counterparts. In the combined APA category, six in ten had at least some college education, 23 percent did not have their high school diploma, and fourteen percent had less than a ninth grade education. For all Californians in 1990, 45 percent had at least some college, 24 percent did not have their high school diploma, and eight percent had less than a ninth grade education.

Language Skills

The Census measures English language proficiency in two ways. First, it separates the ability to speak English by language spoken at home and age. By this measure, in the 2000 Census, 22 percent of adults (age 18 to 64) who spoke an Asian or Pacific Islander language either spoke English not well or not at all. This was a drop from 1990's figure of 26 percent. The percentage of seniors (65 and older) who spoke an Asian or

Per-Capita Income by Race, 1999: California

	United States	California
Total	**$21,587**	**$22,711**
Asian alone	$21,823	$22,050
Black alone	$14,437	$17,447
NHPI alone	$15,054	$15,610
Hispanic alone	$12,111	$11,674
Non-Hispanic white alone	$24,819	$31,700

Source: U.S. Census, SF3, Tables P82 and P157A-I

A community in transition: Little Saigon

On a typical day in an American suburb, people can be seen shopping at grocery stores, eating in restaurants, getting their cars fixed, and visiting their doctors. Although a similar scenario exists in central Orange County, California, the common spoken language is Vietnamese and the majority of individuals are refugees or immigrants.

Twenty-five years ago, very few Vietnamese lived in the United States, and this commercial center, better known as Little Saigon, did not exist. Now this vibrant area boasts approximately 2,500 Vietnamese businesses. It caters to over 400,000 Vietnamese in southern California—the largest population of Vietnamese outside of Vietnam—who gather for shopping, entertainment, dining, and professional services. This is the "capital" of the overseas population (or Viet Kieu) in terms of commerce, culture, and politics.

Revitalizing an aging bedroom community

In the mid-1970s, when the first group of Vietnamese refugees arrived, the bedroom community of Westminster was populated mainly by elderly whites and was known for its aging tract homes, auto yards, trailer parks, small farms, and open lots. Many of the early Vietnamese in Orange County came from nearby Camp Pendleton, a marine base in northern San Diego County, where the first wave of refugees were temporarily placed in 1975. Attracted by the affordable housing and commercial space, second and third waves of refugees joined this first group, quickly enlarging the population and revitalizing the area.

In Orange County in 2000, Asian Pacific Americans comprised 14 percent of the population. The Vietnamese are far and away the largest group with 135,548, an increase of 89 percent from 1990 when they numbered 71,822. That's more than twice the next largest group, the Chinese. There are 27,109 Vietnamese living in Westminster, comprising 31 percent of the city's population, and 35,406 in Garden Grove, comprising 21 percent of the city population. Currently, this increase is a result mainly of births and of Vietnamese migrating from other parts of the United States, not from new immigration. The population includes groups who immigrated through different programs: for war brides, refugees, immigrants, and Amerasians (multiracial Vietnamese).

In 1988, after rallying by the Vietnamese community, the Westminster City Council designated the 1.5-mile stretch of Bolsa Avenue, from Magnolia to Brookhurst, as the "Little Saigon Tourist Commercial District." Technically, Little Saigon includes the cities of Westminster and Garden Grove; however, cluster business districts have nowadays spilled onto surrounding communities including Santa Ana, Fountain Valley, Huntington Beach, and Midway City, covering a total area of over four square miles.

In the beginning, Little Saigon had just four businesses: a pharmacy, a grocery store, an insurance company, and a restaurant. And while it has been labeled an ethnic enclave similar to urban immigrant neighborhoods, it is located in the suburbs and dominated by mini-mall structures. A real estate developer, Frank Jao of Bridgecreek Development Company, is credited with helping to create Little Saigon. He transformed the low-end shopping centers into profitable spaces, of which Asian Garden Mall is the most well known landmark.

Many centers are named after the street locations, while others are given more ethnic names, such as Le Loi Center, Asian Village Mall, Cathay Bank Center, Pearl of the Orient Mall, Little Saigon Village, and Saigon Plaza. In recent years, a controversy has arisen over the perception that Vietnamese of ethnic Chinese descent are dominating Little Saigon, bringing in networks of overseas Chinese investors and pushing for Chinese architectural designs. This was exemplified by the recent conflict over the Harmony Bridge Project, which was eventually scrapped.

Local schools have been transformed by the arrival of the Vietnamese. Asian American, mainly Vietnamese, enrollment has increased to 31 percent in the Westminster School District and 28 percent in

Pacific Islander language and spoke English not well or not at all, remained unchanged at 51 percent.

Linguistic isolation, an oft-overlooked Census category, occurring in households where all members 14 years old and over have at least some difficulty with English. For households where Asian and Pacific Island languages serve as the primary form of communication, 30 percent of households (301,083) were considered as being linguistically isolated in 2000. This can be compared to Spanish-speaking households, where linguistic isolation occurs in 26 percent (2,578,801) of households. In 1990, 33 percent of Asian and Pacific Islander language speaking households (218,169) were linguistically isolated.

Poverty

Under the U.S. Census, the determination of poverty fluctuates from year to year and is related to a number of consumer indexes and weighted averages. In 2000, it was defined as having an income of less than $16,895 for a family of four with two parents and two children. While parts of California's APA populations enjoy some of the highest incomes in the state, the Garden Grove Unified School District. Their presence has impacted the curriculum, with selective incorporation of Vietnamese language classes and Vietnamese American curriculum at these levels. Also, since 1982 the Union of Vietnamese Student Associations of Southern California, a non-profit organization run by college students and alumni, has worked to bridge the cultural and social divide between the generations.

Culturally, the area boasts a thriving center for the media, arts, and entertainment industries. Media outlets, such as *Nguoi Viet Daily News*, *Van Hoa* newsmagazine, Little Saigon Television, and Little Saigon Radio, cater to the ethnic clientele. Singers and artists have created a fertile industry and have a ready-made fan base; however, now the innovative music imported from Vietnam is competing with the more traditional local industry. At local night clubs, such as the Majestic Dancing, Ritz, and MVP (a.k.a. Many Vietnamese People), technopop blends with ballroom music. Songs are sung in Vietnamese, English or French. A New Year's Tet Festival has taken place for more than two decades, with a Tet parade since 1994.

Some problems and politics

The sights, smells, and sounds of a homeland left behind have been recreated in Little Saigon. However, the community also faces social problems. Refugees with limited education and job skills live in poverty, have inadequate access to healthcare, and depend on welfare services. The jobs available to them are low paying service-sector or manufacturing jobs. The area has received negative publicity regarding gang hangouts, drug trafficking, extortion racketeering, and other illicit activities. The community has faced antagonism from white residents, although for the most part other Asian, Latino (mainly Mexican), Middle Eastern, and mainstream American businesses peacefully co-exist side-by-side with the Vietnamese establishments.

Many former Vietnamese military and political leaders, along with former re-education camp prisoners who immigrated through the Humanitarian Operation Program, live in or near Little Saigon. Naturally, the community remains active in fighting for "freedom, democracy and human rights" in Communist Vietnam. A Vietnam War Memorial stands in Westminster commemorating both the South Vietnamese and Americans who served in the war. There have been anti-Communist demonstrations, most notably in 1999, which attracted approximately 15,000 protesters against Truong Van Tran, a local video storeowner who displayed the Communist flag and a picture of Ho Chi Minh.

Little Saigon residents are also emerging on the local political scene. Tony Lam, elected to Westminster City Council in 1992, was the first elected Vietnamese American in the country, and Van Tran, who won his seat to Garden Grove City Council in 2000, was the second.

In the coming years, there are three major concerns that Little Saigon will face, all of which are related to the longevity and vitality of the community. With few new Vietnamese immigrants entering the United States and socio-economically mobile Vietnamese Americans choosing to leave this enclave, how will the area sustain itself? Although Vietnamese are moving outside of the core of Little Saigon, most remain in Southern California and return for shopping, entertainment, religious services, and professional needs, which is quite evident from weekend traffic jams.

Some community leaders want to capitalize on Little Saigon's location—near Disneyland and Knott's Berry Farm amusement parks, and just a few miles from the beach—in order to attract tourism. Debates rage on how to preserve it as a culturally comfortable space for the Vietnamese American population while enhancing it as a mainstream tourist site. There is also concern about growing competition from satellite Vietnamese business districts in the San Gabriel Valley and downtown Chinatown, both located in nearby Los Angeles County. In the near future, Little Saigon's transnational connections will remain, as will its influence in reshaping the perception of what constitutes American society.

—Linda Trinh Võ

poverty amongst the separate Asian and NHPI populations remains close to or higher than the state average (14 percent). Thirteen percent of Asians and 16 percent of NHPIs lived below the poverty line in 2000. On the bright side, that appeared to be a drop from 1990, when 17 percent of the combined APA population lived in poverty, compared to the state average of 19 percent.

Child Poverty

Child poverty remains a significant issue within the APA population in California. In 1990, one in five Asian Pacific Islander children (under the age of 18) lived in poverty. In 2000, roughly one in eight or thirteen percent of Asian children lived below the poverty line in California, whereas, with the NHPI children, the ratio remains closer to the state average of one in five. In averaging the numbers between the Asian and Pacific Islander population, child poverty has remained the same since 1990.

On a statewide level, certain socioeconomic trends have emerged in certain categories while, for others, they have remained the same. However, as one moves from state to county and to city level, the differences in ethnic

Educational Attainment of Asian and NHPI Adults, by Major California Metro Areas

	ASIAN ALONE			NHPI ALONE		
	Total adults over age 25	% without HS diploma	% college graduates	Total adults over age 25	% without HS diploma	% college graduates
Los Angeles	773,327	17.6%	12.3%	14,489	25.9%	3.4%
Oakland*	263,171	17.0%	16.2%	6,663	23.1%	3.9%
Orange County	253,320	18.8%	12.6%	4,737	20.0%	3.4%
San Diego	160,925	18.7%	10.8%	7,805	15.6%	3.4%
San Francisco	283,436	24.4%	11.7%	7,080	31.8%	2.7%

*Includes both Alameda and Contra Costa counties.

Source: U.S. Census 2000, SF3 (Tables 37 and 148 A-I)

and socioeconomic compositions of the APA community become even more pronounced.

Behind the numbers: The new geographies of APAs in California

The diverse geography of Asian Pacific America begins to emerge as one moves from state to county level. In 2000, 85 percent of Asians and 77 percent of NHPIs lived in ten counties, compared to the 72 percent of the general population. These ten counties were predominantly urban and located around major California cities of Los Angeles, San Francisco, Stockton, and Sacramento. Even at a county level, it is clear that the APA population is not uniformly distributed throughout the state and that geography matters.

Regional Differences

We profile the APA populations within five of the largest metropolitan statistical areas (MSAs) in the state—San Francisco, Oakland, Los Angeles, Orange County, and San Diego. In all cases except for Oakland, the MSA corresponds to the county of the same name. In addition to ethnic composition, we will also look at the socioeconomic figures for non-hapa Asians and NHPIs in these five places.

San Francisco

By percentage, the 33 percent Asian composition of San Francisco County is the highest in the state, and the eighth highest for NHPIs (0.8 percent). By gross size, San Francisco County had the sixth largest Asian and the tenth largest NHPI populations in California. The majority of Asians in San Francisco are Chinese, at 51.8 percent, followed by Filipinos at 27 percent and Japanese at 7.1 percent. Sixty eight percent of Asians and four in ten NHPIs were immigrants; the latter is the highest concentration of NHPI immigrants in California.

For both NHPIs and Asians, San Francisco has the largest proportion of individuals over the age of 25 lacking high school diplomas, 24 percent (69,253) and 31 percent (7,080), respectively. Twenty one percent (26,946) of all Asian and 20 percent (549) of NHPI households earn less than $25,000. Conversely, one-quarter of Asian and more than one in five of NHPI households earned more than $100,000, the second largest concentration of high-income households in this regional study.

Oakland

The Oakland MSA, which comprises all of Alameda and Contra Costa Counties, is an interesting parallel. Similar to San Francisco, Chinese are the largest APA ethnicity, at 35 percent (157,069). Filipinos, at 27.6 percent (123,705) are the second largest ethnicity. Replacing the Japanese, however, are the Asian Indians, who make up 13.5 percent (60,570). At 35 percent, the Oakland metro area has the highest percentage of native-born Asians among the five areas we look at here (30 percent of NHPIs in Oakland were native-born). Oakland has the lowest number of Asians over the age of 25 who do not have their high school diplomas, but it has the second highest number of NHPIs individuals over the age of 25 lacking high school diplomas. Oakland has the highest concentration of Asian and NHPI college graduates in the state. With household incomes, 15 percent of NHPI and 19 percent of Asian households earn less than $25,000. 27 percent of Asian and 16 percent of NHPI households earned more than $100,000.

Los Angeles

By raw numbers, Los Angeles County had the largest Asian and NHPI populations. But because L.A. County is so huge (more than 9.5 million), its proportion of Asians and NHPIs is less impressive: 13 percent of L.A. County is Asian (eighth largest), and 0.5 percent of L.A. County is NHPI (18th largest). As in Oakland and San Francisco, the Chinese (29.9 percent or 372,338) and Filipino (23.8 percent or 296,708) populations are the two largest APA subethnicities. Koreans (15.7 percent or 195,150) make up the third largest APA group.

Seventy percent of the Asian and 25 percent of the NHPI populations were immigrants to the United States. Out of the overall Asian and NHPI populations, 18 percent (136,135) of Asians and 26 percent (3,757) of NHPIs lack their high school diplomas, while 12

Photo: Corky Lee

With a family make-up that frequently includes many extended family members, the Filipino American community is the second largest among all APAs in the state.

percent (95,096) of Asians and 3 percent (3,757) of NHPIs have their college degrees. 30 percent (1,962) of NHPI and 12 percent (32,915) of Asian households in the Los Angeles MSA earned less than $25,000 while 17 percent (62,293) of Asian and 12 percent (781) of NHPI households earned more than $100,000.

Orange County

Directly south of Los Angeles, Orange County shares many similar APA socioeconomic characteristics with Los Angeles. However, one major difference is the huge Vietnamese population (33.3 percent of the APA population or 141,164) which is well over twice the size of the second largest APA population of Chinese (16.8 percent or 71,366) with Filipinos being the third largest (at 14.2 percent or 60,000).

Nineteen percent (47,692) of the Asian population and 20 percent (947) of the NHPI population over the age of 25 do not have their high school diplomas while 13 percent (31,807) of Asians and 3 percent (163) of NHPI have their college degrees. 70 percent of Asians and 24 percent of NHPIs were immigrants to the Orange County MSA. 15 percent (317) of NHPI and 20 percent (22,241) of Asian households earned less than $25,000 while 14 percent (289) of NHPI and 23 percent (25,167) of Asian households earned more than $100,000.

San Diego

By raw numbers, San Diego County is home to the second largest NHPI (25,262) population in California and the fifth largest Asian (303,204) population in California. The APA population is dominated by Filipinos (49.1 percent of the APA population or 145,132). Their population is nearly three times that of the Chinese (13.2 percent and 39,103) or Vietnamese (12.4 percent or 36,512).

Nineteen percent of Asians and 16 percent of NHPIs over the age of 25 lack their high school diplomas, while 3.4 percent of NHPIs and 11 percent of Asians have their college degrees. Sixty seven percent of Asians and 10 percent of NHPIs were immigrants to the San Diego MSA. Twenty percent (765) of NHPI and 22 percent (15,794) of Asian households earned less than $25,000 while 11 percent of NHPI and 16 percent of Asian households earned more than $100,000.

What do the numbers really mean?

In comparing the 1990 and 2000 Census figures for California's Asian Pacific American population, a number of policy and research issues emerge.

Alone vs. inclusive: number differences indicating larger trends

As we have seen, what numbers a researcher, policy analyst, or community activist uses has a major impact towards what kind of picture she/he is painting. A striking example of the difference when including

Household Language by Linguistic Isolation, California

	United States	California
Asian and Pacific Islander languages	**2,755,826**	**984,463**
% speaking an APA language	2.6%	8.6%
Linguistically isolated	**804,731**	**301,083**
% speaking an APA language linguistically isolated	29.2%	30.6%

*A linguistically isolated household is one in which no member 14 years old and over (1) speaks only English or (2) speaks a non-English language and speaks English "very well." In other words, all members 14 years old and over have at least some difficulty with English.

Source: Census 2000, SF3 (Table P20)

versus excluding hapas occurs with the Japanese. Looking at only single-race Japanese in 2000, the population appears to have decreased ten percent from 1990. However, when the inclusive numbers are used, the population is seen to have increased by 23 percent! With California's high APA population, interracial and interethnic marriage rates are high; excluding the fast-growing and young population of hapas can have drastic consequences.

The geographies of APA difference and the need for coalitions

California's APAs do not fit neatly into any one cultural, economic, or geographic category. While some have been economically prosperous in the 1990s, there are similarly many who are struggling. Most APAs live in urban areas, but they are spread out throughout the state. With no one subethnic group larger than one-quarter of the overall APA category, diversity is the rule and not the exception within the APA population. From both the 1990 and the 2000 Censuses, it is clear that to adequately represent the APA community requires interethnic coalitions. With funding sources mainly available on a state and a federal level, the need for multiethnic coalitions on a statewide level is all the more important.

Challenging the Model Minority Myth

The relatively high median household incomes and educational attainments of APAs may lead to the belief that APAs face few economic or social barriers or, at least, unlike other racial minorities, seem to be able to overcome them. However, if Census data is examined comprehensively and not on a few myopic indicators, we see that portions of APA communities continue to face social and economic barriers. General and child poverty rates are not significantly below California's averages. Many APA households and seniors are linguistically isolated, making it hard for them to access basic social services or be economically mobile.

Ironically, the most significant implication of the model minority myth is that APAs are invisible to policy makers. Because of their supposed success, APAs are perceived to have few problems and hence, no need for social services, political empowerment, or advocacy. The most disenfranchised portions of the APA population become captives not only of their circumstances, but of a society that denies their existence.

Get to know the Census

Knowledge is power. Information from the Census is not fodder for APA trivia buffs, but can serve as a beacon towards serving APA populations. Big changes in how race and ethnicity were tabulated in the 2000 Census have had major implications towards how these APA numbers can be used. It's more complicated, yet the ability to know how to use Census data has never been more important.

In a 1995 Edmonston and Schultze survey of eighteen State Government data centers, sixteen reported that race in the Census is an "essential" category that is used for such activities as Voting Right Act compliance, grants applications and assessment, and education and employment services. The Census remains one of the key instruments towards how federal, state, and local governments allocate resources to their constituents and provide answers for the questions of who gets what, where and when.

Conclusion

From 1990 to 2000, the APA population in California has changed, and yet remained the same. The APA population has grown, with an influx of immigrants from throughout the Pacific Rim and South Asia, and increased in ethnic diversity. Certain portions of the APA population found prosperity in the booming economy of the 1990s. However, certain issues have remained the same: linguistic isolation and poverty levels have neither significantly decreased or increased. In this paradox of dynamic and static social and economic characteristics, APAs in California and, for that matter, the United States face a present and a future where social and economic diversity is the rule and not the exception.

—Andrew Yan and Paul Ong

The authors would like to thank Jordan Rickles from UCLA's Ralph and Goldy Lewis Center for Regional Policy Studies and Melany dela Cruz from UCLA's Asian American Studies Center for their assistance in assembling the data for this chapter.

Breaking New Ground

Of the four Census-defined regions of the United States, the nine-state Northeast is geographically the smallest. But with its large number of old urban centers like Boston, Philadelphia, and of course New York City—which tend to attract new immigrants, including APAs—the Northeast boasts the second-largest APA population, at more than 2.4 million in 2000.

Around half of Northeastern APAs lived in New York state in 2000. But New Jersey may yet catch up in the next decade or two: the suburbs of the Garden State are attracting middle-class APAs, many of them commuting to well-paid jobs in Philadelphia or Manhattan. New Jersey's median Asian family income was more than $72,000, by far the highest in the country for Asians and the highest for any racial group for any state (outside of whites living in Washington D.C.).

Overall, there were more than a million new APAs in the Northeast in 1990s. That goes contrary to both current and future overall population trends. Demographers say that the Northeast is losing people, mostly whites, to other regions—especially the South and the Rocky Mountain states of the West—as old factories are shut down and moved elsewhere in the country or overseas. But APAs will continue to arrive to the Northeast; the Census Bureau predicts 2.3 million will come between 1995 and 2025.

Socioeconomic status of Asians and NHPIs

Income

Median household

Asians in the Northeast maintained the second highest median household income in 2000 at $51,912 after those in the West ($53,373). Their median household income surpassed the national median ($41,994) by 23 percent, but came close to what the nationwide Asian household population earned ($51,908). States like New Jersey, which had the highest median household income in the Northeast for Asians at $72,224, Connecticut at $61,587, and New Hampshire at $56,344, contributed to the overall high median household earnings for the region. The median household income for Asians was highest among all other racial groups, with the second highest at $48,918 for non-Hispanic whites.

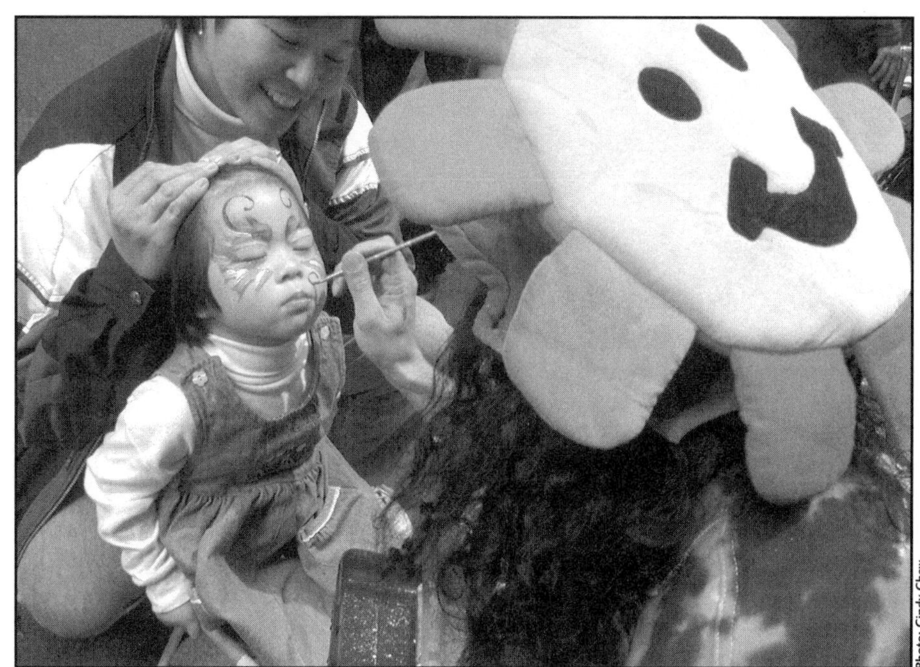

Photo: Cindy Chew

The APA population in the Northeast is expected to more than double between 1995 and 2025 from new immigration and children. That bucks the overall trend, which is seeing many residents, especially whites, move to less-crowded, economically-booming areas in the West and South.

For NHPIs in the Northeast, the median household income, at $35,073, was lower compared than the median for other NHPIs across the nation, $42,717. Still, compared to other groups in the region, they earned the third highest, after Asians and whites. Median household earnings for NHPIs were highest in states like Connecticut ($60,536), New Jersey ($56,080) and Maine ($48,000) and lowest in Vermont ($28,750) and New York ($28,713).

Median family

The median family income for Asians in the Northeast was $58,347, the third highest in the nation. They earned slightly less than the national average for Asians ($59,324) but 16 percent higher than the total population's median income at $50,046. Compared to other races, the median family income for Asians closely followed that of non-Hispanic whites, $59,971, the highest among all groups. Asians in New Jersey again had the highest median family income, at $78,211, while those in Connecticut ($70,007), New Hampshire ($62,176), Massachusetts ($57,893) and Pennsylvania ($53,574) all stayed above the national median. NHPIs for that region had a median family income of $41,716, the lowest among all the regions, and lower than the national NHPI figures ($45,915). However, compared to other groups, NHPIs continued to have higher median family earnings than blacks ($36,758) and Hispanics or Latinos ($32,530) in the Northeast. NHPIs enjoyed higher family incomes in states like Connecticut ($66,500), New Jersey ($64,762) and Pennsylvania ($46,217).

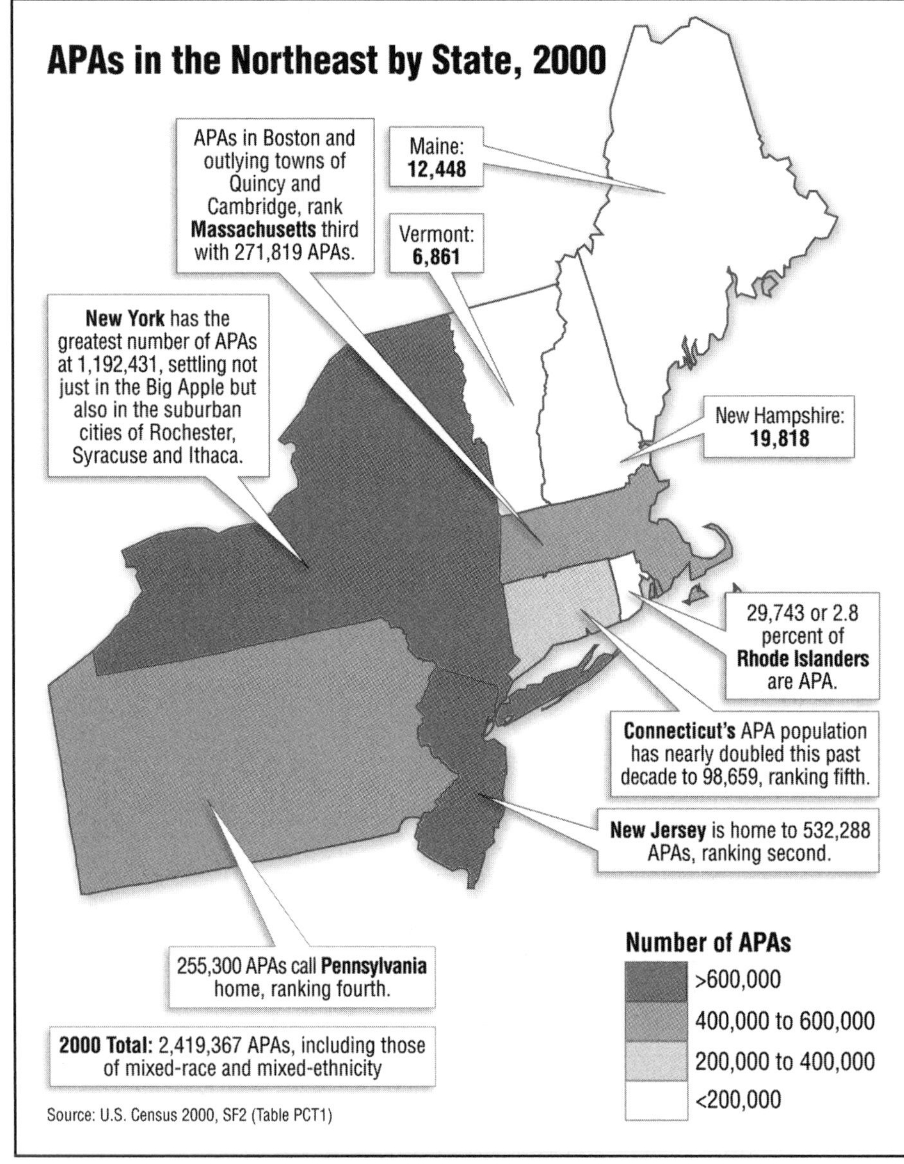

Per capita

Per capita income among Asians in the Northeast at $22,433 was slightly more than the national per capita income ($21,587). Aside from the non-Hispanic whites ($26,850) and Asians who have the second highest per capita income, the per capita income of NHPIs at $15,914 was higher than blacks ($15,602) and Hispanics ($12,994), but still fell 26 percent behind the U.S. figure for all races.

Poverty

The poverty rate among Asians in the Northeast was 14.4 percent and 22.4 percent for NHPIs, highest among all regions for both groups and higher than the 12.4 percent national poverty rate. The poverty rate among Asian children (under age 18) in the Northeast was 15.2 percent. For NHPI children, the poverty rate at 32.4 percent was more than double that of Asians.

Educational attainment

33.6 percent (422,044) of Asians in the Northeast over age three were enrolled in school or college in the Northeast. NHPIs have lagged behind Asians in most cases, but they surpassed Asians in this case as 34.2 percent over age three were enrolled in school, matching closely with the national average at 35.4 percent.

Vermont, with 46.4 percent of people over age three enrolled in school, ranked the highest among the Northeast states. Among states with 100,000 or more people, Pennsylvania

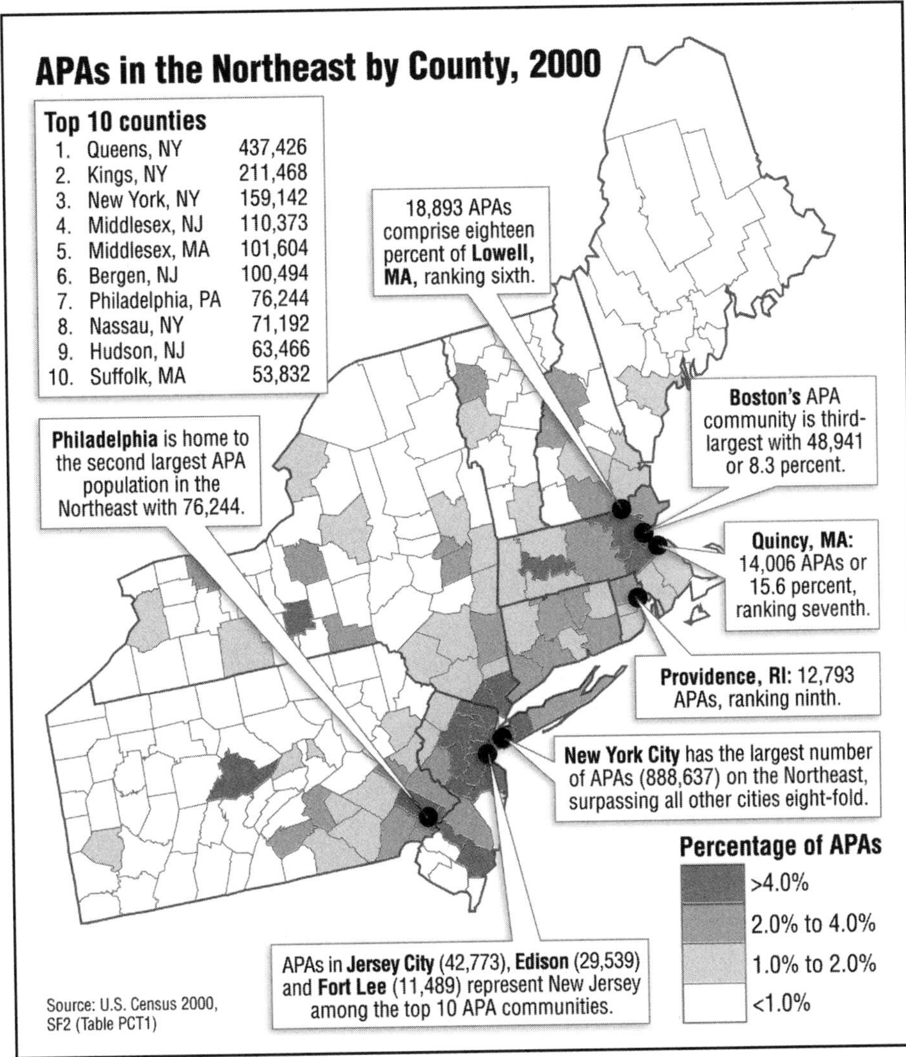

with 37.6 percent and Massachusetts with 37.9 percent ranked highest. For NHPIs, Connecticut had the highest percentage of those enrolled in school over age three with Pennsylvania at 36.7 percent and New York with 35.6 percent rounding out the top three.

In the Northeast, 50.3 percent of Asians in school and 49.7 percent of NHPIs in school attended a private college, an indication of the numerous private educational opportunities in the area. This was higher than the white population at 42.6 percent.

The percentage of Asians with bachelor's degrees, 48.4 percent, is significantly higher than both the national average at 24.4 percent and the regional average at 27.5 percent for all races. New Jersey, Connecticut, New Hampshire, and Vermont have the highest percentages of Asians who have attained at least a bachelor's degree. For NHPIs, 21 percent held a bachelor's, the highest percentage among all regions of the United States. Vermont, New Hampshire and Massachusetts have the highest percentages of NHPIs holding at least a bachelor's degree.

Language

2.5 percent of all people in the Northeast speak an APA language. 34 percent are linguistically isolated, the highest among all regions and higher than the national average at 29.2 percent. The percentage of people who speak an APA language and who are also linguistically isolated is highest in states like New York, Massachusetts and New Jersey, where the Asian immigrant populations are high.

—*Cindy Chew*

Northeast region by the numbers

Total APA population, including hapas of mixed-race and mixed-ethnicity: 2,419,367

Asian population 'alone': 2,119,426

1990 APA population: 1,335,375

Total APA population growth, 1990-2000: 81.2 percent

Largest APA population (nationwide rank): New York, 1,192,431 (2nd)

Smallest APA population (nationwide rank): Vermont, 6,861 (48th)

Fastest growing state, rate (nationwide rank): Vermont, 113.4 percent (12th)

Slowest growing state, rate (nationwide rank): New York, 71.9 percent (42nd)

Highest percent of APAs in population (nationwide rank): New Jersey, 6.33 percent (4th)

Lowest percent of APAs in population (nationwide rank): Maine, 1.0 percent (tie 42nd-44th)

Asian New Yorkers in a 'Majority Minority' City

By the mid-1980s, New York City had become a 'majority minority' city. A driving force in this demographic transformation was the dramatic growth of the Asian Pacific American population. New York City's racial and ethnic diversity is unparalleled in previous historic periods and in other metropolitan locations. The foreign-born population in this quintessential immigrant city has reached levels not seen since the last great immigration wave of the late 1800s. Today, approximately 38 percent of New Yorkers are foreign-born.

New York is second only to California in the numbers of Asian Pacific Americans. The overwhelming majority (75 percent) of the 1.2 million APAs in New York State reside in one of the five boroughs which comprise the city of New York: Kings (Brooklyn), Queens, New York (Manhattan), Bronx, and Richmond (Staten Island). Indeed, with another 150,000 or so APAs living in the counties immediately outside of NYC, nine out of ten APAs in New York state live in or around the New York metro area.

Latinos and African Americans in New York State are similarly concentrated in New York City. In contrast, more than half of non-Hispanic whites reside outside the aforementioned five counties.

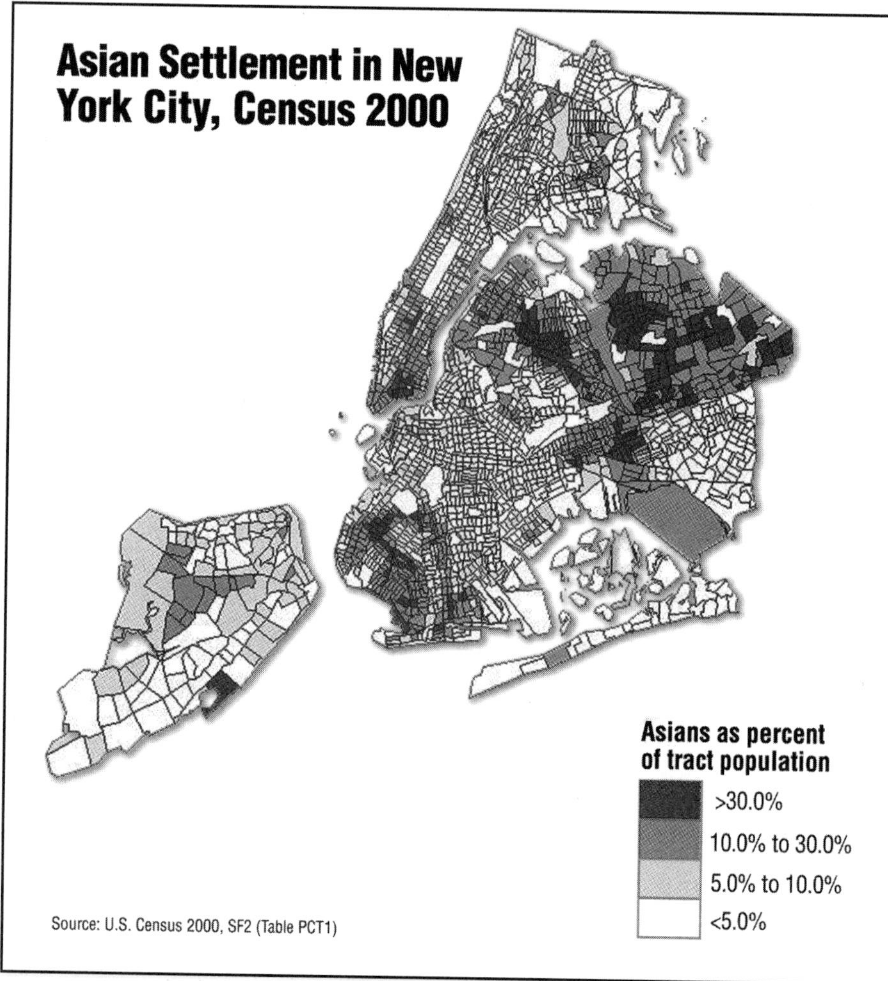

The spatial concentration of Asian Pacific Americans is further underscored by the fact that one in two APAs in New York City resides in the borough of Queens, where they now comprise one-fifth of the total population.

Growth and diversity

New York City is the most dense and populous city in the United States. Numbering more than eight million people in 2000, New York City's population growth is characterized by notable racial shifts as the share of non-Hispanic whites continue to decline while Latinos have surpassed African Americans as the second largest racial group. Asian Pacific Americans continue to be New York City's fastest growing population group increasing their numbers by 74 percent in the past decade.

At 888,637, APAs now comprise 11 percent of New York City's population. This count includes both multiracial and multiethnic of part-Asian or Pacific Islander descent. Counting only Asians and Pacific Islanders who are not of mixed-race, the Census found 792,477 APAs. The recent Census included a new multirace category that provided the opportunity for respondents to check up to six race categories, whereas in 1990, respondents could only check a single-race category. Based on this new race category, the 2000 Census found that three percent of New Yorkers identified as multiracial. Out of nearly 300,000 individuals, 96,160, or about one-third, are part-APA, a figure which accounts for the difference between the two APA totals earlier in this paragraph.

The rich ethnic diversity of Asian Pacific Americans is evident in New York City. While the three largest ethnic groups are Chinese, Asian Indian, and Korean, NYC's APA population includes

significant numbers of Filipinos, Pakistanis, Japanese, and Southeast Asians. It is notable that a relatively smaller ethnic group, Bangladeshis, experienced the greatest growth as their numbers increased threefold, from fewer than 5,000 in 1990 to 19,148 in 2000 (note: due to the unavailability of data at press time, all calculations for APA subgroups in New York City exclude hapas of both mixed-race and mixed-ethnicity). Overall, South Asians including Asian Indians, Pakistanis, Sri Lankans, and Bangladeshis are the fastest growing segment of New York City's APA population and their numbers more than doubled in the past decade to nearly 217,000. Much of the population growth of APAs is driven by immigration. In 1990, more than three in four (79 percent) Asian New Yorkers were foreign-born. Looking just at non-mixed-race Asians in 2000, 78 percent were foreign-born. Out of that population, 57 percent were not citizens.

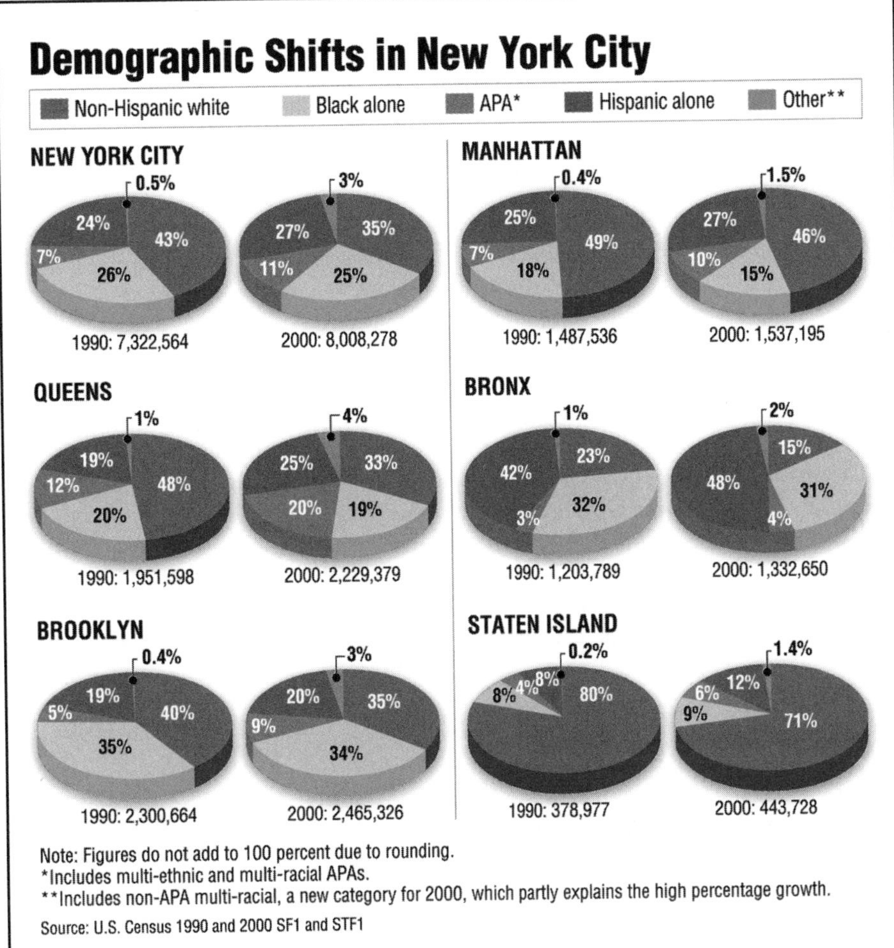

Numbering more than 361,000, the Chinese remain the largest Asian ethnic group in New York City. Unfortunately, Census data does not illustrate the regional and linguistic differences that are increasingly prominent among New York City's Chinese population. While large numbers of Chinese New Yorkers emigrate from Taiwan and Hong Kong, the overwhelming majority come from the People's Republic of China. In addition to historically important provinces in southern China, growing numbers of Chinese New Yorkers are from Fujian, a southeast coastal region. A significant share of the Fujianese are undocumented immigrants and their experiences are recounted by Professor Peter Kwong in a series of articles and his 1996 book, *Forbidden Workers*. Clearly, official enumerations underestimate their numbers evident in the burgeoning neighborhoods of Brooklyn's Sunset Park and Manhattan's Chinatown, where Fujianese immigrants concentrate.

Koreans are NYC's third largest Asian ethnic group at 86,473. In the past decade, the numbers of Koreans grew relatively modestly compared to the Chinese and Asian Indians, and this is reflected in their declining share of the APA population. In 1990, Koreans comprised fourteen percent of NYC's APA population. A decade later, their population share had declined to eleven percent. This trend is also found in NYC's fourth largest APA ethnic group, Filipinos. Similar to Koreans, the growth rate of Filipinos was modest at 20 percent, bringing their numbers to nearly 55,000 in 2000.

As noted earlier, smaller South Asian ethnic groups such as the Bangladeshis and Pakistanis grew dramatically during the 1990s. Although they made up only three percent of the APA population in NYC, the numbers of Pakistanis had nearly doubled to more than 24,000 in 2000. Another example is the Hawaiian and Pacific Islander population, which increased by 148 percent from fewer than 2,200 in 1990 to 5,430 in 2000.

Immigration to New York City in the 1990s

The key force driving APA population trends in New York City is immigration. New York City is the top destination for newcomers to the United States. During the 1990s, nearly one million new immigrants settled in New York City. Immigration to NYC is distinguished by its exceptional diversity of sending countries. In contrast to other "port of entry" cities such as Los Angeles where a majority of newcomers are from Mexico, no one group dominates the immigrant influx to NYC.

The top twenty sending countries account for 75 percent of new immigrants to New York City during the 1990s. The top three sending countries are the Dominican Republic, the former Soviet Republics, and the People's Republic of China. Several Asian countries are among the top twenty sources of new immigrants to NYC such as India, Philippines, Bangladesh, Pakistan, Korea, and Hong Kong.

Immigration from the Caribbean countries of Guyana and Trinidad contributes to NYC's emerging Indo-Caribbean population. Indo-Caribbeans are descendants of Asian Indians who migrated to the Caribbean more than one hundred years ago, many to labor as indentured servants. It is noteworthy that the settlement pattern of Guyanese immigrants is equally divided among those settling in Brooklyn and Queens, suggesting divergent patterns for Indo and Afro Caribbeans who settle in well-established West Indian communities in Brooklyn.

New immigrants from India and Korea concentrate overwhelmingly in Queens, in contrast to Chinese immigrants from the People's Republic of China and Hong Kong who settle in Manhattan's Chinatown as well as "satellite" Chinatowns in Brooklyn and Queens. The settlement patterns of newcomers from Philippines, Bangladesh and Pakistan indicate that in addition to Queens, many settle in Brooklyn or Manhattan.

Chinese in New York City, Census 2000

Number of Chinese

	>300
	100 to 300
	50 to 100
	<50

Source: U.S. Census 2000, SF2 (Table PCT1)

Spatial patterns: immigrant enclaves and ethnic communities

A mere two percent of NYC's more than 2,200 Census tracts are majority Asian. However, it is significant that one-third of Asians in Manhattan reside in one of its seven majority Asian tracts. The spatial concentration of Asians is notable throughout New York City. Mapping this shows several key neighborhood clusters with a majority and/or significant Asian population.

Most APA New Yorkers reside in Queens, Brooklyn, or Manhattan, with the remaining ten percent residing in the Bronx or Staten Island. In fact, as previously noted, one in every two APA New Yorkers calls the borough of Queens home. A spatial analysis of Asian (alone) settlement illustrates two important patterns: (1) Census tracts with a majority Asian population are concentrated in several key NYC neighborhoods surrounded by a much larger area of Census tracts with a significant Asian population; and (2) Asian neighborhoods include historic enclave neighborhoods as well as "global" neighborhoods.

The relatively smaller share of Census tracts with 9 percent or fewer Asians notes the significant presence of Asians in many Queens neighborhoods. In contrast to the other boroughs where the overwhelming majority of Census tracts would be categorized as being "low" in Asian population, less than half (42 percent) of Queens Census tracts are similarly categorized. Asian concentrations are evident in the Queens neighborhoods of Flushing, Elmhurst, Richmond Hill, South Ozone Park, Jackson Heights, Woodside, Sunnyside, Corona, Bayside, Bellerose and Floral Park.

In Brooklyn, the greatest concentration is in Sunset Park, with significant clusters in Sheepshead Bay and Bensonhurst. These Asian neighborhoods are typically comprised of majority Asian tracts that are surrounded by numerous tracts with

Ethnic Diversity and Growth of New York City's APA Population

NEW YORK CITY	1990	2000	Percent change
APA alone†	**510,489**	**792,477**	**55%**
Chinese*	47%	46%	51%
Asian Indian	17%	22%	94%
Korean	14%	11%	21%
Filipino	9%	7%	20%
Pakistani	3%	3%	86%
Japanese	3%	3%	28%
Bangladeshi	1%	2%	319%
Southeast Asian**	2%	2%	16%
Native Hawaiian††	0.4%	1%	148%
Multi-ethnic Asian***	—	2%	—
Other Asian****	3%	3%	28%

MANHATTAN	1990	2000	Percent change
APA alone†	**110,168**	**145,607**	**32%**
Chinese*	66%	60%	20%
Asian Indian	5%	10%	157%
Korean	6%	7%	75%
Filipino	8%	6%	1%
Pakistani	0.5%	1%	89%
Japanese	10%	10%	26%
Bangladeshi	0.4%	1%	81%
Southeast Asian**	1%	1%	53%
Native Hawaiian††	0.6%	1%	59%
Multi-ethnic Asian***	—	1%	—
Other Asian****	3%	3%	12%

QUEENS	1990	2000	Percent change
APA alone†	**238,818**	**392,831**	**64%**
Chinese*	36%	36%	61%
Asian Indian	23%	28%	102%
Korean	21%	16%	24%
Filipino	10%	8%	24%
Pakistani	3%	3%	79%
Japanese	2%	1%	18%
Bangladeshi	1%	3%	348%
Southeast Asian**	1%	1%	24%
Native Hawaiian††	0.2%	0.3%	263%
Multi-ethnic Asian***	—	2%	—
Other Asian****	3%	3%	64%

BRONX	1990	2000	Percent change
APA alone†	**33,696**	**41,503**	**23%**
Chinese*	20%	16%	-2%
Asian Indian	30%	37%	52%
Korean	16%	9%	-27%
Filipino	9%	11%	59%
Pakistani	3%	3%	2%
Japanese	2%	1%	10%
Bangladeshi	1%	4%	277%
Southeast Asian**	13%	10%	-4%
Native Hawaiian††	1%	3%	220%
Multi-ethnic Asian***	—	2%	—
Other Asian****	6%	4%	-24%

BROOKLYN	1990	2000	Percent change
APA alone†	**111,148**	**187,283**	**68%**
Chinese*	62%	64%	75%
Asian Indian	13%	14%	74%
Korean	6%	3%	-7%
Filipino	6%	3%	2%
Pakistani	4%	5%	106%
Japanese	1%	1%	81%
Bangladeshi	1%	2%	364%
Southeast Asian**	3%	2%	18%
Native Hawaiian††	1%	1%	119%
Multi-ethnic Asian***	—	2%	—
Other Asian****	3%	2%	-1%

STATEN ISLAND	1990	2000	Percent change
APA alone†	**16,719**	**25,253**	**51%**
Chinese*	31%	30%	46%
Asian Indian	24%	26%	63%
Korean	19%	14%	10%
Filipino	18%	18%	50%
Pakistani	2%	4%	153%
Japanese	1%	1%	43%
Bangladeshi	0%	0.2%	—
Southeast Asian**	1%	1%	164%
Native Hawaiian††	0.3%	1%	264%
Multi-ethnic Asian***	—	1%	—
Other Asian****	4%	5%	69%

Note: This table includes mixed-ethnic APAs, but excludes APAs of more than one race (up to 6).
*The total number of Chinese includes Taiwanese.
**Southeast Asian includes Cambodian, Hmong, Laotian, and Vietnamese.
***Multi-ethnic Asian is a new subcategory in 2000 Census which includes persons of multiple Asian ethnicities.
****Other Asian includes Thai, Sri Lankan, Malaysian, and Indonesian.
†Asians of more than one ethnicity, i.e. Chinese-Japanese, are counted in the separate multi-ethnic category.
††Includes Pacific Islanders; mono- and mixed-ethnic NHPIs, i.e. Hawaiian-Tongans or Samoan-Guamanians.

Source: 1990 PUMS, U.S. Census 2000 SF1

a significant Asian population suggesting "clustering in adjacent tracts accentuates the ethnic character and reputation of neighborhoods by aggregating more group members in a delimited space." More important, while Asians concentrate in these neighborhoods, these neighborhoods are by no means majority Asian, indicating that in addition to historic enclave neighborhoods such as Manhattan Chinatown, Asian New Yorkers reside largely in multiracial and multiethnic neighborhoods.

The spatial distribution of the three largest Asian ethnic groups also indicates distinct ethnic-specific settlement patterns. As noted earlier in the discussion on new immigrant settlement patterns, Chinese New Yorkers are concentrated in three boroughs. Several Census tracts with high Chinese population constitute the core of New York City's three "Chinatowns"—historic Manhattan's Chinatown, Flushing in Queens, and Sunset Park in Brooklyn. In addition to these well-known concentrations, the Chinese in Queens are also concentrated in neighborhoods with large Asian and Latino populations such as Elmhurst, Jackson Heights, and Woodside.

In Brooklyn, there is a "spine" of high Chinese population tracts along the northern border of Dyker Heights through Bensonhurst connecting to the Chinese cluster in Sunset Park. The surrounding neighborhoods of Bay Ridge, which is largely Italian, and Borough Park, the densest concentration of Hasidic Jews in the United States, have maintained their neighborhood boundaries, which has "directed" the expanding Chinese population to neighborhoods further south. In addition to Bensonhurst, a Chinese concentration is located in Sheepshead Bay comprised of a core tract surrounded by tracts with smaller numbers of Chinese.

Asian Indians largely reside in Queens, forming three spatially concentrated clusters. The largest cluster forms a band across southern Queens from east

Median Household Income by Race and State, 1999: Northeast

	United States	Northeast region	Connecticut	Maine	Massachusetts	New Hampshire
All Non-Family Households	**41,994**	**45,481**	**53,935**	**37,240**	**50,502**	**49,467**
Black alone	29,423	31,791	35,104	30,758	33,727	43,474
Asian alone	51,908	51,912	61,587	37,873	51,273	56,344
NHPI alone	42,717	35,073	60,536	48,000	34,891	36,250
Hispanic alone	33,676	31,678	32,075	36,224	27,300	39,985
White alone, not Hispanic	45,367	48,918	58,564	37,405	53,031	49,746

	New Jersey	New York	Pennsylvania	Rhode Island	Vermont
All Non-Family Households	**55,146**	**43,393**	**40,106**	**42,090**	**40,856**
Black alone	38,513	31,364	27,415	24,973	31,585
Asian alone	72,224	45,402	44,205	36,473	39,630
NHPI alone	56,080	28,713	42,656	29,423	28,750
Hispanic alone	39,609	30,499	26,930	22,851	38,728
White alone, not Hispanic	60,600	49,474	41,742	45,314	41,077

Source: U.S. Census 2000, SF3 (Tables P53, P152B, D, E, H, I)

to west through the neighborhoods of Bellerose and Floral Park, Queens Village, Hollis, Jamaica, Jamaica Hills, Briarwood, Richmond Hill and South Ozone Park. These neighborhoods, in particular Richmond Hill and South Ozone Park, have emerged as the center of New York City's Indo-Caribbean population. Interestingly, this cluster includes the only neighborhoods with notable Asian and African American populations. This pattern may reflect the specific historic and social experiences of Asian Indians who have coexisted with Afro-Caribbeans in their home countries of Guyana, Trinidad and Tobago for many generations.

There are two additional clusters of Census tracts with high numbers of Asian Indians. One cluster in Flushing is often referred to as NYC's second Chinatown, but its demographic composition reflects a pan-Asian community comprised of Chinese, Asian Indians, and Koreans. Another cluster is situated in the neighborhoods of Jackson Heights, Elmhurst and parts of Corona and Rego Park. The businesses and services based in Jackson Heights' Little India serve a regional South Asian consumer market.

Korean New Yorkers are concentrated in a handful of Queens neighborhoods. The neighborhoods with Census tracts containing the highest number of Koreans are located in two Northeastern Queens neighborhoods—Flushing and Clearview. In addition to these

Koreans in New York City, Census 2000

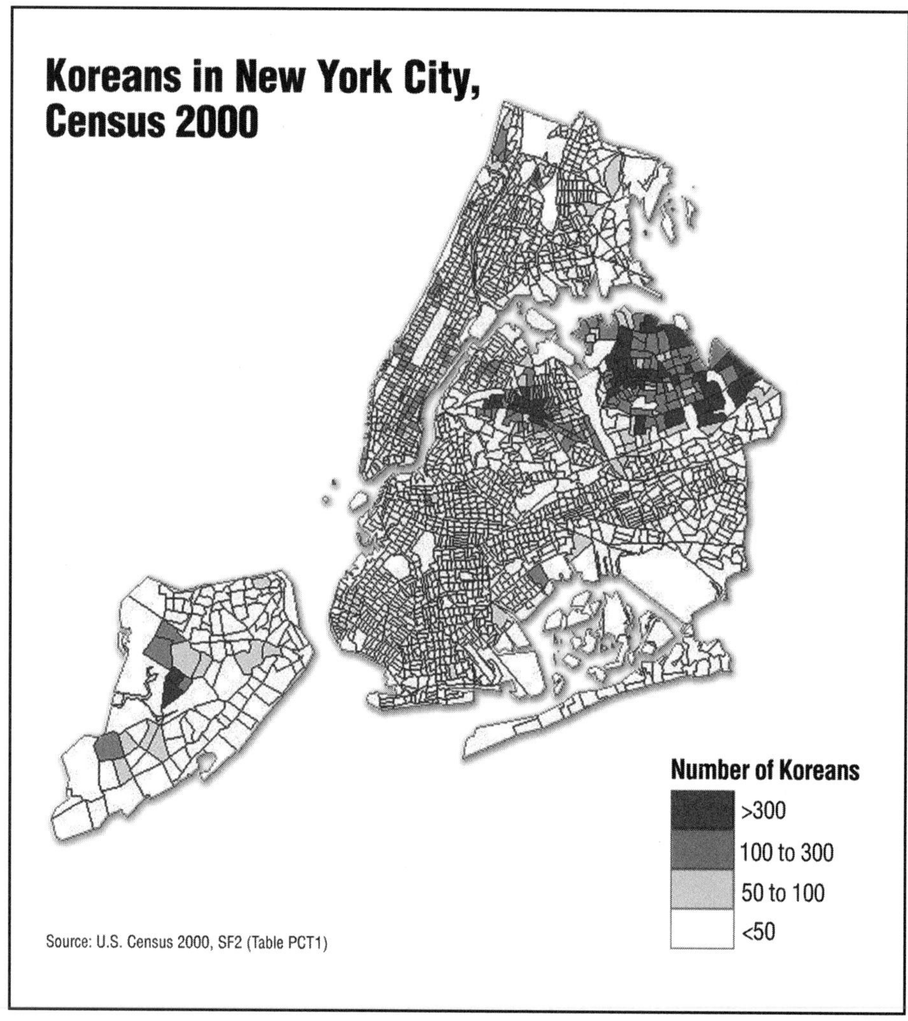

Source: U.S. Census 2000, SF2 (Table PCT1)

concentrations, Koreans are settled in relatively high numbers in Douglaston, Oakland Gardens, Bayside, and Fresh Meadow. Several highly concentrated Korean tracts are also located in Sunnyside, Woodside, and Elmhurst.

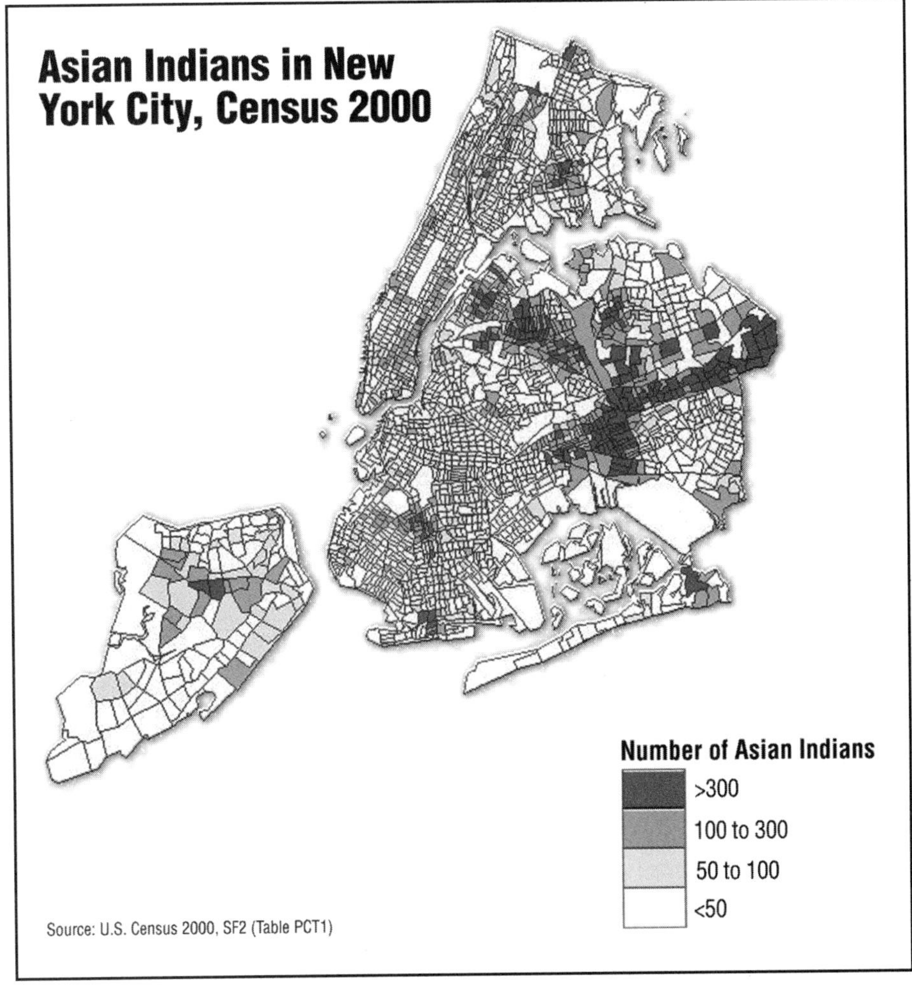

Regional policy and electoral impact
The demographic patterns of Asian New Yorkers underscore several significant regional impacts. An enclave, i.e., an ethnically homogenous neighborhood, is no longer dominant among Asian Pacific Americans. Even the neighborhoods known as NYC's "satellite" Chinatowns are in fact ethnically and racially diverse; APAs comprise nearly half of the total Flushing population, and about a quarter of Sunset Park's. Similar to other concentrated Asian neighborhoods such as Elmhurst and Jackson Heights, majority Asian Census tracts are located within these neighborhoods that typically contain sizable Latino populations. These settlement patterns and neighborhood formations need to be further investigated especially since much research on Asian socioeconomic incorporation relies on concepts of voluntary segregation, ethnic resources, and an enclave economy.

The spatial concentration of Asian Pacific Americans contributed to a historic election in 2001. Despite a historical presence of over 150 years in New York City, no Asian Pacific American had ever been elected to public office. The implementation of term limits resulted in the opening of 35 city council seats, an unprecedented number, in the 2001 elections. Local campaign finance laws provided a one to four matching fund, further enabling many new individuals to run for public office. Thirteen Asian candidates vied for seats on the New York City Council. Their ethnic composition reflects the diversity of the APA population and included three Asian Indians, one Bangladeshi, one Guyanese, one Korean, and seven Chinese candidates. They ran in Manhattan and Queens districts that represented Chinatown-Lower East Side, Flushing, Richmond Hill, and Elmhurst as well as other neighborhoods with sizable Asian populations. The result: the election of the first Asian American, John Liu (District 20-Flushing, Queens), to seat on the New York City Council.

Conclusion
The rapid growth and rich ethnic diversity of the Asian Pacific American population is an integral dynamic in New York City's racial and ethnic transformation into a 'majority minority' city. Undergoing the greatest population growth, Asian Pacific Americans also represent tremendous ethnic, linguistic, and cultural diversity, with national origins rooted in the Pacific Rim as well as the Caribbean. The immigrant experience common to Asians is increasingly more complex as an undocumented influx is becoming more prominent in APA migration processes. The multi-faceted nature of the Asian Pacific American population poses formidable challenges to defining and mobilizing pan-ethnic and pan-racial interests.

The release of the next levels of 2000 Census data will help develop a richer and more complex profile of the APA population in New York City. Based on this preliminary overview highlighting key trends in ethnic composition and growth, spatial patterns and neighborhood concentrations, research should further investigate shared and divergent socioeconomic characteristics and experiences among Asian Pacific American ethnic groups in an increasingly diverse neighborhood and metropolitan context.

—*Tarry Hum*

Spotlight on New Jersey

They're growing something in the Garden State, but it's no longer crops—it's Asian Pacific Americans.

Led by Asian Indians, New Jersey's APA population nearly doubled in the 1990s, as the state added nearly 260,000 APA residents, for a growth rate of 95.3 percent. This outpaced the second-fastest growing group, the Hispanic population, which grew 37.4 percent; the white, non-Hispanic population fell 1 percent.

The home of Bruce Springsteen and The Sopranos may only be the ninth most populous state in the union, but it ranks fifth in APA population, with 532,000 people. The Census Bureau predicts that New Jersey's APA population will cross the one million mark by 2025.

Like most New Jerseyans, APAs are concentrated in the bedroom communities of the state's northeastern corner. In affluent Bergen County, right across the Hudson River from New York City, almost one in eight residents is APA, with Koreans the largest group at more than 40,000. In suburbs close to Manhattan such as Closter, Demarest, Alpine, Tenafly and Norwood, more than one in five residents is APA, according to the local newspaper, *The Record*, while Korean and Indian-owned businesses abound in Palisades Park and Fort Lee.

Demographers also noted a growing belt of affluence in the state's center, as drug and technology companies moved there, bringing professionals to counties such as Middlesex, Morris, and others. APAs are also overrepresented here. Many are highly educated immigrants who are finding jobs with corporations setting up shop in central New Jersey, allowing these immigrants to skip the traditional urban gateways such as Newark, Jersey City and Elizabeth.

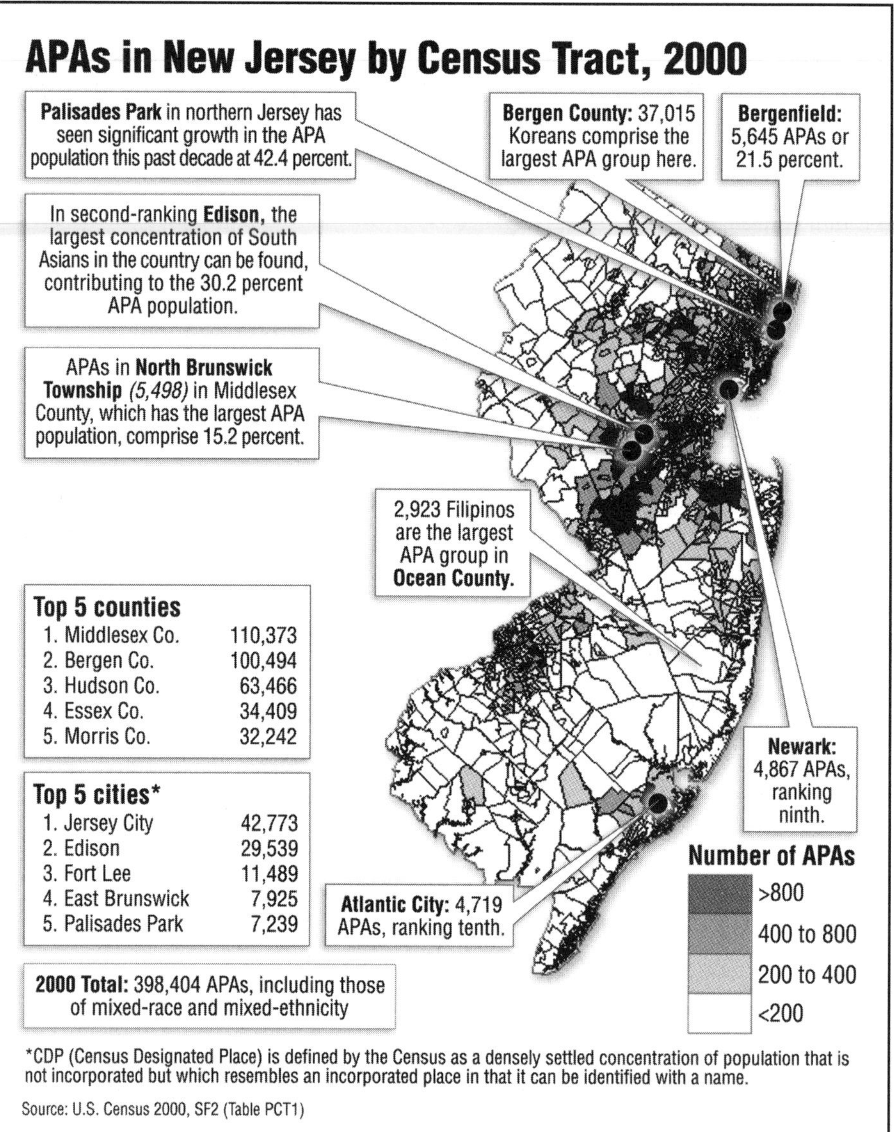

New Jersey boasts high rates of educational attainment among Asians. According to Census 2000, 195,903, or 62.1 percent, of Asians in New Jersey said they had attained at least a bachelor's degree, a rate of almost 40 percent higher than the national average and 20 percent higher than the percentage of Asians nationwide. For NHPIs, whose socioeconomic rates have consistently remained lower than Asians, 21.7 percent held a bachelor's degree. Compared to the 8.9 percent national average, 25.9 percent of Asians and 10.3 percent of NHPIs in New Jersey held a graduate or professional degree.

"Before they would live in an apartment in Newark or New York," Woody Patel, the owner of an Indian restaurant in South Brunswick called Chutney Mary's, told *The New York Times*. "But now they all know computers and right away they get jobs for $60,000, $70,000 and they go straight to the suburbs to look for a house."

Ten Largest APA Groups in New Jersey

	Number of APAs	% of overall APAs
Asian Indian	180,957	34.0%
Chinese	103,229	19.4%
Filipino	95,063	17.9%
Korean	68,990	13%
Japanese	18,830	3.5%
Vietnamese	16,707	3.1%
Pakistani	15,392	2.9%
Native Hawaiian*	10,065	1.9%
Taiwanese	7,034	1.3%
Bangladeshi	2,910	0.5%
Total	**532,288**	

*Includes Pacific Islanders

Note: All detailed group figures include individuals of mixed-race; resulting overlap would cause total to be greater than APA total.

Source: U.S. Census 2000, SF2, PCT1

New Jersey's low poverty rate of 8.5 percent (the national poverty rate was 12.4 percent) sets the stage for that of the state's Asian population—they have the lowest poverty rate, at 6.8 percent, of all other Asians across the nation. The poverty rate among NHPIs in New Jersey, on the other hand, still remains comparatively high at 17.1 percent, though this figure was similar to the national poverty rate among NHPIs.

Lower poverty rates mean higher incomes. Asians in New Jersey had the highest median household income, at $72,224 of all races in the nine northeastern states, while NHPIs earned less at $56,080. NHPIs in New Jersey still had the second-highest median family income among other northeastern states. Median family income for Asians and NHPIs in New Jersey followed a similar pattern, with Asians at $78,211 and NHPIs at $64,762. Regarding per capita income, Asians at $27,581 earned less than whites but more than other races. NHPIs in New Jersey had the highest per capita income ($23,745) of all NHPIs in the Northeast.

Asian Indians are the single largest group in New Jersey, making up more than 180,000, or one-third of the APA population. There are another 20,000 other South Asians. South Asians are probably the most diverse, ranging from new immigrant taxi drivers to well-off Ph.D.-holding engineers. Besides the more urban enclaves of Jersey City, the Central Middlesex County suburbs of Woodbridge and Edison now have an estimated 50,000 South Asians. Several miles of Oak Tree Road have become widely known as Little India for all of the businesses and restaurants.

The Chinese and Filipino populations are the second and third largest in New Jersey. Korean Americans are fourth, while the Japanese, bolstered by the many Japanese corporations moving from Manhattan to New Jersey, ranked fifth.

In a state that has a growing diversity of APAs, language ultimately becomes an important issue. In New Jersey, 105,855 people or 3.5 percent speak an APA language. In the case of linguistic isolation, when all household members over fourteen years old have difficulty with English, 25.4 percent of those that speak an APA language are linguistically isolated. New Jersey ranks sixth among the northeastern states, with the highest rate of people speaking an APA language and who are linguistically isolated.

Highest APA Concentrations in New Jersey, by County

County	Number of APAs	% of overall APAs
Middlesex	110,373	14.7%
Bergen	100,494	11.4%
Hudson	63,466	10.4%
Somerset	26,937	9.1%
Morris	32,242	6.9%

Source: U.S. Census 2000, SF1

Bergenfield has a Filipino American mayor, Robert Rivas, while Franklin Township has an Indian American mayor, Upendra Chivukula. But apart from a few elections of APAs to local school boards, political representation remains pretty low.

'We don't have our own Jesse Jacksons or Al Sharptons. It's contrary to the Asian culture to be aggressive and toot your own horn. But that is what the communities will have to do to gain political recognition," one second-generation Korean American told *The New York Times.*

—Eric Lai

Spotlight on Boston

Boston became a 'majority minority' city in the 1990s, as Latinos, Asians and blacks arrived and tens of thousands of whites left. But Beantown's suburbs also saw an increased Asian presence. For even as whites moved into Boston's Chinatown, Asians moved out to nearby suburbs like Quincy, Worcester, Lowell, Lynn, Lawrence, and Cambridge.

Boston has had a reputation for being a segregated town. During the 1970s, violence flared when courts ordered that the public schools be integrated. But Asians and Latinos appear to be able to break through this color line, moving into areas that still have little black and white mixing.

More than 50,000 APAs resided in Suffolk County, where Boston is located, in 2000. One in twelve Suffolk County residents is of APA descent. But the larger APA population is actually in neighboring Middlesex County, where more than 100,000 APAs live in communities as diverse as academic-minded Cambridge, blue-collar Somerville, and posh Weston.

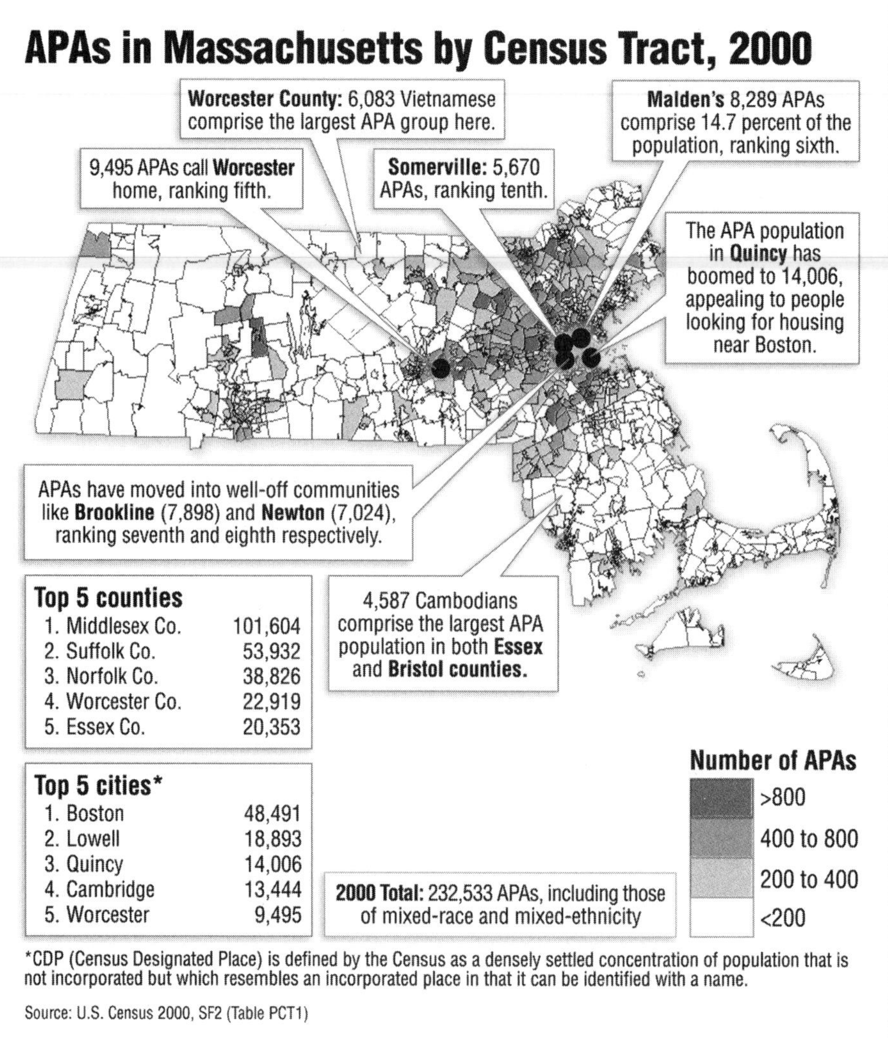

APAs are the largest minority in Cambridge, making up more than one in eight residents. In Weston, fifteen percent of adults speak an Asian language at home, though four out of five of those said they speak English very well, according to Census data cited by the *Boston Globe*. Many moved to Suffolk County to be near jobs along Route 128, the famed highway lined with hi-tech businesses.

The largest Chinatown in Massachusetts outside of Boston proper is in Quincy, where a large Chinese community has existed since the 1970s and today makes up almost one-fifth of the city's population. One in seven Quincy residents speaks Mandarin, Vietnamese, Tagalog, Hindi or another Asian or Pacific Island language at home, the highest percentage in the state, an increase from one in twenty in 1990.

Quincy has boomed because of cheap housing, a large commercial center, and a good location for commuting into Boston. Today, Quincy's police department and hospital all offer translation services for Asians. Nearby suburbs like Randolph also boast substantial immigrant populations, equally split between Asians and Latinos.

From 1980 to 1990, the statewide Asian population increased from 49,501 to 143,392, or 189.7 percent. By 2000, it had grown another 89.6 percent to 271,819, ranking it as the tenth-largest consolidated metropolitan area (CMSA) by APA population (it ranks thirteenth among the overall population). The Chinese are the largest group, nearly double the next largest group, Asian Indians. They are followed by Vietnamese, Cambodians, and Koreans.

Going against the national pattern, Asians lagged behind whites in median family income in Massachusetts. Statewide, Asians and NHPIs had median family incomes in 1999 of $57,893 and $36,429, both behind the statewide non-Hispanic white average of $65,327. Asians in Cambridge had a median family income in 1999 of $43,170, which was much lower than the median non-Hispanic white family income of $76,562. They also lagged in Quincy: $51,352 for Asians versus $62,596 for whites. These figures, along with the relatively high Asian language fluency, indicate the high proportion of recent immigrant arrivals among the Boston APA population.

As Paul Watanabe, co-director of the Institute for Asian American Studies at UMass-Boston, told the Associated Press, the question now is whether the growth of the APA population in Massachusetts will be reflected in growing political and business power.

—*Eric Lai*

Immigration and Imperialism

A Demographic Profile of Asian Pacific Americans in Hawai'i

Hawai'i is clearly the most Asian Pacific American of the fifty states, with some 70 percent of its population being of Asian, Hawaiian, or Pacific Islander descent. This has been true since Hawai'i became the 50th state in 1959 and is a product of its unique history.

History

A series of islands in the middle of the Pacific Ocean, Hawai'i was an independent kingdom populated by an indigenous Polynesian people until forced contact with the West took place in the 18th century. The "discovery" of Hawai'i by British Captain James Cook in 1778 began a chain of events that would see a devastating decline in the indigenous population (hereafter referred to as "Native Hawaiian") and an increasing outside influence on the political and economic life of the islands.

Estimates of the Native Hawaiian population at the moment of contact with the West range from 200,000 to 800,000; by 1893, barely a hundred years later, the Native Hawaiian population stood at 40,000, the population decline due mostly to diseases introduced by the settlers. Wealth and power concentrated in the hands a few, mostly American and European settlers, whose influence led to the illegal overthrow of the Hawaiian monarchy in 1893 and annexation by the United States in 1898. Hawai'i remained a territory of the United States until becoming a state in 1959.

Hawai'i's 19th century economy was based on whaling and the sandalwood trade, and after the Civil War, on sugar exportation. The boom in the sugar industry led to a sugar plantation economy that would control nearly all aspects of life in Hawai'i by the late 19th century. The plantations' voracious need for labor led to successive waves of migrant laborers, mostly from Asia, beginning with the Chinese, followed by Japanese, Koreans and Filipinos. Non-Asian laborers were also brought in, most notably Portuguese and Puerto Ricans. Families and descendents of workers from each of these groups formed immigrant communities, from which contemporary ethnic communities evolved.

Photo: Cindy Chew

Hawai'i is home to different racial groups, including those of Japanese, Korean, Filipino, and other Pacific Islander descent, who make up the state's Asian majority population.

In the mid-1900s, tourism replaced agriculture as the dominant industry,

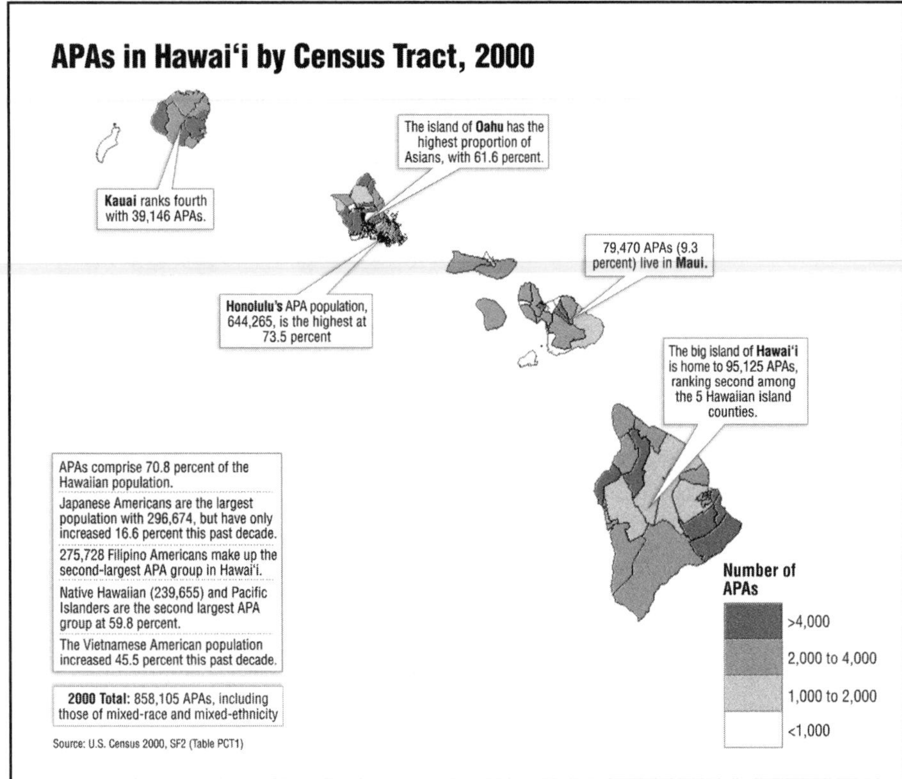

with an annual visitor count in 2001 nearing seven million. Hawai'i also became reliant on military expenditures to an extent approaching that of tourism. Currently, the expenditures from tourism and the military account for approximately half of Hawai'i's gross state product. Being highly dependent on a few industries has made the economy vulnerable to global events, as seen after the decline of the Japanese economy and later after the Sept. 11 terrorist attacks.

Hawai'i has also become one of the most expensive states to live in, with a cost of living estimated to be 27 percent higher than the U.S. mainland. Between 1990 and 2000, there was a net loss in the number of jobs in most occupational categories, but losses were tempered by an increase in government jobs that helped keep the total number up from 1990. Unemployment increased over the decade, from 2.8 percent in 1990, peaking at 6.8 percent in the middle of 1992 and falling to 4.3 in 2000. Paradoxically, personal income increased, possibly due to an in-migration of retirees with high transfer incomes and high-wage workers alongside an exodus of low to medium-wage workers to other states. These economic constraints, along with limited land availability, contribute to the lower population growth rate—nine percent compared to thirteen percent nationally over the past decade.

Hawai'i's "majority minority" population has made it unique among all the states throughout its post-statehood history. The vast majority of the population has always been Asian Pacific American, including Native Hawaiians and Asian immigrants and their descendants. This population was largely disenfranchised in the first half of the 20th century, due to both entrenched *haole* (white) political and economic power and laws prohibiting Asian immigrants from naturalized citizenship.

Plantation bosses also strategically brought in immigrant workers of differing ethnic backgrounds so as to inhibit labor organization that might lead to political organization. But this changed after World War II due in part to successful pan-ethnic labor organizing, large numbers of citizen children of immigrant workers coming of age, and the well-publicized war record of second-generation Asian American soldiers. In the second half of the 20th century, Asian Pacific Americans, particularly those of Japanese ancestry, could be found in corporate boardrooms and the highest political offices in Hawai'i. The first Asian Americans and the first Pacific Islander Americans to hold the highest political offices—United States Senator, governor of a state, and United States Congressperson—could all be found in Hawai'i in the 1960s and 1970s.

Demographic overview

There are 858,105 APAs total in Hawai'i, making it the third largest state population. 70.8 percent of its population is of full or part-Asian or Hawaiian/Pacific Islander descent. Despite having just 0.3 percent of the total U.S. population, 4.9 percent of all single race Asians and 28.5 percent of all single race Hawaiian/Pacific Islanders are in Hawai'i. More specifically, 57 percent of all single race Hawaiians and 25.3 percent of all single race Japanese Americans residing in the US can be found in Hawai'i.

Hawai'i can also be viewed as the "mixed race" state, having by far the largest proportion of people who identify themselves with more than one racial category. The mixed-race population makes up 21.4 percent of the population, compared to just 2.4 percent for the country as a whole. Hawai'i far exceeds the next three highest states of Alaska, California and Oklahoma, where 5.4 percent, 4.7 percent and 4.5 percent identified with two or more races, respectively. 92.8 percent of the multiracial population in Hawai'i, or about 240,000, is hapa, or part-APA.

Median Household Income by Race, 1999: Hawai'i

	United States	Hawaii
All households	**$41,994**	**$49,820**
Asian alone	$51,908	$54,232
NHPI alone	$42,717	$41,779
Black alone	$29,423	$41,032
Hispanic alone	$33,676	$37,704
Non-Hispanic white alone	$45,367	$49,976
Two or more races	$35,587	$44,706

Source: U.S. Census 2000, SF3 (Tables P53 and P152 A-I)

The populations of non-APA racial groups are relatively smaller than those of the United States as whole. 39.3 percent of the population is of full or part European descent compared to 77.1 percent of America as a whole. Just 2.8 percent are full or part black/African American and 2.1 percent American Indian/Alaska Native. 7.2 percent are Hispanic/Latino (of any race), compared with 12.5 percent for the country as a whole.

The state of Hawai'i is made up of many islands, but 99.9 percent of its population of 1,211,537 resides on just five of them: Oahu, Hawai'i, Maui, Kauai, and Molokai. Oahu, on which the capital city of Honolulu can be found, has 876,156 people, or 72.3 percent of the total population. Generally speaking, the island of Oahu has the highest proportion of Asians, with 61.6 percent of the population being of full or part Asian descent. The island of Hawai'i has the largest concentration of European Americans and Hawaiians/Pacific Islanders, with 52.1 percent of full or part European descent and 31 percent of full or part Hawaiian/Pacific Islander descent.

Mixed-race categorization and its implications for Hawaiians

The institution of mixed-race categories on the 2000 Census has led to a dramatically different way of counting Asian Pacific Americans. Nowhere is this more true than in Hawai'i, where more than one in five people is of mixed racial descent. This does not include those of mixed-ethnic ancestry within the Asian racial category, such as those who are Japanese-Filipino, for instance.

One result of the new mixed-race categories is what appeared to be the decline in population of many Asian Pacific American groups. Chinese fell from 68,804 in 1990 to 56,600 in 2000. Koreans fell from 24,454 to 23,537. Native Hawaiians declined from 138,742 to 80,137. Japanese fell from 247,486 to 201,764. The apparent 18 percent decline of the Japanese American population in Hawai'i was part of an apparent nationwide decline in the Japanese American population, prompting Japanese American newspapers to ponder the meaning of a shrinking population.

In fact, the populations really weren't shrinking. Because of the new mixed-race categories, some 199,311 mixed-race Asians are not counted in the single race figures for individual Asian Pacific American groups. The 1990 and 2000 figures for the individual groups are thus not directly comparable. But by looking at the Census Bureau's SF2 data, which includes separate subtotals for both single race and multiracial people, we find that the Japanese American population was actually 296,674.

Similarly, the Chinese population, including multiracial people, grows to 170,628—more than tripling. The Chinese and the Native Hawaiians, in fact, have the highest rate of multiraciality—around two-thirds each group is multiracial. Similarly, about four in ten Samoans, Filipinos and Koreans in Hawai'i are also multiracial.

Asians (including those of mixed-race or mixed-ethnicity) make up some 58 percent of Hawai'i's population. Though there are many Asian American groups in Hawai'i, the vast majority belong to just two groups, Japanese and Filipino. About three-quarters of the APA population is part or pure Japanese or Filipino. About one-fifth of the population is part or pure Chinese, while 5 percent is pure or part Korean.

The largest increases among Asians were among Southeast and "other" Asians, including Vietnamese, Cambodian, Hmong, Thai and others. In 1990, these groups made up 2.4 percent of the Asian population; in 2000, they were about one-tenth of the population, calculating by single race.

Native Hawaiian and Pacific Islander populations

Though they are counted as part of the same "race" in the Census, the Native Hawaiian community and other Pacific Islander communities have very different histories in Hawai'i. As noted above, the Native Hawaiian population was severely depleted in the years after contact with the West. There was much intermarriage between Hawaiians and

Poverty Status by Race, 1999: Hawai'i

% below poverty level	United States	Hawai'i
Total	**12.4%**	**10.7%**
Non-Hispanic white alone	8.1%	9.1%
Black alone	24.9%	8.8%
American Indian alone	25.7%	18.2%
Asian alone	12.6%	7.1%
NHPI alone	17.7%	21.4%
Hispanic alone	22.6%	17.5%

Source: U.S. Census 2000, SF3 (Tables P87, P159 A-I)

Socioeconomic trends in the Aloha State

At a first glance at factors like income, Hawai'i residents appear to be doing be better than their peers around the country. Much of that impression, however, is cancelled out by Hawai'i's high cost of living. Factors like poverty rate and educational attainment confirm the gap long suspected to exist between the Asian and NHPI populations in Hawai'i.

Income

Due to Hawai'i 's high cost of living, nearly all racial groups have higher median household incomes in Hawai'i than elsewhere in the country. For all households, the median household income in Hawai'i is $49,820—around 20 percent higher than the U.S. median. Asians have a median household income of $54,232, which is the highest in the island (though not the highest for Asians throughout the country: in New Jersey, Asians have a median household income of more than $77,000). Native Hawaiians and Pacific Islanders, however, have one of the lowest in the state: $41,779, which is actually under the NHPI national median.

Families are generally larger than households, as the Census defines them, so median family incomes tend to be higher than median household ones. For Asians in Hawai'i, it was $63,222; which is 17 percent higher than the median household figure. For NHPIs, it was $45,293, which is 8.5 percent higher. Compared with other races (alone) in Hawai'i , Asians had the highest median family income. NHPIs ranked just behind whites ($57,927) and multiracial people ($49,297), but higher than blacks, American Indians and Hispanics.

The next level of data showing the breakdowns in income by specific ethnic groups such as Chinese, Samoan, etc. were not available at the time of this writing. But even the data available, such as per-capita income, show that not all APAs are paid-up members of the model minority. For instance, while Asians tend to have higher median household or family incomes, they also have larger households and families (3.61 members per Asian family nationwide, versus an average of 3.14 members per family). NHPIs, with a median age around 8 years younger at both the Hawaiian and national level, have even larger families: 4.05 average members per family nationwide and 4.13 in Hawai'i.

Thus, it's not surprising that by examining per-capita income figures, we see that both Asians and NHPIs on the whole earn less than whites, with NHPIs lagging behind both blacks and American Indians in Hawai'i, though not nationwide. In Hawai'i, non-Hispanic whites had a per-capita income ($30,199) about a third greater than Asians ($22,884) and more than double that of NHPIs ($14,375).

Poverty

The poverty rate in Hawai'i is 10.7 percent. While Asians have a lower poverty rate than the average (7.1 percent), NHPIs have nearly double the poverty rate (21.4 percent), the highest among all the major racial groups. Indeed, nearly three out of ten NHPI children (under age 18) is considered impoverished. The Asian child poverty rate in Hawai'i is less than one in ten.

Europeans/Americans and later between Hawaiians and Asian migrants and their descendants. As a result, the part-Hawaiian population grew larger than the "pure" Hawaiian population. Intermarriage, combined with the decline of Hawaiian culture and language in the face of American annexation, led to a decline in those who identified with being Hawaiian. However, the last two decades have seen a resurgence of Hawaiian language and culture, along with a political movement seeking sovereignty for Hawai'i after the illegal takeover by the United States in 1898.

As with some of the Asian groups, the Hawaiian population apparently declined, going from 138,742 in 1990 to 80,137 in 2000. But employing the statistics from the Census 2000's SF2 dataset, we see that the Hawaiian population, single and multiracial, in 2000 was 239,655—almost 70 percent more than 1990, and encompassing 28 percent of Hawai'i's APA population.

Most of the remaining people in the Hawaiian/Pacific Islander category are Samoan. The 1990 population of 15,034 nearly doubled in 2000, including mixed-race Samoans. There are also small but significant populations of Tongans, Chamorros, Marshellese, and others who trace their ancestry to island states in Micronesia, Polynesia and Melanesia.

Future trends

Hawai'i will undoubtedly remain the most Asian Pacific American state for the foreseeable future. However, the make-up of that population will undoubtedly change. The Japanese will almost certainly continue to decline in relative population (but not necessari-

Household and Family Size and Median Age, 2000: Hawai'i

TOTAL POPULATION	United States	Hawai'i
Median age	27.5	28.8
Average household size	3.6	3.8
Average family size	4.1	4.1
ASIAN ALONE	**United States**	**Hawai'i**
Median age	32.7	42.7
Average household size	3.1	3.0
Average family size	3.6	3.5
NHPI ALONE	**United States**	**Hawai'i**
Median age	35.3	36.2
Average household size	2.6	2.9
Average family size	3.1	3.4

Note: Younger populations tend to have more children, making average household and family sizes larger.

Source: U.S. Census, 2000 SF1 (Table P13 A-I)

Age

Hawai'i's Asians (alone) are the oldest group in the United States, at a median age of 42.7 years. NHPIs, by contrast, are a young population, with a median national age of 27.5 years.

Education

More than one third of NHPIs in Hawai'i over three years or older (35.3 percent) are enrolled in school, confirming the youthfulness of the NHPI population there. A much smaller percentage of Asians (22.3 percent) are enrolled in school—not surprising considering the relatively old Asian population in Hawai'i.

Whites are the most likely to send their children to private schools in Hawai'i , and much more likely than in the rest of the country. Asians and NHPIs are both more likely than their peers on the mainland to send kids to private schools.

In terms of educational attainment, slightly more than a quarter of Asians (26.6 percent) and about one-eighth of NHPIs in Hawai'i have a bachelor's degree or more. Both groups lag behind their peers nationwide—Asians nationwide, for instance, have a 44.1 percent rate of attaining a college bachelor's degree. The same pattern exists for those going on for post-graduate education—Asians and NHPIs are less educated than their peers on the mainland. Only 6.9 percent of Asians in Hawai'i, for instance, have a master's, professional, or doctoral degree, while 17.4 percent of Asians on the mainland do.

The fact that many NHPIs leave Hawai'i for the mainland to attend universities and remain there to work must be taken into consideration when looking at these figures. Prospects of greater educational and job opportunities on the mainland combined with the high cost of living in Hawai'i may be the reason for this apparent "brain drain."

Language

29.1 percent of Hawaiian households speak an APA language, the highest rate in the nation, ahead of California (9 percent) and the national household rate of 2.6 percent. Of those APA-speaking households in Hawai'i , 22.3 percent are linguistically isolated (all members of household 14 years old and over have at least some difficulty with English)—a rate lower than the national median of 29.2 percent.

About 267,000 Hawaiians altogether speak an Asian or Pacific Islander language. While nearly eight out of ten foreign-born ones do speak an APA language, only eleven percent of native-born Hawaiians do. While that's much higher than the rest of the country—the next closest state is California, where one-quarter of the foreign-born population speaks an Asian language but only 2.4 percent of the native-born does—it is an indicator of how integrated most of the Asians in the Hawai'i are, and how it's population size does not depend upon recent immigrants, as other states, chiefly California and New York, seem to do.

—Eric Lai

ly in actual numbers), mirroring national trends. Indeed this process has already begun. Filipinos may well pass Japanese in absolute numbers by the next Census. It seems likely that the Southeast Asian population will continue to grow at a faster rate than that of other Asian groups.

The population of Hawaiians and Pacific Islanders seems likely to grow as well. In the case of Native Hawaiians, political developments and the outcome of lawsuits challenging the special status of Hawaiians will greatly affect the future of the indigenous population and could also impact the number of people who identify with being Hawaiian. As a young and largely immigrant population, the Samoan and other Pacific Islander populations will likely grow at a faster than average rate.

APA Population in Hawai'i by Ethnicity, 2000

	Single race	% of total APAs	Including Multi-race	% of total APAs	% of pop. that is multi-racial
TOTAL APAs	**617,407**	**100.0%**	**858,105**	**100.0%**	**28.0%**
Asian	**503,868**	**81.6%**	**703,232**	**82.0%**	**28.3%**
Japanese	201,764	32.7%	296,674	34.6%	32.0%
Chinese*	56,600	9.2%	170,628	19.9%	66.8%
Filipinos	170,635	27.6%	275,728	32.1%	38.1%
Koreans	23,537	3.8%	41,352	4.8%	43.1%
Vietnamese	7,867	1.3%	10,040	1.2%	21.6%
Asian Indian	1,441	0.2%	3,145	0.4%	54.2%
NHPIs	**113,539**	**18.4%**	**282,667**	**32.9%**	**59.8%**
Native Hawaiians	80,137	13.0%	239,655	27.9%	66.6%
Samoans	16,166	2.6%	28,184	3.3%	42.6%
Tongan	3,993	0.6%	5,988	0.7%	33.3%
Guamanian or Chamorro	1,663	0.3%	4,221	0.5%	60.6%

*Includes Taiwanese.

*Note: Because of double counting of multiethnic and multiracial individuals, subtotals and percentages of detailed groups would combine to equal more than 100 percent of APA, or Asian, or NHPI totals.

Source: U.S. Census 2000, SF2, PCT1

Demographic changes will inevitably impact the balance of politics in the state. Where once the governor and both United States senators were all Japanese American, today only one Japanese American remains among this group. That person, the extremely influential Senator Daniel K. Inouye, who has held his Senate seat since 1962, will be eighty years old by the end of his current term in 2004. Meanwhile, Filipino political representation has markedly increased—the most recent current governor was a Filipino, Ben Cayetano—reflecting the broader demographic change over the past several decades. This demographic shift takes place at a time in which the Democratic Party, which has held power continuously since 1954—due largely to Japanese and Filipino American voters and political leaders—faces its most serious challenge from the Republican Party. Republicans, in fact, are courting Native Hawaiians as a "swing vote" in their efforts.

Hawai'i will also surely remain the state with the largest proportion of those indicating mixed racial ancestry. The question still remains whether Hawai'i actually has a much greater proportion of those with mixed racial ancestry as compared to all other states or whether a higher proportion of the population simply identified with more than one racial category in the 2000 Census. The unique history of the state may explain both the phenomena of interracial families as well as multiple racial identification. This history includes Western colonization, strong labor union movements, the formation of a distinct "local" identity, and political empowerment among a non-white majority. Regardless, as Hawai'i experiences the cultural, social and political developments accompanying racial "fusion" and the ongoing issues of multicultural democracy, it will undoubtedly serve as a laboratory for issues that will come to the forefront in many other places in the decades to come.

—Brian Niiya and Karen Umemoto

Educational Attainment by Race, 2000: Hawai'i

TOTAL POPULATION	United States	Hawai'i
% with college bachelor's degree or more	**24.4%**	**26.2%**
Men	26.1%	26.9%
Women	22.8%	25.5%
% with graduate/professional degree or more	**8.9%**	**8.4%**
Men	10.0%	9.2%
Women	7.8%	7.7%
ASIAN ALONE		
% with college bachelor's degree or more	**44.1%**	**26.6%**
Men	48.2%	27.0%
Women	40.4%	26.3%
% with graduate/professional degree or more	**17.4%**	**6.9%**
Men	22.1%	7.3%
Women	13.2%	6.5%
NHPI ALONE		
% with college bachelor's degree or more	**13.8%**	**11.8%**
Men	14.5%	12.3%
Women	13.1%	11.3%
% with graduate/professional degree or more	**4.1%**	**3.3%**
Men	4.4%	3.1%
Women	3.8%	3.4%

Source: U.S. Census 2000, SF3 (Tables P37 and P148A-I)

What Do Asian Americans Earn?

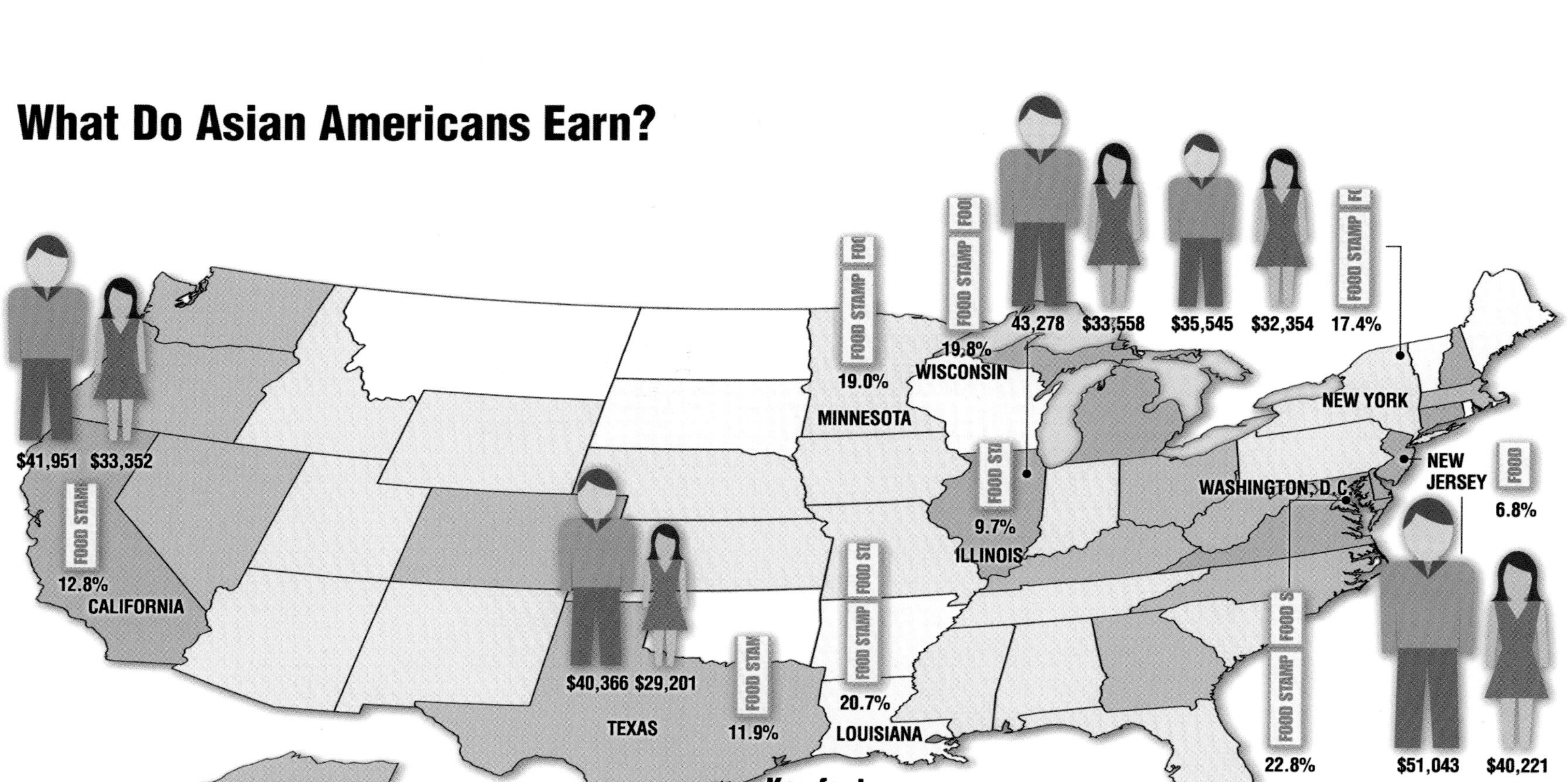

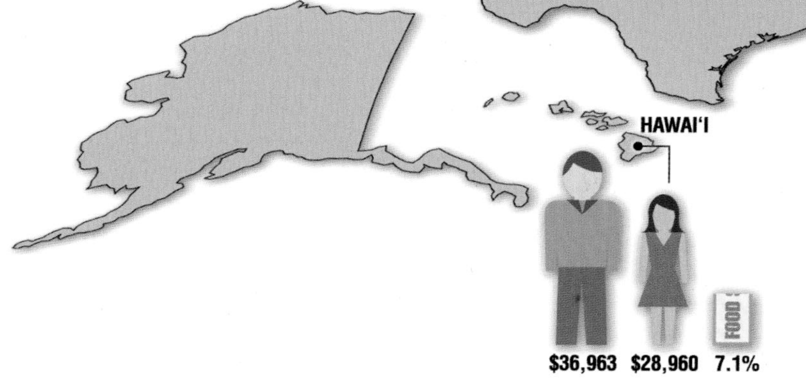

CALIFORNIA
$41,951 $33,352
12.8%

TEXAS
$40,366 $29,201
11.9%

HAWAI'I
$36,963 $28,960
7.1%

LOUISIANA
20.7%

MINNESOTA
19.0%

WISCONSIN
19.8%

ILLINOIS
43,278 $33,558
9.7%

NEW YORK
$35,545 $32,354
17.4%

WASHINGTON, D.C.
22.8%

NEW JERSEY
$51,043 $40,221
6.8%

Key facts

- Asians nationwide had a median household income of $51,908, versus $41,994 for all races. Asians earned the most in New Jersey ($72,224) and the least in Montana ($24,419).
- 1.3 million Asian Americans lived below the poverty line, or 12.6 percent. Non-Hispanic whites had the lowest rate of poverty – 8.1 percent.
- Merced, Calif. had one of the highest poverty rates for Asians in the nation, at 38.8 percent. Only 6.1 percent of Asians in Charlotte, NC were under the poverty line.
- Asian American women earned less than Asian American men everywhere. The gap was largest in West Virginia, where men earned more than twice what women did. The gap was lowest in New York – about $3,000, or 10 percent.
- California had the largest population of Asians in poverty – 466,000.

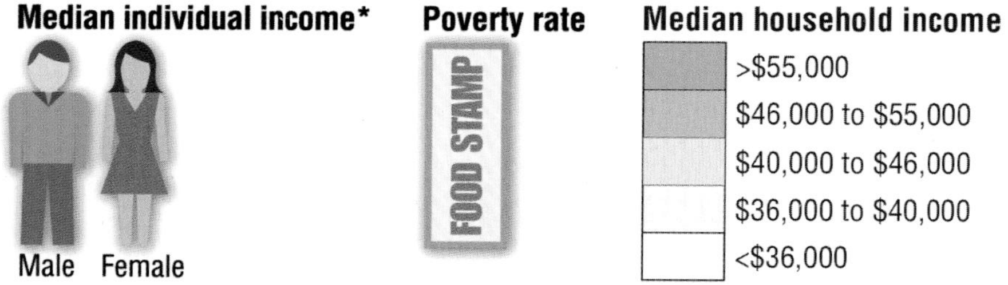

Median individual income*

Male Female

Poverty rate

FOOD STAMP

Median household income

- >$55,000
- $46,000 to $55,000
- $40,000 to $46,000
- $36,000 to $40,000
- <$36,000

*For full-time workers only.

Note: Includes only single-race individuals

Source: U.S. Census 2000, SF3 (Tables P152D, P152E, P159D, P159E, PCT74D and PCT74E)

Design: Olivia Nguyen

What Do Native Hawaiians and Pacific Islanders Earn?

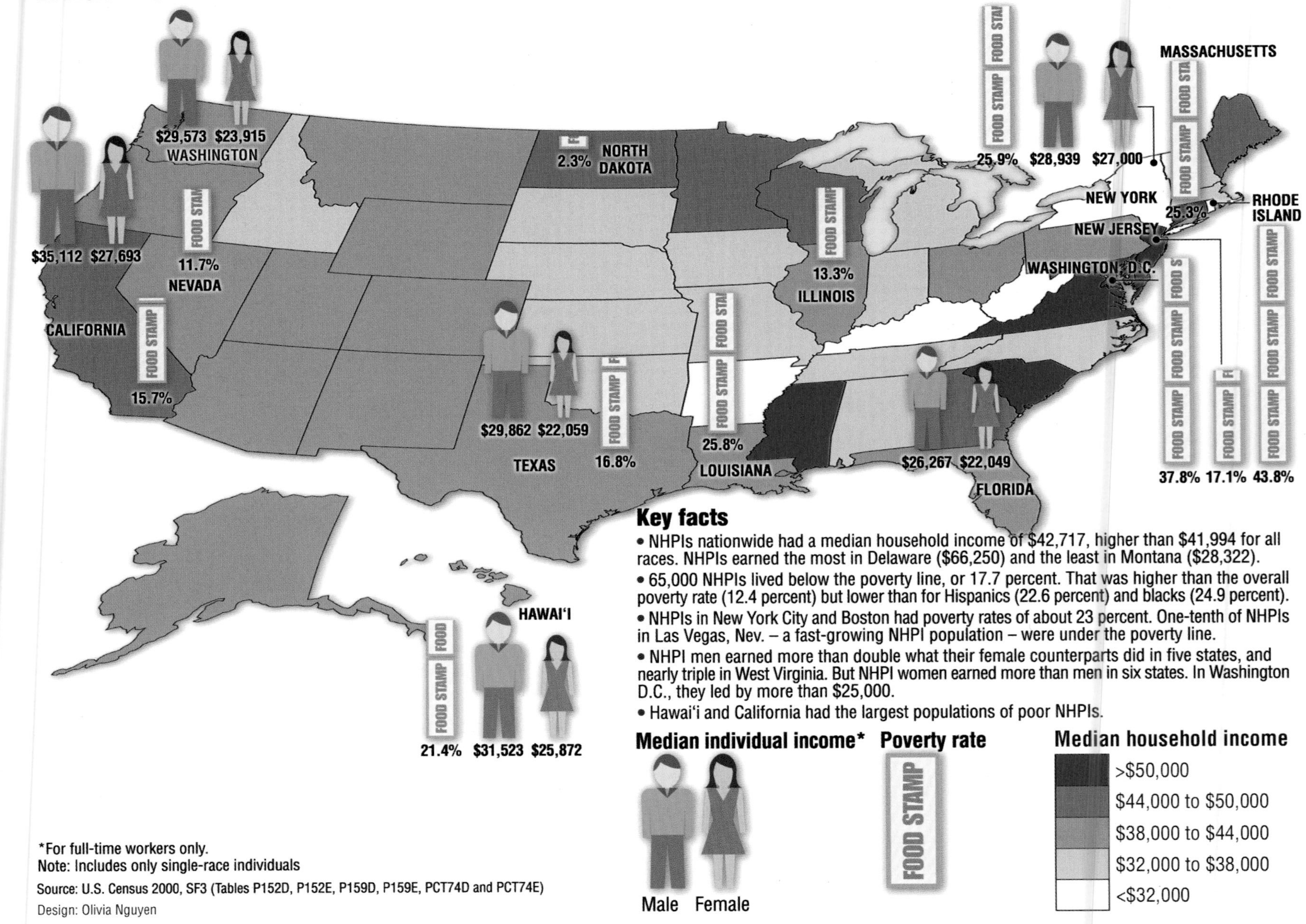

Key facts

- NHPIs nationwide had a median household income of $42,717, higher than $41,994 for all races. NHPIs earned the most in Delaware ($66,250) and the least in Montana ($28,322).
- 65,000 NHPIs lived below the poverty line, or 17.7 percent. That was higher than the overall poverty rate (12.4 percent) but lower than for Hispanics (22.6 percent) and blacks (24.9 percent).
- NHPIs in New York City and Boston had poverty rates of about 23 percent. One-tenth of NHPIs in Las Vegas, Nev. – a fast-growing NHPI population – were under the poverty line.
- NHPI men earned more than double what their female counterparts did in five states, and nearly triple in West Virginia. But NHPI women earned more than men in six states. In Washington D.C., they led by more than $25,000.
- Hawai'i and California had the largest populations of poor NHPIs.

Median individual income*

Male Female

Poverty rate

FOOD STAMP

Median household income

- >$50,000
- $44,000 to $50,000
- $38,000 to $44,000
- $32,000 to $38,000
- <$32,000

*For full-time workers only.
Note: Includes only single-race individuals

Source: U.S. Census 2000, SF3 (Tables P152D, P152E, P159D, P159E, PCT74D and PCT74E)

Design: Olivia Nguyen

Are You Renting or Owning? Asian Americans

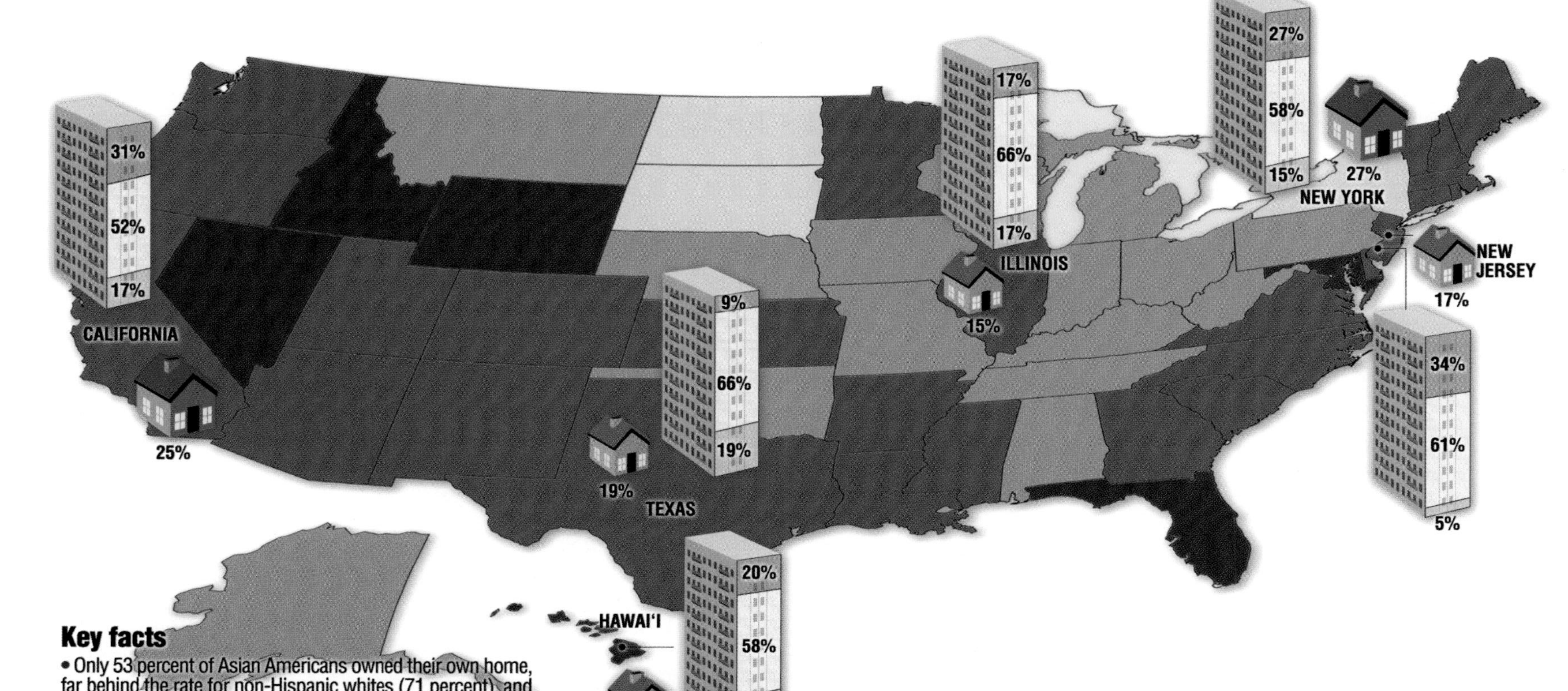

*Indicates homes with an average of more than one person per room. Includes both owner-occupied and rental homes.

Key facts

- Only 53 percent of Asian Americans owned their own home, far behind the rate for non-Hispanic whites (71 percent), and not much higher than the rate for blacks (47 percent).
- Among states with large Asian populations, New York and Texas had the highest proportion of Asian renters, 60 percent and 47 percent respectively.
- One in five Asian homes nationwide was overcrowded. California had the largest number (272,000).
- One reason for overcrowding: the average Asian household had 3.1 members, versus 2.6 members in the general population. The average Asian family was even bigger: 3.6 members, versus 3.1 in the general populace.
- The median gross rent paid by Asians nationwide was $734, versus $602 for renters of all races.

Note: Includes only single-race individuals.

Source: U.S. Census 2000, SF3 (Tables HCT29D, HCT29E, P17D, HCT37D and H63)

Design: Olivia Nguyen

Are You Renting or Owning? Native Hawaiians and Pacific Islanders

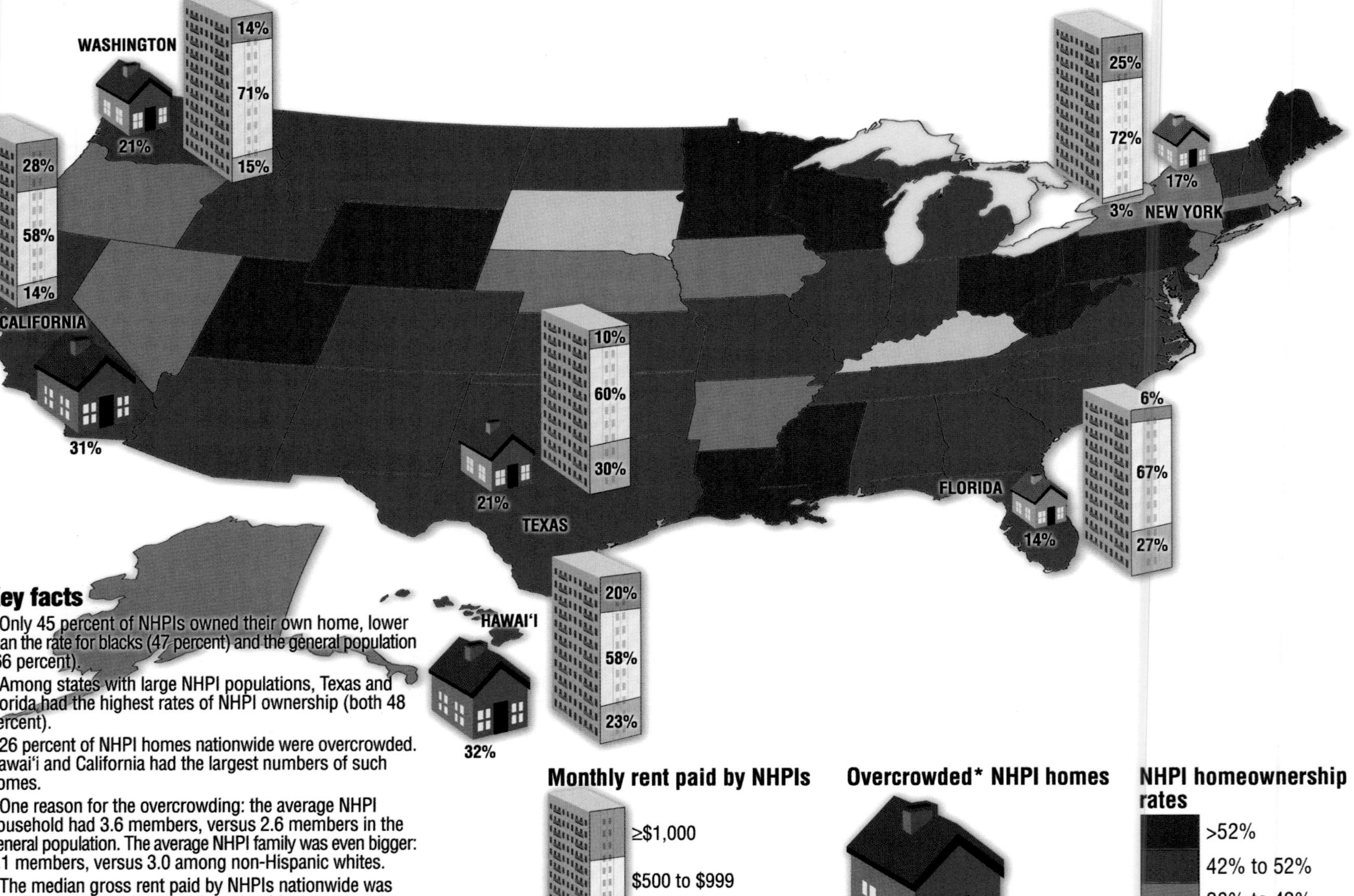

Key facts

- Only 45 percent of NHPIs owned their own home, lower than the rate for blacks (47 percent) and the general population (66 percent).
- Among states with large NHPI populations, Texas and Florida had the highest rates of NHPI ownership (both 48 percent).
- 26 percent of NHPI homes nationwide were overcrowded. Hawai'i and California had the largest numbers of such homes.
- One reason for the overcrowding: the average NHPI household had 3.6 members, versus 2.6 members in the general population. The average NHPI family was even bigger: 4.1 members, versus 3.0 among non-Hispanic whites.
- The median gross rent paid by NHPIs nationwide was $690, versus $613 for non-Hispanic whites.

Note: Includes only single-race individuals.

Source: U.S. Census 2000, SF3 (Tables HCT29D, HCT29E, P17E, HCT37E and H63)

Design: Olivia Nguyen

*Indicates homes with an average of more than one person per room. Includes both owner-occupied and rental homes.

Coming to America: Asian Americans

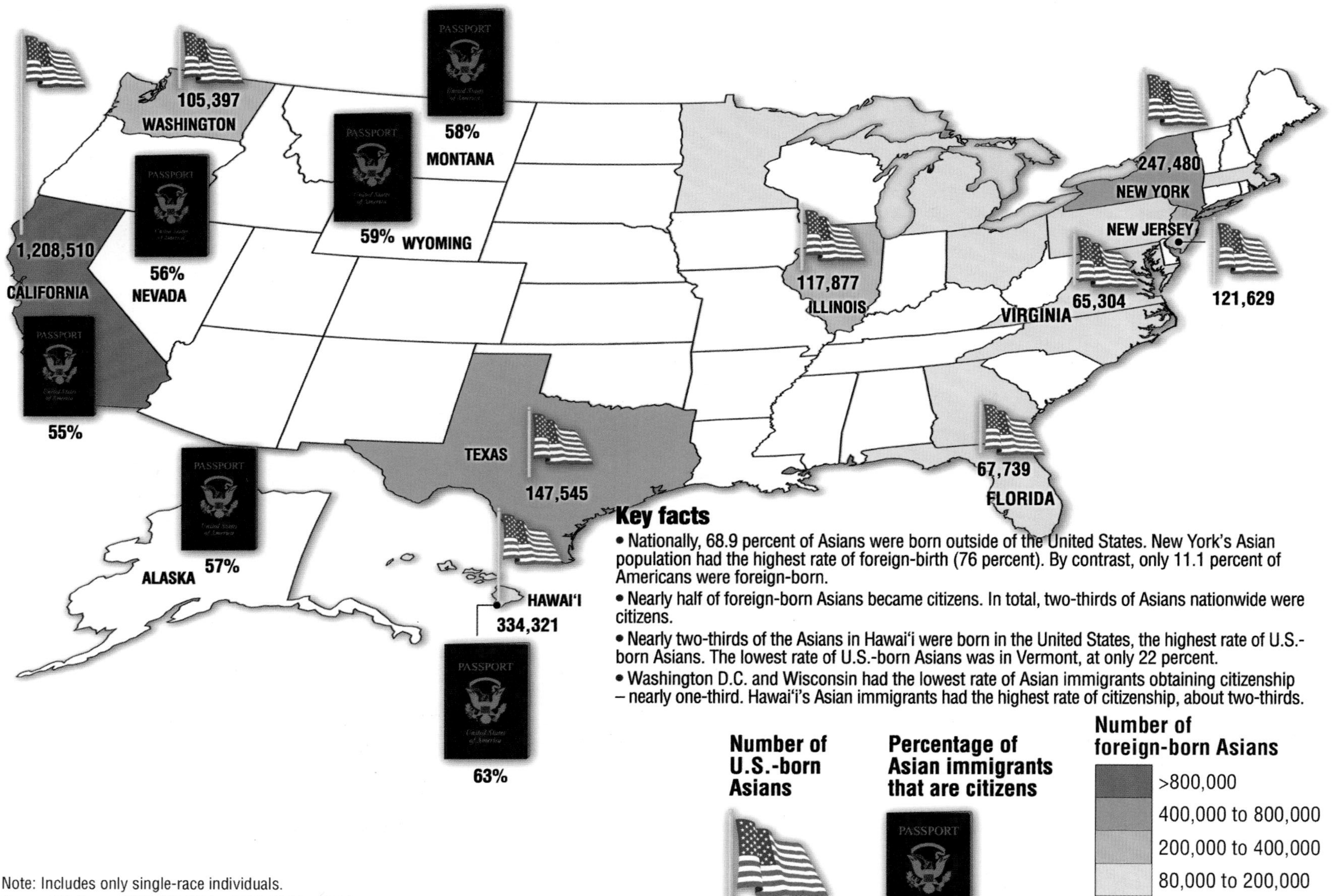

Key facts

- Nationally, 68.9 percent of Asians were born outside of the United States. New York's Asian population had the highest rate of foreign-birth (76 percent). By contrast, only 11.1 percent of Americans were foreign-born.
- Nearly half of foreign-born Asians became citizens. In total, two-thirds of Asians nationwide were citizens.
- Nearly two-thirds of the Asians in Hawai'i were born in the United States, the highest rate of U.S.-born Asians. The lowest rate of U.S.-born Asians was in Vermont, at only 22 percent.
- Washington D.C. and Wisconsin had the lowest rate of Asian immigrants obtaining citizenship – nearly one-third. Hawai'i's Asian immigrants had the highest rate of citizenship, about two-thirds.

Note: Includes only single-race individuals.
Source: U.S. Census 2000, SF3 (Tables P63D, P63E and P21)
Design: Olivia Nguyen

Coming to America: Native Hawaiians and Pacific Islanders

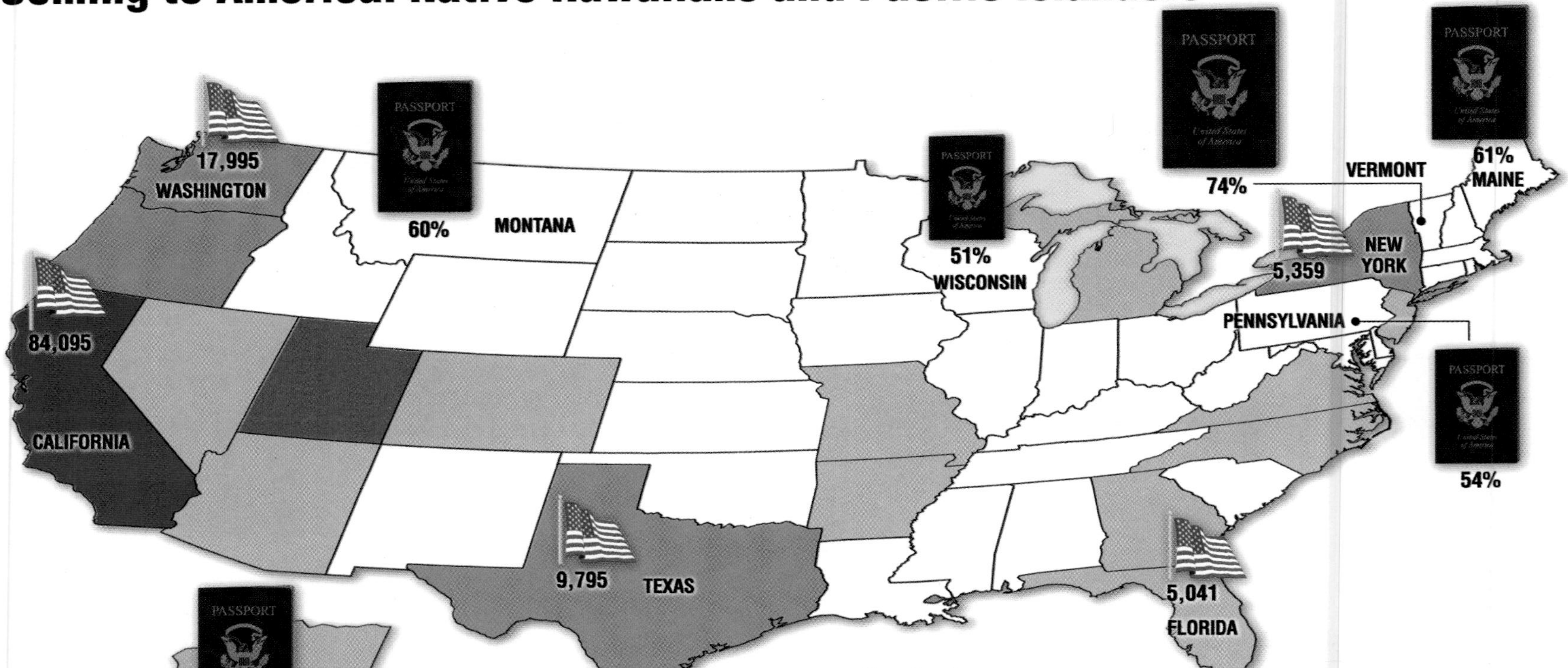

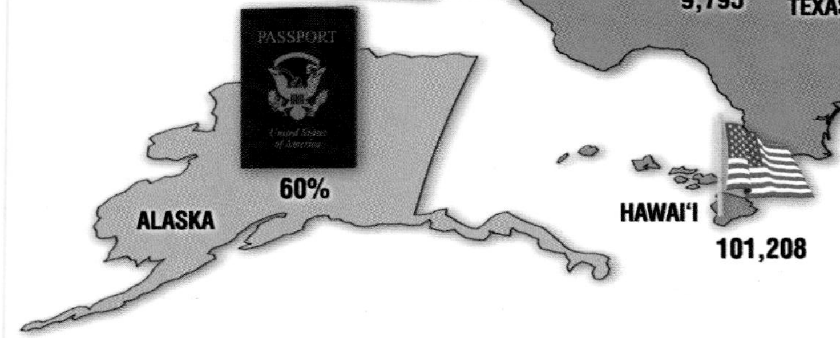

Key facts

- Nationally, only 19.9 percent of NHPIs were born outside of the United States. Of Hawai'i's NHPI population, only one-tenth were foreign-born.
- Four out of ten NHPI immigrants became citizens. The lowest rate was in Vermont, where only 25 percent of NHPIs had citizenship.
- One-third of the NHPIs in New York were foreign-born. The lowest rate was in Mississippi, where only five percent of Asians were foreign-born.
- Rates of obtaining citizenship were highest among NHPIs in Montana and Alaska, and lowest in Georgia and North Carolina.

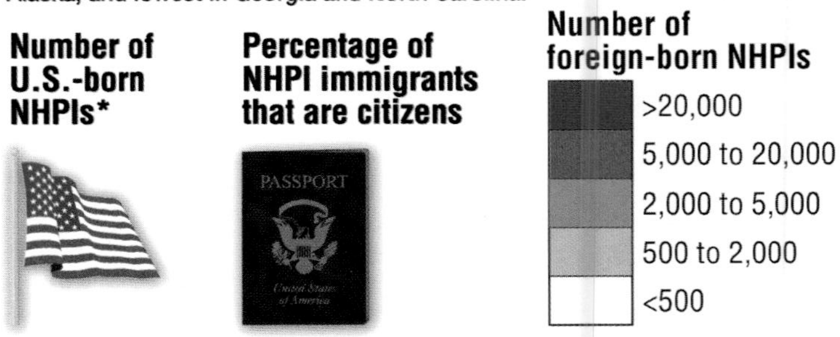

*Includes NHPIs born in U.S. Island areas.
Note: Includes only single-race individuals.

Source: U.S. Census 2000, SF3 (Tables P63D, P63E and P21)
Design: Olivia Nguyen

Employment and Education: Asian Americans

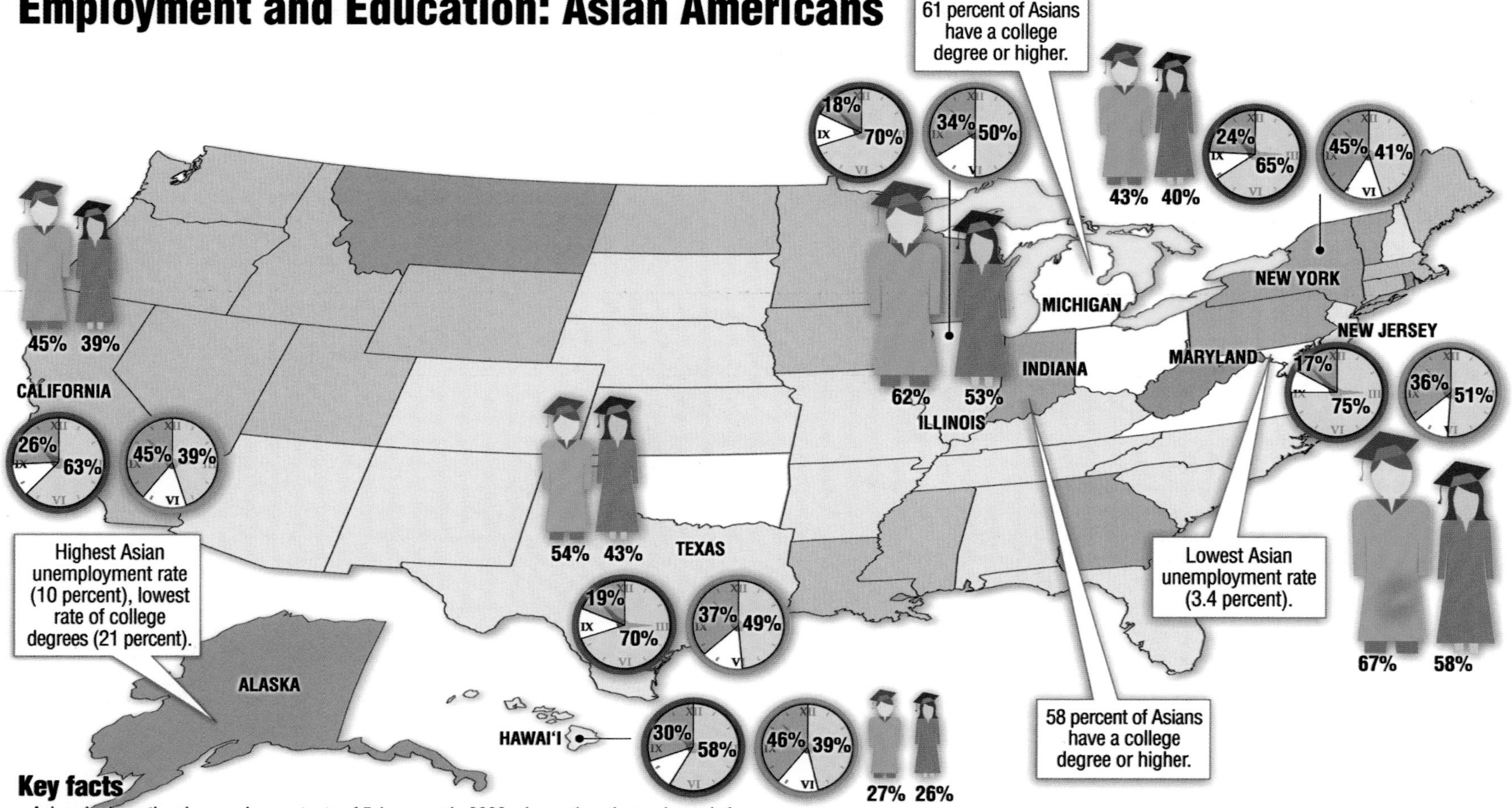

Key facts

- Asians had a national unemployment rate of 5.1 percent in 2000 – lower than the total population (5.7 percent) but higher than non-Hispanic whites (4.3 percent).
- Asians in West Virginia had the highest rates of obtaining a bachelor's degree or higher (64 percent). Nationally, 44 percent of Asians had a college degree or higher, while 20 percent lacked a high school diploma. For non-Hispanic whites, 27 percent had a college degree or higher, while 15 percent lacked a high school degree.
- Reflecting their high proportions of older immigrants, the highest rates of Asians lacking a high school degree were found in Louisiana (32.6 percent) and Rhode Island (30.8 percent). Other states with high percentages of Asian non-high school graduates include Minnesota, Mississippi, Arkansas and New York.
- More than 70 percent of Asians in seventeen states worked more than 35 hours a week, a strong indicator for a high percentage of family-owned or entrepreneurial businesses.

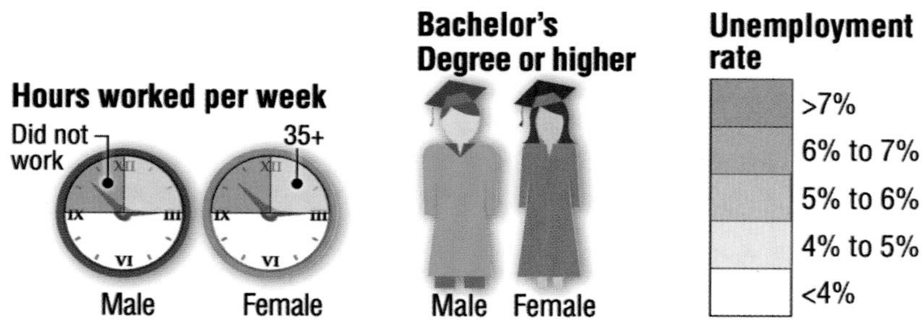

Note: Includes single-race individuals only.
Source: U.S. Census 2000, SF3 (Tables P43, P148D, PCT71D and PCT150D)
Design: Olivia Nguyen

Hours worked per week

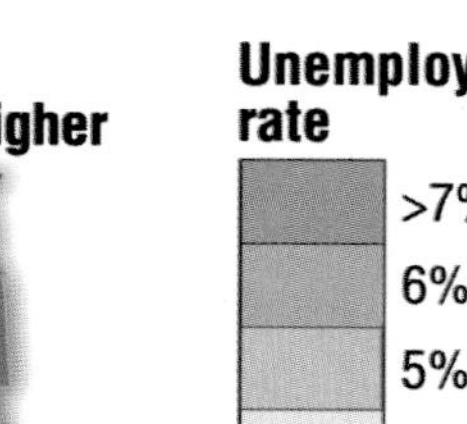

Bachelor's Degree or higher

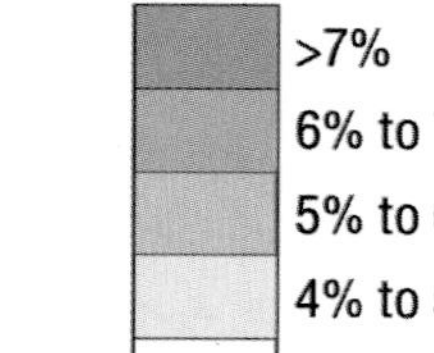

Unemployment rate

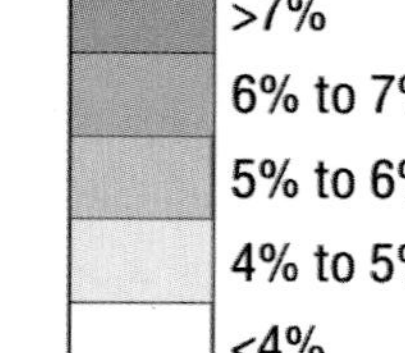

Employment and Education: Native Hawaiians and Pacific Islanders

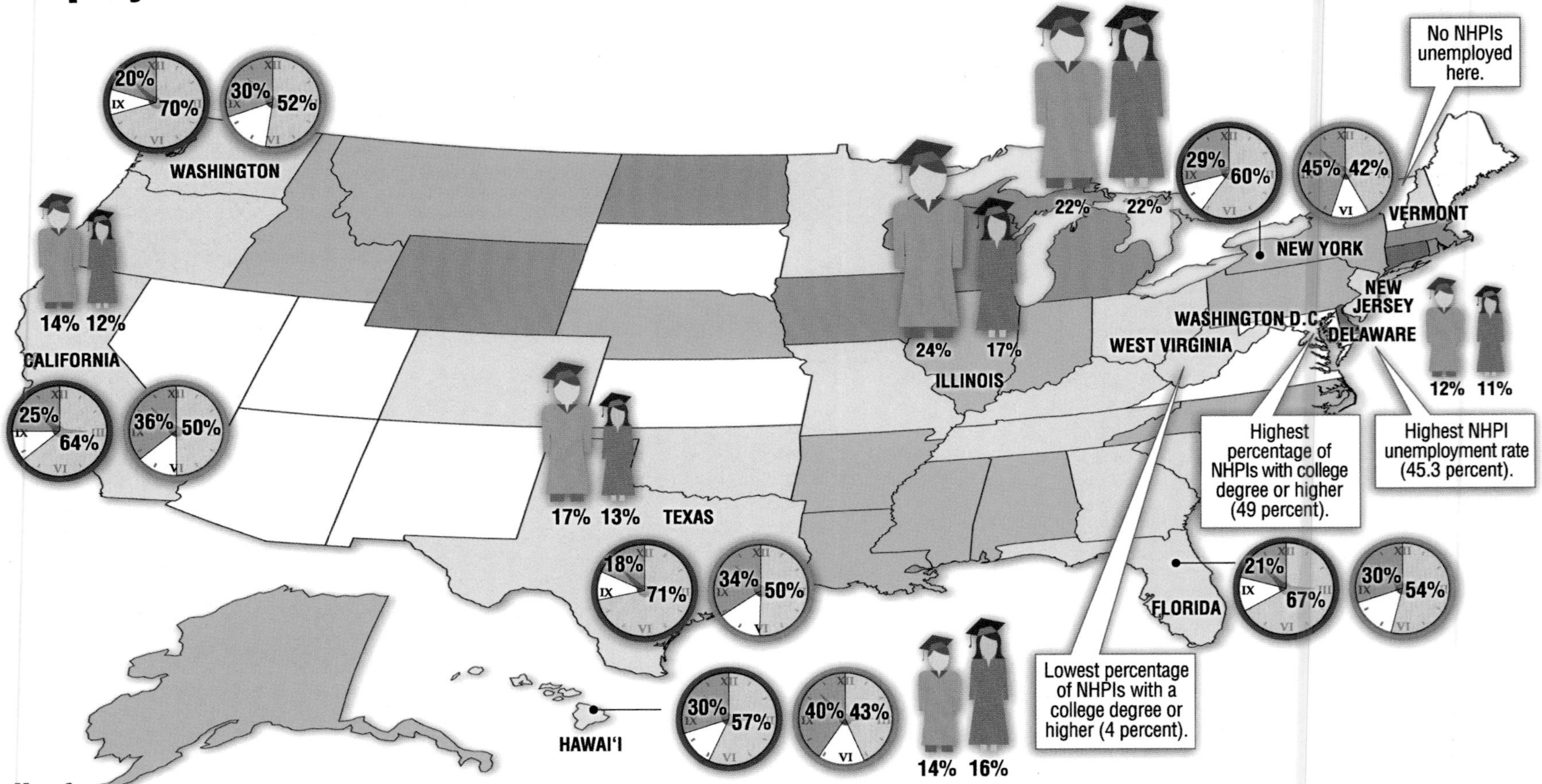

WASHINGTON
20% 70%
30% 52%

CALIFORNIA
14% 12%
25% 64%
36% 50%

TEXAS
17% 13%
18% 71%
34% 50%

HAWAI'I
14% 16%
30% 57%
40% 43%

ILLINOIS
24% 17%

22% 22%
29% 60%
45% 42%

NEW YORK
VERMONT
NEW JERSEY
DELAWARE
12% 11%
WASHINGTON D.C.
WEST VIRGINIA

FLORIDA
21% 67%
30% 54%

No NHPIs unemployed here.

Highest percentage of NHPIs with college degree or higher (49 percent).

Highest NHPI unemployment rate (45.3 percent).

Lowest percentage of NHPIs with a college degree or higher (4 percent).

Key facts

- NHPIs had a national unemployment rate of 10.6 percent in 2000 – higher than the total population (5.7 percent) and Latinos (9.2 percent) but lower than blacks (11.2 percent).
- NHPI educational attainment was highest in the Eastern states: New Hampshire, Vermont and Virginia all had about three in ten NHPIs graduating from college.
- More than four in ten NHPIs in Delaware and Rhode Island lacked a high school degree. Other states with high percentages of NHPI non-high school graduates include Nebraska, New Jersey and Arkansas.
- Nationally, 14 percent of NHPIs had a college degree or higher, while 22 percent lacked a high school diploma. For the entire population, 24 percent had a college degree or more, while 20 percent lacked a high school degree.

Note: Includes single-race individuals only.

Source: U.S. Census 2000, SF3 (Tables P43, P148E, PCT71E and PCT150E)

Design: Olivia Nguyen

Hours worked per week

Bachelor's Degree or higher

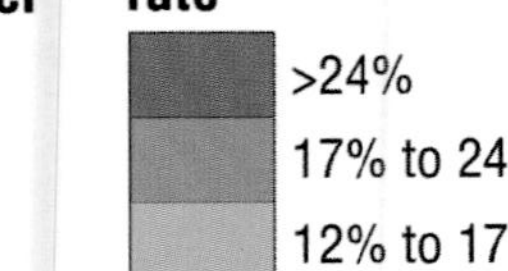

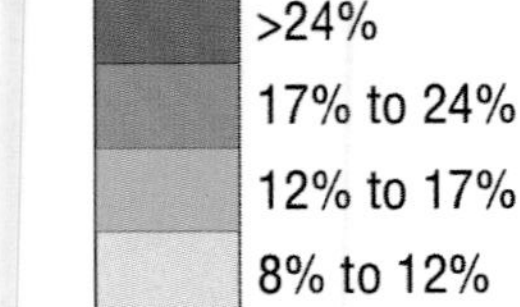

Unemployment rate

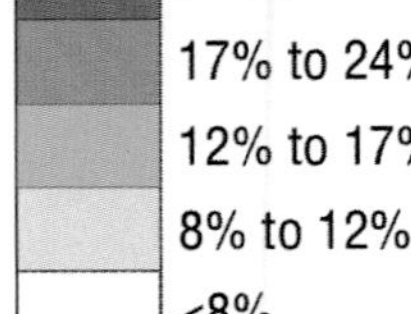

Old Roots and New Growth

When one thinks of Asian Pacific Americans and the American West, California and Hawai'i probably spring to mind. Indeed, more than 82 percent of the 6.3 million APAs living in the Census-defined thirteen-state West in 2000 resided in either California or Hawai'i.

Still, that leaves more than 1.2 million APAs living in states like Washington, Arizona, Colorado, Oregon and others. Their numbers and impact are growing: in Washington, APAs already make up nearly one in twelve residents. In the booming cities of the Rocky Mountain region like Denver, Las Vegas and Phoenix, APA populations doubled during the 1990s, lured by cheap housing and job growth.

Meanwhile, states like California and Hawai'i—ranked first and third by APA population overall—were actually the two slowest-growing states in the whole nation, despite adding 1.65 million APAs between them. Demographers noted that many people left cities with high costs of living in California and Hawai'i for neighboring Western states, and many of them were no doubt APAs. All told, eight Western states out of the thirteen saw their populations more than double.

In the following chapter, we spotlight the fast-growing Pacific Northwest region of Washington, Oregon, and Idaho—which due to its proximity to the Pacific Ocean, has a long history of APA residents and is seeing its populations grow again. Sidebars look into the booming states of Arizona and Nevada, where APAs are flocking in increasing numbers. Due to their size and significance, California and Hawai'i are dealt with separately.

Photo: AsianWeek Archive

About half of all APAs live in the Western states, most in California and Hawai'i. But those populations are increasingly aging, as young APAs move north or eastward in search of jobs and homes

Pacific Northwest: undiscovered country

Beginning in August 2002, King County, Washington, which includes Seattle, has provided Chinese-language voting ballots for those requesting them. The reason? Over 10,000 citizens of the voting-age population reported that they share this Asian language. That's a small but salient example of how the Pacific Northwest, consisting of Washington, Oregon and Idaho, despite not being known for its APA populations like California and Hawai'i, are nevertheless seeing large communities arise. In the state of Washington, there were 428,659 APAs in 2000 (including those of mixed-ethnicity and mixed-race), representing 7.3 percent of the population (ranking third behind Hawai'i and California), Oregon with 139,282 APAs, at 4.1 percent of the population, and Idaho, with 19,590, at 1.5 percent.

The significance of the APA population to the Pacific Northwest, however, belies its relatively small size. APAs have had a remarkable influence in the economic, political and social arenas, an influence that is uneven but will only continue to increase. Although the importance of agriculture is obvious for the region's overall economy, the Cascade mountain range divides the more arid and rural eastern side from the more populous and urban centers of the west. While early APAs were involved heavily in agricultural enterprises, today's APAs live mostly in and around the large metropolitan areas of Seattle, located in King County, Washington; Portland, in Multnomah County, Oregon; and Boise, in Ada County, Idaho. This trend has especially sharpened with the post-1965 arrival of newer APA immigrants and refugees.

APAs in Pacific Northwest

	Washington	Oregon	Idaho
Total APAs*	**428,659**	**139,282**	**19,590**
Total mixed-race APAs	82,371	29,956	6,393
Total mixed-race population	213,519	104,745	25,609
% of APAs that are mixed-race	19.2%	21.5%	32.6%
% of mixed-race population that is part-APA	38.6%	28.6%	25.0%

*Includes mixed-race and mixed-ethnicity
Source: U.S. Census 2000, SF1 (Table P3)

APA population trends 1990-2000, by state

For all three states, while the total population increased during the 1990s, the percentage of whites decreased, the percentage of Hispanics and Latinos grew, while blacks, American Indians, and Native Hawaiians and Pacific Islanders remained about the same. The dramatic decrease in those marking "Other race" from 1990 to 2000 was expected, due to the new ability for respondents to identify themselves as more than one race.

Overall, the APA population is growing fast. In each state, the combined APA population, including multiracial APAs, more than doubled from 1990 to 2000. Their percentage share of the total state population also increased, fastest in Washington (from 4 percent to 7.3 percent). The combined APA population in Washington and Oregon is the second largest minority after Hispanics, and in Idaho, third largest after Hispanics and Native Americans.

Multiracial population

In the 1970s, the Census Bureau started to note the increasing numbers of children living in mixed-race families. The number of mixed-race children grew from half a million in 1970 to nearly two million in 1990. In 2000, around 6.8 million people, or 2.4 percent of the total population, indicated to the Census that they were multiracial. Within the Pacific Northwest, Idaho reports a smaller percentage than the national norm (1.4 percent); Oregon with 2.4 percent is the same; while Washington reported a higher percentage, at 3.0. In the Pacific Northwest, Washington has the largest number of mixed-race APAs while Idaho, with the smallest APA population, has the largest percent of mixed-race persons of the three states. The "APAs in the Pacific Northwest" table shows the high proportion of APAs in the overall mixed-race population in the Pacific Northwest and the relevant counties.

The chart above documents, for the first time, the large percent of mixed-race APAs in the Pacific Northwest and especially the large percentage of mixed race APAs within the mixed-race population in the three Pacific Northwest counties. Barring an unexpected social change, this trend toward APA interracial marriages will continue.

Idaho and Ada County

In the 1870 Census, the Idaho Territory counted 4,274 Chinese, representing 28 percent of the total population. Most worked in the Snake River gold mines and few remained after 1900. In 1942, more than 7,000 Japanese Americans were forcibly brought to Idaho and incarcerated for three years at the War Relocation Authority's Minidoka center in Jerome County.

Idaho's APA population remains small and relatively urbanized. Ada County alone has around four in ten of the state's total APA population. At the state level, all of the major APA ethnicities saw their populations grow, except for the Japanese. The increase was highlighted in Ada County, where most APA numbers doubled from 1990 to 2000, with Asian Indians making the largest gains.

Oregon and Multnomah County
The history of APAs in Oregon dates back to the 1880s. By 2000, the state's APA population, including mixed-race APAs, consisted of 4.1 percent of the total. APAs in Multnomah County, with Portland as its most populous center, made up 4.6 percent of the population in 1990, increasing to 7.3 percent in 2000. Chinese Americans were the largest APA group statewide, with 27,145 (this includes Taiwanese). Vietnamese, Japanese and Filipinos came next, in that order, though their numbers differed by only one thousand each. While APAs nationwide tend to live close to big cities, of the major APA groups only a majority of the Vietnamese lived in Multnomah County. By contrast, four-fifths of Koreans and Asian Indians in Oregon lived outside of Multnomah.

Washington and King County
Seattle was a stopping place for early gold prospectors and laborers to Alaska, and a population terminus for early workers in lumbering, railroad building, and coal mining. The relationship between the early APA immigrants and the white frontier population dates back to the mid-19th century and although it has often been contentious and antagonistic, the influence of APAs in Washington has been strong and continuous.

APAs in 1990 represented four percent of the total state population and by 2000, their numbers increased to 7.3 percent. King County alone in 1990 held 58.3 percent of the state's APA population, which in the year 2000 increased numerically to 228,993 but decreased percentage-wise to 53.4 percent. The populations that grew the fastest include the Asian Indians, Native Hawaiians and Pacific Islanders, Vietnamese and Chinese, all of whom saw their numbers double or grow nearly four-fold at either the state or county level. Japanese American numbers grew the least.

Explanation of growth
Although APAs have been coming to the Pacific Northwest since the mid-19th century, the population recently benefited from the 1965 Immigration Act, which resulted in an influx of skilled and highly educated Asian immigrants. There are also substantial communities of Southeast Asians, many of whom are former refugees who arrived after the end of the Vietnam War. Noticeably absent from this rush of new immigrants were those from Japan, a country that had risen from the devastating ashes of wartime defeat in 1945 to become a major economic power by the 1980s. Consequently, Japanese immigration has been conspicuously limited throughout this period. The following will discuss the listed APA groups in order of their population numbers. Although important, APA groups with fewer numbers such as the Cambodians, Laotians and others, will not be discussed here due solely to the limited available space.

Filipino Americans
Even before the mid-1960s, Filipinos were less likely to create territorial-based communities, as many of the pre-World War II immigrants worked in mobile, labor-based jobs in the farming or fishing industries. Post-1965 immigrants have tended to be more highly skilled and educated. Their community is created through cultural and social activities like family, religious institutions, and community centers. Overall, Filipinos are the largest APA group in the Pacific Northwest (112,975) and are especially numerous in Washington, with 91,765 persons. In Idaho they are third largest but in Oregon, Filipinos numbered fewer than the Japanese did.

As with other APA groups, however, the Filipino influence has been considerable since the end of World War II. Dolores Sibonga was on the Seattle City Council, Robert Santos was a Clinton appointee to the regional Health and Human Services Department; and there are numerous others in various professional fields. The Filipino American National Historical Society today has chapters nationwide, but it was formed in Seattle in 1982.

Even without a physically based area that centers the Filipino American community, its group presence is felt in the many family and social institutions. The ties to the Philippines will continue to be strong as immigrants continue to arrive—a trend that will continue for the foreseeable future.

Western region by the numbers

Total APA population, including mixed-race and mixed-ethnicity: 6,295,680

Asian population 'alone': 5,307,857

1990 APA population: 4,047,970

Total APA population growth, 1990-2000: 55.5 percent

Largest APA population (nationwide rank): California, 4,321,585 (1st)

Smallest APA population (nationwide rank): Wyoming, 4,588 (51st)

Fastest growing state, rate (nationwide rank): Nevada, 225.5 percent (1st)

Slowest growing state, rate (nationwide rank): Hawaii, 25.2 percent (51st)

Highest percent of APAs in overall state pop. (nationwide rank): Hawaii, 70.8 percent (1st)

Lowest percent of APAs in overall state pop. (nationwide rank): Wyoming, 0.9 percent (49th)

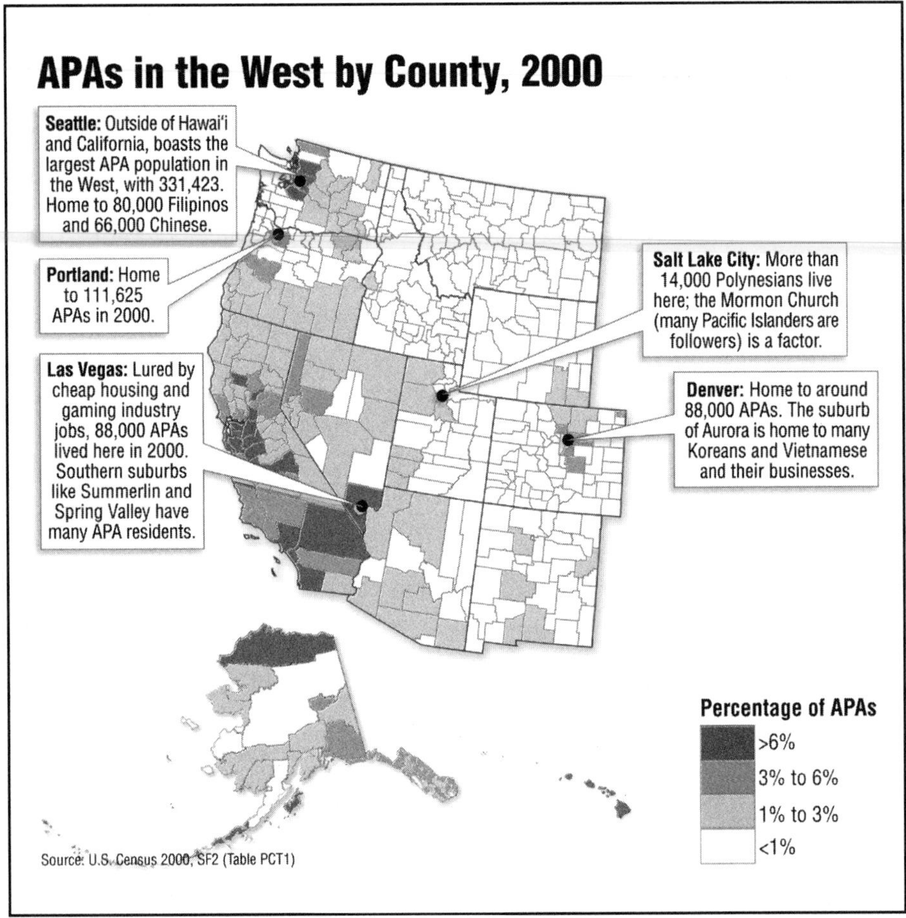

Chinese Americans

The Chinese first came to the Pacific Northwest in 1860 and quickly became an important part of the region's labor pool. They were also early victims of the anti-Asian actions that were crucial in creating and maintaining segregated Chinatowns in Portland and Seattle. These early communities, once populated almost exclusively by Chinese bachelors, changed over the course of the 20th century, as Chinese women were eventually allowed into the United States, resulting in the creation of nuclear families. Chinatowns, wrote sociologist Ivan Light, gradually transformed themselves from late-nineteenth century "vice-districts" to twentieth century "tourist attractions."

Soon after World War II, second-generation Chinese began graduating from college and becoming visible and active in Portland and Seattle civic life. Wing Luke became the first Asian American elected to the Seattle City Council and helped pave the way for others like Ruby Chow, Cheryl Chow, and Art Wang to run successfully for local political office. Current Washington governor Gary Locke is the ultimate example of a successful Chinese American politician supported by many non-APA voters.

Although Chinatowns in Portland and Seattle have had a long history, it is the post-1965 Chinese-speaking immigrants from Hong Kong, Taiwan, Mainland China and Southeast Asia who have dramatically altered the public face of this community. Bringing new capital and business acumen from Asia, these immigrants introduced specialized Chinese cuisine restaurants and numerous small and medium-size businesses, revitalizing crumbling and derelict-ridden areas in both Seattle and Portland in the 1970s. The physical and psychic improvements are obvious.

Government officials eventually realized that these Chinatowns were popular tourist attractions which also brought new tax money into their coffers. The larger society paid for façade upgrades such as pagoda-looking telephone booths and streetlights, liberal use of red-paint for street décor, and approval to erect a Chinese gateway in Portland. These actions symbolize the changed relationship from the 1960s between the APA community and wider society. And as touristy as they've become, these Chinatowns remain vibrant ethnic business centers servicing their numerous APA customers.

There were 106,049 Chinese Americans living in the Pacific Northwest as of 2000, making them second in number to the Filipino Americans. Even as the succeeding generations are becoming more integrated into the American mainstream society, the immigrant Chinese American generation will retain cultural traditions and norms. With the lessening of overt discrimination, today's Chinese Americans are allowed to choose how much they identify with their ethnic heritage. Where once there was little choice, it is now the individual's to make.

Japanese Americans

The issei, or Japanese immigrants, arrived in King and Multnomah Counties after the Chinese and initially worked in lumber, railroad and agriculture. With the arrival of many Japanese women after 1906 and the formation of families, the issei created Japanese communities in Portland and Seattle centering on small businesses, temples and churches and prefectural (Japanese regional) associations. Many worked the farms they were unable to own themselves, due to anti-alien land laws of the early 1920s (which also hurt other early APA settlers). During World

War II, the Issei suffered devastating economic and social losses resulting from their incarceration into America's internment camps.

In King and Multnomah counties, the post-war Japantowns never returned to the vitality and exuberance they had before the war. Since the alien land laws precluded issei land ownership, for most, there were no establishments or farms to reclaim when they returned from the War Relocation Authority camps. Although some nisei (second generation) went back into farming, especially in places such as Ontario, Oregon, or Auburn, Washington, many went instead into civil service, the professions, and other entrepreneurial activities.

Beginning in the 1970s, the media placed the Japanese Americans into the questionable status of an American model minority. It was an overly reductionist label that ignored problematic evidence—for example, per capita earnings were less impressive than total family income (APAs tend to have more workers per household), disregarding issues of under-employment and slighting the existence of an employment "glass ceiling." Still, it was true that education, coupled with their parents' norms and values, helped them move into middle class affluence and gain influence locally in the Pacific Northwest in almost every area of life as high achievers and leaders in a diversity of professions. No longer are they tied to an ethnic community region or base.

The Japanese American population, while not shrinking, is falling behind in size compared to other APA groups due to low immigration and birth rates. In 1970, they constituted the largest APA Pacific Northwest population. By 2000, their Pacific Northwest numbers had nearly tripled to 80,038, but they were now the third largest. Still, the Japanese Americans have not "disappeared" into American society. Instead, many continue to join Japanese American organizations and embrace their ethnicity in religious, social and familial matters. For example, Japanese Americans who are well integrated into the majority society join in the Japanese American Citizens League and Seattle's Nikkei Concern, a non-profit organization helping Japanese Americans and other APAs.

Korean Americans

Up to the 1970s, the local Korean population was scattered and sparse. Small pockets of Korean women married to U.S. servicemen lived around military bases while Korean children adopted by American families after the Korean War

Spotlight on Nevada

During the 1990s, California's loss was Nevada's gain. With home costs and commute times spiraling ever upwards in the Golden State, more and more people—many of them APAs—moved across the border into Nevada, into cities like Las Vegas and Reno, where there was a booming economy, cheap housing, and no income taxes.

"In-migration into Southern Nevada is dominated by people from Southern California," Keith Schwer, director of the University of Nevada-Las Vegas' Center for Business and Economic Research, told the *Las Vegas Sun* newspaper. "And Southern California has historically had a high portion of the Asian and Hispanic population."

Nevada's APA population more than tripled to 124,116 by 2000. It was the fastest-growing APA population in the country, mirroring Nevada's booming overall population. With the seventh-largest APA population in the West, Nevada, at current growth rates, could jump into fourth place by 2010, ahead of Oregon, Arizona, and Colorado.

Filipinos were the single largest group, with more than 50,000. The Chinese population was much smaller, with around 18,000 Nevada residents. Other groups like the Japanese, Koreans, Asian Indians and Vietnamese also had smaller populations. Most of those APAs lived in Clark and Washoe Counties, where Vegas and Reno are located. Some are finding work in the hotel and gaming industry, but many others are starting small businesses and restaurants.

Jim Martin, a member of Reno's Korean Presbyterian Church who has lived in Nevada since 1960, says that the change is noticeable from foods to small businesses with Asian owners.

"You see markets, Filipino shops, jewelry stores. We've seen more ethnic entrepreneurs," he told the Associated Press. "People used to think of Asian as Japanese or Chinese... Now, Reno is a mix of Vietnamese, Cambodians, Laotian."

Las Vegas even has a small, young Chinatown, though due to its newness, it resembles the suburban Asian malls of Orange County more than the kitschy old-fashionedness of San Francisco's Chinatown.

The Associated Press reported that if current growth trends hold true, the APA population in Clark County will at least equal the number of blacks in Clark County by the next Census in 2010.

Spotlight on Arizona: In the desert, an APA population blooms

In one of the fastest-growing states in the United States, Asian Pacific Americans were the fastest-growing ethnic group between 1990 and 2000.

Arizona's population grew more than three times faster than that of the rest of the country during the 1990s, propelling Phoenix from the tenth largest city in 1990 to the sixth largest city, with 1.3 million residents in 2000. While Arizona's population of Asian Pacific Americans was not able to keep pace—it only doubled the nationwide APA growth rate—its growth was still impressive. Arizona added around 75,000 APAs during the 1990s, for a growth rate of 133.7 percent.

Chinese and Filipinos are the two largest groups; each claims more than 25,000 Arizona residents, most of them living in the Phoenix metro area, and many of them lured during the last decade by the plentiful jobs, cheap housing, and sunny weather.

Immigrants from Southeast Asian countries, as well as Asian Indians and Koreans, have also moved to Arizona in increasing numbers, some to work in the technology companies springing up around Phoenix, others to start their own small businesses. Meanwhile, an older Japanese population still thrives.

The history of APAs goes back for more than a century. In the mid-1850s, Chinese men came to work on the railroads. Many stayed to avoid the more overtly racist climate in California at the time, and set up small Chinatowns in Prescott, Tucson and eventually Phoenix. They started the same businesses as in Chinatowns all over—groceries, restaurants, laundries—or they farmed, as the early Japanese and Filipinos did (though Arizona law forbade them from owning the land they worked).

During World War II, more than 35,000 Japanese were relocated to two internment camps in Arizona. In 1946, immediately after the war, Chinese American Wing F. Ong was elected to the Arizona House of Representatives.

Today, few APA Arizonans are involved in farming. Seven out of ten live in suburban Maricopa County, the heart of greater Phoenix. Pima County, where Arizona's second largest city, Tucson, is located, draws most of the rest.

Asians, at least, appear to be doing relatively well in Arizona. In Phoenix suburbs like Chandler, Gilbert and Mesa, Asians sport a higher median household income than whites. In Chandler, Asians had a median household income of $71,621, reported the *Arizona Republic*, versus a median for whites of $59,795. Statewide, Asians had a median household income about $5,000 above the state's $40,558. The poverty rate for Asians also fell during the 1990s.

There is an Asian Chamber of Commerce in Phoenix, and three English publications based there, aimed at different Asian groups.

Still, some APAs realize that with their growing numbers, gaining political representation is the next step.

"We've been real good about paying attention to our families, our kids and our jobs. But we've got to expand our horizons. Nobody knows we even exist in Arizona, and that has to change," one Chinese restauranteur told the *Arizona Republic*.

—*Eric Lai*

were widely dispersed. That changed after immigration restrictions were relaxed. In the Pacific Northwest, there were only a few thousand Korean Americans in 1970 but by 2000, the population had increased to 73,179, making them the fourth largest APA group.

These post-1965 Koreans came with high educational levels, strong job skills, and access to more monetary capital than previous Korean immigrant. Their relatives arrived later, and together, many opened small businesses such as teriyaki take-out restaurants, liquor stores, shoe-repair shops, import-export businesses and Korean restaurants—most of them located outside existing Chinatowns.

Korean American communities tend to form around participation in social institutions, rather than living in close proximity in Chinatown-like neighborhoods. Central to this emphasis are the Korean American churches, business and professional organizations, university and high-school alumni associations and the family or fictive family relationships.

Still, in King County, there are two notable Korean-heavy enclaves—Seattle's University District and the suburb of Federal Way. Chang-Mook Sohn, director of Washington's economic forecast council, told *AsianWeek* that close to 30 percent of the state's 4,000 Korean-owned businesses are based in Federal Way. In 2000, Michael Park was elected as mayor of Federal Way, making him only the second Korean American mayor in the country. Informal Korean sources indicate that the next Census promises further growth, due to an undercount in 2000, and the recent influx of Koreans from the Los Angeles area searching for a more racially-accommodating environment.

Besides Federal Way's Park, other local Korean Americans have made

local political inroads. Martha Choe was elected to Seattle's City Council, Paull Shin is a State Senator from the Edmonds district, and the state economist is a Korean American. There are many Korean businesses and institutions, from doctors, grocery stores, newspapers to television and radio programming.

Vietnamese Americans and Southeast Asians

The 1970 Census reported no Vietnamese Americans in the Pacific Northwest. By 2000, they were the fifth largest APA group in the Pacific Northwest as a whole (72,917), the second largest APA group in Oregon, the largest in Multnomah County, the second largest in Ada County, Idaho and the third largest in King County.

In the Pacific Northwest as elsewhere, the Vietnamese tended to create visible communities. With real estate in Chinatowns already filled with businesses, Vietnamese and other Southeast Asian immigrants and refugees in Portland and Seattle went to other lower-density, low rent areas to open businesses like pho shops, restaurants, contract gardening services, grocery stores, fish-markets, and jewelry stores.

Most of the Southeast Asians are refugees who fled their countries after the Vietnam War. For many refugees from Southeast Asia, America represented a vast unknown place in language, culture, norms and values. By dint of hard work, postponement of immediate gratification, support of the family, emphasis on education and the use of skills they brought with them, this group has prospered in the intervening three decades.

Native Hawaiian and Other Pacific Islanders

Although Hawaiians are the numerically largest Pacific Islander group, there are also populations of Samoans, Guamanians, Tongans, Fujians, and other Pacific Islanders. The aggregate number (63,196) places them in the sixth position numerically, with almost 45,000 Native Hawaiian and Pacific Islanders (NHPI) in Washington alone.

While NHPIs have a higher percentage of out-marriage and mixed-race children, their cultures also maintain strong loyalty and cohesion through family, extended family and the church. These characteristically tightly-knit and cohesive communities are bound by tradition, homeland values and social norms that combine to maintain a more strongly felt group solidarity than is found in other APA groups. As sociable as Hawaiian and Pacific Islander individuals are to others outside the group, the existing centripetal social forces make it difficult for outsiders to enter easily into their inner cultural life.

Asian Indians

Asian Indians have been in the United States from the early 1900s but lacked a sizable population until 1980. In 2000, there were 41,824 Asian Indians in the Pacific Northwest with the majority (28,614) in Washington state and 18,274 of them residing in King County. The popularity of this area was attributed, in part, to the use of a temporary immigrant status under the "H-1B visa" program for skilled workers. For the Pacific Northwest, this program translates into workers needed in the computer and other technology industries. The *Seattle Times* reported in the year 2000 that about 2,000 Indians holding H-1B visas were working at Microsoft alone. Another reason offered for the increased Pacific Northwest numbers centers around the Sikh population's emigration from India's Punjab region. With an estimat-

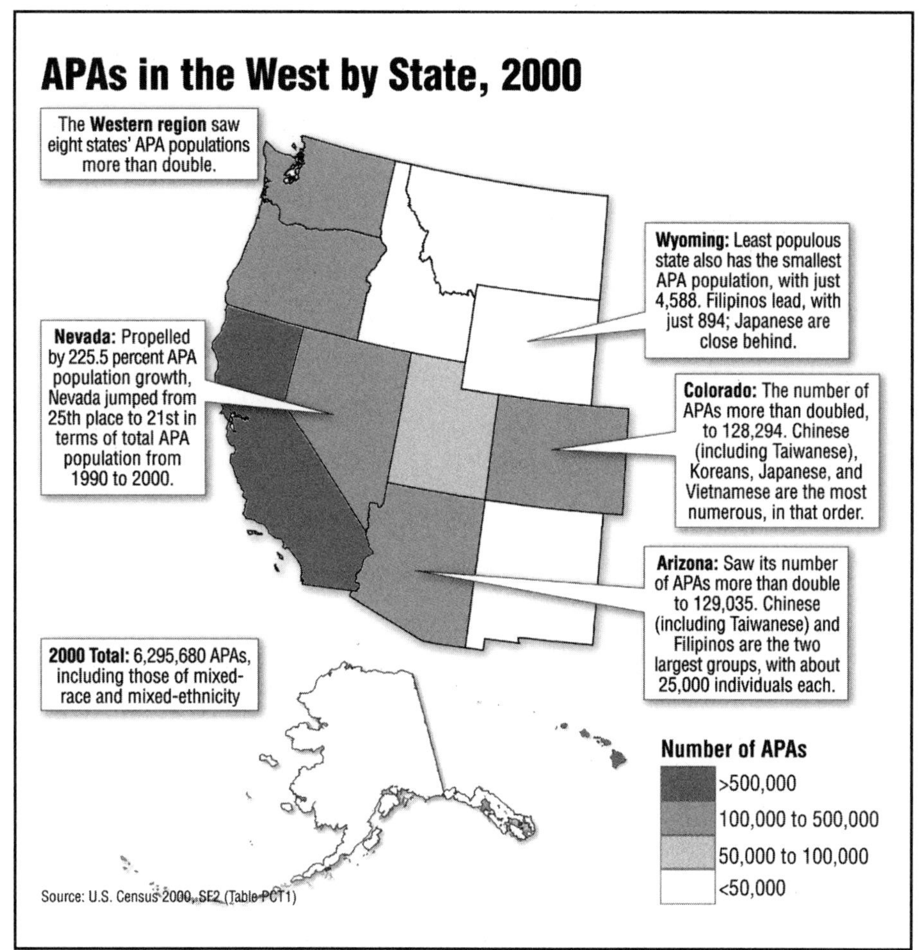

Extremes in Western family incomes by race, 1999

	Total population	Asian alone	NHPI alone
All families	**$15,430,587**	**$1,157,468**	**$62,405**
% of families over $100,000 income	17.1%	23.2%	11.6%
% of families under $20,000 income	14.6%	13.3%	18.2%

Source: U.S. Census 2000, SF3, Tables P76 and P154A-I

ed quarter-million Sikhs in the neighboring Canadian province of British Columbia, many moved to the Pacific Northwest to be near their relatives.

Asian Indians tend not to create recognizable territorial-based communities. One possible explanation for this is the diversity found within the Asian Indian population, in which differentiating identifiers such as province of origin, language or dialect, and religion are exacerbated by educational, occupational and status differences. Sikhs in King County, for instance, include not only a fair number of blue-collar workers but also computer technologists, doctors, medical personnel, entrepreneurs and engineers. The uncertain immigration status of many, as well, makes it difficult to present a cohesive ethnic collective for political or social purposes.

Conclusion

In King County, the completion of the Interstate 5 freeway in 1969 physically divided the then International District/Chinatown in Seattle, resulting in the uprooting of homes and residents and creating environmental problems. The community response was the creation of the International District Improvement Association, known as Inter*Im, by Asian American activists. Inter*Im has, for example, successfully renovated old hotels, offered low-rent subsidy housing, and created community centers and gardens.

Inter*Im is an example of what I believe is fairly unique to the APA community of King County: second and third generation APAs worked together on projects of mutual interest. In the Pacific Northwest, the social and political uses of racism arrived later than in other states and when they did, they did not play as central a role in the state's history as they did, for example, in California. APAs in King County have been able to cross cultural lines and mix more easily, in part, because of their early social interactions, a delimited geographical base and, beginning in the 1970s, a national and regional cooperative spirit.

But the times have also brought changes. Within the APA community, the post-1965 emphasis on immigrants and refugees represents real social and political realities. There are conflicts and clashes in values and cultures between recent immigrants and those of the second or third generation and between the working class and the upper middle class. This is the future challenge for the Pacific Northwestern APAs. The lessons learned from the past and the present successes of Inter*Im, the Filipino American National Historical Society, the Korean American Historical Society, and Nikkei Concerns, for example, offer exemplary models to meet future challenges.

APAs today continue to face disquieting issues, such as a national sentiment which views Asians and Asian Americans as perpetual foreigners. While a substantial number of Russian and other Eastern European immigrants and refugees have also recently arrived in the United States, there is no similar and commensurate attitude about their "alien-ness." This same attitude existed toward the nisei in World War II and one might assert that it appears not to have changed even though six decades later there are now fifth generation Japanese Americans, seventh generation Filipino Americans, and fourth generation Chinese Americans. Seemingly, any APA group could be tarred with the same "alien" label. In many ways, while the nature of racial and ethnic relations has changed for the better in the last half-century, it is still necessary for all Americans to be vigilant and make appropriate responses to counter unacceptable behavior raised against any American group.

—*Tetsuden Kashima*

Asian Experiences in the Canadian Mosaic

Introduction

Although their stories have not been prominent in Canadian history books, people of Asian descent were instrumental in the development of this nation. And like their predecessors who arrived over a century ago, contemporary group members still play an important part in shaping this country, its economy and its social landscape.

This chapter begins in the late 19th and early 20th centuries with the experiences and characteristics of the first reported Asian immigrants to Canada. These entrants came primarily from China, Japan and India. The second part looks at the composition, socioeconomic status and settlement patterns of the post-World War II Asian populations, the majority of whom arrived after 1970.

The social and economic environments encountered by immigrants at the turn of the 20th century are very different from those of the new millennium. Yet current conditions are historically rooted in the experiences of the earlier Asian arrivals. As a result, an overview of Asians in Canada needs to start with the past so that we may better understand the social and economic contexts of contemporary Asian Canada.

Early Asian immigration

Asian migration to Canada commenced at a time when the nation was beginning a period of rapid industrial growth. Immigrants came to this country drawn by the prospects of greater economic opportunities and higher wages than could be found in their homeland.

During the country's early years, the government targeted people of Anglo-Saxon ancestry to settle the country and most new migrants came from the United States or the United Kingdom. Yet many industrialists encouraged immigration from Asia since it provided a cheap source of labor.

The Chinese answered the call of the "Great North" in the mid-1850s. They were followed by the Japanese at the end of the 19th century and the Asian Indians in the early 20th century. Due to their non-white status, these groups

Toronto, home to many fans of the Toronto Maple Leafs hocky team, is also home to the largest Asian community in Canada.

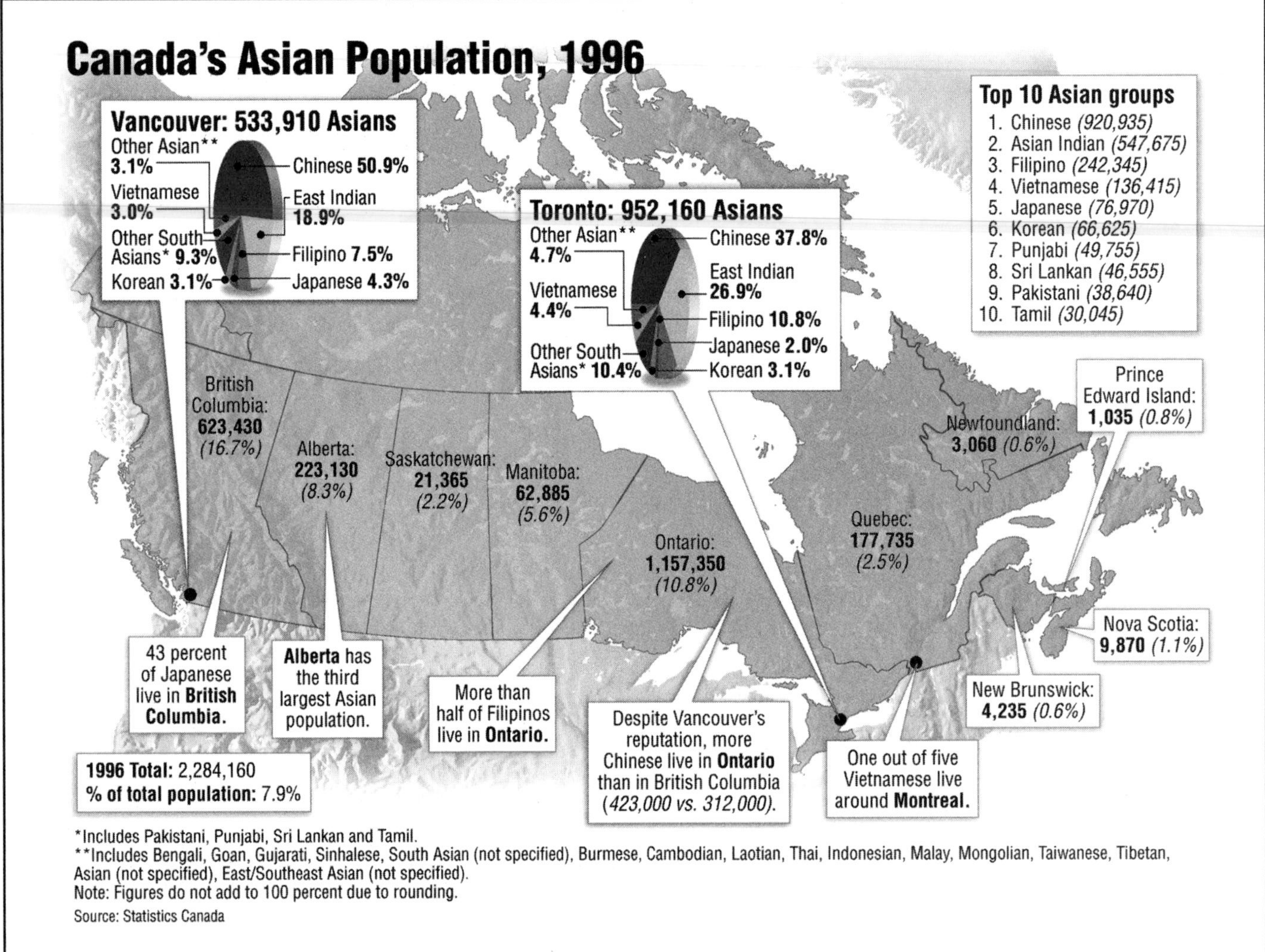

occupied similar subordinate positions relative to the dominant society of the time. Their opportunities for social mobility were restricted by anti-Asian laws and regulations. Group members were often portrayed as threats to the nation's ethnic "purity" and to the economic security of "true Canadians." As well, they were believed to be "unassimilable" and undesirable for permanent settlement in the country. Thus, the early Chinese, Japanese and Asian Indian pioneers experienced similar barriers and frustrations in their position at bottom of the Canadian ethnic "mosaic."

Pre-war Chinese community

Many early Chinese immigrants came to North America lured by the prospect of gold on the West Coast of the United States. When the American gold rush drew to an end in the second half of the 19th century, large numbers made their way up from California to the Fraser Valley of British Columbia, where the Canadian gold rush was at its height.

Immigration direct from China is said to have begun in earnest around 1881. While only 2,326 Chinese were reported to have arrived in Canada by ship between 1876 and 1880, in 1881 the number rose to 2,939. In the following year it reached 8,083, before receding to 2,223 in 1884. Many of those arriving during this period had been recruited to help construct the Canadian Pacific Railway (CPR).

The early pioneers were predominantly male, agricultural workers from the Sze Yap area in the province of Guangdong. Few had much formal education or English-speaking ability. A small minority were merchants. Most of these immigrants had left home seeking financial opportunities to offset the poverty and economic hardship in their regions. They hoped to make their fortunes abroad, then settle comfortably in China. This "sojourner orientation" was not uncommon among immigrants of the time. Yet it is difficult to determine whether many Chinese immigrants were able to fulfill their goal of returning home wealthy.

While working on the CPR, the Chinese endured dangerous conditions and

exploitative wages. It is said that one Chinese worker was killed for every mile of the railway, although some sources have suggested that the number may be as high as three or four per mile, after considering deaths due to exposure, scurvy or malnutrition. The Chinese workers earned $1 a day; this was about half the wage of other workers.

In addition to working on the railway, the Chinese labored in saw mills, fishing canneries and agricultural industries. Prospects for social mobility in the wider community were limited by a myriad of anti-Asian laws. These regulations denied the Chinese many economic opportunities available to other groups in Canada.

The majority of Chinese who arrived in the late 19th century lived in British Columbia, the western province of Canada. Yet many began moving eastward and by the early 20th century, Chinese had settled all across Canada. Ethnic communities soon developed in cities such as Vancouver, Victoria, Montreal and Toronto. These burgeoning Chinatowns provided a variety of economic and social services for their residents. The ethnic ghettos also offered some protection against the animosity of the dominant society. Yet, they were, on occasion, the targets of white violence. In 1907, a mob of anti-Asian demonstrators swept through Vancouver's Chinatown and the nearby Japanese quarters. The riot caused thousands of dollars in property damage and provided justification for the government to limit immigration from Asia.

Yet attempts to restrict Chinese entrants began long before the turn of the century. In 1885, soon after the last spike of the CPR had been driven in, the government passed the Chinese Immigration Act. This law required that people arriving from China pay a C$50 fee, referred to as a Head Tax, before being allowed into the country. The amount was increased to C$100 in 1900 and C$500 in 1903. The tax effectively prevented Chinese family formation in Canada, since most migrants could not afford to bring their wives and children into the country. These restrictions largely contributed to the development of a "bachelor" society among the Chinese. The 1911 Census recorded 27.9 Chinese males for every Chinese female, compared to an overall ratio of 1.58 immigrant males per every immigrant female.

Despite the high entrance fee, the Chinese population experienced moderate growth over the years. By the 1920s, the Chinese community in British Columbia numbered over 20,000—up from an estimated 4,000 in 1860. Yet the increase was small compared to the growth of the province's white population. In the early 1880s, the Chinese were about one-fifth of the size of the white population; 40 years later in 1921 they were less than six percent.

In 1923, the government passed the Chinese Exclusion Act. This further hampered community formation since it prohibited almost all migration from China. Between 1924 and 1946, only eight Chinese immigrants were allowed into Canada. Although the legislation was repealed in 1947, Chinese immigration remained low well into the 1960s.

Pre-war Japanese community

Japanese migration to Canada began later than that of the Chinese. The first known issei immigrant, Manzo Nagano, arrived in New Westminster, British Columbia in 1877 after having stowed away on a British cargo ship. Issei refers to the first-generation pioneers, followed by second-generation nisei born between 1910 and 1945, and third-generation sansei born between the 1940s and 1960s. Migration from Japan was modest until the mid-1890s. Then, between 1897 and 1901, more than 15,000 Japanese arrived in Canada. Many promptly headed south to the United States and in 1901 only 4,738 remained in Canada. The next major influx occurred between 1905 and 1907, when nearly 12,000 Japanese arrived in the country.

A large percentage of these early Japanese immigrants came from four prefectures in Japan: Hiroshima, Shiga, Wakayama and Kagoshima. Most were young, single males from poor farming and fishing villages. Over ninety percent of these new arrivals were literate, much higher than the average immigrant at the time, yet few possessed the ability to read, write or understand English.

Japanese movement abroad, like that of the Chinese, was primarily motivated by economics. At the turn of the 20th century, wages in Canada were, on average, seven times those in Japan. The migrants stayed primarily in British Columbia. They moved throughout the province working mostly in fishing, farming, mining, and lumbering industries.

In the early 20th century, a small, self-contained ethnic enclave developed along Powell Street in downtown Vancouver. This neighborhood, known as Nihon-machi (Japantown) or "Little Tokyo," became the heart of Japanese Canada and it provided housing and services for the ethnic community. In the wake of the 1907 anti-Asian riot in Vancouver, the Canada government entered into the 1908 "Gentleman's Agreement" with Japan where the latter agreed to limit the migration of Japanese laborers to Canada to 400 persons per year. In 1928, the quota was further reduced to 150 people annually.

After 1910 the structure of the Japanese community changed dramatically. Since the wives of those already residing in Canada were initially not counted in the quota, women began immigrating to the country in large numbers. Many arrived under the "picture bride" system, in which they were married by proxy in Japan to men living in Canada. As a result, unlike in the Chinese case,

Japanese families were formed and the population grew steadily. By the 1920s the Japanese community was growing quickly despite reduced immigration. When the net birth rate reached its peak in 1930 it was more than ten times the rate of the population as a whole. On the other hand, immigration from Japan slowed down due to the various entrance restrictions, and by the 1940s it stopped altogether.

December 7, 1941, the day Japan attacked Pearl Harbor, marked a transition point for the Japanese in Canada. On this day all persons of Japanese descent, whether born abroad or in Canada, were labeled "enemy aliens." In the months that followed, the government removed some 22,000 men, women and children of Japanese ancestry, or about 90 percent of all Japanese in Canada at the time, from their homes within 100 miles of the British Colombian coast and sent them to various locations across Canada. In addition, the government sold the internees' property. Homes, boats, cars, land and businesses were liquidated, without the owners' permission, at a fraction of their actual value.

Even after the war ended, the Japanese were not allowed to return to the West Coast. Instead they were forced to choose between deportation to war-torn Japan or dispersal east of the Rocky Mountains. Of the approximately 4,000 people sent to Japan, about half were Canadian born and many were dependent children. For those who remained in Canada, wartime restrictions were not lifted until April 1, 1949. Immigration from Japan, on the most part, did not resume again until the 1960s.

In 1988, one month after President Ronald Reagan signed a bill to give $20,000 to each of over 60,000 surviving Japanese Americans, Canadian Prime Minister Brian Mulroney gave each of approximately 16,000 surviving Japanese Canadians a symbolic C$21,000 in redress.

Pre-war Asian Indian community

The third group of early Asian pioneers in Canada was the Asian Indians. Official Canadian records show that immigration from India started in the early years of the 20th century. When Chinese immigration declined after the Head Tax was increased in 1903, Canadian companies sought new sources of labour from India. Between 1905 and 1908 more than five thousand Asian Indians entered Canada. Most of these immigrants were Sikhs from the Punjab countryside, specifically from the Northeastern districts: Hoshiarpur and Jullundur. They were primarily single males motivated by population pressures back home and desirous of greater economic opportunities. Like the Chinese and Japanese before them, their objective was to earn enough money to help their families and eventually return to India.

Asian Indians, like the Japanese, stayed predominantly in British Columbia during the pre-war years. They were a highly mobile group that spread quickly throughout the province supplying manual labor for the lumber, transportation, farming and railroad industries. Due to their dispersed nature and small size, concentrated pre-war communities did not form. There was no equivalent to "Chinatown" or "Little Tokyo" for the Asian Indian community.

The years 1906 to 1908 brought a large influx of South Asian immigrants into Canada. Approximately 4,700 entered the country during this period. This wave of immigrants added to the anti-Asian hysteria in British Columbia that led to the 1907 Vancouver riot. In the wake of the disturbance, the federal government stepped in to curtail immigration from Asia.

In 1908, the government implemented two regulations that effectively barred immigration from India. One required that immigrants have two hundred dollars upon arrival, a prohibitive sum for most Sikh peasants. The second requirement made it mandatory for immigrants to come to Canada directly from the country of their birth or citizenship. At the time, direct sailings between India and Canada were typically not available. Even fulfilling these requirements did not ensure entry into Canada. One Japanese ship that arrived in Vancouver in 1914 with 374 Asian Indians on board had been specially chartered by the Punjabi passengers to satisfy the continuous passage legislation. Apparently the travelers met the two requirements yet they were not allowed to disembark. After two months of waiting, the ship was sent away.

The restrictions effectively checked the growth of the Asian Indian community in British Columbia. In 1907, when immigration was at its height, the population may have been close to 4,000. But, after that initial period, the province's Asian Indian population declined considerably, as many migrated to the United States or returned to India. In 1911 the Indian population in Canada stood at 2,342.

Community decline continued even after legislation was passed in 1919 granting admittance to the wives and dependent children of Asian Indian immigrants. Few women joined their husbands in Canada. Only two females immigrated in the first year and an average of about 11 arrived per year over the next two decades. At the beginning of World War II there were an estimated 1,100 Asian Indians in British Columbia and no more than fifteen married families. It is likely that many immigrants were reluctant to subject their wives and families to the hostile and discriminatory environment in Canada. As a result, the pre-war Asian Indian community paralleled the Chinese community with its predominately single male population. This continued to be the case up until the 1970s.

Selected Educational Levels by Group, 1996

	Total Canadian population	South Asian	Chinese	Korean	Japanese	Southeast Asian	Filipino
Without High School degree	23%	22%	20%	17%	16%	28%	12%
With University degree	13%	22%	22%	30%	25%	12%	28%

Source: 1996 Census – Statistics Canada ("Visible Minority" variable)

Immigration in the 1960s and beyond

Between 1931 and 1941 the number of Asians in Canada fell by 10,500. Even after World War II, when immigration from other countries began to rise, restrictions kept Asian immigration to a minimum. In the 1960s, growing objection to the limitations placed on non-white immigration and a demand for skilled and professional labor in Canada led to a series of policy changes. In 1968, new legislation was implemented that based admission not on ethnicity or race but largely on demand for the applicant's occupation in Canada. In the years following the new regulations, the number of British and American immigrants to Canada decreased while immigration from Asian countries rose substantially.

Post-1970s immigrants

Changes made to the Canadian immigration policy were crucial to increasing the ethnic diversity of Canada's immigrant population. Fifty seven percent of entrants who arrived in Canada between 1991 and 1996 came from Asia. Nineteen percent were from Europe. These numbers differ quite dramatically from those who arrived under the previous entrance requirements. Of those who immigrated before 1961, only three percent were from Asia while 90 percent came from Europe. High immigration rates from Asia have continued into the 21st century. In the year 2000, 53 percent of people who immigrated to Canada came from Asia-Pacific countries.

Increasing Asian diversity

Since the 1970s, Asian immigrants no longer come exclusively from China, Japan and India. Many other countries and regions in Asia, including the Philippines, Sri Lanka, Korea and certain regions in Southeast Asia, have become sources of sizeable migration. As a result, Asian groups in Canada have been characterized by increased ethnic and regional diversity.

China continues to be an important source of immigrants. Since the 1970s, the Chinese have become one of the fastest growing ethnic groups in Canada. Between 1986 and 1991, they went from 1.7 percent to 2.4 percent of the population (statistics reported in this chapter, unless otherwise stated, come from the 'visible minority' variable of the 1996 Canadian Census. The Canadian Census also collects statistics on 'ethnic origin', which may differ slightly.). In 1996, the Chinese were the largest visible minority group in the country, making up three percent of the total population.

The growth in the Chinese community is largely due to immigration rather than births. In 1996, only 24 percent of the nation's Chinese population was born in Canada. The vast majority of Chinese migrants, 71 percent, arrived after 1980.

Contrary to early immigration patterns, Canada has experienced very little recent migration from Japan. Of the immigrants who arrived in the country after 1970, less than half a percent were of Japanese origin. The Japanese had the greatest representation of non-immigrants out of all the Asian groups considered in 1996. Around sixty-five percent of group members were born in Canada. This is well above the proportion of Canadian-born in other Asian groups—just under 30 percent for South Asians and less than 25 percent for all other Asian groups. Eighty percent of the South Asians in Canada are Indian.

Socioeconomic characteristics among Asians in contemporary Canada

Unlike the pre-war Asian settlers,who were largely poorly educated laborers, more recent migrants show a wider variety of educational and occupational statuses. For example, between 1904-1944, 96 percent of the immigrants from India were manual laborers. In contrast, 30 percent of Asian Indian immigrant men had jobs in professional or management professions in 1991, and 23 percent were in manufacturing.

Educational attainment of post-1970s Asians

Asian immigrants tend to be highly educated. This likely reflects the selection process for independent immigrants, which looks favorably upon applicants with high educational levels. For most Asian-origin groups in Canada, the proportion with a university degree (a bachelor's degree or higher) was well above the national rate of 13 percent in 1996. This was particularly true of Koreans and Filipinos, where 30 percent and 28 percent, respectively, of those 15 years old and over had a university degree. The only exception to this trend was the Southeast Asians where 12 percent had a university degree.

The Asian groups were also generally more likely than the total population to have a high school diploma. Filipinos had the highest high school graduation rate, at about 88 percent, compared to 77 percent in the total population. South Asians had a 78 percent graduation rate, while 72 percent of Southeast Asians had completed high school in 1996.

Post-1970s Asians—an urban phenomenon

Where Asian Canadians Live, by Census Metropolitan Area, 1996

	Percentage of total Asian pop.	South Asian	Chinese	Korean	Japanese	Southeast Asian	Filipino
Vancouver	24%	18%	32%	26%	32%	12%	17%
Toronto	41%	49%	39%	44%	25%	27%	42%
Montreal	7%	7%	5%	5%	3%	22%	6%

Source: 1996 Census – Statistics Canada ("Visible Minority" variable)

Early Asian pioneers were largely concentrated in the province of British Columbia whose resource-rich environment provided work for the predominantly "working-class" immigrants. Asian groups at the turn of the 21st century, on the other hand, typically live in metropolitan areas, such as Vancouver, Toronto and Montreal. This is befitting the groups' more diverse occupational statuses. Immigrants, in particular, tend to gravitate to metropolitan areas where they often find greater economic opportunities and already established communities of fellow ethnics.

Vancouver

In 1996, almost one-quarter of the nation's Asian population lived in the Vancouver metropolitan area as defined by the Canadian Census. One note: the Canadian Census does not have an 'Asian' category. All figures in the text were derived by adding up the Asian groups listed in the 'visible minority' category, including: South Asians, Chinese, Korean, Japanese, Southeast Asian and Filipino. The Canadian Census also collected data by 'ethnic origin', which may differ slightly from 'visible minority' figures.

Vancouver is home to the second largest populations of Chinese, South Asians, Filipinos and Koreans in Canada and the largest Japanese population. About one-third of the nation's Chinese and Japanese populations live in this coastal city as well as 26 percent of Koreans, 18 percent of South Asians, 17 percent of Filipinos and 12 percent of Southeast Asians.

Nearly three out of ten Vancouver residents is Asian. The high representation of Asians is not surprising considering the city's historical role as a port of entry for Asian immigrants and its position along the Pacific Rim (indeed, the high number of emigrants from Hong Kong has led the city to be nicknamed "Hongcouver" by some).

Toronto

Toronto is Canada's biggest and most culturally diverse city. In absolute numbers, it has the largest Asian communities in Canada, for all groups except the Japanese. In 1996, just over 40 percent of the nation's Asian population lived in Toronto. This includes almost half of the South Asian population and about two-fifths of Canada's Chinese, Korean and Filipino populations. Around a quarter of the Japanese and Southeast Asians in Canada made Toronto their home. In 1996, slightly more than one-fifth of Toronto was of Asian origin.

Montreal

The Asian presence is not as strong in Montreal as it is in either Vancouver or Toronto. Still, there are sizeable numbers of Asians among its residents. In 1996, approximately 5 percent of the city's population were of Asian descent.

Seven percent of the Asians in Canada lived in Montreal in 1996. The high proportion of French speakers might explain why 22 percent of Southeast Asians settled in Montreal (with 23 percent of those able to speak French, compared to less than 10 percent for all other Asians in the area). Meanwhile, only 7 percent of South Asians, 6 percent of Filipinos, 3 percent of Japanese and 5 percent of both Chinese and Koreans made Montreal their home.

Income of post-1970s Asians

The high levels of education among Asians generally did not translate into higher incomes. Most Asian groups earned less on average in 1996 than the total Canadian population. This was especially true among those of Korean origin. Although the Koreans were the most likely to have university degrees, this group had an average income well below the national average (C$16,934, compared to C$25,196). Even members of the Southeast Asian group, who had a lower percent of university graduates and higher proportion without a high school certificate, had a higher average income (C$18,114) than the Koreans. The Japanese were the only group whose average income of C$29,815 in 1996 was higher than the national average.

These relatively low wages might reflect the large proportions of recent immigrants in these groups. Asian immigrants who arrived more recently generally have lower income levels. In addition, those who have credentials from abroad typically earn less than those with equivalent Canadian degrees. The combination of being an immigrant and possessing a foreign degree is typically associated with even greater economic disadvantage than any one of these characteristics on

Average Income by Group, 1996*

	Total Canadian population	South Asian	Chinese	Korean	Japanese	Southeast Asian	Filipino
Average income	$25,196	$21,477	$20,490	$16,934	$29,815	$18,114	$20,025

*Includes only individuals 15 years or older.
Source: 1996 Census – Statistics Canada ("Visible Minority" variable)

its own. This likely reflects various labor market barriers encountered by immigrants, including the lower value ascribed to certain foreign degrees. These factors might also explain the higher incomes among the Japanese relative to the other Asian groups, since a much larger proportion of the Japanese in Canada are Canadian-born.

Occupations of post-1970s Asians

In 1996, Asians in Canada occupied a range of employment categories, although some ethnic groups were more highly represented in certain categories than in others. Southeast Asians and South Asians had the largest proportions of manual laborers (around 7 percent for each) in 1996, a statistic which does not include skilled crafts and trade workers. They were the only Asian groups whose members were more likely than the general population (4 percent) to engage in physical labor.

The Koreans had the highest proportion of managers, with around 24 percent occupying this role in 1996. The Japanese and Chinese were also above the general population (9 percent), with 12 percent and 11 percent respectively. The other groups were below the national figure with Filipinos having the lowest proportion of managers (3 percent).

The Japanese had the highest percent of professional workers, with 21 percent of their workforce employed in this category. The Chinese, with 18 percent, was also above the national figure of 14 percent. Filipinos were the least likely of the Asian groups to be in professional fields, with approximately 10 percent of its population thus employed.

Filipinos were highly represented in sales and service jobs. Over 40 percent of their population had jobs in this sector. Koreans were the next highest, with 38 percent, followed by the Chinese, with 30 percent. The other groups were fairly close to the national average of 27 percent.

Conclusion

This chapter outlines both the historical and contemporary statuses of Asian groups in Canada. During the more than 150 years that people of Asian background have lived and worked in this country, their experiences have often been shaped by factors outside their control. Yet Asians have also been active participants in their own destinies. They have frequently resisted attempts of subordination. In so doing they effectively altered the social, political, and economic landscape of Canada.

One of the most prominent examples of this is the Japanese Canadian Redress campaign. In 1988 Japanese Canadians successfully negotiated compensation for the government's actions during and immediately following World War II. This agreement set a precedent for other communities seeking to rectify government mistreatment.

The agreement also resulted in the creation of the Canadian Race Relations Foundation, which was proclaimed into law by the federal government on October 28, 1996. The stated mandate of this foundation is to "contribute to the elimination of racism and all forms of racial discrimination in Canadian society." Thus, this foundation can potentially play a major role in creating a nation hospitable to all ethnic groups.

—Tracy Matsuo and Eric Fong

Selected Occupations of Asians in Canada, 1996*

	Total Canadian population	South Asian	Chinese	Korean	Japanese	Southeast Asian	Filipino
Managers	9%	7%	11%	24%	12%	5%	3%
Professionals	14%	13%	18%	14%	21%	11%	10%
Sales and service	27%	27%	30%	38%	28%	27%	43%
Manual workers**	4%	7%	3%	1%	3%	7%	3%

*Includes only individuals 15 years or older.
**Does not include skilled crafts and trade workers or semi-skilled manual workers.
Source: 1996 Census – Statistics Canada ("Visible Minority" variable)

Making Homes in the Heartland

If there is a new face to Asian Pacific America in the 21st century, then many of its facets are walking the streets of Chicago, working in the boardrooms and on the line in Detroit, tilling family farms in Indiana, attending classes in Ann Arbor, Bloomington, and Evanston, working in nail salons in mid-Michigan shopping malls, enjoying the dance scene in Minneapolis, and relaxing by the lakeshore in Madison, Wisconsin. Much of Asian Pacific America's new face is to be found in the American Midwest.

While it has been neglected, even by APA journalists and scholars, this Midwestern side to Asian Pacific America has been growing in size, diversity, and number of communities: APAs made up 2.3 percent of the Midwestern population, or about 1.45 million people, 2000. The percentage is much higher in some states: in Illinois, there are nearly half a million APAs, making up almost 4 percent of the population. Cook County, where the city of Chicago is located, had more than 262 thousand APA residents in 1999—just ten thousand shy of San Francisco County! There are also numerous APAs in the urban areas of Michigan, Minnesota, Ohio, Wisconsin and others.

APAs also increasingly comprise the institutional "intellectual capital" in the Midwest, as seen in the proliferation of APA studies programs in Midwestern colleges and universities. While this academic surge has been recent, the demographic growth has been proceeding for some time. As a historian, I would go so far to say that the APA presence in the Midwest has been growing steadily, and doing so for a much longer span of time than usually recognized. This chapter will trace those long roots and supply a map to the "third coast" of Asian Pacific America. This "third coast" faces neither the Pacific nor the Atlantic coasts, but somewhere in between.

Where is the "heartland?"

Scholars agree that the notion of the "Midwest" is both familiar and baffling. On the one hand it's the "center," on the other hand, what does that mean? The U.S. Census defines the Midwest as comprising these 12 states: Illinois, Iowa, Indiana, Kansas, Michigan, Minnesota, Missouri, Nebraska, North and South Dakota, Ohio, and Wisconsin.

Photo: AP Wide World

Midwest states like Michigan, Ohio and North Dakota boast a highly educated APA population: one-third of Midwestern Asians had a graduate degree or higher, and educational rates for Midwest NHPIs holding a bachelor's or graduate degree are comparable with the general populace.

APA Population Growth, 1990-2000: Midwest

1990 rank	Region	POPULATION 1990	2000 rank	2000	Pop. growth 1990-2000	% growth 2000-1990	Rank by % growth
	Midwest	768,069		1,425,940	657,871	86.5%	
1	Illinois	285,311	1	482,339	197,028	69.1%	11
2	Michigan	104,983	2	213,552	108,569	103.4%	4
3	Ohio	91,179	4	164,817	73,638	80.8%	9
4	Minnesota	77,886	3	165,779	87,893	112.8%	2
5	Wisconsin	53,583	5	105,436	51,853	96.8%	6
6	Missouri	41,277	6	81,173	39,896	96.7%	7
7	Indiana	37,617	7	76,141	38,524	102.4%	5
8	Kansas	31,750	8	58,411	26,661	84.0%	8
9	Iowa	25,476	9	44,799	19,323	75.8%	10
10	Nebraska	12,422	10	28,149	15,727	126.6%	1
11	North Dakota	3,462	12	5,344	1,882	54.4%	12
12	South Dakota	3,123	11	6,426	3,303	105.8%	3

Source: U.S. Census 2000, SF1 (PCT7 and PCT10)

But does this exhaust the possibilities? This chapter will go with the Census definition for now, but argues that any line drawing will be arbitrary: the "Midwest" is less a thing bordered by rigid state boundaries and more the changing imagined identity that demographers, writers, marketers, regional promoters, and former Midwesterners have invested in a slippery spot on the map of the continental United States.

This attitude has its advantages: it contributes to a dynamic view of the supposedly stolid, stodgy, static (and stagnant?) Midwest. Asian Pacific America diversifies understandings of the "Midwest" not only because it adds to "diversity," but also because APAs were always there in the region, and recalling that historical legacy complicates the comforting (and for some, discomforting) image of heartland sameness. One way to achieve this new view is to look anew at Midwestern history.

Long roots

Asian Pacific America in the Midwest has a history, and the Midwest has figured in the past of Asian Pacific America. The relationship is complementary. This connection is true of all the major Asian Pacific American migrations that have occurred, and the presence of Chinese, Japanese, Filipino, Korean, South Asian, Vietnamese, and Hmong communities on the "third coast" (and its interiors) tell us of a significant development.

It might seem that Hmong communities in Wausau, Wisconsin in 2002 would have little connection with Chinese laundrymen in 1870s Chicago, but the long past of Asian America worked like waves, creating patterns of precedent and attitudes that would affect subsequent Asian community formations. Not the least of these precedences were policy outlooks acquired by 20th century government planners who saw the Midwest as a good place to disperse two waves of Asian American population "unsettlements," first in the 1940s, then in the 1970s.

Possibly the earliest APA settlements occurred after the Civil War in the form of Chinese migration. According to old-timers in Chicago's Chinatown who were interviewed in the 1930s, these pioneers walked from the West Coast and Rocky Mountain regions to the "middle west," eating for food what they caught from streams and carrying their rice in bags slung over their shoulders. Chinese hand laundries would develop in Chicago during the 1870s and 1880s, with the latter decade being the period of considerable growth.

Midwest region by the numbers

Total APA population, including hapas of mixed-race and mixed-ethnicity: 1,432,366

Asian population 'alone': 1,197,504

1990 APA population: 768,069

Total APA population growth, 1990-2000: 86.5 percent

Largest APA population (nationwide rank): Illinois, 482,339 (6th)

Smallest APA population (nationwide rank): North Dakota, 5,344 (50th)

Fastest growing state, rate (nationwide rank): Nebraska, 126.6 percent (7th)

Slowest growing state, rate (nationwide rank): North Dakota, 54.4 percent (49th)

Highest percent of APAs in population (nationwide rank): Illinois, 3.9 percent (12th)

Lowest percent of APAs in population (nationwide rank): North Dakota, 0.8 percent (50th)

Chicago

Though located in the land of corn, the image that comes to mind of Chicago is not of a typical Midwest town. The Chicago area has seen many demographic changes this past decade, one of which is the increase of a minority population, creating a 'majority minority' in an increasingly racially diverse city.

People forget how huge Chicago and its outlying suburbs is: more than 9 million people, or 9,157,540, to be exact. 432,175 Asians and 9,934 NHPIs were settled in this area in 2000. While scattered all over, Asians reside predominantly in Chicago's suburban northwestern Cook County and in parts of DuPage and Lake Counties. One in ten residents in the far western suburb of Naperville is Asian. In the northwest suburb of Schaumburg, about one in seven residents is Asian.

Asians had the highest median household income of all races in Chicago, at $59,376. For NHPIs, the median household income of $42,045 was higher than the national median ($41,994). Though the median family income for Asians at $66,640 was lower than non-Hispanic whites ($70,778), they still earned more than the national median ($50,046). NHPIs jumped over the national median at $51,080, even surpassing the Midwest median. In terms of per capita income in that area, Asians earned $24,594, a figure lower than for non-Hispanic whites ($29,043), but higher than the national per capita figure for the total population. Per capita income for NHPIs was $16,403.

Asians in the Chicago area, similar to the trend in other major metro areas of the United States, had a high rate of educational attainment. Compared to other races, 57.4 percent of Asians attained a bachelor's degree or more, the highest rate among all other races, followed by whites with a 34.4 percent rate. For NHPIs, that rate was 22 percent. For Asians with a graduate or professional degree or more, their rate of 22.6 percent was almost double that of non-Hispanic whites (12.7 percent), who were second highest. 8.8 percent of NHPIs had a graduate or professional degree.

Chicago's Asian population has experienced a relatively low poverty rate at 8.8 percent, second only to non-Hispanic whites with 4.5 percent. The poverty rate among NHPIs is almost double that of Asians, but still lower than that of blacks and Hispanics.

There are 125,208 Asian Indians in the Chicago metro area, comprising the largest APA population. Filipinos (95,928), Chinese (76,793), Koreans (49,972), Japanese (24,094), Pakistanis (18,268) and Vietnamese (17,937) are among the other groups that make up the majority of APAs, along with Thais (6,212) and Laotians (4,055).

Among Chicago's diverse APA population, 2.8 percent of households in the Chicago area speak an APA language, slightly higher than the 2.6 nationwide rate. Of those APA language-speaking households, 26.6 percent are considered linguistically isolated—slightly lower than California.

—*Cindy Chew*

Educational Attainment by Race in Chicago, 1999*

Chicago-Gary-Kenosha, IL-WI CMSA	Black alone	Asian alone	NHPI alone	Hispanic alone	Non-Hispanic white alone
Total	**979,246**	**257,359**	**1,721**	**741,993**	**3,783,185**
% high school graduate	74.3%	86.9%	71.3%	48.6%	88.8%
% with college bachelor's degree or more	15.2%	57.4%	22.0%	8.9%	34.4%
% with graduate/professional degree or more	5.2%	22.6%	8.8%	3.1%	12.7%

*Only for population 25 years and older.

Note: CMSA data is derived from the 2000 Census showing 245 places in the United States with 100,000 or more population. They included 238 incorporated places (including four city-county consolidations) and seven census-designated places that were not legally incorporated.

Source: U.S. Census 2000, SF3 (Tables P148 A-I)

Expansion was accompanied by trouble and by 1883, a newspaper in the South, the *Atlanta Constitution*, would note that the 700-some Chinese in Chicago had requested "Peking" to establish a consulate in the city because the local police had "raided" them "indiscriminately" on the pretense of cracking down on opium dens.

That Chinese Chicagoans requested assistance to ward off or redress local intimidation shows the underside of Asian American Midwestern settlement. Chinese laundrymen often suffered the indignities of regular intimidations by neighborhood teenagers. The latent anti-Chinese sentiment exploded in the most spectacular way in Milwaukee, Wisconsin. In March 1889, the city saw 3,000 of its denizens

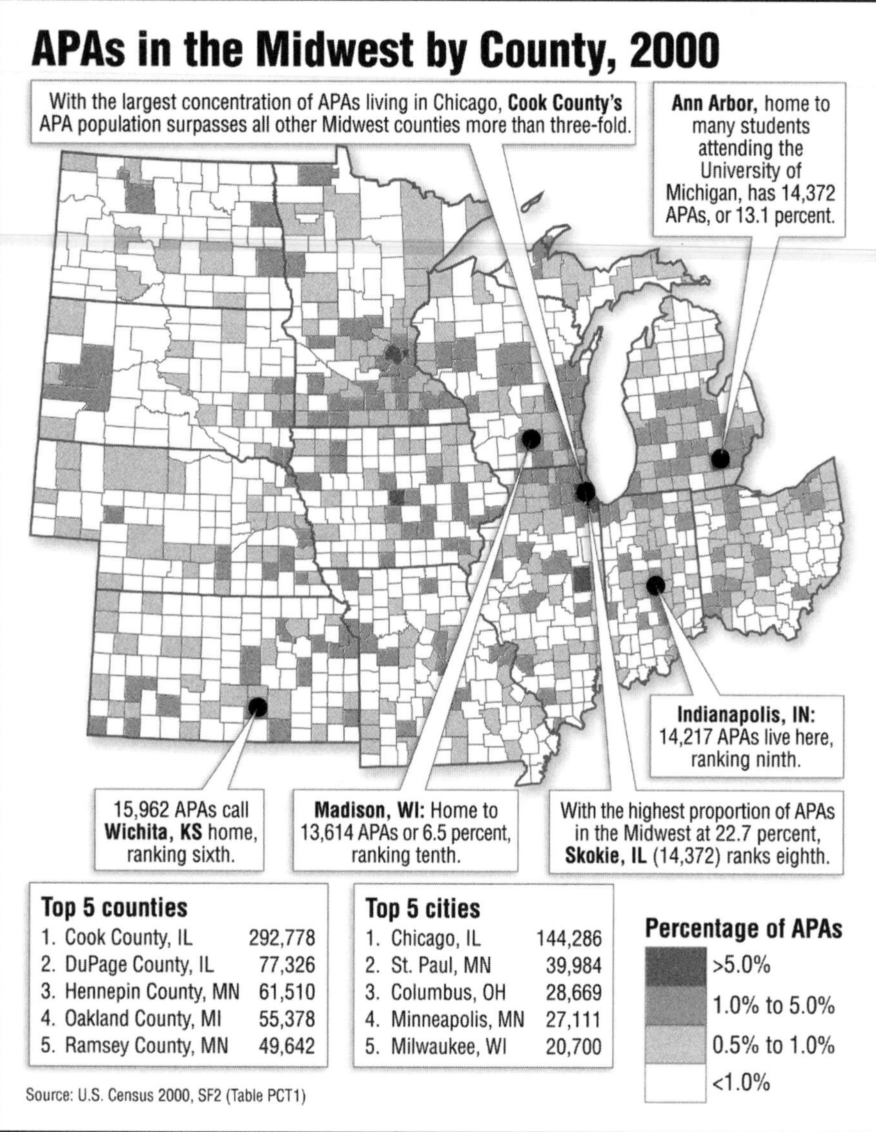

Top 5 counties	
1. Cook County, IL	292,778
2. DuPage County, IL	77,326
3. Hennepin County, MN	61,510
4. Oakland County, MI	55,378
5. Ramsey County, MN	49,642

Top 5 cities	
1. Chicago, IL	144,286
2. St. Paul, MN	39,984
3. Columbus, OH	28,669
4. Minneapolis, MN	27,111
5. Milwaukee, WI	20,700

spend four days protesting the Chinese presence, an outburst that later turned deadly when it transformed into a city-wide anti-Chinese riot.

Second generation arrives

For the rest of the 19th century and continuing into the 20th, Asian American experiences in the Midwest were neither as violent nor as dramatic as the Milwaukee riot. With the passing years, Chinese Midwesterners would be joined by other Asian groups, and by the 1910s and 1920s, an American-born second generation would make itself felt. These small developments took such forms as: 1) issei families starting farms in Wisconsin in 1914; 2) Filipino government scholarship students starting communities in Midwestern college towns and Chicago; 3) Filipino men becoming Pullman porters on lines running from Chicago to Champaign; and a Chinese American teenager who caught the attention of a Madison, Wisconsin newspaper in 1911 because of his prowess on the football field. The newspaper said he was "a terror running through the line."

The Midwest played a role in two of the watershed moments of twentieth century Asian Pacific American history: the forced evacuation and relocation of Japanese Americans during the Second World War, and the formation of Southeast Asian refugee communities throughout the Midwest after the end of the Vietnam War in 1975. During the Second World War, two groups of Japanese Americans who were exempted from the War Relocation Authority camps went to the Midwest. One group consisted of agricultural workers, some of whom worked in agricultural experiment station farms owned by universities near the Great Lakes. The other category consisted of nisei college students, who spent the war years studying at such schools as the University of Wisconsin, the University of Michigan, and the University of Chicago.

With the camps slated for closing in 1946, postwar planners saw a chance to change the face of Japanese America. They looked to the Midwest as the best place to resettle Japanese Americans on a more permanent basis. Hoping to break up the pre-war concentrations of Japanese Americans that allegedly overcrowded Little Tokyo in Los Angeles, postwar planners thought the Midwest would be a good place to disperse the population and promote American assimilation.

This Midwestern history sounds familiar because its spirit was conjured up again thirty years later. In the midst of evacuating and resettling refugees from South Vietnam in 1975, Federal government bureaucrats sought to prevent the concentration of Southeast Asian refugees on the West Coast by locating many of them to the Midwest. Much the same could be said of the Hmong experience in 1980. Many Hmong were initially settled in the Midwest, but an even greater number have voluntarily moved there in the last two decades from other parts of the country. In 2000, more than half of the Hmong population lived in the Midwest. Five of the ten largest Hmong populations were located in Midwestern metropolises: Minneapolis-St. Paul, Minnesota; Milwaukee,

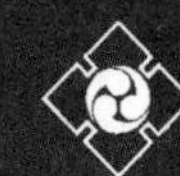

St. Paul's Hmong population moves from city to suburbs

The Hmong began arriving in the Twin Cities area after the Vietnam War, eventually ending up in Frogtown, St. Paul's eastside and other areas with affordable housing. Today, the Twin Cities, and especially St. Paul, are the capital of Hmong America, boasting the largest Hmong population nationwide. And in the above-mentioned areas of St. Paul, nearly one in four residents in these areas are Hmong, many living in close quarters for community support as new arrivals.

In the early 1980s, the Hmong population in the Twin Cities was nearly evenly split between Minneapolis and St. Paul. Over time, more Hmong began moving into St. Paul because there was less crime and cheaper housing.

These days, according to Ilean Her, the executive director of Council on Asian Pacific Minnesotans, Hmong, especially young couples, are filtering out into the suburbs for the better schools and safer streets. Nearly four times as many Hmong own homes in 2000 as did in 1990, according to the Census.

Chao Lee, a member of the 4th District congressional staff in Minnesota, said most of the Hmong residents who continue to live in public housing are the elderly, who lack sufficient English and professional skills to earn enough money to move out. He also said many don't want to move out because of the governmental assistance they receive for living in public housing.

He warned that if a large segment of the Hmong population continues to live in St. Paul's public housing, they will remain voiceless in the community. She said they have been silent in pressuring public officials to improve their area.

"I think the quality of life and the standard of living in the long term may be compromised because they are not socially active," she said. "They can choose to live together, but they don't understand that they have a right to all these perks as citizens and property owners."

—*AsianWeek*

Hmong in Minnesota by Census Tract, 2000

Hmong are beginning to move to the outer suburbs, especially northern ones, such as **Brooklyn Center** and **Brooklyn Park,** and eastern ones such as **Maplewood** and **Woodbury.**

St. Paul and **Minneapolis** are home to over half the total Hmong population in the state.

Rochester: home of famed Mayo Clinic is also home to small but thriving Hmong community.

Top 5 counties

1.	Ramsey County	28,117
2.	Hennepin County	13,727
3.	Washington County	820
4.	Anoka County	720
5.	Dakota County	493

Top 5 cities

1.	St. Paul	26,509
2.	Minneapolis	10,489
3.	Brooklyn Center	1,448
4.	Brooklyn Park	1,292
5.	Maplewood	714

2000 Total: 45,184 Hmong, including those of mixed-race and mixed-ethnicity

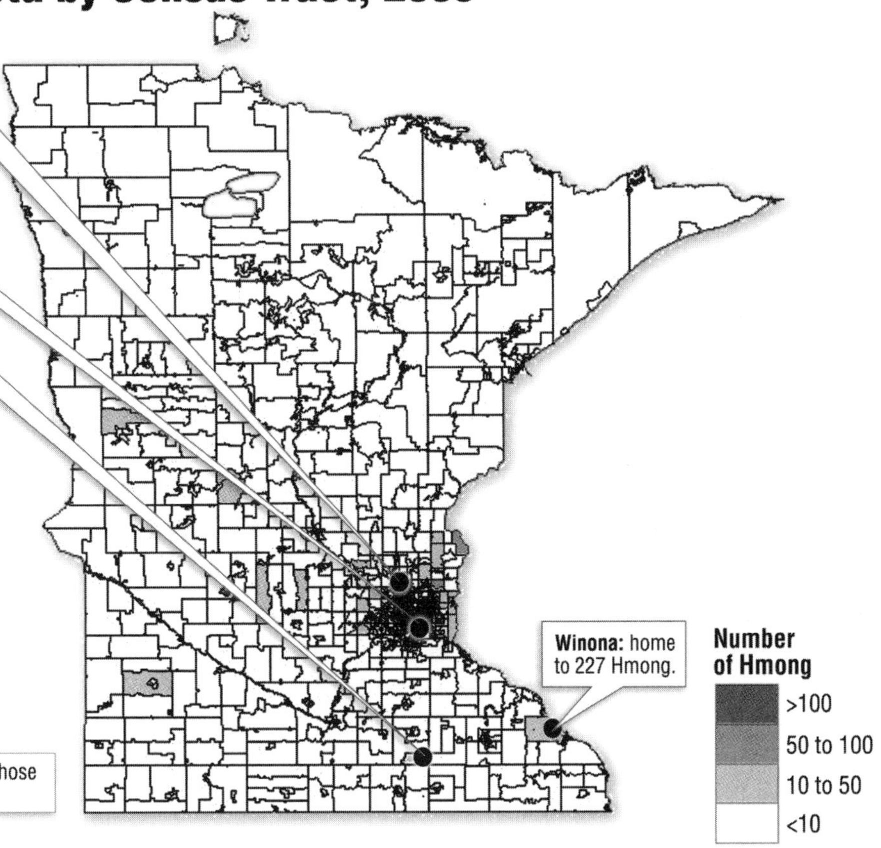

Source: U.S. Census 2000, SF2 (Table PCT1)

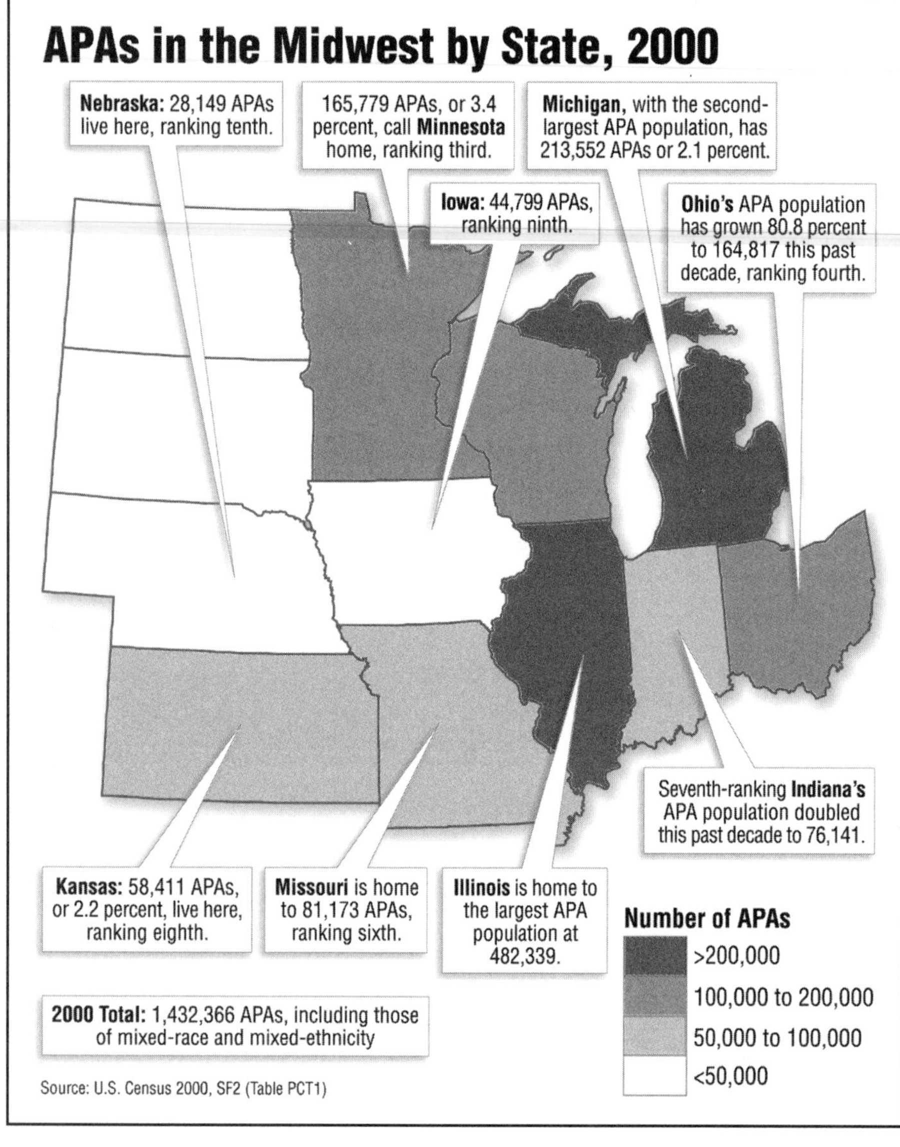

Wisconsin; Appleton-Oshkosh, Wisconsin; Wausau Wisconsin, and Detroit, Michigan.

Here we see the long hand of APA Midwestern history. Asian Pacific America and "Midwest" had connected meanings whose consequences could reach myriad numbers of persons, many of whom had no inkling of either of these connotations, or the Midwestern places they would eventually call home since 1975 and 1980.

Civil rights

But the Midwest is more than a place where things happened to Asian Americans. The Midwest is also where APA activists worked, lived, and advocated civil rights causes. In the 1880s, Wong Chin Foo, the Chinese spokesperson who opposed the Chinese Exclusion laws, spoke at Great Lakes locales such as Chicago and the University of Wisconsin. Foo would settle in Chicago, and his Chinese Midwestern compatriots would form a Chinese American volunteer unit to fight in the Spanish American War in 1898. They never went to Cuba; the war ended before their efforts could proceed very far. In the twentieth century, a Punjabi named Ali pursued a lawsuit in Michigan to test the federal citizenship rule limiting naturalization to free white persons.

In the 1920s, Easurk Emsen Charr, a Chicagoan, would also sue to test the naturalization ban as it affected Korean Americans who had served the United States armed services during the World War I. In the 20th century, Detroit's Grace Lee Boggs would carry the fight against separate facilities by race as allowed during "Jim Crow" America. Later in the 1960s, Asian American students at the University of Wisconsin, Madison and the University of Michigan would become Asian American activists in the Midwest. More recently, the murder of Vincent Chin in 1980s Detroit, and the lax sentencing of his killers, led to a burst of anti-racism activism and Asian American agitation that spread from the Midwest to the rest of the nation.

East of California's hot center

What does Midwestern Asian Pacific America hold for the future of Asian Pacific America? In terms of demographics, one can assume that population growth will continue in various Midwestern cities. While the Midwest has the smallest APA population by region—just around 12 percent of the overall APA population—it is expected to gain 1.13 million APAs during the 30 years between 1995 and 2025, according to the Census Bureau. Still, certain APA groups will increase their numbers much faster. Hmong and certain other Southeast Asian groups have large groups of 1.5 and second generation members who are just now beginning to marry and have children.

Other trends portend benefits for APAs in general. The most intriguing prospect is greater and novel APA self-understanding, especially as it develops in Midwestern APA studies programs. The institutional "intellectual capital" that is accumulating in the APA Midwest—mostly the result of APA student activism—has blossomed into APA Studies Programs at schools such as the University of Wisconsin-

Madison (founded in 1990, the first APA Studies program in the Big Ten academic conference); the University of Michigan Program in American Culture (a program that features a strong emphasis on Asian Pacific Americans); and the very active program currently at the University of Illinois-Urbana Champaign.

These programs, along with faculty hires at other Big Ten institutions (Northwestern University for example), will lead to the Midwest being an extremely productive place for APA studies. It is no stretch to say that the "third coast location" of these programs will allow for new and different perspectives on Asian Pacific America. Already, scholars at the University of Michigan are re-examining Pacific postcolonial relationships, and the Midwestern distance from the Pacific region is enabling new ways to imagine regional relationships and regionality. Not unlike Wong Chin Foo in the 1880s, who found a "space" in Chicago and Wisconsin to agitate against exclusion, so APA scholars in the Midwest will be released to pursue new directions in conceiving and conceptualizing Asian Pacific America in the 21st century.

This is so because they are occupying a new and different vantage from which to view APA, a place at once different from the traditional sites of APA identity making—the West Coast and the East Coast—and connected historically to Asian Pacific America in general.

Back to history, I would argue that the lack of a recognized and remembered history, a lack that afflicts both Asian Pacific Americans and non-Asian Pacific Americans, is debilitating. The ignorance of APA's long Midwestern roots leads to the false assumption that Asians have little invested in the American heartland, that their presence is just an interloping recent event that is illegitimate. Such a position is spurious; the long roots of the APA Midwest more than adequately refute the "forever stranger" recency notion. Unfortunately, such a long view is still unknown.

It is such ignorance that could show itself in the most mundane, everyday, and racist ways, such as was experienced by Ronald Takaki, one of the pioneers of Asian American history and the author of *Strangers From a Different Shore.* While standing on a street corner in East Lansing, Michigan, waiting for the light to change, Professor Takaki was accosted by a drive-by "orientalizing" mockery thrown by some males who slowed down their car to ridicule an Asian-looking fellow. Wider knowledge of Asian Pacific American Midwestern history may not have prevented this instance, or the many episodes like it, but the widespread recognition, teaching, circulation, and acceptance of Midwestern Asian Pacific American history would go some distance to undermining and refuting its base assumptions.

—*Victor Jew*

Socioeconomic trends in the Midwest

Household income

For all racial groups, median household incomes in the Midwest tend to be lower than on the coasts, but higher than the south. For the general population, the median household income in 1999 was $42,414; Minnesota was the highest state ranked eleventh, with $47,111, and Illinois close behind at thirteenth with $46,590. North Dakota had the lowest. NHPIs consistently had lower median household incomes than Asians and the general population in the Midwest, except in three states: Minnesota, Wisconsin, and North Dakota. In North Dakota, the NHPI median household income was more than $10,000 higher than the Asian median! Those results may be blips rather than indicators of an emerging trend: there were fewer than 2,000 single-race NHPIs living in Minnesota and Wisconsin, and only 230 in North Dakota.

Family income

Families are generally larger than households, as the Census defines them, so median family incomes tend to be higher than median household ones.

Extremes in Midwestern Family Incomes by Race, 1999

	Total pop.	Asians alone	NHPI alone	Non-Hispanic white	Black or African American	Hispanic or Latino
% of families over $100,000 income	14.1%	23.3%	10.2%	15.0%	7.5%	7.3%
% of families under $20,000 income	12.7%	12.5%	18.7%	10.2%	30.6%	20.9%

*Includes Alaskan natives alone.

Source: U.S. Census 2000, SF3 (Tables P76 and P154 A-I)

Educational Attainment for Population 25 Years and Over by Race and State, 1999: Midwest

TOTAL POPULATION	United States	Midwest	Illinois	Indiana	Iowa	Kansas	Michigan
Total	182,211,639	41,537,007	7,973,671	3,893,278	1,895,856	1,701,207	6,415,941
% high school graduate	80.4%	83.5%	81.4%	82.1%	86.1%	86.0%	83.4%
% with college bachelor's degree or more	24.4%	22.9%	26.1%	19.4%	21.2%	25.8%	21.8%
% with graduate/professional degree or more	8.9%	7.9%	9.5%	7.2%	6.5%	8.7%	8.1%
	Minnesota	Missouri	Nebraska	North Dakota	Ohio	South Dakota	Wisconsin
Total	3,164,345	3,634,906	1,087,241	408,585	7,411,740	474,359	3,475,878
% high school graduate	87.9%	81.3%	86.6%	83.9%	83.0%	84.6%	85.1%
% with college bachelor's degree or more	27.4%	21.6%	23.7%	22.0%	21.1%	21.5%	22.4%
% with graduate/professional degree or more	8.3%	7.6%	7.3%	5.5%	7.4%	6.0%	7.2%

ASIANS ALONE	United States	Midwest	Illinois	Indiana	Iowa	Kansas	Michigan
Total	6,640,671	717,531	276,697	35,529	20,157	27,227	107,112
% high school graduate	80.4%	83.1%	86.9%	86.2%	74.3%	74.8%	85.6%
% with college bachelor's degree or more	44.1%	53.7%	57.7%	58.0%	42.9%	40.5%	61.0%
% with graduate/professional degree or more	17.4%	25.7%	23.6%	29.7%	24.4%	20.8%	32.3%
	Minnesota	Missouri	Nebraska	North Dakota	Ohio	South Dakota	Wisconsin
Total	68,939	39,231	12,594	2,046	85,861	2,669	39,469
% high school graduate	71.1%	82.2%	77.7%	84.4%	86.6%	72.3%	73.2%
% with college bachelor's degree or more	36.3%	51.5%	42.3%	48.9%	58.6%	39.6%	43.0%
% with graduate/professional degree or more	17.3%	28.6%	20.2%	32.9%	31.9%	20.8%	22.7%

NHPIs ALONE	United States	Midwest	Illinois	Indiana	Iowa	Kansas	Michigan
Total	206,675	10,962	2,172	929	440	714	1,354
% high school graduate	78.3%	77.1%	70.5%	77.0%	78.6%	88.7%	73.5%
% with college bachelor's degree or more	13.8%	19.7%	20.9%	17.4%	21.4%	21.1%	21.6%
% with graduate/professional degree or more	4.1%	7.2%	9.3%	5.8%	9.5%	8.8%	9.5%
	Minnesota	Missouri	Nebraska	North Dakota	Ohio	South Dakota	Wisconsin
Total	1,060	1,630	339	78	1,363	88	795
% high school graduate	78.3%	83.8%	61.9%	76.9%	78.5%	79.5%	78.7%
% with college bachelor's degree or more	21.7%	18.4%	14.5%	9.0%	18.5%	27.3%	17.7%
% with graduate/professional degree or more	3.8%	5.9%	3.2%	5.1%	7.0%	0.0%	6.2%

Source: U.S. Census 2000, SF3, Tables P37 and P148A-I

For the whole Midwest, 23.3 percent of Asian families had annual incomes of more than $100,000 in 1999, while 12.5 percent were under $20,000 in income. That's similar to the overall national Asian figure (23.1 percent and 13.8 percent, respectively), and by this measure, Asians are more prosperous than the general Midwestern population (which has 14.1 percent of the populace above $100,000 income and the same percentage below $20,000 income) and topped non-Hispanic whites on the high side (of whom only fifteen percent were over $100,000 in income) but was worse on the low side (10.2 percent of non-Hispanic whites under $20,000 in income).

The more urbanized Midwestern states had a higher proportion of wealthy Asian families. The percentage of Asian families with more than $100,000 in income was highest in Michigan (29.7 percent), followed by Illinois (26.1 percent) and Ohio (25.9 percent). Minnesota and Wisconsin, despite having overall high incomes for the general populace, had relatively low percentages of wealthy Asian families and higher percentages of low-income Asian families. This can be accounted for by the large populations of Hmong and other Southeast Asians.

Midwestern NHPIs, while generally worse off than Asians and non-Hispanic whites, tended to have higher incomes than other minority groups such as blacks, American Indians, and Hispanics. 10.2 percent of Midwestern NHPIs were above the $100,000 family income mark, while 18.7 percent were below the $20,000 family income mark. The wealthiest and poorest NHPI families were in Michigan—22.8 percent above $100,000, and 21.8 percent below $20,000. Of North Dakota's 26 NHPI

Per Capita Income by Race, 1999: Midwest

	United States	Midwest	Illinois	Indiana	Iowa	Kansas	Michigan
Total	**$21,587**	**$21,438**	**$23,104**	**$20,397**	**$19,674**	**$20,506**	**$22,168**
Non-Hispanic white alone	$24,819	$23,002	$26,975	$21,328	$20,249	$22,023	$23,860
Asian alone	$21,823	$21,803	$24,137	$22,421	$18,279	$18,182	$24,581
Native Hawaiian or Pacific Islander alone	$15,054	$15,702	$15,523	$15,504	$21,436	$17,272	$16,378
Black alone	$14,437	$14,661	$14,747	$15,049	$12,400	$14,206	$15,714
Hispanic alone	$12,111	$12,548	$12,584	$12,921	$10,848	$11,177	$13,889
	Minnesota	**Missouri**	**Nebraska**	**North Dakota**	**Ohio**	**South Dakota**	**Wisconsin**
Total	**$23,198**	**$19,936**	**$19,613**	**$17,769**	**$21,003**	**$17,562**	**$21,271**
Non-Hispanic white alone	$24,494	$21,032	$20,722	$18,434	$22,159	$18,837	$22,548
Asian alone	$15,389	$21,297	$16,739	$21,265	$24,912	$14,528	$14,962
Native Hawaiian or Pacific Islander alone	$16,948	$14,012	$13,670	$45,993	$12,919	$11,353	$15,076
Black alone	$13,741	$14,021	$13,055	$12,468	$14,499	$12,505	$12,186
Hispanic alone	$12,215	$13,051	$10,752	$12,156	$13,544	$10,242	$11,499

Source: U.S. Census 2000, SF3 (Tables P82 and P157 A-I)

families, about one in five were above $100,000. In South Dakota, none were.

Per capita income

The average Midwestern per-capita income of $21,438 was topped by Asians ($21,803) but NHPIs lagged ($15,702). Asians in Ohio had the highest per-capita income ($24,912); South Dakota was lowest ($14,528). NHPIs in North Dakota pulled in an astounding $45,993 per capita; on the low end, South Dakota NHPIs made $11,353 per capita.

Poverty

Of the four regions, the Midwest generally ranks third on measures of income. But in terms of poverty, it ranks the lowest—just 10.2 percent, compared to the national average of 12.4 percent, providing evidence that generally, income inequality and cost of living are lower there than elsewhere in the country.

Among Asians, poverty was highest in Wisconsin and Minnesota, where nearly one in five Asians were deemed so in 2000. Most of them were Southeast Asian immigrants such as Hmong and Laotians. Overall, the poverty rate for Asians in the Midwest is 13 percent; for NHPIs, it was 14.8 percent. The smallest proportion of impoverished Asians was in Illinois (9.7 percent), while for NHPIs it was in North Dakota (2.3 percent).

Educational Attainment

Midwestern Asians may not be the wealthiest in the nation, but they are the best-educated. 53.7 percent of all Asians had a bachelor's degree or high-

Median Household Income by State, 1999: Midwest

State	Total pop.	National rank	State	Asians alone	National rank	State	NHPIs alone	National rank
Minnesota	$47,111	11	**Michigan**	$57,966	5	**Minnesota**	$48,214	9
Illinois	$46,590	13	**Illinois**	$57,333	7	**Wisconsin**	$47,670	11
Michigan	$44,667	16	**Ohio**	$49,266	16	**North Dakota**	$45,875	13
Wisconsin	$43,791	18	**Minnesota**	$45,520	25	**Illinois**	$41,276	22
Indiana	$41,567	22	**Indiana**	$42,933	31	**Ohio**	$40,718	24
Ohio	$40,956	23	**Kansas**	$42,767	32	**Kansas**	$37,788	32
Kansas	$40,624	26	**Nebraska**	$41,945	36	**Michigan**	$35,903	38
Iowa	$39,469	31	**Missouri**	$41,075	37	**Indiana**	$35,625	39
Nebraska	$39,250	32	**Iowa**	$40,348	39	**Iowa**	$35,568	40
Missouri	$37,934	35	**Wisconsin**	$39,847	41	**South Dakota**	$34,293	43
South Dakota	$35,282	41	**South Dakota**	$38,346	43	**Nebraska**	$34,120	44
North Dakota	$34,604	42	**North Dakota**	$35,441	49	**Missouri**	$32,773	45

Source: U.S. Census 2000, SF3 (Tables P53, P152 A-I)

Photo: Corky Lee

Illinois and Michigan saw their Asian Indian communities double in size during the 1990s. Chicago now boasts the third-largest Asian Indian population, behind only New York City and the San Francisco Bay Area.

er, compared to the national Asian figure of 44.1 percent. Notable states were Illinois, Indiana, Michigan and Ohio, where more than six in ten Asian males had a bachelor's degree. In North Dakota, Ohio and Michigan, around a third of Asians had a graduate degree or higher. These all compare favorably with the general population at large and in individual Midwestern states: rates of obtaining bachelor's degrees were generally between 20 to 25 percent—half the Asian rate in many cases.

Midwestern NHPI rates of having a university bachelor's or graduate degree were very similar to the general populace, and higher than other minorities: 19.7 percent with a bachelor's, and 7.2 percent with a graduate degree or higher, respectively.

Language

By region, the Midwest has the lowest percentage of households that speak an APA language, at 1.3 percent (or about half the national rate of 2.6 percent). 27.6 percent of those households fluent in an APA language are linguistically isolated (meaning no one over the age of 14 rated themselves as speaking English well or very well), slightly lower than the national rate of 29.2 percent. The highest rate of APA language fluency was in Illinois, at 2.3 percent, with the lowest in North Dakota, at less than half a percent.

—Eric Lai

Catching Up to California?

Since the Civil War and throughout most of the 20th century, race relations in the South have traditionally referred to the interactions between whites and blacks. To be sure, during this period, there also were Asian Pacific Americans in the South. The "Louisiana Manilamen," probably the first APAs in the South, established villages in the 18th century outside of what is now New Orleans. And in the 19th century, Chinese Americans completed a second transcontinental railroad through Texas. Nonetheless, until relatively recently, the APA population in the South has been so tiny and dispersed that its presence has not received much attention.

The vast majority of APAs have traditionally been in the West. The first major immigration waves from Asia—including Chinese, Japanese, Filipinos, Koreans, and South Asians—began in the 19th and early 20th centuries. These immigrants settled primarily in California and Hawai'i or in a few other areas in the West. On the other hand, most Native Hawaiians were of course already residents of Hawai'i when that area became a U.S. territory and later a state. As late as 1940, nine out of ten APAs resided in the West.

The APA population has experienced a very high level of growth since the Immigration Act of 1965, which again permitted immigration from Asia by nullifying the national origins quota system dating back to 1924. In 1970, APAs numbered 1.5 million, and by 1980 this population size more than doubled to 3.6 million. The APA population in 1990 increased to 6.9 million—almost double the population from the previous decade. By 1990, APAs constituted 2.8 percent of the total American population whereas before 1965 APAs constituted only 0.5 percent or less of the total American population.

Photo: AP Wide World

The appeal of warm weather and greater geographic mobility among younger generations of APAs is expected to contribute to the continued APA growth in the South.

Moving eastward

Due to their high concentration in the West, APAs represented only 1.3 percent of the population of the South in 1990, compared to 7.1 percent in the West. In 1990, most APAs, about 54 percent, lived in the West. The second most populous region in 1990 was the Northeast with 1.3 million (or 19.2 percent) followed by the South with 1.1 million (or 15.8 percent). The Midwest had the fewest APAs, just 800,000. Although 2.8 percent of the total American population was APA in 1990, this figure represents a national average that varied considerably by region.

By 2000 the APA population increased substantially to 12.5 million, or 4.5 percent of the total American population. APAs numbered 2.4 million in the Northeast, 1.4 million in the Midwest, 2.4 million in the South, and 6.3 million in the West.

At this time in APA history, about half of all APAs are living outside of the West, with 18.8 percent residing in the South—nearly caught up to the percentage in the Northeast. Thus, the proportion of APAs living in the West is about equal to the proportion living elsewhere in the nation—which is considerably dispersed compared to the early part of the 20th century.

Southern population boom

Although the APA population grew by 81.6 percent between 1990 and 2000 at the national level, there were differences by region. The growth rate for the APA population was highest in the South (115.2 percent) and lowest in the West (69.8 percent). The growth rates for the Northeast (82.3 percent) and for the Midwest (89.9 percent) are closer to the national APA average.

The growth rate for the APA population is faster outside of the West in part because these figures refer to percentage changes. When the base population is small, then a moderate increase in population size yields a high growth rate. In absolute terms, the West's APA population still grew the fastest, adding 2.6 million APAs during the 1990's, or double the 1.3 million added in the South during this period.

Reasons for migration

Growth rates are still substantively significant because they are more clearly indicative of future changes. Several aspects of the migration context have affected the higher growth rates of APAs outside the West. First, in contrast to the earlier part of the 20th century, employment opportunities for APAs have greatly expanded since the Civil Rights Act of 1964, which prohibits discrimination in the labor market. Improved job opportunities result in more geographic mobility and dispersion. In the early part of the 20th century, labor market discrimination against APAs was fairly extensive. Even tiny numbers of APAs could attract anti-Asian rhetoric and behavior. For example, Texas passed its Alien Land Law in 1921 which was largely intended to prevent the development of a Japanese American agricultural community in that state.

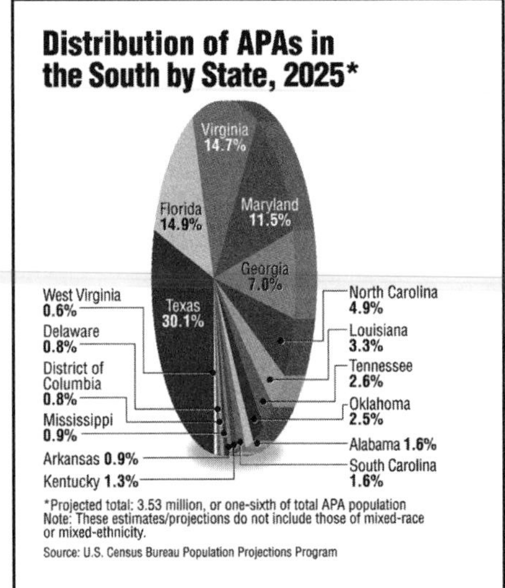

APAs often needed to rely on seeking work in enclaves of people of the same ethnicity. Most of the existing ethnic enclaves were situated in the West. Today, as job discrimination recedes and the economy of the South expands, APAs are taking advantage of opportunities there.

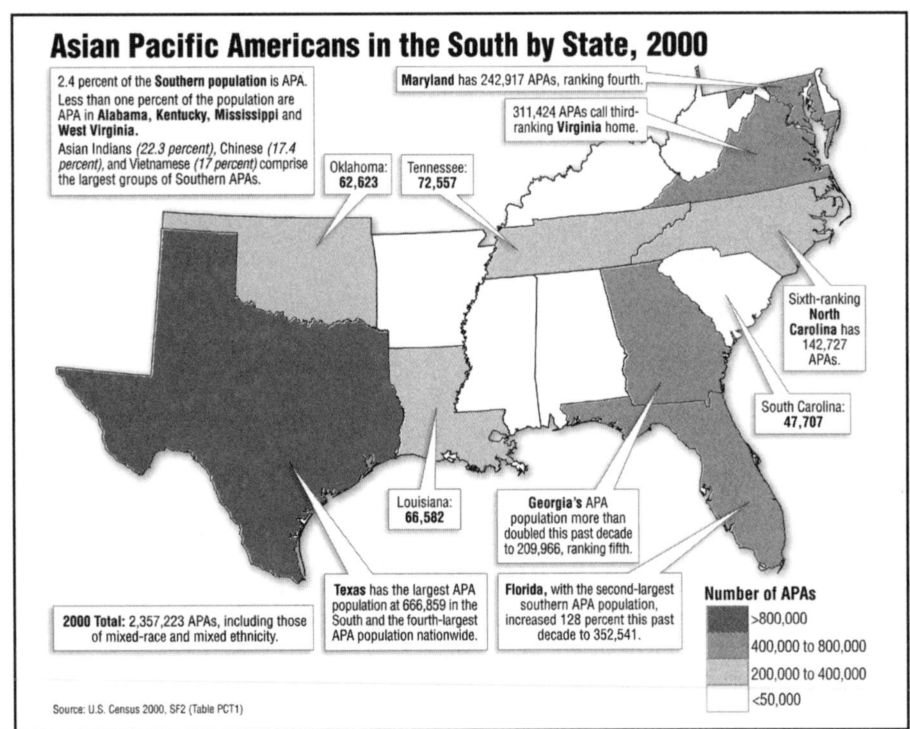

Another aspect of migration is education. More educated persons are more likely to migrate to other regions for employment than are less educated persons, because employers for higher-skilled jobs are more willing to spread their net farther and hire those coming from more distant locales. Asian Americans are more likely to have a college degree than are the members of other ethnic groups. This results in higher mobility for many Asian Americans to migrate out of the West, where they have been previously concentrated. In a similar vein, newly arrived immigrants from Asia are more likely to find jobs and homes outside of the West when they have higher levels of education. Markets for higher-skilled labor tend to recruit workers from a more national pool (due to the reduced supply of such workers) and because the demand for higher-skilled workers

(such as professionals) partly reflects population density and thus is not limited to any single geographic vicinity.

Age is another significant factor: young adults have higher levels of mobility. Because many Asian Pacific Americans came to the United States after the Immigration Act of 1965 and subsequently had and raised children in the United States, the APA population has a relatively large cohort of 'one and a half' and second generation who are now young adults. This age structure of the APA population promotes greater geographic mobility. In fact, among the racial groups, Asian Pacific Americans are the most likely to move between states.

South region by the numbers

Total APA population, including mixed-race and mixed-ethnicity: 2,357,223

Asian population 'alone': 1,922,407

1990 APA population: 1,122,248

Total APA population growth, 1990-2000: 110.0 percent

Largest APA population (nationwide rank): Texas, 666,859 (4th)

Smallest APA population (nationwide rank): West Virginia, 12,565 (45th)

Fastest growing state, rate (nationwide rank): North Carolina, 173.6 percent (2nd)

Slowest growing state, rate (nationwide rank): Louisiana, 62.0 percent (48th)

Highest percent of APAs in overall state population (nationwide rank): Maryland, 4.6 percent (8th)

Lowest percent of APAs in overall state population. (nationwide rank): West Virginia, 0.7 percent (51st)

Top APA Southern states

Regarding population sizes by state, the six Southern states with the largest numbers of APAs are Texas, Virginia, Florida, Maryland, Georgia, and North Carolina. The growth rates for most of these states exceeded the national average. In absolute terms among Southern states, Texas has the largest APA population, at 666,859 in 2000. In fact, the APA population in Texas is the fourth-largest among all states, despite constituting only 3.2 percent of the population of Texas.

In Florida, the APA population increased by nearly 129 percent during the past decade, to a population of 352,541, with the Miami-Dade County APA population swelling to more than 60,000. Most of the new residents are Indian, Filipino, Chinese and Vietnamese.

Since the end of the Vietnam War, many Vietnamese, Cambodians and Laotians have also come to Southern coastal cities (30 percent of all Vietnamese Americans reside in the South). Many find jobs picking crabs and processing shrimp and oysters, while others resume former occupations like fishing. Take the tiny coastal town of Bayou La Batre in Alabama. In this mostly white town of 2,313 residents, one-third are APAs. Although many immigrants now call the bayou their permanent home, it's hard to keep track of the APA fishing population because they move often.

"A lot of them go from Texas, Louisiana, Mississippi to Alabama and Florida. They work this coast. They move," a Bayou La Batre city councilperson told the Associated Press in 2001.

In terms of the overall American population, the South is the most populous region. For this reason, although the growth rate of APAs in the South has been large in recent years, the proportion of the total Southern population that is APA is nonetheless quite small and below the national average. Only 2.3 percent of the Southern population is APA, which is considerably lower than the 10.0 percent figure for the West.

Social impact of APA immigrants

The fact that APAs still make up a tiny, albeit visible, percentage of the South's population often has certain social consequences. First, APAs are less likely to interact with members of their own ethnic group (other than those in their

What defines the South is partly a reflection of historical legacy. Before the Civil War, slavery was legal in the states south of the Ohio River, from Delaware through Texas. This region came to be identified as the South. We use the U.S. Census Bureau's definition of the South, which consists of the following states: Delaware, Maryland, Virginia, West Virginia, Kentucky, Tennessee, North Carolina, South Carolina, Georgia, Florida, Alabama, Mississippi, Arkansas, Louisiana, Oklahoma, and Texas, together with the District of Columbia.

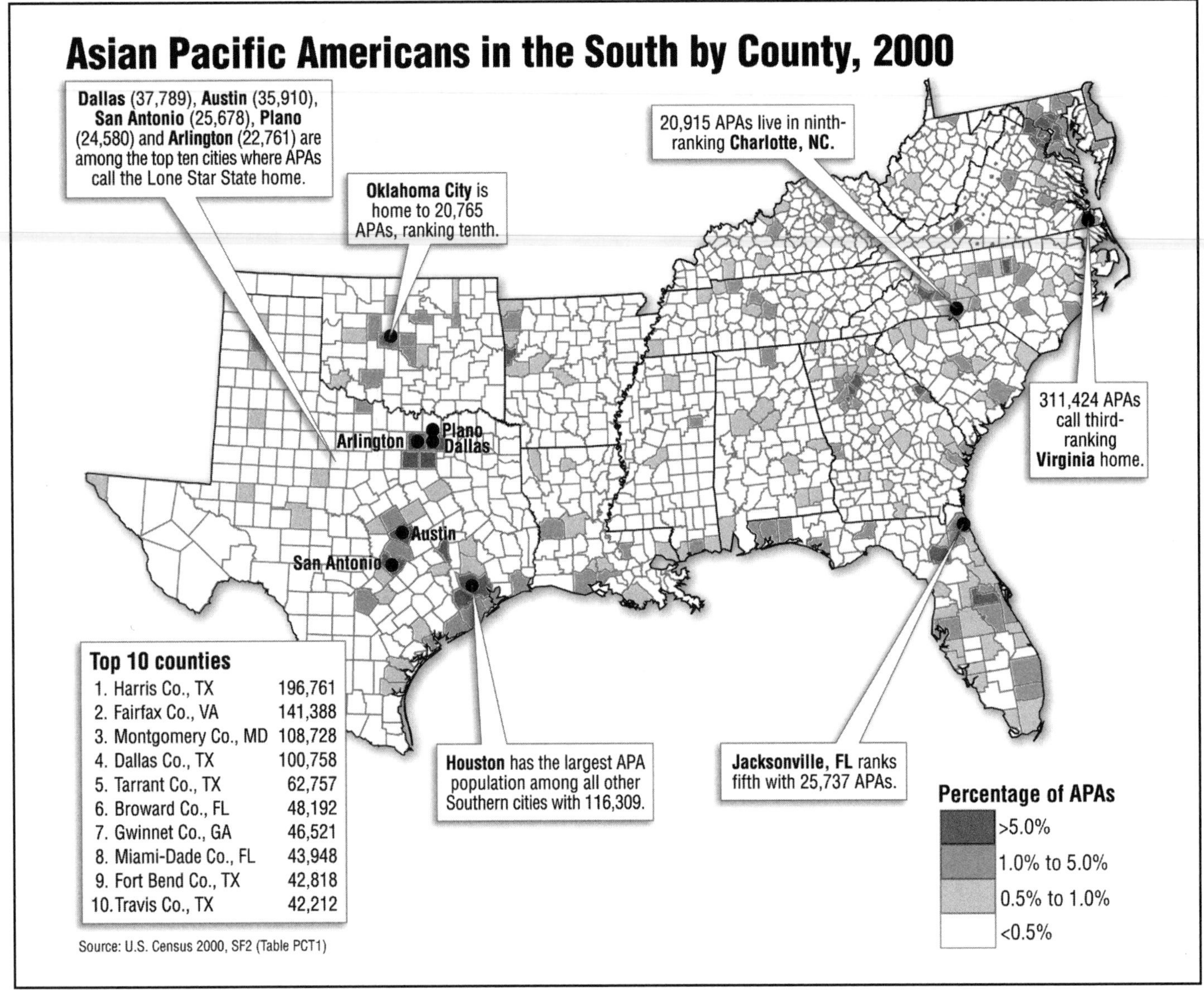

immediate family) and probably do not have access to the substantial ethnic communities that are generally more visible and developed in the West. This may make the development of an ethnic identity more psychologically arduous for the second generation while for the first generation, the adjustment to American society often must be made without less substantial social support from others of the same ethnicity. The latter tend to be far fewer in number as well as more geographically distant in the South as compared to the West.

Second, due to the lower level of social interaction and the lack of substantial and established ethnic communities with high concentrations of APAs in the South, some whites may have a tendency to develop more stereotypical views of APAs or to assume that they are foreigners. For example, a white person in the South is far less likely to have known a native-born APA than is a white person in the West. Third, there may be a tendency for more intermarriage because of the reduced social interaction with other APAs. Related to this phenomenon, 15.2 percent of Asian Pacific Americans in the South are biracial or multiracial—the highest percentage of any region.

Economic transformations

Unlike California, Hawai'i or New York, there are no metropolitan areas in the South that have very high proportions of APAs. However, there are a couple of Southern metropolitan areas that do have proportions that are slightly above the national average. In particular, 6.1 percent of the Washington-Baltimore area is APA and 5.5 percent of Houston-Galveston metropolitan area is APA. Dallas-Forth Worth and Atlanta are two other Southern metropolitan areas that have notable APA populations. In fact, Atlanta's APA population tripled between 1990 and 2000, to around 150,000, lured by the strong economy

Hayfarmin' Henry

More than one in five Korean Americans now reside in the South, according to the 2000 Census. That's not surprising, according to comedian Henry Cho, who grew up as the lone Korean in his Tennessee town during the 70s and 80s. He who says the South isn't as rednecked as you might believe.

Photo: Henry Cho

My parents graduated from the top boys' and girls' schools in Seoul, at the top of their classes. Nowadays they'd go to Harvard, but back then they got to go to Warren Wilson Junior College in Asheville, North Carolina. My dad received his doctorate at the University of Tennessee in Knoxville and worked at Oak Ridge National Labs [home of the world's oldest nuclear reactor] fifteen miles away.

The biggest myth of the South is the prejudice factor. There are prejudiced people everywhere. Growing up in Knoxville, I wasn't the "Asian" guy, I was just a guy. I played all the sports and actually excelled in baseball, basketball and football. There were no other Asians until my junior year in high school. My girlfriend was a blonde cheerleader and a homecoming queen. The two new Asian guys asked me how I did that. I told them that it was because I was an athlete. I know other Asians born in the South who grew up the same way I did. No problems whatsoever.

In my comedy act, I joke about it being tough growing up in Knoxville, since I was the only Asian guy within four states: playing "army" as a kid was tough ... it was the neighborhood against me. Playing "cowboys and Indians" was tough, too ... I was always the cook. Those are just jokes. I was never treated differently, ever.

My buddies and I never thought it was strange that I had a Southern accent until we were in college and some girl from Michigan asked my friend, "Who's that Asian guy?" My buddy replied, "Oh, that's Henry, he's Korean but he's really a Tennesseean." I ended up dating that girl and she got used to my Southern drawl and actually didn't think to tell her parents I was Korean because she didn't see me as a Korean guy, but just as a guy. So when we went to meet her parents, they were a little surprised she didn't mention it, but they didn't think anything about it either after a few minutes.

I think people in the South treat Asians with some degree of respect due to the positive stereotypes: being smart and hard-working, which aren't bad raps in my book. I know that when people go to the hospital, they are actually glad their doctor is Asian ... stereotyping again, but a positive one.

I'm not surprised that a lot of Koreans are moving to the South. With large cities such as Atlanta, Charlotte, Nashville and Birmingham, there are many opportunities. There are also many good colleges in the South, Duke and Vanderbilt, to name just two. I mainly see Korean restaurants. [Otherwise], I haven't noticed any Korean businesses.

Tennessee has a few larger cities, but for the most part it's very rural with small towns a few miles apart. I hope no city in Tennessee ever becomes like Los Angeles. It would take away from the "flavor" of the South for it not to be a white majority. I own a hay farm outside of Nashville, and as far as I know I'm the only Asian farmer in the South ... maybe in the U.S. I know it happens in Asia, but I just can't see a bunch of minorities becoming ranchers and farmers.

there. Most of the APAs are Chinese and Koreans.

Among APAs who reside in the South, the various ethnic groups are fairly equally represented (with the exception of the Japanese, Pacific Islanders, and mixed Asians, who collectively represent only about 8 percent of APAs in the South). The most numerous group of APAs in the South are the Asian Indians, who make up 22.3 percent of the APA population. They are followed by the Chinese and Vietnamese, who make up 17.4 percent and 17 percent, respectively.

While no APA group has its largest populations residing in the South, some come close. Asian Indians and the Vietnamese are the two groups that stand out in this regard with a relatively high proportion of each of these two groups residing in the South. By contrast, only about one out of eight Pacific Islanders lives in the South, and only one out of ten Japanese lives in the South.

During the last quarter of the 20th century, the U.S. economy transformed from an industrial economy to a service economy more heavily based upon professional, business, social, medical and personal service industries. Employment in the manufacturing sector has declined, and the jobs that do remain there are more often engaged in the production of goods for which the main

Socioeconomic status of Asians and NHPIs in the South

The American South is the largest of the four Census-defined regions, including sixteen states and our nation's capital, Washington D.C. Long a less-populated region, it has recently come into favor for many young families and jobseekers as a place to settle, for its low cost of living, plentiful jobs, and good weather. The APA population more than doubled there during the 1990s—the only region to experience such a fast rate of APA growth.

Median household income

While the cost of living in the South is generally lower than in other regions, incomes are also lower, across all races, as a result. The median income for Asians in the South was $49,804. Delaware, famed for its pro-business climate (corporations do not pay state income tax in many cases), has the highest Asian median income, about 30 percent higher than in the South as a whole. On the other end, Asians in Oklahoma have a median income of just $34,547, about 30 percent lower than the Southern median income. NHPIs registered their second-highest median household income by region in the South. Delaware and South Carolina were on the high side, while Arkansas, Kentucky and West Virginia were on the low side.

Median family income

The median family income for Asians in the South was $56,219, higher than the national and regional median and topping all racial groups. In most Southern states, Asian families had lower median family incomes than the Asian national median; major exceptions were Delaware ($70,160) and West Virginia ($75,678), which ranked third and second behind only New Jersey. Unlike New Jersey, which has nearly half a million APAs, both of these states sport tiny APA populations, each under 20,000. The results for Delaware and West Virginia probably indicate a near-uniformity of highly-educated professionals and their families.

NHPIs had a median family income of $42,873, lower than whites and Asians but about one third higher than blacks, Hispanics and Native Americans. The range was wide: the median NHPI family income in Delaware was three times that of Washington D.C., indicating widely-varying socioeconomic statuses of NHPIs residing in each respective location.

Family income distribution

The South has the lowest percentage of families making more than $100,000 (12.9 percent) and the highest percentage of families making less than $20,000 (17.6 percent). Asian families were doing the best among races in the South on this measure: 21 percent of Asian families were above $100,000 in income (versus 15.6 percent for non-Hispanic white families), with 13.3 percent of Asian families below $20,000 in income. The wealthiest concentrations of Asian families were in Delaware and West Virginia, where three out of ten and four out of ten families, respectively, made more than $100,000. The poorest concentrations of Asians were in Washington D.C., where one in four made less than $20,000, and Louisiana, where the rate was more than one in five.

Of Native Hawaiian and Pacific Islanders in the South, 8.4 percent made more

input involves advanced technology and human capital (e.g. computers). The U.S. economy is no longer heavily based on the production of goods that require the input and transformation of substantial quantities of raw materials. Consequently, the U.S. population has shifted out of the traditional industrial centers of the Midwest and Northeast, and during the last decades of the 20th century, net migration has been to the West and South (which are also the regions with the highest growth rates for the overall population).

Eclipsing California?

Regarding prospects for future growth, we anticipate that the South will continue to have a high rate of APA population growth. APAs will continue to move into the South as the economies of Southern cities continue to expand. In general, the political climate of the South is more pro-business, with generally lower taxes, weaker labor unions, less stringent environmental regulations, and greater business

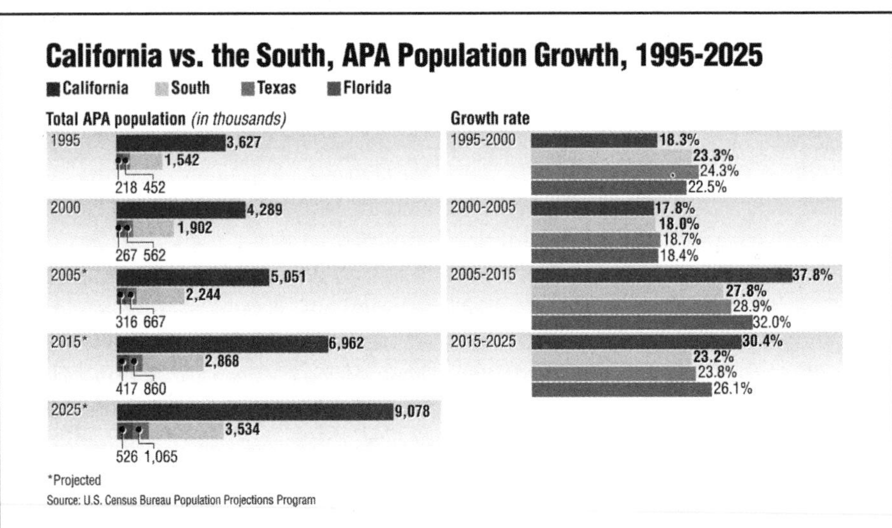

than $100,000 in 1999, while 16.8 percent were below $20,000. The latter was the lowest percentage for NHPIs by any region.

Per capita

In no state or region in the country did Asians actually have a higher per capita income than non-Hispanic whites. Overall, non-Hispanic whites in the South had a per capita income 12 percent higher than Asians ($23,682 versus $21,159). NHPIs had a per capita income in the South of $15,546—higher than all other non-white groups except Asians.

Asians had their highest per capita income of $28,607 in West Virginia, which is around $8,000 higher than the state average. NHPIs had their highest per capita incomes in South Carolina and Virginia—topping the state average and nearly equaling non-Hispanic whites in South Carolina.

Poverty

Despite the generally lower income figures, poverty rates for Asians and NHPIs in the South were not higher than in other regions. The Asian poverty rate was just 11.5 percent, the lowest among the four regions, while NHPIs registered a poverty rate of 16.2 percent, the second-lowest by region. Washington D.C. had the highest poverty rates for both Asians and NHPIs—22.8 percent and 37.8 percent, respectively—which is not surprising considering that the city had the highest poverty rate in the country (about one in five). However, within Washington D.C., NHPIs were the most-impoverished racial group.

Educational attainment

In the general population, the South had the lowest percentage of people with college educations. That was not true for Asians—46.6 percent had bachelor's degrees, versus 39.2 percent of Asians in the West. More than six in ten Asians in Delaware and West Virginia had bachelor's degrees. In states with large Asian populations like Texas and Virginia, the percentage was nearly half.

Almost 17 percent of NHPIs had bachelor's degrees, which like Asians, was also higher than those in the West (12.4 percent). The highest rate of obtaining bachelor's degrees among NHPIs was in Washington D.C., where 48.7 percent had such a degree, followed by Virginia, where nearly three in ten had a degree.

Language

Only 1.4 percent of Southern households speak an Asian or Pacific Islander language, about half the national rate (2.6 percent). Those that do speak an APA language are the least likely to be linguistically isolated (26.8 percent, lower than the national average of 29.2 percent). The largest number of APA language speaking-households was in Texas (more than 150,000, indicating a large recent immigrant population), but the highest percentage was in Maryland, at 2.8 percent. Linguistic isolation was near the national average for APA language speakers in states like Texas, Georgia, Oklahoma, Louisiana, and Washington D.C.

—Eric Lai

incentives for the relocation of major businesses to the area. Inhabitable land is widely available in the South, where energy and land prices are frequently lower than elsewhere in the nation. And as the American population continues to grow older, the mild winters of the South will remain an attraction. With the large overall population size of the South, its opportunities for employment in the various service industries will continue to expand.

While about two-thirds of the growth of Asian Pacific Americans in the West during the 1990s was in California, the growth rate for this state will probably be slowing down. The total population of California is now 34 million, home to 12 percent of the entire American population. As a result of its large population size, however, California has experienced a number of infrastructure problems. There have been major energy shortages in the last couple of years. In urban areas, land prices are exorbitant, while the smog and traffic congestion are among the worst in the nation. Younger APAs and those who are the newest immigrants may find permanent residence in California somewhat difficult if they do not already own a home there. Based on these factors, we predict that population growth will be much greater outside of California.

Newly arriving immigrants from Asia often initially settle in places where they have pre-existing social connections such as friends or family. As more APAs become located outside of the West, then Asian immigration to those places is likely to increase. Furthermore, the continued—if not increased—emphasis on educational credentials as the basis for immigration to the United States is likely to increase the geographic dispersion of APAs because, as was noted above, higher-skilled labor markets tend to have broader geographic boundaries. Although nine out of ten APAs resided in the West in 1940, we predict that a century later, the corresponding figure will be about three out of ten, and that more APAs will reside in the South than in California.

—Arthur Sakamoto and Thao Ha

For research support, we thank the Population Research Center of the University of Texas.

SECTION IV

CULTURE & SOCIETY

Taking the Spotlight

Asian Cinema: Now at a Theater near You

In December 2000, the Chinese-language martial arts film *Crouching Tiger, Hidden Dragon*, capped a decade of increasing influence by Asian film on American culture. The movie, by Taiwanese-born director Ang Lee, achieved massive critical and commercial success, gaining an Oscar nomination for Best Picture, and eventually becoming the highest-grossing foreign-language film in American history (it earned $127 million in the U.S. alone*). The film was just one instance of an American enthusiasm for Asian cinema that percolated throughout the 1990s; more obviously illustrating the impact of Asian filmmaking in Hollywood, and surpassing even *Crouching Tiger*'s success, was the sci-fi action flick *The Matrix* (1999), whose eye-popping blend of martial arts with special effects garnered $171 million, and was temporarily America's highest-grossing film of all time.

Such pop culture success, and the universal audience that it denotes, was a significant change from the previous decade, when Asian films usually were either indie movies or prestige productions, the categories in which foreign films typically reach American audiences. China's "Fifth Generation" filmmakers (named for their class at the Beijing Film Academy) are characteristic imports, whose sumptuous historical pieces, such as *Raise the Red Lantern* (Zhang Yimou, 1991) and *Farewell My Concubine* (Chen Kaige, 1993), were highly praised. Yet the films—and many other Asian releases of the same time, such as the Vietnamese-language film *Scent of Green Papaya* (Tran Anh Hung, 1993)—also were criticized by intellectuals for perpetuating Orientalist and stereotypical images of Asian culture. Thus, although these Asian movies were gaining attention, they did so only by emphasizing the differences between Asia and America. What they certainly were not doing was provoking Americans to explore Asian culture—as had occurred in the late 1970's, when Hong Kong "chopsocky" movies spawned countless American fans of kung fu master Bruce Lee.

Photo: Tai Seng Entertainment

Hong Kong has been recognized in past decades for its action cinema, piquing interest among today's American audiences to explore other genres of Hong Kong film and Asian cinema.

Hollywood, Bollywood, and other Asian crossovers

By the mid-1990s, however, the consolidation of the global economy, and particularly political events in Asia that the United States followed closely, focused more attention on Asian movies. Hong Kong cinema, long one of the world's most vibrant domestic industries, and an industry devastated by the territory's 1997 reunification with China, is a chief example. During this period the desire of numerous Hong Kong film talent to emigrate coincided with Hollywood's relentless search for new ideas. Jackie Chan, the martial artist known for his astonishing stunts; John Woo, Hong Kong's most famed action director; and Chow Yun-fat, Woo's favorite actor (and later star of *Crouching Tiger*), are the best-known gains of this brain drain, but Hollywood also benefited from the two-man empire of Yuen Woo-Ping, the veteran martial arts choreographer of *The Matrix* and *Crouching Tiger*, and his brother Yuen Cheung-yan, choreographer of the girl-power blockbuster *Charlie's Angels* (2000, $125 million). Asian cinema thus became a dominant presence in American popular culture when Hong Kong expertise in action cinema began contributing to Hollywood's single-most profitable genre.

Japan and India, two other Asian countries with prolific domestic film industries, occupy interestingly different positions in this history. "Bollywood" movies, the primarily Hindi-language films from Bombay, had little trouble transitioning from immigrant subculture to pop culture phenomenon: the musical romance, the distinctive film genre of India and Pakistan, had a campy appeal that made Bollywood-style movies briefly popular in urban U.S. nightclubs, and eventually inspired Twentieth-Century Fox's Oscar-nominated *Moulin Rouge* (2001), a musical homage to Bollywood that transformed pop culture back into high art.

By contrast, Japan, perhaps the one Asian cinema to have enjoyed long-standing Western interest and which, given the 1989 acquisition of Columbia Pictures by the Sony Corporation, was well-positioned to profit off of the contemporary taste, seemed to be the era's only loser. With the modest exception of Masayuki Suo's *Shall We Dance?* (1996, $10 million), a Japanese ballroom dance comedy, the 1990s saw no significant crossover hit. Even the American version of the hit anime (a Japanese genre of animated movie adapted from a comic book), *Princess Mononoke* (Hayao Miyazaki, 1997, $3 million), lost money, despite its re-dubbing with an all-star cast of American voices.

Asian directors on the rise

American consumption of Asian filmmaking thus reached unprecedented proportions in the late 1990s, because of Hollywood projects that incorporated ideas or talent drawn from the Asian film industry. While the rash of John Woo blockbusters (*Hard Target*, 1993, $32 million; *Face/Off*, 1997, $112 million; *Mission: Impossible 2*, 2000, $215 million) are the best known collaborations, Ang Lee is also a major player. Before *Crouching Tiger*, it was the success of Lee's two early Taiwanese films—particularly 1993's *The Wedding Banquet*, which had the highest-percentage profit margin of any American release that year—that recommended Lee to Hollywood studios, where he would make A-list films *Sense and Sensibility* (1995), *The Ice Storm* (1997), and *Ride with the Devil* (1999).

One particularly interesting strain of Asian-American partnerships has been the collaborations between Hong Kong and African American talent, as seen in Kirk Wong's *Big Hit* (1998), starring several young African American actors, and *The Replacement Killers* (1998), in which African American director Antoine Fuqua directed Chow Yun-fat. Director Quentin Tarantino, former cult movie fan turned big-time producer, has significantly supported this developments by distributing recent Asian features under his distribution label, Rolling Thunder.

All these movies, however, whether from Asia or made in Hollywood with Asian influences, differ from films about Asia made by Western directors (e.g., *Rising Sun*, 1993), or films by Asian Americans about Asian America (e.g., Wayne Wang, *The Joy Luck Club*, 1993). However, if tracked, those films arguably parallel the changing U.S. taste, from looking at Asia as a strange and distant culture, to one with which Americans of all colors identify. While recent American movies set in Asia such as *Red Corner* (1997) have done dismally at the box office, *The Joy Luck Club* earned a respectable $33 million. And while this American willingness to see Asian people on screen might in part be justified by the growing cultural diversity of the United States, it can't account for all of it. After all, Hollywood hardly is a champion of positive racial representations.

The answer may be that in the 1990s, when the world was poised for what was being hailed as "the Pacific Century," Asian movies were a cultural fashion. Where will this new relationship lead? Currently, Korean films, long obscured from international attention due to rigid censorship and production codes, seem to be the hottest new thing from the East.

—Karen Fang

all box office earnings cited are for U.S. earnings only.

Reality Shift?: America's Changing Perception of the Asian American Experience

All forms of mass media serve to condition and perhaps even create our perceptions of reality. Asian Pacific Americans have long struggled to change the stereotypes present in the mainstream consciousness of America. But with the mass media slow to change during the 1990s, so were the stereotypes.

In the early 1990s, APAs on television and in Hollywood films were, for the most part, nonexistent. According to the Screen Actors Guild, only 1.3 percent of all available roles in 1992 were cast with Asian faces. The prevailing belief in Hollywood was that APAs were all foreigners. Middle America was still associating APAs only with images of fresh-off-the-boat immigrants, gangsters and kung fu experts, and weird foreign exchange students like the infamous Long Duk Dong character in the John Hughes film *Sixteen Candles*.

Stereotypes like these served to create an identity crisis for APAs born in the United States. They were left without readily identifiable images with which to associate their experiences. Many APAs had to be asking the question: "Who am I? We're not foreigners, but we're not easily recognized as being 'Americans.'"

Early 1990s: everybody was kung-ku fighting

As always, in the 1990s the mainstream American media and Hollywood had no interest in showing the real APA experience. Instead, they were still capitalizing on the legend of Bruce Lee and America's fascination with Asian martial arts.

Hollywood cashed in by releasing a wave of martial arts films during the 1980s and 1990s, including teen audience fare like *The Karate Kid* and *Teenage Mutant Ninja Turtles*. The two films and their sequels scored at the box office with over $500 million in domestic gross revenue, but reinforced the same old "chopsocky," kung fu images associated with Asians in American pop culture.

In 1993, Hollywood resurrected the legend of Bruce Lee with *Dragon: The Bruce Lee Story*, a biopic of his early life starring Jason Scott Lee (no relation), while Amy Tan's novel *The Joy Luck Club* hit the big screen with Wayne Wang directing an all-female Asian American cast.

The Joy Luck Club was a huge crossover commercial success, earning over $30 million at the U.S. box office and opening the doors for Asian American actresses in Hollywood, but criticism surrounded the film's portrayal of its Asian American male characters. That same year, Korean American comic/actress Margaret Cho's landmark prime time TV sitcom *All-American Girl* hit the airwaves and flopped after one season.

Although the visibility of APAs in mainstream television shows and Hollywood films increased during the early 90s, Asian American independent filmmakers were the first to break into the limelight, with Steven Okazaki winning an Academy Award in 1991 for his short documentary, *Days of Waiting*.

More acclaim came for Asian American independent filmmakers, with Frieda Lee Mock winning an Academy Award for her documentary *Maya Lin: A Strong Clear Vision* and Jessica Yu winning for *Breathing Lessons: The Life of Mark O'Brien*.

During this same period, gay filmmakers like Gregg Araki (*The Living End*, *Totally Fucked Up* and *The Doom Generation*) and Arthur Dong (*Coming Out Under Fire* and *Licensed to Kill*) pushed into new territory with their seminal works.

Photo: Trailing Johnson Productions

First coming onto the film scene with his 1997 *Shopping for Fangs*, Justin Lin's *Better Luck Tomorrow* created a buzz when it debuted at the 2002 Sundance Film Festival.

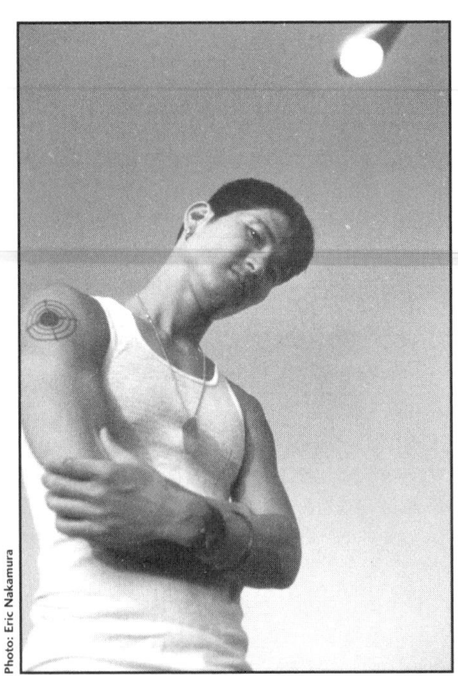

Gregg Araki pushed the limits of indie filmmaking with such provocative works as *The Doom Generation* and *Totally Fucked Up*.

Mid 1990s: indie films break on through

As the mid-1990s approached, APAs were collectively struggling on the margins of Hollywood even as Asian imports like John Woo and Jackie Chan were beginning to prove their crossover box office appeal. Through community-based organizations like the National Asian American Telecommunications Association (NAATA) and Visual Communications (VC), a number of independent feature films found success, including Kayo Hatta's *Picture Bride*, which won the Sundance Film Festival's audience award in 1995. Unable to crack through the Hollywood maze, Asian American independent filmmakers turned more towards community organizations like the NAATA.

Overlooked during this period was the arrival of Filipino American filmmaker David Maquiling with *Too Much Sleep*, a film that raised controversy in the Asian American film community for not featuring any Asian American characters. Thanks to good word of mouth and press reviews *Too Much Sleep* later found a crossover art-house film audience and become the first nationally distributed film by a Filipino American.

As the decade came to a close, Asian American independent film gained momentum, with Tony and Timothy Bui's *Three Seasons* (Sundance Grand Jury Prize in 1999), Karyn Kusama's *Girlfight* (Sundance Grand Jury Prize in 2000), and Emiko Omori's documentary *Rabbit in the Moon* (Sundance Audience Award in 1999 and Emmy Award in 2000).

Hollywood: Where's our story?

But in Hollywood, the real APA experience remained invisible to mainstream audiences. Filmmakers such as part-Japanese Dean Devlin (*Stargate*, *Independence Day* and *Godzilla*), Hong Kong native James Wong (*Final Des-tination* and *The One*) and Asian In-dian American M. Night Shyamalan (*The Sixth Sense*, *Unbreakable* and *Signs*) created some of the decade's biggest Hollywood blockbusters, but weren't easily recognizable as APAs.

Their success as mainstream filmmakers (nearly one billion dollars in combined domestic gross box office revenue) proved that opportunities exist for talented APAs in Hollywood, but as filmmakers they did little to change the stereotypes or increase the visibility of APAs on the screen. According to the Screen Actors Guild, about 2.6 percent of all roles cast in television and film went to Asians and Pacific Islanders in 2000—a doubling from 1992's 1.3 percent figure, but most of those roles remained relatively minor.

On the independent filmmaking front, burgeoning talents like Rod Pulido (his film *The Flip Side* was the first Filipino American film to screen at Sundance), Gene Cajayon (*The Debut*) and Chinese American Bertha Bay-Sa Pan (*Face*) all went the self-distribution route to find an audience for their unique works.

Pan's film attracted a lot of attention from African American audiences: its story, surrounds a Chinese American girl dating an African American DJ against the wishes of her family. The casting of an African American rapper in the film and mixing of Asian Americans with urban hip-hop culture tapped into the popular trend of Hollywood films like Jet Li's *Romeo Must Die* and Jackie Chan's *Rush Hour* movies.

Director Justin Lin pushed the boundaries of Asian American film even further with *Better Luck Tomorrow*, a dark tale of frustrated suburban teens finding an outlet through sex, drugs and violence. The controversial film stirred up debate at the 2002 Sundance Film Festival for its lack of "positive" Asian American characters, prompting film critic Roger Ebert to jump up on a chair to defend the film during a post-screening Q&A sessions with the film's cast and crew.

With its all-Asian American cast, Lin's visionary tale could be the breakthrough film for APA filmmakers. It may herald the total assimilation of APAs into the mainstream American consciousness, helping to accomplish a reality shift in which multiculturalism, mixed-races and alternative lifestyles become the "norm" in Hollywood and the mass media.

—*Ed Moy*

Breaking the Silence: The New Asian Voice in American Music

The 21st century finds the first and second-generation children of Asian immigrants establishing a new identity for themselves in American music. A decade ago, it would have been almost impossible to find any Asian American voices in the music industry. Pop music essentially came from either black or white artists. This void became an increasingly pressing issue, as music is arguably one of the most influential and important interests of many young people.

Making their mark in hip-hop

Today, the Asian Pacific American music scene is still developing and evolving, and a new generation is witnessing history in the making. A growing number of emerging new artists are receiving attention, not just from the Asian community but from an international audience. One of the best examples is in hip-hop. Groups such as the predominantly Filipino DJ crew, the Invisible Scratch Piklz, have gained world-wide recognition as the pioneering masters of "turntablism" (the method of scratching, beat juggling and performing other tricks, using vinyl records and turntables). The Bay Area group helped to bring attention back to the DJ and to legitimize the turntable as an instrument for making, not just playing, music.

It is no exaggeration to say that the Piklz took music to another level, gaining a legendary reputation after winning the DMC (Disco Mixing Club) turntable battles in 1992 and 1993. The event's organizers eventually asked them to retire because they were "too intimidating to competitors." Although no longer officially together, the former members of the Invisible Scratch Piklz (Q-Bert, Apollo, Shortkut, Mix Master Mike, Yoga Frog and D-Styles) continue to redefine and push the boundaries of hip-hop music, working on numerous projects and making varied public appearances.

The growing popularity of DJ culture and turntablism was reflected in the 2002 documentary, *Scratch,* which won rave reviews and awards. The culturally diverse mix of artists featured in the film, which included many APAs, served as a strong reminder of the many talented APA artists who have contributed to the scene.

The roster of APAs in hip-hop currently contains many successful and respected artists who are inspiring newer generations. In *Scratch,* Los Angeles DJ Babu of the prolific Beat Junkies reminisces on growing up as a Filipino kid in America and describes how he had no heroes of his color to look up to in the media. But then he goes on to say that he did have Q-Bert!

The fact that APAs have now become a major force in turntablism and DJ culture—while African Americans seem to now be concentrating on MC-ing or hip-hop vocals—is not necessarily an unusual phenomenon, nor is it an issue to this community of artists. Rather, it is a sign that the hip-hop community is acknowledging talent and skill over ethnicity and cultural background.

What is APA music?

As the roles of Asians in music continue to grow, some questions will frequently arise: What exactly is APA music? Is there a definitive genre of music that is considered APA or are we borrowing from other cultures, for example hip-hop's distinctly African American roots?

Attempting to answer these questions about APA music requires an understanding of the Asian community itself. Asian Pacific Americans' involvement and roles in America's music industry are as complex and diverse as the APA community itself, comprised of many different cultures and languages. For a long period of time, mainstream perception of "Asianness" was based largely on what was coming out of China and Japan. Other Asian Pacific cultures such as Indonesian, Thai, Laotian, Cambodian, or Filipino were relatively unknown.

Hip-hop and R&B are widely considered to be "black music," and rock is thought of as mainly "white music." But outside of that, there is no easily identifiable "yellow music." There is still no real niche for Asian musicians and that is a big barrier to APA recognition in an industry that tends to label and categorize artists. A prime example of this is with Chinese American singer CoCo Lee. Her debut International/English album, *Just No Other Way,* sold more than a million copies worldwide. Her love ballad, "A Love Before Time" from *Crouching Tiger, Hidden Dragon* was nominated twice for a Grammy Award. CoCo is the first Asian singer to actually break into the pop music mainstream. But even with her label, Sony, promoting her on television entertainment shows, she still did not receive the attention that was expected. In

Photo: Dylan Maddux

Bay Area-based producer Dan "The Automator" Nakamura is the producer behind such popular groups as Primal Scream and the Gorillaz.

Greater China and Taiwan, CoCo is a superstar who has dominated the airwaves for over six years and released more than a dozen albums sung in Mandarin. Some critics may argue that the singer's lack of success is due to a cookie-cutter pop persona and lyrics. But even if she isn't particularly groundbreaking or cutting edge, neither are the majority of current American pop icons, such as Britney Spears.

Finding one's identity

The struggle for APA artists is a complex issue in itself. In addition to trying to establish themselves in an industry that is still uncomfortable or unfamiliar with their presence, they must also deal with criticism and lack of support from their own community. DJ Kuttin Kandi, a pioneering female turntablist and member of DJ battle crew The 5th Platoon, speaks of her own struggle as an APA artist: "The Filipino media should have been there from day one. They only began to care when I became vocal, an activist. I was slapped with the label "hip-hop," and the older generation automatically assumed that I represented something negative...I used to be so sad that while hip-hop accepted me, my own community didn't have my back. It hurt until I realized that all that mattered was that at least my mother and sister encouraged me. I'm proud of my race and culture, and I learned (the hard way) that as long as I support my community, it doesn't have to be vice versa."

Undiscouraged by the lack of community support or mainstream recognition, many young artists are taking initiative and releasing their own music through the independent music circuit, supported by a network of people who share the same ideals. In addition to hip-hop and R&B, Asian kids have adopted punk and indie rock into their own musical tastes. The attraction of minority groups to hip-hop is easy to comprehend, as it angrily vocalizes and reflects many of the issues and problems that minority communities face. It has translated itself into a subculture outside of the music world, gaining cross-cultural and global appeal. And the stereotype of punk and indie rock, being an equally angry form of white suburban music, no longer applies, as punk music's do-it-yourself ethic and sound speak to a lot of marginalized groups, including APAs.

Entering into the independent circuit

The number of APA artists in punk and other forms of rock is growing. With a few exceptions like James Iha, guitarist for the former alternative rock band The Smashing Pumpkins, or rap-metal band Linkin Park, which includes a Korean and a Japanese American in its lineup, most artists still remain very much in the underground circuit.

"It's white middle class kids that are going to buy punk rock. So they're not going to sign an Asian fronted band. More than likely that's not going to happen. That's why I say, in hop-hop a lot of the buyers are Asian. So it doesn't hurt to maybe take that chance. Maybe they will sign an [Asian] hip-hop artist. Whether it would be within a group or a solo artist. I could see someone in hip-hop breaking in, but in terms of other music I still have a lot of doubt," explains Mike Park, founding member of the Asian punk band, The Chinkees.

The Chinkees have released a number of albums of their own distinct brand of political, ska-based punk rock. They chose their name as a direct acknowledgement of the reality of racism. The band members themselves admit that the name sometimes makes them feel uncomfortable, but it reflects a relevant point they are trying to illustrate. Along with being a pioneering all-Asian American band, members Mike Park and Miya Osaki also run independent record label Asian Man Records, which distributes 40 other bands.

More outlets for exposure

Audiences now have more opportunities to see APAs in contemporary music where they were never seen before. Music festivals like San Francisco's Pinoise Pop Festival, started in 1998 by Ogie and Jesse Gonzales, members of a hardcore/thrash band from the Philippines called V.O.D. (Valley Of Death), is now held annually and showcases bands from various cultural backgrounds, playing everything from pop and punk to hardcore and thrash metal. It has received a lot of support from both Asians and non-Asians over the years and continues to be a highly anticipated event.

The current state of contemporary music itself is becoming increasingly complex, as hip-hop, punk, and electronica are becoming increasingly global. Countries like Japan and China are now becoming fertile breeding grounds for some of today's most innovative music. Nowadays the more discerning musical ears in America are in tune with Japan's emerging musical talents like the legendary DJ Krush, a Tokyo native who collaborates regularly with heavy hitters in American hip-hop. The genre-defying Japanese female duo of Cibo Matto, Yuka Honda and Miho Hatori, has become a vital part of New York City's underground music scene. They have collaborated with artists like Sean Lennon and the Beastie Boys while continuing to release their own music and working on solo projects.

And as the Asian Pacific American community continues to define its role in American music, they are also attempting to do so on their own terms with success. Music from the South Asian community known as the "Asian Underground," is beginning to gain momentum in U.S. metropolises like New York, Los Angeles, and San Francisco. This fairly new style of music incorporates traditional parts of Indian music with the beats of drum and bass, house, dub and other

electronic musical genres. The "Asian Underground" was originally made popular by artists of Indian or Pakistani descent, such as Talvin Singh and the Asian Dub Foundation, and continues to gain an increasing audience in the urban music scene.

Breaking new ground
As the voices from the APA community continue to crack through the armor of mainstream media, it is becoming easier to imagine the possibilities of the future. And while it still has long way to go, this generation's struggle to define a new voice has made undeniable progress. Pioneers like The Invisible Scratch Picklz and popular producers like Dan the Automator (Dr. Octagon, the Gorillaz) are bringing attention to APAs.

The possibility of mainstream recognition can now be seen with such signs of success from the Neptunes' Chad Hugo, a Filipino American who is one half of a two-man music production team, producing some of the biggest names in pop music, from rapper Jay-Z to boy band N'Sync.

The Asian and APA communities now have more of a voice in music culture than ever before. As the Latin community experienced a "Latin Explosion," perhaps there will finally be an "Asian Explosion." But more than likely, the changes will not occur in such a drastic manner. It still seems doubtful that this will be a phenomenon that the rest of America can easily embrace anytime soon.

But just as the Latin minority continues to establish a place for themselves in a country that is usually seen in only black and white, so too will the Asian minority. There is currently no one type of "yellow music," just as there as there is no one type of Asian people. Their talents and interests are applied to many diverse musical directions. But there is an undeniable Asian influence and contribution to today's music. APAs are becoming key players in a musical landscape that is now global and is bridging gaps between different cultures. With each accomplishment, a new definition is formed of what it really means to be an APA.

—Santi Suthinithet

Photo: Santi Suthinithet

Ska-based punk rock band The Chinkees have paved their own way on the independent music circuit, running their own independent record label, Asian Man Records.

Sports: An APA Field of Dreams

In the year 2002, the forecast for Asian Pacific Americans in the world of sports couldn't be more appealing. Never before have APAs carved their names on so many of sports' most hallowed awards or instigated so much media frenzy over their future prospects.

Just a decade ago, APAs were nearly absent and unnoticed in mainstream American sports. Pioneers such as Masanori Murakami (who pitched for the San Francisco Giants in the mid-1960s) and Paul Kariya (one of the first APAs to strap on skates in the NHL) paved a path toward future success of APAs. But only recently have APAs held a prominent place in the sports world.

Thank Tiger Woods, Michelle Kwan, Apolo Anton Ohno, Ichiro Suzuki, a trio of Chinese basketball sensations, and a host of other APA rising stars. These APA athletes have captured America's attention, elevating APA representation in sports to new heights. No longer are APAs thought of as supporting or role players. It is time for APAs to get star treatment.

Photo: Eric Lai

Short in stature but big in heart, tennis star Michael Chang reached number two status in the world during the 1990s and blazed a trail for other professional APA athletes.

Baseball's new all-American

Ichiro Suzuki, known among fans as the "Wizard," signed with the Seattle Mariners prior to the 2001 season after winning seven consecutive batting titles and Gold Glove awards for the Orix Blue Wave in the Japan League. Suzuki, though, was bombarded with questions regarding his ability to adjust to American pitching and style of play. Before Suzuki signed with the Mariners, Japanese baseball was considered by many to be no better than Double-A minor league baseball in America.

Less than two months into the 2001 season, Suzuki was answering different types of questions: "Do you think you can break Joe DiMaggio's 56-game hitting streak? Do you think you can make it eight straight batting titles?" All hinted at his greatness.

When the 2001 season ended, Suzuki posted up numbers that were considered by many to be the greatest rookie season ever. He hit .350 to win the American League batting title, won a Gold Glove for his play in right field, led the league in stolen bases and won the American League Rookie of the Year and Most Valuable Player awards.

Suzuki was also the integral name at the top of the Mariners line-up. With his speed and scrappy hitting, Suzuki led the Mariners to 116 victories, which matched the major-league record set by the 1906 Chicago Cubs. Not only did Suzuki excel in individual honors, he showed that he could be part of a winning team.

With the arrival of Suzuki and Dodger pitcher Hideo Nomo (who started pitching for Los Angeles in the mid-

Sumo do, sumo don't

Photo: AP Wide World

Hawaiian-born Akebono was recruited into sumo at 18, becoming the most feared wrestler of the 1990s. He was forced to retire in January 2001 because of knee problems.

He is a 6'8", 515 pound mountain of a man who scaled the summit of Japan's most revered sport, sumo. In 1993, Chad Rowan—better known by his sumo name, Akebono—became the first foreigner to win the title of Yokozuna, or Grand Champion.

Rowan's ascent cemented the trail blazed by other American sumo wrestlers—virtually all Samoans from Hawai'i like Rowan—before him. Sumo wrestlers have long been one of Hawaii's biggest exports to Japan. Since 1964, more than thirty Hawaiians have become sumo wrestlers.

Konishiki was Akebono's compatriot in the Makunouchi division—the Sumo version of baseball's Major Leagues. At 6'1"and 650 pounds, Konishiki (whose real name is Salevaa Atisanoe) was, even by sumo standards, massive. Japanese fans nicknamed him "Meat Bomb."

Konishiki won three championships and finished runner-up eight times before retiring in 1997. While attaining the rank of Ozeki (Champion), Konishiki was never promoted to Yokozuna. His critics said he lacked *hinkaku* or dignity. Konishiki grumbled that it was racism.

The controversy that Konishiki's comments generated were rendered somewhat moot by Akebono's ascent to the top rank just one year later. A star basketball player before he was recruited into sumo at age 18, Akebono progressed quickly from clumsy stableboy to the most feared wrestler of the 1990s.

"[Sumo] made me grow up and work hard to be something," Akebono told a Hawaiian newspaper. "In sumo, the only thing you can do is get strong and win. If you don't get strong, you do the dishes and wash the clothes."

While the Japanese shunned Konishiki during his wrestling days, only to embrace him after his retirement in 1997, they immediately warmed to Akebono for his work ethic and humility.

"I never thought of myself as a star," said Akebono, who won eleven tournaments and retired as the seventh most successful sumo wrestler of all-time. "I've just been very fortunate. Somebody up above in the clouds was with me."

All the while, Akebono battled chronic knee problems and fellow Hawaiian sumos like Konishiki and Musashimaru, who followed Akebono and became the second Hawaiian elevated to Yokozuna. The three heavyweights made such an impact that they together won about a third of all sumo tournaments during the 1990s. But by the end of the decade, quota restrictions on foreigners, coupled with declining interest in the sport, had drastically shrunk the number of Hawaiians competing in sumo.

"It will be lonely," Musashimaru said. "There used to be plenty of boys from back home."

—Eric Lai

Photo: AP Wide World

All eyes were on speedskating newcomer Apolo Anton Ohno who won a gold medal for the 1500-meter event at the 2001 Winter Olympics.

1990s), other Japanese and Korean stars started moving to the West Coast. In 2002, the most notable of the new crop of APA players include Los Angeles Dodgers' pitcher Kazuhisa Ishii, San Francisco Giants' outfielder Tsuyoshi Shinjo and Arizona Diamondback closer Byung-Hyun Kim.

Golf's gobal appeal

No teams are necessary when Tiger Woods and Se Ri Pak are on the golf course. Woods, who is half-Asian (one quarter Thai and one-quarter Chinese, the latter coming from both his mom and dad's side), just may be the greatest golfer who has ever lived. Only 26 years old, Woods has already won eight Majors, tying him for fifth all time. Golf legend Jack Nicklaus had 18, a record that is well within reach for Woods.

Aside from his inimitable play, Woods has also become the poster boy of the golf world. One of the most recognizable athletes on the globe, Woods has single-handedly skyrocketed television ratings and revenue for the PGA. Woods has become an athlete many can bank on, but he has also increased APA roles in professional sports.

Pak, the sweet-swinging 24-year-old South Korean, has become LPGA's brightest newcomer in years. Pak is the youngest golfer ever to win four LPGA majors, surpassing the previous mark set by Mickey Wright, who was 25 when she won her fourth. Pak is also one of the most respected players on the course, and is celebrated as a national hero in South Korea.

With Pak and Woods leading professional golf into the 21st century, many Asians here in the United States and the Far East have been picking up golf clubs. A sport once only thought to be for upper-middle class whites, golf has become more global, enticing new APA athletes into the game. The proof is on the PGA and LPGA leader boards week after week.

Olympic achievements

Michelle Kwan and Apolo Anton Ohno were the talk of the 2002 Winter Olympic Games in Salt Lake City. Kwan, who had won four world titles, six national titles and an Olympic silver medal in 1998, was searching for a gold to complete her impressive resume. It didn't happen, but the Olympic world was still thankful for her performance, which earned her a bronze medal. Though Kwan did not get the gold, she could still be considered as one of America's great figure skaters.

Ohno, the short track speedskater sporting the "soul patch" on his chin, did not disappoint in his first Olympics. Just 19, Ohno first came on the scene at the 2001 World Cup, winning the 500 meter, 1,000 meter and the 1,500 meter events. Ohno did not disappoint in the Olympics, winning the gold medal in the 1,500 meters.

Hoop dreams

The landscape of the NBA is changing dramatically. Whether basketball fans or not, APAs have their eyes on Yao Ming, the 7'5" center of the Shanghai Sharks, who was the No. 1 overall pick in the 2002 NBA Draft. Ming's unique combination of size and coordination has made many NBA teams excited, but it was the Houston Rockets who grabbed him. Ming, the first high-profile Asian player in the NBA, might shoulder tough responsibilities (such as learning a new language and bearing the pride of a watchful native country of 1.2 billion people) but he has the skills and potential to be dominant in a couple seasons.

There are already two other Chinese citizens in the NBA: Mengke Bateer of the Denver Nuggets and Wang Zhizhi of the Dallas Mavericks. Both players had successful seasons for their respective teams, but it is Ming who has the physical tools to really put APAs on the basketball map. Zhizhi and Bateer too could eventually become mainstay players in the NBA.

—Ethen Lieser

Kung Fu, Tattoo, Mu Shu: Asian Culture on the Rise

Hybrid Pop Culture

In the past decade or so, magazines and newspapers across the United States have annually run an "Asian culture is the new big thing" article. As evidence, they cite Jackie Chan's Mountain Dew commercials, the latest Japanese toy frenzy at Toys "R" Us, celebrities with Zen fetishes, or Asian language characters tattooed on NBA stars' arms. It's true: the presence of Asian and Asian American popular culture is increasing in mainstream America. And the adoption of Hong Kong movie stars, importation of new cartoons and toys, thirst for new spiritual outlets, and general obsession over Oriental style are significant because they help Asians find bearing in America and improve the cultural gene pool. But that's not necessarily cultural enrichment; it's more like outsourcing.

More interesting than the cases in which mainstream America has tapped Asian culture are the ways that Asian and Asian American popular culture evolves. Consider the Asian pop culture mainstays of kung-fu movies, anime, and toys. These are some of the topics we cover with great seriousness at *Giant Robot* magazine, which I co-edit. Although they belong to pop culture—fine art's stepson, neither fully respected nor realized—they are part of culture nonetheless, and their evolution and importance too often goes unacknowledged.

The art of ass kicking

There were artistic kung-fu movies before Ang Lee's *Crouching Tiger, Hidden Dragon* (2000). King Hu's *A Touch of Zen* (1971) and Tsui Hark's *Once Upon a Time in China* (1991), for example, received ovations from fight fans and film festival judges alike. However, *Crouching Tiger* was the first subtitled martial arts film from Asia to cross over to reach mainstream American moviegoers.

Photo: Manga Entertainment

Anime movies, like the hit Japanese import *Ghost in the Shell*, have found increasing acceptance in American popular culture and influenced artists, within and outside APA community.

In taking a story from a martial-arts serial novel, casting Asian movie gods Chow Yun-Fat and Michelle Yeoh, and employing the legendary martial arts director Yuen Wo-Ping from Hong Kong, Lee wasn't simply plugging Hong Kong stars or directors into a Hollywood blockbuster format. Instead, the Taiwanese director applied his experience with epic period piece dramas and romances to give the martial arts movie production value,

Photo: Giant Robot

Giant Robot magazine has gained success in recent years, covering anything and everything that pertains to Asian popular culture.

character development, and heart. The characters leaped over rooftops and wielded their weapons with balletic grace, but the operatic pacing and emotional relationships were what kept the audiences involved in the story.

Where others saw a simplistic and violent genre, Lee recognized potential. Indeed, the way *Crouching Tiger* combined action, emotions, and style affected the way people saw martial arts movies. It gave the genre credibility, earning Academy Awards for Best Foreign Language Film, Best Cinematography, Best Art Direction, and Best Original Score, in addition to several other accolades. It was also the highest-grossing foreign-language film in America.

In the wake of *Crouching Tiger*, a few Hong Kong films have been released in the United States in hopes of getting a similar response. However, without the hybrid appeal, they have failed to capture a similar audience. In the meantime, Lee looks forward to filming a sequel. "There's part of me that feels unless you make a martial arts film, you are not a real filmmaker," Lee says. "It's pure cinema energy."

Rise of the Superflat

While American *otaku* (Japanese slang meaning obsessive fans or collectors) point to Pokémon on after-school television and *Akira* on the shelves of Blockbuster Video as signs of acceptance of anime in America, in Japan a new generation of artists is using its upbringing with anime as fuel for new art.

Yoshitomo Nara, Aya Takano, Chiho Aoshima, the Groovisions design group, and an artist simply known as "Mr." are part of Takashi Murakami's Superflat collection of artists. The 19 artists' traveling art show, program book/manifesto, and style reflect anime and otaku culture—the world of Japanese animation and technology addicts.

Murakami, who manages the Superflat artists, sculpts hypersexual characters dressed in space-age outfits and creates computer illustrations depicting flying mice, mushrooms with multiple eyeballs, and grinning flowers. Murakami explains that mass-produced popular culture was what inspired him to make his fine art, citing as specific inspiration the explosion scenes from the animated *Battle Cruiser Yamato* film, which he saw as a teenager (and which Americans know as the Star Blazers cartoon, shown on American television in the 1980s).

Yoshitomo Nara paints, sculpts, and sketches youngsters with dreamy looks and a dash of mischief (often evidenced by sharp weaponry). The mixture of danger and cuteness in his work gives it the most universal appeal of the Superflat artists, and it has appeared on American CD artwork for singers and bands such as Jim Black, The Busy Signals, and Shonen Knife. He clarifies where his style came from: "People say, 'You have a big influence from Japanese animation.' No. I have a big influence from my childhood."

The youthful appeal translates well to American art fans, many of whom aren't familiar with the anime touchstones used by the Superflat artists. When on the show's opening day in January 2001 at the new Museum of Contemporary Art in Los Angeles, curator Michael Darling expected 5,000 guests, but saw 8,000 arrive. The promotional banners featuring Chappies (colorful, paper-doll-like characters made by Groovisions) were subsequently used as premiums for new members of MoCA.

New king of figures

There is a lengthy history of Japanese toy collecting in America. Long before the launching of eBay, die-cast and vinyl junkies would swap videotapes and photo albums of their collections and make back-alley transactions with people who used pseudonyms. These expensive collectibles are still highly coveted, but their scarcity and price have kept them from spreading beyond the *otaku* subculture. In their stead, Hong Kong figure makers have quickly found a place in hip American boutiques.

In New York and Los Angeles, limited-edition figurines from Hong Kong depicting actors, rappers, skateboarders, and street characters are displayed under glass. Many of the customers have never heard the music by MC Yan or his Hong Kong rap group Lazy Muthafucka, but they'll spend $150 for his figurine by Michael Lau.

Lau's 12-inch figures are like G.I. Joe figures, but cooler, adorned with tattoos and piercings, and accessorized removable skateboard shoes, skateboards, snowboards, and basketballs. His "crazychildren" series of stylized young rappers, rockers, and skaters molded into vinyl, which was limited to 500, is being released for the second time with different paint jobs. Many are sold on eBay to Japan and the United States.

"Paintings are a lot more difficult to understand," explains the Hong Kong resident. "For the figures, they

Video game champ turned CEO

Tell your job counselor that "video game champion" is your career goal and he's liable to sputter and choke on his coffee. But for 24-year-old Dennis Fong, time spent in front of the computer polishing his skills at *Doom* and *Quake* has paid off handsomely so far.

The young Chinese American has parlayed his fast-twitch skills into world championship titles, hundreds of thousands of dollars in prize money, and his own Internet company.

It was in 1997, when the then-19-year-old Fong won a Ferrari sports car worth $100,000 at a video game tournament that his parents were persuaded by his choice of vocation. Shortly afterwards, Microsoft signed up Fong, better-known in the gaming world by his fearsome alias "Thresh," to sponsor their line of joysticks.

Photo: Jennie Sue

Dennis Fong, a.k.a. "Thresh" to the gaming community, turned his passion for playing video games into a lucrative professional endeavor.

Video games are big business, and Fong, the biggest star in this fledgling sport, is its Michael Jordan. One gaming industry group estimates that as many 145 million Americans, or 60 percent of the population, play video games. In 2001, sales of video games topped $6.35 billion. Hollywood, by contrast, earned $8.35 billion from box-office sales in the same period.

In part because so many video games come from Japan, APAs play a big role in this burgeoning industry, from video game developer to star player. According to Wes Nihei, longtime editor of a popular video game magazine, "if you're not Asian or Caucasian, you're virtually nonexistent."

As the sport's de facto evangelist, Fong leapt easily into the business side of gaming. In fact, these days, the UC Berkeley graduate spends less time playing games and more time running his Internet company, GX Media, which operates two of the biggest Web sites aimed at video game fanatics.

"Gaming is going to be the next big thing, and not only the next big thing—the thing," says Fong. "Eighty percent of teenagers play video games, and it's not just the nerdy kids, but it's also the sports superheroes of the world who play games as well."

—*AsianWeek*

understand. They look at them and their jaws drop. That's why I call my company 'crazysmiles.'"

The appeal of Michael Lau's figures has led to deals with American skateboard and skater clothing companies. In addition, a French company is developing an animated series that will feature his figures.

Another Hong Kong artist, Eric So, sees miniature figures as a way to combine his interests, which include fashion, design, painting and modeling figures. His work, including a series of Bruce Lee dolls and Hong Kong street characters (including gangsters, fish mongers, dim sum waiters, and propane deliverers) are currently being distributed to American comic book stores, expanding on the market once dominated by high-end boutiques.

Pop culture and beyond

Crouching Tiger, Superflat art, and crazychildren are important because they are not merely imported, translated, and sold. Ang Lee, Takashi Murakami, Michael Lau, and Eric So take the popular arts they grew up with (kung fu movies, anime, and toys), revisit them with hindsight, and add a layer of artistic interpretation. Such cultural re-interpretation inspires the imagination not only in Asia but also secures a place even in Middle America multiplexes, art museums, expensive boutiques, and beyond—where their merit is not necessarily validated, but is allowed to affect further cultural change.

—*Martin Wong*

Don't Touch that Dial: APAs in the Media

In the last decade, APA names and faces began to make waves in news radio, television and print media. Along with recognizable television reporters/anchors like Ann Curry, Connie Chung and Lisa Ling, other APAs across the nation are slowly achieving a visible presence in mainstream media, becoming a necessary reflection of America's growing APA population.

True, APAs are making significant contributions to journalism, as they are becoming integral players in the newsroom as reporters, editors, photographers, and managers.

But the reality is that APAs, along with other minorities, are still a small presence in many newsrooms in United States. So the question remains: Is the old-boy's network of traditionally white males in newsrooms fading in the 21st century?

According to a newsroom employment census conducted by the American Society of Newspaper Editors (ASNE), the number of minority journalists working at U.S. daily newspapers in 2002 was 12.07 percent (or 6,567 journalists).

ASNE's initial survey in 1978 revealed that minority journalists comprised 3.95 percent of the newsroom workforce (1,700 out of 43,000). In 2002 Asians Americans made up 2.36 percent (1,283), compared to African Americans at 5.29 percent and Hispanics at 3.86 percent. Sixteen percent (209) of Asian Americans were in supervisor positions.

Coverage depends on diversity

The issue of newsroom diversity goes hand in hand with how communities are represented in the media. For the APA community, media coverage of such events as the Wen Ho Lee case and the backlash against the South Asian community after Sept. 11th have served as shocking reminders of old-but-lingering stereotypes and have forced the mainstream news media to reexamine its responsibilities in reporting.

The ethnic news media has served an important role in telling these stories about the community, at times setting the standard for diverse reporting in community journalism. New California Media, an association of over 400 ethnic publications founded in 1996 by the non-profit Pacific News Service, has worked towards raising the visibility of ethnic publications which can tell the stories the mainstream may ignore.

"As a minority journalist, I recognize the importance of community-based media and the kinds of often unheard voices they can reflect," *The Examiner*'s Annie Nakao told *AsianWeek*.

The challenge of community journalism continues to be its integration into the mainstream news media. Minority media organizations that include the Asian American Journalists Association and the South Asian Journalists Association have gained momentum in recent years, providing support for minority journalists and responding to the lack of newsroom diversity.

Yet accurate APA media representation cannot be judged solely by the numbers in the newsroom, as veteran journalist Bill Wong points out: "The important thing is how our incredibly diverse and fascinating Asian American communities are covered. I have seen improvement there, too—more nuanced coverage, not just tired old stereotypes of minority or gang kids. There is still plenty of that, but there is now greater 'mainstreaming' of Asian Americans into American society."

APA media growth

Such mainstreaming of Asian Pacific Americans is reflected in the growth of

Photo: AsianWeek Archive

APA presence in the mainstream news media has slowly grown this past decade, yet the challenge continues to be accurate media representation of the APA community.

APA media organizations. According to CEO Bill Imada of Imada Wong Communications, a marketing firm specializing in Asian Pacific American communities, over the past decade "the Asian American print media has increased 300 percent, to over 600 print and broadcast in-language (non-English language) media organizations."

Various APA print publications have attempted to carve their own niches in American media this past decade, as several prominent APA publications like *aMagazine, AsianWeek, Filipinas, Giant Robot, KoreAm Journal* and *Yolk* each have set out to address the community's issues, news and culture in a different way.

The diversity among these various APA publications has resulted in both highs and lows in efforts to appeal to mainstream audiences. L.A.-based *Giant Robot*, which launched in 1994 as a xeroxed-zine and is now a full-

San Francisco's Fang Family: Preserving a Legacy, Ensuring Diversity

In 2000, the Fang family of San Francisco completed the purchase of the *San Francisco Examiner* from the Hearst Corporation, thereby not only preserving daily editorial competition in San Francisco, but also precipitating a nearly-unprecedented event: local Asian American ownership and operation of a daily newspaper in a major American city.

"Against the odds, the deal keeps San Francisco in the thin ranks of cities with two competing dailies," reported the *New York Times*.

A year before the sale, *The Examiner* seemed guaranteed to fold. Hearst had clinched a deal to purchase the morning *Chronicle* and made plans to merge the two newspapers if a buyer would not come forward. After months of intense public outcry and antitrust investigations, however, the merger was stalled. Numerous parties—including major newspaper chains such as Knight-Ridder and the Times Mirror Company—were rumored to have bid on *The Examiner*. But when the dust settled, the Fangs secured the deal, becoming the first Asian Americans to own a major daily San Francisco Bay Area newspaper, and the second to own a major daily newspaper nationwide.

The Examiner purchase signified the Fang family's continuing efforts to preserve the late patriarch John Fang's dream of building on a small publishing business he began in San Francisco's Chinatown when he immigrated to the United States from Shanghai during the 1950s.

Under the Fangs' ownership, *The Examiner's* focus reflects the changing needs of the San Francisco's growing APA population. "You'll see more of an involvement, integration, assimilation of Asian American issues as mainstream issues," said company president James Fang.

The acquisition of *The Examiner* also marked an ironic twist in American journalism history. For it was *The Examiner* which, in the middle of the 19th century, made its name by leading the nation's editorial charge against the presence of the Chinese in this country. Through its sensationalist journalism, *The Examiner* played a pivotal role in the passage of the Chinese Exclusion Act, which in essence stopped Chinese immigration to America. Many saw the Fang purchase as poetic justice.

For the diversity-minded media, the Fangs' purchase of *The Examiner* did not come as a shock. The Fangs have owned *AsianWeek* since 1979 and the *Independent* newspaper since 1987. In fact, they were surprised that others were surprised.

"Anybody who is familiar with the work effort of our family and organization should realize that *The Examiner* acquisition was a logical step for our family and community. I think the surprise comes from those who are uncomfortable with Asian Americans expanding into fields they are not traditionally associated with," said James Fang.

Since the purchase, the family has been forced to respond to criticism, sometimes from their publishing peers. With the sale of *The Examiner* by the Hearst Corporation, Hearst "committed some financial resources" to help the family get the paper going for the first few months. But the attacks are nothing new to the family, particularly to James Fang, who shrugs off the criticism.

The success of the negotiations also stemmed from what the Fangs believed was a shared philosophy that San Francisco should remain a two-newspaper town. Indeed, it was the urging of prominent city officials which sparked the Fangs' involvement and ultimate success.

"The time is clearly right for a paper that can serve as a window to Asia and a bourgeoning Asian American community," journalist and author Helen Zia told the alternative weekly newspaper, the *Bay Guardian*. "The Fangs have a real opportunity to open up new avenues of journalism."

—*AsianWeek*

color glossy, has gained a wider readership and gradual success with its pop culture focus.

Meanwhile, *aMagazine*, a lifestyle-oriented glossy that gained acceptance within the APA community during the mid-90s, folded in spring 2002 after financial troubles, leaving the APA community to ask itself exactly what kind of APA publication will succeed in the mainstream media industry?

The question remains and APAs are ready for the prospect of future publications that will reflect and encompass the diversity of the community. Meanwhile, community journalism will continue to have an impact, as more APAs enter prominent newsrooms across the nation. These steps toward diversifying the newsroom will hopefully affect the way news is reported, while the ethnic media continues to work towards finding its rightful place in the American media landscape.

—*Cindy Chew*

Design of the Decade

Asian design in America exists and thrives because it has found a balance between two very different cultures. What was once considered "foreign" is now part of our everyday lifestyle choices—from our "casual Friday" Hawaiian shirts to our flat-screen TVs to our Zen-inspired bamboo gardens. You can even buy tropical rattan furniture at mainstream department stores like Target. Just as U.S. popular culture has invaded Asia for decades, Asian aesthetics and popular culture is now even permeating the American heartland.

The 1990s saw fields like fashion and animation mining Japanese and Chinese popular culture for new influences. Many APA designers and artists were at the fore of introducing these trends. At the same time, many APAs, displaying minimal influence from Asia, are creating compelling new designs that appeal to a global audience. Landscape architect Maya Lin, fashion designer Anna Sui, and Star Wars art director Doug Chiang are some who exemplify that end of the spectrum. Still, what is now obvious is that being an APA designer today means one has the freedom to mine Asian cultural aesthetics without the burden of being expected to do so.

"To a certain extent, Asian influence is 'non-existent' in most design fields today. This is neither a good thing nor a bad thing. It simply means that in certain respects we are becoming a monoculture," says Dung Ngo, a writer and editor of design books as well as a lecturer at California College of Arts and Crafts. "We do not see our surroundings, whether in Beijing or New York, as the only way to define who we are."

A new global architecture

Asian aesthetics have long influenced American architecture, going back to early last century, when elements of traditional Japanese Zen design were adopted in Frank Lloyd Wright's environmental architecture, to modern, contemporary residences and buildings.

"Asia as a culture, which is informed by both a way of life as well as a certain aesthetic, has influenced Western/American culture and design through a special perspective or philosophy on life," says Ngo. "The search for calming spaces, for instance, has its roots in Zen gardens and meditation spaces in the East. The minimalist trend so prevalent in architecture and design in the last 10 years certainly came from this particular root."

One reason for architecture's early embrace is because the field has traditionally been at the forefront of internationalization. The upshot is that leading exponents can design and build projects whose influences are not necessarily tied their birthplace or heritage. This goes for Asian Pacific Americans, too. Take Shanghai-born, American-raised I.M. Pei. Known for realizing his abstract design ideas with modern-looking materials, Pei's resume spans the globe and includes notables like the Rock-and-Roll Hall of Fame and Museum in Cleveland, Ohio, the Pyramide du Louvre in Paris, and the Bank of China in Hong Kong. Ironically, Pei had to brush off criticism that his design for the Bank defied certain Chinese elements of feng shui. Today, the Bank remains one of the most recognizable, modern skyscrapers in Asia.

"The time has passed when an architect who grows up, say, in Seoul will only do projects in and inspired by Seoul," says Terence Riley, chief curator of architecture and design at the Museum of Modern Art in New York City. "Cultures have become aesthetically accessible; national barriers are porous."

At the age of 20, Ohio-born Maya Lin instantly catapulted herself into the

Photo: Corky Lee

Fashion designer Vivienne Tam draws Asian inspiration from her Hong Kong-born roots, but puts a fun twist on her modern clothing designs.

elite of the landscape architecture field with her bold design for the Vietnam Veterans Memorial in Washington D.C. in 1981. Lin, a student at Yale at the time, beat out over 1,400 other submissions—most from well-established professionals in the field—in a national competition. Her recognition did not come without controversy. Lin was forced to defend herself against political and cultural conservatives, who attacked her minimalist design and her Chinese American background.

"Isn't it ironic," one reporter asked her, "that the war in Vietnam was in Asia and you are of Asian descent?" Lin writes in her autobiography, *Boundaries*: "I thought the question was completely racist ... and completely irrelevant. I was as American as anyone else."

Today, the memorial's popularity, as well as Lin's other works—the Civil Rights Memorial at the Southern Poverty Law Center in Alabama, the Women's Table at Yale University, and the Langston Hughes Library in Tennessee—testify to her ability to transcend questions of cultural identity and geographical boundaries.

Shanghai-born I.M. Pei has gained international recognition for his innovative and controversial architecture, from the Louvre in Paris to the Bank of China in Hong Kong.

Made in Japan

In today's technology-driven society, the world looks to Japan for the latest innovations and inspiration in cutting-edge design for electronics products, gaming and animation. What began in 1979 with the invention of the Walkman cassette tape player by Japanese electronics giant Sony, has now become the generational icon for product design. With products that appeal to the gadget-lover in all of us, Sony has shaped global perceptions and continually tests the boundaries of product design with its newest CD players, digital video camcorders, TVs, and now, the Playstation 2 video game player, which threatens to usurp the home personal computer.

The gaming revolution of today can be traced back to 1960s Japan. Popular animated shows—called anime in Japan—from *Astro Boy* and *Transformers* to *DragonballZ* and *Pokémon*, depicting doe-eyed heroes and heroines, or transforming robots, in dramatic plot lines and futuristic settings, have moved from being a cult to having a mainstream intergenerational following. Today, this interest among both young and adult audiences can be seen in the popularity of American animated films like Walt Disney's *Mulan* and *The Power Puff Girls*. *Mulan* not only became a box-office success, bringing in $55 million in ticket-sales within its first two weeks, but it brought to mainstream audiences in Disney's first Asian-themed animated feature.

Elements of cartoons and anime are making their way into American video games and merchandise. The Pokémon craze hit American school children in the late 90s. A total of $1 billion was spent on Pokémon merchandise in 1999—an example of how these industries intersect.

The granddaddy of this cross-over movement is the Japanese company, Sanrio. Its Hello Kitty line of merchandise—which became hugely popular in America despite the obscurity of the actual cartoon—is sold at more than 120 Sanrio boutiques across the United States. Target, the American megastore, even caught onto this Sanrio cuteness a few years ago, carrying pretty pink Hello Kitty products.

Fashion forward

Sanrio's success has inspired American fashion designers. Paul Frank, a Los Angeles designer, created a clothing line featuring Julius the chimp, which like Sanrio gained popularity sans cartoon or animated movie. Not surprisingly, Sanrio is now teaming up with Paul Frank to create a combined Paul Frank/Hello Kitty line of clothing accessories.

Asian-inspired fashion, though, is not just fun and cartoons. Big name APA fashion designers are drawing in varying degrees upon their heritage. Hong Kong-raised Vivienne Tam is known for her kitschy use of Chinese cultural icons – imagine Mao with pigtails – and colorful patterns that are distinctly but postmodernly Chinese.

American-born Anna Sui, on the other hand, has followed her own fashion sense, incorporating her teen passion for rock-music culture into her current fashion ideas. And the man behind Nautica's all-American-looking designs is Taiwanese-born David Chu. Similarly, Vera Wang rose to prominence in the 1990s as the creator of wedding gowns for Hollywood stars. Like Ralph Lauren, another child of immigrants, Wang has been able to capture through her designs the dreams and aspirations of American women, as filtered through the most important day of their lives.

Design in the 21st century
It's easy to say that APA designers have followed one of two paths in their approach to design: returning to a nostalgic Asian past or looking towards an American future. But APAs and other Americans looking to the East for inspiration are no longer limited to nostalgic elements of "old Asia," but can draw upon technology-flavored elements of today's popular culture that is arguably—especially in Japan—setting trends ahead of the United States. As a result, there are many paths ahead for APA designers.

—Cindy Chew

Have You Eaten?

Fried rice and potstickers once defined what mainstream America believed to be typical Asian cuisine. Today, those iconic take-out boxes contain more complicated dining options that reflect the increasing cultural diversity of Asian immigrants in the United States.

Dim sum houses and sushi bars, both trendy eating options in the '80s and '90s, have become as commonplace as the local pizza place or diner. And more than ever, people are boldly seeking the next new Asian dining adventure, hoping to experience the world through food.

"People have always viewed Thailand as a very exotic place, so going to a Thai restaurant is like an adventure," says Yong Chen, History and Asian American Studies professor at UC Irvine, who is working on a book about ethnic food in the United States.

"The core of the American diet is shrinking, and what is expanding is what used to be considered the fringe of American cooking," Greg Drescher, an official at the Culinary Institute of America, told the *Los Angeles Times* in a 2002 article presciently headlined "Vietnamese pho everywhere you go."

And while the search for "authentic" Asian food continues, its evolution, as with all food in America, has proven to be inevitable. Just as Italian and Mexican foods have simultaneously taken upscale and downmarket paths in American food culture, Asian cuisine has taken two paths: "fusion" restaurants that self-consciously marry Asian and Western flavors and ingredients, and the fast food mall courts of suburban America. Both are valid examples of this country's "melting pot" trend of assimilating immigrants and their cultures. Tourists continue to flock to the traditional Chinatowns and Japantowns, yet modern-day Asian "towns" like Monterey Park in Los Angeles and Flushing, Queens, in New York City are forming around new and fast-growing Asian immigrant communities. It is here that you can find racks of steaming Shanghainese soup dumplings, fragrant Malaysian fish head soup, chewy Taiwanese hand-pulled noodles, or oversized bowls of Vietnamese beef pho. It is Asian food as authentic as one can get in the United States, food that clings to its Asian origins despite a movement towards an American lifestyle.

Blazing the trail: Chinese cuisine
The California Gold Rush in the mid-19th century lured Chinese immigrants, who while working on the Central Pacific Railroad also brought their cooking skills and food traditions along. Today, this legacy remains strong, as Chinese restaurants can be found in virtually every corner of the country. Out of 69,903 Asian-owned eating and drinking places in the United States, 54 percent were Chinese-owned, according to the 1997 U.S. Economic Census (see Table). Chinese food is available nearly anywhere and is the most widely accepted of all Asian cuisines. The familiarity of Chinese food has paved the way for a diversity of flavors today—Indian cumin, Vietnamese fresh basil, Thai lemongrass and Korean chili paste—spicing up dishes and opening up a whole new sense in tasting food.

Food, along with pleasing palates, is also big business today. APA-owned food and drink establishments had

sales of $15.8 billion in 1997. Japanese restaurants, not surprisingly, had the highest average 1997 receipts per restaurant—$423,205. Chinese food and drink establishments had average sales of $225,448 in 1997, while Vietnamese-owned locations had average sales of $138,037 each.

APAs also owned 35,796 food stores, generating $17.2 billion in sales, with a definite percentage stocking Asian groceries. But they are getting competition these days from the major supermarkets, where increased demand has caused chains to stock items like Japanese rice wine vinegar and Chinese hoisin sauce. Packaged Asian foods accounted for $650 million in sales at mainstream supermarkets in 2001, according to Information Resources, a Chicago-based food sales research firm. Even that all-American firm, Campbell Soup, is getting ethnic, marketing a refrigerated pho soup aimed at mainstream restaurants.

APA-owned Restaurants and Bars in the United States, 1997

(In billions of dollars)

*Because of low number, data withheld by Census to protect privacy of individual companies.
Source: 1997 U.S. Economic Census

The fast and the fusion

Asian food, for better or worse, has not escaped being influenced by American culture. Some Asian food has become synonymous with "fast food," as scores of take-out restaurants and even Asian chains—think Yoshinoya or Panda Express (which has 400 locations in mall food courts nationwide)—have replaced McDonald's as a quick meal option. More upscale chains like Benihana and PF Chang's have found a niche as dining options for suburban America. Pan-Asian soup-noodle joints like Zao Noodle Bar or Long Life Noodle House assimilate the best of Chinese won ton restaurants, Vietnamese pho joints, and others, into something that caters to the insatiable American demand for choice and convenience in a single location.

"The style and the taste of the restaurant's food are determined by its clientele and also by the perceptions that its customers have of Chinese food," says UC Irvine's Chen, referring to the emergence of these Chinese chain restaurants in very targeted areas of the nation.

Even once-forbiddingly expensive and esoteric food like sushi is not immune to being "Americanized" into a fast food option, which can now be bought at mainstream supermarkets and even warehouse-style megastores Costco. What was once a strict, traditional art in Japan has evolved into a style that caters to uniquely American tastes, incorporating non-Japanese ingredients like cream cheese and smoked salmon into sushi inventions like California, Philadelphia and 49er rolls.

"We didn't have enough material available in the United States so chefs got creative using avocado and crabmeat," wrote Takehiko Yasuda, president of the Northern California Japanese Restaurant Association, in a *San Francisco Chronicle* article.

In Hawai'i, the local favorite Spam has long been a popular sushi filling. Such combinations of East and West have been influencing chefs and appealing to diners for the past two decades. Make way for the fusion revolution…

Asian celebrity chefs

The recent Food Network phenomenon, which sparked a revived interest in food, has somewhat redeemed America's "fast food nation" reputation. The cable television network has also elevated chefs to celebrity status. One such star is Ming Tsai, who owns the Asia-meets-French-bistro restaurant, Blue Ginger, in Boston. On his FoodTV show, "East Meets West," Tsai shows viewers how to create such unusual flavor combinations in dishes like "Foie Gras and Morel Shu Mai" and his "Crab Lemongrass Tartlettes."

Before Ming, came Roy Yamaguchi. His Japanese heritage and Hawaiian

Photo: Photodisk

The rise in popularity of Asian fusion cooking has created a new outlet for restaurants to combine Asian ingredients with Western cooking techniques.

upbringing combined with his cooking experiences at some of the best French restaurants in the United States helped pioneer the Asian fusion trend in the 80s with a style he calls "Euro-Asian."

Trendy foodies know all about Nobu, an upscale Japanese restaurant opened in 1994 by Chef Nobu Matsuhisa and co-owned with actor Robert DeNiro. The restaurant, located in the stylish TriBeCa district of Manhattan, has gained recognition for its unconventional approach to traditional Japanese food—a style that draws from Nobu's experience as a classically trained chef in Tokyo and the years he spent as owner of a sushi bar in Peru.

Ruth Reichl praised Nobu in *The New York Times*: "He follows no rules, topping monkfish liver pate with caviar and floating it in a sweet mustard sauce, or making salad of delightfully herbal Egyptian leaves sprinkled with transparent flakes of dried bonito. He might surprise you by drizzling hot pepper sauce onto raw slices of Japanese sea bass and cilantro. These flavors are edgy, unexpected and often exciting."

Chef Masaharu Morimoto, a.k.a. the Iron Chef, was also a product of Nobu's unconventional training ground. Although he spent years working as a seasoned chef, it was not until the Food Network aired episodes of Japan's popular "Iron Chef" show—the campy cooking competition that pits chef against chef in a timed battle of cooking wizardry—did Chef Morimoto gain widespread fame. The show, which began in Japan in 1990, had spread to the United States by the late 1990s and now holds cult status with many Food Network viewers.

Effects of immigration

California is an obvious example of how food is affected on a local, global and economic level. In the Bay Area, for example, the Silicon Valley boom lured Asian Indian technology workers and their families in droves, causing the population to increase 170 percent during the 1990s. Asian Indian restaurants grew, too, so much that there are now nearly 100 Indian restaurants in the Silicon Valley, according to an online Yellow Pages of Indian businesses.

"In some ways, ethnic cuisine is often more in tune with what's happening with immigration patterns than any survey or study," says Hans Johnson, a demographer with the Public Policy Institute of California.

And in the urban sprawl that is Los Angeles' San Gabriel Valley—a stretch of suburbia that begins with the well-known Chinese suburb of Monterey Park on the west and stretches east all the way to newer suburbs like Walnut and Diamond Bar—is home to the largest concentration of Chinese in the United States. The constant influx of new immigrants, coupled with an established, middle-class Asian community, has breathed new life into Chinese cuisine. The diversity and quality of Chinese food offerings, from Taiwanese to Shanghainese to Szechuan to Cantonese styles, makes it a mecca for those seeking authentic Chinese food in America. Communities such as this have proven that there is no pressure to conform to American tastes.

Food forecast

At the Asian supermarket Ranch 99, shoppers stroll through aisles stocked with all kinds of Asian food products imaginable. With eight U.S. locations so far, mainly on the West Coast, Ranch 99 has set the example for the marketplace, and perhaps even the Pan-Asian food landscape, of the 21st century. There, Thai lemongrass, Vietnamese rice wrappers, Chinese soymilk and Filipino banana ketchup can be found together in harmony under one roof.

As some chefs continue to experiment with their fusion fantasies and Americanized Asian fast food maintains its devoted following, individualized authentic Asian cuisine and flavors will remain a strong part of food culture in America.

So what will be the next new Asian food adventure to hit America? While Vietnamese food is currently hitting a home run with Americans for its light, healthy flavors, cuisines like Korean, Malaysian and Singaporean remain on-deck. These cuisines share a spice factor that Americans are beginning to crave. With all this, the Asian food trend of today might become the Chinese food of yesterday. Yet even this prospect in America leaves optimistic room for Asian food to again reinvent and reintroduce itself in time.

—*Cindy Chew*

Haunted by the Myth of Universal Success

The diversity of the Asian Pacific American population coupled with constantly shifting immigration patterns and public policies ensures that any effort to document and describe their past, present, and future educational experiences will be somewhat if not totally inadequate. At the same time, there are several noteworthy issues that have preoccupied scholars and policy makers during the past decade, which will continue to have implications for virtually every APA either working in or making their way through the educational pipeline. This chapter will highlight some key educational challenges facing what is becoming an increasingly larger and more diverse APA population.

Unfortunately, what is largely driving some of the major challenges is a tired issue that still haunts APAs. The "model minority myth" is alive and well in education and continues to be fueled by simple-minded record keeping of academic achievement. When data are not separated out by individual ethnic groups, the educational achievement and circumstances for APAs almost always look better than they do for any other group, including whites.

For example, figures from the U.S. Department of Education show that in 1997 and 1998, APAs earned approximately six percent of the conferred bachelor's degrees, five percent of master's degrees, ten percent of professional degrees, and five percent of doctoral degrees. These figures are higher than the overall representation of APAs in the general population (between four and five percent). The 2000 Census reported that APAs were more likely than any other racial group to hold either a bachelor's, master's, professional or doctoral degree. According to these figures, approximately 44 percent of APAs had obtained at least a bachelor's degree, compared to 28.1 percent of whites, 16.6 percent of African Americans, and 10.7 percent of Latinos. The fact that this picture looks much different when APAs are disaggregated, however, is still falling on deaf ears. The inattention to the diverse and complex reality of APA academic achievement cannot be attributed to a lack of available information and research.

APAs are more likely than other racial groups to hold a bachelor's, master's, professional or doctoral degree, but the reality is that educational opportunities are distributed unevenly across different APA groups.

A 1997 report by Shirley Hune and Kenyon Chan for the American Council on Education again made clear that educational opportunities are still distributed unevenly across different APA ethnic groups. For example, they showed that Chinese, Japanese, Asian Indian, and Korean Americans are twice as likely as Hmong, Guamanian, Samoan, Hawaiian, and Laotian Americans to be enrolled in college. The college attendance rates of some of the latter groups are among the lowest of any group in the nation. This is just one example and there is certainly no shortage of evidence that counters the characterization of APA educational success. Despite this, the stereotype of APA students as over-achievers with little need for educational intervention, guidance, or support has maintained a strong grip on public perception.

The persistence of this myth continues to result in negative consequences for APAs, particularly the inaccessibility of services and other opportunities within the educational enterprise. Although most issues have implications on all levels of education, each plays out in a unique way with different degrees of significance within the systems. What they have in common is a direct or indirect linkage to the model minority myth.

APA College Enrollment, Aged 18-24, by Ethnicity, 1990

Ethnicity	Percentage
All U.S.	**34.4%**
All APA	**55.1%**
Chinese	66.5%
Japanese	63.5%
Asian Indian	61.9%
Korean	60.3%
Thai	53.1%
Vietnamese	49.3%
Filipino	47.1%
Cambodian	36.3%
Hmong	31.7%
Guamanian	30.6%
Samoan	29.7%
Hawaiian	28.9%
Laotian	26.3%

Source: *Glass Ceilings And Asian Americans* (2000: p.109, Altamira Press), from Hune and Chan 1997: p. 53, using data from 1990 U.S. Census.

Primary and secondary education

There are several key issues in primary and secondary education that should not escape attention. One has to do with calls for greater accountability in schools, which have generated more momentum for "high stakes testing." These standardized tests have "high stakes" because their results are broadly used to make critical decisions about student placement and graduation, as well as about staff promotion and school funding. Although APAs as a whole tend to perform comparably better than other groups, this is a woefully incomplete snapshot.

In a forthcoming study, scholars Pang, Kiang, and Pak argue that APA performance on high stakes tests is greatly misunderstood. According to them, the failure rate on the state exam for APA tenth graders in Massachusetts, which has implications for high school graduation, was 26 percent on the English portion and 40 percent on the math portion. These overall failure rates are alarmingly high, but are even higher in those schools that have larger concentrations of Cambodian and Vietnamese students. Pang, Kiang and Pak also reported that APA scores on another high stakes test, the SATs are much more varied than they are for other groups (e.g., whites, African Americans, Native Americans), suggesting that there are wide discrepancies in performance within the APA population.

These and other examples challenge claims that such tests are the best tools for assessing APA academic achievement and potential. The validity and reliability of these tests notwithstanding, ignoring the variations in test scores and over-generalizing all APAs as high achievers is highly problematic, but the problem is worsened by the nature of high-stakes testing. Under such circumstances, Pang, Kiang and Pak argue, schools not only increase the risk of denying key services to APA students (e.g., programs that develop writing & communication skills), but can also force a disturbingly high number of them out of the schools.

How to educate bilingual and non-native English speakers

Another pressing issue is the education of non-native English speakers. More than half of all APA students do not consider English to be their first language; these non-native speakers bring with them into the classroom a wide range of languages. How best to educate them has been an ideological and political struggle between proponents of bilingual education on one side and English immersion/English-only advocates on another side. APAs played a pivotal role in mandating the accessibility of bilingual education in our nation's schools. A class action suit filed by twelve Chinese Americans led to the landmark 1974 Lau v. Nichols U.S. Supreme Court decision, which legally binds schools to provide Limited English Proficient (LEP) students with equal education through bilingual instruction and support.

Pang, Kiang and Pak worry that the rollback of bilingual educational programs will have serious negative consequences for LEP students. Drawing from a 1992 U.S. Commission on Civil Rights report, they contend that APA immigrant students are already being deprived of equal access to educational opportunities because of the shortage of bilingual/ESL teachers and counselors. Surely, educational opportunities would be compromised even more if bilingual education were eliminated. Additionally, Pang, Kiang and Pak also charge that the lack of bilingual instruction and support would put immigrant students, particularly those from low-income households, at even greater risk of being labeled "learning disabled" because of their poor command of English.

Breakdown of University Degrees Earned by APAs and All Others

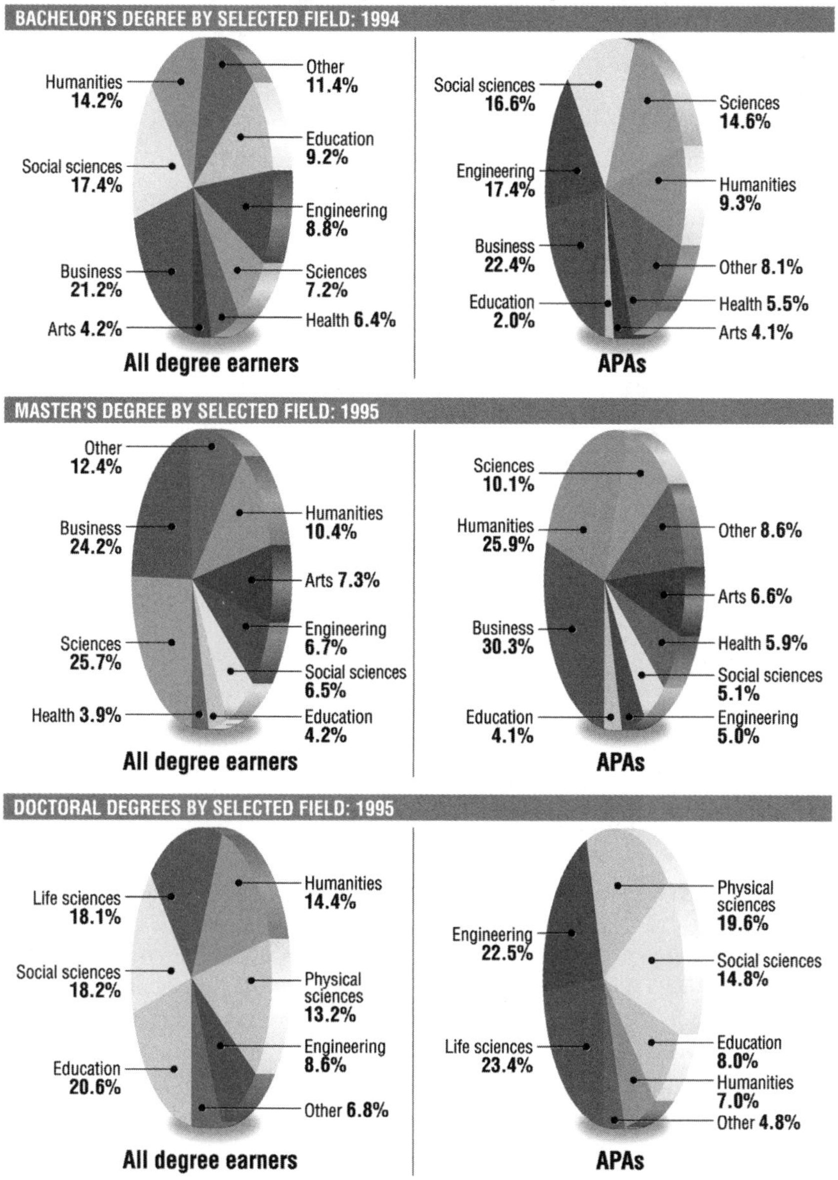

BACHELOR'S DEGREE BY SELECTED FIELD: 1994

All degree earners		APAs	
Humanities	14.2%	Social sciences	16.6%
Other	11.4%	Sciences	14.6%
Education	9.2%	Engineering	17.4%
Social sciences	17.4%	Humanities	9.3%
Engineering	8.8%	Business	22.4%
Business	21.2%	Other	8.1%
Sciences	7.2%	Education	2.0%
Health	6.4%	Health	5.5%
Arts	4.2%	Arts	4.1%

MASTER'S DEGREE BY SELECTED FIELD: 1995

All degree earners		APAs	
Other	12.4%	Sciences	10.1%
Humanities	10.4%	Humanities	25.9%
Business	24.2%	Other	8.6%
Arts	7.3%	Arts	6.6%
Engineering	6.7%	Business	30.3%
Sciences	25.7%	Health	5.9%
Social sciences	6.5%	Social sciences	5.1%
Health	3.9%	Education	4.1%
Education	4.2%	Engineering	5.0%

DOCTORAL DEGREES BY SELECTED FIELD: 1995

All degree earners		APAs	
Life sciences	18.1%	Physical sciences	19.6%
Humanities	14.4%	Engineering	22.5%
Social sciences	18.2%	Social sciences	14.8%
Physical sciences	13.2%	Life sciences	23.4%
Engineering	8.6%	Education	8.0%
Education	20.6%	Humanities	7.0%
Other	6.8%	Other	4.8%

Source: *Glass Ceilings and Asian Americans* (2000, Alta Mira Press), p. 111, quoting Hune and Chan 1997: 53-54, figures 26, 27, and 28; after U.S. Department of Education, National Center for Education Statistics, Integrated Postsecondary Education Data System (PEDS), "Completions" Survey.

There are certainly other social costs to removing bilingual education programs. For example, Lily Wong-Fillmore's 1991 research showed that because language and culture are so inextricably linked, when minority students lose the ability to speak the language of their immigrant parents, it creates greater cultural distance between family members, which subsequently erodes family relations. Given that research tends to support bilingual strategies for promoting the cognitive development and academic achievement of English language learners, APAs will need to think seriously about the elimination of such programs because this can severely limit educational opportunities for a large proportion of the population.

Post-secondary education

APAs will need to monitor closely several key issues in higher education because their outcomes will have widespread ramifications. One of these issues concerns undergraduate admissions practices and policies. Recent attacks on affirmative action have forced colleges and universities to change how they admit students. Aside from state and federal mandates, two other forces are also driving these changes. First, public institutions in particular, because they receive state funding, have an obligation to educate their state's population. Their ability to fulfill this obligation is called to question when certain groups of taxpayers find themselves and their children with limited access to the state's most prestigious public institutions. These concerns can have implications on future funding because they raise questions about whether public monies should be used to support universities which have basically been relieved from the responsibility of educating certain taxpayers in the state. Private colleges and universities are not immune to these concerns because they too depend on tax-based funds and exemptions (i.e., student financial aid, federal research grants, tax exemption status, etc).

Another force driving recent changes in admissions practices is support for educational arguments made in the landmark 1978 U.S. Supreme Court decision, Regents of the University of California v. Bakke. Here the interest is to provide students with an educational atmosphere that encourages speculation, experiment, and creation. Educators believe that a racially diverse student body contributes to this type of environment because it maximizes students' opportunity to exchange ideas with someone who does not share similar viewpoints, which makes for a more robust intellectual atmosphere. Indeed, it is becoming increasingly clear that a racially diverse student body adds value to students' educational experiences and learning. In this way, all students benefit from efforts to enroll a diverse student body, particularly if institutions maximize students' engagement with one another across racial lines.

APAs will need to monitor carefully any redesign of admissions practices because changes in the 1980s were used to systematically limit APA enrollment in some of the nation's most elite universities, without any sincere interest in promoting the educational benefits of diversity. As present and future leaders of a diverse society, APAs undoubtedly benefit from attending institutions that enroll a diverse student body, but admissions practices should not unduly restrict access to APA applicants or overlook them at institutions where APAs are underrepresented. There are currently many alternative admissions practices that have either been recently implemented or are being seriously considered. They include policies that (1) automatically admit a certain percentage of graduating high school seniors primarily on the basis of students' academic ranks within their high school, (2) give greater consideration of other "race neutral" factors such as income, parental educational level, "life challenges," etc., and (3) eliminate altogether the use of standardized test scores.

A recently published study by a professor at the Harvard Graduate School of Education and his colleagues provides some sense of how certain changes in admissions practices might affect the acceptance rates of APAs. They used data from California and a simplified model of the University of California admissions process to explore how various approaches to admissions affect the diversity of the admitted student population. They found that giving preferences to applicants who are either from low-income families, urban and rural areas, high schools with low graduation rates, or whose mothers are less well-educated, did not always substantially increase the admissions rate for African Americans and Latinos, but consistently increased the representation of whites at the expense of APA applicants. These are the types of analyses that should to be conducted in order to find an acceptable balance between enrolling a diverse student body and providing fair access to APA applicants.

APA educators

Another area that deserves close monitoring is the representation of APAs in the faculty and executive administrative ranks. During the last decade, APAs made large gains in entering the faculty ranks. According to the U.S. Department of Education, APAs represent 5.8 percent of the full-time faculty across all institutions in 1998. A large proportion of these APA faculty, however, are likely to be foreign nationals (approximately 40 percent) and male (approximately 80 percent).

The representation of APAs in top-level university or college leadership positions has also improved during the last decade but is still not reflective of their representation in the general population. The U.S. Department of Education reported that APAs represented in 1997 only 1.8 percent of those who held such executive/managerial positions in higher education. The conspicuous absence of APAs in those positions continue to raise concerns about whether they are either being systematically screened out of college and university leadership or hitting a "glass ceiling" in those administrative careers.

Asian American studies thriving

Another issue that deserves attention in post-secondary education is the development of Asian American Studies (AAS). The field has seen a remarkable growth during the last decade. There are 48 universities and colleges with AAS departments or programs, with another 11 offering AAS courses.

The first AAS programs were founded in 1969 at San Francisco State University and UC Berkeley, but California and the West Coast no longer hold a monopoly on AAS. There are programs at elite private universities (University of Pennsylvania, Yale, Stanford), Big Ten universities (Michigan, Wisconsin, Illinois), liberal-arts institutions (Loyola University Chicago, Oberlin, Wesleyan) urban public colleges and universities (Queens College, SUNY Albany, UMass Boston), and even some high schools (Berkeley High, Milton Academy, Brookline High).

In the 1990s, campuses witnessed courageous displays of activism by both students and faculty to establish new programs and sustain older ones. For example, between 1996 to 1998, students at Princeton, Northwestern, Columbia, Stanford, and the University of Maryland, to name a few, demanded institutional support of AAS through sit-ins, occupation of administrative buildings, hunger strikes, and other public demonstrations.

There are two good reasons why this type of campus activism is not likely to disappear in the near future. First, APA student enrollment will continue to grow and certain campuses will experience dramatic increases. Larger enrollments of APA students will most likely trigger interest for new and expanded course offerings in AAS. Second, higher education is already experiencing a period of shrinking resources because

APA College Students, 1990-1999

	Number of APA college students	% of overall student population
1990	572.4	4.3%
1995	797.4	5.8%
1996	828.2	6.0%
1997	859.2	6.1%
1998	900.5	6.4%
1999	909.7	6.4%

Note: Counts U.S. citizens only, in thousands.

Source: U.S. Department of Education, National Center for Education Statistics, Higher Education General Information Survey (HEGIS), "Fall Enrollment in Colleges and Universities" surveys; and Integrated Postsecondary Education Data System (IPEDS), "Fall Enrollment" surveys

In 1997, APAs held only 1.8 percent of executive managerial positions in higher education, according to the U.S. Department of Education.

of recent economic downturns. This trend typically results in the elimination or consolidation of academic programs. Existing programs, units, and departments may find themselves depending on faculty and student activism just to survive in this climate of institutional retrenchment.

Perhaps the negative effect of the model minority myth on the development of AAS is not nearly as obvious as it is on the other issues raised. To clarify this, it is important to appreciate the rich linkage between AAS and civil rights-related interests. AAS has contributed to transforming academic culture by redefining and reshaping the curriculum, the nature of scholarship, the practice and methods of research, the expectations for pedagogy, the empowerment of diverse students, and the engagement with communities. The pursuit of those interests can be undermined when educators cling onto the myth of APA educational success because the myth obscures APA interests in those struggles, particularly when compared to African Americans and Latinos. With resources shrinking even more in higher education in the foreseeable future, this stereotype can prevent access to and development of AAS.

Racism on campus

Uncritical examination of the model minority myth also contributes to campus inadequacy in preventing and addressing racial animosity expressed against APAs. Records show that racial incidents on college campuses continue to be a persistent problem for APAs. Some examples include an e-mail message sent to Asian American students and staff members at the University of California at Irvine, warning them to leave the university, and threatening that if they did not, "I personally will make it my life career to find and kill every one of you personally" (October, 1996); the word "chink" sprayed on the door of two Asian American students at Dartmouth College (February, 1996); and explicit pornography depicting Asian females printed on the front page of the student newspaper at the University of Massachusetts Boston (November, 1997).

Effective strategies and adequate services may not be available to address these problems, let alone prevent them, when campuses are blinded by the myth of APA educational success. The underestimation of the seriousness and pervasiveness of racial animosity perpetrated against APAs and the inadequacy of services to address this problem are of course a much bigger issues because racism is not limited to just higher education.

Conclusion

Given the diversity of the APA population, it is difficult to gauge precisely what is truly in the best interest of APA communities. There exists a diversity of opinions within the APA population regarding the issues raised above, and regardless of the outcome for each issue, some APAs will perceive themselves to be losers, whereas others will be perceived as winners. Despite this, the ubiquity of education will ensure that all APAs will either be directly affected by those issues or have a very small degree of separation from them.

The outcomes of these educational issues will not have a monolithic effect on APAs. All the same, APAs cannot afford to just sit back and take a neutral position because each issue has serious implications regarding race and race relations, which invariably affects all APAs.

UC Freshman Admits from California by Ethnicity, 1997-2002

	1997	1998	1999	2000	2001	2002
American Indian	307	292	275	255	271	292
Black	1,435	1,193	1,331	1,328	1,508	1,620
Chicano/Latino	5,494	5,084	5,607	5,753	6,801	7,316
Subtotal	*7,236*	*6,569*	*7,213*	*7,336*	*8,580*	*9,228*
Asian	12,771	12,625	14,358	14,306	15,554	16,350
Non-Hispanic white	15,527	13,815	17,162	15,968	17,433	18,500
Subtotal	*28,298*	*26,440*	*31,520*	*30,274*	*32,987*	*34,850*
Other	941	595	795	785	826	752
Decline to state	1,953	5,618	3,224	3,395	3,737	3,539
Subtotal	*2,894*	*6,213*	*4,019*	*4,180*	*4,563*	*4,291*
TOTAL	**38,428**	**39,222**	**42,752**	**41,790**	**46,130**	**48,369**

Note: (1) Data are from the Management Reports: 4/2/97 for Fall 1997, 4/1/98 for Fall 1998, 3/30/99 for Fall 1999, 3/24/00 for Fall 2000, 3/28/01 for Fall 2001 and 3/28/02 for Fall 2002. (2) Counts for out-of-state, international and referral students are excluded from this report. (3) Asian Americans include Chinese, East Indian/Pakistani, Filipino, Japanese, Korean, Vietnamese and other Asians; Latinos represent 24 percent of the Chicano/Latino group for 2002; Other includes students who chose category "Other" on the admissions application; and Decline to State includes students who did not provide information on their ethnic identity in the admission application.

Source: UC Office of the President, Student Academic Services, OA&SA, March 2002 (f02/preadm-Cal Fr)

Dr. Chang-Lin Tien: His Golden Bear Years

When Chang-Lin Tien, former chancellor of UC Berkeley, died on Oct. 29, 2002 at the age of 67, he left huge shoes to fill within the Asian Pacific American community. As chancellor of the University of California's flagship Berkeley campus, the mechanical engineering professor had been the first APA to head a major American university. Credited with transforming UC Berkeley from a large and uncaring institution into a more unified and intimate campus, the upbeat and spirited Tien was known for his frequent strolls around campus and fervent sideline cheering at Cal football games.

However, in July 1996, when Tien announced his plans to step down as chancellor, few were very surprised. The popular administrator had clashed with UC regents over the controversial dismantling of affirmative-action programs, and during the search for a new president for the entire nine-campus University of California system, Tien was not even granted an interview.

But those close to the chancellor speculated that aside from "shabby treatment" by the regents, Tien was in the running for a presidential Cabinet appointment as Clinton's Energy secretary—something that did not materialize after he was tainted by the 1996 campaign finance scandal involving illegal donations to the Democratic party by overseas Asians.

In his first year as chancellor, Tien had to deal with two crisis situations: a fraternity-house fire killed three students, and a gunman held 30 people hostage at a nearby hotel, killing one student and injuring seven others before being shot to death by police. Two years later in 1992, a Berkeley activist with a history of mental illness broke into Tien's campus residence wielding a machete. Police on the scene shot and killed Tien's would-be assassin in the chancellor's master suite. Tien's sensitive handling of those situations helped to establish his commanding presence in the local community.

The choice to leave UC Berkeley was a difficult one for Tien. One of the most successful chancellors ever to lead the university—raising a total of more than $780 million for the financially ailing campus—Tien invested most of his 38-year career in academia at UC Berkeley. With the exception of a two-year stint at UC Irvine, Tien spent his entire professional career at UC Berkeley, as a teacher, department chair, vice-chancellor and chancellor.

Chang-Lin Tien was the first Asian American to head a major U.S. university, as chancellor of UC Berkeley.

Photo: AsianWeek Archive

"This decision has not been an easy one," Tien said in an announcement of his resignation from Berkeley. "Cal is so much a part of me, my wife, Di-Hwa, and our three children, who have grown up here and are all UC Berkeley graduates. I know we will always be a part of Cal."

Tien continued to be involved in APA political circles until his death, always encouraging factions within the community to unite for the common good.

—*AsianWeek*

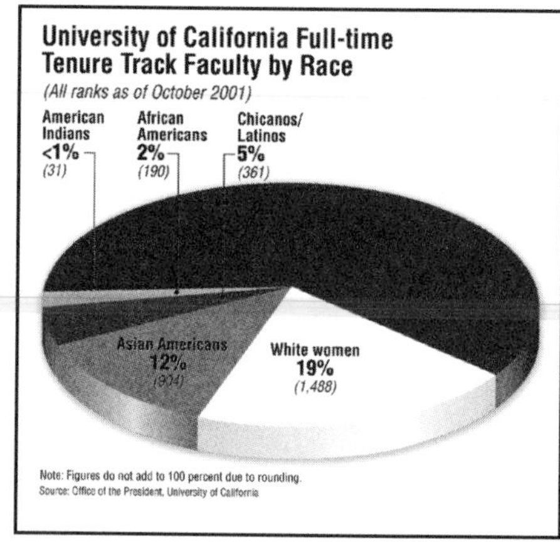

Since stakes are incredibly high, APAs have to think beyond immediate winners and losers and find strategic points of solidarity so that a combined effort can be advanced to make a lasting positive difference. One promising unifying point is to dismantle racism by vigilantly contesting and resisting the use of stereotypes that oversimplify educational practices and policies. Although APAs have made huge gains in education, those gains will always require an unhappy footnote unless racist stereotypes are eradicated.

—*Mitchell Chang*

The Political Incorporation of Asian Pacific Americans

At the dawn of the third millennium, Asian Pacific Americans are becoming a political force whose potential cannot be ignored. While few activists would claim that APA political progress has been sufficient, the gains are striking. For the first half of the 20th century, most Asian immigrants had been denied the right to naturalize, and many could not even own property. During World War II, over 100,000 Japanese Americans were imprisoned against their will, guilty only of Japanese ancestry. Today, however, APAs can be found in the Cabinet, Congress, governors' mansions, and many other government offices.

The Immigration Act of 1965 proved to be a watershed. Conditions had improved considerably in the 1950s and early 1960s, but Asian Pacific Americans still had minimal political presence outside of Hawai'i. The 1965 legislation helped to open the door to large-scale immigration from Asia (and Latin America), particularly through the unanticipated phenomenon of "chain migration." With the increased numbers of APAs, plus their concentration in politically important states such as California and New York, the raw material for political influence was in place.

Another important development came in the late 1960s, when many third- and fourth-generation Asian Americans coalesced in the Asian American Movement. Although it faded in the 1970s, the movement left a legacy of young leadership that was instrumental in establishing Asian American Studies programs at universities, interest groups, and a host of other organizations that built the infrastructure necessary for effective political efforts.

Although the APA population had reached a potent political size by the 1980s, much of it was composed of recent immigrants who were still adapting to their new country. By the late 1990s, however, the second generation and those who arrived as children were coming of age, and they began to move into the political arena in significant numbers.

The greater political presence of APAs was hard to miss by 2000, when President Bill Clinton named the first-ever APA cabinet secretary, Norman Mineta, to head the Department of Commerce, and Gary Locke (the nation's first Chinese American governor) was elected to his second term in the state of Washington. The following year, President George W. Bush chose two APA cabinet secretaries, Mineta for Transportation, and Elaine Chao for Labor.

Photo: AP Wide World

Minnesota State Sen. Mee Moua became the first Hmong elected to a state legislature in the U.S. Moua was born in Laos and lived in a refugee camp in Thailand before her family came to the U.S., 23 years ago.

The political future remains unclear, however. The rapidly growing APA population has the potential for significant political clout, but that influence can be greatly diluted through internal differences. Significant challenges continue to face APAs, but it remains to be seen whether APAs will be able to mount the unified response needed to meet them effectively.

Growth in elected officials

The increasing importance of APAs is demonstrated in part by the growth of APA elected officials. In 1978, when comprehensive records were first compiled, there were only 120 APA elected officials in key local, state, and federal offices, from members of Congress and governors all the way down to school board members. By 2000, there were 328.

Also notable is the expanding diversity among APA officials. Three decades ago, APA elected officials were primarily of Chinese and Japanese ancestry. The picture has changed to include men such as Hawai'i's U.S. Senator, Daniel Akaka (Native Hawaiian); St. Charles, Louisiana councilmember Ganesier "Ram" Ramchandran (Asian Indian American); and Lowell, Mass. councilmember Chanrithy Uong (Cambodian American); and women such as Minnesota State Sen. Mee Moua (Hmong American), Washington State Rep. Velma Veloria (Filipina American), and Garret Park, Md. councilmember Nguyen Minh Chau (Vietnamese American).

Another important development is the success of candidates outside Hawai'i, a longtime bastion of APA political success. California, with the largest APA population in the United States, has the most extensive roster of APA officeholders, but APA elected officials can today be found in almost half the states.

Particularly notable was Gary Locke's 1996 election as governor of Washington, a state where APAs comprise less than six percent of the population. Locke, a Democrat who was reelected in 2000, is the first APA to be elected governor of a mainland state, and the first Chinese American governor. APA

Effects of Immigration

Immigration and naturalization affects large numbers of APAs. Congress continues to revisit the issue, with the last major revisions of immigration quotas coming in the Immigration Reform and Control Act (IRCA) in 1986, and the Immigration Act of 1990. IRCA was intended to control illegal immigration, but is widely viewed as a failure, creating an incentive for further reform of immigration law.

The 1990 act has been more consequential for APAs, because it increased the allotment for skilled workers. In 2000, Asian immigrants comprised 31.2 percent of all legal immigrants, but they were awarded 54.4 percent of employment-based preference visas, according to the Immigration and Naturalization Service. Also, although the Immigration Act of 1990 lowered the number of legal immigrants allowed under the various preferences, it continued to apply no limit to immediate family members (parents, spouses, and unmarried children under the age of 21) of U.S. citizens. Because of the high naturalization rate of immigrant APAs, the lowered immigration caps may have only a modest effect on total APA immigration.

Many APA immigrants continue to gain naturalization status in the United States, despite lowered immigration caps implemented by the Immigration Act of 1990.

Photo: Judi Parks

In 1990, Congress also passed legislation granting U.S. citizenship to Filipinos who fought during World War II. Congress did not grant them veteran's status, however, and the struggle continues to gain that status—and the benefits that go with it—for the Filipino veterans now living in the United States.

In 2000, Congress passed two immigration-related bills of great importance to

governors preceding Locke were George Ariyoshi (1974-86) and Ben Cayetano (1994-2002), both Democratic governors of Hawai'i. Locke, whose grandfather immigrated to the United States, also served in the Washington House of Representatives, and as the elected chief executive of King County, which includes Seattle. Locke's was the most notable instance of a trend of APA candidates winning elections in areas with relatively few APA voters.

Two years after Locke was first elected, Taiwanese-born David Wu was elected to the U.S. House of Representatives from Oregon's 1st District. As with Locke, Wu had a very small APA base (about five percent of his district), requiring him to appeal effectively to a broader range of voters.

APA representation in Congress, however, continues to be modest. As of summer 2002, there were only eight APA members of Congress. Currently, there are only eight APA members of Congress (MCs), or about 1.5 percent of the total membership, not including representatives from territories like American Samoa and Guam. However, MCs are elected by state, and the APA population continues to be very small in most states (under five percent of the population in all but five states). In addition, congressional seats are usually highly prized, and an effective campaign often requires political experience. The growing numbers of APAs in local and state office is creating an expanding pool of veteran candidates who are likely to be able to mount effective campaigns for higher office.

APAs in Congress

	APA Senators	APA Representatives
American Samoa	0	1
California	0	2
Guam	0	1
Hawai'i	2	1
Oregon	0	1
Total*	**2**	**6**

Note: 107th Congress (2001-02). American Samoa and Guam have only one congressional delegate and no senators. States not listed have no APA senators or representatives.

Source: Asian American Action Fund, http://www.aaa-fund.org

another small APA group—Hmong immigrants who fought for the United States in the Vietnam War. Coming from an agricultural society which did not even have a written language prior to the mid-20th century, many adult Hmong immigrants struggled with English and adaptation to American society, and found it difficult to pass citizenship tests, which were administered in English. The Hmong Veteran's Naturalization Act, passed in May, and its extension approved in November, allowed Hmong veterans and their spouses to take the citizenship test in the language of their choice and in a simplified form.

Another issue of great concern to some APAs was the furor over H-1B visas, which are given to workers in certain specialty occupations, most notably "computer-related" work (accounting for almost 54 percent of all H-1B petitions from October 1999 to February 2000). Although H-1B holders are technically classified as non-immigrants, many recipients view H-1B status as a foot in the door to the United States, hoping that they can later convert to permanent resident status. In the mid-1990s, some began to assert that H-1B workers were being used by some employers to undercut the wages of American citizens. Prospective immigrants, attracted by higher pay or by the possibility that they might later be able to convert to permanent resident status, were willing to work for wages much lower than comparably-trained domestic workers could command. Employers successfully fended off efforts to reduce H-1B allocations, countering that they could not find adequately trained workers in the United States, forcing them to rely on immigrant labor to meet their needs. Whichever was the case, it was clear that Asian Indian immigrants were receiving large numbers of the H-1B visas. From October 1999 to February 2000, 42.6 percent of all H-1B petitions approvals went to Asian Indian applicants.

What remains unclear is the long-term impact of Sept. 11 on immigration. Regardless, however, Asian interest in immigration to America is likely to remain very high, so U.S. immigration policy will continue to play an important role in shaping Asian Pacific America.

Immigration – Fiscal Year 2000

Region of birth	% of total legal immigration	% of immigrants allowed under employment preferences
Europe	15.6%	15.9%
Asia	**31.2%**	**55.5%**
Africa	5.3%	4.1%
Oceania	0.6%	0.8%
North America	1.9%	6.9%
Caribbean	10.4%	2.4%
Latin America	34.9%	14.3%

Source: Calculated from Immigration and Naturalization Service, Fiscal Year 2000 Statistical Yearbook

Political Participation & Influence

As the 20th century drew to a close, the APA political presence had become substantial. An extensive "infrastructure"—i.e., groups and networks that enable effective political action—had developed, and an effort was undertaken to maximize the clout of APA voters. APAs had also developed a reputation as generous campaign contributors, although that image was probably exaggerated. Despite the gains, however, APA political participation and influence was still very much a work in progress, and the next decade could see considerable gains.

Currently, APAs continue to vote at relatively low rates (substantially below black and white voters). Low voting rates are in part because considerable numbers are immigrants who have not yet naturalized, or have not yet reached voting age. For instance, in 2000, only 59 percent of APAs residing in the United States were eligible to vote, i.e. were citizens 18 years and older. But that doesn't explain the low voting rates among those who are able to vote. In 1998, a non-presidential election year, only 32.4 percent of eligible APAs voted, down from 39.4 percent in 1994, and far lower than the 46.3 percent voting rate among eligible whites in 1998. In 2000, 43.3 percent of eligible APAs voted. That's the lowest among all ethnic groups, and far below the 60.5 percent rate among eligible whites.

Among those who are American citizens and registered to vote, APAs turn out at rates lower, but still close to whites. In November 2000, a presidential election year, 83 percent of registered APAs voted, compared to 86 percent of whites.

Among some APA immigrants, interest in U.S. politics is probably overshadowed by a continued interest in the politics of the country of their birth. APA immigrants maintain substantial contacts with their country of origin, and many have been active in issues affecting their native lands. In the coming decade, then, APA levels of political participation should grow, as the increasing percentages of American-born APAs will no longer be faced with the barrier of naturalization, and will have diminishing interest in the homeland of their ancestors.

While APA voting rates continue to lag, APA interest groups are proliferating. Organized interests are critical to wielding political influence in America, and APA influence in Washington D.C. and elsewhere is greatly enhanced by the growth of this political infrastructure. Events that are seen as attacks on APAs—such as the Wen Ho Lee case—are increasingly likely to be met with swift responses that are only possible from organized groups with sufficient resources. Furthermore, these groups provide ready-made avenues for political involvement, greatly reducing the difficulty of making one's voice heard.

In the past 20 years, long-established APA groups such as the Japanese American Citizens League (1929) and the Organization of Chinese Americans (1973) witnessed the founding of numerous additional APA groups, such as the Southeast Asian Resource Action Center (founded in 1979 as the Indochina Refugee Action Center), the Korean American Coalition (1983), the Asian Pacific American Legal Center (1983), the Asian & Pacific Islander American Health Forum (1986), the National Asian Pacific American Legal Consortium (1991), and the Asian Pacific American Institute for Congressional Studies (1995). These and dozens of other advocacy, educational, legal, professional, and student groups have helped create a massive political infrastructure for APAs.

Another important avenue for APA political participation has been campaign contributions, but the image of APAs as fountains of money seems to be more myth than reality. The limited available evidence suggests that APA donors give primarily to APA candidates, and are not lavish contributors to all types of candidates. Nevertheless, perceptions of APAs as deep-pocketed donors helped to create one of the most bitter APA political experiences of the 1990s.

As the 1996 campaign approached, many politically active APAs had felt that the coming election might mark a watershed for APA political influence. Instead, however, they found themselves reeling after allegations surfaced late in the year that the Clinton campaign had accepted illegal contributions from Asian sources. The key player was John Huang, a Democratic National Committee fundraiser and former Com-

Some APA elected officials have moved into leadership positions, which should help them, should they choose to run for higher office. As of Summer 2002, Sharon Tomiko Santos was the Democratic Whip in the Washington State House of Representatives, and Democrat Majority Whip Wilma Chan was named to be the new majority leader in the California State Assembly. In the Fall 2002 elections, Democrat Stan Matsunaka, president of the Colorado State Senate, ran a closely followed, though ultimately unsuccessful campaign, for the open seat in the 4th Congressional District.

In addition, whether or not they have moved into leadership positions, mainland APA office-holders must usually build robust interracial coalitions. Even with the rapidly growing APA population, there are only a handful of areas where it would be possible to assemble a majority APA state or local legislative district, and nowhere outside Hawai'i do APAs have sufficient geographical concentration to constitute a majority of a U.S. congressional district. Compounding the challenge for APA candidates is the fact that the voting rate of APAs is still relatively low. As a result, mainland

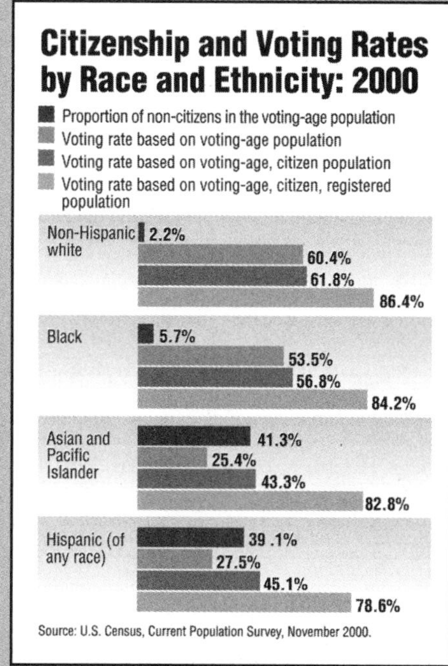

Source: U.S. Census, Current Population Survey, November 2000.

merce Department official, who served as a conduit for money from foreign sources forbidden from contributing to U.S. campaigns. Over the next year, the media was filled with stories about Asian contributors and Asian American intermediaries. Interest heightened when charges surfaced that China was the source of some of the donations, and Chinese nationals had sought to gain access to government secrets in exchange for their contributions. Although only a few Asian Americans were involved, reports began to surface that all APAs were being treated with suspicion, signaled out for heightened scrutiny and asked if they were citizens. To some, it felt depressingly like a resurgence of the image of APAs as "forever foreigners," aliens who could never become Americans. Perhaps the most infamous portrayal was the March 24, 1997 *National Review* cover which featured a caricature of Bill and Hillary Clinton, with the president and first lady drawn with stereotypical Asian features, implying that Asian connections were antithetical to American interests.

But some things had changed. With the growing network of APA groups, and increased incorporation into American society, outraged APAs responded, criticizing the caricatures and stereotypes that emerged in the media coverage of the scandal. Although the controversy left many APAs with a bad taste for politics, it also showed that the expanding APA political infrastructure would respond forcefully.

Another example of the increasing APA political engagement could be seen in the controversy over the 1997 nomination of Bill Lann Lee to be assistant attorney general for civil rights under President Clinton. Reacting to the strong opposition Lee faced from conservative groups, APA groups rallied to push for his confirmation. Although Clinton was unable to overcome the opposition of some Senate Republicans, he placed Lee in the post as acting Assistant Attorney General.

In the 2000 presidential election, the growing APA political significance was again apparent. Democrat Al Gore carried California with strong support from Latino, Asian American, and African American voters, overcoming the majority of whites who voted for Republican George W. Bush. A CNN exit poll showed APAs voting for Gore over Bush by a 55-41 percent margin, while a *Los Angeles Times* exit poll found a wider margin, 62-37 percent. California is by far the most important prize of presidential election politics, with over a fifth of the electoral votes needed for victory. Comprising a little over 10 percent of the population, Californian APAs have the potential of providing a critical swing vote.

Of course, APA clout will be enhanced if there is greater unity. Recognizing this, the 80-20 movement was started in 1998, seeking to deliver 80 percent of the APA vote to a single presidential candidate in 2000. Led by former Delaware Lieutenant Governor S.B. Woo, 80-20 attracted a significant amount of media interest (primarily from the California press), and gained the attention of the major candidates. The 80-20 goal was very ambitious, and no one was surprised when it fell short, but the tactic helped to highlight the influence APA voters could wield if they vote in a bloc. While it remains doubtful that any candidate can command the support of 80 percent of the diverse APA population, efforts such as 80-20 illustrate the increasingly sophisticated political efforts which are likely to translate into growing political influence for APAs.

APA candidates must appeal to the interests of non-APA voters in order to be elected—experience that increases their chances of success if they choose to run for higher office.

Economic challenges

Despite the "model minority" image that portrays APAs as all highly educated and prosperous, substantial numbers of APAs are in poverty. Southeast Asian immigrants in particular have struggled economically, so they stand to be strongly affected by reductions in government assistance (in 1990, the poverty rate for Southeast Asian Americans was over 25 percent).

In 1996, Congress passed landmark welfare reform legislation. Although the focus of the legislation was on ending the 50-year-old Aid to Families with Dependent Children program and replacing it with the Temporary Assistance for Needy Families (TANF) program, the legislation also dramatically reduced benefits for non-citizens. Illegal immigrants were already ineligible for most government benefits, but now, most legal immigrants were cut off from Supplemental Social Security (SSI), food stamps, and TANF (the successor to AFDC).

APA Elected Officials, 2001-2002

	Federal	State	Local	Total
California	2	4	136	142
Hawai'i	3	56	36	95
Washington	0	5	20	25
New York	0	0	11	11
Maryland	0	3	1	4
Massachusetts	0	0	4	4
Oregon	1	1	2	4
New Mexico	0	0	3	3
Texas	0	0	3	3
Alaska	0	0	2	2
Colorado	0	1	1	2
Illinois	0	0	2	2
Michigan	0	0	2	2
Minnesota	0	2	0	2
Ohio	0	0	2	2
West Virginia	0	1	1	2
Louisiana	0	0	1	1
Nebraska	0	0	1	1
Nevada	0	0	1	1
North Dakota	0	0	1	1
Wisconsin	0	0	1	1
Total	**6**	**73**	**231**	**310**

Source: Don T. Nakanishi and James S. Lai, 2001-02 *National Asian Pacific American Political Almanac* (Los Angeles: UCLA Asian American Studies Center, 2001); and Asian American Action Fund, http://www.aaa-fund.org

There were actually two bills passed, the Personal Responsibility and Work Opportunity Reconciliation Act of 1996 (PL 104-193, sometimes referred to as the Welfare Reform Act, or WRA), and the Illegal Immigration Reform and Immigrant Responsibility Act of 1996 (Immigration Reform Act, or IRA for short). The former had the greatest impact on welfare benefits for immigrants. Much of the IRA was devoted to efforts to reduce illegal immigration, although it also established the first income requirements for sponsors of immigrants, requiring the sponsors to have an income of at least 125 percent of the federal poverty level.

Congress later moderated some of the harshest provisions, but large numbers of APAs still faced benefit cutoffs. The extremely strong economy of the late 1990s probably greatly reduced the impact of these cutoffs, but poor APAs now face the dual challenge of a weaker economy at a time when even those eligible for aid may be reaching their five-year lifetime limit. With the confluence of these factors, the legacy of welfare reform will continue to pose a serious challenge for economically disadvantaged APAs in the early twenty-first century.

Political and social challenges

Anti-Asian violence has been a major focus of many prominent APA interest groups, including the Asian Law Caucus, Asian American Legal Defense and Education Fund, and the National Asian Pacific American Legal Consortium. The case of Vincent Chin, a Chinese American killed in 1992 by attackers who saw him as a "Jap," was a major impetus to the building of more pan-ethnic ties between the different Asian Pacific American ethnic groups. In the 1990s, though, anti-Asian violence became a more complicated issue.

In late April 1992, the nation's attention was riveted to the torrent of rage that followed the acquittal of the police officers charged with beating Rodney King. As the flames subsided, it became clear that Korean Americans were among the chief victims of the destruction. Indeed, so searing was the memory that many Korean Americans came to identify the events simply as *Sa-i-gu*, Korean for April 29. This particular instance of anti-Asian violence was much more complicated, however, since it was not perpetrated primarily by white Americans, but rather by other persons of color. APA interest groups were accustomed to interracial alliances that sought to improve conditions for different minority groups, but they had little experience with efforts to reduce tensions between communities of color. Indeed, in the immediate aftermath of April 29, many Korean Americans felt a notable lack of support from prominent APA groups.

Somewhat similar although less devastating conflicts occured on the other side of the country, in New York City, where Korean American grocers also found themselves in conflict with some African Americans (although the initial tensions developed with Afro-Caribbean immigrants, not native-born African Americans). Again, APA groups were faced with the challenge of navigating tensions in a more complex, multiracial society.

Most recently, South Asian Americans have found themselves the target of those seeking to vent their anger after the attacks of Sept. 11. Although the facts are still being determined in some of these cases, the violence suggests that APAs continue to be viewed as "foreign" by many, and that there will continue to be a struggle for acceptance and full incorporation into American society.

The challenge of pan-ethnic unity

Although anti-Asian violence usually encourages pan-Asian American unity, ethnic identity may predominate in other circumstances. Evidence suggests that APAs, when asked to identify themselves, are more likely to use ethnic labels (e.g., "Vietnamese American" or "Chinese American") than a pan-ethnic one (e.g., "Asian American"). However, although an ethnic identity is often the first choice of APAs, many also see themselves as Asian Americans, indicating some level of support for the pan-ethnic identity as well, as shown by the groundbreaking work of Professor Pei-te Lien and her colleagues. Also, for APAs, as for most people, one's stated identity probably varies somewhat with the context, so one might identify oneself as a Japanese American in a group of APAs of different ancestries, but as an Asian American in a group composed primarily of Americans of European and African descent. Still, ethnic identity is likely to be an impediment to pan-ethnic unity among APAs.

Furthermore, like any sizeable group, APAs have many political differences. Although world changes have diminished the relevance of some issues, Southeast Asian immigrants often bear a strong hostility to the communist

Wen Ho Lee:
A Clear and Present Danger?

Beginning in the spring of 1999, the quiet life of nuclear scientist Wen Ho Lee was turned upside down and pushed into public scrutiny. In March, *The New York Times* ran a story reporting concern that China might have stolen U.S. nuclear weapons secrets. The article said that FBI suspicions had focused on a Chinese American scientist at the lab, but it did not name the scientist. (*The New York Times* would later publish an editorial in September 2000 that acknowledged its coverage had been flawed.) Bill Richardson, the Secretary of Energy at the time, leaked to the press that the prime suspect was Lee, who was involved in computer codes used in the simulated tests of nuclear weapons.

Lee maintained throughout his ordeal that it was normal practice to make backup tapes of files in case of possible computer crashes. But two days after the *New York Times* article, the Energy Department fired Lee from Los Alamos National Laboratory on grounds that connected him with a three-year espionage investigation involving leaks of U.S. nuclear weapons secrets to China.

It was only half a year later, after months of trial by media, that Lee was arrested at his New Mexico home and indicted on 59 felony counts that charged him with transferring secret nuclear weapons data to unsecured computer terminals and computer tapes—the only evidence the government could find against him on charges of breaching national security.

Lee's arrest prompted nationwide attention and political action among the APA community. On June 8, 2000, hundreds of APAs across the country gathered at Day of Outrage rallies held in cities across the nation, protesting Lee's treatment, calling for due process for Lee and urging government officials to free him on bail. Lee's supporters contended that the Taiwanese-born, U.S. citizen of 25 years was targeted because he is Asian American. Some demanded a presidential pardon and an apology, despite denials of racial profiling by the FBI and U.S. Attorney General, Janet Reno.

Photo: AsianWeek Archive

Despite intensive FBI investigations, there was no evidence to suggest espionage or that Lee had passed classified information to foreign agents. On September 13, 2000, Wen Ho Lee was freed after spending nine months in solitary confinement. In a political hearing days later, FBI Director Louis Freeh testified that prosecutors could have sent Lee to prison for years, but agreed to let him plead guilty to a single charge out of fear that atomic weapons secrets would become public at trial. Lee was not charged with spying and denied giving information to China, though he eventually pleaded guilty to one felony count of downloading sensitive material.

"I think the Wen Ho Lee case has encouraged Asian Pacific Americans to be more politically involved," said Assemblywoman Judy Chu of Monterey Park, Calif. "People are starting to realize to be treated fairly, they have to have a political voice. This was a real wake-up call."

At a book reading in Los Angeles for his autobiography, *My Country Versus Me*, Lee admitted he seldom read newspapers and did not vote before this ordeal happened to him. He encouraged a largely APA crowd to not make the same mistakes.

"You should pay more attention to politics," said Lee. "Speak out when you can. If you want people to respect us, you must respect yourself first."

—*AsianWeek*

regimes of their native countries, an attitude that contrasts sharply with that of some third- and fourth-generation APAs. Native-born APAs also often hold liberal social views that differ from those of immigrants, who are often socially conservative. And although foreign-born APAs may share a common interest in liberal immigration policy, some native-born APAs cast a critical eye toward more recent immigrants. In addition, the enormous economic diversity in the APA community probably helps produce considerable disagreements over social welfare policies as well.

At times, APAs may simply have different political interests. In these cases, political conflict is replaced by apathy, with each APA group taking little interest in the primary concerns of the others. For example, immigrant APAs are often still strongly drawn to the politics of their country of origin. This, of course, has the potential for importing historical enmities into the United States—for

Hawaiians

Hawai'i is a unique case for those interested in APAs. In the last half-century, Asian Americans have become the dominant influence in Hawaiian politics, leading to greater influence at the national level through the efforts of the Hawaiian congressional delegation. However, the other, smaller element of the Asian Pacific American population—Pacific Islander Americans—do not always see Hawai'i as a success story.

Far from the view of most of the mainland media, Native Hawaiian—those descended from ancestors who resided in Hawai'i prior to 1778—activists have been working to transform politics on the islands. The economic, social, and political concerns of many ethnic Hawaiians are more similar to those of Native Americans than they are to those of Asian Americans. Like Native Americans, Hawaiians lost control over their lands to outsiders, and today many struggle with poverty, health problems, and other ills. In recognition of this, the Hawaiian state government created the Office of Hawaiian Affairs (OHA), governed by a board elected by Hawaiians and responsible for improving conditions for Native Hawaiians.

In February 2000, however, the U.S. Supreme Court overturned the OHA election process and boosted efforts to transform the legal status of Hawai'i's indigenous people. Limiting voting to those of Native Hawaiian ancestry was tantamount to limiting voting to members of one race and therefore unconstitutional, the Court ruled. This has raised concerns over further challenges to special provisions for Native Hawaiians. In response, Senator Daniel Akaka and others have introduced legislation which would recognize a "native Hawaiian governing entity," thereby allowing Hawaiians to form a semi-sovereign government and negotiate benefits with the state of Hawai'i and the federal government. At this writing, the fate of the bill is uncertain.

Political activists differ over what is needed to address the challenges facing Hawaiians. Groups such as Ka Lahui Hawai'i focus on the creation of a "nation within a nation," similar to the relationship enjoyed by federally recognized Native American tribes. Ka Lahui leaders have been highly critical of some state-sponsored efforts, such as the Hawaiian Sovereignty Elections Council, seeing it as a vehicle for undermining efforts to gain greater control for Native Hawaiians. Other groups, such as Ka Pakaukau, are unsatisfied with any continued membership in the United States and favor an independent Hawaiian nation. Still others seem primarily to favor greater government assistance for Native Hawaiians.

The 1990s have sometimes seen political tension between some Native Hawaiians and Asian Americans, particularly Japanese Americans. Because Japanese Americans have been politically dominant in Hawai'i for much of the post-World War II era, some Native Hawaiian activists see Japanese American politicians as part of the power structure which has perpetuated the mistreatment of the indigenous peoples and prevents Native Hawaiians from gaining the political power they deserve. Although some Asian Americans have supported the efforts of Hawaiian activists, political gains for the latter must sometimes come at the expense of the former, so tensions are likely to continue in the foreseeable future.

example, the hostility that many Koreans have toward Japanese—but, more likely, it simply draws APAs away from issues that might unite them. For instance, APAs of different ancestries can come together much more easily over domestic issues such as bilingual ballots, adequate working conditions, or anti-Asian violence, than over issues such as political corruption in South Korea or continuing unrest in Kashmir. The vast APA category encompasses groups whose shared interests may not be obvious: for instance, South Asian Americans and East Asian Americans are not always certain as to how much they have in common.

The future—individuals and the community

And so, as the 21st century unfolds, the political future remains unclear. APA candidates are experiencing growing success, most notably in districts where APA voters are a small minority, and APA interest groups are gaining experience and influence. As American-born voters grow in number, and immigrants become more accustomed to American politics, APAs are likely to make up a growing percentage of the electorate.

However, the very idea of "Asian Pacific American" cannot be assumed. Indeed, native Hawaiians have spearheaded an effort to remove Pacific Islander Americans from the "APA" category, seeing their interests as different—and sometimes even opposed—to those of Asian Americans. Relatively high rates of APA intermarriage demonstrates increasing societal acceptance, but it also means that there will be increasing numbers of children whose ethnic identity must be chosen rather than assumed.

It seems certain that many individuals of APA ancestry will prosper. Indeed, many are already economically successful, and growing numbers are advancing in politics. Whether most APAs—and most people of color—will be able to enjoy the same success is the subject

Photo: Corky Lee

South Asian Americans found themselves the target of anti-Asian violence after the Sept. 11 attacks on the United States.

of an extensive and sometimes bitter debate among scholars. But regardless of who is right, an APA politics will only be able to exist if millions of individuals see themselves as sharing some sort of common Asian Pacific heritage.

—*Andrew Aoki*

Disparities in Giving to APA Communities

Asian Pacific Americans today receive only 0.3 percent of total foundation and charitable giving in the United States. That percentage is disproportionately low given the size, diversity, and needs of one of the fastest growing and most diverse racial groups in the United States. APAs comprise nearly 4.5 percent of the total population, and include 28 different Asian ethnic groups and 19 different Pacific Islander ethnicities, each with different socioeconomic characteristics.

As APA communities experience this ongoing population growth, many of the problems identified in a landmark 1992 Asian Americans/Pacific Islanders in Philanthropy (AAPIP) report, *Invisible and In Need: Philanthropic Giving to Asian Americans and Pacific Islanders*, continue to be major obstacles to a decent quality of life. Racially-motivated crimes, unmet health care needs, poor working conditions for those in low-wage jobs, and domestic violence are just a few examples of the problems that still have a particularly serious impact on APA communities. In California, for example, 23 percent of Southeast Asians live in poverty, according to the Public Policy Institute of California report of October 2001.

Despite these dramatic increases in population and the persistent nature of the serious economic, social, and health problems facing APA communities, philanthropic investment in meeting the needs of APA communities was and continues to be inadequate. In 1990, APAs accounted for 2.9 percent of the national population. However, between 1983 and 1990, only 0.2 percent of national philanthropic dollars went to nonprofit organizations serving APA communities.

Even in California, where APAs are numerous and the high-tech economic boom during the 1990s provided unprecedented wealth, philanthropic giving to APA communities continues to lag behind population growth and size. At the same time, the assets of, as well as the resources allocated by, California foundations for philanthropic giving reached an all time high:

• In 1999, California grant-makers awarded $2.9 billion to recipients, representing a 224 percent growth in giving for California foundations since 1991.

• In 1999, California grant-makers had assets of $68.3 billion, a 249 percent growth in California foundation assets since 1991.

As of 2000, APAs comprised 13 percent of California's total population, or nearly 4.4 million, including those of mixed-ethnicity and mixed-race (i.e. the "Asian alone or in combination" category). Despite this APA population explosion and the increase in foundation assets and

Missing Charity

California non-profit groups serving APAs get disproportionately less funding from foundations...

	1991	1999
California foundation donations to California non-profits serving APAs	$2.6 million	$ 10.9 million
Percentage of overall giving to California non-profits	0.7%	1.1%
U.S. foundation donations to California non-profits serving APAs	$ 3.4 million	$ 18 million
Percentage of overall giving to California non-profits	0.5%	1.2%

...this despite the fact that APAs make up thirteen percent of California's population and that many groups remain in need. Twenty-three percent of Southeast Asian households in California remain in poverty.

Source: Asian Americans/Pacific Islanders in Philanthropy

giving in California, only $18 million out of $1.5 billion, or 1.2 percent of all giving by U.S. foundations to California non-profits, was given to California groups that served APA communities in 1999. Only 1.1 percent of giving by California foundations, or $10.9 million, benefited these same APA-serving California organizations.

Why APAs are ignored

Explanations for low philanthropic investments to APA communities are complex and under-researched. Foundation executives, public policymakers, and the general public often uncritically accept the notion that APAs are a "model minority" that has succeeded in spite of societal barriers. In fact, the APA population is bi-polar, occupying extreme ends of the spectrum, from wealth to marginal daily survival, advanced education to illiteracy.

But research and data on APAs often are not separated out to show the existences of both rich and poor. The resulting data is skewed to portray Asian Americans as uniformly successful and conceal the issues facing those APAs at the bottom of the economic ladder. Consequently, APAs are not perceived to have pressing needs that should be addressed by philanthropy.

There are some robust APA community organizations that have attained significant successes. But unable to access major sources of foundation funding, APA communities have some of the weakest national infrastructures and institutions compared to their counterparts in other communities of color. Another explanation for low funding rates to APAs is that many APA organizations depend heavily on large government grants and are unable to garner much funding from private foundations.

Within the philanthropic field, APAs continue to face racism. Foundations put APA communities low on their funding priorities. And there are few APAs in leadership positions at foundations. Although hiring APA staff does not guarantee funding to APA communities, diversifying the philanthropic field is one aspect of foundations' accountability to the communities they support.

New challenges

At the time this article was written, post-Sept. 11 national priorities were shifting toward the so-called "war on terrorism" and "homeland defense." Two major challenges face APA communities (and all communities of color) and make it crucial to examine how philanthropic resources are being invested. First, people of color, and APAs in particular, are the targets of worsening hate violence and racial profiling in the wake of Sept. 11. Second, national resources are increasingly being spent on defense and national security, at the expense of health and other human and social services benefiting APA communities. This political climate coupled with the historic disparities in giving to APA communities, creates a deeper barrier for changing these inequities.

We at AAPIP continue to advocate and recommend these policies to foundation and corporate grantmakers:

Recognize the needs of APA communities and direct more resources to organizations that empower communities;

Fund language-appropriate and culturally-appropriate programs;

Fund problem-identification and documentation efforts;

Provide technical assistance to APA community organizations; and

Increase representation of APAs on boards of trustees and staffs of philanthropic organizations.

—Maria Kong and Peggy Saika

Maria Kong is program director and Peggy Saika is executive director of Asian American/Pacific Islanders in Philanthropy, a San Francisco-based group dedicated to building ties between APA communities and philanthropists.

Labor, Workplace, and the Glass Ceiling

Asian Pacific Americans have been part of the U.S. workforce for the past 150 years. Asians built the Transcontinental Railroad, worked in the sugar plantations of Hawai'i, and planted some of the first crops in the fields of California. APA immigrant workers over the years have been forced to work in some of the most difficult jobs with low wages and poor working conditions. While there has been much progress, the situation still exists today. In this chapter, we examine two phenomena: the ongoing existence of APAs, mostly blue-collar immigrants, working under sweatshop-like conditions, and the unions which once excluded them but are now attempting to help APAs; and the glass ceiling in Corporate America which subtly but firmly continues to hurt many APAs' hopes for advancement.

Labor and the Workplace: A Call to Action?

With the lifting of racially restrictive immigration policies in the 1960s, the influx of APA immigrant workers increased dramatically. About 62 percent of APAs are immigrants; 42 percent emigrated to the United States in the last ten years. Forty-five percent of APAs live in inner cities, and many Asian immigrants have settled in urban ethnic enclaves. Asian Pacific American workers are also frequently clustered in racially segregated occupations. Asian workers today are concentrated in service industries such as restaurants, hotels, retail stores and maintenance; health service and health care; in garment, electronics and other light industries; in supermarkets and food production; and in public sector government jobs.

Due to culture and language barriers, many Asian workers are unaware of their basic labor rights. Exploitation and abuse among Asian immigrant workers are common, including minimum wage, overtime, health and safety violations. Many Asian immigrant workers lack health insurance, vacation and sick pay or retirement plans.

Contract labor is pervasive in APA communities, and community groups continue to fight against such abuses as unfair wages and poor working conditions for contract employees.

Due to the myth of the "model minority," certain political leaders and media reports have projected an image of Asians as a model of educational and economic success. This stereotype is a dangerous fallacy that obscures the reality of working and living conditions within many Asian communities. The true picture is somewhat more complicated. Many Asian Americans have attained levels of educational and economic success. Some Asian Americans have family roots in this country dating back many generations, and have succeeded over the years in spite of historic barriers. Among more recent immigrants, some are business

Nearly 11 percent of APA households were under the poverty line in 2000. That's higher than the white population's poverty rate of 9.4 percent, and significantly higher than the white, non-Hispanic poverty rate of 7.5 percent.

people or educated professionals who have come to this country with existing economic resources.

The APA community has the largest gap between rich and poor. The median household income for APAs in 2000 was $48,614, the highest of any racial group, and nearly $9,000 above the national average for all populations. But 10.8 percent of APA households were under the poverty line in 2000, which was approximately a household income of $18,000 for a family of four. That's higher than the white population's poverty rate of 9.4 percent, and significantly higher than the white, non-Hispanic poverty rate of 7.5 percent. Nearly one in five (19.4 percent) of APA non-citizen immigrants was under the poverty line. The vast majority of these low-income households include wage earners that work full-time. Many APA immigrant workers face long hours, low wages, and few if any job benefits. Language and cultural barriers keep APA workers trapped in ethnic ghettoes.

Immigrant workers' dilemma

About half a million APAs—out of a labor force of about 3.9 million—are members of unions. That rate—about 12 percent—is slightly lower than the 14 percent national average of unionized workers in the workforce. The overall rate of unionization among APAs is not much lower than the general populace. But certain segments of Asian workers, especially immigrants, disproportionately lack union representation while facing difficult working conditions.

For APA workers employed by APA bosses, the employer-employee relationship that develops sometimes mirror class relationships that existed in their native countries. Asian immigrant workers may feel in debt to their employer for the opportunity to work. Bonuses for hard work, or special gifts during holidays, are methods used by Asian employers to foster loyalty. In addition, the APA business class has historically dominated community and social functions, maintaining extensive influence over many aspects of workers' lives.

Contract labor is also pervasive in APA communities. This has been used extensively in the garment industry, in janitorial services and building maintenance, and in construction. Through contract labor, payment is handled through piecework or on a project-by-project basis. This exacerbates the problems of a transitory work force, and allows employers to be even less accountable to workers' needs.

The abuse of contract labor was graphically illustrated during a raid on an El Monte garment factory in August 1995. Seventy-two Thai immigrant garment workers were freed from virtual slavery by state and federal law enforcement agencies. For up to seven years, these immigrants had been forced to sew garments for U.S. manufacturers and retailers from morning to night, 6 days a week, and were paid about $1.60 per hour.

APAs and unions go way back

APA workers throughout the years have demonstrated a willingness to organize worker associations and unions to improve their working and living conditions. Chinese workers, protesting unequal pay with the Irish immigrant workers, launched labor strikes during the building of the Transcontinental Railroad. Asian immigrant workers in Hawai'i have a long history of organizing in the sugar plantations and on the docks.

The Filipino farm workers in the Central Valley of California launched the historic Delano Grape Strike, which ultimately led to the birth of the United Farm Workers Union, a merged organization that brought together Filipino and Mexican farm workers. The struggles of the Filipino cannery workers in Alaska protesting segregated, racially discriminatory conditions made national news, and have invited U.S. Supreme Court and

Photo: Jem Lew

About half a million APAs are members of unions, but some Asian workers, especially immigrants, lack union representation while facing difficult working conditions.

Joann Lo: Sweatshop Labor Organizer

"Doing what I do is both mentally and physically fulfilling," says Joann Lo. The young Taiwanese American works for the United Garments Center, a Los Angeles-based nonprofit group helping to fight for the rights of workers, mostly Asian or Latino immigrant women, in clothing sweatshops. As a labor organizer, Lo tries to increase the wages of exploited workers or reduce their hours on the job.

"Several manufacturers pay their workers less than minimum wage," Lo says. "They can commit this crime for two reasons. Firstly, the government doesn't do enough to enforce labor laws. Secondly, most of the workers are illegal immigrants. They don't speak out for fear of being deported."

Even though California workers are comprised of many races, APA labor organizers are a rarity. Lo is bent on breaking the social barriers that exist within the job. Many Latino workers, for instance, are nervous when they speak to her. Often, she says, their boss is Asian American.

"That's why they are amazed when I speak to them in Spanish," Lo chuckles. "But all races come together when fighting for the rights of employees."

Demand for labor organizers is growing. The salary ranges widely: according to the Bureau of Labor Statistics, mid-range wages in 1998 were between $28,000 and $50,200, and $34,300 to $59,000 in California.

"The pay depends on who is being represented," Lo notes. "If the union stands for richer patrons, the pay can be quite high, but if you are representing minimum wage workers, the salary is lower."

There isn't any particular field that must be studied in college, though a bachelor's degree is usually required. Lo studied environmental biology at Yale, but she was also heavily involved in student activism.

Photo: Joann Lo

As labor organizer for the United Garment Workers, Joann Lo's task is to represent workers and improve labor conditions.

Lo has strong, if not cautionary, words of encouragement for anyone who plans on becoming a labor organizer. "I find my job physically and mentally fulfilling, but you have to be committed to social change to be successful as a labor organizer."

—*AsianWeek*

Congressional response. In the 1980s, garment workers organized rallies that brought 20,000 workers onto the streets of New York's Chinatown. Also in the 1980s, Asian American hotel workers in San Francisco played a leading role in significant strikes.

While Asian workers have a proud tradition of organizing resistance against employers, unions over the years have been reluctant to embrace APA workers within their ranks. In years past, American labor unions were at the forefront of advocating for racist immigration laws and exclusionary policies that kept Asians out of unions. Going back to the late 19th century, the "union label" campaign was launched by the cigar maker's unions as a way of distinguishing "union-made" products from "Chinese-made" products.

New beginnings

A critical development in the advancement of APA workers within the U.S. labor movement came with the formation of the Asian Pacific American Labor Alliance (APALA) on May 1, 1992. This historic gathering drew 500 Asian Pacific unionists from around the country, including garment workers from New York, hotel and restaurant workers from Honolulu, longshore workers from Seattle, nurses from San Francisco, and supermarket workers from Los Angeles. This was the first time a national APA labor organization was established within the ranks of the AFL-CIO.

Within the APA community, APALA has emerged as an advocacy voice for worker's rights and civil rights. APALA has forged significant alliances between

Asian American women earn 80 cents for every dollar made by an Asian American man. Census numbers indicate that women of all ethnicities and races on average make 72 cents for every dollar earned by men.

Source: Estimate by the Asian Pacific American Labor Alliance.

In the Bay Area, there are 20,000 garment sweatshop workers, women from Hong Kong and China. In New York, APA women make up the majority of sweatshop workers; in Los Angeles, some 15 percent of sweatshop workers are API.

Source: Sweatshop Watch.

labor and Asian community on issues such as immigrant rights, affirmative action, hate crimes, and economic justice. Within the labor movement, APALA has emerged as an advocacy voice for APA workers, and has advanced greater participation of APA rank and file union members, leaders, and union staff. APALA has also worked hard in the political arena, strengthening political power and participation of APA workers.

Organizing APA workers remains low on the priority list for most unions. So APALA started a program in 1992 to recruit and train APA union organizers. Prior to APALAs founding, there were only a handful of APA union organizers across the country. Since then, dozens of new organizers have been recruited and trained through a program initiated by APALA and the AFL-CIO Organizing Institute. A new generation of APA union organizers have brought into the labor movement tremendous energy and enthusiasm, as well as language skills in over a dozen Asian languages, and cultural knowledge and relationships with many different APA communities.

A significant transformation within the AFL-CIO occurred in 1995. For the first time, there was a contested election for the leadership of the labor movement. John Sweeney of the Service Employees International Union launched an insurgency campaign against the old guard leadership and was elected President.

Along with the change in the presidency, a sizable number of people of color and women were elevated to the leadership slate. A special seat of Executive Vice President was created, and Linda Chavez Thompson was elected, the first woman and first person of color ever to hold a top leadership post in the AFL-CIO. In addition, Sumi Haru from the Screen Actors Guild was elected as the first APA ever to serve on the AFL-CIO Executive Council. This change was a symbolic step forward, and represented the growing role of people of color and women within the labor movement.

The change in leadership within the AFL-CIO, however, was more than symbolic.

The new leadership has taken dramatic steps to change the direction of the American labor movement. This includes allocating greater resources to organizing, restructuring the labor movement to strengthen its effectiveness, improving the public image and profile of unions, and strengthening alliances with its natural allies, such as communities of color, women, gays and lesbians, religious leaders, and progressive academics.

In the last few years, unions have been involved in the struggle for a living wage, linking with religious leaders and community organizations to demand more than a "minimum wage." Although the beneficiaries have generally not been union members, the campaign reflects labor's broader agenda to support economic justice for all.

APALA emerged as one of the first organizations within the AFL-CIO to call for defense of immigrant rights, a repeal of employer sanctions (civil and criminal penalties against employers for hiring undocumented workers), and a new amnesty program. While initially, this position was unpopular within the AFL-CIO, in February 2000, the AFL-CIO Executive Council adopted a new policy on immigration that also called for amnesty for undocumented workers and a repeal of employer sanctions. This new position reflected a major breakthrough for the immigrant rights movement and a huge victory for APALA.

In May 2002, the California State Assembly held the first ever hearing of Asian Pacific Islander Workers. APALA played a major role in recruiting worker testimony for the hearing. What was significant was the large numbers of organizing campaigns involving Asian Pacific Islander workers, an impressive development over the last few years.

A number of key issues emerged during the course of the hearing.

Discrimination: Because many APA workers do not speak fluent English, have limited rights as immigrants, or limited employment opportunities, employers often assume they will not assert their work place rights. Some business and industries target Asian workers for exploitation. Fueling this form of discrimination is the stereotype that Asian workers are particularly hardworking and passive.

Poverty jobs: Many APA immigrant workers are concentrated in industries that pay minimum wage or below, and struggle to support their families. Sweatshop conditions exist in numerous industries and are perpetuated because of barriers due to language, culture and immigration status.

Immigration: Many APA workers face additional challenges due to their immigration status. Undocumented workers are particularly vulnerable, as threats of deportation may keep them

APA Labor Pioneers

Philip Vera Cruz
One of the founders of the United Farmworkers of America and the highest-ranking Filipino within the union.

Karl Yoneda
A Japanese American community activist, socialist, and the leader of the International Longshore and Warehouse Workers Union.

Art Takei
A leader of the United Food and Commercial Workers Union who dedicated years of his life after his retirement to build Asian Pacific American Labor Alliance.

Sue Embrey
A leader of the American Federation of Teachers and a Japanese American community activist who has worked over the years to support education on the Japanese American internment and to demand redress and reparations.

George Wong
Founder of the Asian American Federation of Union Members in San Francisco and longtime leader in the Graphic Communications Union.

Photo: Steve Louie

Philip Vera Cruz organized a successful strike of Filipino grape harvesters in 1965, an event that contributed to the formation of the United Farm Workers Union.

Ah Quan McElrath
A social worker and union supporter in Hawai'i, who has dedicated her life to social justice.

Morgan Gin
A veteran New York community activist and trade unionist from the Newspaper Guild.

from reporting employment violations. Many workers who testified decried the 2002 U.S. Supreme Court ruling in Hoffman Plastics v. NLRB, which determined that even when workers are illegally fired for reasons such as discrimination or union activity, employers do not have to pay back wages if the worker is undocumented.

Indentured work and slavery: Thousands of APA workers are either indentured or incarcerated. From sweatshop workers to high technology workers, many are trapped in exploitative or abusive work situations. The case of the Thai garment workers in El Monte received national publicity, but the problems persist. Many cases go unreported because workers who manage to escape or report violations to law enforcement face deportation. Another major area of indentured work and slavery exists in the sex industry, of which Asian immigrant women constitute a high percentage of victims in the United States.

Right to organize: More and more Asian American workers are unionizing because they want to have a voice at work. Companies often hire professional "union-busters" and seek legal and illegal ways to prevent workers from exercising their right to organize. Harassment and intimidation of pro-union workers are common. In one-third of union organizing campaigns, workers are illegally fired for their union activity. Some companies also drag out the legal process for years, denying workers their basic democratic right to form and join unions. As an example, 150 workers at the *Chinese Daily News* newspaper in Los Angeles voted in March 2001 to join the union. In spite of this, over a year after the election was held, management still refuses to bargain in good faith and refuses to sign a union contract. Instead, they have retained the services of an anti-union consultant who has systematically harassed and intimidated pro-union workers.

A new chapter of APA labor history is being written. Asian Pacific American workers throughout history have demonstrated a commitment to form and join labor unions. Only recently, however, has the American labor movement begun to open its doors to APA workers. Today there are unprecedented opportunities to organize APA workers, to forge new alliances between unions and the APA community, and to build a new labor movement that represents the interests of workers of all colors.

—*Kent Wong*

Nearly one in five non-citizen APA immigrants were under the poverty line.

Glass Ceiling: a Wake-Up Call for APAs?

Qualified Asian Americans continue to experience the dissatisfaction of being overlooked for upper management positions because of the artificial barriers of the "glass ceiling."

In the early 1990s, before California voted to end affirmative action, then-Governor Pete Wilson and University of California Regent Ward Connerly argued that Asian Americans were being "hurt" by race-based affirmative action policies that gave preferential treatment to African Americans and Latinos. Whether APAs could personally benefit from the ban (being then promoted simultaneously by Proposition 209 and the UC Regent's SP-1 Resolution) is debatable: there is a high variability in terms of which programs, and which Asians, are included in affirmative action programs. One study by William Kidder that appeared in the *Asian Law Journal* in 2000, however, has clearly documented how in terms of applicants to UC Law Schools, whites were the main beneficiaries of such a ban on race-based affirmative action. Relatively little known is the fact that the majority of Asian Americans who went to the polls in 1996 opposed the controversial ballot measure, as reported by the *Los Angeles Times*.

In 2002, Connerly sponsored the Racial Privacy Initiative, with the intention of preventing the state from gathering racial data in areas related to public education, public health, and hiring and contracting in the workplace. Again, the publicly stated reason is that race-conscious practices thwart the realization of a color-blind society. However, in a remarkable parallel to their response to Prop. 209, most Asian Americans in a field poll are opposed to this ballot initiative as well, the *Sacramento Bee* reported.

Discrimination during the 1990s
While Connerly and his backers argue that a color-blind society can best be achieved by ignoring race, there was abundant evidence in the early 1990s that racial discrimination was not only alive and well but that a corporate culture of racial discrimination was prevalent. In 1994, the Denny's restaurant chain agreed to pay $54.4 million to settle federal class-action lawsuits filed in California and Maryland by black customers who had been unfairly denied service and in other ways shown that preferential treatment was reserved for whites. The settlement constituted the largest ever since the Public Accommodations Act was passed in 1964, forbidding separate facilities, seating, etc. for whites and non-whites.

Also in 1994, six Texaco employees brought a discrimination suit against their employer on behalf of themselves and at least 1,500 other African American employees, claiming they had been denied promotions because of their race. Settled in March 1997 for $176.1 million, the case is the largest settlement of a racial discrimination suit in U.S. history. Equally significant is that it is an exceptional case of disclosure. Secretly tape-recorded discussions indicated racially disparaging remarks and plans to shred documents linked to the suit, the tip of an iceberg that included secret lists of which employees could become senior managers.

It is therefore under exceptional rather than routine conditions that racial bias "behind closed doors" is exposed. It was, in fact, such backstage discrimination *in the workplace* that prompted the first efforts at affirmative action. Thus, in 1965 it became a government-mandated policy that not only firms but universities and all other organizations holding government contracts must review their workforce composition to ensure that it reasonably drew upon the available pool of qualified minorities. Because documenting such problems was beyond the reach of employees, greater accountability was imposed on management, and the keeping of workforce statistics by race was a first step in this direction.

Discriminated against for your accent? It's not legal

M. Chow (full name withheld for privacy reasons) had worked at a Bay Area marketing research firm for two years, receiving accolades and raises for her job performance. But when a new supervisor began to subject her to daily "tutorials" to correct her pronunciation, Chow was baffled.

"Every day, he asked me to sit with him for half an hour to practice reading the questionnaire," Chow recalled. "It was stressful because he monitored me every day, telling me that I did something wrong here, didn't say certain words right."

Eventually, he told Chow, hired as a bilingual English and Cantonese interviewer, that because "she didn't speak English so well," she should work only one hour a day and focus only on Cantonese interviewing assignments.

Chow quit the company but later filed a complaint with the Equal Employment Opportunity Commission with the help of the American Civil Liberties Union.

"So long as she could be understood, there were no communication problems, she could ask questions and get information for her survey, she was qualified," said Ed Chen, the director of the ACLU's Language Rights Project and Chow's lawyer. "We saw no documentation that anyone ever had difficulty understanding her. Her supervisor wasn't pleased with her enunciation, her tone, sometimes the choppiness of her pace, as he described it."

The EEOC is handling a growing number of accent discrimination cases as the population itself diversifies. One in three California workers speaks a foreign language at home; the national ratio is one in fourteen, according to U.S. Census figures. More than one quarter of residents of Asian descent speak limited English, according to the Census.

Employers generally are prohibited from discriminating on the basis of accent, Chen said, adding that workers cannot be fired simply because an employer or customer does not like the sound of an accent.

"Employers cannot rely upon prejudices of customers," Chen explained. Just as an employer cannot hire only men just because clients want it to, he said, "if customers prefer to deal with someone with no accent, simply because of those preferences, you can't give into that either."

Chow, who speaks with a discernible but understandable accent, eventually settled with the company in court in 1999 for $55,000 in lost wages and damages.

"Employers should be on notice," said Chen. "An employer may not harass or terminate an employee solely because the employee speaks with an accent or uses a foreign language at work. Those that do are at risk of having to pay for their actions."

—*AsianWeek*

Subtle barriers

Racial slurs are only the most blatant form of bias. Other forms of bias are more subtle and invidious, not always intentional nor even motivated by racial antipathy. Although Title VII of the 1964 Civil Rights Act explicitly prohibits discrimination based on race, color, religion, sex and national origin, it has its greatest efficacy in cases where discrimination can be narrowly construed as intentional discrimination, thus excluding discriminatory practices or policies which are on the surface race-neutral. The Federal Glass Ceiling Commission brought renewed attention to structural or institutional forms of discrimination when it identified artificial barriers keeping minorities and women out of senior-level management positions in 1995.

As the metaphor suggests, a glass ceiling is an invisible barrier, one generally not seen, let alone experienced, until one runs right into it. Second, the barrier is defined as an artificial one, i.e., not due fundamentally to a lack of qualifications. Third, it is a barrier into management. Thus, the U.S. Department of Labor stated in 1991 that "the glass ceiling is most clearly defined as those artificial barriers based on attitudinal or organizational bias that prevent qualified individuals from advancing upward in their organization into management level positions." Although the phenomenon circulated into popular consciousness when women encountered such barriers in the corporate world, there is evidence that Asian American professionals experienced such career blocks as early as the 1920s.

Asian Americans are more highly educated than all other racial groups, including white males. They already have a disproportionate share of professional workers. And they are projected to make up an increasing percentage of the total labor force in the next few decades. Yet, numerous studies point to recurring patterns of

Exit Poll of California Voters on Proposition 209 Banning Affirmative Action

	Yes	No
White	63%	37%
Black	26%	74%
Latino	24%	76%
Asian	39%	61%

Source: *Los Angeles Times*, November 7, 1996

Executives, Managers, and Administrators in Major U.S. Industries, by Ethnicity

	HISPANIC		ASIAN*		BLACK		WHITE	
	Male	Female	Male	Female	Male	Female	Male	Female
Business services	5.2%	3.2%	1.7%	1.2%	3.5%	0.5%	51.6%	32.8%
Finance	3.4%	5.0%	1.8%	2.6%	2.6%	2.6%	44.8%	37.6%
Communications	6.1%	3.4%	1.7%	0.3%	2.4%	1.0%	58.4%	25.6%
Insurance	2.0%	4.2%	0.5%	1.7%	3.2%	3.0%	44.0%	40.7%
Retail trade	2.8%	2.0%	3.5%	1.7%	2.3%	2.6%	41.7%	39.1%
Utilities	3.1%	0.7%	0.0%	0.8%	3.1%	0.8%	71.9%	17.2%
Transportation	6.1%	3.4%	1.7%	0.3%	2.4%	1.0%	58.4%	25.6%
Wholesale trade	2.7%	2.1%	2.4%	1.8%	1.2%	0.3%	53.4%	36.2%

*Includes Pacific Islanders.

Source: Chinese for Affirmative Action, 1995

underemployment, blocked mobility, and overall lower returns on their education than other groups. A college degree for an Asian American offers seven times less protection from poverty than it does for whites. As managers, Asian Americans are underrepresented in a number of occupational sectors, including private employment, both public and private institutions of higher education, and all levels of government.

Public sector no haven

In the San Francisco city government, Asian Americans were found clustered in "dead-end technical positions," such as finance or operations. The Department of Public Works epitomized the "ghettoization of Asian American professionals," according to studies by Chinese for Affirmative Action in 1989 and 1992, and the entire city's civil service was labeled a "giant white-collar sweatshop"—exploiting Asian expertise but limiting advancement. Since education and work experience are the two most important criteria for both hiring and promotion in federal employment, it is surprising that complaints focused on being passed over by those with far less education, training, and years of experience. In a 1993 speech in front of the Chinese American Librarians Association, Joy Cherian said:

"If it is not the glass ceiling then I don't know what it is when an Asian American with extensive supervisory experience, with two masters degrees, with highly successful performance in the same position on an acting basis, is denied a permanent position as Division Chief at the GS-14 level in a federal government agency by the same selecting official who had rated him highly successful. That Asian American was passed over in favor of a white male with a high school education and little managerial experience . . . . The evidence showed that the same selecting official had earlier passed over another Asian American with almost identical qualifications, in favor of . . . another white male with a high school education."

At XYZ Aerospace, the government research site where I conducted my own study, I learned that the agency had documented a glass ceiling since the early 1970s, and that as late as 1997 few if any "Asian American Pacific Islanders" were in senior management. Employees identified the "old boy network" as a major reason for preferential treatment towards less qualified white males. Inferences about mobility based on educational attainment alone therefore can be misleading.

Discrimination in hi-tech

Although far more Asian Americans have been attracted to careers in industry than in government, this employment sector has also been the site of many glass ceiling complaints. In the Silicon Valley, white males are concentrated at the upper end of the occupational scale. When professional status is controlled for, white men were two times more likely than Asian males to be officials or managers. Dissatisfaction was greatest in the electronics industry, where despite stereotypes as mere "technical grunts" and "hi-tech coolies," 75 percent of Asians expressed an interest in managerial work, according to a 1993 study by Asian Americans for Community Involvement. The disparity with whites could also not be explained by recency of arrival, poor English language abilities, differences in cultural assimilation, work experience, formal business training, or greater occupational concentration in undesirable fields or sectors of the economy, according to various studies.

The corporate culture and the informal old boy network constitute two major artificial barriers to advancement. Although "communication skills" or "leadership skills" are on the surface neutral criteria or standards, American corporations following the idea of the "one best model" have generally organized themselves along the lines of a top-down, "command-and-control model," leaving little room for other forms of leadership. Ironically, though many Asian Americans are disinclined toward self-promotion, not being part of the old boy network means that to succeed they have to actually be even more aggressive than white males, because they lack the mentorship and sponsorship of higher-ups who can facilitate their transition into critical assignments that will gain them the wider visibility necessary for further advancement.

In sum, while the Texaco suit exposed what Barbara Reskin terms "pervasive outgroup antipathy" towards blacks, APAs have experienced the glass ceil-

ing in terms of "pervasive ingroup favoritism," cognitive biases and preferences that may be "nonconscious" rather than intentional. In either case, the discriminatory effects are the same: these daily "micro-acts of discrimination" consistently, repeatedly, and cumulatively disadvantage certain groups over others. An Asian American manager at XYZ noted a negative impact on the organization as well:

"Promotion is not on merit but through social circles ... The criterion is not ability but friendship. I don't think people are out to "get" Asians. I just think that Asians aren't in these social circles. You can quote me on that ... It's my perception that what had happened in the old days was that the old white boy network reserved the managerial jobs for themselves. That was their preserve, they didn't want to let any minorities in."

In his immediate work sphere, he observed that his supervisor promoted only a small coterie of individuals: "all his white male friends ... got to be deputy directors, directors, branch chiefs, division chiefs, despite some of them being very, very poor administrators and very poor researchers."

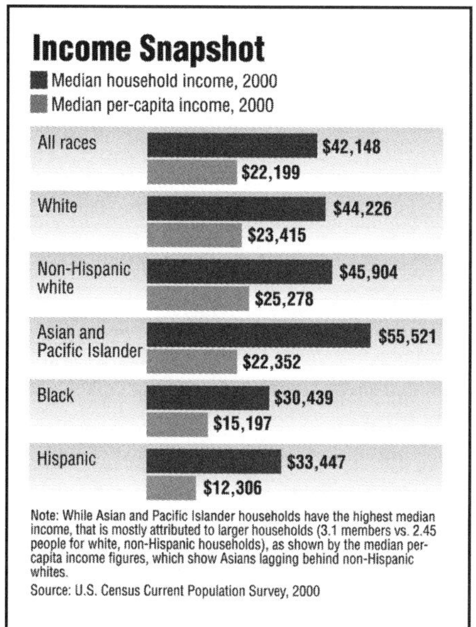

Potential for mobilization

Exclusionary rationales cloaked in the language of merit and universalistic criteria have often been merely pretexts for exclusion, arbitrary claims intended to perpetuate the existing structure of privilege. When given the opportunity, blacks admitted to elite schools through affirmative action have been far more civically minded or socially active than their former white classmates, assuming leadership "in virtually every type of civic endeavor," according to *The Shape of the River*, a 1998 book by two former Ivy League university presidents, William Bowen and Derek Bok. Because their study did not include APAs, we do not know what happened to these graduates. We do know that those APAs who sit on corporate boards as directors, or serve as appointed government officials and military leaders, have largely attended elite schools and their politics tends to be conservative, consistent with their origins in wealthy, high-status families. If there is to be a transformation of APA consciousness, it will most likely come from other segments of the APA population, including those professionals who have faced a glass ceiling.

The potential for mobilizing around glass ceiling issues has never been greater. As professionals, Asian Americans form a highly skilled and important segment of the workforce. They are also a critical mass. The only question is whether they respond to blocked mobility as artificial barriers—as an injustice that is deeply felt and widely shared—or as individual deficits, requiring further investments in education or training. In either case, they should not expect much, if anything, from Secretary of Labor Elaine Chao. Although she concentrated on advancing the hi-tech job sector as president of the United Way, her service was in the interests of big business, not workers. In her present job as Secretary of Labor, she has been unsympathetic to glass ceiling issues, affirmative action and the use of industry funds for training workers, and has been chided for

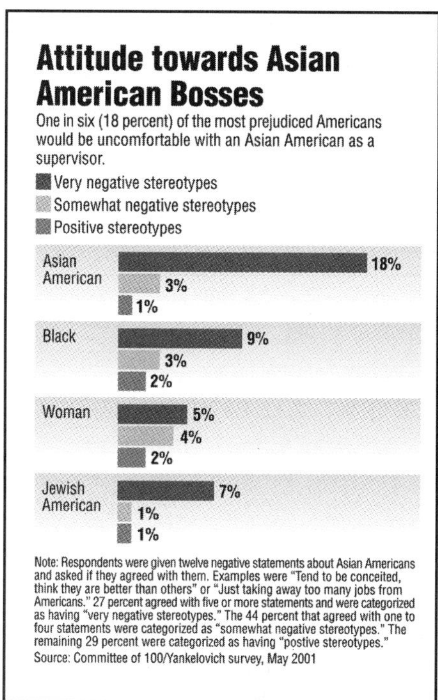

failing to address sweatshop conditions in garment factories swiftly.

Echoing supporters of Prop. 209 in California, Chao has said that Asian Americans are being "tremendously damaged by affirmative action." This attitude towards affirmative action is hypocritical: prior to becoming Secretary of Labor, Chao had no experience or expertise in labor. Since Chao serves an administration that has sought to drastically reduce federal oversight of domestic economic affairs, her policies have been basically pro-business, specifically pro-big business. We should not be surprised that her response to corporate corruption in the securities industry has been to endorse President Bush's emphasis on voluntary, "personal responsibility" and less aggressive forms of accounting reform.

Shattering the ceiling

Asian Pacific Americans seeking to break through the glass ceiling may try pressing Chao on this issue. Despite her explicitly anti-affirmative action stance, she is not averse to courting the vote of certain constituencies. Thus, she announced in early 2002 an

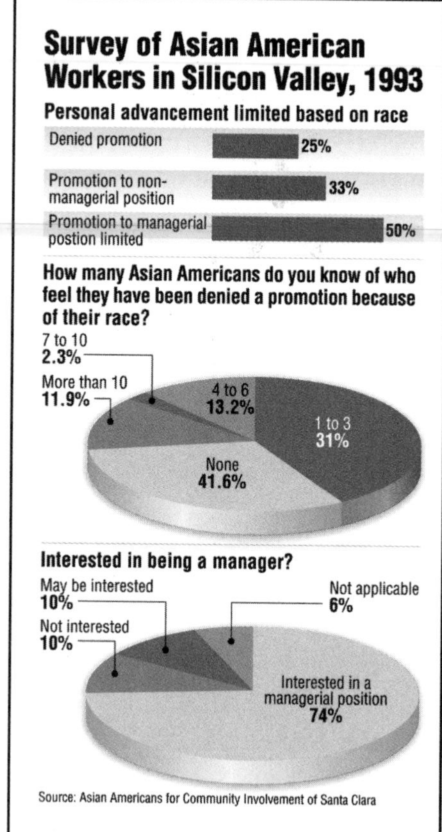

initiative to increase the number of Hispanics who are senior federal executives: "You have my commitment that we can and will do better. The community is indeed underrepresented, but I promise we will work hard to change that. We are committed to realizing Hispanics' potential." Such an initiative falls short of an overarching policy of affirmative action, and any similar stance towards APA concerns would depend on how much political clout APAs can bring.

At another level, breaking through the glass ceiling will also mean grappling with two major currents associated with globalization—the broadening of requirements for senior executives, and the way certain segments of the professional workforce are being turned into a new *proletarian* class—white-collar factory workers with little hope for advancement. Strategic leadership, in the former instance, extends beyond one's commitment to a specific agency or profession. Communication skills are becoming paramount, and they now require "the ability to explain, advocate and express facts and ideas in a convincing manner, and negotiate with individuals and groups internally and externally ... the ability to develop an expansive professional network with other organizations, and to identify the internal and external politics that impact the work of the organization," said the U.S. Office of Personnel Management in 1998.

This orientation is reinforced by mergers and acquisitions, which involve shepherding employees through organizational upheavals and the reshuffling of personnel. Even if professionals were to opt out of executive careers because of these more demanding expectations, professional careers themselves are more uncertain than ever in a turbulent environment where work cultures are continually being dismantled and restructured.

Reliance on foreign workers has added another dimension to the problem. The United States has sought to satisfy its demand for highly skilled workers from abroad. Between 1972 and 1988, as many as 200,000 Asians in science-based professions entered the United States from India, South Korea, the Philippines and China, according to a 1992 study by Ong, Cheng, and Evans. The 1990 Immigration Act doubled work visas from 54,000 to 120,000, with 80,000 for high-level professionals and their families. That same year, Congress also established the H-1B visa, a temporary visa for immigrants with just a bachelor's degree or equivalent. The original H-1B quota was 65,000 but that was increased to almost 200,000 by 2000, according to a 2001 study by Matloff.

The implications of this can be seen in computer science and computer engineering, where the industry's repeated calls for increases in the quota of foreign workers have been linked to underemployment. Specifically, software employers have refused to retrain U.S. workers for the specific skills they require, preferring to avail themselves of cheap foreign labor. Although industry lobbyists have responded defensively by arguing that most H-1Bs possess U.S. Ph.D.s, this is not the case among computer science Ph.D.s, who receive 40 percent of these degrees but are only a small portion of the H-1B population. The consequence of this selectivity has been short-lived careers for domestic programmers and de facto "indentured servitude" for foreign workers. Asian Pacific Americans fall into both these categories. Globalization thus creates a depressing effect on professional salaries that invites expanding the classic meaning of glass ceiling to include new forms of artificial barriers as well as creating new forms of potentially serious political mobilization.

—Deborah J. Woo

The "Healthy Minority?"

Emerging trends are shattering the stereotype of Asian Americans as the "healthy minority." For example, Asian American women are more likely to die of cancer that any other racial and ethnic group in the country. Asian Americans and Pacific Islanders not only experience a wide variety of health problems, but also barriers to care. This chapter will cover the key health issues facing the APA community in the 21st century, as well as the challenges and barriers facing APAs in receiving quality health care.

Health Status

Cardiovascular disease

Among Asian American men, cardiovascular disease—diseases of the heart and stroke—is the number one cause of death, followed by cancer. Among Asian American women, cancer is the number one cause of death, followed by heart disease and stroke. Among Asian Americans, stroke is the leading case of death among Chinese, Filipinos and Japanese. Although stroke is the leading cause of death for many Asian American subgroups, there is a lack of information and data about risk factors in these subgroups and additional research is needed. Moreover, even though cardiovascular disease represents one of the major causes of death for Asian Americans, there are disparities that persist among Asian Americans. This is especially true among limited English speakers, who may have less access to information on the importance of preventative screenings and on the medical advances made against cardiovascular disease.

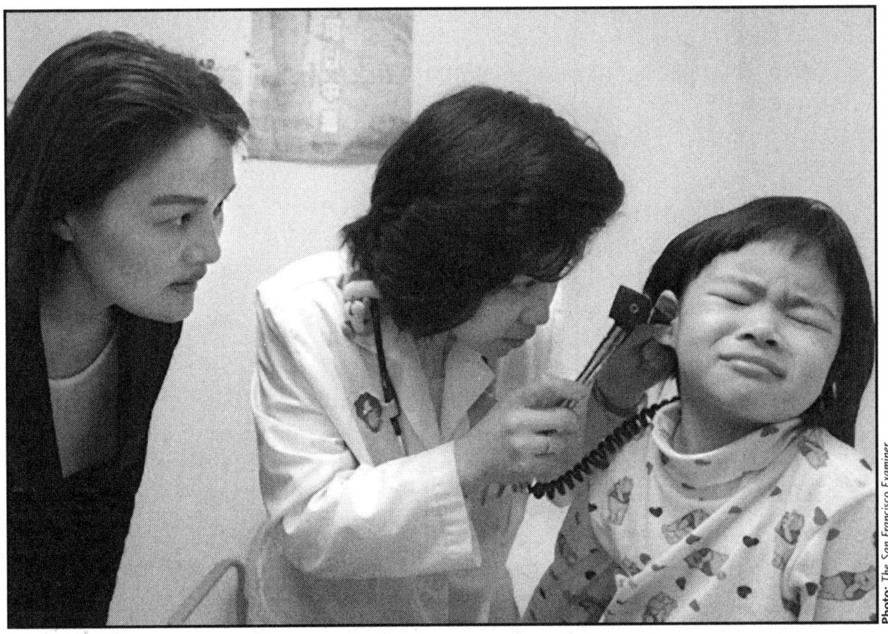

Photo: *The San Francisco Examiner*

Many APAs fail to get the regular checkups that are needed for good long-term health. One major reason: 30 percent of Asian immigrants lack health insurance, with Koreans and Southeast Asians the most likely to be uninsured.

For Asian Indians, Filipinos, Japanese, Chinese, and Korean, heart disease caused over 23 percent of all deaths. The known risk factors for heart disease include high blood cholesterol, high blood pressure, diabetes, physical inactivity, nutrition, tobacco use and exposure. High cholesterol increases an individual's risk for coronary heart disease. Studies on serum cholesterol levels of Asian Americans are limited. Moreover, only a limited number of studies have included cholesterol levels of Asian Americans. The limited studies that do exist show that Asian Americans do not

Although Asian Americans represent four percent of the population, they account for over half of the 1.3 million chronic hepatitis B cases in the United States.

Source: *www.asianlivercenter.org*

regularly get blood cholesterol exams. For instance, a 1993 study showed tha only 44 percent of APAs had had their blood cholesterol level examined within the past two years, compared with 54 percent of the total population.

High blood pressure is also a risk factor for both heart disease and stroke. High blood pressure, or hypertension, is defined as condition in which the systolic blood pressure is equal to or exceeds 140 mmHG, or the diastolic blood pressure is equal to or more than 90 mmHG. A high intake of salt and sodium can lead to increases in blood pressure. Like cholesterol screenings, there is a lack of information in the Asian American community on the importance of blood pressure screenings. In a study of Cambodian, Laotian and Vietnamese immigrants, 94 percent had no knowledge of the importance of blood pressure screenings and 85 percent did not know how to prevent heart disease.

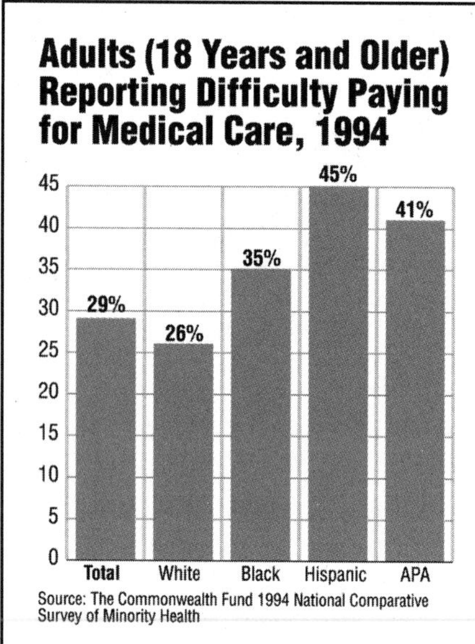

Source: The Commonwealth Fund 1994 National Comparative Survey of Minority Health

In addition to the above-mentioned risk factors, cigarette smoking is also a known risk factor for cardiovascular disease. Asian American men between the ages of 22 and 44 have the highest smoking rate of any demographic group. A lack of physical activity also contributes to the development of cardiovascular disease. Overall, Asian Americans engage in less physical activity than the general population. Among Vietnamese Americans in California, 40 percent of Vietnamese males and 50 percent of Vietnamese females were not exercising, compared to 24 percent of men and 28 percent of women in the general population. A 1997 Center for Disease Control and Prevention (CDC) study of Korean Americans in Northern California found that 31 percent of the respondents did not exercise, compared to 21 percent of the total California population.

Cancer

There is a stereotype that Asian Americans do not get cancer because their diets are soy-based and thus low in red meats. The truth is that Asian Americans do get cancer. Between 1980 and 1993, Asian Americans experienced the highest increase in cancer deaths for all racial and ethnic groups. The cancer death rate for Asian American and Pacific Islander women increased by 240 percent, and the rate for Asian American and Pacific Islander men increased by 290 percent, according to National Center for Health statistics.

Asian Americans are not a homogenous group and certain subgroups have different group rates. Among Asian American women, there is an alarming increase in the overall cancer mortality rate. More troubling is that Asian American women are the least likely racial and ethnic group to get screened for cancer. According to the most recent reports from the American Cancer Society (ACS), National Cancer Institute (NCI), and the CDC, overall cancer incidence rates have been declining for all racial and ethnic groups—with the notable exception of Asian American and Pacific Islander women. And while overall cancer death rates declined by an average of about 0.7 percent per year between 1990 and 1995, the only group dying more often from cancer was Asian and Pacific Islander women. For Asian American and Pacific Islander women, cancer has been the leading cause of death for as long as these statistics have been collected.

There is a myth inside and outside the Asian American communities that breast and cervical cancers affect white women only. However, as Asian Americans acculturate to the United States, their risk for eventually getting breast cancer equals that of white women. Further, Asian American women, as compared to white women, are diagnosed at more advanced stages of breast cancer. Japanese, Vietnamese, Filipino and Korean women are all diagnosed with cervical cancer at later stages than white women. One big reason: Asian American women have the lowest screening rates for pap smears and mammogram examinations. Yet early detection in these cancers is crucial for women, because detection

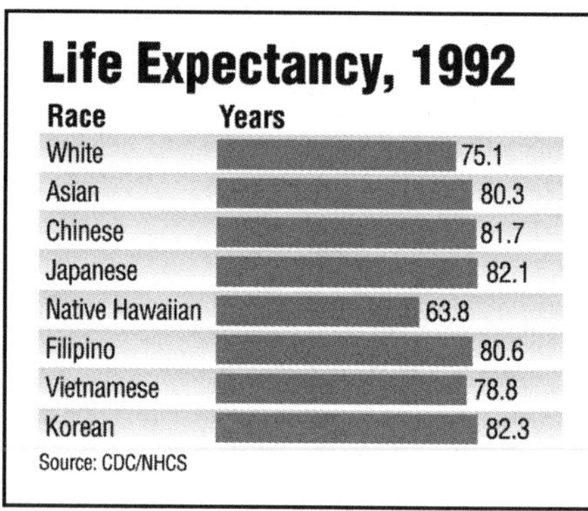

Source: CDC/NHCS

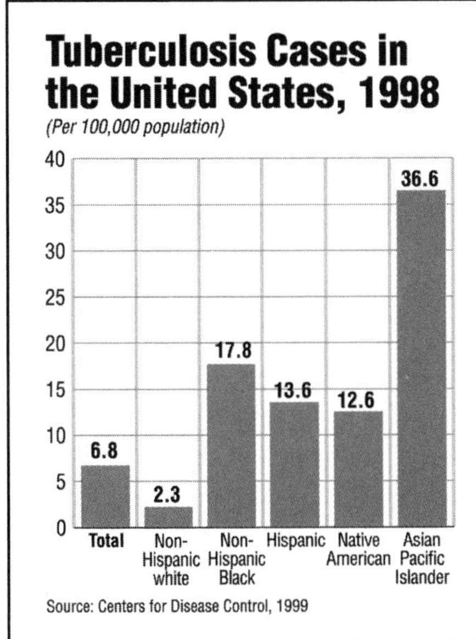

at a later stage may mean higher mortality and lower survival rates. 30 percent of all Asian American women over the age of 40 have never had a mammogram, according to a 2000 study, while only 21 percent of all Asian American women have had a pap smear. The result? Vietnamese American women have the highest cervical cancer rates of any ethnic group in the United States—43 cases per 100,000, versus 8.7 cases per 100,000 in the general population, according to the National Cancer Institute, as reported in *AsianWeek*. Cultural factors, poverty, and insufficient health insurance play a part in whether Asian American women obtain pap smears and mammographic examinations. Asian American women with better educations and English fluency are more likely to get breast cancer screening tests than their less educated or less English-fluent peers.

Together, Asian Americans also experience the highest rates of liver and stomach cancer of any racial and ethnic group in the United States. Korean American men experience the highest rate of stomach cancer of all racial and ethnic groups, and a five-fold increased rate of stomach cancer compared to white American men. A risk factor associated with the development of stomach cancer includes the consumption of foods that are preserved by drying, smoking, salting, or pickling, as is common in many Asian cuisines. Recent studies also indicate that a type of bacteria, Helicobacter pylori, which plays a role in stomach inflammation and ulcers may also be an important risk factor for this cancer.

Liver cancer strikes Asian Americans more than any other racial and ethnic group in the United States, and most often it strikes Asian American men. Vietnamese American men have the highest rates of liver cancer for all racial and ethnic groups. The incidence of liver cancer in Chinese, Filipino, Japanese, Korean, and Vietnamese American populations are 1.7 to 11.3 times higher than rates among white Americans. About two-thirds of liver cancers are hepatocellular carcinomas (HCC), which are associated with hepatitis B and hepatitis C viral infections and cirrhosis. Although Asian Americans represent four percent of the population, they account for over half of the 1.3 million chronic hepatitis B cases in the United States.

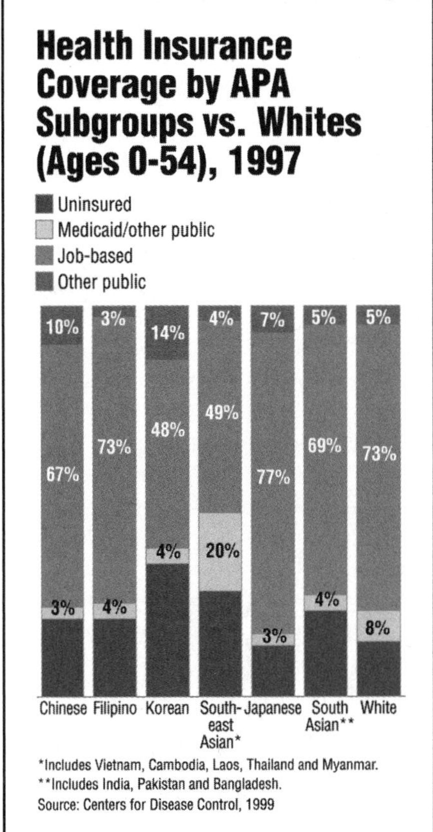

Transmission of the hepatitis B virus among Asian Americans is most often transmitted from mother to infant. Although the hepatitis B vaccination, can provide life-long immunity, Asian American children in the United States were found to have low vaccination rates despite national vaccination guidelines and availability.

Access to health care

Despite these troubling trends in health status among Asian Americans, a more significant problem is that many Asian Americans do not have access to health care and health insurance. One in five Asian Americans lack health insurance. Compared with whites, Asian Americans are more likely to be uninsured. Koreans, followed by Southeast Asians, have the lowest rates of health insurance coverage. Koreans lack job-based coverage because many are self-

Most Commonly Diagnosed Cancers among Asian American Women, 1988-1992

Rank	Chinese	Filipino	Japanese	Korean	Vietnamese
1	Breast	Breast	Breast	Breast	Cervix/Uteri
2	Colon/Rectum	Colon/Rectum	Colon/Rectum	Colon/Rectum	Breast
3	Lung/Bronchus	Lung/Bronchus	Stomach	Stomach	Lung/Bronchus
4	Corpus Uteri	Thyroid	Lung/Bronchus	Lung/Bronchus	Colon/Rectum
5	Ovary	Corpus Uteri	Corpus Uteri	Cervix/Uteri	Stomach

Source: Miller et al., 1996

Caring Overseas: Overview of Filipino Nurse Immigration

In the late twentieth century, the Filipino nurse has become a familiar face in hospitals and clinics worldwide. The World Health Organization estimates that the Philippines has exported 250,000 nurses to alleviate critical shortages in countries in North America, Europe, and the Middle East. The United States has always been the leading destination.

Although this migration is often mistaken for a contemporary phenomenon, its origins go back to the U.S. colonial presence in the Philippines in the early twentieth century. During this period, the U.S. colonial government established Americanized hospital schools of nursing that trained primarily young Filipino women. This training, which included the study of English, prepared Filipino nurses to practice nursing in the United States. The U.S. colonial government also established the *pensionado* program, which enabled an elite group of Filipino nurses to study abroad at U.S. universities and colleges. Although most of these nurses returned to the Philippines to assume leadership positions in U.S.-established hospitals, a few remained in the United States.

History

While these colonial education programs facilitated the first wave of Filipino nurse migration to the United States, the Filipino nurses who participated in them were few in number. In the 1950s and 1960s, U.S. educational exchange programs such as the Exchange Visitor Program (EVP) ushered in the first mass migration of Filipino nurses to the United States. Although the program included exchanges between the United States and many countries and involved persons of various occupational backgrounds, by the late 1960s, the exchange of Filipino nurses dominated the program. Between 1956 and 1969, over 11,000 Filipino nurses participated in the program. Given the colonial interaction between the United States and the Philippines and their Americanized professional training, many Filipino nurses were eager to visit and further their education in the United States. Furthermore, critical nursing shortages after World War II motivated U.S. hospital administrators to search for labor overseas and to use the exchange program as a way to facilitate the migration of foreign-trained nurses.

Filipino exchange-nurses were supposed to return to the Philippines after two years, but many of them attempted to avoid going back. Despite reported abuses of the EVP by some U.S. hospital administrators—for example, assigning them work as registered nurses while paying them minimal exchange stipends—low wages and poor working conditions in the Philippines contributed to the growing desire of Filipino nurse migrants to remain in the United States. In 1965, watershed U.S. immigration legislation facilitated the permanent residence of Fiipino nurses by favoring the immigration of professionals with needed skills. By the late 1960s, the Philippines was sending more nurses to the United States than any other country, ending decades of numerical domination by European and North American countries. Paul Ong and Tania Azores estimated that at least twenty-five thousand Filipino nurses migrated to the United States between 1966 and 1985.

Today

Filipino nurses continue to provide a critical source of labor for large metropolitan and public hospitals, primarily in the states of New York, New Jersey, California, Texas, and Massachusetts. In New York City, Filipinos comprise eighteen percent of the registered nurse staff in the city's hospitals. There are also many Filipino nurses in Midwestern urban areas, such as Chicago. Wages can be good, compared to the Philippines. *Filipinas* magazine recently reported that the average nurse's wage in California is $35 per hour, compared with an average monthly salary of $200 to $300 in the Philippines.

Despite the important role that Filipino nurses have played in alleviating critical U.S. nursing shortages, they have also encountered prejudice and discrimination in multiple forms. Some Filipino nurses have criticized their hospital nursing supervisors for assigning better working conditions to white American nurses, at Filipino nurses' expense. Some have charged that they have been paid begin-

employed and do not opt to buy health insurance. Altogether, about 30 percent of Asian immigrants are uninsured. The higher rates of uninsurance in these groups are attributed to their lower rates of job insurance rates.

Being uninsured plays a major role in the community's inability to access health care services. However, changing federal and state Medicaid policies for immigrants have also prevented access for low-income Asian immigrants. Because of federal welfare reform, the changes in eligibility and the later clarifications have caused confusion: low-income Asian legal immigrants may not use public-funded health services because of fears of deportation and concerns about jeopardizing their immigration status. These fears become powerful deterrents to the use of health services. Moreover, because of changing policies, they may be unclear as to whether they qualify. Even though Asians have higher rates of poverty than whites, the same fears over immigration status and deportation have translated into fewer low-income Asian Americans getting Medicaid. For example, only 13 percent of low-income Chinese have Medicaid coverage compared to 24 percent of low-income whites.

Several studies have documented that the lack of health insurance hurts access to health care. As a result, delays in seeking health care because of uninsurance have

One in five medical school graduates today is Asian Pacific American. More than four in ten students at the five medical schools in the University of California system are Asian Pacific American.

Source: Association of American Medical Colleges, UC San Francisco newsletter

ning nurses' salaries despite their substantial professional nursing experience in the Philippines. Others have claimed that U.S. nurse licensure examinations are culturally biased and that English-only policies at hospital workplaces unfairly target Filipino nurses.

Historically, Filipino nurses have refused to be victims of prejudice and discrimination. Beginning in the 1970s, they organized three Filipino American nurse organizations—the Philippine Nurses Association of America, the National Alliance for Fair Licensure of Foreign Nurse Graduates, and the Foreign Nurse Defense Fund—to ameliorate their working conditions. In the late 1970s, after being wrongly accused of conspiracy, poisoning, and murder at the Veterans' Administration Hospital in Ann Arbor, Michigan, Filipina Narciso worked on her defense, sometimes up to twelve hours a day, in her basement. In the late 1980s, Aida Dimaranan charged Pomona Valley Hospital of California with work discrimination that violated Title VII of the 1964 Civil Rights Act and received back pay and fringe benefits after her challenge of a no-Tagalog policy at the hospital led to a demotion.

A century of Filipino nurse migration to the United States has made the Filipino nurse seemingly ubiquitous in U.S. hospitals. Despite legislative attempts to curtail this phenomenon such as the 1989 Immigration Nursing Relief Act—which made it more difficult for U.S. hospitals to recruit Filipino and other foreign nurses—the aggressive recruitment of Filipino nurses overseas continues unabated in the new millennium. Previously conceptualized as more of an East and West Coast phenomenon, the recruitment of Filipino nurses in the first years of the twenty-first century has penetrated the heartland of America. In 1999, several Twin Cities health organizations started nurse recruiting efforts in the Philippines to ease severe nursing shortages, spending five to ten thousand dollars to relocate each new nurse. Despite some immigration process delays, the first of these Filipino nurses arrived in May 2002.

A century of the incorporation of Filipino nurse migrants has also produced experienced Filipino American nurse leadership for the new millennium. For example, Lolita Compas is president-elect of the New York State Nurses Association. Compas immigrated to the United States in 1969 and served as president of the Philippine Nurses Association of America from 1998 to 2000.

In the new millennium, the global dimension of Filipino nurse migration overseas has made the United States similar to other developed countries, like Great Britain and Norway, which also recruit Filipino nurses to alleviate their nursing shortages. Philippine government officials contribute to this phenomenon by promoting a nursing labor force (among other occupations) for export. With overseas Filipino workers sending $6.2 billion back to the Philippines in 2001 and with multiple countries vying for Filipino nurse recruits, one can expect Filipino nurses to continue to care for overseas populations in the twenty-first century.

—*Catherine Ceniza Choy*

major health implications for immigrant communities. Cancer, heart disease and diabetes are health conditions that can get worse if diagnosis is delayed and thereby reduces effective treatment and management. Access barriers reduce the use of preventative services. Moreover, several studies have documented that Asian immigrants without insurance were more likely to forego mainstream health care services and instead utilize traditional Asian medicine. Insured immigrants were more likely to use mainstream health services, especially preventative care like cancer screenings.

Conclusion

Still, there are some positive notes for Asian Americans health-wise. For one, Asian American babies are more likely to be born of normal birth weight. The number of Asian Americans infected with HIV are also relatively low compared to the rest of the population.

There are also a growing number of organizations and individuals are becoming involved to address health disparities among racial and ethnic groups in the United States. A key health advocate for the Asian American community in Washington D.C. and in California is the Asian Pacific Islander American Health Forum (APIAHF). Based in San Francisco, the mission of the APIAHF is to promote improvement in the health status of all Asians and Pacific Islanders in the United States. As an

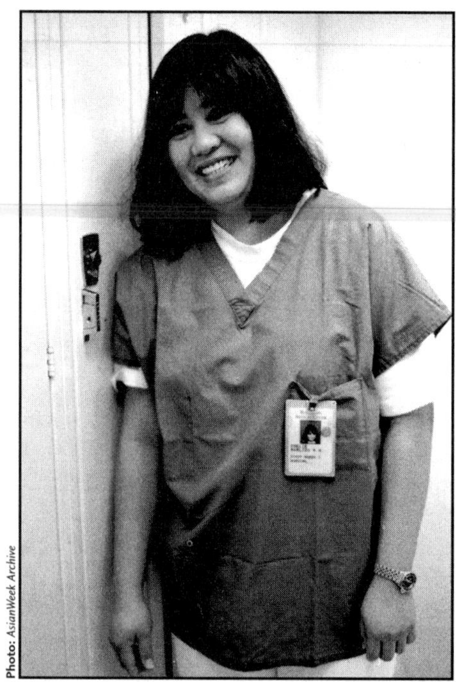

Photo: AsianWeek Archive

APAs such as this Filipino nurse increasingly dominate the medical profession. One in five medical school students today is APA.

advocacy organization, it dedicated to promoting policy, program, and research efforts to improve the health and well being of Asian American and Pacific Islander communities.

The alarming increase in cancer deaths among Asian Americans in the United States is of concern; moreover the lack of research on cancer and Asian Americans is also disturbing. The National Cancer Institute has provided new research initiatives to understand these disparities. Under the leadership of Dr. Moon Chen, a faculty member at the UC Davis School of Medicine, the Asian American Network for Cancer Awareness, Research and Training (AANCART) seeks to build partnership and programs to increase cancer awareness and cancer research among Asian Americans throughout the United States.

—*Grace J. Yoo*

Electric Dreams: APAs in Hi-Tech

The engineer born in Taiwan. The programmer from Seoul. The scientist educated at the Indian Institute of Technology. APAs, particularly immigrants, have made their mark since the late 1960s as some of the brightest scientists and engineers working on college campuses and in corporate labs around the United States. Nowhere has this been truer than in the hi-tech industry.

APA executives remained a rarity, though, until the decade-long hi-tech boom of the 1990s. For the first time, APAs were moving into the CEO's chair in significant numbers. In places like Silicon Valley—the epicenter of the Internet revolution—APAs were breaking through the corporate glass ceiling—or sidestepping it by starting their own companies.

The bursting of the Internet bubble economy in 2000 has had a dampening effect on the hi-tech industry and on entrepreneurs of every ethnicity. Still, prospects look good for APAs to continue to increase their numbers in the management and ownership ranks of what is now arguably America's premier industry.

"Work horses, not race horses"

The dirty truth is this: a disproportionately large number of APAs, especially immigrants, *are* math whizzes, big-brained scientists, computer geeks, etc. Instead of genetics, though, credit a key mid-1960s change in U.S. immigration policy.

In 1960, there were only 877,934 APAs, representing less than one percent of the U.S. population. Growth was slow: restrictive quotas allowed most Asian countries to send only a maximum of 100 immigrants to the United States per year. In 1965, Congress passed the Hart-Cellar Act. This immigration reform not only greatly increased the number of immigrants allowed into the United States per year, it granted visas to those with family ties to existing U.S. citizens and permanent residents, and, crucially, to immigrants possessing scarce skills or training—which translated in many cases into scientists and engineers.

Photo: Kingston Technology Company

Chinese Americans John Tu (left) and David Sun started leading Orange County, California-based chipmaker, Kingston Technology. At their Christmas party in 1996, the two founders gave $100 million to be shared among their then-500 employees.

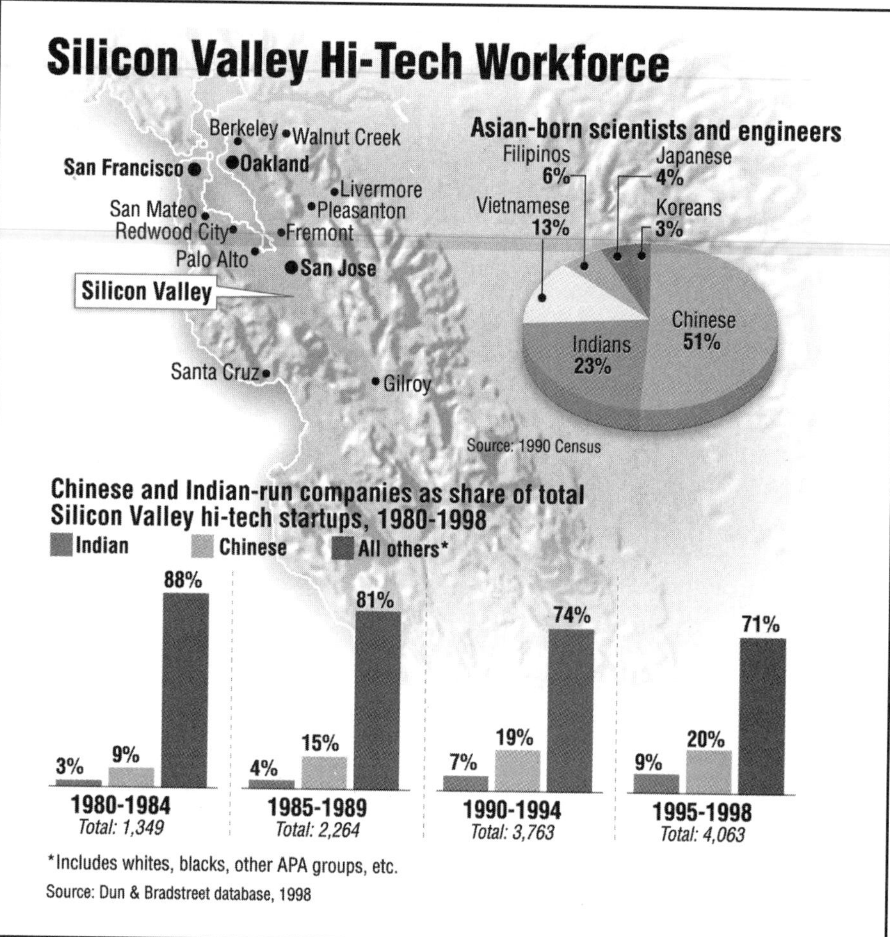

The results were immediate and dramatic. Take Taiwanese Americans, of whom there were virtually none in America before Hart-Cellar. In 1965, 47 scientists and engineers emigrated to the United States from Taiwan. Two years later, the number was 1,321. According to the 2000 Census, there are 144,795 Taiwanese Americans, many of them technologists or their children. Other ethnic populations that boomed as a result of Hart-Cellar included Koreans, Indians and other South Asians, Filipinos (due to a huge influx of nurses and other medical professionals), Chinese from both Hong Kong and mainland China, and others.

In places with concentrations of hi-tech companies, like Boston, Austin, Los Angeles, and, of course, Silicon Valley, APA scientists and engineers were a fact of life by the 1970s and 1980s. For instance, the 1990 Census showed that more than 20 percent of Silicon Valley's scientists and engineers were Asian immigrants. Of that group, most were Chinese or Taiwanese (51 percent), or Indian (23 percent).

But APAs, for all of their success at research and development, still found promotion into the management ranks difficult. For instance, the same 1990 Census showed that only 15 percent of Indian techies working in the Silicon Valley were managers, while 26 percent of whites were.

Rightly or wrongly, APAs were stereotyped as lacking in the language and leadership departments. They were viewed as "work horses, not race horses" as one Chinese American engineer put it. Success stories like An Wang of Boston-based Wang Computer were a rarity (see sidebar).

Benefiting from trans-Pacific links

AnnaLee Saxenian, a sociology professor at UC Berkeley who has extensively studied Asian immigrants in the Silicon Valley, writes that at least on one count —income—APAs did not appear to lag behind their white colleagues. But she agrees that APAs generally had to overcome more hurdles than their white counterparts to be promoted at large, established companies.

"Although these immigrants have achieved income and occupational status comparable to their native counterparts in professional jobs, their opportunities for advancement to management occupations appear more limited, suggesting the possibility of a 'glass ceiling' or invisible barriers to career mobility," she wrote in a 1999 study.

The Silicon Valley ethos has always encouraged both technical smarts and freewheeling verve. So frustrated APAs began to take matters into their own hands. Take David Lam, who left a solid position at Hewlett-Packard in 1979 after being passed over for a promotion. He started a chipmaking company called Lam Research. It has grown into a phenomenal success. In 2001, Lam had more than $1 billion in sales. In 2002, it was worth more than $3 billion on the stock market.

Firms started by Chinese or Taiwanese Americans tend to be in areas like computer and electronic hardware manufacturing. Companies started by Indians, by contrast, tend to be in the areas of software and business services. The difference is partly due to language skills: first-generation Chinese immigrants are less proficient in English than Indians, for whom it is one of the official languages of their native country. Of course, there are plenty of exceptions, such as Jerry Yang, the Stanford wunderkind behind the Yahoo! website; Charles Wang, the billionaire CEO of software maker Computer Associates International; and Vinod Khosla, co-founder of hardware giant Sun Microsystems.

But the differences in specialization between the Chinese and Indians were also due to the emergance of connections to their native countries that helped entrepreneurs get a start, and a leg-up on their competition. Long a center of low-cost electronics manufacturing, Taiwan embarked on a modernization scheme in the 1980s that included creating a Silicon Valley-style research zone in the Taipei suburb of Hsinchu. Thousands of Taiwanese American engineers returned to set up companies. Those who stayed in the United States benefited from relationships with their Hsinchu counterparts. By 1999, Taiwan was the third largest producer of computer hardware, behind only the United States and Japan, much of it destined for the Silicon Valley.

Meanwhile, the Indian city of Bangalore had by the mid-1990s earned a reputation as one of the world's leading centers of software development. Many of the companies were founded by Indians returning from completing postgraduate degrees in the United States. Just as common was the reliance on outsourced contracts from Indian-run companies in the Silicon Valley. No longer was there simply a "brain drain" from one country to another, but, as Saxenian called it, a "brain circulation," whereby skills, technology, and money flowed between Asia and the Silicon Valley.

The curry network

APAs also realized that the traditional, white "old boys club"

Photo: Yahoo! Media Relations

Taiwanese-born Jerry Yang was one of the Internet boom's poster children: he founded Yahoo! while a graduate student at Stanford University in the mid-1990s.

Computers, not laundries

Long before Yahoo! or Computer Associates, there was a hi-tech giant started by a Chinese American: Wang Laboratories Inc. Its founder, An Wang, lived the prototypical immigrant's dream, starting with next to nothing and becoming a billionaire. Born in 1920, Wang lost most of his family in China during World War II. After he earned a Ph.D. in applied physics from Harvard in just three years, the Shanghai native started his own company. Wang said: "I founded Wang Laboratories to show that Chinese could excel at things other than running laundries and restaurants."

Wang Laboratories became one of the biggest computer firms of the 1970s and 1980s, a household name that rivaled IBM or Hewlett-Packard. For a time, nearly every office owned a Wang word processor. In the 1980s, Wang Laboratories shifted gears yet again, earning billions from manufacturing mini-computers (which were, in reality, about the size of a closet).

The heart of Boston's burgeoning hi-tech scene, Wang's company was responsible for numerous inventions: the predecessor to RAM computer memory, the 5.25-inch floppy disk, and more.

Wang's initial $600 investment paid him back many times. He was once estimated to be worth $1.6 billion, making him the fifth richest person in the United States at the time. Wang's Confucian ideals led him to donate millions to universities and institutions. He also helped create thousands of jobs by building factories in depressed areas of Boston.

He credited his success to perspiration, not inspiration. "Success is more a function of consistent common sense than genius," Wang said.

At its peak in 1986, Wang Laboratories was a $3 billion company that employed 30,000 people. But even then, the company was already in trouble. Wang had retired and turned his company over to his son. Faced with the growing popularity of the PC, the company tried many strategies, none of them successful.

Wang died of cancer in 1990. His namesake company filed for bankruptcy in 1992. After reorganizing, Wang Laboratories recovered financially, but the firm was just a ghost of the exciting market trendsetter it had been. The Wang era—and name—came to an end in 1999, when it was swallowed by a rival.

tended to lock them out of promising business opportunities. So they created their own "old boys clubs": groups like the Asian American Manufacturers Association, the Chinese Software Professionals Association, and The IndUS Entrepreneurs (TIE), aimed at South Asians.

"From networking with people at the monthly meetings, I got inspiration," one Indian entrepreneur told a Silicon Valley business magazine. "When you are talking face-to-face with people who sold their companies for $400 million, it shifts your perspective on how high to aim."

Senior members take their responsibility as mentors seriously. One, a chairman of a major telecommunications hardware firm, holds an "open house" at his Boston home every Sunday morning to advise up-and-coming entrepreneurs.

Founded in the early 1990s, TIE, was so successful by the late 1990s that it had more than a thousand members in chapters throughout North America. Members joked that they were part of the "Indian Mafia," or the "Curry Network."

These networking groups remain important today, according to Saxenian, "for the same reason that networking groups exist within the white community. Success in hi-tech is dependent on cross-cutting institutions and relationships that allow people to learn quickly from one another."

From computer geek to dot-com hero

Still, perhaps what leveled the playing field most for APAs was the 1990s hi-tech boom. Not only did it make it easier for APAs to get funding to start their own companies, but the fact that so many APAs were leaving for startup companies forced big corporations to promote talented APAs to keep them.

Crowed an Indian American entrepreneur, "In the 1970s, they never promoted Indians to be managers. In the 80s, some were moving into sales, marketing, and finance. Today, it's a non-issue—Indians are in senior management at Sun Microsystems, Microsoft, Cisco."

Chinese and Indian CEOs ran 13 percent of Silicon Valley tech firms started between 1980 and 1984. Of all Valley hi-tech firms started between 1995 and 1998, 29 percent were started by Chinese or Indians.

"I quickly realized that being foreign-born was no barrier. It was only a barrier in my mind," said Sabeer Bhatia in a 1999 *Wall Street Journal* article. Bhatia co-founded the popular Internet e-mail provider, Hotmail, which was sold to Microsoft Corp. for more than $300 million.

Brash, young, APA techies like Bhatia and Yahoo!'s Jerry Yang were also glamorized in the mainstream media. Once perceived simply as computer geeks, technologically-minded APAs were now viewed as dot-com zillionaires-in-waiting.

Small, foreign and female

Silicon Valley lore tends to glorify the inventors and the buccaneer bosses. But it was APA women—in particular, Filipino and Vietnamese women—who comprised much of Silicon Valley's blue-collar workforce, making the chips and building the computers for low wages and under often-unhealthy conditions.

"The way this industry arose was on the backs, hands and strained eyesight of immigrant women," says Karen Hossfeld, a sociologist at San Francisco State University. The title of her book, *Small, Foreign, and Female*, comes from an expression some Silicon Valley employers had for the ideal factory worker. Asian women fit all of those traits, the employers told Hossfeld, because they "work very hard, are loyal, and they are smart, but they won't use their smarts to rebel or bring in their own ideas."

The boom in hi-tech manufacturing and assembly jobs in the Silicon Valley during the late 1960s lured many Filipino immigrants and, in the late 1970s, Vietnamese refugees. By the 1980s, 47 percent of the assemblers and 42 percent of the laborers in Santa Clara County factories were Asian women, virtually all of them Vietnamese or Filipina.

Granted, many of the women were grateful for the jobs, which were better-paid than those in their homelands and helped thousands of immigrant families leap into the middle class. But by American standards, they were not well-paid. According to 1990 Census figures, Vietnamese and Filipino women working in electronics and hi-tech jobs earned the lowest average salaries in the Valley – less than $22,000 per year. By contrast, white men in the electronics industry earned more than $54,000 per year on average.

And the jobs had plenty of drawbacks. The pace and sheer repetition often led to eyestrain and injuries. More dangerous was the exposure to chemicals like the now-regulated chemical Freon, which maskless workers commonly sprayed to clean computer circuit boards. Studies have shown that female APAs working in Silicon Valley chip plants suffered a higher rate of miscarriage and birth defects as a result.

"It's almost reverse discrimination," said Khosla, who after leaving Sun Microsystems has had a wildly successful career as a Silicon Valley venture capitalist. "People almost assume that if you're Indian or Chinese you're smarter, and you get the benefit of the doubt."

Not to suggest that ethnicity and business connections alone were guarantees of success. The hallmarks of rising immigrants—sacrifice and hard work—were necessary. Take Chong-moon Lee, a Korean-born former hi-tech CEO. Lee lost his home, his family, and nearly bankrupted himself while running Diamond Multimedia. Suicidal, and at one point so poor and in debt that he could only afford meals of instant noodles, Lee turned his company around, eventually selling a majority stake in Diamond for $92 million.

Future remains bright

By the late 1990s, Silicon Valley APAs were credited with owning and managing more than 3,000 companies with total sales of nearly $17 billion—around one-quarter of all Silicon Valley firms—greater than the economy of many small nations.

"When local technologists claim that 'Silicon Valley is built on ICs' they refer not to the integrated circuit but to Indian and Chinese engineers," wrote Saxenian.

The figures also suggest that skilled APA immigrants, far from taking away jobs from native American workers, add jobs and boost the economy overall. This remains a point of contention, as the U.S. government continues to wrestle with whether to increase or decrease the number of H-1B visas granted to foreign immigrants with hi-tech educations.

Despite their success, APAs still have a way to go before the glass ceiling of Silicon Valley is truly shattered. For instance, the percentage of APAs on the corporate boards of Silicon Valley's ten largest public companies remains just one in twelve.

The economic slump that began in 2000, and as of this writing in mid-2002 remains in full effect, also hurts. Indian tech workers, lured to Silicon Valley by the recently ended economic boom have suffered especially from the layoffs. Still, immigrant chutzpah combined with thriving cross-Pacific links and well-established ethnic networking groups are all factors that are helping APAs become Silicon Valley's New Establishment.

"We tend to work really hard and are not easily stopped by hardship or failure," said one Vietnamese American computer startup executive. "The [stock market] crash is just part of our learning curve."

—*Eric Lai*

And there was the lack of job protection, which was exposed when the computer industry slumped in the 1980s and companies began moving chip plants out of state or overseas. The APA women, lacking union protection, were among the first to be laid off. When the industry recovered in the early 1990s, the market had changed. Many of the new jobs were in designing, rather than manufacturing, computer goods, or in areas like the Internet. Some, mostly Filipinas, left the hi-tech industry for fields like nursing. Those who stayed and retrained for these higher-paid jobs thrived.

But those who went back into manufacturing had to find work with small subcontractors, assembling on behalf of bigger, better-known firms, run in most cases by fellow APAs. For the workers, job security was still lacking, and wages and working conditions were often worse. In the 1999 case Mao v. Top Line Electronics, a Cambodian immigrant claimed that he was paid piece rates—amounting to as little as $1 an hour—to assemble computer parts at his home, using unhealthy chemicals. The case was settled out of court, though the company admitted no wrongdoing. But a *San Jose Mercury News* investigation in 2000 found at least fourteen Silicon Valley companies that paid workers per piece for electronics assembled at home, contravening labor and minimum wage laws.

Despite it all, many of the women look back upon their old jobs with a mixture of pride and nostalgia. "Filipinas were hard workers and we seldom made mistakes," one woman told the *Mercury News* in 1995. "We didn't complain, because our boss was nice and treated us good."

Born for Business

In small businesses around America, APAs are having a huge impact. In 1997, APA-owned companies generated $307 billion in revenue and employed more than 2.2 million people. New Asian immigrants have moved seamlessly off the boat, or jet, into retail businesses like "mom and pop" convenience stores, laundromats, etc. So many are family-run firms that more than two-thirds (68 percent) of APA-owned companies don't have any paid employees! But APA businesses also include some of America's largest publicly traded Fortune 1000 companies, employing several hundred thousand workers in high-wage jobs, generating tens of billions in revenue for the U.S. economy.

Only a few years ago, when immigrant quotas were being proposed, immigrants were blamed for many of America's economic problems. Today, APA entrepreneurs are being recognized for their contributions to the U.S. economy. In 1997, the number of APA-owned businesses reached nearly 913,000—up 30 percent from half a decade prior in 1992. Sales, meanwhile, were up 68 percent to the aforementioned $307 billion. During that five-year period, the number of new APA-owned firms grew more than four times faster than the rate of all new firms throughout the United States. Similarly, sales at APA-owned firms grew 70 percent faster than those of all U.S. companies, and nearly 39 percent faster than combined Hispanic and African-American firms.

Finding niches and thriving

Much of that growth stems from the way some APA immigrants are coming to dominate certain small business sectors. For example, Vietnamese immigrants, primarily women, own 30 percent of the 22,000 nail manicure salons in the United States. Nationwide, nearly four out of ten Vietnamese businesses were in personal services—nail salons, beauty shops and dry cleaners—compared with a rate of just over 10 percent

Averages Sales of Businesses Owned by Asian and Pacific Islander Groups, 1997

Group	Average sales
All Asian and Pacific Islander	$336,195
Japanese	$511,364
Other Pacific Islander	$493,519
Chinese	$420,453
Asian Indian	$404,849
Korean	$338,837
Other Asian	$268,332
Native Hawaiian	$144,760
Filipino	$131,047
Vietnamese	$95,361

Source: U.S. Census Bureau

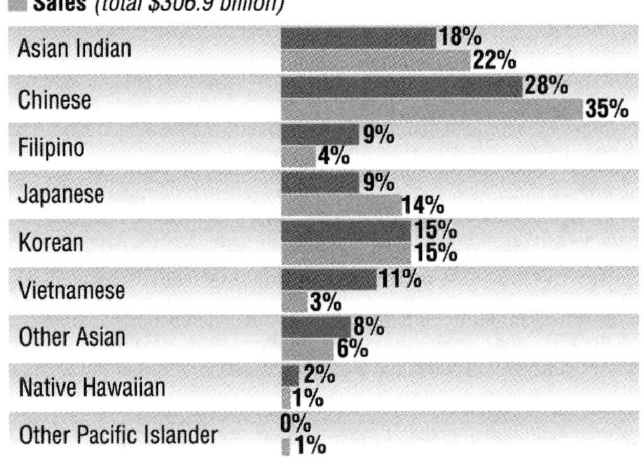

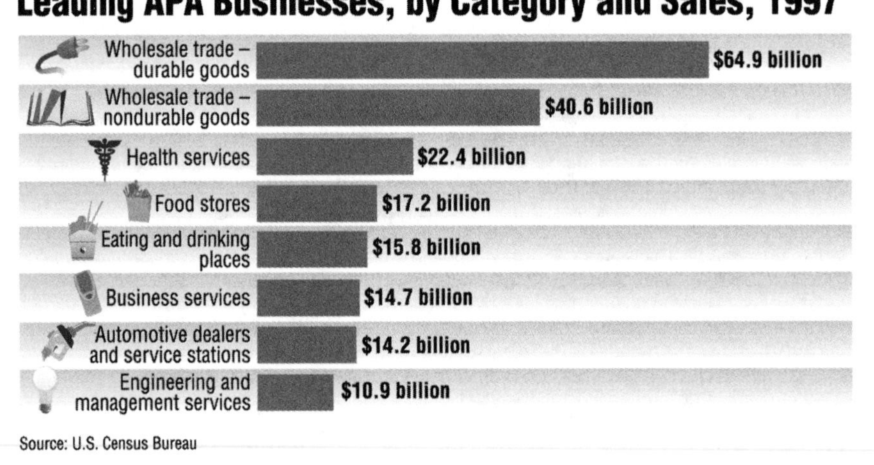

Asian- and Pacific Islander-owned firms, 1997

As a percent of total firms in each state.

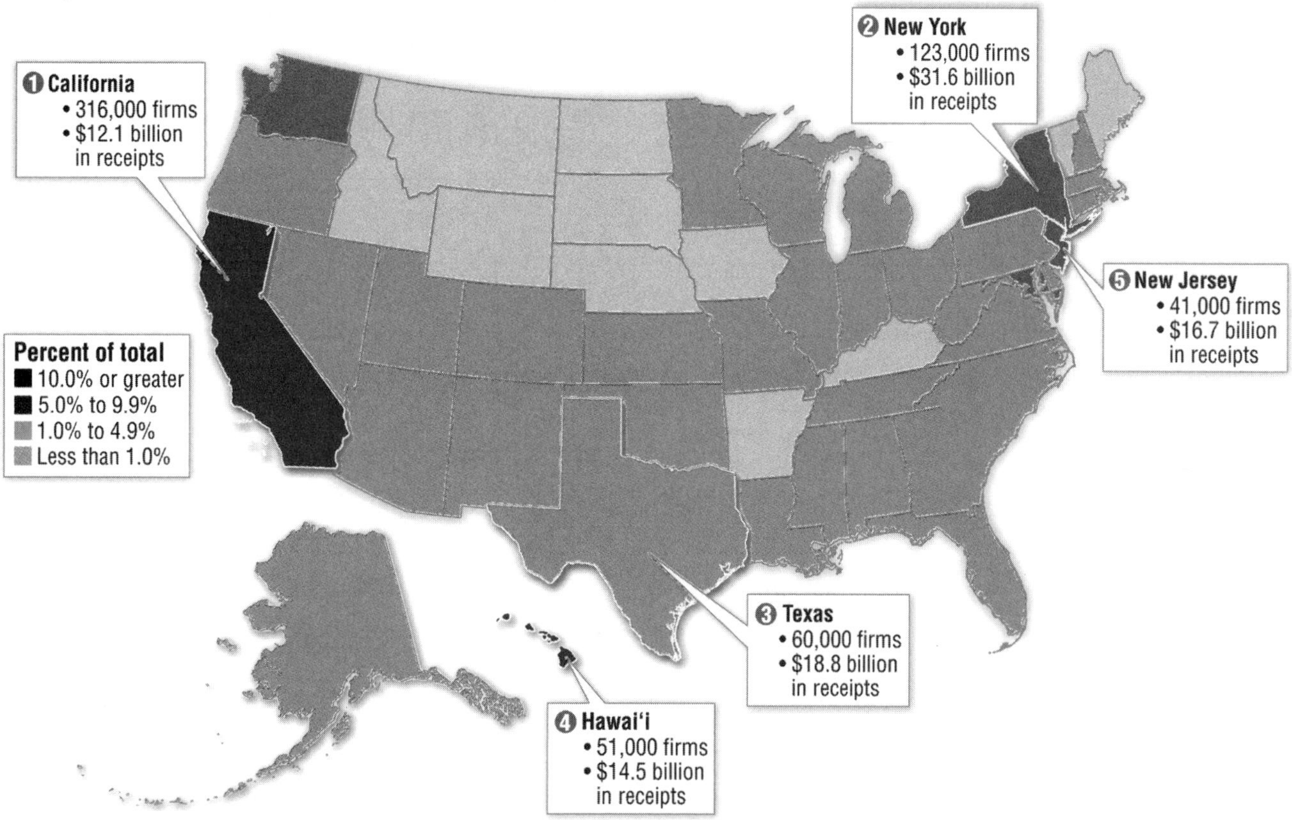

METRO AREA	NO. OF FIRMS	TOTAL RECEIPTS (in billions)	LEADING APA GROUP(S)
Los Angeles-Long Beach	114,000	$55	Chinese, Korean
New York	102,000	$26	Chinese, Indian, Korean
Orange County	45,000	$15	Mix
Honolulu	39,000	$12	Japanese
San Francisco	35,000	$12	Chinese

Source: 1997 U.S. Economic Census

among all APA-owned businesses, according to 1997 Census data. In *The Contemporary Asian American Experience* in 1998, Timothy Fong wrote:

"[Nail care] is an industry operated top to bottom largely by Vietnamese. Even supplies such as nail polish, buffing pads and shop furnishings are from Vietnamese businesses."

Since the 1980s, Cambodian immigrants and refugees have become major owners or operators of donut shops in California. One estimate puts the number of independent, non-chain donut shops in California at around 50,000, with as many as 90 percent of those run by Cambodians, according to an article in the *San Jose Mercury News*.

Or take Asian Indians, who dominate the nation's budget hotel and motel sector. Despite making up less than 1 percent of the total U.S. population, Indian Americans own 46 percent of the nation's economy hotels and motels, and 26 percent of all lodgings in the country. The Asian American Hotel Owners Association, whose members collectively control nearly 12 million rooms in 20,000 hotels, is dominated by Indians from the northern province of Gujarat, with a huge proportion of them sporting the surname Patel (prompting wags to dub this sprawling network the "Patel Motel Cartel").

There are plenty of other examples. Koreans, for instance, have taken over from the Chinese and now run many laundries and dry cleaning businesses in cities around the United States. Koreans have also proliferated in businesses like corner grocers and liquor stores.

Donuts, anyone?

"It is odd that Cambodians are doing this work-considering that most Asians don't eat donuts and prefer noodles," said Mann Lee, who, like thousands of other Cambodian immigrants in California, has been frying donuts, brewing coffees, and frothing milk for decades.

But the attraction is clearly there. Of the more than 50,000 independent donut shops in California, Cambodians and Chinese Cambodians operate as many as 90 percent of them, according to one estimate. In Los Angeles alone, there are more than 1,800 independent Cambodian- or Korean-owned donut shops, according to another.

Donuts were invented in Holland more than 400 years ago, but Cambodians only began making them in the mid-1970s, all due to one enterprising Cambodian Chinese ex-army major, Ted Ngoy. Inspired by a short stint working at the Winchell's donut chain, Ngoy borrowed some money, opened several donut shops in Southern California, and got his relatives to work for him. As his donut empire grew, Ngoy sold off some stores to fellow Cambodians, even as others independently got into the business hoping to emulate his success.

"Ngoy is the one who found a way for Cambodian immigrants to become part of the American dream of owning their own business," said Dennis Wong of the Asian Business Association.

Donut shops appealed to Cambodians for other reasons. The initial outlay for a donut shop—various estimates put it between $40,000 and $100,000—fell within the affordability range of new but enterprising Cambodian immigrants.

Also, "getting hired at a place where your boss and colleagues speak Chinese was a real incentive for my wife and I [to] take on this work," said David Chau, who runs a shop in downtown San Francisco.

Nonetheless, running a donut store is arduous work. "As a family we are working seven days a week, the store is open 24 hours, and we have no family time. It's tiring," said one twenty-something Chinese American woman.

The often rough urban locations—coupled with the lack of a protective umbrella of a big chain like Krispy Kreme or Dunkin' Donuts—also translates into difficult customers. Nonetheless, selling donuts has paid off for many Cambodian families. Lee, for instance, owns two donut shops, which each reap $60,000 in profits annually.

While existing Cambodian donut shops continue to thrive, fewer Cambodians are entering the business.

"Donuts are not as commercially viable as they used to be," said Victor His, who works at the South East Asian Community Center in San Francisco. "Changes in people's food choices are changing towards healthier things. And donuts aren't the healthiest thing to eat."

—*AsianWeek*

Photo: AsianWeek Archive

Cambodians dominate the donut shop business in California, running up to 90 percent of non-chain shops.

Why do members of the same ethnic group tend to congregate in the same industries? Theories abound. Some point out that in a close-knit immigrant community, the success of one member or relative can catch on like wildfire and encourage others to enter the same business. Others see strength in numbers: Korean retailers in Oakland, California, for instance have leveraged their ability to collectively purchase products in bulk to become the leading sellers of beauty and haircare products aimed at black women.

APAs in hi-tech

Beyond these areas, APA immigrants are broadly involved in a variety of businesses. In certain technology-dependent industries, APAs have been able to make major contributions as employers, subcontractors, and entrepreneurs. They include such areas as computers, communications, multimedia, biotechnology, and medical devices, and run the gamut from hi-tech to low-tech.

APA participation in these industries can be felt in all the nation's centers for high technology research, development and manufacturing: Silicon Valley; the multi-media gulches of Los Angeles and San Francisco; North Carolina's "Research Triangle" of Durham, Raleigh and Chapel Hill; Fairfax County in Virginia near Washington D.C.; and Austin, Texas. For instance, nearly one in five engineers at leading chipmaker Intel Corp. is a Chinese immigrant. One quarter of the technical staff at IBM's research labs in Yorktown, New York are APAs.

APAs also work at or manage many of the hi-tech subcontractor firms that have made Silicon Valley and other hi-tech centers so efficient. These companies typically manufacture chips or components for "brand" name companies like IBM, Intel, and Cisco Systems. The heavyweight of the bunch is Solectron Corporation. It was co-founded by Winston Chen and Roy Kusomoto in 1977, and has, since 1992, had a Japanese American CEO, Koichi Nishimura. Its revenues for 2001 topped $18.7 billion.

Whether by leaps and bounds, or by baby steps, APA firms have come a long way, while contributing significantly to America's economic vitality. "Mom and pop" facilities and businesses have revitalized many deteriorating cities in the United States, while hi-technology businesses have kept America competitive in the global marketplace and insured its continued technological leadership.

—Gelly Borromeo

Key Facts about APA Businesses

- Of 912,960 APA-owned companies, five percent had more than $1 million in sales. Twenty eight percent had less than $10,000 in sales.
- The average APA-owned company had sales of about $336,000, compared with around $410,000 for all U.S. firms (excluding public corporations and firms whose owners' race or ethnicity could not be determined).
- APAs (of non-mixed race) had purchasing power of $296.4 billion in 2002, up 152% from 1990. That will grow 53% to $454.9 billion by 2007. APAs in California had the most buying power—$104.1 billion—but APA buying power is growing fastest in Nevada, Georgia and North Carolina.
- Only 32 percent of APA-owned firms had paid employees. Seventy one percent of APA-owned companies were sole proprietorships.
- In 2002, APA women owned 30 percent of the 1.2 million businesses run by women of color in the United States.
- Three out of four APA-owned hotels were owned by Asian Indians.
- Two out of three APA-owned fishing, hunting and trapping firms were owned by Vietnamese.
- About half of APA-owned apparel and accessory stores were owned by Koreans.

Source: 1997 U.S. Economic Census, Center for Women's Business Research, Selig Center for Economic Growth. Note: APA ownership based on race or ethnicity of 51% or greater.

Flexing their Economic Muscle

As Asian Pacific Americans continue to climb the economic ladder, they are also making their presence known as consumers. APAs possessed $296.4 billion in buying power in 2002, according to the Selig Center for Economic Growth, a thinktank at the University of Georgia. APA buying power is defined by Selig as after-tax income held by APAs (excluding mixed-race individuals).

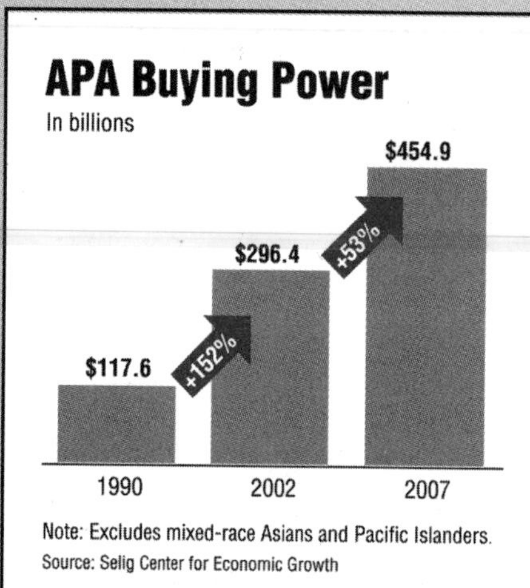

Note: Excludes mixed-race Asians and Pacific Islanders.
Source: Selig Center for Economic Growth

Although the collective buying power of APAs does not yet substantially outweigh their population presence—both are about four percent—the purchasing power of APAs is growing faster than the overall population's, and faster than all other racial groups except for Hispanics. By 2007, APA buying power will reach $454.9 billion—an average annual increase of 16.4 percent from 1990 to 2007. For whites, the increase is less than half—7.8 percent compound annual growth over the same time period.

According to the Selig Center, APA buying power is being propelled by a number of factors, including the large proportion of well-educated APAs, many in management or technical jobs, and others that are successful entrepreneurs. A relatively-large proportion of APAs are adults in early stages of their careers.

APA buying power is growing especially fast in economically-booming states in the West and South to which APAs are migrating for jobs and cheap housing.

In states such as Nevada, Georgia, and North Carolina, APA purchasing power has more than quadrupled in twelve years.

Still, for marketers wishing to cater to APA consumers, they can look primarily at a few states.

Indeed, the five and ten largest states accounted for 62.7 percent and 77.3 percent of APA purchasing power in 2002. By contrast, the five and ten largest states represented 38.2 percent and 56.2 percent of the American population's total buying power. Though California alone accounted for over a third of nationwide APA buying power, APAs actually only had a tenth of total purchasing power within the state. In Hawai'i, APAs account for 49 percent of the consumer market in 2002, though that is actually expected to fall more than eight percent by 2007.

With these demographic and socioeconomic trends, however, it remains to be seen whether mainstream American businesses will begin to develop and market products and services catering to APAs—something corporate America for the most part continues to fail to do.

—*Eric Lai*

States with the Largest APA Buying Power in 2002

State	In Billions
California	$104.1
New York	31.9
New Jersey	18.0
Texas	16.6
Hawai'i	15.3
Illinois	13.4
Washington	8.6
Virginia	7.5
Florida	6.9
Massachusetts	6.9

States with the Fastest-Growing APA Buying Power

State	Pct. Change, 1990-2002
Nevada	362%
Georgia	358
North Carolina	325
Minnesota	268
Texas	256
Nebraska	241
Tennessee	240
Colorado	231
Massachusetts	228
New Hampshire	223

Building Community in Los Angeles and Elsewhere

The U.S. Census frustrates the lesbian, gay, bisexual and transgender Asian Pacific American community. To begin with, we are not a category. And since Census data is often the impetus for policymaking, our communities could only be bound by other people's less scientific estimates. Depending on whether the government wants to ignore us or to contain us, we are either freakishly minuscule or menacingly taking over the world.

In very broad strokes, this essay paints an interpretive evolution of the queer APA community in Los Angeles; particularly how we as queer APAs have come to relate to each other and to other communities in the new millennium. Los Angeles is by no means the only hub of activity for queer APAs in this country. There are a handful of other urban centers that can claim just as vibrant a history. Los Angeles is simply what I know best, having adopted it as my home in the early 1980s and having come of age here sexually, racially and politically. Hopefully, I can provide insight that reflects on issues that extend to the queer APA community as a whole.

In May 2002, a national gay and lesbian organization put on its website, for the first time and in honor of Asian Pacific American heritage month, information about the queer APA community. Under "Issues affecting LGBT Asian Pacifics," the website lists: visibility and stereotypes, family, language, religion and HIV/AIDS. For the most part, this information does not stray from the truth: these are issues that affect many queer APAs. But they are also the same issues that affected our community fifteen or twenty years ago. In fact, the website could have transposed literature from the 1980s and it would not have been much different. Does that mean our community has not advanced in the last twenty years? No. The problem lies in the way a community is too often defined by its needs, which don't change easily. When we focus on needs, we fail to see the evolution that takes place otherwise. Instead, we need a historical

Photo: Kieran Ridge and Hiromi Oda

Gay and lesbian families, including APAs, are on the rise, as evidenced by Census figures showing a large increase in unmarried, same-sex partner households in 2000 over 1990.

telescope to situate these needs in a larger context of human actions.

Bridging sexuality and race

There have always been lesbian and gay APAs who participated in activist Asian American or lesbian and gay communities, but there was not always an articulated identity or politics that connected both their sexuality and race. That is, until the First National Third World Lesbian and Gay Conference in 1979. For much of the 1970s and 1980s, many in the Asian American Movement considered homosexuality as deviant as drug addiction or prostitution. Likewise, it is still a common complaint today that the mainstream gay and lesbian movement has not adequately addressed racism and discrimination in our own community. Even though lesbian and gay APAs recognized their own individual fate as a minority regardless of where they called home, twenty years ago there was not the sense that they could organize as both lesbians or gay men *and* APAs.

For APAs, the notion of pan-ethnicity was still relatively new and many tensions and barriers existed to organizing by race. New waves of immigrants arriving after the relaxing of immigration laws in the sixties had not yet developed a pan-ethnic consciousness, as made evident by the pervasive ethnic segregation often found in bars frequented by gay APA men in the 1970s.

Asian/Pacific Lesbians and Gays (A/PLG), the first organization of its kind in Los Angeles, was founded in 1980 on the unique vision of a handful of lesbian and gay APAs. Some of them did not even know each other at the time, but many shared a connection—gay activist Morris Kight. Kight has been an iconoclastic leader in the history of progressive gay and lesbian movement in Los Angeles; his battle scars are many. Most of the A/PLG founders had fought side by side with Kight on various struggles. In 1980, Kight called a meeting among his network of Asian comrades in his Hollywood abode, and from that discussion—and a few others that followed—A/PLG was born.

Before A/PLG, many lesbian and gay APAs saw each other the way dominant gay society saw them: invisible, passive, or foreign. By organizing along both racial and sexual identities, the founding of A/PLG disrupted the internalization of these stereotypes and represented a major cultural transformation away from this marginalization.

Because there had not been an organized network of lesbian and gay APAs before A/PLG, the organization had an open membership policy. Non-APA men accounted for half of its member-

Your Tongzhi Body*

Russell C. Leong

I see a brown tongzhi
body-
Neither female nor
male
Eyes from Beijing
Lips from Hong Kong
Spleen from Guizhou
Belly from
Guangzhou
Feet from Singapore

I touch a smooth
tongzhi body-
Without day, month,
or year of birth
Whose fingertips
Reach to Canada and
America
Whose thighs and
calves stretch to
Malaysia
Whose toes touch
Thailand and
Vietnam
Whose body travels
from Italy to
Australia.

I hear a tongzhi body
speak out-
A voice sings, cries,
and prays
As she/he tells stories
of love and lust
Of homelessness and
lonliness.

I know a tongzhi
body like yours-

Who is HIV positive
And HIV negative
But I will kiss you on
the lips anyway
And on every part of
your body
For everyone's love
and nobody's fault.
For I possess this
brown tongzhi
body-
And so do you, and
You, and you.
For we are one, or
are we not?

**Tongzhi is Hong Kong slang for gay or queer; it also means comrade in Cantonese.*

from *A New Reader on Chinese Tongzhi: Essays and Conference Proceedings*, Russell Leong and John Loo, editors, Hong Kong: Worldson Books, 1999

APA Lesbians Coming Out, Coming Together

When 20-year-old Linda Tran finally decided to come out to her mother last summer, she got a response along the lines of: "I would rather be dead than have to listen to this."

Emotions and empathy ran high as Tran relayed her personal coming-out story to a room full of other Asian Pacific American lesbian, bisexual, queer and transgender women sharing their ongoing struggles of being queer and APA—a "double minority."

"We are most concerned about our family and the huge fear of rejection we may face," says Trinity Ordona, co-founder and co-coordinator of the API-PFLAG Family Project, which provides "coming out" resources to families of APA queers.

Photo: Kieran Ridge and Hiromi Oda

The lesbian APA community is working towards bridging what it means to be queer and APA, and expressing the community's concerns and issues with a strong voice.

Ordona says it is difficult it is to make PFLAG resources available to APAs because the whole idea of coming out "breaks the number one rule we have in our families: which is to never talk about our problems." She said that often the parent goes deep into denial, and the resulting tactics of silence and rejection wreak havoc on the entire family.

Hate crimes, workplace discrimination and same-sex domestic violence (which has been long overlooked by mainstream organizations) are among the other issues at hand for the lesbian APA community.

"We need a new theory, not just a copied model of the heterosexual domestic violence model, and real community intervention to deal with this problem," said Hediana Utarti, of the San Francisco Asian Women's shelter. Immigrant women who have been battered, in particular, are more vulnerable because of both language and cultural barriers.

The lesbian APA community continues to struggle with the old heterosexual models that affect other aspects of government policy. Sasha Kokha of the National Network for Immigrant and Refugee Rights maintains that immigration policies are often based on the model of a heterosexual nuclear family that dates back to the 19th century, saying that "there needs to be a serious review of the asylum process and the way sexual and gender issues are dealt with."

Alma Beck, a San Francisco attorney, remembers meeting and falling in love with a woman in Korea. But because her girlfriend could not attain a visa to come to America, their relationship was subsequently destroyed by both distance and immigration bureaucracy. Her story is one of many who must deal with the futile battle to gain immigration status for their same-sex partners.

"The media assumes all queer people are white and male," says journalist and author Helen Zia. "But look at the Hawai'i Marriage Law: why did this law pass in this majority Asian American state first? I believe the same-sex law passed in Hawai'i because of the importance of family in API heritage. But we must bring these parts of our community together because even today we can still be APIs in one space and queer in another. We must change the status for all APIs."

—*AsianWeek*

ship for most of the organization's life. While some of these members genuinely supported the growth of the organization, others were only interested in dating or "cruising" Asian men. This engendered a lot of bad feelings among A/PLG members.

Turning the organization into a mere alternative to gay bars derailed the political ambitions of early A/PLG leadership. The founders had wanted this space to build self-esteem of lesbian and gay APAs, develop their leadership, and stake a claim of representation in the mainstream APA community. They had made some headway, but the reputation of A/PLG as a pick-up place between white and Asian men preceded anything else. More and more, the leaders encountered new members who did not share this vision. This transformation of A/PLG in its early years once again altered the cultural landscape for lesbian and gay APAs—in two ways.

First, the cruising among men discouraged participation of APA lesbians in A/PLG. Further inspired by a burgeoning national network of APA lesbians and bisexual women (thanks in no small part to a landmark 1979 conference in Washington), the women in A/PLG organized separately as Asian/Pacific Lesbians and Friends and later formally as Los Angeles Asian Pacific Islander Sisters (LAAPIS) in the mid-nineties, organizations which lasted half a decade. Around the same time, A/PLG dropped the "lesbian" in its name and changed to Asian/Pacific Gays and Friends. Today, former LAAPIS members and other APA lesbians and bisexual women continue networking through an online group called LOTUS.

Second, those Asian men who were not interested in dating white men felt alienated by the organization. When a new gay APA men's group began in Long Beach in 1984, they jumped ship. The group, Gay Asian Rap Group, started only informally as a social group and had an exclusively Asian membership. In 1989, they became incorporated as Gay Asian Pacific Support Network (GAPSN), which still exists today.

The emergence of co-gender and ethnic specific organizing

By the early nineties, the community offered very few opportunities for co-gender organizing. Around the same time, a handful of queer APA student organizations sprang up in universities across Southern California. This was in part fueled by the growth of women's studies, ethnic studies and gay and lesbian studies on larger campuses. Another factor was affirmative action, which opened the door of higher education to many APAs, making college campuses a hotbed for people-of-color activism. I came out in this generation. Not that the men in our generation were any more enlightened, but these campus groups were all co-gender by varying degrees. Only after we graduated and became active in the community, where men and women organized separately, were we asked to choose.

Fortunately, there was one last bastion of co-gender community building: HIV/AIDS organizing. The epidemic represented yet another cultural transformation of the queer APA community. Although co-gender organization does not imply immunity to sexism, Asian Pacific AIDS Intervention Team (APAIT), developed in 1987 out of a sub-committee of A/PLG, nevertheless gave many young lesbian and gay APAs an opportunity to work together on an issue that had struck the community hard. Many of us flocked to it as staff or volunteers. More than that, AIDS activism had contributed to a queer APA cultural renaissance in Los Angeles. Many writers, poets, visual artists and performance artists made their living as community organizers by day and honed their craft at night, or vice versa. There was only a thin line separating their community activism and cultural work. The stories they told were the stories of the community. Not too long after, however, HIV work became professionalized, and the make-up of the staff reflected this transformation.

The mid and late nineties also witnessed the birth of many ethnic-specific queer APA organizations: Barangay (Filipino), China Rainbow Association, Chingusai (Korean), Gay Vietnamese Association, JUST (Japanese), O Moi (Vietnamese), and Trikone L.A. (South Asian). Their emergence reflected the increasing sophistication of immigrant communities. Some of these organizations conducted their meetings in their respective Asian languages. Paradoxically, some came into being because of under-representation in the pan-ethnic A/PGF, LAAPIS or GAPSN, even as the leadership of these smaller organizations received training from these larger groups.

The future

Today, many of these groups have disappeared, though the informal networks still prevail. Even for those that continued, their membership roles generally could not match the heyday of the nineties. Likewise, the pan-ethnic groups also suffered the same decline.

I believe a major reason that some of these supportive social spaces have lost their appeal is that they have been operating on an outdated community-building model based on safe spaces. These organizations began with the idea that queer APAs needed their own space where they could feel safe to explore their racial and sexual identities. However, a younger generation of APA college students has already developed those spaces on campus. Others have even been involved in multi-issue organizing that eschews preoccupation over one's identity. By the time they graduate, they are not interested in sitting around and discussing coming out or dating. They are looking for more. Some of these progressive-minded young people find their place among the community and continue their activism as teachers, labor organizers, community workers, advocates, and artists.

The traditional organizations, on the other hand, have always been leery of political activism because of its alleged potential to alienate men and women who are just coming out. Unwittingly, they fail to appeal to this younger generation. There is no infusion of new blood, the leaders play musical chairs, and the median age of the membership grows at the same rate as that of their leadership.

To be sure, these traditional organizations are not obsolete. Not every queer APA has gone through college, and there will always be people just on the

verge of coming out, for whom these safe spaces will still be lifesavers. After twenty years of providing safe space, however, the community needs more innovative strategies. Asian Pacific Islanders for Human Rights, founded in 2000, has developed a strategic plan that includes components of leadership development, social service and advocacy. These strategies are tried-and-true, but long overdue in the Los Angeles queer APA community.

The cultural transformation that I hope will bring our community truly into the new millennium is the potential of queer youth of color organizing, and it is already underway in Los Angeles. These youth are looking at issues that connect multiple communities. If successful, they can provide a fresh model of multiracial organizing and can change the political dialogue in a city that has a spotty record of coalition building.

This organizing is only in its nascent stage, and these youth, representing a handful of organizations, are small in number. But you already know what I think about numbers.

—Eric Wat

The author would like to acknowledge Alice Y. Hom and Eric E. Reyes, who contributed valuable insights to early drafts of this essay.

Queer APA Households by the Numbers

The Census Bureau does not ask individuals their sexual preference; in today's climate, that would be considered by most a gross invasion of privacy. However, the Bureau has for the last two decennial Censuses attempted to count the number of gay and lesbian households in America. It does this by asking respondents in the short form (SF1 and SF2 data in the 2000 Census) what kind of household they live in, whether or not they are married, if not married whether one of their fellow householders is their partner, and the gender of that partner.

NHPI Unmarried Same-sex Partner Households by Metro Area, 2000

Rank	Metro area	Number of households
1	Honolulu, HI*	284
2	San Francisco-Oakland-San Jose, CA**	211
3	Los Angeles-Riverside-Orange County, CA**	193
4	New York-Northern New Jersey-Long Island, NY-NJ-CT-PA**	132
5	Seattle-Tacoma-Bremerton, WA**	79
	Percent male-male relationships	46.9%
	Percent female-female relationships	53.1%
	Total	**2,050.0**
	Percent	*0.9%*

*MSA: Stands for Metropolitan Statistical Area.
**CMSA: Stands for Consolidated Metropolitan Statistical Area.
Source: U.S. Census 2000, SF2 (Table PCT22)

In 1990, the Census counted 145,000 unmarried same-sex households, of which 56 percent were of two male partners. At 0.2 percent, they were a tiny percentage of the overall number of American households. Unmarried same-sex households involving an APA partner were even fewer: just 2,192, or about 1.5 percent of the unmarried same-sex household total.

By 2000, the numbers of unmarried, same-sex households in general and those involving Asians or Pacific Islanders had grown dramatically. There were 594,000 such households in total; of that, about 17,000 involved an Asian partner (this and NHPI figure includes those of both mixed-race and mixed-ethnicity) and 2,000 involved a Native Hawaiian or Pacific Islander partner.

Growth rates between 1990 and 2000 appear dramatic. The number of gay and lesbian households, at first glance, appears to have quadrupled during that time period. But the Census Bureau cautions against making direct comparisons. While factors such as greater comfort by same-sex couples to identify themselves and clearer Census form instructions in 2000 were no doubt a factor, the Bureau's method of counting unmarried same-sex couples also changed. In 1990, same sex couple respondents who marked their relationship as 'spousal' had their responses treated as errors and converted to some other relationship. In 2000, such responses were converted to same-sex, unmarried partner household relationships. According to the Galip Gazette, the newsletter for Gays and Lesbian members of the American Planning Association, the Defense of Marriage Act prevents the Census Bureau from

Asian Unmarried Same-sex Partner Households by Metro Area, 2000

Rank	Metro area	Number of households
1	New York-Northern New Jersey-Long Island, NY-NJ-CT-PA*	2,653
2	Los Angeles-Riverside-Orange County, CA*	2,534
3	San Francisco-Oakland-San Jose, CA*	2,366
4	Honolulu, HI**	679
5	Chicago-Gary-Kenosha, IL-IN-WI*	580
6	Seattle-Tacoma-Bremerton, WA*	553
7	San Diego, CA*	395
8	Boston-Worcester-Lawrence, MA-NH-ME-CT**	368
9	Philadelphia-Wilmington-Atlantic City, PA-NJ-DE-MD*	366
10	Houston-Galveston-Brazoria, TX*	290

Rank	Metro area	% of total households
1	Honolulu, HI*	0.24%
2	San Francisco-Oakland-San Jose, CA**	0.09%
3	Stockton-Lodi, CA*	0.06%
4	Los Angeles-Riverside-Orange County, CA**	0.05%
5	Sacramento-Yolo, CA**	0.04%
6	Salinas, CA*	0.04%
7	San Diego, CA*	0.04%
8	Seattle-Tacoma-Bremerton, WA**	0.04%
Tie (9-13)	Fresno, CA*	0.03%
	Las Vegas, NV-AZ*	0.03%
	Modesto, CA*	0.03%
	New York-Northern New Jersey-Long Island, NY-NJ-CT-PA**	0.03%
	Reno, NV*	0.03%

*MSA: Stands for Metropolitan Statistical Area.
**CMSA: Stands for Consolidated Metropolitan Statistical Area.
Source: U.S. Census 2000, SF2 (Table PCT22)

recognizing same-sex relationships as spousal.

Unmarried same-sex Asian households still only make up half a percent of all Asian households; the percentage for NHPIs is 0.9 percent. Male-male partner households make up 53 percent of all unmarried, same-sex Asian households; female-female partner households make up the same percentage for NHPI unmarried same-sex households.

As for the metropolitan areas with the largest number of Asian or NHPI unmarried same-sex partner households, New York, Los Angeles-Orange County, the San Francisco Bay Area, Chicago, and Boston led the way among the general population. For Asians alone, it was the same cities, with Honolulu easing ahead of Chicago for fourth largest. For NHPIs, the five largest metro areas were Honolulu, the San Francisco Bay Area, Los Angeles-Orange County, New York, and Seattle, in that order. Among Asian ethnicities, Chinese and Filipinos had the largest number of identified unmarried same-sex households, which may not be surprising considering they are the two largest populations overall.

Of course, there are caveats about the statistics: it is likely that the Census continues to undercount gay and lesbian households reluctant to identify themselves, and certain that the Census ignores the entire population of single gays and lesbians.

—Eric Lai

A Divergence of Faiths

Introduction

Finding comprehensive, detailed and accurate information on the religious beliefs of Asian Pacific Americans is nearly impossible. As Pyong Gap Min and Jung Ha Kim note in the introduction to their 2002 anthology, *Religions in Asian America: Building Faith Communities*, there are a number of reasons for this. First and foremost, one of the bedrock freedoms guaranteed by the Bill of Rights is the freedom of religion. As a result, the U.S. Census is prohibited from surveying respondents about their religious beliefs.

Second, attempts at non-governmental nationwide surveys on religion usually sample too few APAs to provide accurate results. Third, research on immigrants tends to ignore their cultural lives in favor of economic adjustment issues. Fourth, most research on APAs and religion has been based on ethnographic-style field work, rather than large-scale demographic surveys.

Finally, Gap and Min write, Asian American studies has lately emphasized cultural studies with a Marxist, postcolonial, postmodernist and feminist stance. These tend to discount the importance of religion or associate them with Western missionary and colonial activities.

Still, a number of facts—all taken from the preceding anthology—are known about APAs and religion:

– Japanese immigrants established the Young Men's Buddhist Association of San Francisco in 1898, the first "Pure Land" Buddhist organization in the continental United States.

– There are an estimated 3 million Buddhists in America, virtually all of them of Asian descent.

– In India, around 80 percent of the population is Hindu. Among Asian Indian Americans, the percentage may be as low as 65, as religious minorities like Sikhs and Christians are overrepresented in the United States.

Photo: Corky Lee

A Tibetan Buddhist candlelight ceremony marks the end of a 49-day mourning period after death. Buddhism is the fourth largest religion in the world, following Christianity, Islam and Hinduism.

– The majority of Indian immigrants from the province of Kerala are Christians. The Orthodox Syrian Christian Church of India is the most popular denomination.

– Pakistanis and other South Asians accounted for about one quarter of the six million Muslims in the United States in 1999.

– The first Sikh temple in the United States was established in Stockton, Calif. in 1912.

– About 25 percent of Koreans in Korea are Christian. In America, the ratio is reversed, as around 75 percent of Koreans are Christians, mostly Protestants.

– One-third to two-fifths of Vietnamese refugees in the United States are Catholic.

– One out of five Chinese immigrants in New York City is Christian, with 11 percent of them Protestant and 9 percent Catholic.

In this chapter, we feature two pieces on two different aspects of APA religiosity. The first is a look at Korean American churches, particularly those with mostly younger, one-and-a-half or second generation members, which are opening their doors to people of different ethnic backgrounds. The second is a look at the Mormon Church, which is winning many APA followers, especially among Pacific Islanders.

A New Generation of Korean American Churches

It's well documented that Christianity has been widely embraced by Koreans both in Korea and in the United States. Four of the ten largest churches in the world are located in South Korea; the largest in the world, Yoido Full Gospel Church, boasts an active membership of 900,000.

Close to 30 percent of South Korea's population today is Christian. However, Korean immigrants in the United States appear to be even more Christian than their counterparts in the old country. According to a recent survey, close to 80 percent of Koreans in Los Angeles attend a Korean church every week. In Los Angeles, where the largest numbers of Korean immigrants reside, there are approximately 800 Korean churches, serving 250,000 Koreans. The church is by far the most influential institution in the Korean American community.

For decades, Korean immigrant churches primarily served the Korean-speaking immigrant population. However, beginning the late 1980s with the increasing population of second-generation Korean Americans, the churches have had to grapple with a whole new set of inter-generational conflicts and tensions. American-born Koreans began to express their discontent with the immigrant-led church and demanded that their unique needs be met within the church. Frustrated that their demands fell on deaf ears, many second-generation pastors left to launch their own autonomous, second-generation Korean American churches, taking followers with them.

In Los Angeles, 26 second-generation churches have been created in the past ten years and the majority of these new churches are growing and thriving. Second-generation churches are also appearing in cities like Boston, Washington D.C., Chicago, and New York. The rapid proliferation of new ministries and churches that target second-generation Korean Americans in Los Angeles is an unparalleled social phenomenon. No other immigrant group in the United States has witnessed its second-generation reinventing and replanting ethnic churches at the same level as Korean Americans have had.

To go solo or multiethnic?

Second-generation churches emerged largely as a response by younger Korean Americans to the generational tensions within immigrant churches and a host of issues associated with "not belonging" or feeling "different" within mainstream religious institutions. However, within these newly constructed spaces, the second-generation has had to grapple with a whole new set of internal challenges and tensions, chiefly important and shared dilemmas of identity and mission.

Some second-generation ministers are determined to keep their churches Korean-only, similar to African American churches in the South. They advocate the importance of retaining culture and the development of a Korean American spirituality. Other ministers, however, are intentionally widening their ethnic "Korean" boundary to also encompass other Asian Americans. They argue that the similarities in life experiences and cultural orientation among different Asian American groups, largely derived by their shared status as children of immigrants and as racial minorities, serve as the common denominator that binds them together.

Lastly, convinced that the Protestant faith mandates racial reconciliation and unity, there are second-generation ministers who are determined to attract people of all races in order to transform their churches from Korean American institutions to multiracial ones.

This internal tension provides important insights into the ways in which the boundaries of these new churches can and do shift in response to changes in the vision and values of the second-generation. In addition, it points to the

Asian Mormons: Knockin' On Heaven's Door

In 1997, three Mormon missionaries, looking to spread the word, greeted Minh Mao at his doorstep. Before that visit, "I had an idea of God," recalls Mao, a young San Francisco native whose parents—Vietnamese immigrants of Chinese descent—had reared him in Buddhist traditions.

Photo: Andrew Chow

Chinese Vietnamese immigrant Minh Mao converted to the Mormon faith after being visited by missionaries. He joins the 600,000 other Asian Pacific Mormons around the world.

By year's end, Mao, now 22, had joined more than 600,000 others of Asian and Pacific Islander ethnicity, both in the United States and overseas, and elected to embrace the Church of Jesus Christ of Latter-day Saints.

The eleven million-member church now boasts a veritable rainbow congregation. As of 2002, half of Mormon members live outside of the United States, particularly in the Asia-Pacific region. More than half a million people in Asian and Pacific Island nations were baptized as Mormons each year throughout the mid-1990s, according to church statistics. In 2000 alone, 750,000 people from the Asia-Pacific region joined the Mormon Church.

The three most commonly spoken languages by Mormon members are English, Spanish and Portuguese. But Asian and Pacific Islander tongues round out the top ten: Tagalog, Cebuano (both spoken in the Philippines), Japanese, Samoan, Ilokano (another Filipino language), Korean and Tongan.

There are no statistics on what percentage of Mormons in the United States are APAs. But in the Bay Area, Mormon churches conduct separate services in Filipino, Samoan and Chinese language dialects. In Salt Lake City, where the Mormon church is based, five Tongan branches exist alongside those that serve Chinese and Japanese speakers.

The Mormon lifestyle includes abstaining from alcohol, caffeine and premarital sex, along with adhering to traditional family roles. The emphasis on education and traditional family values appealed to Shirley Tong, a Japanese American born in Hawai'i, where some 60,000 Mormons reside.

For other Asian converts, however, joining the Latter-day Saints represented an opportunity to come to the United States. Without them, "I would be in New Zealand now, maybe," says Moli Vaivaka, a Tongan native who now lives in Utah.

Some outsiders label the Latter-day Saints a "cult" that propagates sexist and racist doctrines. APA Mormons dismiss those claims. "We wouldn't have members in 160 countries if we were racist," Mao says flatly.

As the diversity of the Mormon fold increases, so does devotion. Many of the Church's immigrant members depend on the Church and fellow members to learn new languages, get job contacts, and obtain support from others in the community—all of which strengthen the spiritual bonds.

"It's not just a religion," Mao says. "It's a way of life."

—*AsianWeek*

reality that change, or in the case of the second generation what emerged as a "solution" in the face of multiple tensions, is itself laden with contradictions and instability.

Church's role for preserving Korean culture

Several of the pastors argue that Korean churches will not and should not evolve into multiethnic organizations and they strongly advocate a mono-ethnic congregation on two related grounds. First, they believe that the ethnic church is the main institution responsible for preserving the Korean culture and passing it down to the next generation. They argue that the church should not just limit itself to spiritual activities but should embrace a more holistic approach to ministry that includes promoting cultural awareness and identification among the second generation. Secondly, they argue that there is a distinct "Korean American" spirituality and it is the responsibility of Korean American churches to be carriers, preservers, and in some cases re-interpreters of this spirituality.

Regarding culture, some ministers believe that Korean churches should serve as a site of resistance against the accommodative forces and pressures of the American mainstream. Resistance, in the case of the Korean churches, takes the form of affirming one's cultural heritage. That means that American-raised Korean Americans must continue to be bound by cultural traditions, practices, and values from Korea that serve as a basis for ethnic solidarity. They argue that Korean churches must intentionally play an active role in preserving, fostering, and shaping Korean American culture. In other words, say these mono-ethnic advocates, although all Christians are called to unity, it should not come at the expense of ethnic identity and ethnic difference.

Pan-Asian—not just a cuisine, but a church, too

For advocates of pan-Asian churches, the similarities in life experiences and cultural orientation, largely derived from their shared status as children of immigrants and as racial minorities in the United States, draws different Asian American groups together at these new churches. They argue that cultural preservation should come second in importance to evangelizing the lost.

In casting their nets of evangelism, these second-generation Korean American churches have largely attracted and pulled in other Asian Americans. The fact that the majority of non-Korean Asian members were introduced to their churches through their friends indicates that among second-generation Koreans in Los Angeles, friendship networks are largely constructed along racial lines. Treated as members of the same race, Asian Americans tend to experience the same types of racist or racialist behavior, such as stereotypes for being "nerdy," "foreign," and "passive."

In Los Angeles, pan-ethnicity is playing a significant role in the formation and growth of Asian American churches. While not sharing a common history or national roots, Asian Americans do share common experiences as children of immigrants and as racial minorities in the United States and a common value system that is derived largely

Photo: Charles Ku

The Christian church is a focal point for the Korean community. In the Los Angeles area, home to the largest Korean American community, there are close to 800 Korean churches.

from Confucian culture. These commonalities increase the level of connection, identification, and camaraderie that bind Asian Americans together at these new churches.

Widening the boundary

In emphasizing the centrality of faith and the Christian identity, several other churches have consciously and intentionally allowed ethnic traditions, sensibilities, and expressions to fade. Many pastors see widening their racial boundary as just one necessary step in the steady movement from a mono-ethnic to a multiethnic congregation. They reject ethnic-specific congregations as inherently problematic for those who adhere to a Christian worldview; after all, doesn't the Bible clearly teach that within the church, "there is neither Jew nor Greek, slave nor free, male nor female, for you all one in Christ?"

To these pastors, those who want to remain within respective ethnic congregations do so simply out of convenience and comfort—motivations which they believe are inherently self-centered, narrow minded, and "un-Christian." However, while these second-generation churches advocate the inclusion of different ethnic and racial groups into their congregation, memberships have remained predominately Asian American. Nonetheless, convinced that a multiracial congregation is a God-given and achievable goal, ministers with a fierce determination have employed various strategies in order to attract more non-Asians into their churches. Heeding the advice of recent church growth experts who have argued that churches essentially attract people with the same profile as the leadership, one strategy has been to intentionally diversify the ethnic make-up of the church leadership. A few of the churches have also made intentional efforts to incorporate different cultural forms and expressions of praise music.

Conclusion

In the area of ethnic composition, second-generation churches are currently in a stage of experimentation and flux. It is well known that individuals and groups create boundaries as a way of differentiating themselves from the larger society and as a way of affirming their unique identities. This is playing out among second-generation churches: some churches draw tighter, more-fixed boundaries around ethnicity while other churches embrace looser, more fluid boundaries that change in response to the ethnic and racial composition of their membership.

Observing what happens provides important insights on the role of religion and religious organizations in the adaptation process of the offspring of post-1965 immigrants. Unlike the second-generation of European immigrants, second-generation Koreans are not simply assimilating into mainstream churches. They are creatively replanting and reinventing sacred spaces where their religious, ethnic, racial, and generational selves intersect.

Although at some churches there has been a natural progression in the ethnic composition of their congregations, I believe that not all churches will follow this progressive path. Mono-ethnic churches will continue to exist as long the Korean culture and identity is important for the members of these churches. The pastors and leaders of these churches, as spiritual and cultural entrepreneurs, play a large role in strengthening the ethnic identity among their congregation members. In short, ethnic churches and ethnic identity will continue to remain strong, for each works to promote and strengthen the other.

For Asian American churches, it is yet to be seen if they can successfully move from an organization that is bound by race to one that is solely bound by religion. At this juncture, there appears to be a desire to cross over the racial divide and become simply Christian churches. But if they do successfully cross the racial divide, will these churches be essentially identical to mainstream churches that are led by Caucasian Americans, or will there remain some distinguishable "Korean" or "Asian" roots? Is the planting of new ethnic churches a distinctly second-generation phenomenon? Will the next step invariably be an assimilated church? What will the ethnic church look like for the third generation—will Korean Americans follow in the steps of African Americans, previous white immigrants, or chart out an entirely new course altogether? In fifteen to twenty years, with the emergence of third-generation Korean Americans, we will be better equipped to answer these questions.

Nonetheless, the phenomena of Korean American churches moving between the identities of "Korean" to "Asian" to "multiethnic," demonstrates the fluid and flexible nature of a group's self-definition.

—*Sharon Kim*

Sources

(Note: some sources have been omitted where they are mentioned in more than one chapter.)

Section I – Overview

Chapter 1 – APA Demographics

Barnes, Jessica S. and Bennett, Claudette E. *The Asian Population: 2000*. Washington DC: Bureau of the Census, 2002.

Barringer, Herbert R. et al. *Asians and Pacific Islanders in the United States*. New York: Russell Sage Foundation, 1995.

CBS News/NY Times Poll, 7-10 December 2001. <http://pollingreport.com/race.htm>.

Chan, Sucheng. *Asian Americans: An Interpretive History*. New York: Twayne Publishers, 1991.

"County: English is Official Language." *New York Times*, 18 July 2002.

Crawford, James. "Language Legislation in the U.S.A." 15 July 2002. <http://ourworld.compuserve.com/>.

Immigration and Naturalization Service, 2000 Statistical Yearbook of the Immigration and Naturalization Service: Immigrants, Table 2: Immigration by Region and Selected Country of Last Residence Fiscal Years 1820-2000 (Washington, DC: Immigration and Naturalization Service, 2000) 6.

Logan, John R. "From Many Shores: Asians in Census 2000," Report by the Lewis Mumford Center for Comparative Urban and Regional Research. Albany, NY: University of Albany, 2001, unpublished, 3.

McGregor, Davianna. E-mail to Loh Sze-Leung, 26 September 2002, citing Stannard, David. *Before the Horror: The Population of Hawai'i Before Western Contact*. Honolulu: Social Science Research Institute, University of Hawai'i, 1989.

Office of Hawaiian Affairs. "Native Hawaiian Databook 1998," <www.oha.org/>.

Ong, Paul and Hee, Suzanne. "The Growth of the Asian Pacific American Population: Twenty Million in 2020," in *The State of Asian Pacific America: Policy Issues to the Year 2020*, eds. Hokoyama, J.D. and Nakanishi, Don T. Los Angeles: LEAP Asian Pacific American Public Policy Institute and UCLA Asian American Studies Center, 1994.

Toosi, Nahal. "English-only measure approved." *Milwaukee Journal-Sentinal*, 18 July 2002, <http://www.jsonline.com/>.

U.S. Bureau of the Census, "A Report of the Seventeenth Decennial Census of the United States, Census of the Population: 1950, Volume II, Characteristics of the Population," Washington, D.C., Government Printing Office, 1953.

U.S. Bureau of the Census, Population Division. Race and Hispanic Origin of the Population by Nativity. <http://www.census.gov/>.

U.S. Bureau of the Census, Population Projections Program, Population Division, "Projections of the Resident Population by Race, Hispanic Origin, and Nativity: Middle Series, 1999 and 2000."

U.S. Bureau of the Census. Public Use Micro Samples tables, 1960-1990.

U.S. Bureau of the Census, "Thirteenth Census of the United States Taken in the Year 1910, Volume III, Population 1920," Washington, D.C., Government Printing Office, 1913.

Zhou, Min and Gatewood, James. *Contemporary Asian America: A Multidisciplinary Reader*. New York: New York University Press, 2000.

Chapter 2 – Census / Mixed Race

Alphonso, Pinkney. *Black Americans*. Prentice-Hall: 2000.

Chang, Edward T. and Leong, Russell C. *Los Angeles--Struggles toward Multiethnic Community: Asian American, African American and Latino Perspectives*. University of Washington Press, 1994.

Chew, K., Eggebeen, D. and Uhlenberg P. "American children in multiracial households." Sociological Perspectives. Vol. 32 (1989): 65-85.

Chuman, Frank. *The Bamboo People: The Law and Japanese Americans*. Del Mar: California Publisher's Inc., 1976.

Der, H. Statement of Henry Der, National Coalition for an Accurate Count of Asians and Pacific Islanders in Review of Federal Measurements of Race and Ethnicity; Hearing before the Subcommittee on Census, Statistics, and Postal Personnel. House of Representatives, Serial No. 103-7. Washington, D.C.: U.S. Government Printing Office. 1994.

Fong, Timothy P. *The Contemporary Asian American Experience: Beyond the Model Minority*. Prentice-Hall, 1998.

Fong, Timothy P. and Shinagawa, Larry H., eds. *Asian Americans: Experiences and Perspectives*. Prentice-Hall, 2000.

Espiritu, Yen Le. *Asian American Panethnicity: Bridging Institutions and Identities*. Philadelphia, PA: Temple University Press, 1992

Fong, C. and Yung J. "In Search of the Right Spouse: Interracial Marriage Among Chinese and Japanese Americans." *Amerasia Journal*. Vol. 21, No. 3: 1995, pp. 77-98.

Hirabayashi, Lane Ryo, ed. *Teaching Asian America: Diversity and the Problem of Community*. Lanham, MD: Rowman & Littlefield Publishers, Inc., 1998.

Houston, Velina Hasu, and Williams, Teresa Kay. "No Passing Zone: Artistic and Discursive Writings By and About Asian-Descent Multiracials." *Amerasia Journal*. No. 1, Vol. 23, 1997.

Hune, Shirley. "An Overview of Asian Pacific American Futures: Shifting Paradigms" in *The State of Asian Pacific America: Policy Issues to the Year 2020*. LEAP Public Policy Institute and UCLA Asian American Studies Center, 1993.

Jacobs, J. and Labov, T. "Sex difference in intermarriage: Asian exceptionalism reconsidered." Paper presented at American Sociological Association Meeting, Washington. 21 August 1995.

Leong, Russell, ed. *Asian American Sexualities: Dimensions of the Gay and Lesbian Experience*. Routeledge, 1996.

Lott, Juanita Tamayo. Asian Americans: From Racial Category to Multiple Identities. Altamira Press, 1999.

Lowe, Lisa. *Immigrant Acts: on Asian American Cultural Politics*. Duke University Press, 1996.

Okihiro, Gary Y. *Margins and Mainstreams: Asian American History and Culture*. Seattle: University of Washington Press, 1994.

Root, Maria P.P., ed. *The Multiracial Experience Racial Borders as the New Frontier*. Thousand Oaks, CA: Sage Publications, 1996.

Saito, Leland. *Race and Politics: Asian Americans, Latinos and Whites in Los Angeles*.

Suburb University of Illinois Press, 1998.

Shinagawa, L. H. and Pang, G.Y. "Asian American Panethnicity and Intermarriage." *Amerasia Journal*, Vol. 22, No. 2, 1996, pp. 127-142.

Smith, J.W. and Worden, W.L. "They're Bringing Home Japanese Wives." *Saturday Evening Post*. 12 January 1952, pp. 26-27.

USA Today. "In the future, diversity will be the norm." 7 September 1999, p. 13A.

Valverde, Caroline Kieuline. "From Dust to Gold: The Vietnamese American Experience." In Maria P.P. Root, ed. *Racially Mixed People in America*. Thousand Oaks, CA: 1992.

Williams, J. "Amerasian Experience: Within, Between, and Beyond the Limits of Race, Culture, Community." *Rafu Shimpo*. 20 December 1990.

Williams-Leon, Teresa and Cynthia L. Nakashima. *The Sum of Our Parts: Mixed Heritage Asian Americans*. Temple University Press, 2001.

Chapter 3 – Immigration

Columbia University Web site, <http://www.columbia.edu/>.

Gardner, Robert; Robey, Bryant; and Smith, Peter C. "Asian Americans: Growth, Change, and Diversity." *Population Bulletin*, Vol. 4, No. 4, October 1985.

"Immigrants to U.S. by Country of Origin." <http://www.infoplease.com/>.

Immigration and Naturalization Service data, released through Inter-University Consortium for Political and Social Research.

Lee, Dong Ok. "Koreatown and Korean Small Firms in Los Angeles: Locating in the Ethnic Neighborhood." *Professional Geographer*, Vol. 47, No. 2, 184-195, May 1995.

Lee, Sharon M. "Asian Americans: Diverse and Growing." *Population Bulletin*, Vol. 53, No. 2, 1998.

Modarres, Ali. *The Racial and Ethnic Structure of Los Angeles County: A Geographic Guide*. Los Angeles, CA: Edmund G. "Pat" Brown Institute of Public Affairs, 1994.

Modarres, Ali. "Two Decades of Immigration: Has the Sky Fallen Yet?" *State of Immigration*. Los Angeles, CA: Edmund G. "Pat" Brown Institute of Public Affairs, 2000.

U.S. News and World Report. "More Asians Pour into U.S. Melting Pot." 13 October 1975. pp. 70-71.

Chapter 4 – Socioeconomics

Asian Pacific American Legal Center (APALC), et al., "Immigrant and Refugee Children Left Behind" Focus Group Study. Los Angeles: APALC, 2002.

Borjas, George J. *Homeownership in the Immigrant Population*, 2002. Boston, MA: Research Institute for Housing America, 2002.

Joint Center for Housing Studies of Harvard University. *The State of the Nation's Housing 2002*. Harvard University, 2002.

LEAP & API Small Business Program, *Dollars & Sense: Policies for Growing API Small Businesses*, 2001.

National Coalition for Asian Pacific American Community Development, Report to White House Initiative, 2001.

President's Advisory Commission on Asian Americans and Pacific Islanders. "A People Looking Forward: Action for Access and Partnerships in the 21st Century." Interim Report to the President and the Nation. Jan 2001, p.86.

Rumbaut, R.G. & Ima, K. "The adaptation of Southeast Asian refugee youth: A comparative study." San Diego, CA.: Southeast Asian Youth Study. Department of Sociology, San Diego State University, 1988.

Schoenholtz, Andrew I., and Kristan Stanton. *Reaching the Immigrant Market*, Washington, DC: Fannie Mae Foundation, 2001.

Smith-Hefner, N.J. "Language and identity in the education or Boston-area Khmer." *Anthropology and Education Quarterly*, 21(3), 250-268, 1998.

UCLA Asian American Studies Center & LEAP Public Policy Institute, *Beyond Asian American Poverty*, 1993.

U.S. Department of Commerce, Economic and Statistics Administration. U.S. Census Bureau. Asian and Pacific Islanders, 1997 Economic Census, Survey of Minority Owned Business Enterprises, Company Statistics Series. May 2001.

U.S. Department of Commerce, Economics and Statistics Administration. U.S. Census Bureau. Fertility of American Women: June 2000. October 2001.

Section II – Ethnicity

Chapter 1 – Chinese

Chan, Sucheng. *Asian Americans: An Interpretive History*. New York: Twayne Publishers, 1991.

Lee, Rose Hum. *The Chinese in the United States of America*. Hong Kong: Hong Kong University Press, 1960.

Logan, John R. with Jacob Stowell and Elena Vesselinov. 2001. "From Many Shores: Asians in Census 2000." Lewis Mumford Center for Comparative Urban and Regional Research Report, State University of New York at Albany <http://mumford1.dyndns.org/>.

Lyman, Stanford M. *Chinese Americans*. New York: Random House, 1974.

U.S. Immigration and Naturalization Service. Statistical Yearbook of the Immigration and Naturalization Service, 1998. Washington D.C.: U.S. Government Printing Office, 2000.

Wong, Morrison G. "Chinese Americans," pp. 58-94 in Pyong Gap Min, ed., *Asian Americans: Contemporary Trends and Issues*. Thousand Oaks: Sage Publications, 1995.

Zhou, Min. *Chinatown: The Socioeconomic Potential of an Urban Enclave*. Philadelphia, Pa.: Temple University Press, 1992.

Zhou, Min, "Chinese: Divergent Destinies in Immigrant New York," pp. 141-72 in Nancy Foner, ed., *New Immigrants in New York*. New York: Columbia University Press, 2001.

Chapter 2 – Filipinos

Agbayani-Siewert, P. and Revilla, L. "Filipino Americans." In Pyong Gap Min, ed., *Asian Americans: Contemporary Issues and Trends*. Thousand Oaks, California: Sage Publication, 1995.

Alonso-Zaldivar, Ricardo and Oldham, Jennifer. "New Airport Screener Jobs Going Mostly to Whites." *Los Angeles Times* 24 September 2002: 18. Nation Section <http://www.latimes.com>

Bennett, Claudette. "Racial Categories Used in the Decennial Censuses, 1790 to the Present." *Government Information Quarterly*, Volume 17, Number 2, (2000): 161-180.

Cheng, Lucie. "Part II: Immigration Patterns Introduction". In Ong, Bonacich, and Cheng's, eds. *The New Asian Migration in Los Angeles and Global Restructuring*. Philadelphia: Temple University Press, 1994: 39.

Espiritu, Yen Le. *Filipino American Lives*, Temple University Press, Philadelphia, 1995:14.

Empeno, H. "Anti-miscegenation laws and the Pilipino." In Jesse Quinsatt, ed., *Letters in Exile*, pp. 133-209. 1972.

Gathright, Alan. "San Jose Airport Hiring Screeners." *The San Francisco Chronicle*, 18 July 2002: A21, Bay Area Section, <http://www.sfgate.com/chronicle>

Kitano, H.H.L. *Race Relations*. New Jersey: Prentis Hall, 1997.

Mangiafico, L. *Contemporary American Immigrants: Patterns of Filipino, Korean, and Chinese Settlement in United States*. New York: Praeger, 1988.

Mathews, Joe. "The New Import: Teachers; First it was Nurses." *Los Angeles Times* August 10, 2002: 1. Metro Desk Section, <http://www.latimes.com>

Melendy, H.B. *Asians in America: Filipinos, Koreans, and East Indians*. Boston: Twayne Publishers, 1977.

Ng, F. & Wilson, J. *The Asian American Encyclopedia*, Volume 2-5: Philippines, Republic of the U.S.–China Relations. New York: Marshall Cavendish Corporation. 1995.

Pido, A. L.L.L. *The Pilipinos in America: Macro/micro dimensions of immigration and integration*. Staten Island, NY: Center for Migration Studies, 1986.

Posadas, Barbara M. *The Filipino Americans*. Westport, Connecticut: Greenwood Press, 1999.

Rodis, Rodel. "Unprecedented Deportation of Filipinos." *Philippine News*. 10 June 2002. New California Media. Pacific News Service. <http://news.ncmoline.com/>.

Sassen, Saskia. *Globalization and its discontents*. New York: New Press, 1998.

Takaki, Ronald T. *Strangers from a Different Shore: A History of Asian Americans*. Boston: Little, Brown, 1989.

U.S. Immigration and Naturalization Service. Statistical Yearbook for the Immigration and Naturalization Service, 2000. U.S Government Printing Office: Washington, D.C., 2002.

Chapter 3 – Asians Indians

Abdel-Latif, Omayma. "Asian Indians are maintaining their ethnic identity in U.S." *Detroit News*, 19 Aug 1994, Sec B, p7N col1.

Amarasingham, Lorna Rhodes. "Making friends in a new culture: South Asian women in Boston, Massachusetts." In *Uprooting and Development: Dilemmas of Coping with Modernization*. Coelho, P. Ahmed, and Yuan, eds. New York: Plenum, 2001.

Burr, Jeffrey. "Household status and Headship among unmarried Asian Indian women in later life." *Research on Aging*, 14(2), 1992.

Chung, L A. "S.F. Includes Asian Indians in Minority Law." *San Francisco Chronicle*. 25 June 1991, Sec A, p14 col4.

Dinnerstein, L. and D.M. Reimers. *Ethnic Americans*. New York: Harper & Row, 1982.

Fernandez, M. and W. Liu. 986. "Asian Indians in the United States: Economic, Educational and Family Profile from the 1980 Census." In *Tradition and Transformation: Asian Indians in America*, Brown and Coelho, eds. Williamsburg, VA: College of William and Mary, 1986.

Franklin, Donald E. "City hires law firm to inquire about hiring of Indians, Asians." *St. Louis Post-Dispatch*. 9 Dec 1994, Sec D, p9 col2.

Gosine, Mahin and Narine, Dhanpaul. "Sojourners to settlers: the Indian migrants in the Caribbean and the Americas." <http://www.saxakali.com/>.

Klein, Easy. "The Asian-American Market: Climb aboard the Orient Express." *D&B Reports* 1990, v38n6, Nov/Dec p38-40.

LaBrack, Bruce. "South Asians." In *Our Cultural Heritage: A Guide to America's Principal Ethnic Groups*. Greenwood Press, 1997, <http://www.lib.ucdavis.edu/>.

O'Hare, W.P. and J.C. Feldt. "Asian Americans: America's fastest growing minority group." *Population Trends and Public Policy*. No. 19, Washington, DC.: Population Reference Bureau, 1991.

Oh, Tai K. *The Asian brain drain: A factual and causal analysis*. San Francisco: R&E Research Associates, 1977.

"Pioneer Asian Indian Immigration to the Pacific Coast," UC Davis Library Web site, <http://www.lib.ucdavis.edu/>.

Rao, K.V. "Growth and Structure of Asian Indians in the United States, 1980-1990." *Demography India*. 1996.

Rao, V.N, V.V. Prakasa Rao, and M. Fernandez. "An exploratory study of social support among Asian Indians in the USA." *International Journal of Comparative Sociology*. 27(3-4), 1990.

Sandalow, Marc. "S.F. May Add Asian Indians to Minority Business List." *San Francisco Chronicle*. 18 June, 1991, Sec A, p15 col1.

Saran, Parmatma. "Patterns and adaptation of Indian immigrants: Challenges and strategies." In *Uprooting and Development: Dilemmas of Coping with Modernization*. Coelho, P. Ahmed, and Yuan, eds. New York: Plenum, 1980.

Seenarine, Moses. "Boundaries and Community: Indo-Caribbean Identities in the US." <http://www.saxakali.com>.

Singh, G.K. "Immigration, nativity and socio-economic assimilation of Asian Indians in the United States." Ann Arbor: University Microfilms International, 1991.

Strozier, Matthew. "Each year, hundreds of thousands participate in the West Indian American Day parade in Brooklyn." <http://www.indiainnewyork.com>.

Taub, Richard P. "American Sentiments towards India and Indians." Unpublished paper, University of Chicago, Chicago. National Opinion Research Center Survey, 1978.

U.S. Bureau of the Census. 1983. We, the American Asians. Census 1980 Brief. US Census Bureau.

U.S. Bureau of the Census. 1991. Studies in American fertility, Current Population Reports, Series P-23, No. 176, U.S. Government Printing Office, Washington, DC.

U.S. Bureau of the Census. 1993. We, the American Asians. Census 1990 Brief. US Census Bureau.

U.S. Bureau of the Census. 2002. The Asian Population: 2000. Census 2000 Brief. US Census Bureau.

Xenos, P., H. Barringer, and M. Levin. 1989. "Asian Indians in the United States: A 1980 Census Profile", No. 111, Papers of the East-West Population Institute.

Chapter 4 – Koreans

Abelmann, Nancy and Lie, John. *Blue Dreams*. Cambridge, Mass.: Harvard University Press, 1995.

Bonacich, Edna. "The Social Costs of Immigrant Entrepreneurship." *Amerasia Journal* Vol. 14 No.1, 1988.

Bonacich, Edna "The Role of the Petite Bourgeoisie Within Capitalism: A Response to Pyong Gap Min." *Amerasia Journal*. Vol. 15 No.2, 1989:195-203.

Bonacich, Edna and Light, Ivan. *Immigrant Entrepreneurs: Koreans in Los Angeles 1965-1982*. Berkeley and Los Angeles: University of California Press, 1988.

Bonacich, Edna, Hossain, Mokerrom, and Park, Jae-hong. "Korean Immigrant Working Women in the Early 1980s." In *Korean Women in Transition: At Home and Abroad*, ed., Yu, Eui Young and Phillips, Earl. Los Angeles: Center for Korean-American and Korean Studies, California State University, Los Angeles, 1987, pp. 219-47.

Bonacich, Edna and Jung, Tae Hwang, "A Portrait of Koreans Business in Los Angeles: 1977." In *Koreans in Los Angeles: Prospects and Promises*, eds., Yu, Eui-

Young, Phillips, Earl, and Yang, Eun Sik. Koryo Research Institute and Center for Korean-American and Korean Studies, California State University, Los Angeles, 1982, pp. 75-98.

Chang, Edward T. "Myths and Realities of Korean-Black American Relations." In Eui-Young Yu ed. *Black-Korean Encounter: Toward Understanding and Alliance.* Los Angeles: Institute for Asian American and Pacific Asian Studies, 1994:83-89.

Chang, Edward T. "The Los Angeles Riots: A Korean American Perspective." *Korean and Korean-American Studies Bulletin.* Vol. 4 No. 3 Summer/Fall 1993: 10-11.

Hurh, Won Moo and Kim, Kwang Chung. "Employment of Korean Immigrant Wives and the Division of Household Tasks." In *Korean Women in Transition,* pp. 199-218.

Hurh, Won Moo and Kim, Kwang Chung. *Korean Immigrants in America: A Structural Analysis of Ethnic Confinement and Adhesive Adaptation.* Rutherford: Fairleigh Dickinson University Press, 1984.

Kang, Connie. "40% of Koreans in Poll Ponder Leaving" *Los Angeles Times.* March 19, 1993: B1.

Kang, Connie. "Korean Riot Victims Still Devastated, Study Finds Urban Problems" *Los Angeles Times.* July 23, 1993: B-3.

Kim, Elaine. "Home is Where the Han Is: A Korean-American Perspective on the Los Angeles Upheavals." In Gooding-Williams, ed., *Reading Rodney King/Reading Urban Uprising.*" 1993: 219.

Kim, Warren. *Koreans in America.* Seoul: Po Chin Chai, 1971.

Lee, Daniel Booduck. "Marital Adjustment Between Korean Women and American Servicemen." In *Koreans in America: Dreams and Realities,* ed. Hyung-chan Kim and Eun Ho Lee. Seoul: The Institute of Korean Studies, 1990, p. 102.

Min, Pyong Gap. *Caught in the Middle: Korean Communities in New York and Los Angeles.* Berkeley, University of California Press, 1996.

Min, Pyong Gap. "Problems of Korean Immigrant Entrepreneurs." Paper presented at the Annual Meeting of the Asian Studies Association, San Francisco, March 26, 1988.

Min, Pyong Gap. "The Social Costs of Immigrant Entrepreneurship: A Response to Edna Bonacich." *Amerasia Journal.* Vol.15 No.2, 1989:187-194.

Patterson, Wayne. *The Ilse: First-Generation Korean Immigrants in Hawai'i, 1903-1973.* Honolulu: University of Hawai'i Press, 2000.

Patterson, Wayne. *The Korean Frontier in America: Immigration to Hawai'i, 1896-1910.* Honolulu: University of Hawai'i Press, 1988.

Rivera, Carla. "Korean-American Looking Elsewhere After Riots." *Los Angeles Times.* 24 December 1992: A-3.

Schoenberger, Karl. "Moving Between 2 Worlds." *Los Angeles Times,* 12 July 1992: A24.

Sheppard, Harold L. "The Potential Role of Behavioral Science in the Solution of the 'Older Worker Problem'." *American Behavioral Scientist* XIV-1 (Sept-Oct 1970), pp. 71-80.

Stewart, Ella. "Ethnic Cultural Diversity: Ethnographic Study of Cultural Study of Cultural Differences and Communication Styles between Korean Merchants and African American Patrons in South Los Angeles." M.A. thesis, Department of Communications, California State University Los Angeles, 1989: 9.

Yu, Eui-Young. "Korean Communities in America: Past, Present, and Future," *Amerasia* 10:2 (1983), pp. 23-35.

Yu, Eui-Young. Korean Community Profile. Los Angeles: *Korea Times,* 1990, pp. 9-10.

Yu, Eui-Young. "Koreatown in Los Angeles: Emergence of a New Inner-City Ethnic Community." Bulletin of the Population and Development Studies Center Vol. XIV (Seoul National University, 1985), p. 37.

Chapter 5 – Vietnamese

Cao, Lan. *Monkey Bridge.* New York: Viking, 1997.

Chang, Pao Min. *Beijing, Hanoi and the Overseas Chinese.* Institute of East Asian Studies, University of California, Berkeley, 1982.

Dinh, Linh. *Fake House.* New York: Seven Stories Press, 2000.

Duong Van Mai Elliott, *The Sacred Willow: Four Generations in the Life of a Vietnamese Family.* New York: Oxford University Press, 1999.

Hayslip, Le Ly with James Wurts. *When Heaven and Earth Changed Places.* New York: Doubleday, 1989.

Hess, Gary R. *Cultural Identity and Diaspora.* Oxford, Policy Press, 1990.

Huynh, Jade Ngoc Quang. *South Wind Changing.* Saint Paul, MN: Gray Wolf Press, 1994.

Mong Lan. *Song of the Cicadas.* Massachusetts: University of Massachusetts Press, 2001.

Nguyen Ngoc Ngan with E.E.Richey. *The Will of Heaven: One Vietnamese and the End of His World.* New York: E.P.Dutton, 1982.

Nguyen, Kien. *The Unwanted.* Boston: Little, Brown and Company, 2001.

Nguyen Qui Duc. *Where the Ashes Are: the Odyssey of a Vietnamese Family.* Reading, Mass: Addison-Wesley Pub. Co., 1994.

Pham, Andrew. *Catfish and Mandala: A Two-Wheeled Voyage through the Landscape and Memory of Vietnam.* New York: Farrar, Straus and Giroux, 1999.

Tran, Khanh. *The Ethnic Chinese and Economic Development in Vietnam.* Institute of Southeast Asian Studies, Singapore, 1993.

Tran, Truong and Hoang Chuong. *The Book of Perception.* San Francisco: Kearny Street Workshop, 1999.

Trinh T. Minh-ha. *Woman Native Other.* Bloomington, Indianapolis: Indiana University Press: 1989.

Truong, Monique Thuy-Dung. "The Emergence of Voices: Vietnamese American Literature 1975-1900." *Amerasia Journal* 19.3 (1993): 27-50.

Truong Nhu Tang with David Chanoff and Doan Van Toai. *A Vietcong Memoir.* New York: Vintage, 1985.

Weinberg, Meyer. *Asian-American Education: History Background and Current Realities.* Mahwah, New Jersey: Lawrence Erlbaum Associates, Publisher, 1997.

Chapter 6 – Japanese

Aratani, Lori. "As their numbers shrink, Japanese-American heritage thrives," *San Jose Mercury News.* 6 July, 2001.

Associated Press, "Census Data Shows Changes in California's Asian Population" *Rafu Shimpo.* 5 May 2001.

Associated Press, "With Population in Decline, Japanese Americans Look to Future" *Rafu Shimpo.* 19 June 2001.

Brownstone, David M. and Irene M. Franck, *Facts About American Immigration,* New York & Dublin: The H.W. Wilson Company, 2001.

Gibson, Campbell J. Emily Lennon, "Historical Census Statistics on the Foreign-born Population of the United States: 1850-1990." Population Division Working Paper No. 29. U.S. Bureau of the Census, 1999. <http://www.census.gov/>.

U.S. Immigration and Naturalization Service. Fiscal Year 2000 Statistical Yearbook. <http://www.ins.usdoj.gov>.

Chapter 7 – Native Hawaiians

Akaka, Daniel. Statements on Introduced Bills and Joint Resolutions, April 6, 2001 to U.S. Senate.

Department of Interior and Department of Justice. "From Mauka to Makai: The River of Justice Must Flow Freely, Report on the Reconciliation Process Between the Federal Government and Native Hawaiians." Washington D.C., 23 October 2000, p. 56.

"Hawaiians in the 2000 U.S. Census." Ke Alii Pauahi Foundation & Policy Analysis & System Evaluation, Kamehameha Schools.

Kanahele, George S. *Current Facts and Figures About Hawaiians*. Honolulu: Project WAIAHA, 1982.

Chapter 8 – Pacific Islanders

Baron, Debra. "Who are the Pacific Islanders?" *The Asian American Almanac*. Gall, Susan and Natividad, Irene, ed. Gale Research Inc., 1995.

Grieco, Elizabeth. "The Native Hawaiian and Other Pacific Islander Population: 2000 Census Brief." U.S. Census Bureau, December 2001.

"Guam History." <http://www.lonelyplanet.com/>

Miller, Ted. "American Football, Samoan Style." <http://espn.go.com/>

Orwell, George. *Animal Farm*. London: Secker and Warburg, 1945. Reprint, New York: Harcourt Brace, 1983.

"Samoan football players in the NFL." <http://espn.go.com/>

"Samoa's Past." <http://www1.visitsamoa.ws/samoa/past.htm>

"South Sea Islanders in Utah." <http://www.media.utah.edu/>

"The Lone Ranger Was Not Alone." Christian Outfitters website. <http://www.christianoutfitters.com/>

"Trust Territory of the Pacific Islands." <http://libweb.hawaii.edu/>

Chapter 9 – Southeast Asians

"Asian Americans and Representation Issues." <http://www.stthom.edu/>.

Associated Press. "Cambodia, U.S. Govts Sign Repatriation Agreement" May 3, 2002.

Bulk, J.D. "American Hmong on the Move: An Explanation of Very Distinctive Secondary Migration." *Hmong Forum* (St. Paul, MN: Haiv Hmoob, 1996): 3-28.

Cheng Mae M. and Richard Dalton. "Count Is Questioned: Hispanic groups say unclear query led to inaccurate numbers." <http://www.mumford1.dyndns.org/>.

Dahlburg, John-Thor. "Sweatshop Case Dismays Few in Thailand." *Los Angeles Times*. 27 August 1995: A4.

Gardiner, Debbie. "Donuts Anyone? Cambodians Own some 90 percent of California's Donut Shops." *AsianWeek*, 22-28 June 2000.

Kiernan, Ben. *The Pol Pot Regime: Race, Power, and Genocide Under the Khmer Rouge, 1975-1979*. New Haven: Yale University Press p.16, 1996.

Martorell, Chancee. Phone interview by Rahpee Thongthiraj. Los Angeles, CA. 7 June 2002.

Nako, Joyce. "The Thai Association: Keeping the Community in Touch With the Homeland." *Gidra*, 20th Anniversary Issue, 1990.

Office of Refugee Resettlement Report Annual Report to Congress 1999. Washington D.C.: U.S. Government Printing Office, 2000.

Panichpant, Nampet. "Visible But Unheard: A Thai Community Profile." *AsianWeek*. 5 March 1993.

Pfeifer, Mark E. "Census Shows Growth and Changing Distribution of the Cambodian Population in the United States" Asian American Press, St. Paul, MN, Copyright by the Author. St. Paul, MN. <http://www.hmongstudies.org/>.

Pran, Dith. "The Cambodian Killing Fields" Woodbridge, NJ, 1997. <http://www.dithpran.org/killingfields.htm>.

Southeast Asia Resource Action Center. 2001. *Opportunities and Challenges of Advocacy in Southeast Asian American Communities*. Washington D.C. 2001.

Thongthiraj, Rahpee. In the "Thai American Experience" classes, UCLA, Los Angeles, 1994, 1995, 1999, 2000.

U.S. Census Bureau. The Cambodian Community of Long Beach: An Ethnographic Analysis of Factors Leading to Census Undercount. Ethnographic Evaluation of 1990 Decennial Census Report Series, Report No. 9. Center for Survey Methods Research Bureau of the Census. Washington, D.C., 1992.

Chapter 10 – South Asians

Administration for Children and Families, Office of Refugee Resettlement. Refugee Resettlement Program, Report to the Congress. Washington, DC: U.S. Department of Health and Human Services, January 31, 1992.

Del Valle, Fidel F. "Who's Driving New York? A Profile of Taxi Driver Applicants." *MigrationWorld*. Vol. XXIII, No. 4(1995): 12-15.

Ghosh, Krittika. Phone interview with author. Asian American Legal Defense and Education Fund, New York, 7 August 2002.

Kershaw, Sarah, "Queens to Detroit: A Bangladeshi Passage." *New York Times*. 8 March, 2001: A:1, B:6.

Khandhar, Parag. Phone interview with author. Asian American Federation, New York, 14 August 2002.

Nepal Association of Oregon, Mission Statement, <http://www.geocities.com/>.

"People of South Asia in America Exhibit." Unpublished exhibit narrative. Center for South Asia Studies, University of California at Berkeley, 1984.

"Redistricting Update: Keeping Communities Together." *Righting Wrongs*. Bulletin of Asian American Defense and Education Fund, May 2002.

Chapter 11 – Hapas

Ang, Ien. *On Not Speaking Chinese: Living Between Asia and the West*. New York: Routledge, 2001.

Chung, Sheila. *Hapa Issues Forum* Press Release: "Over One in Ten Asian Pacific Islanders in California are Multiracial, Census Data Show." 17 July 2002.

Eaton, Edith. *Mrs. Spring Fragrance*.

Fulbeck, Kip. *Paper Bullets: A Fictional Autobiography*. Seattle: University of Washington Press, 2001.

Hagedorn, Jessica. *Dogeaters*. New York: Pantheon Books, 1990

Hall, Bruce Edward. *Tea that Burns*.

Hara, Marie and Nora Okja Keller, eds. *Intersecting Circles: The Voices of Hapa Women in Poetry and Prose*. Honolulu: Bamboo Ridge Press, 1999

Leach, Emily. *Email*, July 16, 2002.

Lee, Sky. *Disappearing Moon Café*.

"Roots in the Sand" (video, 2000)

Spickard, Paul "Injustice Compounded: Amerasians and Non-Japanese in World War II Concentration Camps." *Journal of American Ethnic History*. Spring 1987.

Section III – Geography

Chapter 1 – California

Aguilar-San Juan, Karin. "Creating Ethnic Places: Vietnamese American Community-Building in Orange County and Boston." Ph.D. Thesis, Brown University, 2002.

DeWilde, Steven R. "Vietnamese Settlement Patterns in Orange County's Little Saigon." M.A. Thesis, California State University, Long Beach, 1996.

Do, Hien Duc. "The Formation of a New Refugee Community: The Vietnamese Community in Orange County, California." M.A. Thesis, University of California, Santa Barbara, 1988.

Edmonston, B. and Schultze, C. eds. Modernizing the US Census. Washington, D.C.: National Academy Press, 1995.

Kicon Viet Space, <http://vietspace.kicon.com/>

Mazumdar, Sanjoy, Shampa Mazumdar, Faye Docuyanan, and Colette Marie McLaughlin. "Creating a Sense of Place: The Vietnamese-Americans and Little Saigon," *Journal of Environmental Psychology*. 20: 319-333, 2000.

McLaughlin, Colette Marie and Paul Jesilow. "Conveying a Sense of Community along Bolsa Avenue: Little Saigon as a Model of Ethnic Commercial Belts." *International Migration*, Vol. 36 (1): 49-63, 1998.

Michaels, Robert Daniel. "The Structure and Spatial Morphology of the Ethnic Commercial Enclaves of Little Saigon and Koreatown in Orange County, California: A Comparative Study." M.A. Thesis, California State University, Long Beach, 2000.

Nguoi Viet Daily News, <http://nguoi-viet.com/>.

Orr, Elisabeth. "Living Along the Fault Line: Community, Suburbia and Multi-Ethnicity in Garden Grove and Westminster, CA 1900-1995. Ph.D. Thesis, Indiana University, 1999.

Reyes, Adelaida. *Songs of the Caged, Songs of the Free: Music and the Vietnamese Refugee Experience*. Philadelphia, PA: Temple University Press, 1999.

Southeast Asian Archive. University of California, Irvine, <http://www.lib.uci.edu/>.

The Vietnamese Community in Orange County: An Oral History. Santa Ana, CA: The Vietnamese Chamber of Commerce in Orange County and Newhope Library.

Union of Vietnamese Student Associations of Southern California, <http://www.vnet.org/>.

Chapter 2 – Northeast

Atkins, Kimberly. "Census finds more Asians calling Quincy home." *Boston Globe*. 26 May 2002.

Cowen, Richard. "Far East meets north Jersey many Asians here, but few hold office." *The Record*. 12 March, 2001.

Gold, Jeffrey. "New Immigrants Build a Gold Coast." Associated Press in *AsianWeek*, 16-22 March, 2001.

Johnson, Paul H. "Census to show a bigger New Jersey population gains keep pace with U.S." *The Record*. 28 December, 2000.

Johnson, Paul H. "Growing diversity in north Jersey census estimates show Asian boom." *The Record*. 30 Aug, 2000.

Kasinitz, Philip. *Caribbean New York: Black Immigrants and the Politics of Race*. New York: Cornell University Press, 1992.

Kim, Yung. "Asian-American coalition seeks political power in north Jersey." *The Record*. 4 July, 2001.

Kwong, Peter. *Forbidden Workers: Illegal Chinese Immigrants and American Labor*. New York: New Press. 1996.

Logan, John R., Richard Alba, and Wenquan Zhang. "Immigrant Enclaves and Ethnic Communities in New York and Los Angeles," *American Sociological Review*, 67, April 2002: 229-322.

Massey, Joanna. "Census puts Randolph at top in percentage of foreign-born." *Boston Globe*. 2 June 2002.

Most, Doug and Kane, Paul. "Ethnic mix of north Jersey changes numbers of Asians, Hispanics up sharply. *The Record*. 15 Sept 1999.

Peterson, Iver. "Newest Immigrants Head Straight to New Jersey's Suburbs." *New York Times*. 10 March 2001.

Reid, Alexander. "Towns farther from Boston growing faster, Census finds." *Boston Globe*. 9 Sept 2001.

Rodriguez, Cindy and Dedman, Bill. "Census finds a world of differences from Weston's affluence to Springfield's poverty." *Boston Globe*. 27Aug 2002.

Rodriguez, Cindy. "Census shows a Boston still divided blacks, whites remain apart despite progress." *Boston Globe*. 20 April 2001.

Rodriguez, Cindy. "City, state take on new cast minorities are hub majority, Census finds." *Boston Globe*. 22 March 2001.

Rodriguez, Cindy. "Suburbs drawing Boston blacks Census: Whites shift toward I-495." *Boston Globe*. 4 April 2001.

Scott, Janny. "Foreign-Born in US at Record High," *New York Times*, 7 February 2002.

Scott, Janny. "Minorities Changing Landscape of New Jersey." *New York Times*. 9 March 2001.

Stancavish, Don. "Shifting fortunes N.J.'s wealth moving west and south." *The Record*. 27 Dec 2000.

Weil, Lynne. "Asians, the State's Fastest-Growing Minority, Are Changing the Face of New Jersey." *New York Times*. 22 October 2000.

Chapter 3 – Hawai'i

Beechert, Edward D. *Working in Hawai'i: A Labor History*. Honolulu: University of Hawai'i Press, 1985.

Daws, Gavan. *Shoal of Time: A History of the Hawaiian Islands*. Honolulu: University Press of Hawai'i, 1968.

Department of Business, Economic Development and Tourism, State of Hawai`i. State of Hawai`i: Facts & Figures. 2000.

Fuchs, Lawrence H. *Hawai'i Pono: A Social History*. New York: Harcourt, Brace & World, 1961.

Kent, Noel J. *Hawai'i: Islands Under the Influence*. New York: Monthly Review Press, 1983.

Okamura, Jonathan. "Why There Are No Asian Americans in Hawai`i." *Social Process in Hawai'i*. 35 (1994): 161-78.

Standard, David E. *Before the Horror: The Population of Hawai'i on the Eve of Western Contact*. Honolulu: University of Hawai'i Press, 1989.

Chapter 4 – West

Cohn, D"Vera and Darryl Fears, "1 in 3 Americans is a minority: Census shows diverse nation." *Seattle Times*. 13 March 2001.

Fugita, Stephen S. and David J. O'Brien. *Japanese American Ethnicity: the Persistence of Community*. Seattle: University of Washington Press, 1991.

James, Ronald L. *Ruins of a World: Chinese Gold Mining at the Mon-Tung Site in the Snake River Canyon*. Washington D.C: U.S. Department of the Interior, Bureau of Land Management, Idaho Cultural Resources, Series IV, October 1995.

Kamman, Jon and Ryan Konig, Peter Ortiz and Stephanie A. Miller. "Valley Blacks, Asians gain in income." *Arizona Republic*. 4 Sept 2002.

Kang, K. Connie. "Poll: Many don't trust people of Chinese descent (Los Angeles Times)." *Seattle Times*. 25 April 2001.

Kang, K. Connie. "Report: Asian Americans still treated as 'aliens' in U.S. (Los Angeles Times)." *Seattle Times*. 2 March 2000.

Kashima, Tetsuden and Frank Miyamoto and Stephen S. Fugita. "Religious Attitudes and Beliefs Among Japanese Americans: King County, Washington and Santa Clara County, California." *Behaviormetrika*. 29:2 (2002): 203:229.

Kotchek, Lydia. "Ethnic visibility and Adaptive Strategies: Samoans in the Seattle

Area." *Journal of Ethnic Studies*. 4:4 (1976) 28-38.

Light, Ivan. "From Vice-District to Tourist Attraction: The Moral Career of American Chinatowns, 1880-1940." *Pacific Historical Review*. 43 (August 1974): 367-94.

Lindlom, Mike. "Asian Indian Population Growing Fast." *Seattle Times*. 28 May 2001.

Mattern, Hal. "Valley job growth top in U.S. in '99." *Arizona Republic*. 2 May 2001.

"Nevada sustains status as fastest-growing state." *Las Vegas Sun*. August 30, 2000.

Rozemberg, Hernán. "State's Asian population fastest-growing racial group," *Arizona Republic*. 11 January 2002.

University of Arizona Library. <http://dizzy.library.arizona.edu/>.

Yanagisako, Silvia J. *Transforming the Past: Tradition and Kinship Among Japanese Americans*. Stanford: Stanford University Press, 1985.

Chapter 5 – Canada

Adachi, Ken. *The Enemy That Never Was*. Toronto: McClelland & Stewart Inc. 1991.

Avery, Donald. *Reluctant Host: Canada's Response to Immigrant Workers, 1895-1994*. Toronto: McClelland & Stewart, 1995.

Basran, G.S. "Indo-Canadian Families: Historical Constraints and Contemporary Conditions." *Journal of Family Studies*. 24:3 (1993): 339-352.

Beaujot, Roderic P. "Immigration and Demographic Structures." *Immigrant Canada: Demographic, Economic and Social Challenges*. Shiva S. Halli & Leo Driedger (eds.) Toronto: University of Toronto Press, 1999.

Boyd, Monica & Michael Vickers. "100 Years of Immigration in Canada". *Canadian Social Trends. Statistics Canada*. Cat. No. 11-008. Autumn (2000): 2-12.

Canadian Race Relations Foundation Act. 1991. < http://laws.justice.gc.ca/>.

Chadney, James G. "India's Sikhs in Vancouver: Immigration, Occupation and Ethnic Adaptation". *Population Review*. 29:1/2. (1985): 59-66.

Chard, Jennifer & Viviane Renaud. "Visible Minorities in Toronto, Vancouver and Montreal." *Canadian Social Trends. Statistics Canada*. Cat. No. 11-008. Autumn. (1999): 20-25.

Citizenship and Immigration Canada. *Facts and Figures 2000: Immigration Overview*. Ottawa: Minister of Public Works and Government Services. Cat. No. MP43-333/2001E. 2001.

Citizenship and Immigration Canada. *Immigration Research Series: Profiles India*. Ottawa: Minister of Supply and Services Canada. Cat. No.: Ci62-2/3-1996. 1996.

Costa, Rosalinda & Viviane Renaud. "The Chinese in Canada." *Canadian Social Trends*. Statistics Canada. Cat. No. 11-008E. Winter (1995): 22-26.

Dirks, Gerald E. *Controversy & Complexity: Canadian Immigration Policy During the 1980s*. Montreal & Kingston, ON: McGill-Queen's University Press, 1995.

Fong, Eric. "A Comparative Perspective of Racial Residential Segregation: American & Canadian Experiences." *Sociological Quarterly*. 37:2 (1996): 501-28.

Fong, Eric & Emi Ooka. "The Social Consequences of Participating in the Ethnic Economy." *International Migration Review*. 36:1. (2002): 125-46.

Harvey, Edward B., Bobby Siu & Kathleen D.V. Reil. "Ethnocultural Groups, Period of Immigration and Socioeconomic Situation." *Canadian Ethnic Studies*. 31:3. (1999): 93-104.

Isajiw, Wsevolod. *Understanding Diversity: Ethnicity and Race in The Canadian Context*. Toronto: Thompson Educational Publishing, Inc., 1999.

Johnston, Hugh J.M. *The East Indians in Canada*. Ottawa: The Canadian Historical Association, 1984.

Khan, Shahnaz. "Influences Shaping Relations between the East Indians and the Anglo Canadians in Canada: 1903-1947." The *Journal of Ethnic Studies* 19:1. (1991): 101-16.

Kobayashi, Audrey. "Regional and Demographic Aspects of Japanese Migration to Canada". *The Canadian Geographer*. 32:4. (1988): 356-60.

Li, Peter S. *The Chinese in Canada*. Don Mills, ON: Oxford University Press, 1988.

Li, Peter S. "The Market Worth of Immigrants' Educational Credentials." *Canadian Public Policy*. 27:1. (2001): 23-38.

Miki, Roy & Cassandra Kobayashi. *Justice in our Time: The Japanese Canadian Redress Settlement*. Vancouver: Talonbooks, 1991.

Simmons, Alan B. "The Case of Asian Immigration to Canada". In *The Silent Debate: Asian Immigration and Racism in Canada*. Eleanor Laquian, Aprodicio Laquian and Terry McGee (eds). Vancouver, BC: The University of British Columbia Institute of Asian Research, 1998.

Takata, Toyo. *Nikkei Legacy: The Story of Japanese Canadians from Settlement to Today*. Toronto: NC Press Limited, 1983.

Tan, Jin & Patricia E. Roy. *The Chinese in Canada*. Ottawa: The Canadian Historical Association, 1985.

Vibert, Dermot. "Asian Migration to Canada in Historical Context." *The Canadian Geographer*. 32:4 (1988): 352-4.

Waldinger, Roger & Jennifer Lee. "New Immigrants in Urban America." In *Strangers at the Gates: New Immigrants in Urban America*. Roger Waldinger (ed.) Berkeley & Los Angeles, CA: University of California Press. 2001.

Ward. W. Peter. *The Japanese in Canada*. Ottawa: Canadian Historical Association, 1982.

Ward, W. Peter. *White Canada Forever: Popular Attitudes and Public Policy Towards Orientals in British Columbia*. Montreal & Kingston: McGill-Queen's University Press, 1990.

Chapter 6 – Midwest

Jew, Victor. "'Chinese Demons': The Violent Articulation of Chinese Otherness and Inter racial Sexuality in the U.S. Midwest, 1885-1889." *The Journal of Social History*. Dec 2003.

Posadas, Barbara. "Ethnic Life and Labor in Chicago's Pre-World War II Filipino Community," in Robert Asher and Charles Stephenson, eds., *Ethnicity and American Labor*. Albany: State University of New York Press, 1987.

Barbara Posadas and Roland L. Guyotte, "Aspiration and Reality: Occupational and Educational Choice among Filipino Migrants to Chicago, 1900-1935," *Illinois Historical Journal* 85 (Summer 1992): 89-104.

Koltyk, Jo An. *New Pioneers in the Heartland*. Hmong Life in Wisconsin. Boston: Allyn and Bacon, 1998.

Lieser, Ethen. "St. Paul's APA Population Labeled Most Segregated." *AsianWeek* 11-17 January 2002.

McKeown, Adam. *Chinese Migrant Networks and Cultural Change: Peru, Chicago, Hawai'i, 1900-1936*. Chicago: University of Chicago Press, 2001.

Peterson, David. "Minnesota's Hmong buy homes at brisk pace." *Minneapolis Star Tribune*. 10 April 2002.

Siu, Paul. The Chinese Laundryman. A Study in Social Isolation New York: New York University Press, 1997.

Skertic, Mark. "Diversity is gaining in white suburbs." *Chicago Sun-Times*. 8 April 2001.

Skertic, Mark. "Once-white suburbs now more mixed." *Chicago Sun-Times*. 15 March 2001.

Sumida, Stephen H. "East of California: Points of Origin in Asian American Studies." *Journal of Asian American Studies* 1 (1998): 83-100.

Chapter 7 – South

Barringer, Herbert R., Gardner, Robert W., and Levin, Michael J. *Asians and Pacific Islanders in the United States*. New York: Russell Sage Foundation, 1993.

Farley, Reynolds. *The New American Reality*. New York: Russell Sage Foundation, 1996.

"Hispanics, Asians Fuel Population Growth." *St. Petersburg Times*. 25 April 2002.

Mitchell, Garry. "Bayou Is Alabama's Window on Asian Culture." Associated Press in *AsianWeek*. 23-29 March, 2001.

Rhoads, Edward J. M. "The Chinese in Texas." *Southwestern Historical Quarterly*. 81:1-36, 1977.

Section IV – Cultural and Society

Chapter 1 – Arts and Entertainment

Aderer, Konrad. "A Sundance 2002 interview with Bertha Pan director of Face." <http://www.asianamericanfilm.com/>.

"Asian American Film." <www.AsianAmericanfilm.com>.

"Better Luck Tomorrow." <www.betterlucktomorrow.com>.

"Bomb Hip-Hop." <http://www.bombhiphop.com/>.

Garcia, Roger, ed. *Out of the Shadows: Asians in American Cinema*. Olivares, 2002.

Hammond, Stefan. *Hollywood East: Hong Kong Movies and the People Who Make Them*. New York: Contemporary Books, 2000.

Hsu, Hua. "Cuckoo for CoCo." *AsianWeek*, 9 March 2000.

Hueston, Dave. "Akebono looks back on his career as a sumo champ." *Kyodo News Service*, 3 Sept 2001.

"Internet Movie Database." <www.imdb.com>.

Kehr, Dave. "In Theaters Now: The Asian Alternative." *New York Times*. 14 January 2001.

Lewis, Ferd. "Akebono retires," *Honolulu Advertiser*, 25-28 Sept 2001.

Maquiling, David. "Festival Director New Filmmakers." <www.newfilmmakers.com/>.

"National Asian American Telecommunications Association." <www.naatanet.org>.

Park, Eunice. "Kuttin kandi." *AsianWeek*, 27 July 2001.

Park, Mike, of the Chinkees. Interview by Santi Suthinithet. June 2002.

Rayns, Tony. *Seoul Stirring: 5 Korean Directors*. Bloomington: Indiana University Press, 1996.

Schilling, Mark. *Contemporary Japanese Film*. Trumbull, CT: Weatherhill, 2000

"Scratch." <http://www.scratchmovie.com/>.

"Screen Actors Guild Diversity study." <www.sag.org/>.

Server, Lee. *Asian Pop Cinema: Bombay to Tokyo*. San Francisco: Chronicle Books, 1999.

Silbergeld, Jerome. *China into Film: Frames of Reference in Contemporary Chinese Cinema*. London: Reaktion Books, 2000.

Sumo World. Published in Tokyo, Japan. <http://www.sumoworld.com>.

"The Debut." <http://debutfilm.pinoynet.com>.

"The Flip Side." <www.flipsidemovie.com>.

Vasudivan, Ravi S., ed. *Making Meaning in Indian Cinema*. Oxford: Oxford University Press, 2000.

"Visual Communications." <http://www.vconline.com>.

Wang, Oliver. "DeclarAsians of Independence." *AsianWeek*. 17-23 May 1996.

Wong, Al. "Why the Joy Luck Club sucks." <http://www.olagrande.net/>.

"World Wide Box Office." <http://www.worldwideboxoffice.com>.

Chapter 2 – Popular Culture

American Society of Newspaper Editors website. <http://www.asne.org>.

Chen, Yong. Phone interview by Cindy Chew. 13 June 2002.

Dang, Janet and Ma, Jason. "Changing Hands." AsianWeek. 23, March 2000.

Darling, Michael. Phone interview by Martin Wong. March 15, 2001.

Davis, Robin. "Sushi American Style." *San Francisco Chronicle*. 1 December 1999. <http://www.sfgate.com>.

Fong-Torres, Shirley. "Hawai'i's love for Spam is handed down." *San Francisco Chronicle*. 10 September 1995. <http://www.sfgate.com>.

Gardiner, Debbi. "Asian American Print Media—Proliferation and Problems." AsianWeek. 4 May 2000.

Harber, Randall. "Ming Tsai makes 'fusion' out of 'confusion' when East meets West" CNN Interactive. 20 March 2000. <http://www.cnn.com/2000/FOOD/>.

Iyer, Pico. "The Beauties of Double Exposure." *Time Asia*. October 1996. <http://www.time.com/time/asia>.

Ko, Claudine. "Ang Lee." *Giant Robot*. 20 (2000): 20-21.

Poon, Bill. "So Fun." *Giant Robot*. 25 (2002): 32-35.

Lufty, Carol. "Design." *Time Asia*. October 1996. <http://www.time.com/time/asia>.

Nakamura, Eric. "Punk Art." *Giant Robot*. 20 (2000): 24-28.

Nakamura, Eric. "Superfly." *Giant Robot*. 21 (2001): 24-28.

Namkung, Victoria. "Hello Kitty's Got a Brand New Bag." *AsianWeek*. 21-27, September 2001. <http://www.asianweek.com/>.

Ngo, Dung. Email to Cindy Chew, 25 June 2002.

Patten, Fred. "Anime in the United States." Lent, John ed. *Animation in Asian and the Pacific*. United Kingdom: John Libbey Publishing, 2001.

Severson, Kim. "Sushi's Raw Appeal." *San Francisco Chronicle*. 1 December 1999. <http://www.sfgate.com>.

Severson, Kim. "The Changing Face of Bay Area Cuisine." *San Francisco Chronicle*. 24 April 2002. <http://www.sfgate.com>.

"Statistics for Asian- and Pacific Islander-Owned Firms by Major Industry Group and Ethnicity." Minority-owned Business Enterprises, U.S. Census Bureau, 1997 Economic Census. 10 May 2001.

Wong, Martin. "Garden Party." *Giant Robot*. 21 (2001): 20-23.

Wong, William. Email interview by Eric Lai.

Chapter 3 – Education

Bowen, W. G., & Bok, D. *The shape of the river: Long-term consequences of considering race in college and university admissions*. Princeton, NJ: Princeton University Press, 1998.

Chan, S., & Wang, L. "Racism and the model minority: Asian-Americans in higher education." In P. G. Altbach & K. Lomotey (Eds.), *The racial crisis in American higher education*. Albany, NY: SUNY Press, 1991.

Chang, M. J. "Does racial diversity matter?: The educational impact of a racially diverse undergraduate population." *Journal of College Student Development*. 40 (4), 377-395, 1999.

Chang, M. J. The educational implications of affirmative action and crossing the color line. *Amerasia Journal*. 26 (3), 67-84, 2001.

Chang, M. J., & Kiang, P. N. "New challenges of representing Asian American students in U.S. higher education." In W. A. Smith, P. G. Altbach, & K. Lomotey Eds., *The racial crisis in American higher education: Continuing challenges for the twenty-first century.* Albany: State University of New York Press, 2002.

Escueta, E., & O'Brien, E. *Asian Americans in Higher Education: Trends and Issues.* Washington D.C.: American Council on Education, 1991.

Gurin, P. Expert report of Patricia Gurin, in the compelling need for diversity in higher education. Gratz et al. v. Bollinger, et al., No. 97-75321 (E.D. Mich.) Grutter et al. v. Bollinger, et al., No. 97-75928 (E.D. Mich.). Ann Arbor: University of Michigan, 1999.

Hakuta, K., & Pease-Alvarez. "Special issue on bilingual education." *Educational Researcher*, 21(2), 1992.

Hirabayashi, L. R., & Alquizola, M. C. "Asian American Studies: Reevaluating for the 1990s." In K.A.-S. Juan Ed., *The State of Asian America: Activism and resistance in the 1990s.* Boston, MA: South End Press, 1994.

Hsia, J., & Hirano-Nakanishi, M. "The demographics of diversity: Asian Americans and higher education." *Change.* Nov/Dec, 20-27, 1989.

Hune, S., & Chan, K. S. "Special focus: Asian Pacific American demographic and educational trends." In D. Carter & R. Wilson Eds., *Minorities in higher education* (Vol. 15, pp. 39-107). Washington, D.C: American Council on Education, 1997.

Koretz, D., Russell, M., Shin, C. D., Horn, C., & Shasby, K. "Testing and diversity in postesecondary education: The case of California." *Education Policy Analysis.* Archives, 10(1), 2002.

Nakanishi, D., & Nishida, T. Y. Eds.. *The Asian American Educational Experience.* New York: Routledge, 1995.

Orfield, G., & Whitla, D. "Diversity and legal education: Student experiences in leading law schools." In G. Orfield & M. Kurlaender Eds., *Diversity challenged: Evidence on the impact of affirmative action.* Cambridge, MA: Harvard Education Publishing Group, 2001

Pang, V. O., Kiang, P. N., & Pak, Y. K.. "Asian Pacific American Students: Challenging a Biased Educational System." In J. Banks Ed., *Handbook of Research on Multicultural Education* (2nd ed.). San Francisco: Jossey Bass.

Suzuki, B. H. "Asian Americans as the "Model Minority" outdoing whites? Or media hype?" *Change.* 2-19, 1989.

Suzuki, B. H. "Asians." In A. Levine Ed., *Shaping higher education's future: Demographic realities and opportunities, 1990-2000.* San Francisco, CA: Jossey-Bass, 1989.

Takagi, D. Y. *Retreat from race: Asian-American admissions and racial politics.* New Brunswick, NJ: Rutgers University Press, 1992.

Trueba, H., Cheng, L., & Ima, K. *Myth or reality: Adaptive strategies of Asian Americans in California.* Washington, DC: Falmer Press, 1993.

Wang, L. "Asian American Studies." *American Quarterly.* 33(3), 339-354, 1981.

Wong, S. C. "The language needs of school-age Asian immigrants and refugees." In W.A.V. Horne Ed., *Ethnicity and language.* Madison, WI: University of Wisconsin System: Institute of Race and Ethnicity, 1987.

Wong-Fillmore, L. "When learning a second language means losing the first." *Early Childhood Research Quarterly.* 6, 323-347, 1991.

Chapter 4 – Politics and Civil Rights

80-20 Initiative. "Unity is Power." <http://www.80-20.to/unity1.html#SectionA>.

Baraka, Jessica L., Huber, Gregory A., Espenshade, Thomas J. "Implications of the 1996 Welfare and Immigration Reform Acts for US Immigration," *Population and Development Review.* 23, no. 4, December 1997: 769-801.

Chang, Edward T. "America's First Multi-ethnic 'Riots'," in *The State of Asian America: Activism and Resistance in the 1990s*, ed. Karin Aguilar-San Juan. Boston: South End Press, 1994.

"Characteristics of Specialty Occupation Workers (H-1B): Oct 1999-Feb 2000." <http://www.ins.usdoj.gov/>. June 2000.

Delgado Richard and Stefancic, Jean. *Critical Race Theory: An Introduction.* New York: New York University Press, 2001.

Dirlik, Arif. "Asians on the Rim: Transnational Capital and Local Community in the Making of Contemporary Asian America." *Amerasia Journal* 22 (1996): 1-24.

"Do Native Hawaiians Count?" *AsianWeek.* 6-12 July 2001. <http://www.asianweek.com/>.

Eljera, Bert. "Apologies from the DNC." *AsianWeek.* 12-18 September 1997, <http://www.asianweek.com/>.

Espiritu, Yen Le and Omi, Michael. "'Who Are You Calling Asian?': Shifting Identity Claims, Racial Classifications, and the Census." *The State of Asian Pacific America: Transforming Race Relations*, ed. Paul Ong. Los Angeles: LEAP Asian Pacific American Public Policy Institute and UCLA Asian American Studies Center, 2000: 68-9.

Geron, Kim, et al., "Asian Pacific Americans' Social Movements and Interest Groups." *PS: Political Science & Politics.* XXXIV, no. 3. September 2001: 619-24.

Glazer, Nathan. *Affirmative Discrimination: Ethnic Inequality and Public Policy.* Cambridge, Mass.: Harvard University Press, 1987/1975.

Greenwald, John. "The Cash Machine: Was Huang a Maverick or Part of a Scheme to Shake Down Foreign Tycoons?" *Time.* 11 November 1996, 39-42.

Hing, Bill Ong. *Making and Remaking Asian America Through Immigration Policy, 1850-1990.* Stanford, Ca.: Stanford University Press, 1993.

"Hmong Veterans Naturalization Act of 2000." <http://www.ins.usdoj.gov/>.

Hosenball, Mark and Isikoff, Michael. "The Man in the Middle." *Newsweek.* 21 July 1997: 40.

Jones, Stacey. "From Obscurity to Scapegoat." *Editor & Publisher.* 130, no. 35. August 30 1997: 7.

Kim, Claire Jean. *Bitter Fruit: The Politics of Black-Korean Conflict in New York City.* New Haven, Conn.: Yale University Press, 2000.

Kim, Elaine H. "Home is Where the 'Han' is: A Korean American Perspective on the Los Angeles Upheavals." *Social Justice.* 20, no. 1-2. Spring-Summer 1993: 1-21.

Lai, James, et al. "Asian Pacific-American Campaigns, Elections, and Elected Officials." *PS: Political Science & Politics.* XXXIV, no. 3. September 2001: 613.

Lee, Anne Feder and Meller, Norman. "Hawaiian Sovereignty." *Publius: The Journal of Federalism.* 27, no. 2. Spring 1997: 167-85.

Lichtblau, Eric. "Clinton Bypasses Congress to Install Civil Rights Chief." *Los Angeles Times.* 4 August 2000. <http://proquest.umi.com/>.

Lien, Pei-te, et al., "Asian Pacific-American Public Opinion and Political Participation." *PS: Political Science & Politics.* XXXIV, no. 3. September 2001: 625-30.

Lien, Pei-te. *The Making of Asian America Through Political Participation.* Philadelphia: Temple University Press, 2001.

Lien, Pei-te, et al., "The Mosaic of Asian American Politics: Preliminary Results from the Five-City Post-Election Survey," paper presented at the Midwest Political Science Association. Chicago, Illinois. April 2001.

Lind, Michael. *The Next American Nation: The New Nationalism and the Fourth American Revolution*. New York: Free Press, 1995.

Locke, Gary. Biography. <http://www.governor.wa.gov/>.

Logan, John R. "From Many Shores: Asians in Census 2000," State University of New York at Albany, Lewis Mumford Center for Comparative Urban and Regional Research, <http://mumford1.dyndns.org/>. 6 October 2001.

Lowe, Lisa. "Heterogeneity, Hybridity, Multiplicity: Marking Asian American Differences." *Diaspora*. I. Spring 1991: 24-44.

Nash, Phil Tajitsu and Wu, Frank. "Asian-Americans Under Glass: Where the Furor Over the President's Fundraising Has Gone Awry—and Racist," *The Nation*. 31March 1997.

Pennybacker, Mindy. "Should the Aloha State Say Goodbye? Natives Wonder." *The Nation*. 12/19 August 1996.

Pilot Study of the National Asian American Political Survey. *National Asian Pacific American Political Almanac*, ed. Don T. Nakanishi and James S. Lai Los Angeles: UCLA Asian American Studies Center, 2001.

Saito, Leland T. *Race and Politics: Asian Americans, Latinos, and Whites in a Los Angeles Suburb*. Urbana, Ill.: University of Illinois Press, 1998.

Statham, E. Robert Jr. "Ethnic Nationalism Versus American Constitutionalism: The Impact of Rice v. Cayetano." *World Affairs* 164, no. 3 Winter 2002: 135-44.

Takaki, Ronald. "Reflections on Racial Patterns in America," in *From Different Shores: Perspectives on Race and Ethnicity in America*, ed. Ronald Takaki. New York: Oxford University Press, 1987: 26-37.

Tilove, Jonathan. "Activists Move to Unify Asian-American Voters in Fall Campaign." Newhouse News Service, <http://www.newhousenews.com/>.

Trask, Haunani-Kay. "Settlers of Color and "Immigrant" Hegemony: "Locals" in Hawai'i," *Amerasia Journal*. 26, no. 2. 2000: 1-24.

Trask, Mililani B. "Hawaiian Sovereignty," *Amerasia Journal*. 26, no. 2. 2000: 31- 36.

Tuan, Mia. *Forever Foreigners or Honorary Whites? The Asian Ethnic Experience Today*. New Brunswick, N.J.: Rutgers University Press, 1998.

Wang, Wayne. Chan is Missing.

Waters, Mary C. *Ethnic Options: Choosing Ethnic Identities in America*. Berkeley: University of California Press, 1990.

Watanabe, Paul. "Global Forces, Foreign Policy, and Asian Pacific Americans." *PS: Political Science & Politics*, XXXIV, no. 3. September 2001: 639-44.

Wei, William. *The Asian American Movement*. Philadelphia: Temple University Press, 1993.

Weisskopf, Michael. "Phantom Witness," *Time*. 14 July 1997.

Wu, Frank. "Have You No Decency? An Analysis of Racial Aspects of Media Coverage of the John Huang Matter." *Asian American Policy Review*. VII 1997: 1-37.

Wu, Frank. "Lee Appointment Turns Ugly," *AsianWeek*. 6-12 November 1997. <http://www.asianweek.com/>.

Wu, Frank. "Senate Stalls Lee Confirmation," *AsianWeek*. Oct 30-Nov 5 1997, <http://www.asianweek.com/>.

Zia, Helen. *Asian American Dreams: The Emergence of an American People*. New York: Farrar, Straus and Giroux, 2000.

Chapter 5 – Work

Aguilar-San Juan, Karin. *The State of Asian America: Activism and Resistance in the 1990s*. South End Press, 1994.

American Management Association International. Senior Management Teams: Profiles and Performance, 1998 AMA Survey. New York, New York. 1998.

Asian Americans for Community Involvement. *Qualified But...: A Report on Glass Ceiling Issues Facing Asian Americans in Silicon Valley*. San Jose: Asian Americans for Community Involvement of Santa Clara County, Inc., 1993.

Bronfenbrenner, Kate. *Organizing To Win: New Research on Union Strategies*. Cornell University, 1998.

Barringer, Herbert, Robert W. Gardner, and Michael J. Levin (eds.). *Asians and Pacific Islanders in the United States* New York: Russell Sage Foundation, for the National Committee for Research on the 1980 Census, 1995

Cabezas, Amado, Tse Ming Tam, Brenda M. Lowe, Anna Wong, and Kathy Owyang Turner. "Empirical Study of Barriers to Upward Mobility of Asian Americans in the San Francisco Bay Area." In *Frontiers of Asian American Studies: Writing, Research, and Commentary*. Pullman, WA: Washington State University Press, 1989.

Carlino, Bill. "Denny's Pays $54M to Settle Bias Suits." *Nation's Restaurant News*. 6 June 1994.

Carter, Deborah J. and Reginald Wilson. *Minorities in Higher Education: Fifteenth Annual Status Report, 1996-97*. Washington, D.C.: American Council on Education, April 1997.

Cheng, Mae M. "Immigrant's Success Story; Labor Nominee has Queens Roots." *Newsday*. 14 January 2001.

Cherian, Joy "Asian Americans: An Emerging Force to Break the Glass Ceiling." New Orleans, Louisiana, Remarks at the 1993 Annual Program of the Chinese-American Librarians Association. 28 June 1993.

Chinese for Affirmative Action. *The Broken Ladder '92: Asian Americans in City Government*. San Francisco, Ca., May 1992.

Chinese for Affirmative Action. *The Broken Ladder '89: Asian Americans in City Government*. San Francisco, Ca., June 1989.

Department of Labor, "Statement by Emily Stover Derocco, Assistant Secretary for the Employment and Training Administration on Fiscal Year 2003 Request for the Employment and Training Administration." 7 February 2002.

Duleep, Harriet Orcutt and Seth Sanders. "Discrimination at the Top: American-Born Asian and White Men." *Industrial Relations* 31 (3) 1992: 416-432.

Duster, Troy. "The Structure of Privilege and Its Universe of Discourse." *The American Sociologist* 11 (2) May 1976: 73-78.

Escueta, Eugenia and Eileen O'Brien. "Asian Americans in Higher Education: Trends and Issues." Research Briefs, American Council on Education 2 (4) 1991: 1-11.

Ezorsky, Gertrude. *Racism and Justice: The Case for Affirmative Action*. Ithaca, New York: Cornell University Press, 1991.

Federal Glass Ceiling Commission. *Good For Business: Making Full Use of the Nation's Human Capital, A Fact-Finding Report of the Federal Glass Ceiling Commission*. Washington, D.C., March 1995.

Fong, Pauline and Amado Cabezas. "Economic and Employment Status of Asian-Pacific Women." U.S. Department of Education, Conference on the Educational and Occupational Needs of Asian-Pacific-American Women. Washington, D.C.: U.S. Government Printing Office, October 1980.

Fullerton, Jr., Howard N. "New Labor Force Projections, Spanning 1988 to 2000." *Monthly Labor Review*. November 1989: 3-12.

Gordon, Marcy. "Labor Secretary Testifies at Enron Hearings." Associated Press. 6 February 2002.

Greenhouse, Steven. "U.S. Sues a Sweater Factory After a Pop Singer Assails It." *New York Times*. 2 May 2002.

Guadalupe, Patricia. "A Place for More Hispanics?: The Push to Get More Hispanics on the Federal Payroll Gains Momentum." *Hispanic Business*. March 2002.

Holmes, Steven A. "Texaco Settlement Could Lead to More Lawsuits." *New York Times*. 17 November 1996.

Hymowitz, Carol and Timothy D. Schellhardt. "The Glass Ceiling: Why Women Can't Seem to Break the Invisible Barrier that Blocks Them from the Top Jobs." *Wall Street Journal*, sec 4. 24 March 1986.

Ichioka, Yuji. *The Issei*. Free Press, 1988.

Kidder, William C. "Situating Asian Pacific Americans in the Law School Affirmative Action Debate: Empirical Facts about Thernstrom's Rhetorical Acts." *Asian Law Journal* 7 (29): 43, Dec 2000.

Lee, Chisun. "Chao Time." *The Village Voice*. 6 February 2001.

Lee, Don. "Asian Americans Finding Cracks in the Glass Ceiling." *Los Angeles Times*. 15 July 1998.

Los Angeles Times, "Elections '96; State Propositions: A Snapshot of Voters." *Los Angeles Times*. 7 November 1996.

Loury, Glenn C. "The Racism We Condemn." *New York Times*. 26 November 1996.

Marquis, Christopher. "Woman in the News: A Washington Veteran for Labor–Elaine Lan Chao." *New York Times*. 12 January 2001.

Matloff, Norm. Debunking the Myth of a Desparate Software Labor Shortage. Testimony to the U.S. House Judiciary Committee, Subcommittee on Immigration. 5 September 2001. <http://heather.cs.ucdavis.edu/>.

Milkman, Ruth. *Organizing Immigrants: The Challenge for Unions in Contemporary California*. Cornell University, 2000.

Milkman, Ruth and Kent Wong. *Voices From the Front Lines: Organizing Immigrants in Los Angeles*. UCLA Labor Center, 2000.

Mulligan, Thomas S. and Chris Kraul. "Texaco Settles Race Bias Suit for $176 million." *Los Angeles Times*. 16 November 1996.

Mantsios, Gregory. *A New Labor Movement for a New Century*. Monthly Review Press, 1998.

O'Hare, William P. and Judy C. Felt. *Asian Americans: America's Fastest Growing Minority Group*. Washington, D.A.: Population Reference Bureau, No. 19, February 1991.

Ong, Paul and Evelyn Blumenberg. "Asian Pacific Scientists and Engineers." In Paul Ong ed.. *The State of Asian Pacific America: Economic Diversity, Issues and Policies*. LEAP and UCLA Asian American Studies Center, 1994.

Ong, Paul M., Lucie Cheng, and Leslie Evans. "Migration of Highly Educated Asians and Global Dynamics." *Asian and Pacific Migration Journal* 1 (3-4) 1992: 543-567.

Ong, Paul and Suzanne Hee. "Work Issues Facing Asian Pacific Americans." in *Asian Pacific America: Policy Issues to the Year 2020*. Los Angeles: LEAP and UCLA Asian American Studies Center, 1993.

Ong, Paul and John M. Liu. "U.S. Immigration Policies and Asian Migration." Paul Ong, Edna Bonacich, and Lucie Cheng ed. *The New Asian Immigration in Los Angeles and Global Restructuring*. Philadelphia: Temple University Press, 1994.

Reskin, Barbara F. "Retheorizing Employment Discrimination and Its Remedies." Mauro Guillen, Randall Collines, and Paula England ed.. *The New Economic Sociology*. New York: Russell Sage, 2002.

Reskin, Barbara F. "Employment Discrimination and Its Remedies." Ivar Berg and Arne L. Kalleberg, ed. *Sourcebook of Labor Markets: Evolving Structures and Processes*. New York: Kluwer Academic/Plenum Publishers, 2001.

Ries, Paula and Delores H. Thurgood. "Summary Report 1992: Doctorate Recipients from United States Universities." Washington, D.C.: National Academy Press, 1993.

Rosener, Judy B. *America's Competitive Secret*. New York/Oxford: Oxford University Press, 1995.

Saxton, Alexander. *The Indispensable Enemy: Labor and the Anti-Chinese Movement in California*. Berkeley: University of California Press, 1971.

Scharlin, Craig and Lila Villanueava. *Philip Vera Cruz: A Personal History of Filipino Immigrants and the Farmworkers Movement*. UCLA Labor Center and Asian American Studies Center, 1992.

Siegel, Larry (ed). *Global Electronics*, No. 116. October 1992.

Skrentny, John D. "Inventing Race." *Public Interest*. Washington, Winter 2002.

Tang, Joyce. "The Glass Ceiling in Science and Engineering." *Journal of Socio-Economics* 26 (4): 383-406, 1997.

Tang, Joyce. "Whites, Asians, and Blacks in Science and Engineering: A Reconsideration of Their Economic Prospects." *Research in Social Stratification and Mobility*. Vol. 12. JAI Press Inc., 1993.

Wong, Kent. *Voices for Justice: Asian Pacific American Organizers and the New Labor Movement*. UCLA Labor Center, 2001.

U.S. Commission on Civil Rights. Civil Rights Issues of Asian and Pacific Americans: Myths and Realities. Washington, D.C.: U.S. Government Printing Office, 8-9 May 1979.

U.S. Commission on Civil Rights, Economic Status of Americans of Asian Descent: An Exploratory Investigation. Washington, D.C.: U.S. Commission on Civil Rights, 1988.

U.S. Department of Labor. A Report on the Glass Ceiling Initiative. Washington, D.C.: U.S. Government Printing Office, 1991.

U.S. Office of Personnel Management. Guide to Senior Executive Service Qualifications. 24 February 1998.

U.S. Office of Personnel Management. Qualifications Standards Handbook: For General Schedule Positions. Washington, D.C.: Government Printing Office, 1993.

Wasserman, Jim. "Racial Privacy Initiative Likely Won't Qualify for November Ballot." *The Sacramento Bee*. 30 May 2002.

Wong, Paul and Richard Nagasawa. "Asian American Scientists and Engineers: Is there a Glass Ceiling for Career Advancement?" *Chinese American Forum* 6 (3), January 1991.

Woo, Deborah. *Glass Ceilings and Asian Americans*. Walnut Creek, Lanham, New York, Oxford: Altamira Press 2000.

Yoneda, Karl. *Ganbatte: Sixty-Year Struggle of a Kibei Worker*. Los Angeles: UCLA Asian American Studies Center, 1983.

Zweigenhaft, Richard L. and William Domhoff. *Diversity in the Power Elite: Have Women and Minorities Reached the Top?* New Haven: Yale University Press, 1998.

Chapter 6 – Health

American Cancer Society. 1998. *Cancer facts & figures for minority Americans*, 1998. Atlanta, GA: American Cancer Society, 1998.

Asian Liver Center, Stanford University. Hepatitis B Statistics. <http://www.asianlivercenter.org/>.

Brown, R., Ojeda, V., Wynn, R., Levan, R. *Racial and ethnic disparities in access to health insurance and health care*. Los Angeles: UCLA Center for Health Policy Research, 2000.

Centers for Disease Control and Prevention. *Chronic Disease in Minority Populations*. Atlanta: Centers for Disease Control and Prevention, 1992.

Centers for Disease Control and Prevention. "Behavioral risk factor survey of Korean Americans–Alameda County, California, 1994." *Morbidity and Mortality Weekly Report*. 46(33): 774-77, 1997.

Chen, M., Kuun, P., Guthrie, R., Wen, L., et al. 1991. "Promotion heart health for Southeast Asians: a database for planning interventions." *Public Health Reports*. 106: 304-09.

Choy, Catherine Ceniza. *Empire of Care: Nursing and Migration in Filipino American History*. Durham, NC: Duke University Press, forthcoming 2003.

Euler, Gary. "Changing the Legacy for Asian Americans and Pacific Islanders." *Asian American and Pacific Islander Journal of Health*. 6(2): 304-10, 1998.

Hoyert D.L., Kung, H.C. Asian and Pacific Islander Mortality, 1992. Monthly Vital Statistics Report. 46(1): *Supplement*, 1997.

Jenkins, C.N., Le, T, McPhee, S., Stewart, S., and Ha, N.T. "Health Care Access and Preventative Care among Vietnamese Immigrants: Do Traditional Beliefs and Practices pose Barriers?" *Social Science and Medicine*. 43(7): 1049-56, 1996.

Kagawa-Singer M, Pourat N. "Asian American and Pacific Islander breast and cervical carcinoma screening rates and healthy people 2000 objectives." *Cancer*. 89(3): 696-705, 2000.

Ku, L. and Blaney, S. *Health coverage for legal immigrant children: New Census data highlight importance of restoring Medicaid and SCHIP coverage*. Washington DC: Center of Budget and Policy Priorities, 2000.

Ma, G.X. "Between Two Worlds: The Use of Traditional and Western Health Services by Chinese Immigrants." *Journal of Community Health*. 24(6): 421-37, 1999.

Massachusetts Department of Public Health. Massachusetts Health Status Indicators by Race and Ethnicity. Massachusetts Department of Public Health, Bureau of Health Statistics, Research and Evaluation, 1996.

Mayeno, L, Hiraota, S. "Access to health care." In N. Zane, D. Takeuchi, & K. Young eds., *Confronting critical health issues of Asian and Pacific Islander Americans*. Newbury Park, CA: Sage Publications, 1994.

Miller, B.A., Kolonel, L., Bernstein, L. Young, J. *Racial/ethnic patterns of cancer in the United States 1988-1992*. Bethesda, MD: National Cancer Institute. NIH Publication No. 96-4104, 1994.

National Center for Health Statistics. National Health Interview Survey. Hyattsville, MD: Public Health Service, 1993.

National Heart, Lung and Blood Institute. *Addressing cardiovascular health in Asian Americans and Pacific Islanders*. Bethesda, MD: National Heart, Lung and Blood Institute. NIH Publication No. 00-3647, 2000.

Ong, Paul and Tania Azores. "The Migration and Incorporation of Filipino Nurses." In *The New Asian Immigration in Los Angeles and Global Restructuring*, ed. Paul Ong, Edna Bonacich, and Lucie Cheng. Philadelphia: Temple University Press, 1994.

Park, L., Sarnoff R., Bender C., Korenbrot C.C. "Impact of Recent Welfare and Immigration Reforms on Use of Medicaid for Prenatal Care by Immigrants in California." *Journal of Immigrant Health*. 2(1), 2000.

Park, L and Yoo G. *Impact of Public Charge on Immigrant Women's Access to Medi-Cal*. Final report for California Program on Access to Care/California Policy Research Center.

Pourat, Nadereh; Lubben, James; Wallace, S.P.; Moon, Ailee. "Predictors of Use of Traditional Korean Healers among the Elderly Koreans in Los Angeles." *The Gerontologist*. 39(6):711-19, 1999.

Stanford, J.L., Herrington, L.J., Schwartz, S.M., Weiss, N.S.. 1995. "Breast cancer incidence in Asian migrants to the United States and their descendants." *Epidemiology*. 6(2):181-3, 1995.

Tang T.S.; Solomon L.J.; Yeh C.J., Worden J.K. "The role of cultural variables in breast self-examination and cervical cancer screening behavior in young Asian women living in the United States." *Journal of Behavioral Medicine*. 22: 419-36, 1999.

Westermeyer, J.; Vang, T.F.; Neider, J. "Refugees who do and do not seek psychiatric care: An analysis of premigratory and postmigratory characteristics." *Journal of Nervous & Mental Disease*. 171:86-91, 1983.

Wingo PA; Ries LA; Rosenberg HM; Miller DS; Edwards BK. "Cancer incidence and mortality, 1973-1995: a report card for the U.S." *Cancer*. 82(6):1197-207, 1998.

Yatsu, F.M. "Strokes in Asians and Pacific-Islanders, Hispanics, and Native Americans." *Circulation*. 83(4):1471-2. 1991.

Yoo, G. Federal Welfare Reform and Asian Pacific Islander Communities in California: A view from the grassroots. Paper presented at the Pacific Sociological Association Meetings, San Francisco, 1998.

Yu, E.S., Chen E.H. Brintnall, R.A. "Breast and Cervical Cancer Screening among Chinese American Women." *Cancer Practice*. 9:81-91, 2001.

Chapter 7 – Business and Hi-Tech

"Asian American Hotel Owners Association." <http://www.aahoa.com>.

Evenson, Laura. "Chong-moon Lee profile." *San Francisco Chronicle Sunday magazine*, 5 November 1995.

Gardiner, Debbi. "Asian American Small Businesses Benefit from Going Online." *AsianWeek*. 6 April 2000.

Varadarajan, Tunku. "A Patel Motel Cartel?" *New York Times Magazine*. July 4, 1999.

Dang, Janet. "High Tech's Low Wages." *AsianWeek*. December 23, 1999.

Files, Jennifer. "Valley firms making strides on diversifying." *San Jose Mercury News* 26 April, 2002: A1.

Ha, K. Oanh. "Piecework lawsuit settled claims over man's home assembly of electronics." *San Jose Mercury News*. November 14, 2000.

Johnson, Jean M. and Regets, Mark C. "International Mobility of Scientists and Engineers to the United States–Brain Drain or Brain Circulation?" National Science Foundation Issue Brief, NSF 98-316, 22 June 1998.

Junker, Thomas. "The Unofficial Wang VS Information Center." September 1995, <http://www.tjunker.com>

Lai, Eric and Viloria, Theresa C. "Immigrant Job Machine." *San Jose Mercury News*. 27 August 1995, 1D.

Luening, Erich and Mike Ricciuti. "Wang name comes to an end." 4 May 1999. <http://www.news.com>

Lundstrom, Meg. "East Meets West Meets East: Chinese Networking in Silicon Valley." *BusinessWeek*, 12 January 2000.

"National Inventors Hall of Fame." <http://www.invent.org> 23 May 2002.

Richardson, Vanessa. "The 'Indian Mafia' muscles onto the Web." *Red Herring* 14 December 1999.

Salkever, Alex. "The Curry Network." The *Industry Standard*, 24 January 2000.

Saxenian, AnnaLee. *Silicon Valley's New Immigrant Entrepreneurs*. Public Policy Institute of California, 1999.

Thurm, Scott. "Asian Immigrants Help to Reshape Silicon Valley as Entrepreneurs." *The Wall Street Journal*, 24 June 1999.

Chapter 9 – Religion

Min, Pyong Gap, and Kim, Jung Ha eds. *Religions in Asian America*. Walnut Creek, CA: AltaMira Press, 2002.

Index

C

D

E

F

G

H

I

J

K

Q

R

S

About the Contributors

Andrew L. Aoki is a political science professor at Augsburg College in Minneapolis, Minnesota. He has published works on Asian Pacific American politics, immigration, and multiculturalism, and is a co-founder of the Asian Pacific American Caucus (APAC) of the American Political Science Association.

Dennis Arguelles is the assistant director of the UCLA Asian American Studies Center. An urban planner by training, he has worked on numerous research projects focused on the Asian Pacific American community, poverty, housing and economic development. He is a former president and executive director of the Asian Pacific Policy and Planning Council.

Pauline Agbayani-Siewert has focused much of her research on cross-cultural mental health practice and service delivery, with an emphasis on Asian and Filipino American populations. A former caseworker for the elderly and juvenile offenders, she currently teaches at California State University, Los Angeles.

Gelly Borromeo is the publisher of *Asian Enterprise* magazine. Based in Southern California, *Asian Enterprise* (http://www.asianenterprise.com) is the largest circulation magazine focusing on Asian Pacific Americans in small business.

Edward T. Chang is associate professor of ethnic studies and a former director of the Center for Asian Pacific America at UC Riverside. His research interests include Korean American-African American Relations, Asian-Latino relations, immigration, and race relations.

Mitchell J. Chang is assistant professor of higher education and organizational change at UCLA and a faculty advisor for the Asian American studies program. His research focuses on the educational efficacy of diversity-related initiatives on college campuses and how best to apply those practices toward advancing student learning and democratizing institutions.

Cindy Chew is a freelance photographer and writer who has contributed to *AsianWeek, Doubletake* and *The Villager*. A San Francisco native, she received her B.A. from UC Berkeley and her M.A. in journalism from New York University.

Porthira Chhim is a consultant with Cambodian Community Development, Inc. in Oakland, California. A graduate of the City University of New York School of Law, he has worked for the Southeast Asia Resource Action Center (SEARAC) and the Southeast Asian American Advocacy Initiative. He arrived in the United States from Cambodia as a refugee in 1975.

Chuong Hoang Chung is a professor in the department of Asian American studies at the City College of San Francisco. His books include *The Amerasians from Vietnam: A California Study* and *The Book of Perception*.

Melany dela Cruz received her M.A. in Urban Planning at UCLA's School of Public Policy and Social Research. Currently, she runs the Asian Pacific American Community Development Data Center, a joint project of UCLA's Asian American Studies Center, the National Coalition for Asian Pacific American Community Development and the U.S. Census Bureau's Census Information Center Program.

Catherine Ceniza Choy is assistant professor of American studies at the University of Minnesota and is the author of the forthcoming book *Empire of Care: Nursing and Migration in Filipino American History*. Her current research focuses on the history of international adoption of Asian children in the United States.

Wei Ming Dariotis is assistant professor of Asian American studies at San Francisco State University. She is faculty advisor to SFSU's Hapa Club and Women's Center, as well as co-founder and facilitator of the SF Chapter of the Hapa Issues Forum. She is working on several projects relating to mixed heritage identity, including a book on hapa artists and a novel featuring a bisexual hapa vampire protagonist. She is also currently president of the board of the Asian American Theater Company.

Karen Fang is assistant professor of film and literature at the University of Houston where she teaches Hong Kong, Asian, and world cinema. She received her B.A. from the University of Pennsylvania, and her Ph.D. from Johns Hopkins University.

Eric Fong is an associate professor of sociology at the University of Toronto and a research associate at the Centre for Urban and Community Studies. His research interests include race and ethnic residential patterns and ethnic economy. He has published in various academic journals, including *Demography*, *Social Forces*, and *Sociological Forum*.

Thao Ha is a graduate student in the department of sociology at the University of Texas, Austin. Her research interests include Asian American studies and racial/ethnic relations.

Tarry Hum is an assistant professor in the department of urban studies at Queens College, City University of New York. She has a Ph.D. in urban planning from UCLA's School of Public Policy and Social Research, and an M.A. in city planning from MIT. She is currently working on a research project funded by the Ford Foundation on New York City's multi-ethnic Asian-Latino neighborhoods.

Victor Jew is an assistant professor at Michigan State Unversity. He received his Ph.D. in U.S. history from the University of Wisconsin-Madison. He specializes in U.S. legal and constitutional history and Asian American history. His co-edited volume, *Total War and the Law*, is about to be published and his own book-length study of the social and cultural history of arson in the United States is under contract with the University of Pennsylvania Press.

Tetsuden Kashima, formerly the director of Asian American studies at UC Santa Barbara and the University of Washington, is currently a professor in the department of American ethnic studies at the University of Washington. His publications include the forthcoming book *Judgement With Trial: The Imprisonment of Japanese Americans during World War II.*

Sharon Kim is an Irvine Foundation Post-Doctoral Fellow of Sociology at Occidental College in Eagle Rock, California. Her dissertation, "Replanting Sacred Spaces: The Emergence of Second Generation Korean American Churches" examines the ways in which second generation Korean Americans are carving out new institutional niches to accommodate the intersection of race, generation, and ethnicity in the context of their Christian faith. She has also taught courses on Asian American religions at UCLA.

Eric Lai is a journalist who writes about Asia and Asian America, popular culture, technology and business. A graduate of Pomona College and UC Berkeley's journalism program, he has written for publications such as the *Asian Wall Street Journal*, *Reuters*, the *San Jose Mercury News*, and the *South China Morning Post* in Hong Kong, where he was technology editor.

Corky Lee is a self-taught photographer who has been documenting the APA community for over 30 years. His work has appeared in APA publications such as *AsianWeek*, *Filipinas* Magazine, *KoreAm Journal*, mainstream publications like *Time*, *The New York Times*, and *The Village Voice*, as well as exhibitions throughout America. Lee is a second-generation Chinese American and the eldest child of a "paper son" laundryman and a seamstress. He is a graduate of Queens College and lives in Queens, New York.

Russell Leong is an award-winning poet, essayist, critic, short story writer and documentary film maker. His most recent work, *Phoenix Eyes*, received the 2001 American Book Award from the Before Columbus Foundation. He is also a recipient of the PEN Oakland Josephine Miles award. Leong is the senior editor of the *Amerasia Journal* and managing editor of the UCLA Asian American Studies Center Press.

Ethen Lieser is a former staff writer for *AsianWeek*. A graduate of the University of Iowa, he was born in Pusan, South Korea, and grew up in Minneapolis, Minnesota. He is a lifelong Minnesota Vikings, Timberwolves and Twins fan.

Ji Hyun Lim has written for *Korea Times* (English edition), *Korean Culture Magazine* and *KoreAm Journal*. She has also worked with Social and Public Art Resource Center, a non-profit arts organization that worked with communities in Pico Rivera, Koreatown and South Central after the Los Angeles riots. She is currently a staff writer for *AsianWeek*.

Loh Sze-Leung graduated from Harvard with a degree in East Asian Studies and has a master's in public policy from UCLA. She is manager of marketing and corporate relations for the Los Angeles Youth Opportunity Movement, a U.S. Department of Labor-funded, City of Los Angeles-managed agency helping inner-city, at-risk teenagers get jobs and stay in school.

Tracy Matsuo is a doctoral student in the Sociology Department at the University of Toronto. Her areas of interest include race/ethnicity, culture and community. She is currently researching the interaction between collective memory and ethnic identity among people of Japanese descent in Canada.

Davianna Pomaika'i McGregor is a historian of Hawai'i and the Pacific and teaches as an associate professor of ethnic studies at the University of Hawai'i, Manoa. She is Native Hawaiian from the islands of O'ahu and Hawai'i who, as a member of Kaho'olawe 'Ohana, has been active in Hawaiian movements to reclaim sacred Hawaiian land.

Ali Modarres is associate director of the Edmund G. "Pat" Brown Institute of Public Affairs at California State University, Los Angeles and a professor in the department of geography and urban analysis. He specializes in urban geography and his primary research and publication interests include immigration, race and ethnicity in American cities.

Ed Moy is a freelance writer in the San Francisco Bay Area. He was recipient of the Leukemia & Lymphoma Society's National Print Media Award in 2000 for his series of articles about their Team in Training Fundraising program. His writing has appeared in *AsianWeek*, Oakland's *Urbanview* and *Triathlete* magazine.

Olivia Nguyen is a graphic artist for the *Sacramento Bee* newspaper. Prior to that, she worked at the *Modesto Bee* and *The Austin American-Statesman*. She is a graduate of the University of Texas at Austin.

Tram Nguyen is executive editor of *ColorLines* (www.colorlines.com) magazine, a progressive quarterly publication about race, culture and organizing, based in Oakland, California. An UCLA graduate, she was part of the collective behind the reborn *Gidra Magazine* (www.gidra.net), a pioneering APA publication started in the 1970s.

Brian Niiya is a writer and editor specializing in Japanese American and Asian American topics. A former curator at the Japanese American National Museum in Los Angeles, he has curated exhibitions on Japanese American sport history and on sumo. He is the editor of the *Encyclopedia of Japanese American History* (2001) and is also a columnist for the *Pacific Citizen* newspaper. He lives and works in Honolulu, Hawai`i.

Joyce Nishioka is former editor-in-chief of *AsianWeek* and a two-time winner of New California Media awards in multicultural journalism for her reporting on APA issues. She is currently a features writer for the *San Francisco Examiner*.

Paul M. Ong is a professor at UCLA's School of Public Policy and Social Research and Director of UCLA's Ralph and Goldy Lewis Center for Regional Policy Studies. He has done extensive research on immigration, racial inequality, low-income workers and welfare reform. His publications include *The New Asian Immigration in Los Angeles and Global Restructuring, Impacts of Affirmative Action: Policies and Consequences in California, Transforming Race Relations: The State of Asian Pacific America,* and *The State of California Labor.*

Isabelle Thuy Pelaud is an assistant professor of Asian American studies at San Francisco State University and is co-director of the Vietnamese American Studies Center at SFSU. She is currently working on a book-length manuscript on Vietnamese American literature. Her essays have been published in *Making More Waves, Tilting the Continent, Of Vietnam: Identities in Dialogue and Mixed Race Literature.*

Mark E. Pfeifer earned his Ph.D. in geography at the University of Toronto. An expert on the adaptation of Southeast Asian immigrants and refugees in North America, he is the director of the Hmong Resource Center in St. Paul, Minnesota. He is also editor of websites devoted to Vietnamese studies and Hmong studies (www.vstudies.org and www.hmongstudies.org). He was recently named co-editor of the *Hmong Studies Journal* (http://members.aol.com/hmongstudies).

Toon Phapphayboun arrived in the United States as a refugee in 1981 and earned her bachelor's and master's degrees in English and American literature from UC Santa Cruz and California State, Dominquez Hills, respectively. She is a member of *Satjadham: An Internet Lao Literary Project* (www.satjadham.net), on staff at *Lao Vision Magazine* (www.laovision.net), and teaches English at Western Piedmont Community College in North Carolina.

K.V. Rao is a demographer at Bowling Green State University with research and teaching interests in Asian American issues, technology and society. He is the founder and president of the nonprofit India Network Foundation. He currently chairs the Census Advisory Committee on Asian Americans that reviews and advises the Census Bureau on race and ethnic issues.

Arthur Sakamoto is associate professor of sociology and an affiliate of the Center for Asian American Studies at the University of Texas, Austin. His research interests include racial/ethnic relations and social stratification. His recent publications include "Wages Among Native-born Asian Americans at the End of the 20th Century," and "Relative Deprivation, Efficiency Wages, and Labor Productivity in Taiwanese Manufacturing Industries."

Jane Singh is a lecturer of comparative ethnic studies at UC Berkeley. Her research and writing focuses on comparative immigration history, Asian American and immigrant women, nationalism and identity in expatriate communities, and South Asian American historical and contemporary issues.

Santi Suthinithet is a freelance photographer and writer whose work has been published in *Urb, Thrasher, Vapors,* and *Beautiful Decay*. An East Coast transplant to San Francisco, he has also been exhibited in different venues and shows throughout San Francisco, including the Artists Uncovered group show at Cell Space.

Minh-hoa Ta is an assistant professor of Asian American Studies and a co-director of the Vietnamese American Studies Center, San Francisco State University. Before joining SFSU, Minh-hoa was an academic advisor and Asian American studies instructor at CCSF. She is a first-generation American of Chinese-Vietnamese heritage.

Rahpee Thongthiraj has a bachelor's and master's degree from UCLA, and a Ph.D. in American culture from the University of Michigan. Her main interests are in Asian American literature and history, as well as Thai Americans. She has taught Asian American studies courses at UCLA, University of Michigan, and California State University, Northridge.

Dean S. Toji is assistant professor in the department of Asian and Asian American studies at California State University, Long Beach. His research includes poverty among APAs and the geography of racial formation, and he is now working on several projects to strengthen the research, service and learning linkages between universities and APA communities. He has been involved in APA issues for three decades.

Karen Umemoto is an associate professor of urban and regional planning at the University of Hawai'i, Manoa and a faculty affiliate with the Asian Pacific Islander Youth Violence Prevention Center. She has a Ph.D. in urban studies from MIT. Her general area of interest is planning and governance in a multicultural society, with a focus on race relations. Her areas of research include hate crimes, gang violence, and community building.

Linda Trinh Võ received her Ph.D. in sociology from UC San Diego and is an Assistant Professor in the Department of Asian American studies at UC Irvine. She co-edited a book entitled *Contemporary Asian American Communities: Intersection and Divergences* (2002).

Eric C. Wat has taught Asian American studies at UCLA and California State University, Northridge and is currently a research analyst at the Los Angeles County Children and Families First Commission. In 2002, he published *The Making of a Gay Asian Community: An Oral History of Pre-AIDS Los Angeles.*

Teresa Williams-Leon is associate professor and associate chair of the Asian American studies department at California State University, Northridge. She has a B.A. from the University of Hawai'i in Japanese, and an M.A. and Ph.D. in sociology from UCLA. She helped compile an annotated bibliography of mixed-race Asian Americans and co-edited the anthology *The Sum of Our Parts: Mixed Heritage Asian Americans.* She has served on the board of Multiracial Americans in Southern California and the Amerasian League, and helped found the Southern California chapter of the Hapa Issues Forum.

Kent Wong is director of the Center for Labor Research and Education at UCLA, where he teaches labor studies and Asian American studies. He previously served as staff attorney for the Service Employees International Union #660. He served as the founding president of the Asian Pacific American Labor Alliance, AFL-CIO, and in 2001 published a book entitled *Voices for Justice: Asian Pacific American Organizers and the New Labor Movement.*

Martin Wong has co-edited the Los Angeles-based Asian pop culture magazine *Giant Robot* since its inception in 1994. The UCLA graduate has also edited textbooks for McGraw-Hill and written articles for magazines such as *Dirt, Slap, Flipside,* and *AsianWeek.*

Deborah J. Woo is a sociologist and professor of community studies at UC Santa Cruz. She is author of *Glass Ceilings and Asian Americans: the New Face of Workplace Barriers* (2000).

Andrew Yan is the Census data manager for the Asian American Federation of New York. He holds an urban planning masters degree from UCLA and was a predoctoral fellow of the Institute of American Culture at UCLA's Asian American Studies Center. He specializes in revitalization strategies, geographic information systems, community development, and multicultural planning. His most recent work has been focused on revitalization strategies in Chinatowns across North America.

Grace J. Yoo is an assistant professor of Asian American studies at San Francisco State University. She received her Ph.D. from UC San Francisco in medical sociology and her M.S. in public health from Loma Linda University. She is currently a principal investigator on a National Cancer Institute-funded study examining risk factors associated with cervical cancer among young Asian women. She has also investigated changing health policies and their impact on Asian and Latino immigrants in California, and consulted on health and aging issues for Asian Americans.

Eui-Young Yu is professor emeritus at California State University, Los Angeles, currently in charge of the Census Information Center for the Korean American Coalition. He is co-author of *East is America.*

Min Zhou is professor of sociology and chair of the Asian American studies interdepartmental degree program at UCLA. Her areas of research include immigration and immigrant adaptation, immigrant youth, Asian Americans, ethnic and racial relations, ethnic entrepreneurship and enclave economies, the community, and urban sociology. She is the author of *Chinatown: The Socioeconomic Potential of an Urban Enclave*; co-author of *Growing up American: How Vietnamese Children Adapt to Life in the United States*; and co-editor of *Contemporary Asian America.*